MW01629193

BUDDHIST ART OF
MYANMAR

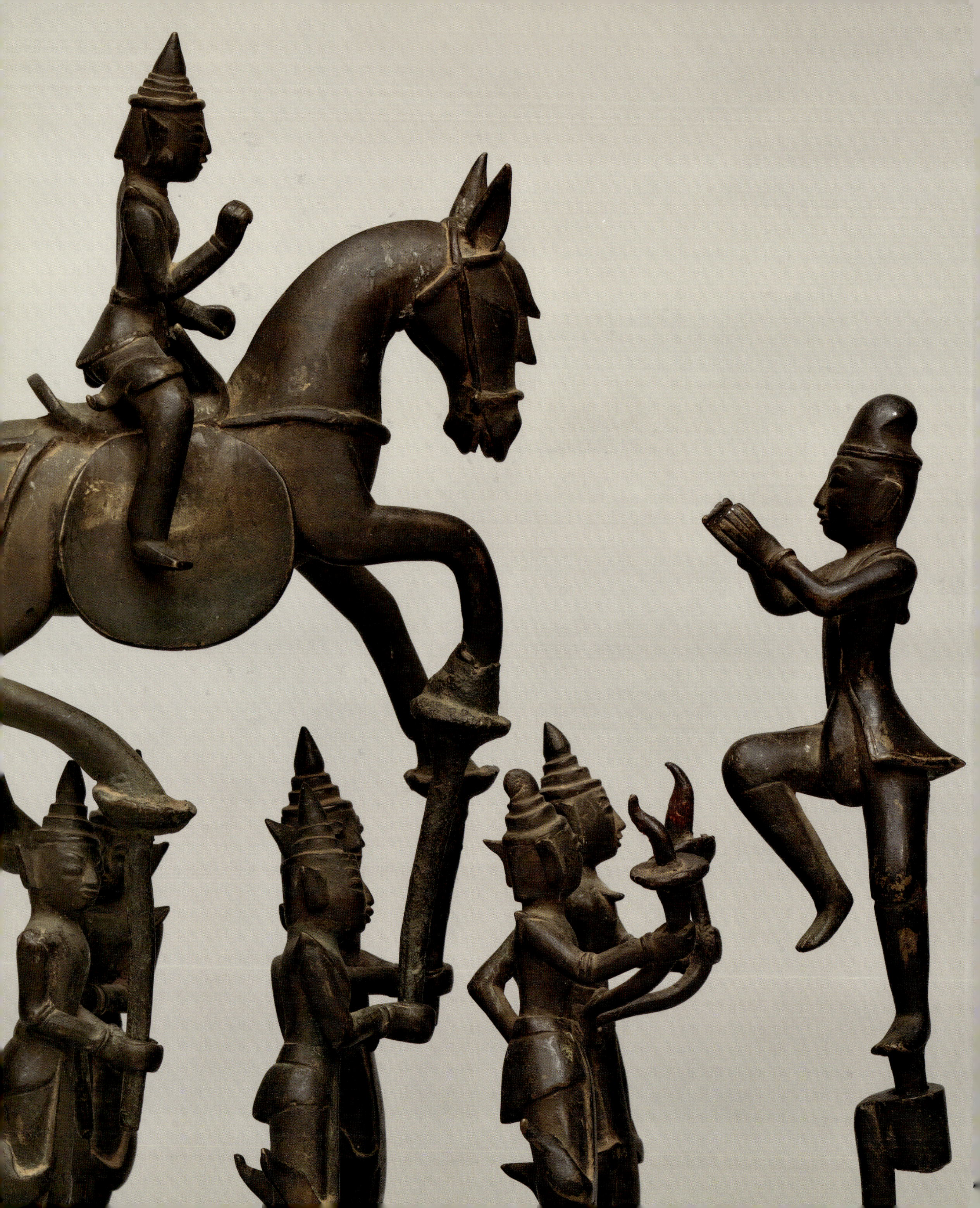

BUDDHIST ART OF MYANMAR

Edited by

Sylvia Fraser-Lu and Donald M. Stadtner

Asia Society Museum

in association with

Yale University Press, New Haven and London

Published on the occasion of the exhibition
Buddhist Art of Myanmar, organized by Asia Society Museum.

Asia Society Museum, New York
February 10–May 10, 2015

Published by
Asia Society
725 Park Avenue
New York, NY 10021
AsiaSociety.org

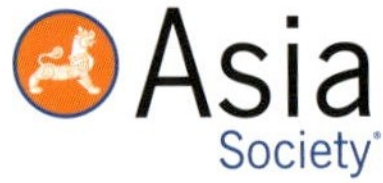

Yale University Press
P.O. Box 209040
302 Temple Street
New Haven, CT 06520-9040
yalebooks.com/art

Yale

Designed by Anjali Pala, Miko McGinty Inc.
Set in Kievit by Tina Henderson
Printed in Hong Kong by Asia One

Library of Congress Control Number: 2014942696
ISBN 978-0-300-20945-7

A catalogue record for this book is available from the British Library.

The paper in this book meets the requirements of ANSI/NISO Z39.48-1992 (Permanence of Paper).

10 9 8 7 6 5 4 3 2 1

Cover illustrations: *(front)* Detail of cat. no. 12; *(back)* Detail of cat. no. 60
Page ii: Detail of cat. no. 43
Page vi: Detail of cat. no. 65
Page x: Cat. no. 26
Pages 228–29: Maps designed by Anandaroop Roy

This book is dedicated to

John Guth

(1924–2014)

Asia Society has lost a great friend and champion. He will be remembered for his friendship, generosity, and support of Asian arts.

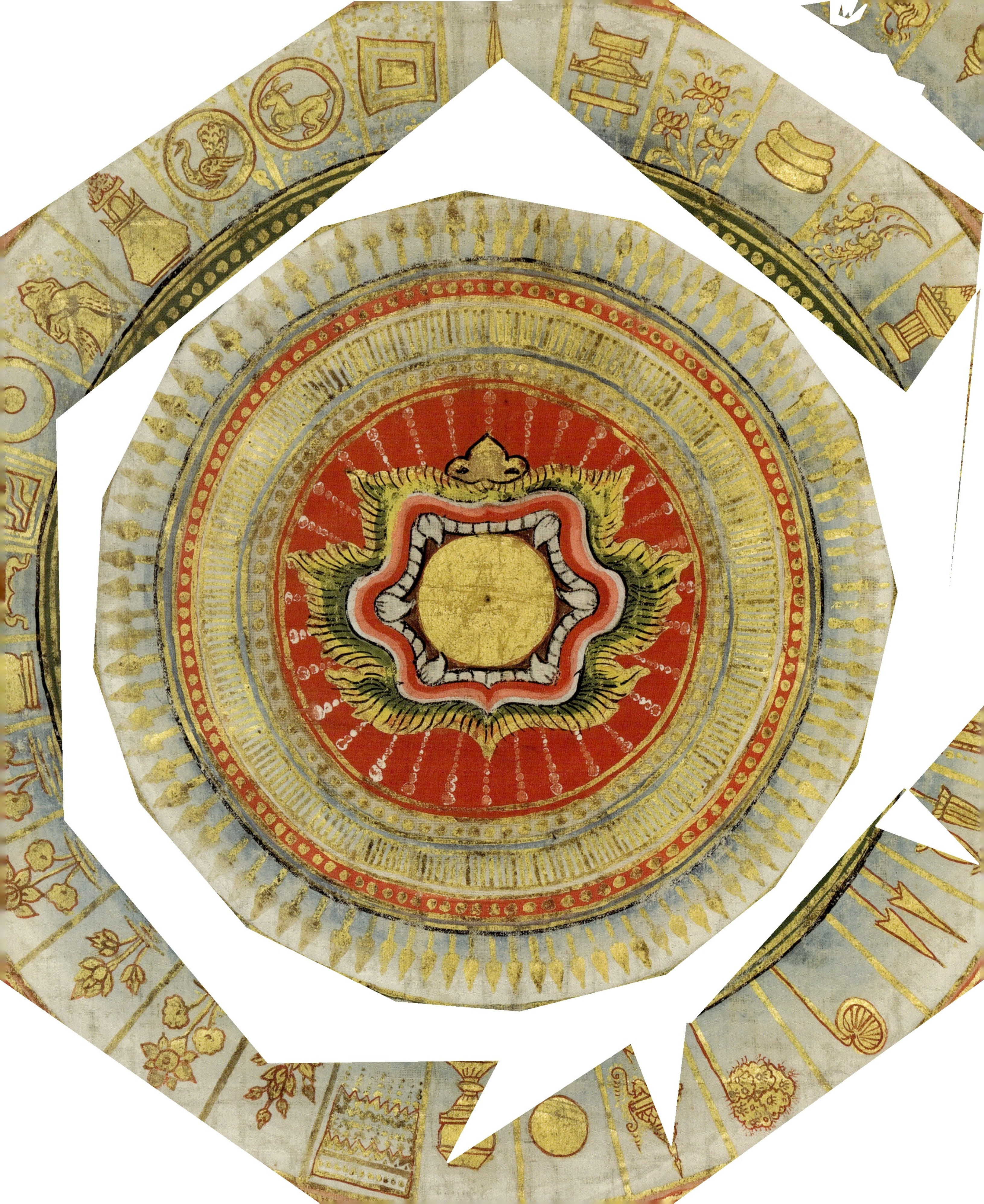

Contents

President's Foreword

This exhibition, "Buddhist Art of Myanmar," is the first major presentation in the United States devoted solely to the art of Myanmar. The majority of artwork on loan in this exhibition has been drawn from five museums across Myanmar and represents a significant occasion in the history of relations between the United States and Myanmar during the past twenty years. The exhibition had its genesis three years ago when President Thein Sein gave a public address at Asia Society in New York and expressed interest in fostering cultural exchange between Myanmar and the United States. Two months later Melissa Chiu, former Museum Director and Senior Vice President of Global Arts and Cultural Programs and current Director of the Hirshhorn Museum and Sculpture Garden, visited Myanmar to pursue the productive collaboration with officials in Myanmar in the Ministry of Culture and Ministry of Religious Affairs that would become the present exhibition.

Asia Society Museum has a long history of developing exhibitions that explore less familiar areas of Asian art. Whether exquisite treasures of the little-known Liao dynasty (907–1125) concurrent with the better studied Song dynasty (906–1279); the dazzling gilded figures of the Densatil Monastery at its height from the thirteenth to fifteenth century, but destroyed during the twentieth century; or overlooked masterworks of revolutionary China or modern Iran, the Museum's mission has been to introduce audiences to the best art from Asia. This has often included the organization of major first-time loan exhibitions such as one of extraordinary art of Gandhara from museums in Pakistan, or a historical survey of art and antiquities from Vietnam, representing more than twenty years of cultural diplomacy that predated normalization of relations between the United States and Vietnam. Like those projects, the present exhibition provides insight into the culture of Myanmar at a time of its renewed engagement with much of the world. The project would not have come to fruition without the inexhaustible efforts and enthusiasm of Melissa Chiu and I congratulate her and applaud her achievement. Asia Society is deeply grateful for her energy for this project, as for so many groundbreaking efforts the Museum has undertaken during her tenure.

Many individuals in Myanmar offered critical support for this project. They include H. E. U Aye Myint Kyu, Union Minister for Culture; H. E. Daw Sanda Khin, Deputy Minister; U Kyaw Oo Lwin, Director General, Department of Archaeology and the National Museum; U Aung Naing Myint, Head of the Office of the Ministry of Culture; U Thein Lwin, Deputy-Director General, Department of Archaeology and the National Museum; Daw Nu Mra Zan, Museum Consultant and Deputy-Director General-retired, Department of Archaeology and the National Museum; Daw Mie Mie Khaing, Director, International Relations, Department of Archaeology and the National Museum; U Ngwe Tun Myint, Director, National Museum, Yangon; U Myint Zaw, Director, National Museum, Nay Pyi Taw; Daw Htay Htay Swe, Deputy Director of the Ministry Office; Daw Mie Mie Thet New, Deputy Director, National Museum, Yangon; Daw Aye Aye Thinn, Deputy Director, National Museum, Nay Pyi Taw; U Naing Win, Director, Bagan Archaeology Branch, Department of Archaeology and the National Museum; Daw Baby, Deputy Director, Bagan Archaeological Museum; U Win Kyaing, Principal of the Field School of Archaeology, Pyay; U Myo Tint Aung, Deputy Director, Pyay Archaeological Branch, Department of Archaeology and the National Museum; and Daw Myint Myint Thein, Assistant Director, Sri Ksetra Archaeological Museum, Hmawza. Similarly, from the Union of Myanmar Ministry of Religious Affairs we thank H. E. U Sant Sint, Union Minister for Religious Affairs; U Khaing Aung, Director General, Department of Promotion and Propagation of Sasana; Daw Yin Yin Myint, Deputy Director, External Missions; and Daw Nwe Nwe, Assistant Curator, Kaba Aye Buddhist Art Museum. Among the others who were most helpful in our efforts to realize this project are Terry Tan, Serge Pun, and Judy Ko. I also would like to thank Alan Chong, Director of the Asian Civilisations Museum and the Paranakan Museum, Singapore, for his early support.

We hope that a greater awareness of the history of Buddhism in Myanmar will contribute to our deeper understanding of Myanmar's developing role in the twenty-first century.

Josette Sheeran
President and CEO

Museum Preface

We are proud to present "Buddhist Art of Myanmar," an exhibition and catalogue which provide a framework for serious understanding of the role of Buddhist art throughout many centuries in Myanmar. The artworks included in this presentation reflect the country's rich and varied ethnic populations and religious practices, as well as its long history of international trade and cultural exchange.

We have sought the most experienced scholars to illuminate our understanding of the subject of Buddhist art in Myanmar and are grateful for the guidance of the exhibition curators, Sylvia Fraser-Lu and Donald M. Stadtner, for their commitment and enthusiasm for the project and the extraordinary scholarship that has resulted in this exquisite exhibition. They have been ably supported by Adriana Proser, John H. Foster Senior Curator for Traditional Asian Art, as well as by the contributors to this catalogue, and we appreciate the work of Robert L. Brown, Jacques Leider, Patrick Pranke, Catherine Raymond, Heidi Tan, U Thaw Kaung, and U Tun Aung Chain.

Thanks also are due to the many public and private lenders to this exhibition whose efforts were an important part of the realization of this project and deserve our deep appreciation (see page xiv). This exhibition would not have been possible without the support of major donors who are listed elsewhere in this catalogue (see page xiv). We would like to make special mention of John and Polly Guth for their long-standing commitment to and patronage of exhibitions of this kind—without them this important project would not have been possible.

This exhibition has benefited greatly from the commitment of Asia Society's staff. We want to recognize the leadership of Josette Sheeran, President and CEO, and Melissa Chiu, former Museum Director and Senior Vice President of Global Arts and Cultural Programs, and others on the Asia Society team who were so helpful in realizing this project, including Suzanne DiMaggio, former Vice President of Global Policy Programs, and Rachel Cooper, Director of Global Performing Arts and Special Cultural Initiatives. Particular thanks go to the museum team: Adriana Proser, John H. Foster Senior Curator for Traditional Asian Art, who worked closely with the curators to shape the exhibition and publication; Clare McGowan, Senior Registrar and Collections Manager, who coordinated the loans and transport and installation arrangements; John Gatti, Installation Manager; Leise Hook, Museum Publication Coordinator, for her work on the book and interpretive materials; Nick Pozek, Manager of Museum Digital Strategy; Nancy Blume, Head of Museum Education Programs; Donna Saunders, Executive Assistant; and Laili Paksima, former Manager of Global Museum Events and Special Initiatives. In addition to Rachel Cooper, La Frances Hui, Anne Kirkup, and Rachel Rosado also have contributed to the exhibition and catalogue in different capacities. Thanks also are due to our copublisher, Yale University Press; to Alicia Turner for her expert editorial assistance with the manuscript; to Miko McGinty and Anjali Pala for the truly beautiful book design; and to Clayton Vogel for the exceptional exhibition design. Others at Asia Society who should be thanked for their support include Tom Nagorski, Executive Vice President; Elaine Merguerian, Director of Communications and Marketing, and their team for public relations and marketing; Christine Davies, Linsey LaFrenier, and the External Affairs team for their fundraising efforts; and Dan Washburn, Megan MacMurray, Tahiat Mahboob, and Jeff Tompkins for their contributions to the website production.

We hope you will enjoy this exhibition and catalogue.

Peggy Loar
Interim Vice President for Global Arts and Culture

Marion Kocot
Museum Deputy Director

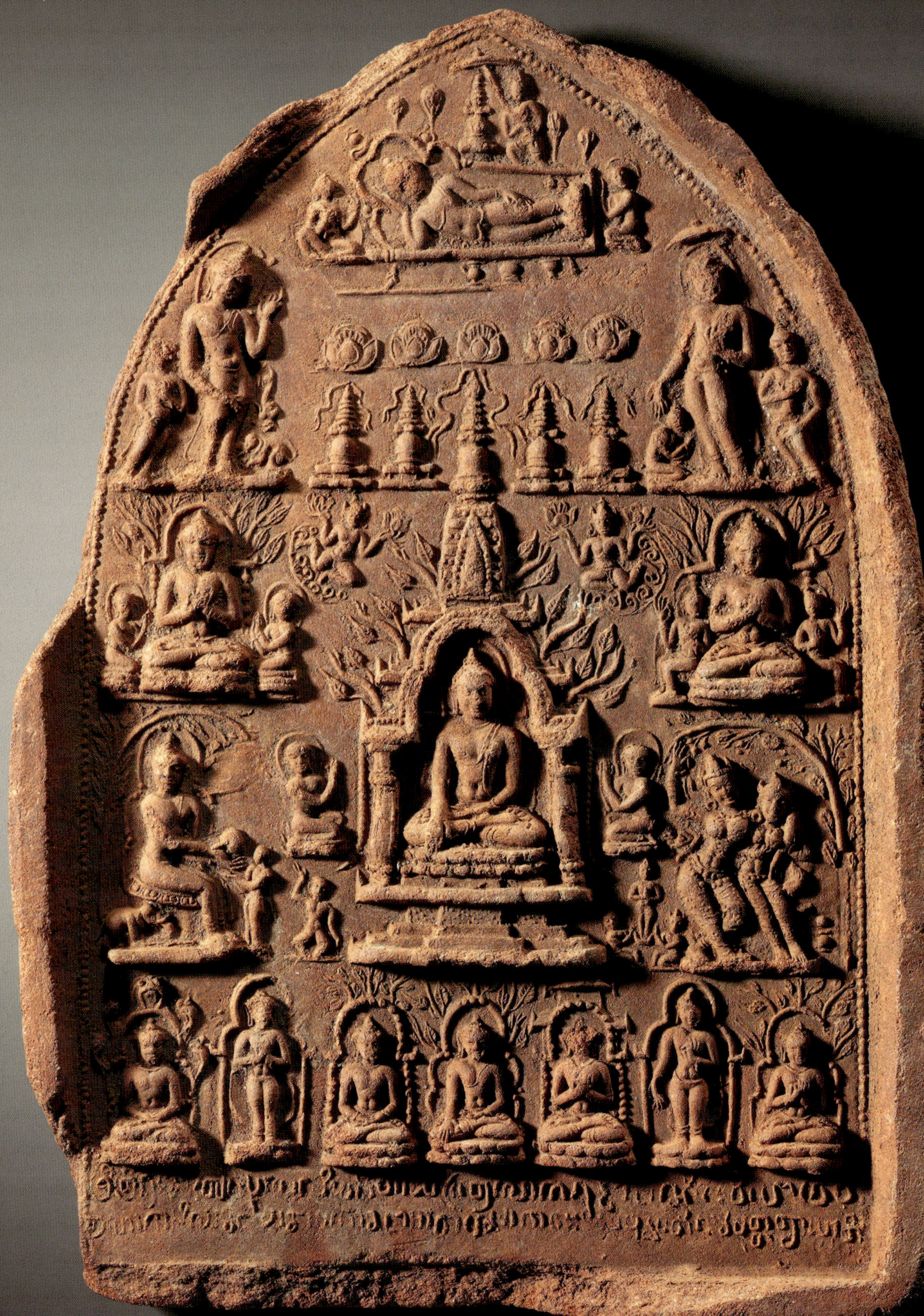

Statement: Ministry of Culture, The Republic of the Union of Myanmar

On behalf of the Ministry of Culture of the Republic of the Union of Myanmar, I wish to offer my deep appreciation and heartfelt gratitude to Josette Sheeran, President; Melissa Chiu, former Museum Director; and the trustees of Asia Society for organizing the exhibition "Buddhist Art of Myanmar," scheduled to be shown at Asia Society, New York, in February 2015. I would also like to express deep appreciation to Asia Society Museum curator Adriana Proser, cocurators Sylvia Fraser-Lu and Donald M. Stadtner, and staff members for the profound expertise and boundless energy they brought to this exhibition project.

Myanmar is rich in ancient cultural heritage as well as admirable traditional customs, which are mostly based on Buddhism. Museum collections of Myanmar include archaeological artifacts and art objects of specific localities, which are explored in "Buddhist Art of Myanmar." This exhibition will showcase the superb craftsmanship of Myanmar from successive historical periods.

We expect that the people of the United States of America will understand and pursue the value of "Buddhist Art of Myanmar" and its important role among Theravada Buddhist countries. We are also convinced that this achievement will foster the long-lasting and ever-closer friendship of America and Myanmar, will further strengthen the foundation of cultural diplomacy, and will promote people-to-people engagement.

H. E. U Aye Myint Kyu

Union Minister for Culture
The Republic of the Union of Myanmar

Curators' Acknowledgments

Early in 2013 we were approached by Asia Society to jointly create an exhibition devoted to Buddhist art from Myanmar. We were both thrilled by the prospect of a show with loans from Myanmar and dedicated to the rich artistic production of that country. Tumultuous years had led to an inward-facing Myanmar, but this isolation, decades in duration, unexpectedly ended about four years ago. A new Myanmar is now emerging and enthusiastically embracing the global community. We are delighted now to have the opportunity to help share some of Myanmar's great cultural achievements with the outside world.

Shortly after our decision to serve as cocurators for the exhibition, we joined colleagues in the field for an advisory meeting. Together we fine-tuned and expanded some of our ideas for the exhibition. We are grateful to this esteemed group, which included Robert Brown, Professor, Department of Art History, University of California, Los Angeles, and Curator, Department of South and Southeast Asian Art, Los Angeles County Museum of Art; Phyllis Granoff, Lex Hixon Professor of World Religions, Department of Religious Studies, Yale University; Patrick Pranke, Assistant Professor of Religious Studies, Department of Humanities, University of Louisville; Catherine Raymond, Director of the Center for Burma Studies, Northern Illinois University; and Kit Young, Artistic Director for the Alliance for New Music-Theatre, Washington, D.C. In addition to Melissa Chiu and Adriana Proser, the following Asia Society staff attended the meeting and contributed to the discussions: Nancy Blume, Head of Museum Education Programs; Rachel Cooper, Director of Global Performing Arts and Special Cultural Initiatives; Marion Kocot, Museum Deputy Director; La Frances Hui, Assistant Director of Cultural Programs and Film Curator; and Clare McGowan, Senior Registrar and Collections Manager.

As we refined our exhibition object list in Myanmar in the summer of 2013, we were overwhelmed by warm receptions at each of the museums and institutions we visited. We would like to thank all the staff of the Republic of the Union of Myanmar Ministry of Culture and museums, noted previously in the President's Foreword, who understood the importance of this exhibition and generously provided us with assistance.

We would also like to offer our heartfelt thanks to those who have made it possible to include some additional loans from public and private collections in the United States. These include Emily Kass, Director, Ackland Art Museum; Jay Xu, Director, and Forrest McGill, Chief Curator, Asian Art Museum, San Francisco; University of North Carolina at Chapel Hill; Catherine Raymond, Center for Burma Studies, Northern Illinois University; Sherry Harlacher, Director, Denison Museum; Christoph Heinrich, Frederick and Jan Mayer Director, and Ronald Otsuka, Dr. Joseph de Heer Curator of Asian Art, Denver Art Museum; Michael Govan, CEO and Wallis Annenberg Director, and Stephen Markel, The Harry and Yvonne Lenart Curator and Department Head of South and Southeast Asian Art, Los Angeles County Museum of Art; Thomas P. Campbell, Director, and John Guy, South Asian Curator, Metropolitan Museum of Art; Malcolm Rogers, Ann and Graham Gund Director, and Jane Portal, Matsutaro Shoriki Chair, Art of Asia, Oceania, and Africa, Museum of Fine Arts, Boston; Margaret Glover, Division of Art, Prints and Photographs, New York Public Library; Lynne M. Thomas, Curator, Rare Books and Special Collections, Northern Illinois University Rare Book Collection; Ronald L. Krannich; and the private collectors who wish to remain anonymous.

We are also very grateful to all of the catalogue authors. Numerous colleagues contributed by reviewing the essays and catalogue entries. For the two essays covering the first millennium and the Pagan period, we wish to thank Robert L. Brown, Phyllis Granoff, and Pamela Gutman. Also, we must thank Catherine Raymond and Jacques Leider for generously taking on the extra tasks of writing the entry for the Rakhine bronze Buddha from the National Museum, Nay Pyi Taw, and creating the chronology for this catalogue, respectively. Also helpful throughout the project was Forrest McGill, who shared his insights; Tilman Frasch, who made valuable suggestions for the essay covering Pagan; and Bob Hudson and Elizabeth Moore, who were always there to answer questions about the first millennium and reviewed our essay on that topic.

For the essay and entries on the post-Pagan periods, we wish to thank U Zaw Win, who helped translate materials pertaining to the exhibition, and U Thaw Kaung for assistance with the manuscripts, or *parabaiks*, in the exhibition. Patricia M. Herbert, Former Curator, Southeast Asia Collections, British Library, kindly reviewed our essay on the post-Pagan period. Christian Bauer, Humboldt University, Berlin, provided assistance with the Mon inscription on our glazed tile from Pegu. Additional thanks go to Beth Bjorneby at the Center for Burma Studies, Northern Illinois University; Marcia Selva and Ronald L. Krannich for their boundless enthusiasm and support for the project; and the late Dr. Sarah M. Bekker, whose love of Myanmar art and generous donations to many U.S. museums have increased awareness of Myanmar's rich cultural heritage in the United States.

We offer our thanks to Alicia Turner, who with grace and enthusiasm provided immensely helpful specialized editorial work on the manuscript at the eleventh hour. Sean Dungan is to be commended for his wonderful photography of loan objects in Myanmar under less than ideal conditions. We are grateful to Alex Jamison for the new photography of the loan works from private collections in the United States, and Perry Hu for generously sharing his beautiful photographs of Myanmar. We also wish to extend our thanks to Richard Cooler, Pamela Gutman, Paisarn Piemmattawat, Kay Simon, and U Win Maung for providing additional images.

At Asia Society, special thanks go to Melissa Chiu, former Museum Director and Senior Vice President for Global Arts and Cultural Programs, whose recognition of the importance of this exhibition has enabled it to become a reality; Adriana Proser, John H. Foster Senior Curator for Traditional Asian Art; Marion Kocot, Museum Deputy Director; Leise Hook, Museum Publication Coordinator; and Clare McGowan; Senior Registrar and Collections Manager.

Sylvia Fraser-Lu and Donald M. Stadtner

Funders of the Exhibition

Critical support for "Buddhist Art of Myanmar" comes from The Partridge Foundation, A John and Polly Guth Charitable Fund.

Major support has been provided by Fred Eychaner Fund and Henry Luce Foundation.

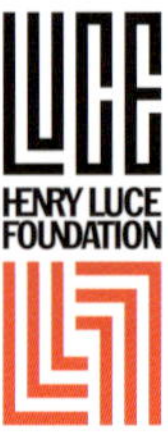

Additional support provided by E. Rhodes and Leona B. Carpenter Foundation and Lisina M. Hoch.

Support for Asia Society Museum is provided by Asia Society Contemporary Art Council, Asia Society Friends of Asian Arts, Asia Society Traditional Art Council, Arthur Ross Foundation, Sheryl and Charles R. Kaye Endowment for Contemporary Art Exhibitions, Hazen Polsky Foundation, New York State Council on the Arts, and New York City Department of Cultural Affairs.

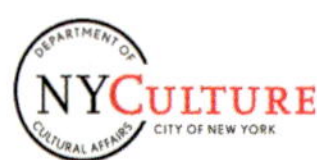

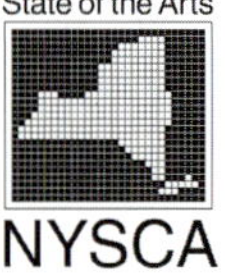

Lenders to the Exhibition

Ackland Art Museum, University of North Carolina at Chapel Hill
Asian Art Museum, San Francisco
Bagan Archaeological Museum
Center for Burma Studies at Northern Illinois University
Denison Museum
Kaba Aye Buddhist Art Museum
Ronald L. Krannich
Los Angeles County Museum of Art
The Metropolitan Museum of Art
Museum of Fine Arts, Boston
National Museum, Nay Pyi Taw
National Museum, Yangon
New York Public Library
Southeast Asia Collection, Northern Illinois University Libraries
Sri Ksetra Archaeological Museum, Hmawza

We also acknowledge with gratitude those lenders who prefer to remain anonymous.

Note to the Reader

As an aid to the reader, please note the following:

The word "Myanmar" is used throughout this book as an adjective and a noun, indicating both the country and the language. The word derives from "Mranma," which has been in use since the twelfth century or earlier. In 1989, the government formally replaced "Burma," which had been the standard English-language name for the country during the British period, with "Myanmar." Here, "Myanmar" is also used to describe the country's people. The Myanmar people have long been ethnically diverse and are made up of various ethnic groups including Bamar, Mon, Rakhine, Karen, and Shan, among others.

Myanmar names and words in this book are transcribed in the Roman alphabet. Several systems exist for transcription; this book opts for spellings that are either more commonly recognized by English readers or are closer to English phonetics, while preserving as much of the original spelling as possible. The place names used are generally the more familiar names used for most of the twentieth century (Moulmein rather than Mawlamyine), followed at the first use by the more recent, official names. Alternate spellings and place names are cross-referenced in this volume's glossary. Recent, official museum names and their official spellings are used.

Pali and Sanskrit names and words are transcribed, without diacritical marks. Full scholarly, linguistic transliterations for Pali and Sanskrit terms appear in the glossary. Thai is rendered in the Royal Thai General System of Transcription; Chinese, in the Pinyin romanization system.

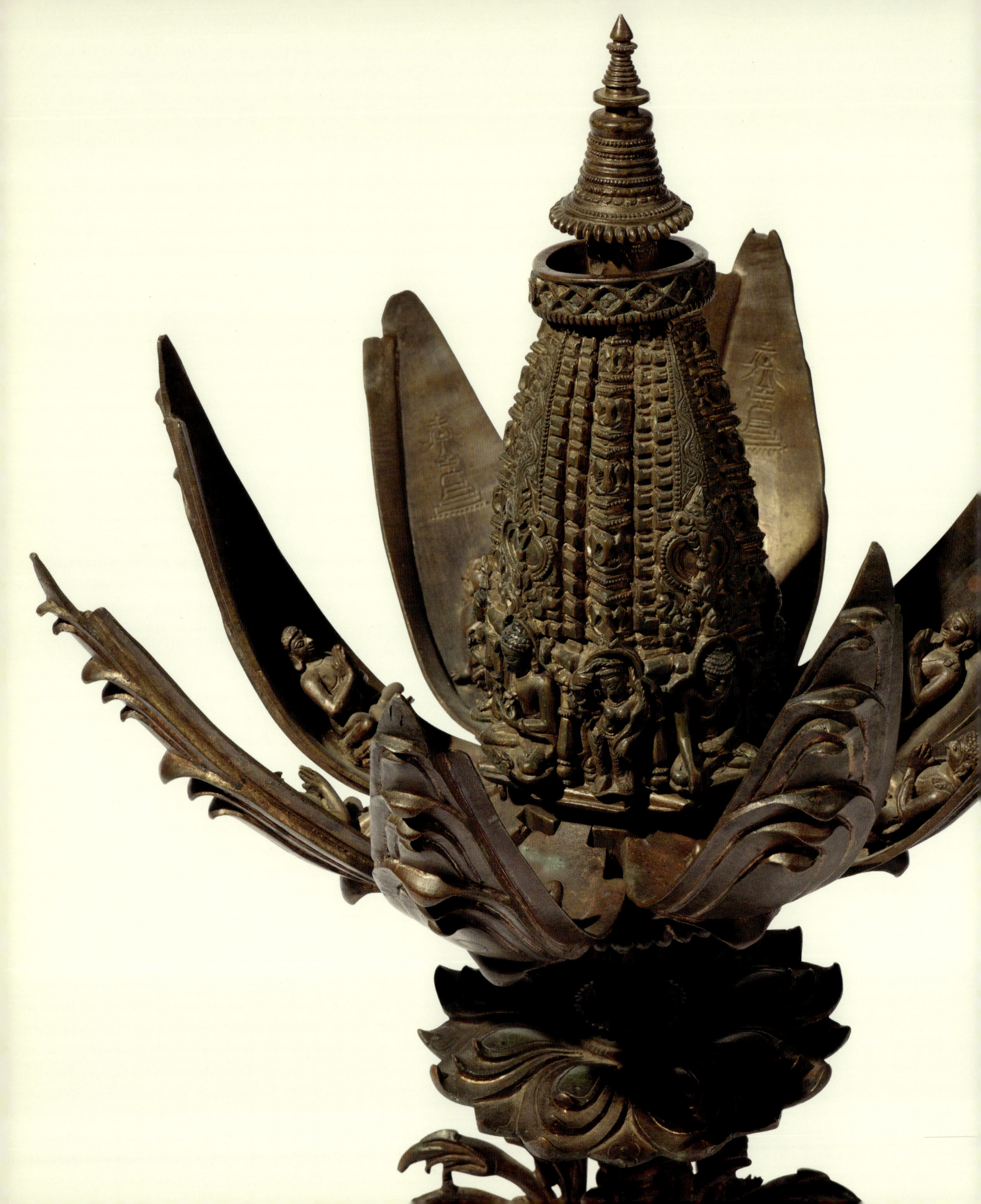

Essays

OPPOSITE Detail of cat. no. 24

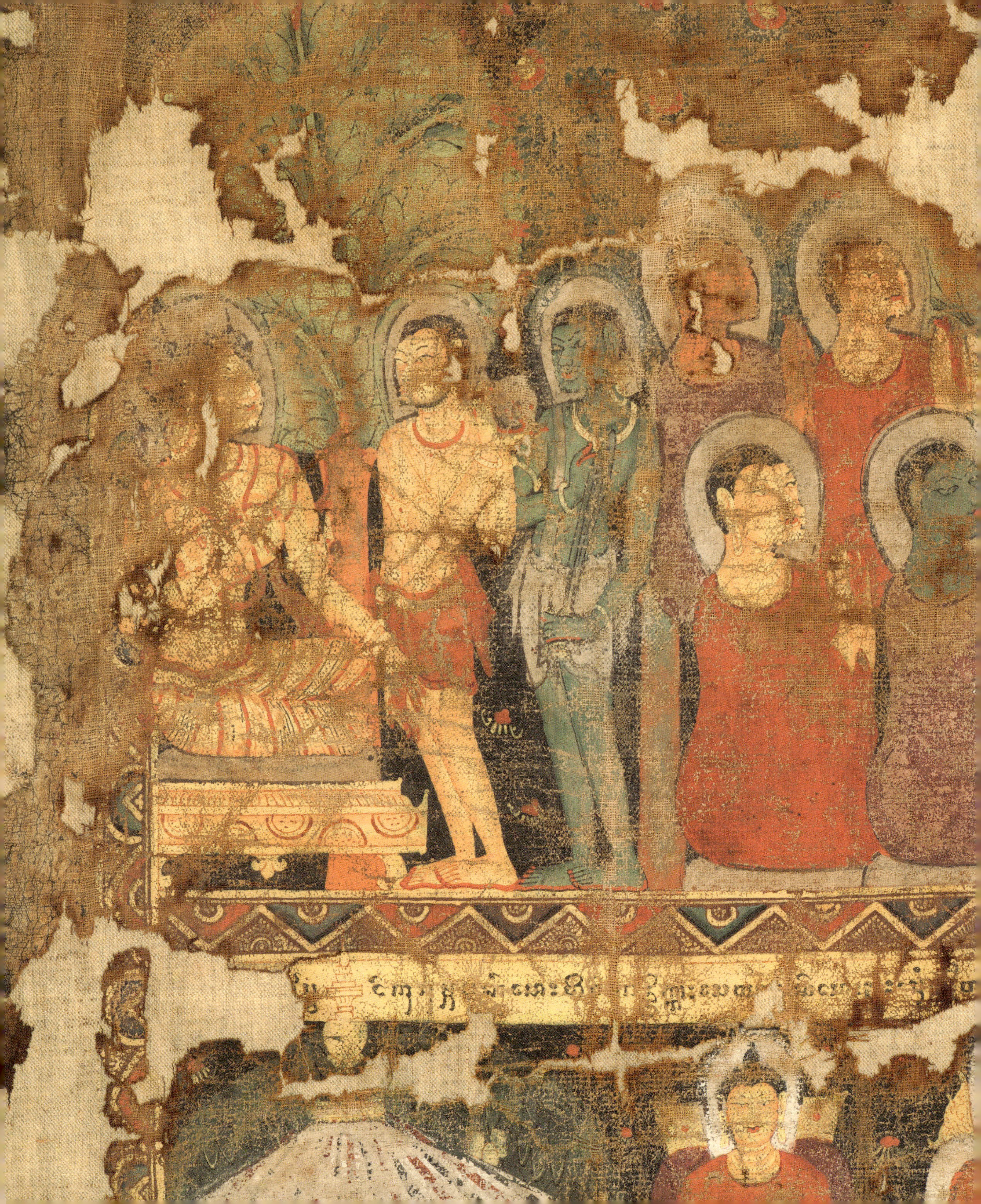

Myanmar
Forging a Nation

Sylvia Fraser-Lu and Donald M. Stadtner

Myanmar is one of the most ethnically diverse countries on earth. Today the nation is home to 135 officially recognized ethnic groups, each with its own distinctive way of life, language, and adherence to a variety of beliefs including Buddhism, Islam, Christianity, Hinduism, and animism. Our decision to present an exhibition with a focus on Myanmar's Buddhist art stemmed from its long and continuous presence in the country. Even to this day nearly ninety percent of the population are devout followers of the Theravada Buddhist faith. Adherents include the Bamar ethnic majority, the Shan, Rakhine, and Mon, who collectively comprise around eighty-five percent of the present-day population. This catalogue and exhibition provide a starting point from which to begin a deeper appreciation of Myanmar's unique Buddhist culture and to stimulate further exploration of the country's rich and extraordinary diversity.

In June 1795, a freshly captured white elephant was sent upriver to Pagan, the ancient capital since the beginning of the second millennium. Descending on the Irrawaddy River was King Bodawpaya (r. 1782–1819), who took possession of the elephant amid great pageantry on June 23. Indeed, an albino elephant in the royal stable was an indispensable symbol of kingship in Buddhist Southeast Asia (fig. 1). Nearly a thousand years earlier, another white elephant had participated in the consecration of a king's palace at Pagan, or Bagan.[1] Today, white elephants on public view in Yangon and the new capital, Naypyidaw, are tethered not by kings but by the Myanmar government. However, such symbolism, extending over a millennium, is a reminder that the past inescapably envelops the present in Myanmar and that the secular and Buddhist worlds blend effortlessly.

A BRIEF HISTORY

The Myanmar-speaking people of today are descendants of those who came down onto the plains of Upper Myanmar toward the close of the first millennium CE, probably from Yunnan, China. The Myanmar were therefore originally outsiders to the region in much the same way that the Thai immigrated to Thailand by the thirteenth century from southern China. These newcomers, in both Myanmar and Thailand, gained ascendency over earlier inhabitants whose diverse regional and ethnic traditions were forged together over centuries into a modern nation. This is not to say that Myanmar was born from a single cloth. The country is in fact more like a quilt, patched together in comparatively recent times from pieces still retaining much of their original character. To appreciate the interaction of diverse peoples one has only to think of the European settlement of the New World.

OPPOSITE Detail of cat. no. 25

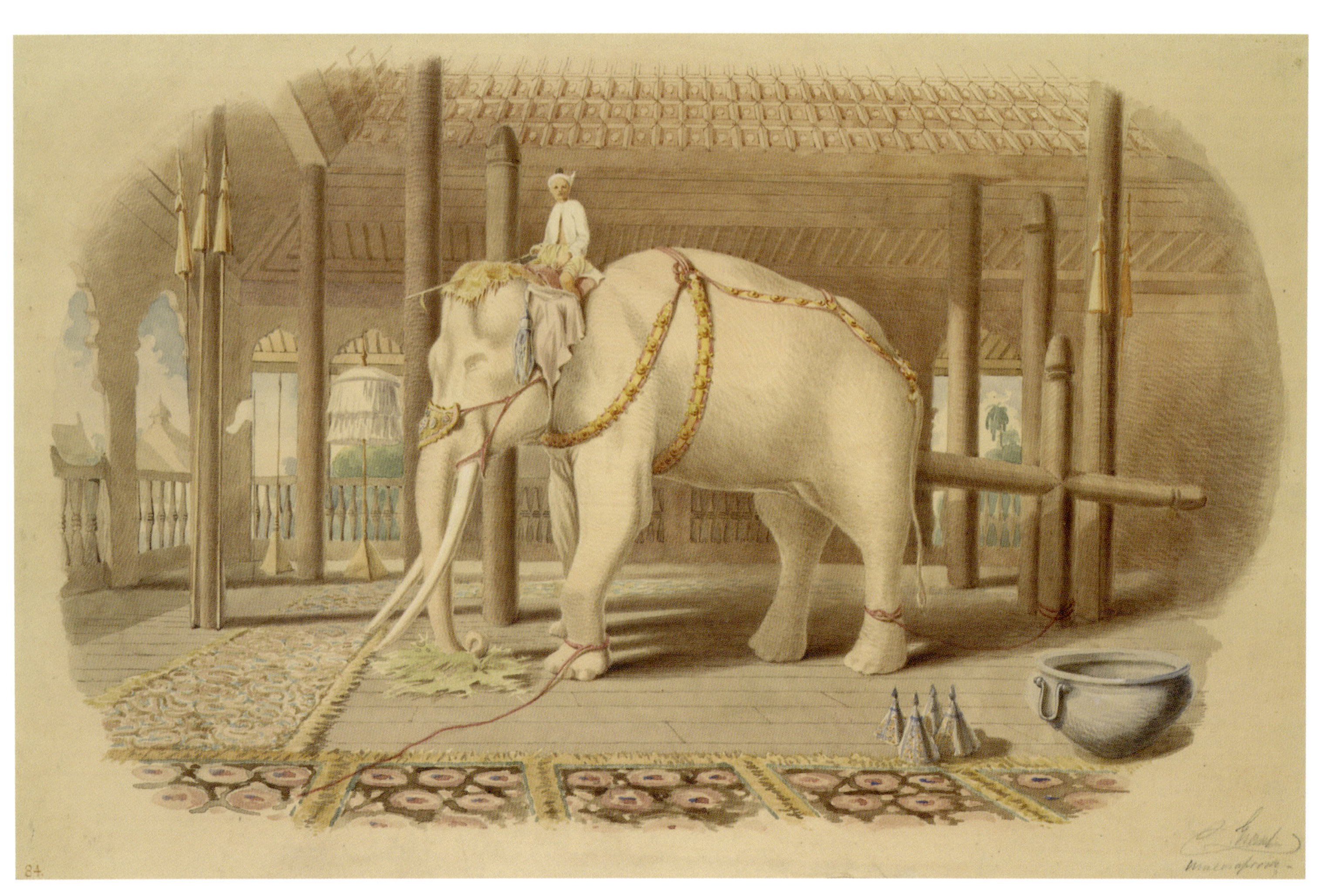

FIG. 1. The royal white elephant at Amarapura, Upper Myanmar. 1855. Watercolor, with pen and ink. By Colesworthy Grant (1813–1880). British Library

Myanmar participated in the remarkable rise of civilization that swept the entire mainland of Southeast Asia in the first millennium, seeded by influences mainly from India. Within the country's present-day borders, three major regional centers emerged at approximately the same time, each flourishing after the middle of the first millennium. All three regions put up huge brick-walled cities, and each minted distinct coin series, underscoring the independent nature of these polities.

Of these three regional groups, the Pyu people, who inhabited Upper Myanmar from the middle to nearly the end of the first millennium, have left the most artifacts and so have furnished the majority of the earliest objects included in this exhibition and its catalogue. Lower Myanmar was in the hands of the Mon throughout the first millennium, and its remains are far fewer but of equal quality. Western Myanmar, or Rakhine state, enjoyed no less rich a history. Northeastern Myanmar has never been properly investigated, but by the fourteenth century Shan speakers descended into this region from Yunnan. The vast hill tracts surrounding Myanmar's modern borders have probably been inhabited by numerous smaller ethnic groups since the first millennium, as they are today.

Buddhism and Hinduism arrived in Myanmar from India in the first millennium, together with various Indian scripts that were soon adapted for the indigenous Pyu and Mon languages. These influences most probably were transmitted not through conquest or colonization but by Indian traders and priests; Sri Lanka also likely played a role, as a fountainhead of Theravada Buddhism. Each of the regions of Myanmar, however, developed a distinctive flavor of Buddhism.

The Pyu were largely eclipsed toward the close of the first millennium, if not earlier, but reasons for their decline are uncertain. The Mon continued to flourish in Lower Myanmar, and their culture contributed to the formation of Pagan, whose roots took hold by the eleventh century. Pagan has been called the country's first capital, since Myanmar-speaking people controlled much of what encompasses the country today; Pagan's "classic age" spanned the eleventh, twelfth, and thirteenth centuries. Although Rakhine was never subject to Pagan's political orbit, it experienced no less of an awakening by the middle of the second millennium.

Pagan was replaced as the capital in the fourteenth century by Ava, or Inwa, near modern Mandalay. The Mon continued to rule in Lower Myanmar, with their center in Pegu, or Bago, but by the sixteenth century the Mon succumbed to Myanmar forces from the north. In Rakhine a separate dynasty arose in the fifteenth century, with Mrauk-U as its capital. Shan speakers inhabited northeastern Myanmar and formed numerous small kingdoms, most of which became subject to Myanmar control over the centuries.

A collective sense of Myanmar, as we know it now, took many centuries to build, beginning in earnest in the Konbaung Period (1752–1885) and accelerating greatly in the English colonial period, which was marked by three wars in the course of the nineteenth century. However, it was not until the fall of Mandalay in 1885 that the entire country fell to British rule, and it was annexed in the following year. During the colonial era, Chinese and Indian immigration was encouraged, and these communities now form significant minorities, especially in urban populations. The Indians were largely Hindus, Muslims, and Christians. Religious, regional, and ethnic conflicts have continued to come to the fore since independence in 1948, but conflicts are now framed within the context of a modern state.

BEGINNINGS OF MODERN ARCHAEOLOGY IN MYANMAR

Archaeology in Myanmar owes its origins to an official visit to the province in 1901 by Lord Curzon (1859–1925), Viceroy of India. Noted for his support of the Archaeological Survey of India, and possessing a personal interest in historic preservation, Curzon was appalled at the sorry state of the Mandalay Palace following the annexation of Myanmar in 1886. He promptly issued detailed orders for the maintenance, custody, and restoration of a number of the most important buildings and decreed that the British Upper Burma Club and Christian churches located within the palace area were to find new premises (fig. 2).[2] The Archaeological Survey of Burma, founded in 1902, was administered by the Archaeological Survey of India, whose annual publications included reports that covered Myanmar. The initial interest focused on epigraphy. As primary sources providing key information on Myanmar's history, a large number of inscriptions urgently needed to be read, catalogued, and preserved in a safe environment.[3] Looting of sites was also a problem—one that continues to this day and compounds the difficulties of provenance and dating for many Myanmar art objects.

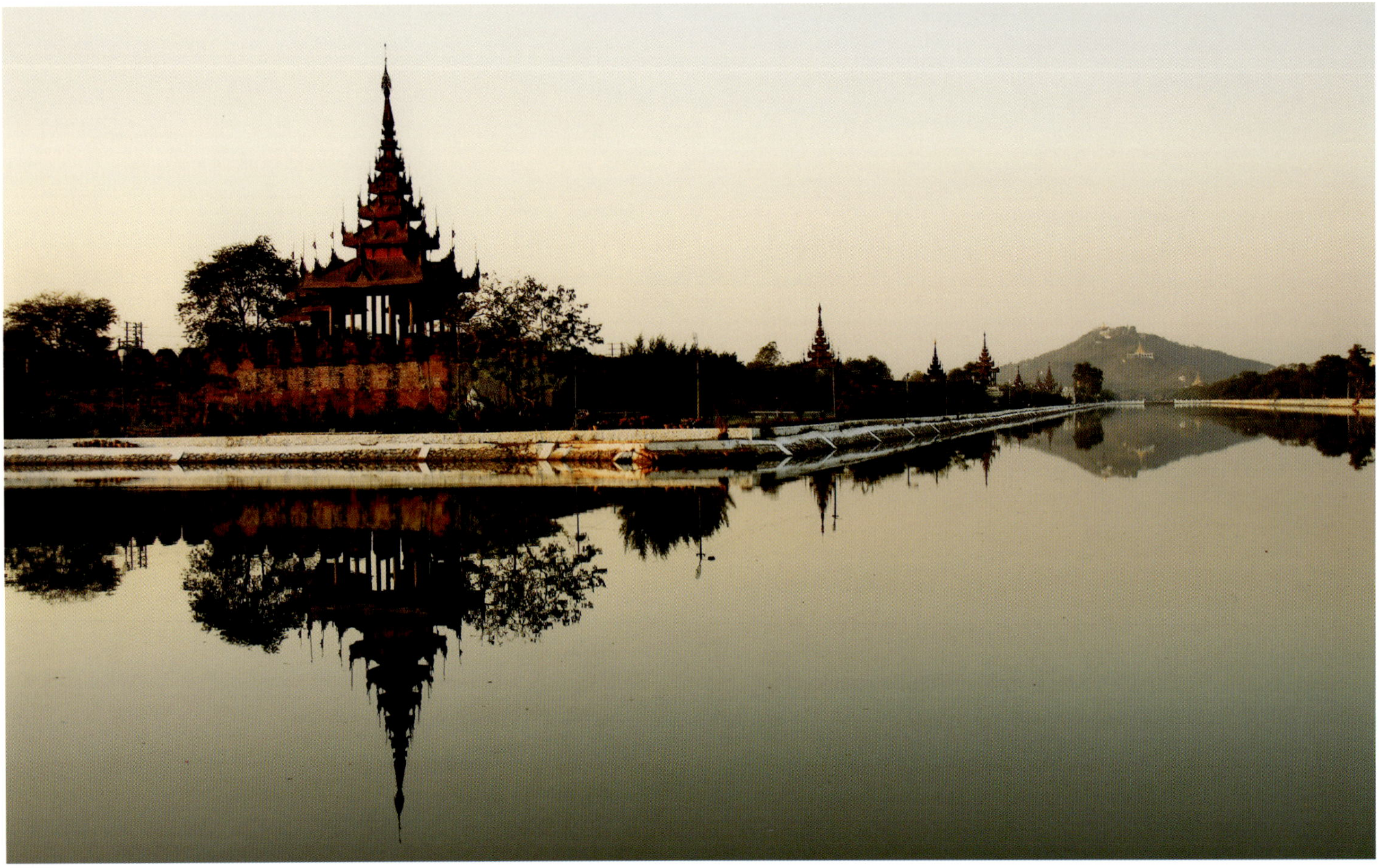

FIG. 2. The wall and moat encompassing the Mandalay Palace, founded in the 1850s. Photo: Paisarn Piemmattawat, River Books, Bangkok

The first director of the survey was Emil Forchammer (1851–1890), a Pali scholar and epigraphist who earlier had written on Myanmar law and the antiquities of the Rakhine state. He was succeeded by Taw Sein Ko (1864–1930), a civil servant of Sino-Bamar descent, who during a distinguished career often served as an interlocutor between the people of Myanmar and those of the colonial administration. Earlier, in 1893, as Assistant Secretary of Burma, he had toured the Mon areas and on his return advocated the preservation of the Mon artifacts in museums such as the Phayre Museum in Rangoon (fig. 3).[4] As Director of Archaeology, Taw Sein Ko also opened Myanmar's first archaeological museum in a small building adjacent to Pagan's Ananda Temple in 1904 to display stone inscriptions and sculpture. He was succeeded as director by Charles Duroiselle (1871–1951), a noted Pali scholar and epigrapher, who also published monographs on

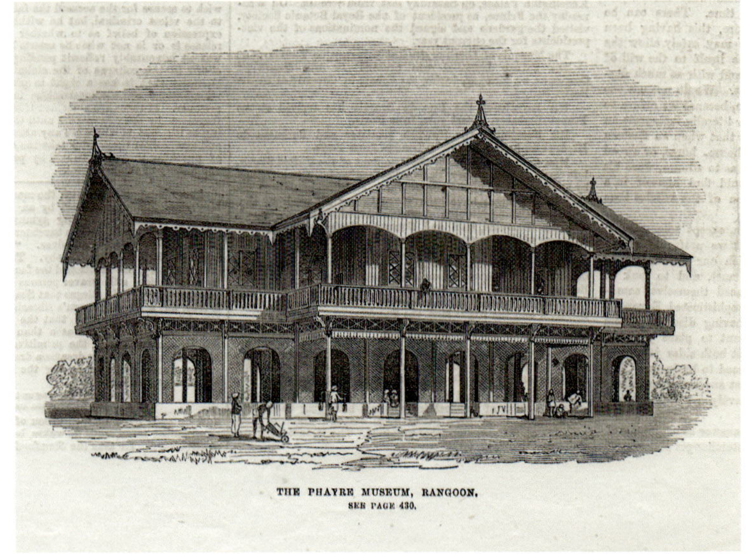

FIG. 3. Phayre Museum, Yangon, from the *Illustrated London News*, 1872

the Mandalay Palace and *jataka* tiles at the Hpetleik Stupas among other subjects.[5] Lu Pe Win (1919–1958), Duroiselle's successor in 1940, occupied the position for the remainder of the colonial period.

THE BURMA RESEARCH SOCIETY

On March 29, 1910, a quartet of talented individuals, all of whom were to make outstanding contributions, founded the Burma Research Society. Gordon H. Luce (1889–1979), a former member of the Bloomsbury group, served as lecturer in English literature at Government College, Rangoon. He devoted the remainder of his life to a study of Myanmar's history and languages, and to the history of Pagan.[6] Pe Maung Tin (1888–1973) was a Pali scholar who, with Luce, translated a key Myanmar text, *The Glass Palace Chronicle*. J. S. Furnivall (1878–1960) later became famous for his writings on colonial policies, while J. A. Stewart (1882–1948) became a Myanmar language expert and also compiled a Myanmar-English dictionary. He later became Professor of Myanmar language at London University and one of the founders of its Department of Southeast Asian Studies at the School of Oriental and African Studies (SOAS).[7]

The Burma Research Society provided a forum for the "investigation of literature and the encouragement of art, science, and literature in relation to Burma and neighboring countries." It held regular meetings where, uniquely in its day, local Myanmar people and foreigners met as equals. Academic papers on a wide variety of topics were presented and published in the *Journal of the Burma Research Society*.[8] Apart from during the period of Japanese occupation, the journal was published regularly from 1911 until 1977, when it was abruptly shuttered by Myanmar's president, Ne Win.[9]

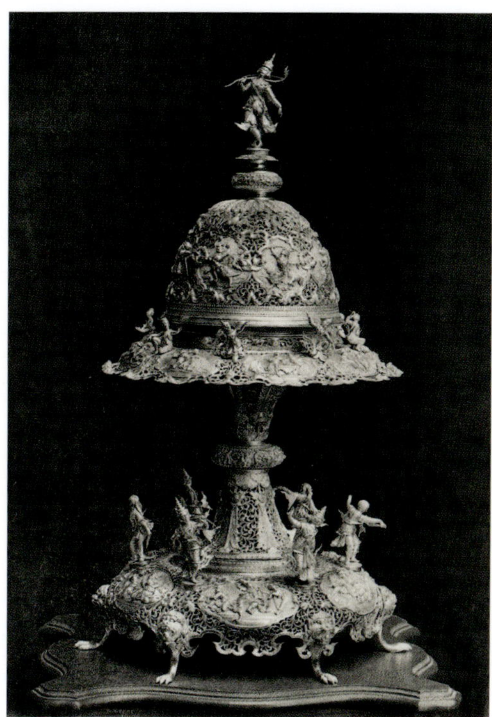

FIG. 4. An elaborate centerpiece for an administrator's table made by Maung Yin Maung, who was awarded a gold medal for his work at the British Exhibition at Delhi in 1903–4. (Tilly and Klier, *Wood-Carving of Burma*, pl. IV.)

THE BIRTH OF COLLECTING MYANMAR ART IN THE WEST

Colonial policies did little to encourage the continuation of small-scale "native manufacturing," which had previously supplied the entire population with basic necessities such as cloth, ceramics, and tools. Myanmar's crafts were often criticized by so-called visiting experts for their "lack of finish" compared with Chinese and Japanese work. Myanmar artistic forms were on occasion even considered "barbaric" and designs "finicky." An earnest desire to improve native handicrafts led to exhibitions of arts and industries held regularly throughout India and also in Rangoon, or Yangon. Despite the perceived shortcomings, Myanmar lacquer artisans, woodcarvers, and silversmiths received many prizes (fig. 4). At imperial and international expositions held during the late nineteenth and early twentieth centuries, beautifully carved Myanmar wooden pavilions brimming with a wealth of products and attractive crafts were always a favorite with visitors.[10]

Among the most outstanding objects in the Victoria and Albert Museum's collection of Myanmar art are purchases from the Colonial and Indian Exhibition of 1886, a popular event in London that showcased the glories of empire and introduced Myanmar, the empire's newest possession, to the British public.[11] Not surprisingly, over the years the British Library, the British Museum, and many provincial museums in the United Kingdom have amassed good collections of Myanmar art, much of it donated by former colonial administrators and their heirs.[12] Prior to World War I, a number of German specialists worked for the colonial administration in Myanmar and as a result a few German ethnographic museums also have impressive collections of Myanmar art.[13] In the United States, initial interest in Myanmar came largely through missionary endeavors. The Myanmar art collection at Denison University, Granville, Ohio, was begun in the 1960s with donations of ethnic costumes and other artifacts from former missionary families in the U.S. Midwest.[14] The other notable Myanmar art collection in the United States is that of the Burma Studies Foundation at Northern Illinois University, De Kalb. Established in the mid-1980s with a donation of Myanmar Buddhist art from Konrad and Sarah Bekker, the collection today consists of a wide range of secular and sacred objects.[15]

INDEPENDENCE AND BEYOND

Upon Myanmar's independence in 1948, the new leaders who felt that their way of life had been eclipsed by an alien regime wasted no time in reasserting the primacy of Myanmar and Buddhist culture. In addition to encouraging the wearing of national dress, Myanmar was made the national language, and the newly established Sarpay Beikman (Burma Translation Society) set about translating western writings on technological and scientific subjects into Myanmar language; this culminated more than twenty years later in the publication of a fifteen-volume *Encyclopaedia Birmanica* in Myanmar, paradoxically issued with a Latin title. The Ministry of Union Culture, formed in April 1952, established the Cultural Institute in Jubilee Hall and gave it the responsibility of developing and maintaining the National Library (the former Bernard Free Library), the National Museum, the National Gallery of Art, and State School for Fine Arts and Music, Drama and Dancing. At various times since independence, the Ministry of Culture has undergone reorganization according to changing government directives.

During the Ne Win era (1962 until the mid-1980s), Myanmar was virtually cut off from the outside world. By contrast, neighboring, newly independent nations, anxious to join the international community, proudly held exhibitions and promoted cultural exchange to make their art and commercial products better known. Sadly, during this period Myanmar art came to be known largely through examples smuggled out of the country for sale and a burgeoning reproduction industry, which flooded the art market with replicas.

Despite a lack of funding and trained personnel, the Department of Archaeology has performed surveys and excavations throughout the country since independence. Since 1970, priority has been given to conservation and restoration, especially following the Pagan earthquake in 1975 where damage was repaired under UNESCO guidance. Since the 1990s the government has ordered the Department of Archaeology to reconstruct former palaces and to refurbish many monuments at Pagan—a policy that has created much consternation and controversy both locally and abroad. Large new museums have been opened at Yangon (1996) and Pagan (1998), to display a wide range of objects, and a school of archaeology was founded in 1995.

Recent changes in Myanmar may, it is hoped, herald the dawn of a new era where through open communication, cultural exchange, and further joint research projects the world may once again come to appreciate the achievements and the distinctive cultural identity found in the Buddhist art of Myanmar that inspired this exhibition and catalogue.

NOTES

1 Blagden, "Mon Inscriptions Nos. IX–XI," 51.

2 The Minute by Lord Curzon, the Viceroy, on the preservation of the palace at Mandalay has been included as Postscript I, in O'Connor, *Mandalay and Other Cities of the Past in Burma*, 417–21. For Lord Curzon's views on imperial heritage building, see Keck, "'It Has Passed Forever into Our Hands,'" 49–83.

3 Aung-Thwin, "Burma before Pagan," 1–2.

4 For two excellent articles on Taw Sein Ko, see Edwards, "Relocating the Interlocutor," and Keck, "Recovering a Lost Genealogy."

5 Duroiselle's notable publications as Superintendent of the Archaeological Survey, Burma Circle, include "The Talaing Plaques on the Ananda Texts and Plates," *A List of Inscriptions Found in Burma*, "Note on the Pictorial Representation of Jatakas in Burma," "Stone Sculptures in the Ananda Temple at Pagan," *A Guide to the Mandalay Palace*, "Pageant of King Mindon Leaving His Palace on a Visit to the Kyauktawgyi Buddha Image at Mandalay," and *A Practical Grammar of the Pali Language*.

6 Besides numerous articles in the *Journal of the Burma Research Society*, Luce's seminal publications include the three-volume *Old Burma—Early Pagan* and the two-volume *Phases of Pre-Pagan Burma*.

7 Furnivall's publications include *Introduction to the Political Economy of Burma*, *Fashioning of Leviathan*, *Colonial Policy and Practice*, and *Government of Modern Burma*.

8 Examples of art-related articles published in the *Journal of the Burma Research Society* include Luce, "Greater Temples of Pagan" and "Smaller Temples of Pagan"; both reprinted in Burma Research Society, *Fiftieth Anniversary Publications* 2: 169–90. Also, Morris, "Lacquerware Industry of Burma" and "Pottery in Burma."

9 Like most organizations in Myanmar, the Burma Research Society became subject to government regulation in 1962 following the military takeover. Student protests following the coup d'état led to reprisals and resulted in the Student Union Building (the site of many protests in colonial times) being dynamited by the military. Although the Burma Research Society continued publishing intermittently and held a very successful Seventieth Anniversary conference in 1980, the society and its facilities were closed by the government later that year.

10 For views on the economic, cultural, and social forces that contributed to the image of Britain and its empire, see Hoffenberg, *Empire on Display*.

11 Franklin, Singer, and Swallow ("Burmese Kalagas," 57–58) note that some of the wall hangings in their collection were purchased from the 1886 exhibition.

12 Blackburn (*Report on the Locations of Burmese Artifacts in Museums*) lists museums holding Burmese artifacts.

13 Two Germans became notorious for sending Pagan artifacts to Germany. One was Fritz Noetling, a German geologist employed by the British authorities as superintendent of the Geological Survey of India, who from 1881 onward sent objects from Pagan and elsewhere to the Berlin Museum of Ethnology and the Hamburg Museum of Ethnology. The other, Theodor Heinrich Thomann, a professional treasure hunter, ended up being expelled from Myanmar for chiseling off paintings from the Wetkyi-in Kubyaukgyi Temple in Pagan. He also wrote a book on Pagan entitled *Pagan, Ein Jahrtausend buddhistischer Tempelkunst*, published in 1923. For an account of Germans in Myanmar see Zollner, "Germans in Burma 1837–1945."

14 For details of the Myanmar art collection at Denison University, see Green, *Eclectic Collecting*.

15 For the Center for Burma Studies collection at Northern Illinois University at De Kalb, see www.grad.niu.edu/burma/collections/index.shtml.

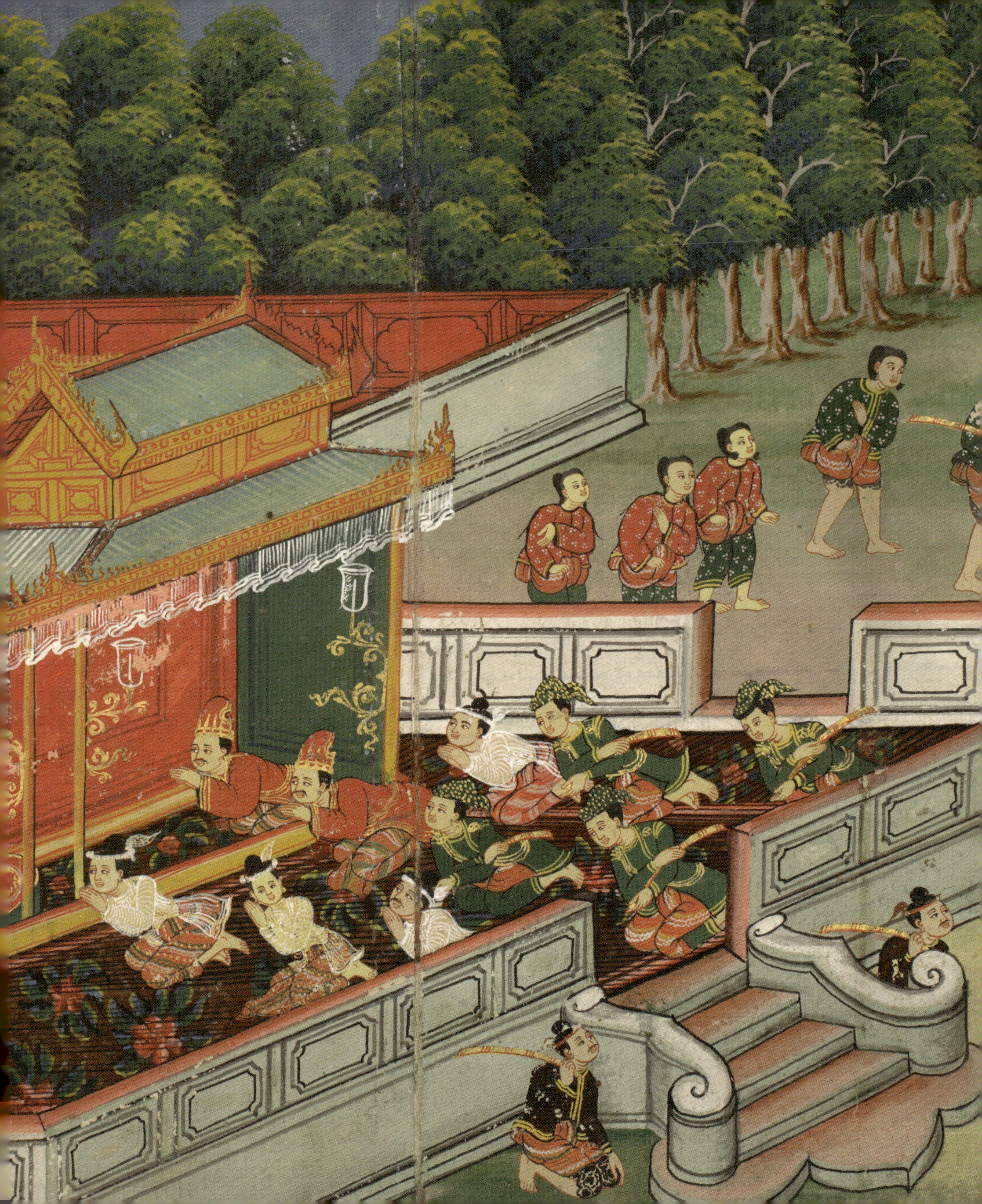

Foundation Myths of Myanmar

Patrick Pranke and Donald M. Stadtner

Despite a bewildering diversity of myths in Myanmar, only a handful of core legends have shaped the nation's identity. These key myths were confined to separate regions centuries ago but coalesced into an overarching national vision during the last several hundred years, in step with the country's political and cultural integration.

The major myths first appeared in the fifteenth and sixteenth centuries; most are based on narratives drawn from the Pali canon, its commentarial literature, and the Pali chronicles of Sri Lanka. Other foundation stories have Sanskrit antecedents, while still others are of uncertain origin. These myths, taken together, underpin the most sacred sites in Myanmar today, namely, the Shwedagon Pagoda in Yangon, the Kyaikhtiyo Golden Rock Pagoda in Lower Myanmar, the Shwesettaw Golden Footprint Pagoda in Upper Myanmar, and the Mahamuni Buddha image, which connects the myths of Rakhine and Upper Myanmar.

In addition, there was a mythic claim that dynastic lines in Myanmar descended from the family of the Buddha, or the Sakya clan in India, and this linked the regions together. This theme developed during the Konbaung period (1752–1885) and stemmed from Pali literature in which the Sakyas were nearly decimated by a neighboring kingdom.[1] A Sakyan king, fleeing from the carnage, was identified by later Myanmar chroniclers as the king who established the nation's first capital at Tagaung, a walled city north of Mandalay. The king's name was Abhiraja but he is unknown in classical Pali sources. Tagaung became linked to all subsequent capitals of Myanmar, such as Pagan, or Bagan; Ava, or Inwa; and even nineteenth-century Mandalay.

THE EARLIEST FOUNDATION MYTH

The earliest recorded myth in Myanmar is from Pagan and is known from stone inscriptions belonging to the reign of King Kyanzittha (ca. 1084–ca. 1112). The Buddha himself prophesied that at the time of his death a sage named "Bisnu" would establish the city named Sri Ksetra and that 1,630 years after that, in a future existence, he would be reborn as none other than Kyanzittha, the king of Pagan.[2] The father of Kyanzittha belonged to the solar dynasty, a royal patrimony borrowed from Indian mythology, and his mother perhaps descended from the fruit of a wood apple tree (*Aegle marmelos*).[3] This early myth underscored the importance of attaching a kingdom's foundation to a much wider Buddhist world, a leitmotif in all the country's later traditions. In this inscription the Buddha uttered his prophesy in India, but in most later foundation myths the Buddha himself traveled to Myanmar and usually converted the king and the local inhabitants and bestowed tokens of himself for worship, such as hair relics.

OPPOSITE Detail of cat. no. 59

FOUNDATION MYTH OF THE BAMAR KINGDOM OF AVA

The key foundation myth of the Bamar in Upper Myanmar is first attested in a royal chronicle, the *Yazawin-gyaw* (Celebrated Chronicle), composed at Ava in 1520.[4] The myth is drawn from a Pali commentary on a canonical text, the *Punnovada Sutta*. The Pali narrative takes place in western India in a region named Sunaparanta, which included the Nammada River, or the modern Narmada; these same locations were transposed to Myanmar in the Bamar version. For example, Upper Myanmar was identified as Sunaparanta, and the Nammada was taken to be the Mann River, a tributary of the Irrawaddy River. The myth is presented in an abbreviated fashion in the *Yazawin-gyaw* but is found in an evolved form in the early-nineteenth-century *Glass Palace Chronicle*, presented below.

Two related episodes form the myth, each giving rise to separate sacred sites not far from each other. The first site is the Sandalwood Monastery, which is now commemorated by a stone stupa in the village of Legaing, a mile or two from the west bank of the Irrawaddy, between Pagan and Prome, or Pyay. The second is the Shwesettaw, literally "Golden Footprint," honoring two footprints incised in the natural stone, one in an outcropping protruding into the river and the other on top of a rocky crag overlooking the river. The Shwesettaw, about twenty miles west of Legaing, is a major pilgrim destination, attracting more than twenty-five thousand people to its annual festival.

The legend opens with two disciples of the Buddha named Mahapunna, an *arahant*, and Culapunna, who invite the Buddha to visit their country of Sunaparanta in order to receive a gift of a sandalwood monastery being built for him there. After receiving the gift of the monastery and converting the local population, the Buddha began his return journey to India. On the way he stopped on the bank of the Mann River and impressed on a stone a footprint for a snake-king, or *naga-raja* (Sanskrit/Pali) (fig. 5). A second footprint was impressed on top of a nearby hill for a newly converted disciple named Saccabandha. These footprints, like all relics, are worshiped as representations of the Buddha.

When exactly the Shwesettaw and the Sandalwood Monastery were established as sacred sites is unknown, but they were likely in existence at the time of the early-sixteenth-century *Yazawin-gyaw*. In later Myanmar chronicles, the footprints became lost as a result of the vicissitudes of war and were only rediscovered by a pious ruler, King Thalun (r. 1629–1648).

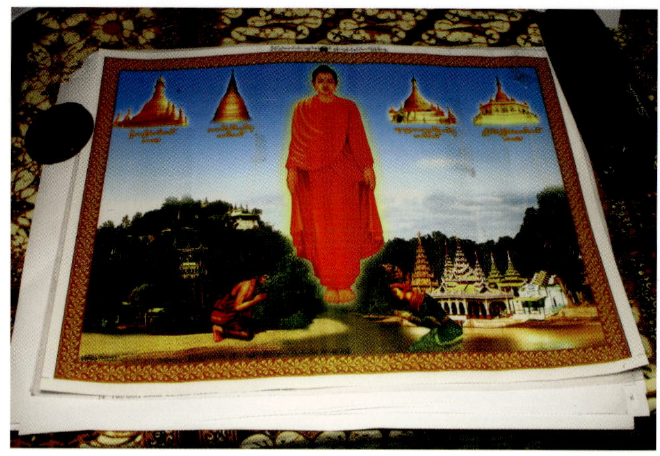

FIG. 5. The Buddha bestows a footprint for a snake-king, right, and a disciple. Modern laminated poster

Yazawin-gyaw also contains a brief reference to Sri Ksetra. However, much later, by the eighteenth century, the same Sri Ksetra was directly tied to the Buddha's visit to Upper Myanmar. After establishing the two footprints and before returning to India, the eighteenth-century myth relates that the Buddha continued south to the Prome area and prophesied the founding of Sri Ksetra and its first king, Duttabaung. The prophesy was issued from a hill top, known as Hpo-u, on the west bank of the Irrawaddy near Prome.[5]

THE MON KINGDOM OF PEGU

The earliest extant Mon foundation legends are known from a dozen or so stone inscriptions erected during the reign of King Dhammazedi (r. 1472–1492) or perhaps slightly earlier.[6] Three important legends emerge from these inscriptions. One centers on a disciple of the Buddha named Gavampati, an *arahant*, who in a previous life was a native of Lower Myanmar, which is called Suvannabhumi, or the Golden Land, in the inscriptions—a legendary region drawn from Pali literature. The basic inspiration for Gavampati is traceable to a Sanskrit Buddhist text widely known throughout South and Southeast Asia, the *Mahakarmavibhanga*.[7]

According to this myth, the first king of Suvannabhumi was Gavampati's kinsman in his previous life. Gavampati persuaded the Buddha, with a retinue of 20,000 saints, to

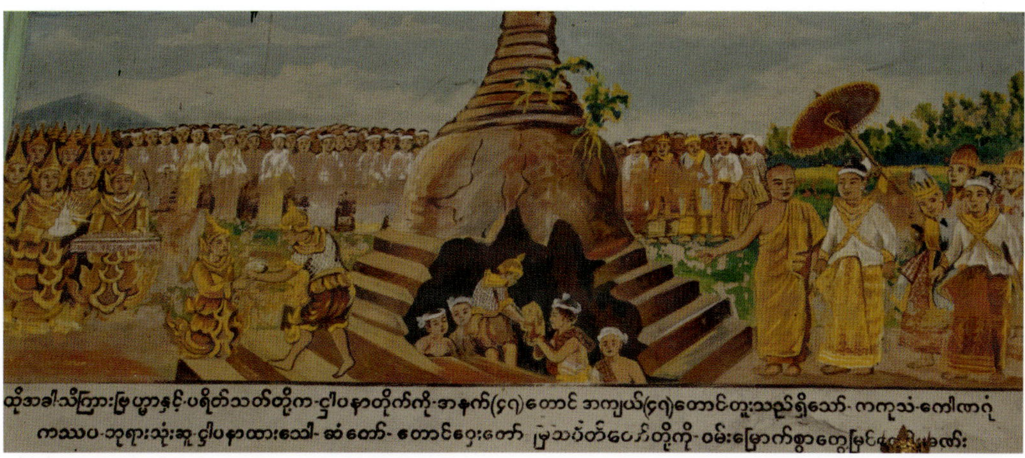

FIG. 6. The King of Thaton directing the interment of relics in a once lost, derelict stupa, a recurring theme in early Mon myths. Modern mural. Shwesayan Pagoda, Thaton

visit the king's capital, Thaton, and to preach to the king and the inhabitants. At this time, the Buddha promised the king the tooth relic that Gavampati would collect from the Buddha's funeral pyre in India. This relic then multiplied to create a total of thirty-three tooth relics. The king enshrined each in a separate stone stupa in his capital, Thaton (fig. 6). The episode of removing a tooth from the Buddha's funeral pyre is almost certainly modeled on the lore surrounding the tooth relic in Kandy, Sri Lanka.

During the same visit to Thaton, the Buddha presented six hair relics to six hermits, according to the fifteenth-century inscriptions. Each hermit returned from Thaton to his individual hermitage and erected a stone stupa over his relic. Only one of these locations can be positively identified, a restored stupa on top of Mount Kelasa, north of Thaton. Later, by the sixteenth century, this core legend associated with hair relics became attached to the Golden Rock Pagoda at Kyaikhtiyo.

Both the tooth-relic and hair-relic narratives recorded in the Mon inscriptions conclude with a description of Buddhism's decline in Suvannabhumi following the death of the Thaton king. The same Mon inscriptions then skip 236 years after the Buddha's death to the age of the Third Buddhist Council at the time of India's Emperor Ashoka. Two missionary monks, named Sona and Uttara, were dispatched at the conclusion of the council from India to Suvannabhumi to convert the local inhabitants. During their sojourn there, they discovered the lost stupas and restored them, with the local king. The missionary activity of these two monks is celebrated in the early Sri Lankan historical chronicles, the *Dipavamsa* and *Mahavamsa*, and the Mon legend of their visit is based upon these Pali sources. The hair-relic stupas were restored in their original locations by Sona and Uttara, but the thirty-three tooth relics were removed from the derelict stupas and dispersed by the two monks throughout the realm. The only monument that can be associated with this dispersal is the Shwemawdaw Stupa, in Pegu, or Bago.[8]

The third fifteenth-century Mon myth was the most significant because it underpinned the Shwedagon Pagoda, which is believed to enshrine eight hair relics given by the Buddha as gifts to two brothers named Tapussa and Bhallika (fig. 7). The myth is recorded on three stone panels dating to the last quarter of the fifteenth century. Each stone is incised in a separate language: Mon, Myanmar, and Pali. The panels were removed from their original location on the eastern slope of the hill on which the Shwedagon sits and are now on the pagoda's platform.

The legend's roots stem from one brief episode in the Pali canon in which the two brothers presented the Buddha with food offerings but received nothing from the Buddha. However, later Pali commentaries from the fifth and sixth centuries expanded upon this narrative by claiming that Tapussa and Bhallika obtained eight hair relics from the Buddha. In these early Pali sources, the brothers are said to

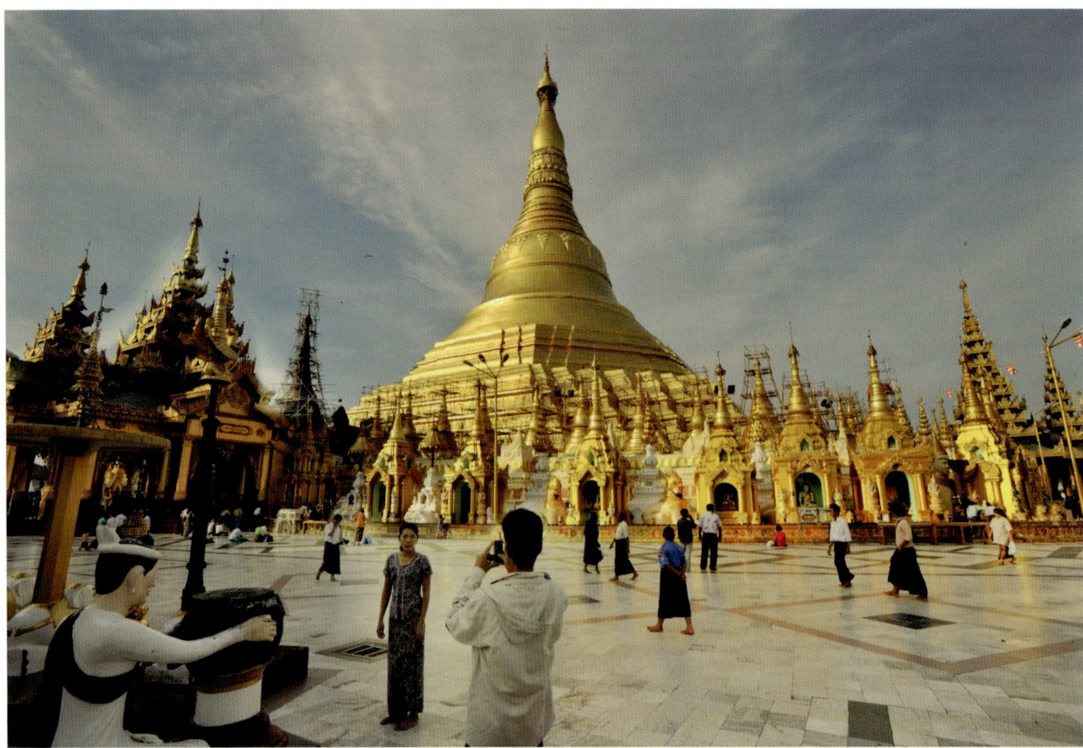

FIG. 7. The Shwedagon Pagoda, Myanmar's most sacred site, containing eight Buddha hair relics

be from Ukkala, or modern Orissa state in India, but by the fifteenth century the brothers were associated with Suvannabhumi in Lower Myanmar. In the Shwedagon Inscription, two of the eight hairs were stolen by a snake-king named Jayasura, a caper taken directly from a tenth- or eleventh-century Sri Lankan chronicle, the Pali *Nalatadhatuvamsa*. The Mon in the fifteenth century therefore believed that there were six hairs enshrined within the stupa. In subsequent centuries, this basic myth was greatly expanded.[9]

THE SIXTEENTH CENTURY: A TURNING POINT

The early sixteenth century saw the dramatic conquest of the Mon of Lower Myanmar by invading Bamar forces from the north. The Mon population slowly dwindled, but key fifteenth-century Mon myths were enthusiastically embraced. Bamar kings from Upper Myanmar, for example, impressively refurbished the ancient Shwedagon in Yangon and the Shwemawdaw in Pegu. At the same time, the core Mon myths from the fifteenth century became greatly embellished by the mixed Mon and Bamar population of Lower Myanmar. The origin of these additions to the myth is difficult to determine, since the majority of the Mon and Bamar chronicles from the sixteenth century onward are usually in general agreement and are often undated.[10] However, a collective sense of Myanmar identity was inexorably developing out of these myths.

The Shwedagon myth illustrates how the basic legends were stretched in new directions. For example, in addition to the two hairs stolen by the snake-king, recorded in the fifteenth-century inscription, the new legend describes how two more hairs were lost to an avaricious king on the return journey from India. The most important addition, however, was that the Buddha prophesied to the two brothers that the eight hair relics would be interred along with relics belonging to three previous Buddhas who had visited Yangon in earlier eons. The brothers returned to Yangon and were greeted by King Okkalapa, whose name derived from the Pali Ukkala, the coastal state of Orissa in India.

The king performed a miracle that resulted in the restoration of the four missing hairs. The relics of the three previous Buddhas who had visited Yangon had long been lost, but

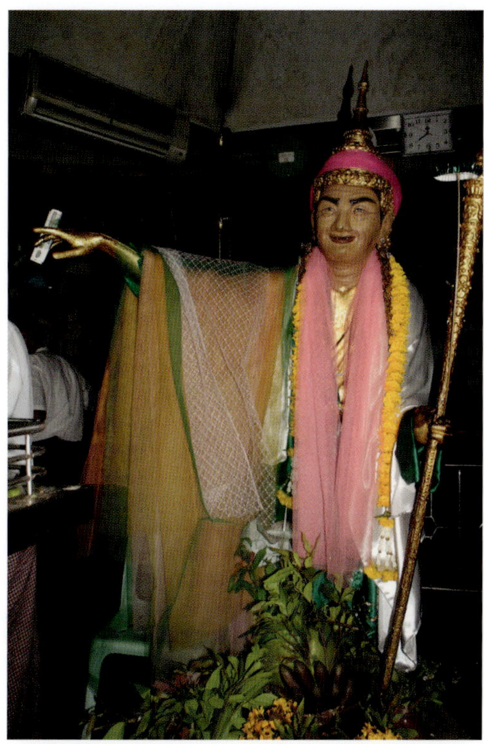

FIG. 8. Sule Bo Bo Gyi pointing toward the Shwedagon Pagoda and the lost relics. Modern sculpture. Sule Pagoda, Yangon

the king and two brothers, with essential help from converted ogres, were able to discover the hidden relics, thereby enabling the Buddha's prophecy to be fulfilled. One converted ogre emerged as more important than the others by the mid-nineteenth century, and he is today worshiped at the Sule Pagoda, a monument forming the hub of downtown Yangon. His life-size statue, known as Sule Bo Bo Gyi, shows him pointing with his outstretched right hand in the direction of the Shwedagon, evoking the episode where he directed the search for the hidden relics (fig. 8).

The fifteenth-century myth centered on the six hair relics associated at an unknown stage with the Golden Rock at Kyaikhtiyo. The Golden Rock is thought to contain one or more of these sacred strands. The modern myth speaks of three hermits, while in earlier versions six hermits were described. The king of Thaton is now thought to be hatched from an egg, the product of a union between a snake-goddess and a wizard. His queen, with a similar parentage, died a violent death and is worshiped today at Kyaikhtiyo as a *nat*, or spirit.[11]

Unlike many of the early Mon myths, which continue to flourish, the tradition stemming from the thirty-three teeth has been largely forgotten. The tooth-relic legend attached to the Shwemawdaw Stupa in Pegu in the fifteenth century was at some point completely lost, replaced by the current legend about two brothers visiting the Buddha in India and receiving two hair relics.

RAKHINE AND SHAN FOUNDATION MYTHS

The defining myth in Rakhine featured the Buddha's conversion of the local king named Chandrasuriya. He asked the Buddha to leave a token of his person, and the king then received permission from the Buddha to cast a metal image in the Buddha's likeness. The bronze was then brought to life by the Buddha by breathing upon it, infusing energy into cold metal. The earliest surviving text in which this myth is found is perhaps dated to the sixteenth century, but the core of the legend and the worship of the image probably grew up in tandem in the fourteenth or fifteenth century.[12]

This metal image grew to symbolize the Rakhine realm, and it was for this very reason that it became the target for King Bodawpaya (r. 1782–1819), who annexed Rakhine and removed the image to its current location outside his capital of Amarapura (now within the present day city of Mandalay). It is now called the Mahamuni Buddha and is the most sacred Buddha image in Myanmar (fig. 9).

Another myth links the very foundation of the Rakhine kingdom to a Pali *jataka* (no. 454). In this *jataka*, ten brothers conquered an Indian city known as Dvaravati, which was identified with modern Sandoway in Rakhine. The brothers' sister, Anjanadevi, settled in Vesali, also in India but identified with a walled city of the same name in Rakhine. This kernel from the Pali *jataka* provided the myth's raw outline, but the remainder of the myth reflected local lore. Anjanadevi's descendants, for example, married a king who was the issue of a brahmin hermit and a female deer. This king founded Dhannavati, identified in Rakhine as the walled city containing the temple that housed the Mahamuni bronze Buddha. The story concluded with a member from this dynasty wedding a prince fleeing from India who belonged to the Sakya lineage, the Buddha's royal family.[13]

The Shan entered Upper Myanmar by the fourteenth century from southern China. There was never a single Shan dynasty but more than twenty independent kingdoms; some

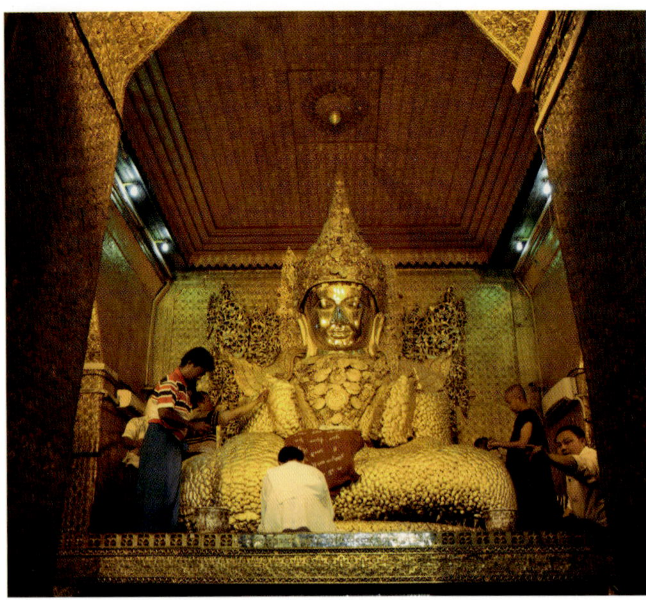

FIG. 9. The Mahamuni, Myanmar's most sacred Buddha image. Bronze covered in gold leaf. Southern Mandalay

were enormous, of a size comparable to modern Belgium, while others were miniscule. The Shan and the Bamar of Upper Myanmar were always in a contentious relationship, with the Bamar generally gaining the upper hand, beginning with the northern conquests of King Bayinnaung (r. 1551–1581). The Shan courts, however, enjoyed great autonomy as tributary states, first to the Bamar and then to the British. Original Shan myths no longer survive, but the extant Shan state chronicles from the late eighteenth and nineteenth centuries contain myths that were largely modeled on Bamar legends but cleverly adapted to local circumstances.[14] Shan courts, for example, traced their origins to the same Sakyan migration to Upper Myanmar but claimed that one Sakyan division split into numerous Shan clans, a concept borrowed from Bamar chronicles.

The most well-known Shan legend centers on five Buddha images enshrined within the Paung Daw Oo Temple at Inle Lake; the lake was part of the Shan kingdom of Nyaungshwe. The myth surrounding the images is a conflation of episodes found in the classic Bamar royal history, *The Glass Palace Chronicle*, but much was completely domesticated to Inle Lake.[15] The myth featured an ogress whose son was saved from drowning in a lake by Pagan's King Alaungsithu (r. 1113–1169). The lake, set on a mythical island in the Bamar version, was transposed to Inle Lake in the local chronicles. This ogress thanked a deity for her son's rescue and received in return four sandalwood logs and a piece of the "southern branch" of the Bodhi Tree. These wooden treasures were presented to Alaungsithu, who sculpted five Buddha images upon his return to Pagan. The king then placed the images on his royal barge, and, after cleaving a passage in the mountains surrounding Inle Lake, hid them in a cave. Discovered by the royal family of Nyaung-shwe in the fourteenth century, the five Buddhas have been worshiped by the royal family and the inhabitants of the lake area ever since. This myth probably arose only in the eighteenth or early nineteenth century and at that time entered the local chronicles. The buddhas are now completely concealed in gold leaf, applied over decades by devotees (fig. 10). In the twentieth century, with far easier access to Inle Lake, these five images have entered what might be called the national pantheon.

THE AGE OF CONSOLIDATION

By the late eighteenth century Bamar writers of monastic chronicles, or *thathanawin* (Myanmar), began to assemble many of the local legends about the Buddha's visits to Myanmar and incorporate them systematically into a history of Buddhism that was truly national in character. Perhaps the best example of this trend is the *Thathanalinkara-sadan*, or the *Ornament of the Religion*, written in 1831. It organizes the significant events in the history of Myanmar's diverse regional kingdoms, both legendary and actual, into chrono-

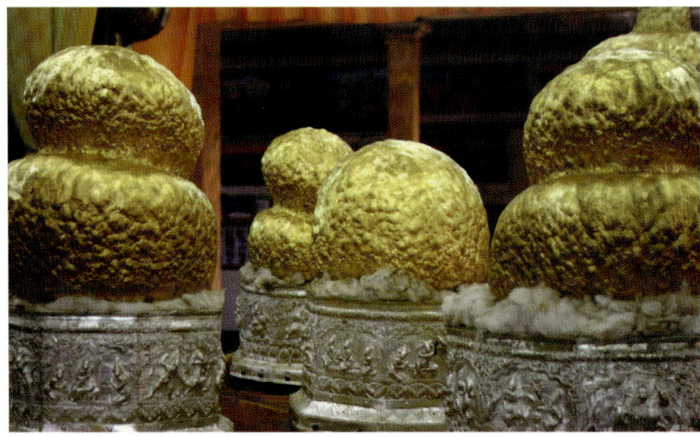

FIG. 10. Five Buddha images concealed by many layers of gold leaf applied by devotees, associated with an ogress from Inle Lake and a king from Pagan. Paung Daw Oo Pagoda, Inle Lake

logical order. This inclusive history encompassed Myanmar's most prominent nationalities of the time, namely the Mon, Bamar, and the Shan.[16] The Buddha is understood as having transmitted his teachings to each nationality while sanctifying their respective homelands with his physical presence. The text does not portray the histories of these diverse regions as separate traditions but rather as facets of a single dispensation that encompassed the entire Myanmar kingdom of the time, which extended well beyond what we know as the borders of Myanmar today. The *Thathanalinkara-sadan* was a widely used text in the nineteenth century and continues to influence the writing of Myanmar Buddhist history even today.

The strategy of linking together the Buddhist foundation stories of different ethnic groups witnessed in Konbaung-era *thathanawins* was not without precedent. The fifteenth-century Kalyani Inscription erected in Pegu by the Mon king Dhammazedi (r. 1472–1492), for example, contains an extended narrative that traces the Buddhism of Pagan in the eleventh century to the more ancient Buddhism of the Mon in Lower Myanmar. It further describes how in subsequent centuries the Buddhism of both Upper and Lower Myanmar came under the influence of a singular reformed Buddhist tradition emanating from Sri Lanka.[17]

The practice of integrating Mon and Bamar legendary and historical material first found in the Kalyani Inscription was embraced and expanded, beginning in the sixteenth century, by the Bamar Taunggu conquerors of Lower Myanmar. The Taunggu kings, having reunited Upper and Lower Myanmar for the first time since the Pagan period (ca. 11th–13th century), consciously adopted Mon Buddhist traditions along with the refinements of Mon culture as a means to legitimate their rule. During the next two and a half centuries, local Buddhist foundation legends continued to evolve until their consolidation under a single overarching historical rubric in the *thathanawins* of the Konbaung era. This consolidating trend continued and even accelerated in the colonial and postcolonial periods, encouraged in part by the introduction of printed editions of these texts. Cumulatively, these developments had a profound impact on the creation of the modern Myanmar state, which despite persistent regional and ethnic differences and even conflicts, is conceived of as a single political and cultural entity whose unity is expressed largely in Buddhist terms.

NOTES

The authors wish to thank U Tun Aung Chain, Yangon, for his patient guidance over the years. His erudition and wisdom are matched by his modesty.

1 Granoff, "Karma, Curse or Divine Illusion." This tradition of invoking the fleeing Sakyas to promote the legitimacy of dynasties outside of India was also true for early Sri Lanka, where a Sakyan princess married a descendant of the island's mythical founder (*Mahavamsa*, VIII. 18).

2 Duroiselle, *Epigraphia Birmanica*, 90–129, 147–68. The legend of Kyanzittha, named in the inscriptions as Tribhuvanaditya-dhammaraja, is likely based on the founding of Sri Lanka by Vijaya, who was forecast to arrive in Sri Lanka on the very day the Buddha died, sharing direct affinities to Sri Ksetra's creation. The Sri Lanka myth also included Vishnu, whom the Buddha appointed guardian of Sri Lanka.

3 Duroiselle, *Epigraphia Birmanica*, 151.

4 Pranke, "'Treatise on the Lineage of Elders,'" 23. For the *Yazawin-gyaw*, see Mahasilavamsa, *Yazawin-gyaw*, 121–23. For the myth, especially its treatment in the Pali commentaries, and its connection with the site in Myanmar, see Duroiselle, *Note on the Ancient Geography of Burma*.

5 Saya Pwa, *Mahazayawin-gyi*, vol. 1.

6 Ibid.

7 The *Mahakarmavibhanga* version does not contain the episodes of the tooth or hair relics. Shorto, "Gavampati Tradition in Burma"; Strong, "Gavampati in Pali and Sanskrit Texts."

8 Stadtner, "Lost Legend of the Shwemawdaw Pagoda."

9 Pe Maung Tin, "Shwe Dagon Pagoda."

10 Ibid.

11 Stadtner, *Sacred Sites of Burma*.

12 Forchhammer, *Report on the Antiquities of Arakan*. The text is named *Sappadapakarana*.

13 Leider, "Emergence of Rakhine Historiography"; Charney, "Centralizing Historical Tradition in Precolonial Burma."

14 Sao Saimong Mangrai, *Padeaeng Chronicle*; Robbine, "Early Myanmar Myths and History."

15 Sao Saimong, "Phaungtaw-U Festival."

16 Mahadhamma-thingyan, *Thathanalinkara-sadan*. The *Thathanalinkara-sadan*, written in 1831, included Lampang and Chiang Mai, now cities in northern Thailand, within the boundaries of the Myanmar kingdom. The two cities were, in fact, former vassals of the Konbaung crown, having thrown off Myanmar overlordship decades earlier in the late eighteenth century.

17 See Taw Sein Ko, *Kalyani Inscriptions*, 3–4, 49–51.

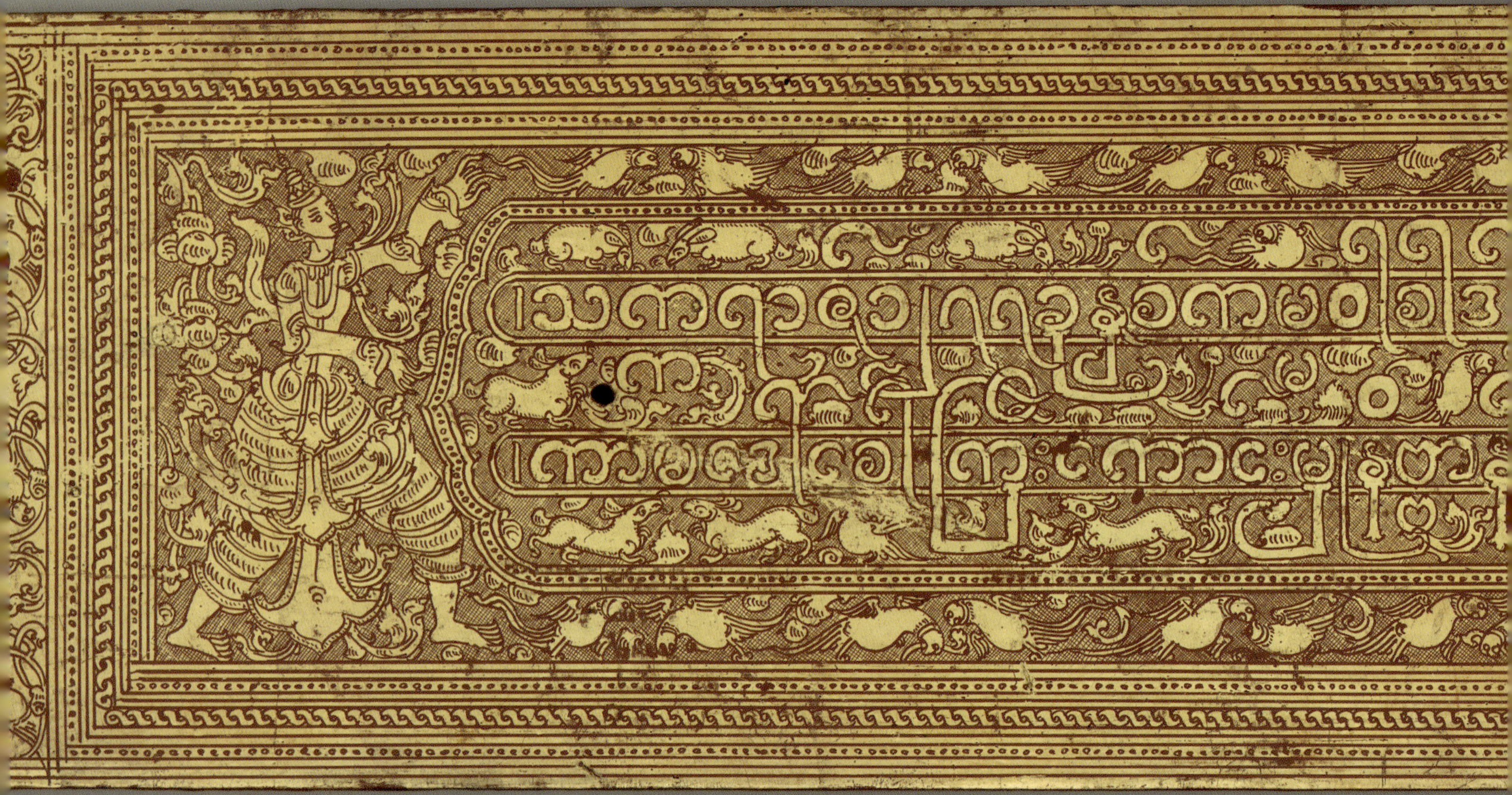

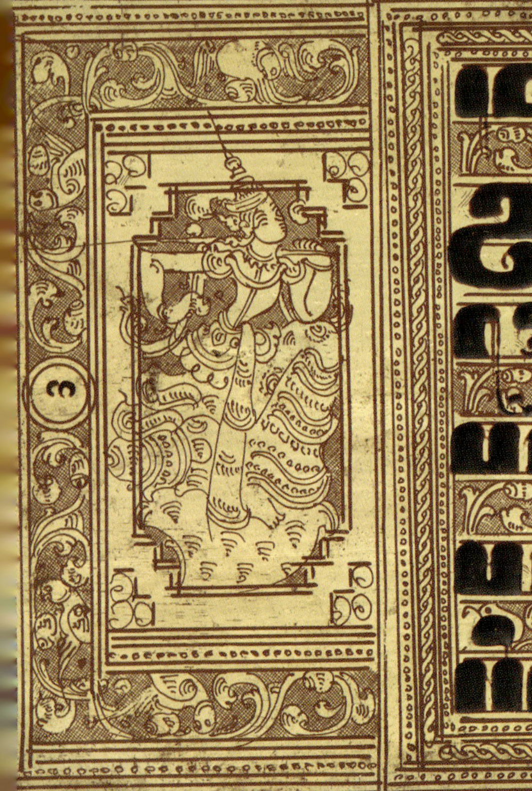

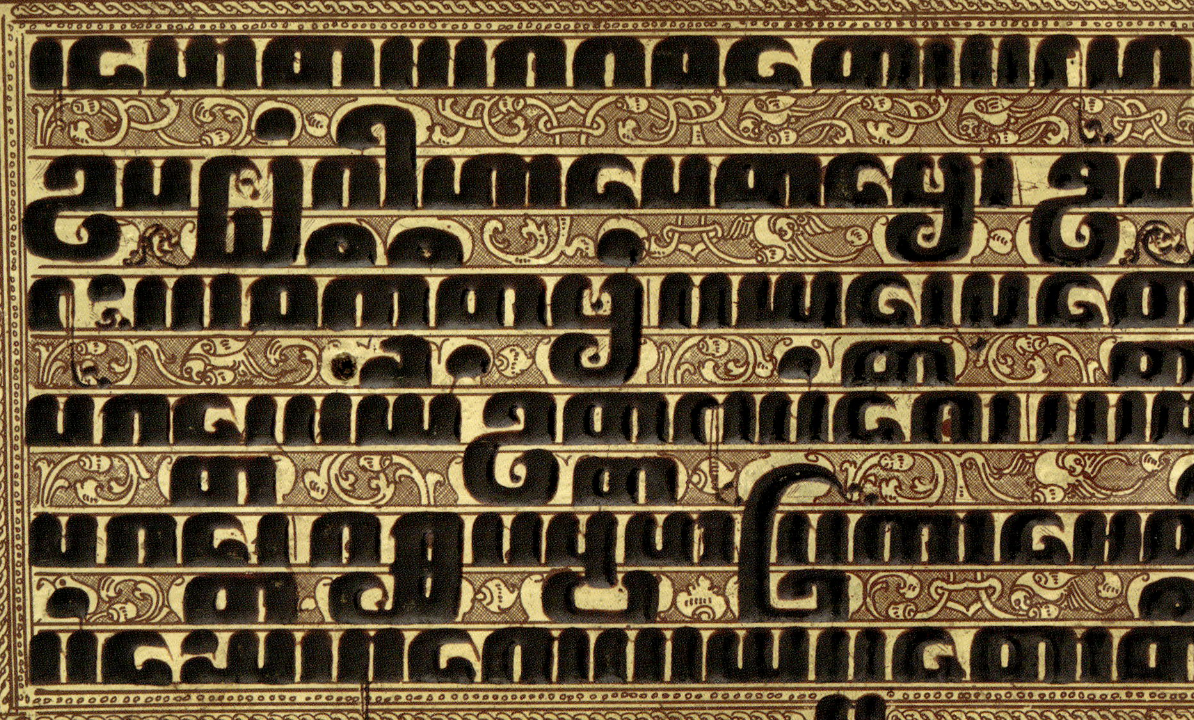

Inscriptions and Chronicles
The Historiography of Myanmar

U Tun Aung Chain

Myanmar's boundaries have changed and fluctuated in the course of time, but the constant heartland of its history has been the valley and delta of the Irrawaddy, or Ayeyarwady, River and the territory around the Gulf of Martaban, east of the delta. Three peoples, distinguished from each other by language, have been dominant in that heartland: the Pyu, the Mon, and the Bamar.

The Pyu were the first to create an urban civilization; their city of Beikthano began to flourish in the first century CE. Pyu cultural remains are impressive, especially at Sri Ksetra, the most extensive of the ancient cities, unusual in its circular plan, and which flourished from the second to the ninth century. Despite this early activity, the Pyu as a people have disappeared altogether. The reason for their disappearance remains a mystery; historians have yet to provide a satisfactory explanation. The Pyu language was first partially deciphered in 1911 with a Pagan, or Bagan, inscription from the early twelfth century; however, Pyu writings are rare and little information can be gleaned from them. Some stone burial urns bearing inscriptions have been recovered from Sri Ksetra. The inscriptions are short, as for example "Harivikrama died ninth day second month year 41 aged 52 years 7 months 42 days"; all that they establish is the fact that a line of kings with the dynastic name Vikrama ruled in Sri Ksetra, nothing more. Even the period in which these kings flourished is uncertain because the era referenced in the urn inscriptions is not clearly known.[1]

Unlike the Pyu, the Bamar and the Mon possess historical accounts. The Bamar were established in the northern part of the heartland, the Mon in the south. The two were in contention for much of the time, with the Mon on the defensive against the Bamar, who were trying to gain territory to the south and secure access to the sea, an action the Mon could not allow for they derived their wealth from trading on the Indian Ocean. The Bamar had a natural handicap in that the rainfall in their part of the heartland was inadequate for the cultivation of rice; however, the handicap was overcome early with the development of an irrigation system, which was so effective it even allowed for two harvests per year. The creation of a strong agricultural base allowed the Bamar to have a large population settled on the land, and this enabled them to put larger armies into the field than the Mon. Having established the kingdom of Pagan, the Bamar claimed an initial victory against the first Mon kingdom of Thaton in the middle of the eleventh century, and—after a period of Mon revival following the decline of Pagan and the establishment of the Mon kingdom of Hanthawaddy, or modern Pegu, or Bago, in the fourteenth century—the Bamar won a final victory over the Mon in the sixteenth century.

OPPOSITE Detail of cat. no. 57

Just as the Bamar dominated the history of Myanmar from the sixteenth century onward, Bamar chronicles dominate the historiography of Myanmar. There are a fair number of Mon inscriptions because Dhammazedi (r. 1470–1492), the Mon king of Hanthawaddy who greatly promoted Buddhism, took care to record his acts of merit in this way. Of particular note are the Shwedagon Inscription, which provides a chronicle of the Shwedagon Stupa and the efforts of the Mon kings of Hanthawaddy to rebuild and enlarge it, and the Kalyani Inscription, which records Dhammazedi's effort to establish the Theravada Buddhist Mahavihara monastic tradition of Sri Lanka in Hanthawaddy. Although the Kalyani Inscription has suffered damage, most of the Mon inscriptions on durable stone have endured. On the other hand, Mon chronicles printed on the less durable surface of palm leaves, which require periodic recopying, have been more severely affected by time and the lack of court patronage.

The best known of the Mon chronicles is the *Struggle of Rajadhiraj*, which provides a detailed account of the efforts of King Rajadhiraj (r. 1384–1420) to repel the invasion of the Mon country by Mingaung, the Bamar king of Ava (r. 1401–1422) as well as an account of Wareru (r. 1287–1307), founder of the Mon kingdom of Martaban and the lineage of kings there. The author of this chronicle is unknown but perhaps was living at the time of Rajadhiraj. There is a Myanmar translation of the chronicle, which was generally available, while the Mon original became obscure and unavailable in Myanmar until a copy was retrieved in the 1950s from the Mon community that had emigrated to Thailand.[2] *A Chronicle of the Mons*, another Mon chronicle by an unknown author and probably dating to the late sixteenth century, is available only in its Myanmar translation, since the Mon original has been lost.[3] Another chronicle, *A History of Kings*, on the other hand, exists in Mon but does not have a Myanmar translation. It was written by the abbot of Acwo, or Athwo, Monastery and finished in December 1766.[4] The work was left untranslated, probably because it was a later work written when the Bamar had already established their dominance and Bamar kings had lost much of their interest in Mon texts.[5]

The Bamar were much influenced by the Mon in their early development. The language of the Bamar was more similar to that of the Pyu, which also belonged to the Tibeto-Burman subfamily of the Sino-Tibetan language family, while the Mon belonged to the Mon-Khmer subfamily of the Austro-Asiatic family. The Bamar occupied an area in which Pyu cities had previously flourished, which may explain the linguistic connection between the two. Nevertheless, the Bamar adopted the Mon script rather than the Pyu, and at Pagan, inscriptions in Mon precede those in Myanmar. While the Bamar were thus indebted to the Mon in their early writing, Myanmar chronicles surpass existing Mon chronicles in their volume and in the details they provide of court life and royal actions.[6]

The earliest extant Myanmar chronicle—the *Yazawingyaw* (Celebrated Chronicle), written by the monk-poet Mahasilavamsa (1452–1520) and completed in 1502—notes that there was an earlier chronicle that traced the succession of kings to Kalekyetaungnyo (r. 1426). There must have been quite a number of early chronicles, mostly local, but they have been overshadowed by U Kala's monumental *Mahayazwingyi* (Great Chronicle), of the early eighteenth century. U Kala began his chronicle with the kings of Sri Ksetra, whose ruined structures still stood impressively at the time of his writing, and ended the chronicle in his own time. The son of a merchant, U Kala was a private citizen, but his mother came from an official family that traced its service to the king back to the late sixteenth century. This connection to the court allowed him to use court materials for the later part of his chronicle. For the beginning of the chronicle, however, he was dependent on earlier works and popular legends, so there is much that is fanciful.

Following the Great Chronicle, the development of the Myanmar chronicle was based on royal patronage. In the late eighteenth century, King Bodawpaya (r. 1782–1819) commissioned his former tutor Mahasithu (1726–1806) to revise the Great Chronicle by incorporating material from other sources. In addition, he was assigned another task: collecting and reinscribing donative inscriptions to aid Bodawpaya in restoring religious lands that had lapsed into secular use. As a result, Mahasithu had about six hundred inscriptions close at hand when he wrote his chronicle.[7] His *Yazawinthit* (New Chronicle), which began with the account of the Great Chronicle and continued to the end of the second Ava, or Inwa, dynasty in 1752, represented a new departure in the writing of chronicles; inscriptions were used for the first time—mainly for the revision of details—as well as interruptions in the narrative to accommodate annotations.

To continue royal patronage of chronicle writing, later kings established Royal Commissions for the task: the first in 1829, the second in 1867, and the third in 1883. The first commission produced two works: the First Chronicle, *Hmannam Mahayazawin-gyi*, which became popularly known as *The Glass Palace Chronicle*, named after the Commission's meeting place, and was a further revision of the Great Chronicle;[8] and the Second Chronicle, which was a continuation of the First Chronicle and provided a record of the ruling dynasty from its establishment in 1752 to its current state of affairs in 1821. The first work made a notable addition to previous chronicles, which began their histories of Myanmar with a history of Majjhimadesa, the Buddhist heartland of India, without establishing any direct connection between the two. *The Glass Palace Chronicle*, by contrast, provided a history of the first kingdom of Myanmar, Tagaung, beginning with a prince of the Sakya clan in Kapilavastu who fled from conflict in his kingdom in India and took refuge in Myanmar, where he founded the first Myanmar kingdom and its line of thirty-three kings. With the connection established, the kings of Myanmar were made lineal descendants of the kings of Majjhimadesa and of the Sakya clan of which the Buddha was a member. The second commission extended the Second Chronicle to cover events in 1854. The third commission, formed to extend the Second Chronicle still further, failed miserably in its task. Perhaps reflecting the circumstances of a dynasty in decline, it produced only a draft account of the first year of the reign of King Thibaw (r. 1878–1885). The draft was left to a very distant cousin of Thibaw, U Maung Maung Tin (1866–1945), who first resisted the British but then entered colonial service to continue the work of the second commission and provide the remainder of the dynastic chronicle.[9]

The chronicles of both the Mon and Bamar were written in a Buddhist context. The earliest evidence of Buddhism can be found among the first-millennium sites in Myanmar, but Dhammazedi's Kalyani Inscription pushes the arrival of Buddhism to the Mon country further back to the third century BCE and attributes it to the missionary effort following the Third Buddhist Council convened by the Maurya emperor Ashoka (r. 273–232 BCE) to rid Buddhism of false monks and heretics and to finalize the Pali canon. The chronicles also position Myanmar as a Buddhist realm through their mythic accounts of the Buddha's visit to Myanmar. In the Mon version, the Buddha's visit was brought about by twin brothers, one of whom became king in the city of Thaton, while the other died young, was reborn in Majjhimadesa, and became a disciple of the Buddha known as Gavampati. During his visit to Thaton, the Buddha gave six hair relics to six hermits who each enshrined his relic in a stone stupa (fig. 11). Following the fifteenth century, this myth became attached to the Golden Rock at Kyaikhtiyo, a huge boulder balanced on a cliff in a fairly remote location, which became a place of pilgrimage in later years (fig. 12).

In the Bamar version, the Buddha went to Legaing, a city on a trade route between central Myanmar and Rakhine in the west, where two brothers built and offered him a sandalwood monastery (fig. 13). He left behind two footprints, the Shwesettaw (Golden Footprints) beside Mann River, as a sign that his religion would flourish in Myanmar in the future.

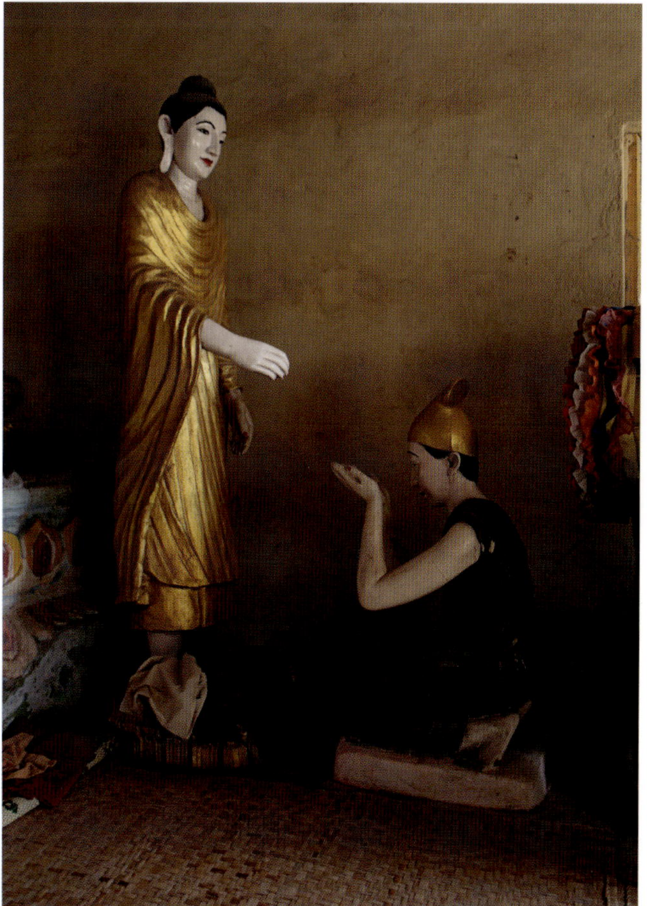

FIG. 11. The Buddha presents a hair relic to a hermit at Thaton. Modern sculpture. Mount Kelasa Pagoda

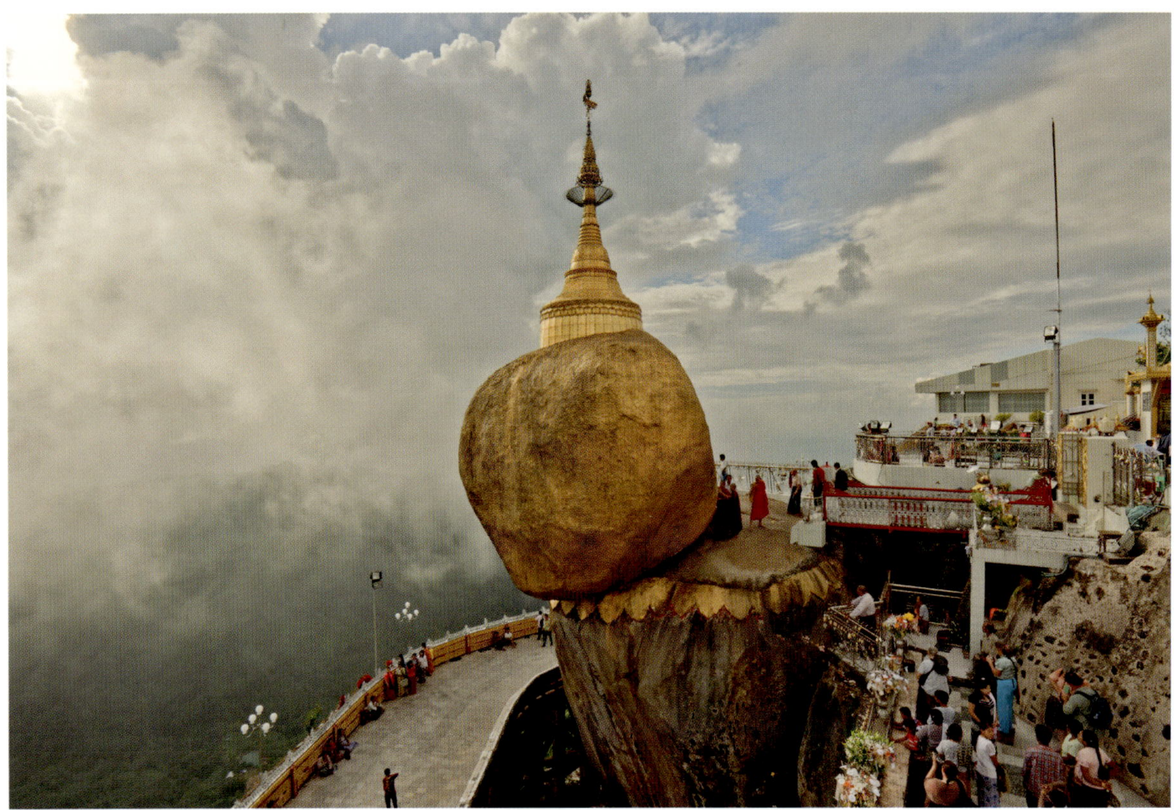

FIG. 12. The Golden Rock, balancing on a cliff side, according to legend supported by a hair relic of the Buddha. Kyaikhtiyo

The Shwesettaw, like the Kyaikhtiyo, has become a popular place of pilgrimage.

Kings lie at the heart of both the Mon and Bamar chronicles. The main type of chronicle—known as *yazawin* in Myanmar and *rajawan* in Mon, from the Pali *rajavamsa* (the lineage of kings)—dealt with the reigns of a succession of kings, usually of a particular city. A subsidiary form—*ayedawbon* in Myanmar and *akruin* in Mon, literally "an account of royal affairs"—dealt in detail with a single reign, such as that of King Bayinnaung (r. 1551–1581) and that of King Alaungpaya (r. 1752–1760).[10] The chronicles gave kings legitimacy by presenting their reign in the context of a prophecy from the Buddha. The earliest instance of this occurs in an inscription of Kyanzittha, king of Pagan (r. ca. 1084–ca. 1112), which includes the Buddha prophesying that an ascetic named Vishnu would go through several existences and be reborn in the future as a king of Pagan who would greatly uphold the religion of the Buddha and bring prosperity to the people. In the account presented by the chronicles, the Buddha's visits to Myanmar provide the setting for a number of prophecies regarding the future kings and royal cities of Myanmar (fig. 14).

In the Mon chronicles, the Buddha, while travelling from Thaton to Martaban, or Mottama, was offered a stone slab as a seat by Sumana and seven other ogres, on which the Buddha prophesied, "In this place the city of Martaban will be founded and Sumana will be the first in a succession of eight kings to rule here. They will be great in glory and my religion will flourish brilliantly." Seventeen other ogres also made him offerings of fruit and cordial, and the Buddha prophesied that they too would be future kings in Hanthawaddy.

In the Bamar chronicles, the Buddha, departing Legaing and the Man stream, travelled up the Irrawaddy and stopped at Sri Ksetra, Pagan, and Ava. At Sri Ksetra he was offered a clod of earth by a small mole, and he prophesied, "In time to come, there will be a great city here, this little mole will rule it as the incomparable three-eyed king Duttabaung, and

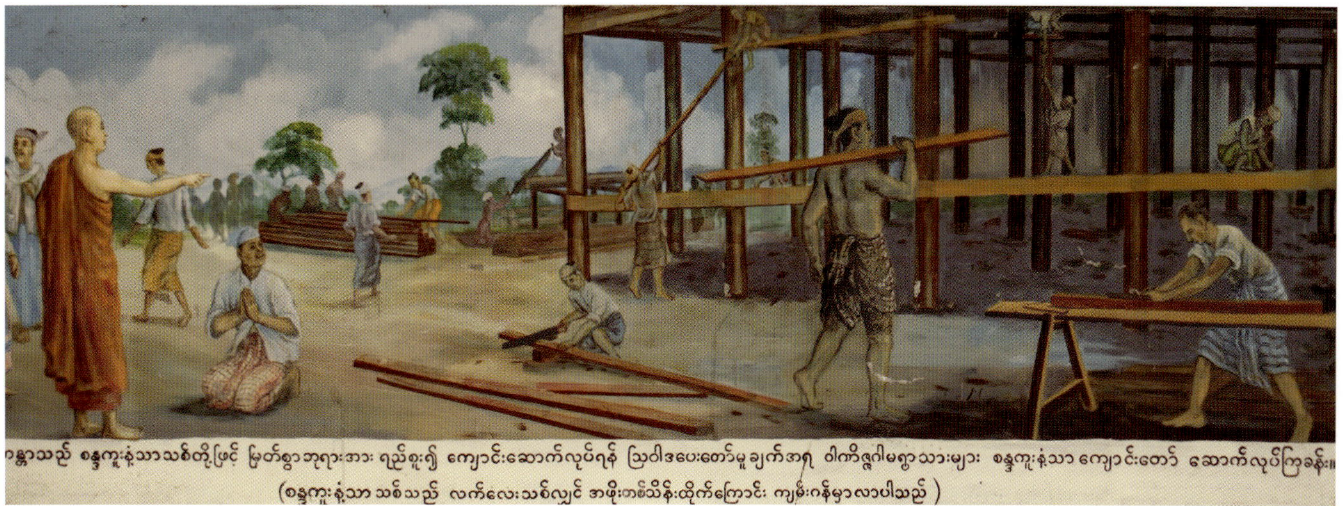

FIG. 13. One of the two brothers supervising the construction of the Sandalwood Monastery. Modern painting by Ma Thin Mi. Sandalwood Monastery, Legaing

my religion will flourish greatly during his reign" (fig. 15). At Pagan, seeing a *pauk* tree with various creatures in it, he prophesied that in time a great city would stand in that place; that the egret and the crow at the top of the tree signified the presence in the city of those who keep the precepts and those who do not; that the fork-tongued lizard in the middle of the tree signified that the citizens would live by trade and speak falsehoods; and that the frog at the base of the tree signified that the people would live comfortable lives, their bellies cool.

Although the prophecies of the Buddha provided legitimacy to kings and cities, the chronicles also referred to kingship as an institution antedating the historical Buddha. In the chronicles, the *brahmas* (celestial beings) who became human beings inhabiting the world turned into degenerates over time, and theft and quarrels occurred. They therefore met in assembly and, approaching the future Buddha, made him king with the title Mahasammata (The Great One of Common Consent) and gave him the power to rule them and to punish misdeeds. In return, they provided him with one tenth of their produce. With Mahasammata as the first king, the kings of Myanmar considered themselves lineal descendants of Mahasammata, ruling in the interest of the people. This concept of the Mahasammata was borrowed from Pali traditions.

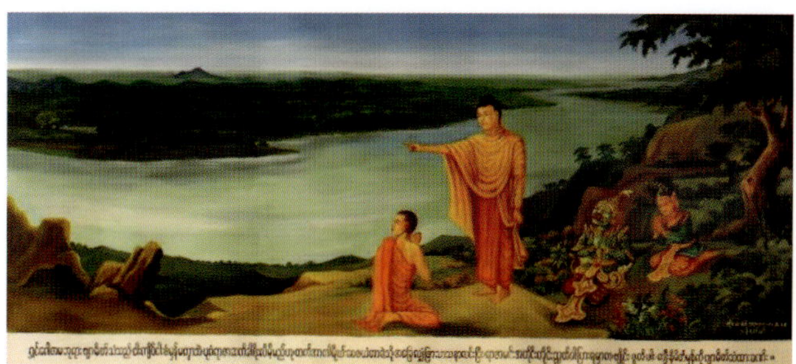

FIG. 14. The Buddha prophesying the foundation of Pagan, while Ananda, a converted ogre, and a snake-goddess look on. Modern painting. Mount Tangyi Pagoda

The Buddhist character of kingship is also indicated in the chronicles by their reference to the ten rules of kingship. First mentioned in the inscription of King Kyanzittha (r. ca. 1084–ca. 1112), the rules were enunciated in the Mahahamsa Jataka, when the King of the Hamsa Birds tells the future Buddha the rules by which he governs his subjects. More moral virtue than principle of government in the strict sense, the rules were: almsgiving, morality, liberality, straightness, gentleness, self-restraint, nonanger, nonhurtfulness, forbearance, and nonopposition.

The chronicles depict a great range of the activities and actions of kings: the building of royal cities; the performance

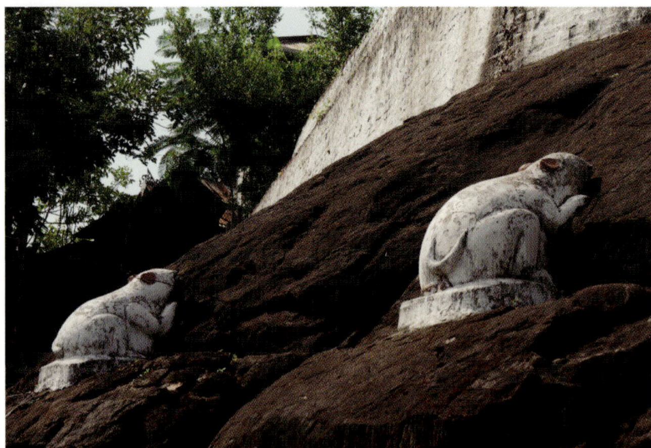

FIG. 15. Two moles that are reborn as the first royal couple of Sri Ksetra. Modern sculpture. Hpo-u Hill, near Prome (Pyay)

of royal ceremonies, in particular the ceremony of royal consecration; the granting of positions, titles, and benefits; the dispatch and reception of missions; the suppression of uprisings; and the fighting of wars. But there is also an emphasis on the king performing a variety of acts of merit to sustain Buddhism: the building and renovation of shrines; the making of images of the Buddha in reverence to the Buddha; the copying of the Pali canon and promotion of Buddhist teaching in reverence to the *Dhamma*; and the granting of positions and the offering of the requisites of monasteries, robes, food, and medicine to monks in reverence to the *Sangha*, or the Buddhist community of monks.

The chronicles pay particular attention to building and renovating shrines, and they give vivid life to these royal actions. *A History of Kings* relates that Queen Shinsawbu (r. 1453–1470), reigning queen of Hanthawaddy, moved her residence to Yangon in order to reconstruct the Shwedagon Pagoda. She increased the size of the pagoda, paved the platform with stones, added stone lamps, and planted palms and coconut trees between the encircling walls, which she rebuilt and strengthened. She also donated a three-ton bell, provided her weight in gold (90 pounds) to regild the pagoda, installed a new umbrella, and assigned five hundred people to the service of the pagoda. The chronicle also relates that as she lay dying, Shinsawbu gazed at the glowing form of the Shwedagon and, with her mind tranquil and calm, drew her last breath.

With endless cycle of death and rebirth in mind and the royal aspiration to Buddhahood, there was indeed a strong compulsion to carry out royal works of merit. The Great Chronicle relates how, while he was building the Mingalazedi Pagoda, King Narathihapate (r. 1256–1287), was told by his wise men that Pagan would suffer utter destruction at the time of the pagoda's completion. The king therefore stopped construction. After ten years had passed, he was reproached by the elder monk Panthagu, "O foolish King, you are a king who has received the prophecy of the Buddha, yet you follow after the kingdom of greed and do not meditate on impermanence. There is no one more foolish than you if, after having made a work of merit, you continue to be concerned for the safety of the kingdom. And will you and your kingdom have no end?" The chronicle then relates that, thus admonished, Narathihapate was grateful to the monk for looking after his spiritual welfare and resumed the building of the pagoda until it was completed.

That other responsibility of kings—administering justice and looking to the welfare and prosperity of the people in the tradition of Mahasammata—receives less attention in the chronicles. Nevertheless, *A Chronicle of the Mons* relates that the Mon king of Hanthawaddy, Banya Barow (r. 1446–1450), hung a bell in front of the palace for subjects to ring when they needed him to administer justice. Whenever the bell was rung he rendered justice accordingly, without partiality or favor. With justice established, there was no theft or banditry, no domineering officials within the kingdom, and Hanthawaddy became like Tavatimsa, the realm of the *devas*. The final act of the king on behalf of the people was a reform of the calendar, for which he knowingly paid the price for such acts: a life cut short.

Bamar kingship came to an end on November 29, 1885, when King Thibaw was deposed. U Maung Maung Tin, recounting the event, described the scene of Thibaw being taken away into exile in an ox-drawn cart along the road south of the royal city, a road that kings had always traveled in pomp: "The Burmese populace, men and women watched him along the course and, lamenting and grieving their loss, cried, 'They are taking away our King,' and kept on wiping away the tears from their eyes."

With the king's departure a new kind of historiography developed. This was influenced by colonial rule and the western ideas and methods that came to Myanmar with it.

The chronicles, too, took on a new character. As palm leaf manuscripts, they had been mainly restricted to the court and to the larger monasteries since making copies was always an arduous task. It was only bits and pieces, mainly anecdotal, that spilled out into oral tradition. Printing changed this completely. The earliest chronicle to be published commercially—the Bamar version of the Mon chronicle *Struggle of Rajadhiraj*—was printed in Rangoon in 1883. This was followed by the publication in Mandalay in 1899 of the Second Chronicle, the work of the first and second Royal Commissions. With the addition of a concluding section, U Maung Maung Tin's *Chronicle of the Konbaung Dynasty* was published in 1905. The First Chronicle, which was first printed by Thibaw in 1883 in the Mandalay Palace, was commercially published as *The Glass Palace Chronicle* in 1908. The commercial publication of the main chronicles made them available to a wider, eager reading public.

U Kala, in his preface to the Great Chronicle, referred to the *Digha Nikaya*, the Pali canon's collection of long discourses of the Buddha, and mentioned the scriptural stricture that says discussing kings is contrary to the attainment of Nirvana. He then declared, "The chronicle which I am writing is for meditating on such matters as impermanence and should therefore be of benefit to good men." He further emphasized the chronicle's theme of impermanence by relating the episode of the minister Anandathuriya, who was unjustly condemned to death by the king, composing a last poem in which he likened the ease enjoyed by kings to a bubble floating up on the surface of the sea, lasting only a brief instant. But the new readers of the chronicles read them in a different light. They were members of an emerging middle class determined to create a new Myanmar identity in a society that had come to have new and strange elements. They became solely responsible for sustaining the Buddha's *sasana*, or religion, in the absence of king and court. They made Buddhism the core of Myanmar identity and attempted to create a Buddhist space through various methods, such as putting up signs at the entrances of pagodas that read, "FOOTWEARING PROHIBITED," which deterred the British from entering. The chronicles fit into this effort by providing a memory of past glories and the efforts of the kings to sustain Buddhism and create its great monuments. Kingship had succumbed to the law of impermanence, but the chronicles endured.

NOTES

1 For a brief survey of Pyu urn inscriptions, see Tun Aung Chain, "Kings of the Hpayahtaung Urn Inscription."

2 For a translation of the Bamar version of *The Struggle of Rajadhiraj*, see the translation by San Lwin in *Campaigns of Razadarit*.

3 For a translation, see Tun Aung Chain, *Chronicle of the Mons*.

4 For text and translation, see Halliday, "Slapat Rājāwan Datow Smin Ron."

5 For a brief review of Mon historiography, see Tun Aung Chain, *Chronicle of the Mons*, Introduction.

6 For a brief survey of the Bamar chronicles, see U Tet Htoot, "Nature of the Burmese Chronicles."

7 For an account of Mahasithu, see U Thaw Kaung, *Aspects of Myanmar History and Culture*, 43–62.

8 Pe Maung Tin and Luce, *Glass Palace Chronicle*, a translation of the chronicle of the fall of Pagan, is a classic work of great literary merit.

9 For a brief review of the work of the commissions and U Maung Maung Tin, see Tun Aung Chain, "Yadanabon Remembered."

10 For a study of the *ayedawbon*, see U Thaw Kaung, *Aspects of Myanmar History and Culture*, 13–42.

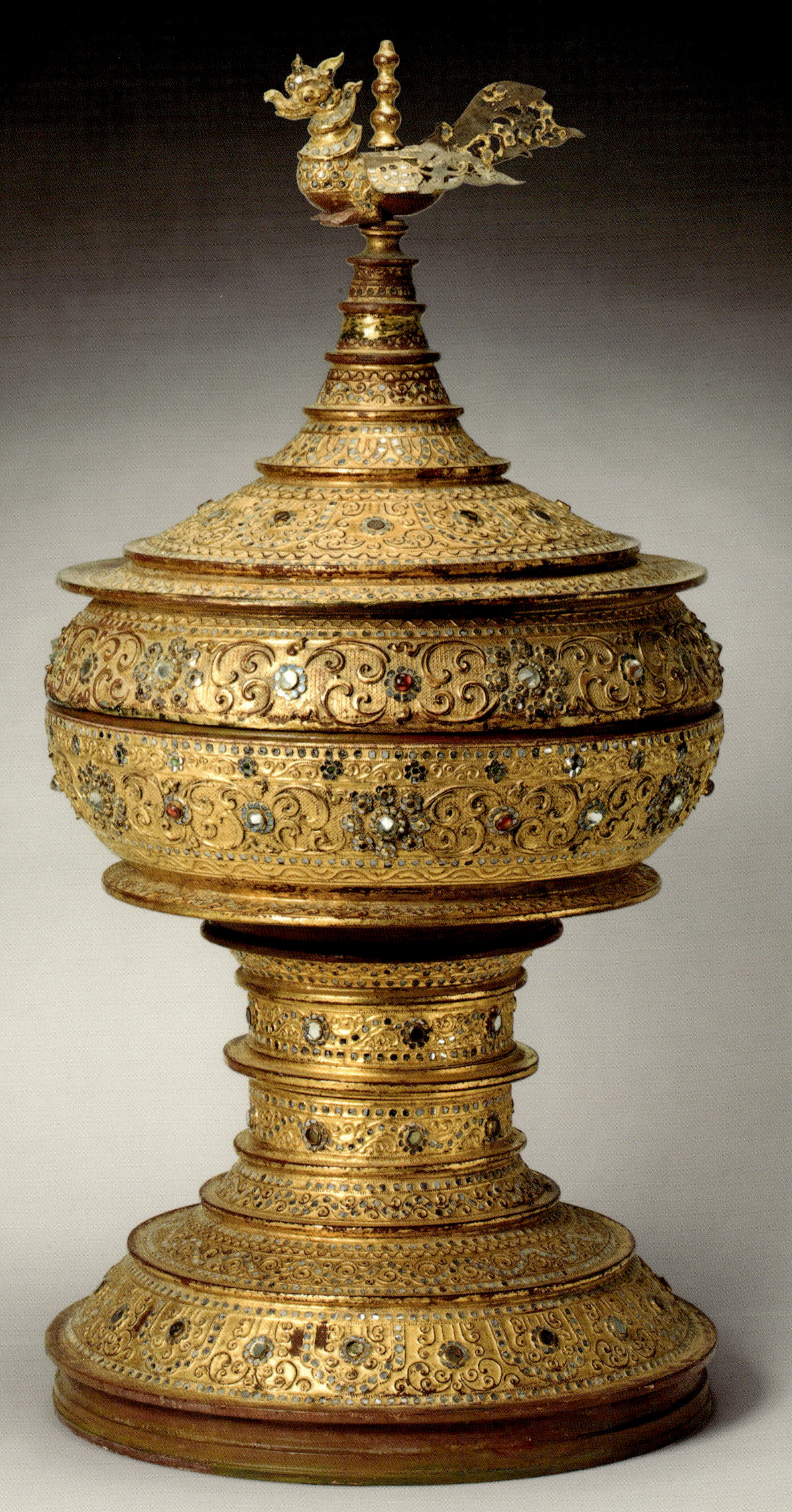

Buddhism and Its Practice in Myanmar

Patrick Pranke

THE THREE JEWELS

If in the early morning in Yangon you set out to visit the Shwedagon Pagoda, along the way you are likely to encounter Buddhist monks—*bhikkhu* (Pali) or *yahan* (Myanmar)—and novices—*samanera* (Pali) or *koyin* (Myanmar)—walking barefoot and silent on their alms rounds (fig. 16). Wrapped tightly in their dark ocher robes and with eyes downcast, they gather food offerings from the faithful, who often will be standing at the roadside waiting for the monks' arrival. The offerings, which are placed in the monks' alms bowls, are made in complete silence—except for a short blessing if the donors request it—and then the monks walk on. This daily encounter, moving in its simplicity, is the most important ritual interaction between the Buddhist *Sangha*, or community of ordained monks, and the Buddhist laity, for it cements and symbolizes the reciprocal dependency of each upon the other. The monks rely on lay donors for their daily sustenance, while the donors, in turn, rely on the monks as religious teachers and as fields of merit in which they can sow the seeds of their generosity that bring good fortune in this life and one day will ripen in a happy rebirth.

Continuing on, you may hear chanting emanating over loudspeakers from one or more of the *dhammayons*, or preaching halls, that cluster along the avenues leading up to the Shwedagon. This architectural arrangement, with preaching halls, monasteries, and other religious buildings surrounding a main shrine—typically becoming more densely spaced as you near the center—is a common feature of many of Myanmar's major pagodas. The chanting you hear will be a melodious sing-song, alternating between passages recited in Pali, the ancient canonical language of Myanmar's Theravada Buddhist scriptures, and translations and commentaries in vernacular Myanmar expressed in such a way that everyone, even children and the uneducated, can easily understand. Every generation, it seems, has produced its own pantheon of famous preaching-monks, renowned for their sonorous voices and for the poetry of their commentaries.[1] You will often see photographs of contemporary preachers set up on altars in household shrines or hanging from the rear-view mirrors of taxicabs—extending their blessings and protection, as it were, through the mere presence of their images.

The sermons these monks preach will always ultimately be based on the *Tipitaka* (Three Baskets), the name given to the collection of canonical texts that comprise the Buddha's teachings. His teachings are called the *Dhamma*, a term that means, depending on the context, "the Truth," or "Righteousness," or simply "Reality." Tradition holds that the teachings and their preservation are the foundation upon which the Buddha's religion, or *sasana*, rests and is made

OPPOSITE Cat. no. 69

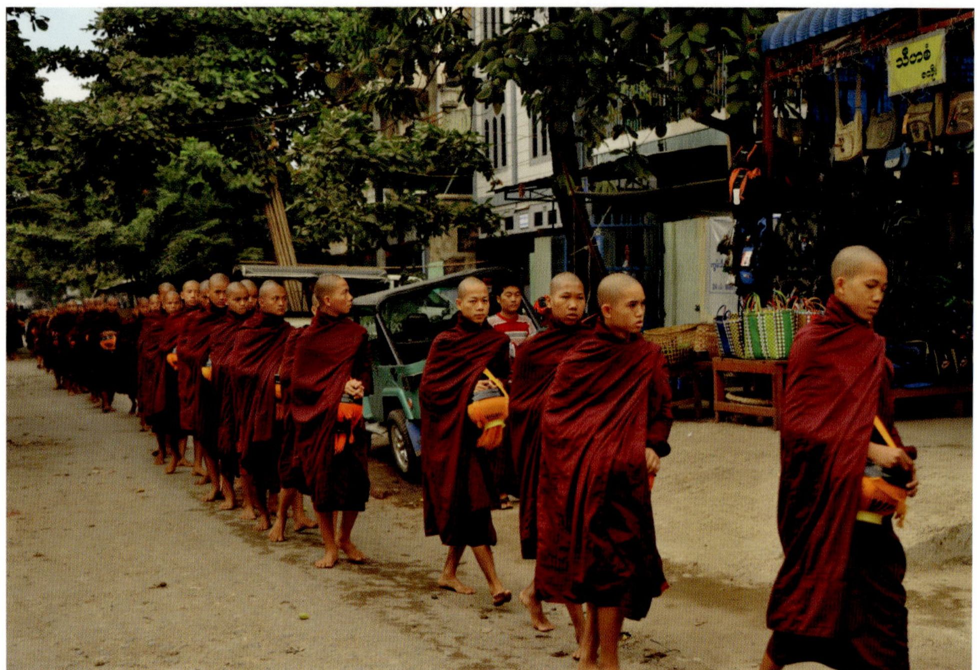

FIG. 16. Buddhist monks on the way to gather alms in the morning

able to endure through time. Composed of the three scriptural collections or "baskets" (*pitaka* in Pali) of the *Vinaya* or monastic rules, the *Sutta* or sermons and discourses, and the *Abhidhamma* or higher philosophical teachings, it is the *Dhamma* that provides guidance for proper religious practice, for ethical behavior, and for right understanding that alone leads to happy rebirth and ultimately to the end of suffering in *nibbana*—a state of transcendence beyond the cycle of birth and death. It is their preservation of the Buddha's *Dhamma* through the study of scripture, through living in accordance with its prescriptions, and through preaching of the *Dhamma* to others, that the monks of the Buddhist *Sangha* are deemed by the faithful to be a valuable field of merit worthy of donations.

Looking toward the Shwedagon from a distance you will see that it sits atop a hill with covered stairways aligned to the cardinal directions leading up to the pagoda at its summit. As you reach the foot of the hill, especially if you approached from the eastern or southern sides, the relative quiet of early morning gives way to noise and bustle as this most sacred of Myanmar's Buddhist shrines wakes up to receive pilgrims from every part of the country as well as tourists from abroad. Ascending the covered stairway that leads to the pagoda platform, always barefoot to show respect, you will see Bamar, Shan, Mon, Kayin, Rakhine, and Pa-o, to name just a few of the more than one hundred nationalities of Myanmar who regularly come to worship at the Shwedagon. Lining both sides of the stairway will be shops selling every imaginable type of religious object and paraphernalia: prayer books, scriptures, icons, prayer beads (*badi* in Myanmar), monks' robes and bowls, flowers for offering, paper flags, CDs of sermons, incense, photographs of living saints and Buddhist wizards (*weikza* in Myanmar), and on and on. Situated strategically among the shops will be astrologers' clinics where clients can go for horoscopes, advice on personal matters, or to ask for lucky numbers. Looking upward you will see that the walls of the covered stairway are occasionally pierced by arches that open onto more secular spaces outside, where there are tea shops and small restaurants selling noodles and snacks. There it is again permissible to wear sandals and shoes and in the relaxed atmosphere you will see old folks resting in the shade gossiping, children playing, and teenagers flirting while listening to music on their radios. Further along these same side paths you will come upon monastic residences housing novices and young monks studying for their state-administered

Pali examinations. Resuming your climb, as you reach the platform summit and exit the relative darkness of the covered stairway, you will be struck by the brilliant light that reflects off the Shwedagon Pagoda's colossal gilded dome, almost blinding in the morning sun. And just as suddenly you will again sense a palpable quiet, broken perhaps by the deep sound of a bronze gong being struck or by the tinkle of wind chimes that hang from the golden umbrella, or *hti* (Myanmar), that crowns the pagoda spire.

Here at the top of the stairs visitors come into the physical presence of the historical Buddha, Gotama, in the form of his bodily relics, or *saririka-ceti* (Pali), buried deep inside the pagoda structure. Inspired by faith, pilgrims feel this intuitively. Bodily relics are of various kinds, such as bones, teeth, or crystallized ash. In the case of the Shwedagon, the relics are eight strands of hair, or *san-daw* (Myanmar), said to have been a gift given by the Buddha to two traveling merchants, Tapussa and Bhallika, shortly after his enlightenment some 2,600 years ago.[2] Native sons according to local Mon legend, upon returning home from their sojourn in India the two merchants interred the relics in a modest shrine atop this hill where, over the course of centuries, and through countless acts of devotion and royal patronage, it grew into the monumental gilded pagoda it is today.[3]

In the *Mahaparinibbana Sutta* (Discourse on the Great Passing Away), the Buddha recommended, shortly before his death, that devotees venerate his relics as a way to make tranquil their minds and earn a rebirth in heaven.[4] Besides bodily relics, relics of use or contact, *paribhoga-ceti* (Pali), such as the Bodhi Tree (the tree under which the Buddha attained enlightenment), and relics of commemoration, or *uddissa-ceti* (Pali), such as images crafted in the Buddha's likeness, may also be worshiped for the same purpose and effect. As you circumambulate the Shwedagon Pagoda, you will encounter hundreds of Buddha statues of various sizes representing a range of historical periods and styles, among which nine are especially prized for their wish-fulfilling properties. Known as the Nine Wonders, or Ambwe ko-pa (Myanmar), each is associated with a legend of its creation. Some statues are alleged to be of ancient origin, such as the San-daw Dwin image that marks the spot where the Buddha's hair relics were washed before being enshrined, while others are more recent such as the Bo Bo Aung Paya image named after a famous nineteenth-century Buddhist wizard, or *weikza*, Bo Bo Aung, who is said to have created the statue through his magical powers. Finally, as you reach the southeast corner of the platform you will come upon a venerable old Bodhi Tree, a relic of use, claimed to be a descendant of the very tree that sheltered the Buddha in ancient India.

Devout Myanmar Buddhists will say that by merely visiting the Shwedagon Pagoda and seeing what you have seen, you will have been immeasurably blessed by your encounter with the three most precious things in the world, namely: the Buddha, the *Dhamma*, and the *Sangha*. These are the Three Jewels, *Tiratana* (Pali), that lie at the heart of Buddhist faith and devotion, and simultaneously are the Three Refuges, *Tisarana* (Pali), that are invoked by the faithful for protection at the beginning of every prayer and religious observance:

Buddham saranam gacchami
I take refuge in the Buddha
Dhammam saranam gacchami
I take refuge in the Teachings
Sangham saranam gacchami
I take refuge in the Monastic Community

DEVOTIONS AT THE SHWEDAGON

The prayers and rituals that you witness on the platform of the Shwedagon are representative of the range of practices that make up Myanmar's diverse Buddhist tradition. On a typical day, the pagoda's four main sanctuaries will fill with scores of lay yogis, seated in lotus posture and often dressed in brown. Some practice insight meditation, or *vipassana* (Pali), in the hope of attaining enlightenment, while others practice tranquility meditation, or *samatha* (Pali), with the aim of gaining supernormal powers. Outnumbering both of these are ordinary worshipers who devote themselves to reciting protective spells, or *paritta* (Pali), that fill the atmosphere with thoughts of loving kindness, or *metta* (Pali), and through this good intention ward off present and future dangers. Among the practitioners will be Buddhist nuns—*thila-shin* (Myanmar)—distinguishable by their shaved heads and peach-colored robes (fig. 17), and Buddhist hermits—*yathei* (Myanmar)—wearing monklike robes and conical hats. Special reverence is shown to these religious women and men, for while they are not members of the *Sangha*, nuns and hermits nevertheless are held in high esteem by

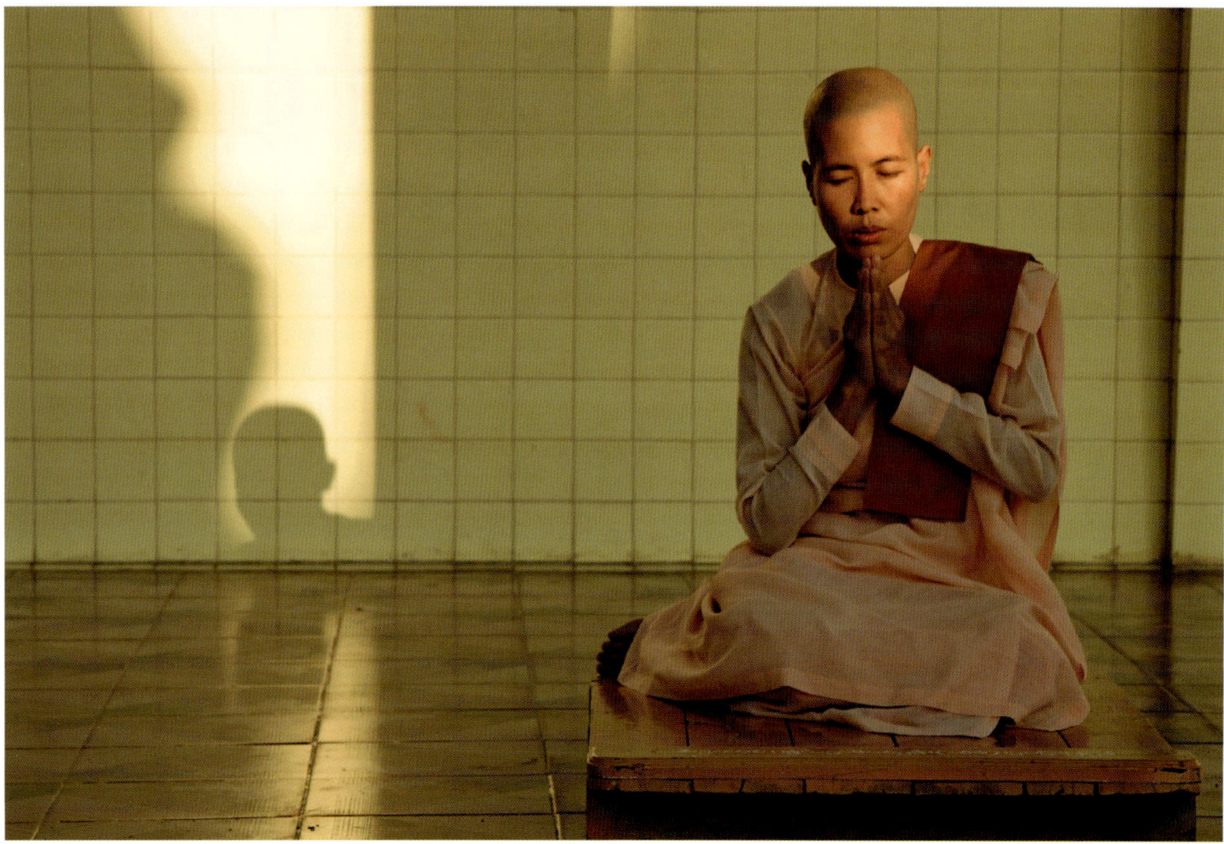

FIG. 17. Buddhist nun practicing meditation. Myathalun Pagoda, Magwe

the laity for their piety and in the case of nuns especially, for their religious learning.[5]

At the end of their devotions and before leaving the pagoda platform, visitors will typically stop at one or another of eight planetary posts installed around the Shwedagon's octagonal base that mark the eight days of the Myanmar week.[6] Each planetary post is equipped with a water basin and a marble Buddha statue that persons born on that day lustrate while making wishes (fig. 18). This ritual is thought to be especially efficacious when done on one's birthday. Besides images of the Buddha, there are hundreds of fantastical statues of gods and spirits ornamenting the pagoda platform that represent figures from both Buddhist and non-Buddhist mythologies. Collectively known as *nats*, these may be local spirits of place such as Bo Bo Gyi, a generic guardian of pagoda platforms, or grandly powerful deities, such as Thagya-min, or Sakka (Pali), the king of the gods according to both Hindus and Buddhists, who dwells in Tavatimsa, the Heaven of the Thirty-three, atop Mount Meru.[7] Worship of *nats* is always inferior to worship of the Three Jewels and is usually done for some mundane worldly objective rather than for a nobler religious goal. For this reason, *nat* veneration is sometimes eschewed and even criticized by the more orthodox in Myanmar. Besides images of the Buddha and *nats* the pagoda complex is filled with a host of colorful figures from Myanmar folklore such as flying alchemists, or *zawgyi* (Myanmar); a variety of wizards such as Bo Min Kaung and Bo Bo Aung (fig. 19), fanged ogres, or *bilu* (Myanmar); half-bird half-human nymphs, or *kinnara* (Pali); dragons, or *naga* (Pali/Myanmar); and colossal guardian lions, or *chinthe* (Myanmar). Most of these figures serve a purely ornamental function similar to gargoyles, but sometimes these fanciful beings are arranged into dioramas and tableaus that recount well-known legends or serve as admonishments against doing evil.

The quiet solemnity of the Shwedagon platform is on occasion broken with seasonal festivities, two of the most prominent of these celebrations occurring at the beginning and end of the Buddhist Lent. The Lenten season lasts from the Myanmar lunar months of Waso to Tazaungmon, a four-month period of monsoon rains that corresponds roughly to July through November of the western calendar. For the duration of this period monks are forbidden to travel and so are more or less continuously resident in their monasteries. It is customary during this time that families will have their sons take temporary ordination as novices. Novice ordinations, or *shin-pyu* (Myanmar), are celebrated with great fanfare, and candidate boys are dressed up as princes in imitation of Prince Siddhattha, the *bodhisatta* or Buddha-to-be, before he abandoned the palace in his quest for enlightenment. Surrounded by family, friends, and neighbors, the boys in their regalia are paraded around the Shwedagon amidst singing and merrymaking before being handed over to the monks for their tonsure and a temporary life of simplicity and rudimentary Buddhist training (fig. 20). Girls at this time celebrate the ear-piercing ceremony for which they too are dressed in royal attire and, like the boys, are feasted and pampered by their families. The end of Lent is marked by the *kathina* ceremony during which the laity makes offerings of new robes to the monasteries. These *kathina* robes are distributed to monks who have observed the Lenten retreat. At the Shwedagon a special robe-weaving contest is held at this time; looms are set up to weave fresh sets of robes called *matho thingan* (Myanmar) for the four central Buddha images housed in the pagoda's main sanctuaries. Teams of women representing various lay associations work the looms in shifts, cheered on by spectators, to complete the robes on time with the winning teams receiving a prize.

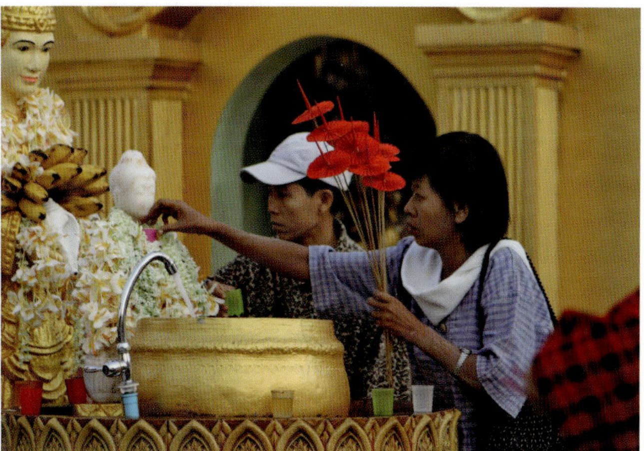

FIG. 18. Worshiper pouring water on a Buddha image at a planetary post at the Shwedagon Pagoda

THE BUDDHA OF THE MYANMAR

At the Shwedagon, as elsewhere throughout Myanmar, the Buddha is encountered and known through his physical representations, or *kou-za* (Myanmar), in the form of relics and icons. But more important than these objects of veneration are the many stories from the Buddha's life, which imbue the objects with meaning and render them sacred in the Myanmar imagination. Many of the stories and narrative cycles popular today can be traced back to a series of Buddha chronicles, or *bodawin* (Myanmar), biographies of the Buddha, composed during the Konbaung Dynasty (1752–1885), the last royal period before British conquest. Written

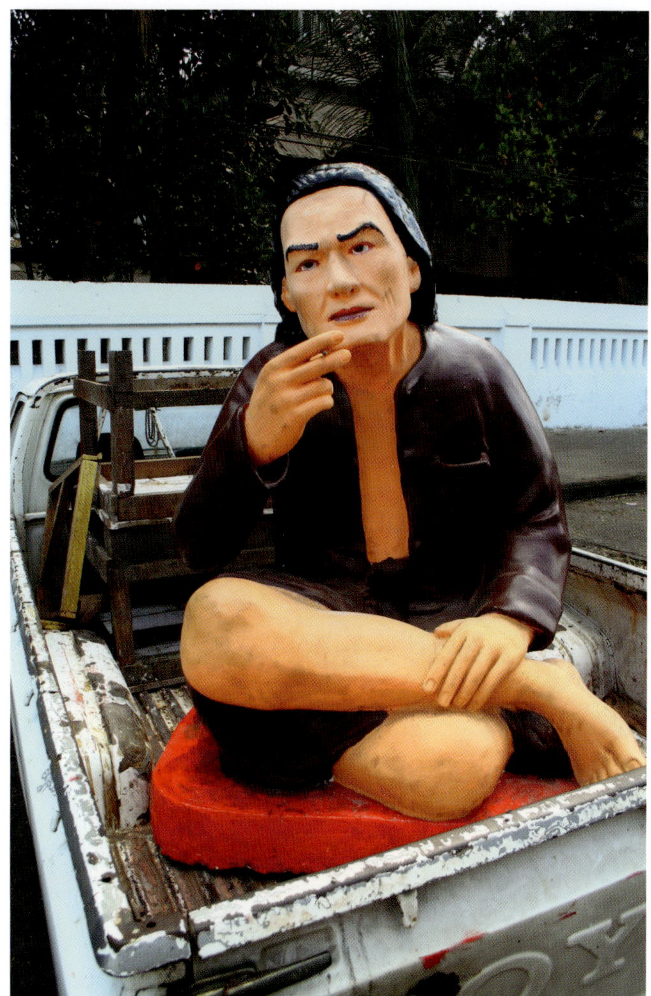

FIG. 19. A sculpture of Bo Min Kaung, a famous twentieth-century wizard, transported in the back of a truck

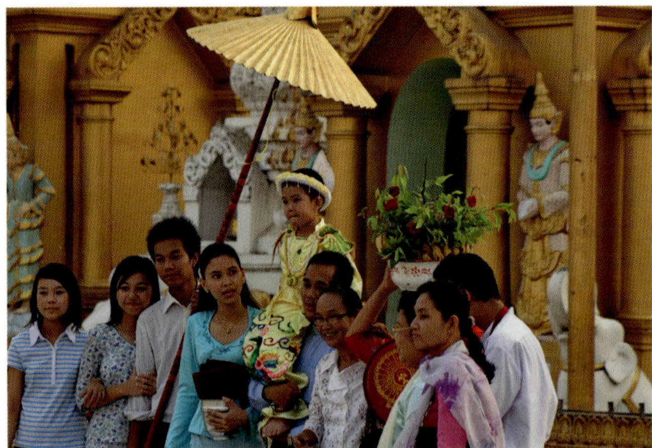

FIG. 20. A novitiate with his family at the Shwedagon Pagoda before entering the monastery

in Myanmar rather than Pali to appeal to wider audiences, these works are characterized by their wealth of detail as well as by their voluminous size, the longest of them, the *Tathagata-udana-dipani*, occupying over a thousand pages in its printed edition.[8] All of the Buddha chronicles of this period share a common outline and trace the Buddha's life from his nativity and royal upbringing, through his renunciation and enlightenment, to his final passing away in *parinibbana*. The presentation of a complete biography of the Buddha from birth to death appears to have been an eighteenth-century innovation in Myanmar Theravada literature, for there are no extant examples from earlier centuries. Prior to that, the Buddha's biography was always presented in discrete segments, some of which could be quite extensive, but none encompassing his entire life. It was during the Konbaung period that authors for the first time began to assemble the many episodes and chapters of the Buddha's life that were scattered throughout Pali literature and weave them together into a contiguous, full life story.

This is not to say that the people of Myanmar have not been keenly interested in the life of the Buddha since the dawn of their civilization. Numerous votive plaques have been recovered from the ancient Pyu city of Sri Ksetra (fifth to ninth century) near Prome, or Pyay, that depict the eight scenes of the Buddha's life, a motif borrowed from the Buddhist iconography of the contemporaneous Pala Dynasty (eighth to twelfth century) in North India.[9] At Pagan, or Bagan, Myanmar's first imperial capital (ninth to thirteenth century), similar plaques have been discovered, some of which incorporate along with the eight scenes, depictions of the seven weeks of the Buddha's enlightenment story as given in Pali sources. Some historians have suggested that the combination of these two narrative sequences in votive plaques represents an iconographic innovation in Pala Dynasty tourist art that was specially designed to appeal to Myanmar pilgrims from Pagan (see cat. no. 28).[10] The twelfth-century Ananda Temple at Pagan contains a series of no fewer than eighty sculptures, each in its own niche, that recount the life of the Buddha in detail from his miraculous conception and birth up to his enlightenment, but abruptly stop there. The Ananda series follows the narrative outline of an incomplete biography of the Buddha found in the *Jataka-nidana*, the introductory chapter of a fifth-century Pali commentary on the canonical *jatakas*, or *Birth Stories of the Buddha*, written by the famous commentator Buddhaghosa.[11] Depictions of later events in the Buddha's life up to his *parinibbana*, taken from other Pali sources, are placed elsewhere in the temple, but occur as isolated tableaus rather than being linked to a larger narrative or arranged into a chronological order.[12]

As the examples mentioned above suggest, all of the basic elements that make up the standard outline of the Buddha's biography as it is known today were already in use at Pagan. It was in the eighteenth and nineteenth centuries that Myanmar chroniclers arranged these elements into the carefully planned sequence of episodes characteristic of the Konbaung-era *bodawins*.[13] Into this basic framework were inserted additional stories and an overall elaboration in narrative detail based on Pali sources that had not yet been used at Pagan.[14] The biographical core of the resulting *bodawins* was typically prefaced with an account of the Buddha's previous lives and followed by an epilogue detailing events after his death. These additions to the main narrative vary in length from text to text depending on the preferences of the authors, but all of them remain securely based on the *Tipitaka*, its commentaries, or other orthodox Pali sources. This conservatism in terms of content and source material is characteristic of Myanmar's Buddhist scholastic tradition, which for centuries has prided itself on its close adherence to, and expert exegesis of, Pali textual authorities. But it also means that Myanmar's standard *bodawins*, however richly detailed they may be, restrict themselves to only narrating the legendary life of the Buddha as it was lived in India, since that is the entirety of what the ancient Pali sources contained. As a consequence *bodawins* typically do not include much if any of the many colorful, and for devout Myanmar Buddhists, often deeply meaningful popular native accounts of the Buddha's frequent visits to Myanmar, where he is shown time and again defeating demons, performing miracles, making prophesies of great import, and converting the masses and leading them to salvation through his teachings.

These localizations of the Buddha's biography in Myanmar are almost always identified with major pilgrimage sites, whose legends are preserved in a wide variety of indigenous sources, such as pagoda histories, or *thamaing* (Myanmar), dedicatory inscriptions, pilgrims' guides, and the foundation legends of important cities and kingdoms contained in royal chronicles, or *yazawin* (Myanmar). Because they are tied to particular locales, these legends of the Buddha's visitations are usually associated with specific political domains and ethnicities, and because of this they often are also closely linked to Buddhist kingship. Historically, kings and queens were the major patrons of Myanmar's most famous Buddhist shrines—an unavoidable requisite of monarchy in a country where the prestige and legitimacy of every royal house, both in the eyes of its subjects and in the eyes of neighboring kingdoms, was measured chiefly by the generosity it could muster and display in support of the religion. In Myanmar, as elsewhere in Theravada Southeast Asia and Sri Lanka, Buddhist polity was conceived to be a kind of giant merit-making enterprise, where every good deed was for the good of all, and where the Buddhist monarch, as chief among lay donors, served as the main instrument through which everyone in the kingdom, from aristocrat to slave, participated in, and benefited from, royal acts of merit.

NOTES

1 See for example the account of the famous nineteenth-century monk Thingazar Sayadaw, who preached throughout British-controlled Lower Myanmar in the 1870s. Maung Htin Aung, *Burmese Monk's Tales*, 3–36. A contemporary example is the Ven. Sitagu Sayadaw, Ashin Nyanissara, the most well-known preaching monk in Myanmar today.

2 According to Theravada calculation, the Buddha attained enlightenment at the age of 35 in 589 BCE. He died 45 years later at the age of 80 in 544 BCE.

3 The Myanmar legend of Tapussa and Bhallika as it is known to pilgrims today is the product of centuries of narrative elaboration. The earliest iteration of the legend occurs in the Pali *Vinaya-pitaka* where even the hair relics, the focus of devotion at the heart of the Shwedagon, are not yet introduced into the story line.

4 Walshe, *Long Discourses of the Buddha*, 264–65.

5 The Buddha established a *Sangha* of ordained nuns (*bhikkhuni* in Pali) along with the *Sangha* of ordained monks (*bhikkhu* in Pali) although in Theravada countries the nuns' ordination lineage is believed to have died out about a thousand years ago. Lacking an ordination, the Buddhist nuns of Myanmar occupy the position of lay religious women much like nuns in the Roman Catholic tradition. Organized into orders, they typically live in convents and observe ten rules of conduct patterned after those of novice monks. Nowadays, it is not uncommon for nuns to out-perform monks in the state-administered Pali examinations, a fact that contributes to their prestige. Buddhist hermits are lay religious men who likewise pattern their conduct after that of Buddhist novices. They are typically wandering ascetics and often are associated with esotericism and occult arts—practices normally eschewed by the monkhood as disallowed by the *Vinaya*.

6 In the Myanmar calendar, there are eight days in the week, with Wednesday being counted as two days—the morning counting as one day, and the afternoon and evening counting as a second day.

7 See Stadtner, *Sacred Sites of Burma*, 92.

8 See Sirisaddhammabhilankara, *Tathagata-udana-dipani-kyam*. Three Buddha biographies from this period proved to be most influential: *Tathagata-udana-dipani* (ca. 1772), *Malalankara-vatthu* (1798), and *Jinattha-pakasani* (ca. 1865). Originally composed on palm leaf, all three were published in the early twentieth century.

9 The eight scenes show some variation in content but always include the nativity, enlightenment, and *parinibbana*, and so in a sense represent in superficial form a complete biography of the Buddha, albeit in a very abbreviated form. It is significant that the motif is Pala in origin. The Pala Dynasty patronized Mahayana Buddhism, which preserved its scriptures in Sanskrit. Unlike the Pali literary tradition of the Theravada, which never produced a complete biography of the Buddha, the Sanskrit Buddhist tradition produced a complete biography already in the second century CE with Ashvaghosa's poetical masterpiece, the *Buddhacarita*.

10 Donald Stadtner, personal communication, December 2013.

11 While not containing a complete biography, the *Jataka-nidana* gives the most extensive account of the Buddha's life found in classical Pali sources. It is divided into three chapters arranged according to time frame. The first chapter covers the Buddha's previous lives as a bodhisattva, from his life as the ascetic Sumedha when he first vowed to become a Buddha, up to his penultimate life as the god Setaketu in Tusita Heaven. The second chapter describes his nativity and life as a prince and continues up to his enlightenment, and the third chapter records events in the Buddha's life following his enlightenment up to his accepting the Jetavana Grove as a donation some twenty years later. The Ananda Temple's series of eighty sculptures represents an iteration of the *Jataka-nidana*'s second chapter. See Jayawickrama, *Story of Gotama Buddha*, 63–101.

12 For a discussion of the Buddha biography as represented at Pagan, see Luce, *Old Burma—Early Pagan*, 1: 147–84.

13 Special attention was given in these *bodawins* to the precise dating of events in the Buddha's life. This emphasis on chronology facilitated the synchronizing of the Buddha's biography, which was constructed from Pali sources, with legendary episodes from Myanmar's own ancient history.

14 Chief among these works were the *Mahavamsa-tika* (ca. eighth–ninth century) and *Extended Mahavamsa* (ca. ninth–tenth century), both elaborations on the fifth-century *Mahavamsa*.

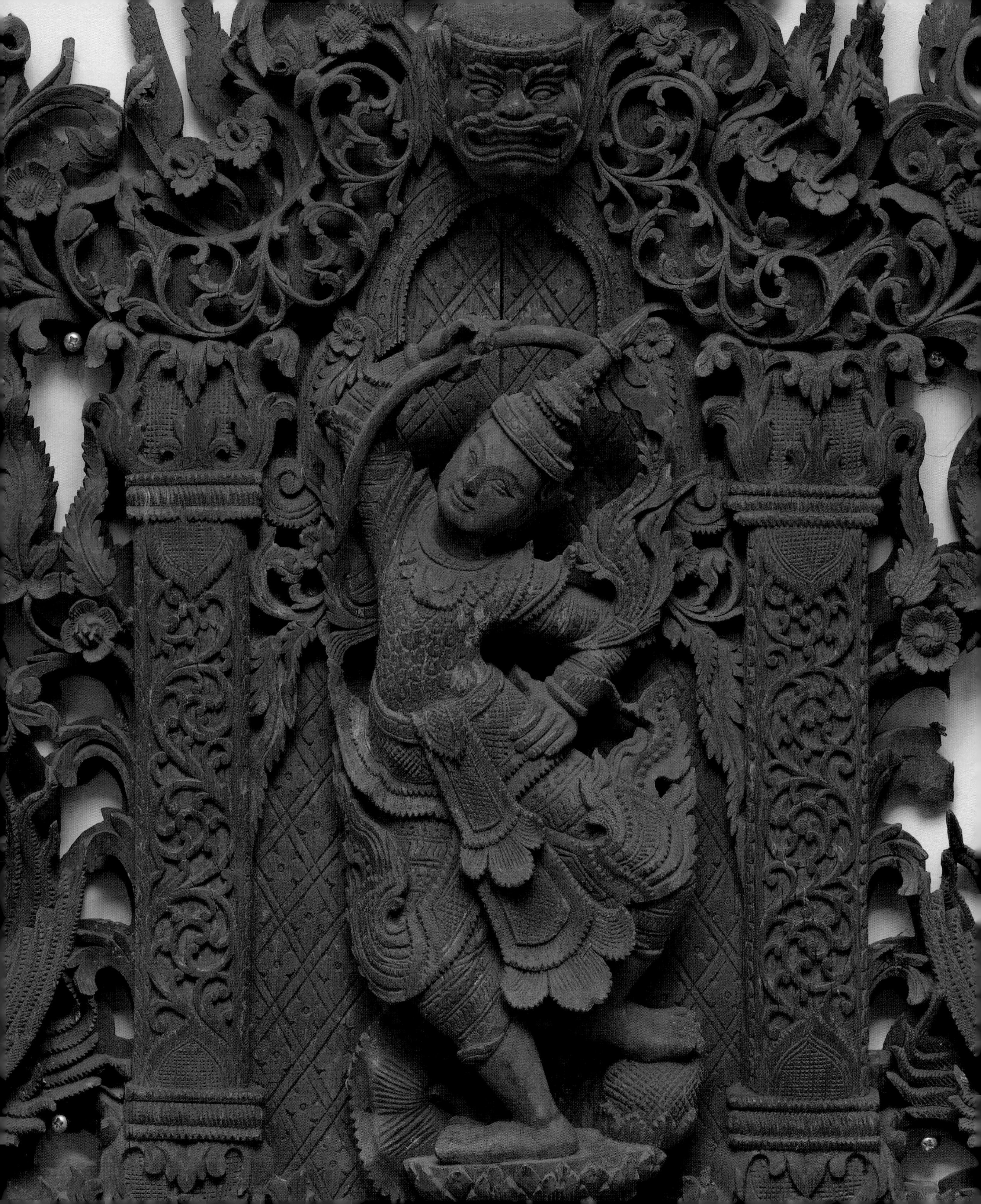

Myanmar and the Outside World

Jacques Leider

Buddhism and trade have been Myanmar's most important interfaces with the outside world, but their importance in shaping external relations has varied greatly. Traders and missionaries were instrumental during the first millennium CE in expanding the teachings of Buddhism and laying the foundation for the country's mature civilization under the kings of Pagan, or Bagan. Exploring Buddhism in its practice and in its art and architecture, one is inevitably drawn in two directions: to the inside toward Myanmar's self-perception and cultural identity and to the outside toward the multiple genealogies from which the country's religious, ritual, and intellectual traditions are derived or have been connected over the centuries. Understanding and defining the inside seems to be the easier task. Buddhism has been the dominant cultural matrix of the country, and Buddhist markers—including artistic forms, concepts, ways of thinking, and social practices—outline a cultural and religious space that has structured Myanmar's historical trajectory throughout the geographical center of the Irrawaddy, or Ayeyarwady, Valley for the last thousand years and longer. This interest in Myanmar has therefore favored a scholarly perception of Buddhism as an intrinsic part of Myanmar's identity rather than being, by itself, a historical agent.

The conventional approach of western scholars has been to look at Myanmar and trade from the outside, in keeping with the perspective of archival sources that adopt the viewpoint of often malcontent Portuguese, Dutch, or English merchants trading Indian cloth, teak wood, rice, rubies, betel nuts, or elephants in Myanmar or Rakhine ports. In this it is too easy to forget the breadth of interests of Myanmar's kings, elites, and traders that nurtured trade relations with the outside world. As the people of Myanmar were neither seafaring nor were they running caravan trade through Inner Asia, historians have often argued that they did not pay much attention to foreign trade. Still, Myanmar's regions were integral parts of both land and maritime trade networks. Nor should one overlook that in the past Myanmar was not a state with fixed borders but included, during most of its precolonial history, several political centers, conventionally known to precolonial Europeans as Rakhine, or Arakan, a coastal kingdom integrated in the Bay of Bengal maritime network; Ava, or Inwa, a place connected both to the riverine and the inland trade; and Pegu, or Bago, a longtime inland port connected to the sea ports of Martaban and later Syriam.

Nonetheless, while one could approach the topic of Myanmar and the outside worlds through themes of Indianization, colonization, or modernization, this would suggest that Myanmar people and their leaders were recipients of foreign influence rather than agents of their own historical

OPPOSITE Detail of cat. no. 54

destiny. They would confirm G. E. Harvey's perception, as he wrote in 1925, of the Myanmar people as "living in a world of their own," who did not "visit other lands" while "nobody from other lands came to them, except a few shipmen and some tribal immigrants." For this colonial historian, "Myanmar knew nothing of international affairs save through bazaar rumor and through the tales, usually anti-English propaganda, of Armenian and Mahomedan merchants."[1] The cliché of Myanmar's marginality seems to find further confirmation in the country's recent reputation gained through decades of outcast status and self-inflicted isolation under authoritarian regimes between 1962 and 2011. Moreover, common textbook characterizations of Myanmar as being a "part" of Southeast Asia or a land "between" India and China, convey no particular sense of homegrown developments. The old-fashioned colonial view that "the existence of the Burmese as a powerful and widespread race [was] due to Indian immigration," peremptorily stated in the *Census of India* of 1911, has long ceded its place to Paul Mus's insight that "Indian culture is complementary . . . not imposed, [but] called for from within Southeast Asia."[2] Postcolonial scholars have not only refined the concept of Indianization but have also integrated the archaeological and inscriptional evidence of the influence of Brahminist and Buddhist ideas within dynamic, local urban communities.

An excellent example of how Buddhism and trade gave essence to Myanmar's relations with the outside world is the territorial expansion under the early Konbaung kings (1782–1819) when, following a secular trend, external relations were at their peak. The second half of the eighteenth and the early nineteenth century were a crucial period in world history. It was an important time in Myanmar as well, when following seventeen years of internecine wars (1740–57), the country moved through a phase of territorial consolidation in the middle of the century toward a period of vibrant expansion. One hallmark of the early Konbaung dynasty was its aggressive policy of conquests that enlarged the kingdom considerably beyond the Irrawaddy Valley. Following the fall of the city of Pegu in 1757, King Alaungpaya, also known as Alaungmintaya, the dynasty's founder, reunified the northern and southern parts (the Myanmar-dominated Ava and the predominantly Mon kingdom of Hamsavati, or Pegu). The conquest of Manipur in 1758–59 gave the Myanmar king a foothold to intervene in Assam after 1805, while a well-prepared invasion of Thailand by land and sea in 1759–60 laid the ground for the conquest of Tenasserim, which would come under full Myanmar control in 1793. In 1785, a decisive campaign against Rakhine put an end to this old Buddhist kingdom on the border with Bengal that had enjoyed independence since 1430.

This vast territorial expansion was read in negative terms by colonial historians, who considered Myanmar's conquests barbarous and lacking inspiration in state building.[3] Contemporary scholarship has nonetheless rehabilitated the statesmanship of early Konbaung kings from Alaungpaya (r. 1752–1760) to Bodawpaya (r. 1782–1819). Due to an increasingly centralized royal administration, Konbaung capitals such as Ava or Amarapura boasted efficient political control over the country's river plains and their close, mountainous periphery. With the growing commercialization of the economy and the existence of an intricate money-lending system, this was, in historian Thant Myint-U's words, the time when "a common language, a common religion, a common set of legal and political ideas and institutions, and even a shared history existed throughout the core area."[4] Myanmar was perceived by British geographers of the early nineteenth century as second only to China's military power in Asia. Still, this was not a territorially unified kingdom, as borders were largely undefined or rapidly changing. A set of maps of Myanmar, drawn in 1795 at the request of Dr. Francis Hamilton, conveys the idea of a central corridor of river valleys with strings of interconnected urban centers, surrounded by far-flung outlying regions that were separated and divided by vast, sparsely inhabited zones. Under the early Konbaung kings, the kingdom's geographical body was undergoing tremendous change, growing toward the west and the south, receding in the northeast, and blocked from expanding toward the east.

Relentless warfare against Thailand between 1759 and 1812 overstretched Myanmar's human resources, but resulted in the conquest of Tenasserim and the control of its trade ports Mergui (together with the inland city of Tenasserim) and Tavoy, or Dawei, which had been key possessions of Ayutthaya's transpeninsular commercial network. Together with the control of Rakhine, the territorial expansion toward the south roughly tripled Myanmar's coastline on the Indian Ocean, unifying its maritime frontier and creating challenging new opportunities. The conquest of Rakhine facilitated

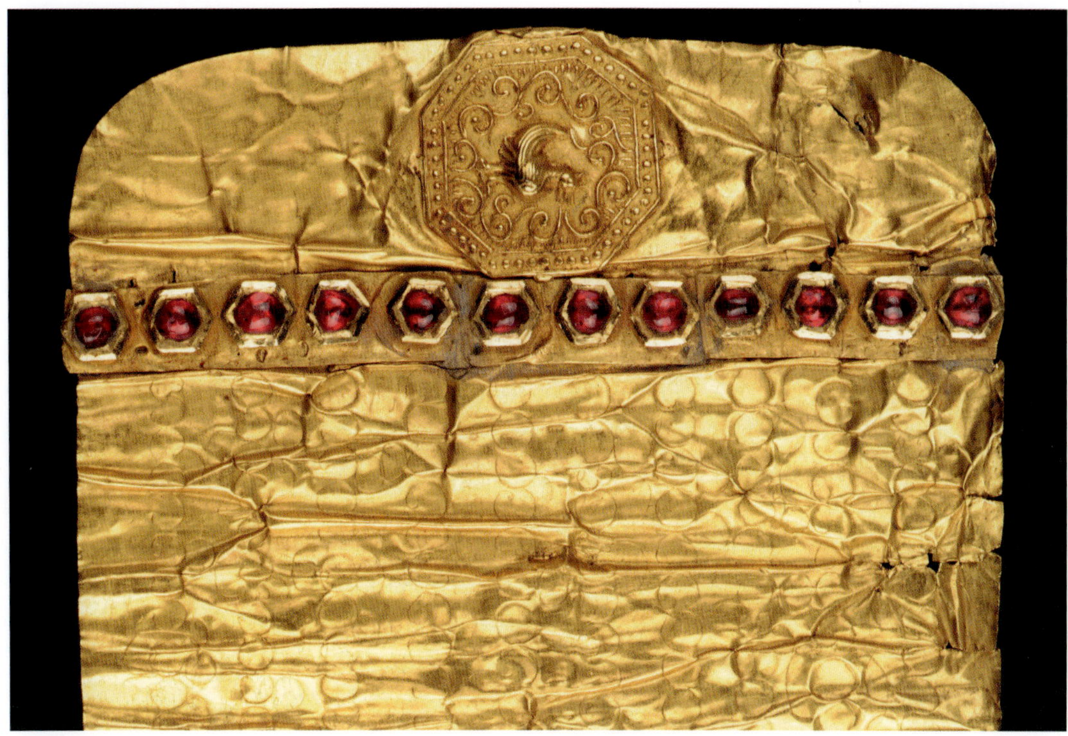

FIG. 21. Golden Letter from King Alaungpaya of Myanmar to King George II of Great Britain, May 7, 1756. Gold plate; gold purity between 95 and 98 percent. H. 3⅜ x W. 21½ x D. 1/125 in. (8.5 x 54.7 x 0.02 cm). Adorned with 24 egg-shaped Mogok rubies fixed in 6 x 6 mm hexagonal settings on two gold ribbons. Inserted seal with *hamsa* bird. Total weight: 100 g. Gottfried Wilhelm Leibniz Bibliothek–Niedersächsische Landesbibliothek, Hanover, Germany: Ms IV, 571a.

contact with Bengal, and soon an inland trade road developed—crossing Rakhine by the Am Pass northward to Hsinbyugywan—which bypassed the long voyage up the Irrawaddy and its numerous tax posts. The often brutal eradication of local power that followed military conquest—a tactic to avoid losing these territories shortly after conquest—and the pressure on the conquered population to support Myanmar's warfare through providing recruits and provisions, often resulted in huge demographic losses. Subjected people would flee en masse to more peaceful areas; for example, numerous Mon fled to Thailand, and the people of Rakhine resettled in Chittagong. Thai historians have shown that, starting with King Alaungpaya's 1759 campaign against Ayutthaya, or Yodaya (Myanmar), Myanmar's southward expansion was motivated by the rapidly growing exports of tin and pepper produced in the Malay peninsula. The lucrative export of Bengali opium to the peninsula and the Indonesian archipelago, as well as the trade of bird nests controlled by the sultan of Kedah, fit into the same picture of expansion fueled by trade, where Myanmar competed not only with the Thai, but also with the British, who had opened a port at Penang in 1786. Successive Myanmar attacks against Thalang, or Phuket, failed, while the Thai, in turn, consolidated their possessions on the eastern side of the Malay peninsula, taking possession of Pattani and reasserting their control over the sultan of Kedah.

British sources testify to the existence of royal trade at the beginning of the Konbaung Dynasty. In an exquisite golden letter adorned with twenty-four rubies sent to King George II in 1756, King Alaungpaya declared that he was keen to seal friendship with the British and made friendly overtures for stable business relations with the East India Company (fig. 21). King Alaungpaya founded the port of Yangon, or Rangoon, in 1754 and heavily lobbied both French and English traders to move their trade from Pegu's Syriam, or Thanlyin, to his new port. The damage his own ship suffered at the hands of Thai authorities in Tavoy was allegedly one of the events that triggered the invasion of Thailand in 1759.[5]

The 1767 conquest of Ayutthaya by King Hsinbyushin (r. 1763–1776) is considered a crucial moment in Thai national history because of its destructive impact—the fall of the city, the loss of its treasures, and the end of a dynasty—and the subsequent establishment of a new political order by the Chakri rulers based in Bangkok. The Myanmar did not intend to rule the center of Thailand, but deported several tens of thousands of people from Thailand to Ava. Resettled alongside the Chinese, Muslim, and Manipuri quarters, the Thai brought huge change to Myanmar's visual arts as musicians and dancers. They made the dramatic performance of the *Ramayana*, an epic story that was not wholly unknown in Myanmar, hugely popular as a drama. In 1789, a translation committee was tasked with translating the dance-drama, as well as other literary works from Ayutthaya and northern Thailand. The introduction of western perspective in Myanmar painting, as well as the use of gilding techniques, has been attributed to these Thai, "Yodaya" painters.[6] Thus skilled Thai, but also Manipuri, craftsmen, musicians, and artists had a long-lasting impact on Myanmar's dance, song, and orchestral music.[7] Furthermore, the people from Ayutthaya revived the building of sand pagodas and established it as a distinctive tradition practiced by several monasteries in Mandalay.[8] Still, cultural inputs from the ethnic-Tai world, beyond the Thais of the Ayutthaya, under Myanmar's political control largely predated the Konbaung period to at least to the seventeenth century. Alexandra Green summarizes the complexity of this development stating, "the transfer of religious stories and practices into central Myanmar from Lan Na, the Shan States, and Sipsong Panna was the result of trade, religious exchange, and pilgrimages, royal and monastic interconnections, warfare, and the expansionist efforts of the Burmese."[9]

Besides the commercial drives connected to the coastal expansion in the Andaman Sea already described, the political motives for Myanmar's unrelenting warfare against Thailand between 1775 and 1812, most notably King Bodawpaya's "nine-army war" of 1785–86, were linked to the reassertion of Myanmar's control over areas situated along the Upper Mekong as well as in Lan Na, where Chiang Mai had regained its autonomy with the rise of the ruler Kavila in 1774.[10] During confrontations that took place between 1803 and 1808, the Myanmar were able to defend Chiang Tung and keep a hold on the Tai principalities in southern Yunnan, but in 1804 they lost the strategic fortress Chiang Saen, which was situated on the Mekong, and with it all reasonable hope to reach out once more for control of northern Laos.

King Bodawpaya was an overconfident monarch who not only wanted to demonstrate his power through projects of territorial expansion, but also sought to excel as protector of Buddhism and a benefactor of holy Buddhist sites. What distinguished Bodawpaya from many other kings was that, from early on he took an extremely critical stance toward the state of religion and public morals, in particular the monkhood's observance of its own disciplinary norms. He put an end to a ferocious monastic debate regarding the wearing of the robe by novices, a conflict that represented at its core a competition between monastic factions that had lingered for decades. Bodawpaya failed to reestablish the monkhood, or *Sangha* (Pali), according to his own norms and moral standards, but he reset the local monastic hierarchies by enforcing reordinations throughout the kingdom with a focus on the peripheral zones. In Rakhine, Myanmar missionary monks faced local resistance when they performed reordinations to align the local *Sangha*. Surprisingly, they were also duty bound to convert the hill minorities to Buddhism. One of the king's worries touched upon the correct setting and observation of dates in the religious calendar. He scolded leading monks for their astronomical incompetence and checked land claims and chronicle accounts against the evidence of stone inscriptions that he had collected and copied. The king's father, King Alaungpaya, a newcomer to royal power, had followed the recommendations of court members and ceremonial masters of the previous Ava dynasty to establish his court. Bodawpaya, on the other hand, did not want simply to reestablish and follow ancient tradition; he wanted to go back to its roots in the textual foundations of kingship, the royal ablution ceremonies, and ritual ceremonies at the court.

The early Konbaung kings ambitiously claimed to be born to rule a domain that was not limited to what historians or geographers would define as Myanmar. Ideally, this domain would be referred to as Majjhimadesa—the Middle Land from Buddhist canonical texts, the part of central India where the Buddhist teachings flourished in Buddhism's early

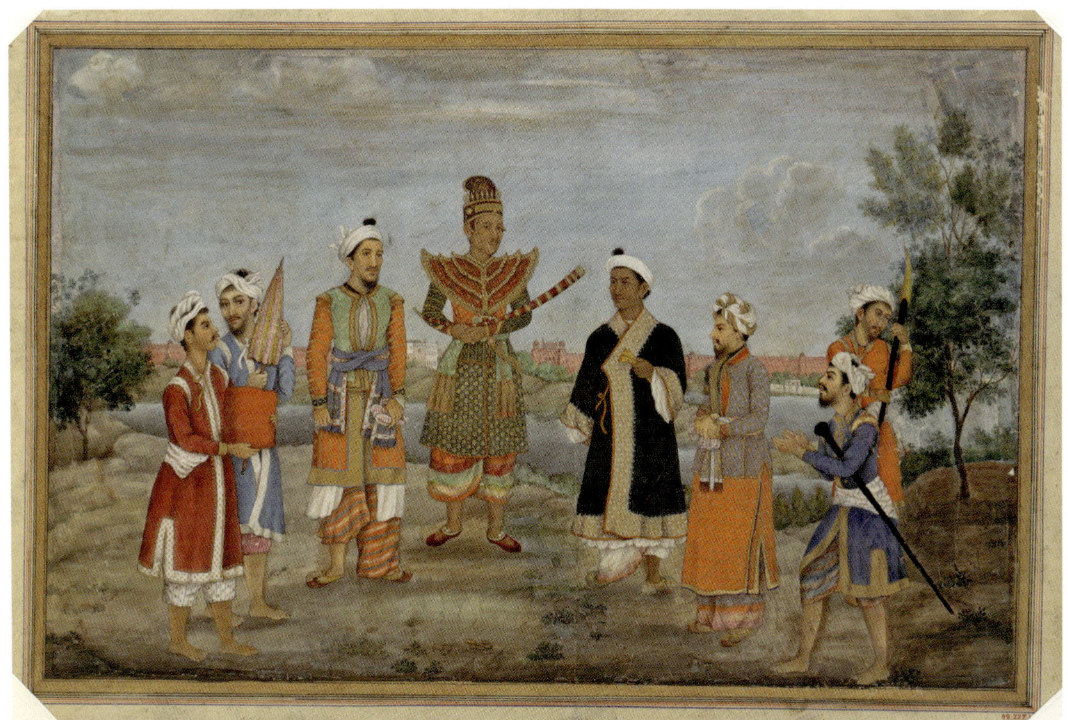

FIG. 22. The communication between Myanmar and India during the Konbaung period (1752–1885) is captured in this anonymous painting, *Eight Men in Indian and Burmese Costume*. Delhi, India. 19th century. Opaque watercolor, ink, and gold on paper. H. 10 x W. 15½ in. (25.4 x 39.4 cm). The Metropolitan Museum of Art: Gift of Dr. Julius Hoffman, 1909, 09.227.1

stages. It is also, in Indian mythology, a part of Jambudipa, the continent where humans reside. In Bodawpaya's intuitive understanding, Myanmar was a part of this imaginary-cum-historical Majjhimadesa because of the belief that not only Gotama but also previous Buddhas had paid visits to Myanmar in former cosmic cycles. It is in this context that one can interpret the king's alleged project to conquer India not simply as a political fantasy but as a logical move within his vision of cosmic duty as a Buddhist world-ruler and protector of Buddhist sites.[11] Visiting the places where Buddhism had its origins is defined in religious terms as a pilgrimage, but it was also part of what one scholar has called the preservation of the religion by "pristinification."[12] In 1811, a Myanmar dignitary sent by King Bodawpaya visited the temple ruins of Bodh Gaya, like many visitors from Myanmar before him. A year later, during his own visit, Francis Hamilton learned of this Myanmar mission and made the following comment: "Hence we may infer that the old man [the Burmese king] . . . has been induced to set up the doctrine afresh. In the year 1795, the priests of Buddha were seriously alarmed at the influence which the Brahmins had then acquired." Hamilton also reports that already some years before two royal messengers had paid a visit to India "in search of the holy places rendered remarkable by the actions of Gautama" using "books, by the assistance of which they pretended to trace the holy places and to detail their history."[13] Missions were also sent to Varanasi, or Benares, to recruit competent Brahmin astrologers to revise the ceremonial calendar of the court and bring back Sanskrit texts to authorize such changes (fig. 22).

Bodawpaya's huge intellectual curiosity with regard to kingship and tradition was also demonstrated in his demands for ritual expertise and medical and historical texts from Rakhine after the Myanmar conquest. The foremost trophy from the 1784–85 campaign was the Mahamuni Statue, the paragon of the Rakhine kings taken to Amarapura, an invaluable statue that materialized and confirmed the king's self-acclaimed supernatural status as a predestined monarch.

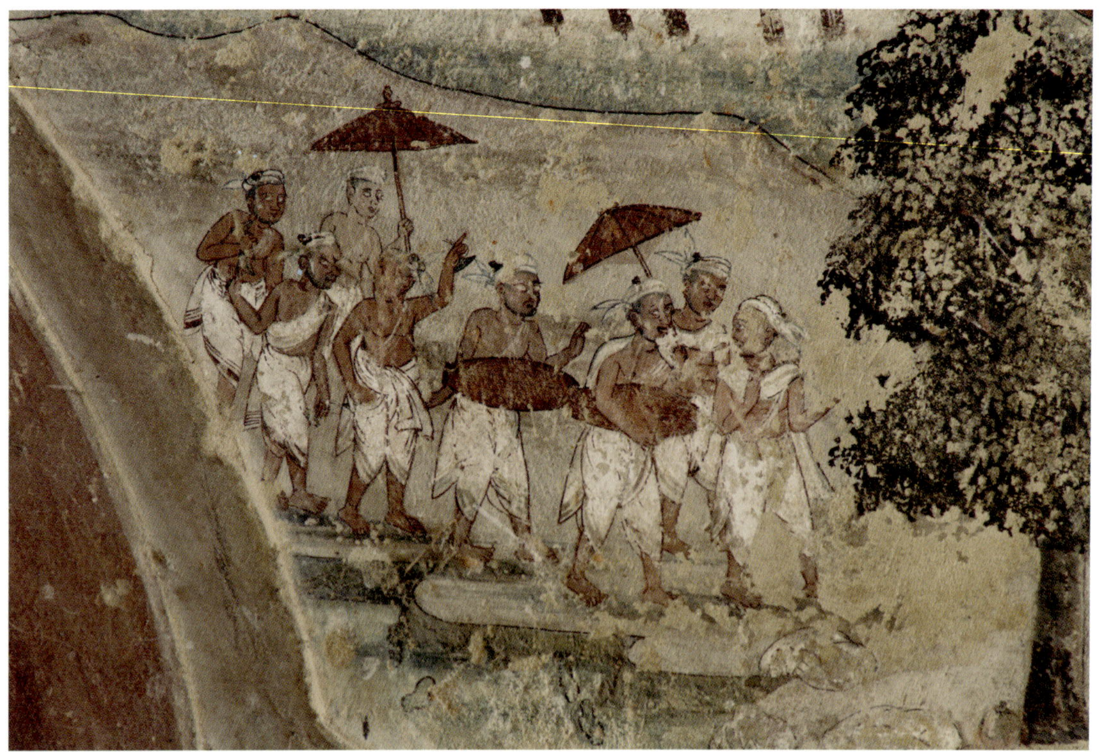

FIG. 23. Indians, clad in white, were probably a common sight in Upper Myanmar in the Konbaung period (1752–1885). Mural. Ca. 1850. Kyauktawgyi Pagoda, Amarapura

The king also deported the entire Rakhine court elite to Amarapura. Among them, the *ponnas* (court Brahmins) from Rakhine replaced existing ritual experts and formed a new elite at the Konbaung court during the nineteenth century. For the court in Amarapura, conquest was not only about territorial expansion and wider access to the trade in the Bay of Bengal; the cultural appropriation of Rakhine's ritual and ceremonial knowledge was part of what the king saw as a restoration of Buddhist kingship and royal ritual in conformity with Brahminic standards (fig. 23). The royal library contained translations of chronicles from Chiang Mai, Manipur, Pegu, and Laos, lands that had been or were still part of the kingdom. Rakhine's integration into the kingdom is notably reflected in historiography with the adaptation and integration of a part of the former kingdom's historical record in the royal court chronicle.

The early Konbaung court's interest in the old Buddhist world of northern India was paralleled by the continuity of the kingdom's secular, monastic links with Sri Lanka, from which Myanmar Buddhism drew its identity, historical foundations, and canonical teachings. Though the textual evidence is sparse, it is nonetheless revealing. When Francis Hamilton returned from Amarapura to Calcutta at the end of 1795, he met a man from Tavoy whom Bodawpaya had sent to Sri Lanka "to bring an account of the Temples at Anuradhapura, the ancient capital of the island."[14] Although there is no other information on this remarkable visit, the object of the mission was clearly to show the king's attention to ancient Buddhist history and topography. It is well known that Myanmar Buddhist orthodoxy traces its origins back to the textual tradition cultivated at the Mahavihara monastery in Anuradhapura.[15] But there is much more to the story. In late eighteenth-century Sri Lanka, Anuradhapura—an ancient archaeological site of religious significance—remained hugely important to the king of Kandy as a site of remembrance. Religious sites were generously maintained, monastic communities were revived, and roads to the old city were repaired.[16] This revival of Anuradhapura calls for a comparison with restoration done simultaneously in Pagan. Bodawpaya's son, the crown prince, intended to make Pagan his future capital and initiated restoration at several temple sites, notably at the Lokananda Pagoda, which was witnessed by the mission led by Captain Michael Symes, envoy of the East India Company to the Court of Amarapura in 1795. The existence of numerous Konbaung-era temples and libraries in Pagan, as well as eighteenth-century mural paintings in many of its temples, is also of particular interest. Pagan's architectural, artistic, and spiritual revival during the early Konbaung period should thus be reimagined within the wider context of a Buddhist nostalgia for religious sites of memory, a feeling shared in Sri Lanka, Myanmar, and eventually beyond, further stressing Pagan's cultural and historical significance in the Buddhist world. Moreover, the revival of religious activities in Pagan and Kandy underscores the indissoluble links that exist between the intimate political and spiritual ambitions of King Bodawpaya on the one hand, and a wider Buddhist endeavor for reform and textual purity that was shared by leading Buddhist figures. Many were worried and frightened by the decline of the Buddhist teaching and institutions.

While trade and pilgrimage remained constant elements of Myanmar's presence in the Indian Ocean over the centuries, the development of Myanmar's relations with the outside world during the second half of the eighteenth century has traditionally been interpreted in light of the shifting balance of maritime power in the Indian Ocean. Still, while the power of the British grew in India, Myanmar's own steady expansion was nourished by maritime trade interests and ambitions to either maintain or extend its territorial control. Between 1761 and 1795, due to the destruction of the Negrais trade settlement, there was no more official contact between the East India Company and the Myanmar court.[17] They were not yet on a collision course, although early signs of future confrontations appeared along the Bengal-Rakhine border, years before the British mission to Amarapura in 1795.

Similar to Myanmar's western maritime borders, the integration of parts of the country into transregional networks of trade and exchange help elucidate its relations with China. The renaissance of Myanmar's official interaction with China was a major aspect of Myanmar's relations with the outside world during the early Konbaung period. Local and regional interests emerged as the initial drivers of diplomatic action, and relations with the Chinese empire should be understood from the angle of commercial interests and Yunnan border affairs before regarding them as a matter of prestige.

In 1750, a Chinese trader named Wu Shangxian, who exploited a silver mine in the Shan-Wa border zone, led a trade delegation sent by King Mahadhammayazadhipati of Ava to the court at Beijing. The Myanmar king was led to believe that the mission, referred to as a tributary mission by the Chinese court, could ensure the support of Chinese troops for his plans, while the Chinese miner wanted to see an easing of trade conditions between Myanmar and Yunnan. As a result, Ava was foreseeably registered as an imperial vassal, but unfortunately Mahadhammayazadhipati, the last king of the Nyaung-yan dynasty, lost his power when, a year later, the capital fell into the hands of an invading army from Pegu. Still, during the previous hundred years, Myanmar kings and Chinese emperors had quietly ignored each other at the highest level, as neither side was driven by expansionist ambitions. In fact, the official objective of Wu's mission sheds some light on transregional commercial interests that had been increasing with the growth of autonomous and wealthy Chinese communities along the unclearly defined border.

The importance of this local episode pales in comparison with the events that took place fifteen years later when the Qing Empire waged war on the kingdom of Myanmar (1765–70). This was, as Yingcong Dai wrote, "the most disastrous frontier war that the Qing dynasty had ever waged."[18] While the reasons that triggered the outbreak of violence are contested, the deep causes were related to a reaffirmation of Myanmar rule over Tai-Yuan principalities (now located in the Sipsong Panna or Xishuangbanna Dai Autonomous Prefecture of China) that had for a long time accepted rule by China and Myanmar, paying tribute to both sovereigns. During their first encounter in Puer, Yunnan, the Myanmar troops routed the Qing provincial garrisons led by the Yunnan governor. Three ensuing campaigns put into the trusted hands of eminent Chinese and Manchu generals similarly ended in disasters despite the lessons learned during various offensives in 1766 and 1767, namely that the threat of lethal diseases, the transport of provisions, and the difficult terrain were insurmountable challenges. King Hsinbyushin (r. 1763–1776) successfully defended the border against the imperial invaders, who ultimately failed to restore the "dignity" of the Empire.[19] With the retreat of the Chinese army and the signing of a treaty, the Myanmar court hoped that the border trade would instantly resume; regrettably, however, the Chinese trade embargo lasted until 1790.

The relationship softened only after 1787, when a bogus mission, probably again initiated by Yunnan traders, was sent to Bodawpaya's court. The king then sent a mission to the Qing court, which Emperor Qianlong interpreted as a tributary mission, henceforth putting an end to the embargo. Trade with China was demonstrably of foremost concern to the Myanmar side, and Bodawpaya made great efforts to nurture relations with the Qing court.[20] Altogether five royal letters, written on sheets of gold, were sent to the Chinese emperor between 1787 and 1792. The magnificent reception of Chinese delegations at the court in Amarapura was self-gratifying to Bodawpaya who reveled in the Emperor's friendship. Still, some Chinese missions, dressed up as imperial delegations, may actually have been regional missions sent from Yunnan where the local government was pulled into action by the importance of the border commerce. In 1790, the Chinese also sent the king a tooth relic of the Buddha, the most valuable present they could possibly give in the eyes of the king.[21] This form of Buddhist diplomacy was revived in recent decades to underscore the cordiality of both countries' relations: in 1955, 1994, 1996, and 2011, Buddha's tooth relic, kept in the Lingguang Temple in Beijing, was taken to Myanmar for temporary visits, and a copy is now kept in a pagoda built north of Yangon.

It is this tremendous success story of territorial expansion, unchallenged achievements on the battlefield, prestigious relations with China, symbolic appropriation of Indian Buddhist sites, and cultural enrichment that lay the groundwork for the court of Myanmar's overly self-confident stance by the time it had to face the threatening British power in Assam and on the Chittagong-Rakhine border. The crushing defeat Myanmar experienced in the First Anglo-Burmese War (1824–26) set the kingdom on a difficult track of adjusting itself to a rapidly changing international context, as its military prowess and capacity to negotiate the control of widely distant lands were insufficient to face the challenges of western imperialism. Nonetheless, the British invasion came at a huge cost for the British invaders, even provoking an economic crisis in India a few years later. Though the scope of Myanmar's international action was vastly diminished during the nineteenth century, Myanmar was far from

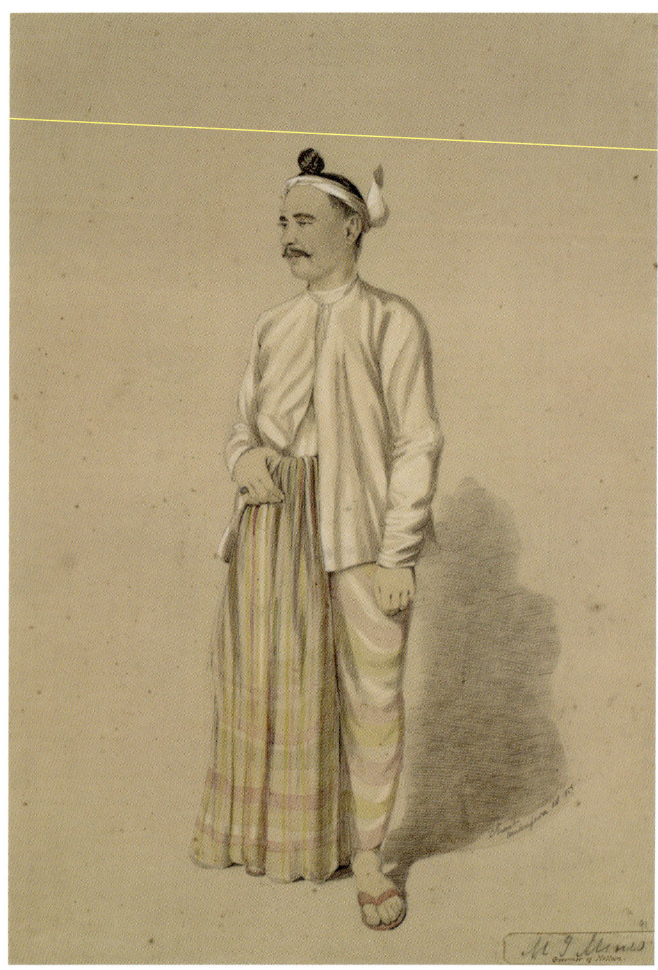

FIG. 24. Portrait of Mr. Mackertich J. Mines, an Armenian official in the court of King Mindon (r. 1853–1878), painted during Arthur Purves Phayre's mission to Upper Myanmar, 1855. Watercolor with pen and ink. By Colesworthy Grant. British Library, London

isolating itself or becoming isolated (fig. 24). The singular focus of western observers on Myanmar's often weak kings has unfortunately affected the general perception of the late Konbaung kingdom (fig. 25). Though it could not, ultimately, ensure its own survival, one should note that the political and ideological reform promoted by clear-minded advisers at the Konbaung court pushed the kingdom closer to modernity. Moreover, the activities of Myanmar monasticism within the Theravada Buddhist world were never interrupted, and the flourishing of Buddhist art and architecture during the nineteenth century and beyond are proof that Myanmar's cultural identity remained strong and creative. Still, it is not just in the framework of present political bor-

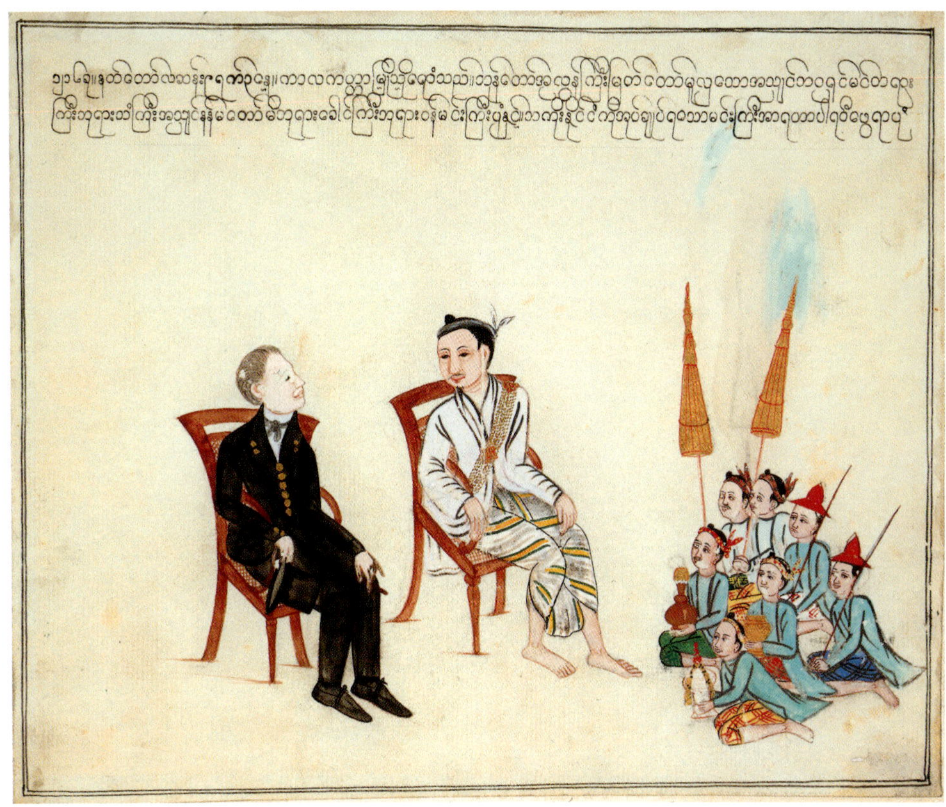

FIG. 25. Arthur Purves Phayre and a Burmese Minister meeting in Calcutta, 1854. Watercolor on paper. H. 8 1/16 x W. 9 5/8 in. (20.5 x 24.5 cm). Victoria and Albert Museum, London, IS 181-1950

ders but in the often neglected, yet connected, transregional histories, and the memories of multiple ethnic pasts in the country's shifting frontiers that scholarly efforts may be rewarded with a fuller and deeper understanding of Myanmar's relations with the outside world and the genealogy of its art and culture.

NOTES

1 Harvey, *History of Burma*, 284, 290.
2 *Census of India 1911, Volume IX, Burma, Part 1*, 74–75; Mus, "Lecture at Yale," November 8, 1966.
3 More recently, Konbaung expansionism and warfare have not played much of a role in Myanmar's nationalist historiography because postcolonial leftist governments and regional realpolitik were hardly sympathetic to triumphalist myths of conquest and neighborly invasions.
4 Lieberman, *Burmese Administrative Cycles* and *Strange Parallels*. Thant Myint-U, *Making of Modern Burma*, 88.
5 King Alaungpaya's main foe, King Banya Dala of Pegu, was a trader to South India, as his correspondence with the East India Company in Madras reveals.
6 Green, "From Gold Leaf to Buddhist Hagiographies."
7 Beemer, "Creole City in Mainland Southeast Asia," 212–46.
8 Ibid., 185–92.
9 Green, "From Gold Leaf to Buddhist Hagiographies," 337.
10 A term used by Thai historians and not widely used outside Thai historiography, "nine-army war" reflects the war from the Thai perspective, with invaders coming from nine directions.
11 This explanation does not exclude alternate interpretations. During the second half of his rule, the king lacked restraint with regard to the way he dealt with the Buddhist *Sangha*, which he considered as fully corrupted. In 1801, he ordered the monks to earn their own living, forbidding people to offer them food. See Poungpattana, "King Bodawhpaya of Konbaung."
12 Frasch, "Making of a Buddhist Ecumene."
13 Hamilton, "Description of the Ruins of Buddha Gáya."
14 Hamilton, "Account of a Map," 228.
15 Frasch, "Making of a Buddhist Ecumene," 385.
16 Sivasundaram, "Buddhist Kingship, British Archaeology," 117.
17 Fort Negrais was a trade settlement that the East India Company had erected in 1752 at Cape Negrais, the southwestern point of the Irrawaddy Delta.
18 Dai, "Disguised Defeat," 145.
19 Ibid., 151–58.
20 Grabowski and Wichasin, *Chronicles of Chiang Khaeng*.
21 Harvey, *History of Burma*, 279; Pasquet, "Quand l'Empereur de Chine écrivait à son jeune frère."

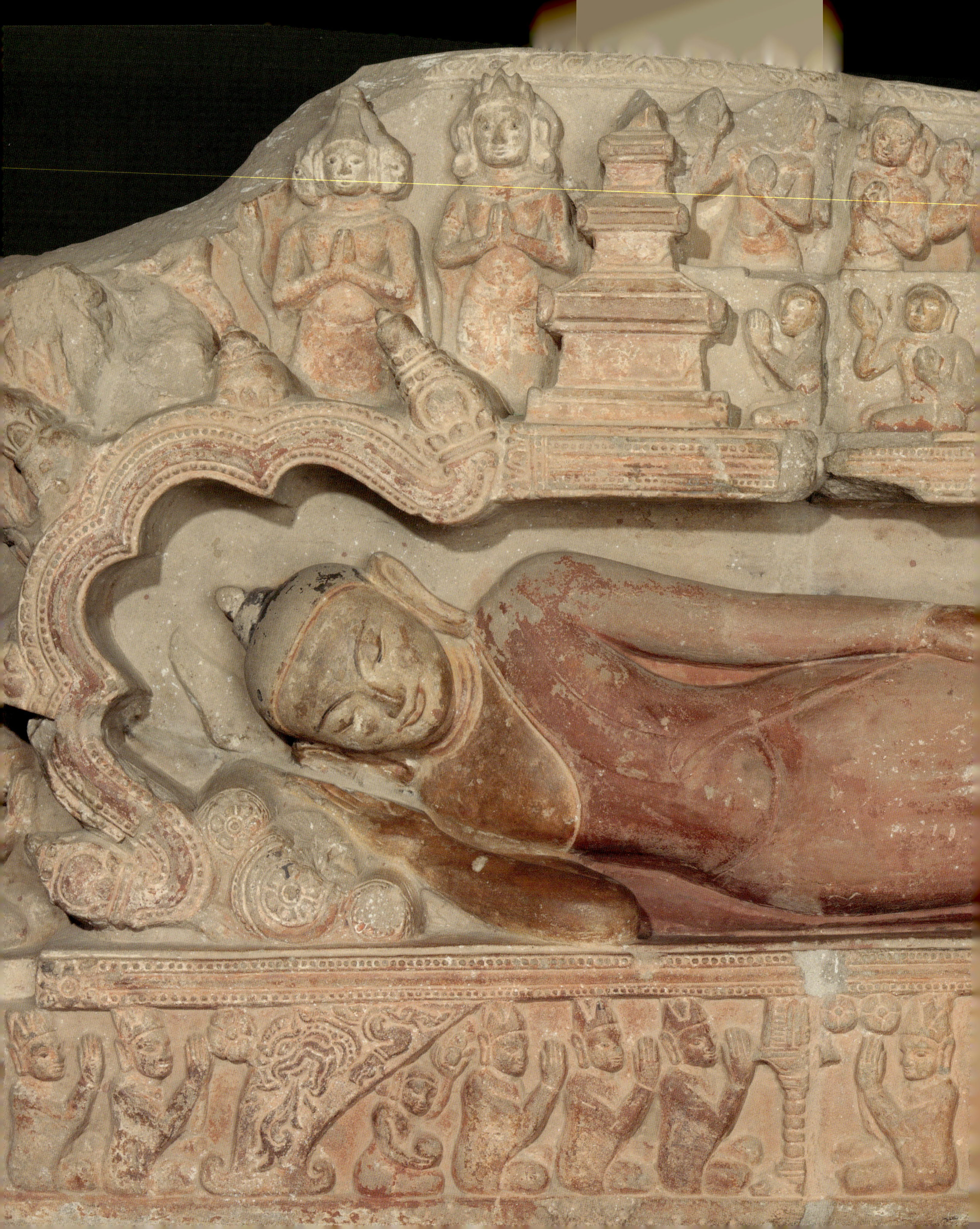

The Buddha's Smile
Art of the First Millennium

Robert L. Brown and Donald M. Stadtner

The Buddha smiled, prompting his disciple Ananda to ask, "For what reason does my Lord smile?"[1] The Buddha then prophesied that a sage named Vishnu would build a city named Sri Ksetra and that a king named Kyanzittha (who did indeed rule ca. 1084–ca. 1112) would be reborn as the founder of Pagan, or Bagan. Pagan was one the foremost Buddhist centers in the second millennium, and Sri Ksetra was the largest first-millennium walled city in Southeast Asia. Both these ancient sites were among the first in a long lineage of successive capitals recorded in historical chronicles into the nineteenth century. This very early history has come to shape how people in Myanmar perceive themselves. Indeed, it explains why new archaeological discoveries are covered so enthusiastically by the country's media.

Myanmar's early history is checkered with numerous gaps, since the number of dated inscriptions from the first millennium can be counted on one hand. By contrast, India's epigraphs from the same period number in the thousands. The first millennium in Myanmar's history also presents a complicated pastiche of times and places, but current scholarship is moving forward quickly, with new archaeological finds challenging old interpretations.[2] Later chronicles describe events that purportedly took place in the first millennium, but these are set in mythological contexts that cannot be confirmed.

PYU BEGINNINGS: EARLY HINDU AND BUDDHIST ART

Myanmar chronicles from the second millennium refer to peoples known as the Pyu and describe their civilization as the forerunner to the great age of Pagan. Chinese sources also mention the Pyu, usually as "Piao." However, according to a Pagan inscription, the name that these people may have used for themselves was "Tircul." This elusive group was believed to be purely mythological until the early twentieth century when the archaeologist's spade brought its civilization out of the shadows, starting at Sri Ksetra. Among the earliest excavators was a colorful Frenchman, General Léon de Beylié, whose 1907 report on Sri Ksetra included his observations on the dinner menu at the recently opened Strand Hotel in colonial Rangoon, or Yangon.

The term "Pyu" is highly controversial, since beyond the archeological evidence it is now used to designate an ethnic or linguistic group, and even a style of art. Each definition has been challenged, and scholars recognize that early Myanmar was diverse, with different languages and cultural traditions. The major early Pyu sites include Beikthano, Halin, Sri Ksetra, and Maingmaw. Criteria for identifying a Pyu site have recently been established.[3] Inscriptions in the Pyu language found at many of the major sites strongly suggest that the ruling elite were Pyu speakers. It also appears that the major sites were confined to Upper Myanmar and were situated near the Irrawaddy River.

OPPOSITE Detail of cat. no. 17

These four major sites were established at different times during the first millennium, with Beikthano considered the earliest site and Halin the latest. Beikthano was established some time between the second century BCE and the fourth century CE; Halin was established between the second and ninth centuries CE; Maingmaw between the fourth and fifth centuries CE; and Sri Ksetra between the sixth and seventh centuries CE.[4] Beikthano's early establishment makes any cultural relationship with India unlikely, thus arguing for an indigenous foundation before Indian Buddhist relationships began to form, perhaps in the second century CE. It is believed Beikthano was largely destroyed—and there is evidence of fire—in the fourth century.[5] According to Chinese histories, Halin likewise may have been destroyed by invading Nanzhao rebels in 832, but no archaeological or epigraphical evidence supports this.[6]

While the Pyu seem to have declined by the end of the first millennium, a handful of Pyu inscriptions indicate that Pyu speakers played some role at Pagan early in the second millennium. One short Pyu inscription at Pagan has been dated as late as the thirteenth century, but the Pyu were quickly lost to history thereafter. The most important Pyu record is Rajakumar's quadrilingual inscription, from about 1112, duplicated on two four-sided stone pillars; each face features writing in Mon, Pali, Myanmar, and Pyu.

Pyu history in the first millennium relies on five types of evidence: inscriptions, Chinese histories, Myanmar chronicles, archaeology, and art. The brief Pyu epigraphs are important for their content and their linguistic and paleographic features. Pyu seems to be a member of the Tibeto-Burman subfamily of the Sino-Tibetan language family, but it has largely defied translation. Pyu inscriptions appear to be among the oldest Southeast Asian inscriptions—some perhaps as old as the fourth century—and are written in their own variety of Indic script.[7]

Dating the inscriptions on the basis of their paleography has been problematic. Luckily, inscriptions on four stone burial urns from Sri Ksetra contain dates. These urns vary from about two to three feet in height, and each has a stone lid.[8] The urns are ossuaries from a dynasty at Sri Ksetra, for kings whose names end in "vikrama," a dynastic appellation known in India and used in other parts of early Southeast Asia. The name of the king and the year of his death are identified on his urn. C. O. Blagden suggested that the dating belonged to an era that began in 638,[9] which most scholars accept. This dating system, later called the Chulasakaraja, was adopted in other parts of Southeast Asia, which is perhaps another indication of the importance of the Pyu in the region.

These four Pyu urn inscriptions range in date from 673 to 718. We can therefore perhaps conclude that the seventh to the eighth century at Sri Ksetra was an important period in the city's development and a firm anchor for scholars to form a chronology for Pyu art. This significant political and cultural period in Sri Ksetra is supported by references from two Chinese monks, Xuanzang and Yijing, who traveled in Southeast Asia. While neither visited Sri Ksetra, they had heard of it and placed it in the context of Southeast Asian geography. Other Chinese texts refer to the Pyu, perhaps as early as the fourth century; Chinese histories also record the ninth-century decline of the Pyu with the destruction of a northern Myanmar city that scholars identified as Halin.[10] But it is only Sri Ksetra that is described as a Pyu city in the Chinese sources. Unfortunately, little information contained in the Chinese chronicles can be corroborated by archaeological or epigraphic evidence within Myanmar.

The third source is Myanmar chronicles, in particular *The Glass Palace Chronicle*, commissioned in 1829 by King Bagyidaw.[11] The earliest extant Myanmar chronicles belong to the middle of the second millennium, so the sources for compiling the *Chronicle* all originated after the disappearance of the Pyu people. The Pyu have an important role in the *Chronicle*, as they are considered the founding kings of Myanmar, whose dates start in the fifth century BCE, about 100 years after the Buddha's death. The *Chronicle* can be read with a variety of intentions, but its value as an ancient historical document is problematic.

For the scholarship presented in this catalogue and the exhibition it accompanies, archaeology and art objects are the most important sources. The four sites mentioned have been partially excavated.[12] The excavation at Beikthano was limited to twenty-five specific sites, a small portion of the overall site. Halin and Maingmaw likewise have not been fully excavated, and questions of dating and sequencing monuments and objects remain unanswered.[13] What is common among all three sites is a striking absence of art. There are many clay jars that functioned as containers for either cremated remains or bones, recalling the Sri Ksetra royal stone urns mentioned above. The excavation also uncovered some coins, beads, and a seated bronze Buddha, but few art objects. The three sites are thought to have been influenced by Indian religions, both Buddhist and Hindu systems of thought that are heavily visual in nature. What underscores the absence of visual material at the three sites is the fourth Pyu site, Sri Ksetra, because in stark contrast to the other sites it is abundantly rich in predominantly Buddhist visual material. There are three monumental brick stupas at Sri Ksetra: the Payagyi (h. 164 ft.; 50 m) and the Payama (h. 99½ ft.; 30.3 m) are shaped like elongated, conical beehives, a shape unlike any other Buddhist stupa in South or Southeast Asia, while the Bawbawgyi (h. 153 ft.; 46.6 m) is in the shape of a cylinder slightly tapered in the center with a large interior circular shaft. It vaguely resembles the Dhamekh Stupa at Sarnath and was likely built around the same time—between the sixth and seventh centuries. According to later chronicles, King Anawrahta, or Aniruddha (r. ca. 1044–ca. 1077) opened the Bawbawgyi Stupa and removed a relic to enshrine at Pagan. This cannot be verified, but two of his votive tablets were discovered inside the shaft of the stupa. Hundreds, if not thousands, of Pyu-period votive tablets still remain within the inner shaft, proving that the Bawbawgyi stupa is from the first millennium.

There are several small brick temples at Sri Ksetra. Gordon Luce (1889–1979) called them "small vaulted chapels" and "prototypes of the great temples of Pagan."[14] Several scholars today question the theory that the temples were prototypes because they believe the temples probably date to the Pagan period; this would mean that we have no extant Pyu temple architecture, apart from ground plans found at Pyu sites.[15] Nevertheless, the stone sculptures placed within some of the Sri Ksetra temples are Pyu in date, suggesting that if the temples are of the Pagan period then earlier images were installed in them.

THE KHIN BA TROVE

The most significant group of sculptures found at Sri Ksetra was discovered in 1926–27 by Charles Duroiselle. He excavated five nearby sites based on several surface finds of sculptures. The sites were mounds of bricks, and Duroiselle found a number of objects during the excavations, but one turned out to be a phenomenal discovery: a relic chamber packed with material that had not been disturbed by treasure seekers. Known as the Khin Ba trove (named after the farmer on whose land the mound was found), the relic chamber contained 430 objects, including bowls, caskets, and bells, mostly in gold and silver, and images of buddhas and bodhisattvas, loose stones and jewels, and even a small silver-gilt duck. Duroiselle's report described the chamber's contents and appended an inventory to his report.[16]

The "Buddhist Art of Myanmar" exhibition includes several Pyu-related sculptures, two of which are from the Khin Ba trove (see cat. nos. 2 and 4). A round silver reliquary also was found at the same site, on the floor in the center of the relic chamber. On the flat lid was a removable object representing a Bodhi Tree, which was broken and in pieces. The reliquary has no bottom, suggesting that it was meant to cover another, now-lost container, and including the tree was nearly three feet tall. Encircling the reliquary are four seated buddhas together with attendant monks, all fashioned in repoussé. Along the rim are brief excerpts from Pali texts interspersed with inscriptions in Pyu and Pali that place the name of each buddha above its respective image: Konagamana, Kakusandha, Kassapa, and Gotama. The names of the attendant monks are written under their feet: Kassapa, Moggallana, Sariputra, and Ananda. Finally, around the bottom rim of the reliquary is a third inscription that names the artwork's donors, Sri Prabhuvarma and Sri Prabhudevi, apparently the king and his queen. Varma, like Vikrama, is another dynastic name known from ancient India, but any connection between these two royal lineages remains uncertain.

An equally spectacular and unique object is a manuscript of gold, which is made up of twenty pages between two covers and is held together by a gold wire placed through two holes in the covers and each page, and then wound around the book. Carved on the gold pages are brief excerpts from eight Pali Buddhist texts.[17] This manuscript and silver reliquary were the focus of a 1995 symposium held by four scholars—Oskar von Hinüber, Harry Falk, Richard Gombrich, and Janice Stargardt—which uncovered an amazing discovery: in a list of fourteen types of knowledge that the Buddha possesses (*buddhananas* or *nanas*), two (the ninth and tenth) were missing from the gold plates. Then, on the rim of the lid of the reliquary, these two missing *nanas* appeared randomly inserted among the other inscriptions. In other words, it appears that when the two items in the book quotation were discovered to be missing, the two missing passages were added to the inscriptions on the reliquary, perhaps in order to insure the efficacy of the interment. Thus the two objects, the gold book and the silver reliquary, are in some way linked.[18]

One impediment to interpreting the Khin Ba material is the poor recording of the excavation—for example, the omission of the dimensions of the relic chamber from the final report. A considerable amount of new information on the Khin Ba monument has come from an archaeological training course sponsored by the Ministry of Culture in 2012.[19] Although the site has been heavily looted, the training course still collected new information, including the size of the relic chamber (13 ft. 1½ in. x 13 ft. 1½ in.; 4 x 4 m). The excavation also demonstrated that the monument itself was a stupa, an assumption previously made by scholars but without solid evidence. Indeed, the design of the stupa was traced, and the form and decorations of the lower sections of the walls, decorated with curved bricks and terracotta figures, were found.

The use of Pali in the textual extracts in the Khin Ba gold book and on the silver reliquary raises the issue of the nature of the Buddhism practiced at Sri Ksetra. The simple division of Hinayana and Mahayana schools of Buddhism has been abandoned by scholars, although no new categories have replaced them. Pali is the language of the Theravada traditions found in Sri Lanka, and the appearance of Pali inscriptions suggests a clear connection. Peter Skilling has argued that Pyu Buddhism was in fact related to Theravada, yet in a helpful twist he suggested it is a Theravada that "evolved independently of the Ceylon schools."[20] This localization of Pyu Theravada Buddhism allows scholars to temper the sometimes disjointed search for influences and sources in early South Asian Buddhism with identifiable connections in Myanmar, and look to Southeast Asian links. Skilling suggests this himself by relating Pyu and Dvaravati (Mon culture in Thailand) writing, "we find remarkable resonances between the two cultures, separated by several river valleys and mountain ranges, and epigraphic practices unknown in Sri Lanka."[21] This looking inward to Southeast Asia has been suggested for Pyu art as well by Charlotte Galloway.[22]

THE MON OF LOWER MYANMAR

Lower Myanmar participated fully in the expansion of civilization that swept up mainland Southeast Asia during the first millennium. Indeed, the terracotta roundel with animated musicians, now in the collection of the National Museum in Naypyidaw (see cat. no. 11), is proof that the art of Lower Myanmar rivaled that of the Pyu and neighboring Thailand. The richest remains were found in a vast arc facing the Gulf of Martaban. This area was home to three large brick-walled cities: Thaton, Kyaikkatha, and Aythema.

The majority of inhabitants most likely spoke Mon, a language belonging to the Mon-Khmer subfamily of the Austro-Asiatic family. The Mon in Myanmar were probably related linguistically and ethnically to the Dvaravati Mon in Thailand, but features most characteristic of Dvaravati art, such as stone wheels atop pillars, are not found in Myanmar. No names of early Mon kings or dated inscriptions have come to light from the first millennium in Myanmar, and evidence proving any formal connections among the Mon, the Pyu, and the Dvaravati Mon is unavailable.

Few artifacts or monuments have turned up in Lower Myanmar, in part because excavations have been slow to start. The inscriptional record is also meager, restricted to a few words in Mon incised on a handful of terracotta tablets recovered at Winka, a brick monastic site north of Thaton datable to the middle of the millennium.[23] A stone inscription found in Lower Myanmar, however, with passages from the *Paticcasamuppada Sutta* suggests that the Mon favored the same texts that were popular among the Pyu and the Dvaravati Mon.[24] It also points to a common Buddhist substratum uniting these diverse civilizations.

Lower Myanmar was perhaps ruled by some form of polity, judging from a coin series unique to this region and probably current during the middle of the first millennium.[25] If Lower Myanmar had a capital, then it may have been Thaton, in light of that city's size and its antiquities from the early second millennium. The Yangon area was the site of ancient habitation, evidenced by hundreds of terracotta votive tablets, or sealings, recovered when debris was cleared from the Botataung Pagoda after it was destroyed by a bombing in 1944. Many of the sealings reflect typical Mon types, while others indicate Pyu influence, suggesting that the Mon and the Pyu coexisted in the Yangon region during the middle of the first millennium. Overall, the Mon enjoyed metal working traditions that matched the quality of those of the Pyu of Upper Myanmar (fig. 26).

By the beginning of the second millennium, however, the historical record for Lower Myanmar fills out dramati-

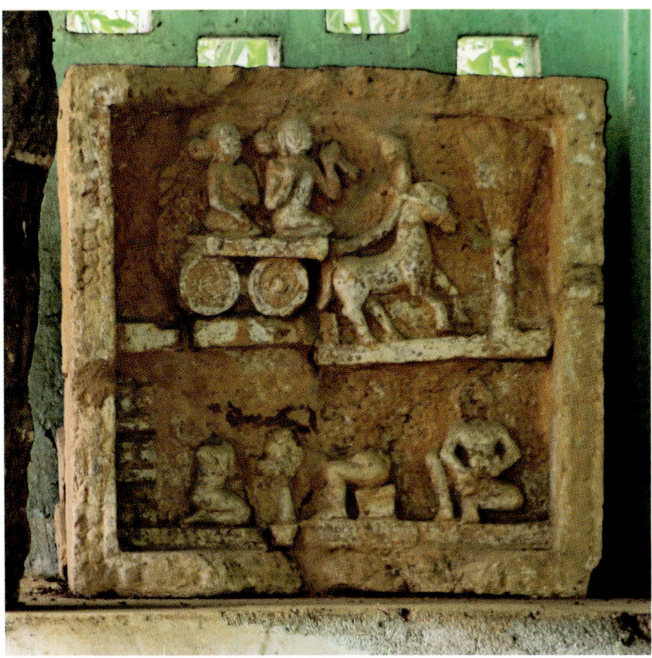

FIG. 27. *Mahosada jataka* plaque original to the Thagya Stupa, Thaton. Ca. 1050. Terracotta. Shwesayon Pagoda, Thaton

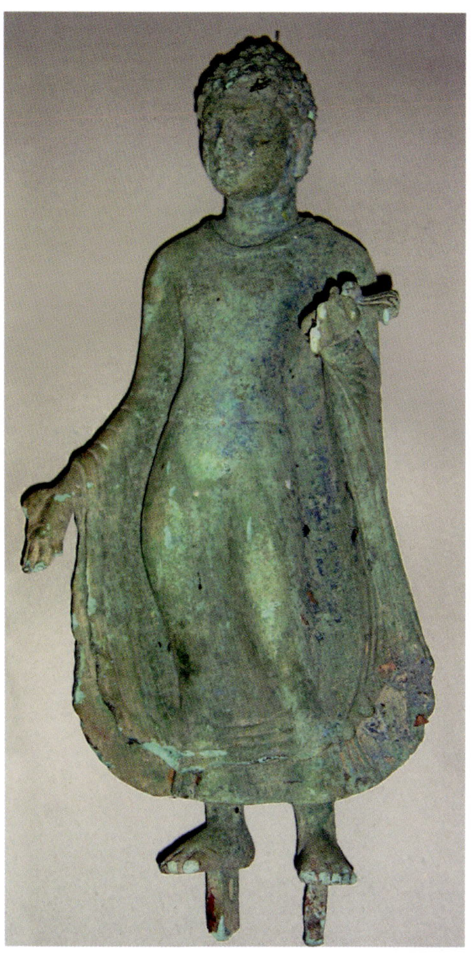

FIG. 26. Standing Buddha discovered in 2005 near Yangon. Ca. 5th–7th century. Bronze. H. 15 in. (38.1 cm). Tagondaing village

cally. Mon royal inscriptions at Thaton, for example, from around the middle of the eleventh century, record Buddhist donations and refer to a king, perhaps named Makata. Also from this period in Thaton are perhaps the earliest depictions in Myanmar of *jatakas*, or stories of the Buddha's previous births. The famous last ten *jatakas* are captured in relief sculpture on boundary pillars that likely surrounded an ordination hall. Another set of the last ten *jatakas* is found on large terracotta panels placed within niches set into a terraced stupa faced with laterite (fig. 27).[26]

A handful of Hindu stone sculptures have been found in and around Thaton, probably from the end of the first millennium, suggesting either small Indian trading communities or more likely a fluid religious milieu in which the native inhabitants worshiped both Hindu and Buddhist deities. The most provocative is a Vishnu recumbent upon the serpent Ananta, a familiar theme in Indian art, though Vishnu's consort, often shown at the god's feet, is replaced by the elephant-headed Ganesha (fig. 28). Other peculiarities suggest that local craftsmen may have based their creations on small imported images from India or more likely foreign pattern books, elements of which were mixed and matched without a full understanding of the underlying iconography.

The Pagan kingdom extended some degree of influence over Lower Myanmar around the middle of the eleventh century, a fact dramatically revealed by more than a dozen huge Buddhist terracotta tiles, each nearly three feet in height and incised with the name of the Pagan king Anawrahta.[27] These tiles were loosely placed against the upper terraces of a brick stupa, implying that the plaques were never part of the stupa's original plan. The stupa was therefore probably constructed by the Mon, and the tiles, placed later on the stupa, were designed to underscore the fresh presence of the Pagan kingdom in Lower Myanmar. This stupa, located between Twante and Yangon, is an important

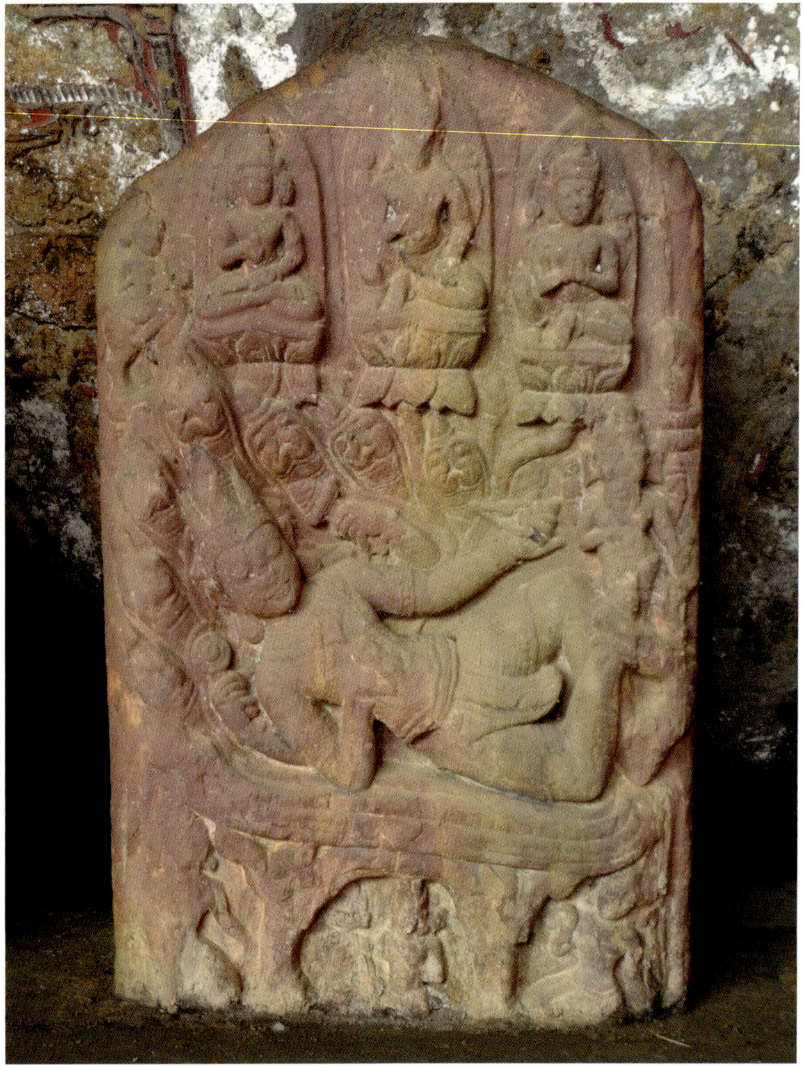

FIG. 28. Vishnu recumbent upon serpent Ananta. Second half of the first millennium. Stone. Kawgun Cave

surviving example of monumental architecture created by the early Mon. Important monuments from the first millennium located just north of Thaton include a large stupa base faced with laterite blocks at Zothoke, and the nearby brick monasteries at Winka.

Pagan's continued presence in Mon country is confirmed by a handful of Mon inscriptions belonging to King Kyanzittha in Thaton and nearby. However, the Mon eventually reasserted control of Lower Myanmar from their capital of Pegu beginning in the fourteenth century. Mon kings then patronized the Shwedagon Pagoda in Yangon and the Shwemawdaw Stupa in Pegu. The three glazed tiles included in the exhibition belong to this period (see cat. nos. 29, 30, and 31). By the middle of the sixteenth century the Mon kingdom fell to Myanmar forces from the north and soon Pegu was home to a brick-walled city built by the Myanmar King Bayinnaung (r. ca. 1552–ca. 1581). Despite a brief revival of fortunes in the second half of the eighteenth century, Mon civilization inexorably waned, and the population gradually diminished and became assimilated. Today Mon speakers number no more than a million in Thailand and Myanmar.

RAKHINE

The western part of Myanmar, Rakhine State, or Arakan, bordering Bangladesh, is the original home of the celebrated Mahamuni Buddha, a large bronze image removed by invading Myanmar forces in 1784 and enshrined just south of Mandalay. The most sacred image in Myanmar today, it is believed to have been cast by Rakhine's first king at the time of the Buddha's visit to his court. This legend arose probably no earlier than the fourteenth century, but the Buddha's visit to Rakhine unites a legendary past with the present for Rakhine Buddhists. The original home of the large bronze is thought to be a restored modern temple built upon an ancient terraced base situated within the walls of a first-millennium city known as Dhannavati, about fifty miles from the coast.

Myths from the second millennium connected Dhannavati with another ancient walled city known as Vesali, about six miles north of Mrauk-U, which is about forty miles from the coast. These legends placed these two ancient walled enclosures into a broad Buddhist context stretching back to India and were based on Pali sources, specifically one key *jataka*, number 454. The story concerned ten brothers and a sister, Anjanadevi, who settled in Vesali and whose descendant wed a king from Dhannavati, thus linking the two first-millennium cities in a continuous narrative based loosely on the Pali *jataka*. Other late legends record the migration to Rakhine of descendants belonging to the Buddha's family, the Sakyas, a leitmotif also found in Bamar and Shan chronicles.[28]

An early eighth-century Sanskrit inscription preserved on a pillar at Mrauk-U is the longest and most informative inscription from the entire first millennium in Myanmar. It describes the king as a Buddhist layman (*upasaka*) who produced buddha images in various materials, such as ivory, wood, and stone, and who also patronized two Hindu monasteries (*mathas*), one associated with Vishnu and another with Shiva.[29] Such eclecticism is underscored by the diverse surviving sculptural material in Rakhine, such as a twelfth-century sculpture of Vishnu and Lakshmi.

A set of five small stone panels once surrounding a ruinous brick stupa reveals the unique qualities that mark the art of Rakhine.[30] One depicts the Buddha delivering his first sermon at the Deer Park, while another shows the death of the Buddha (fig. 29). Another features a standing figure who is likely a bodhisattva. This stupa stood on a hill known as Mount Selagiri, and it was on this very hill that the Buddha was said to have met the legendary first king of Rakhine.

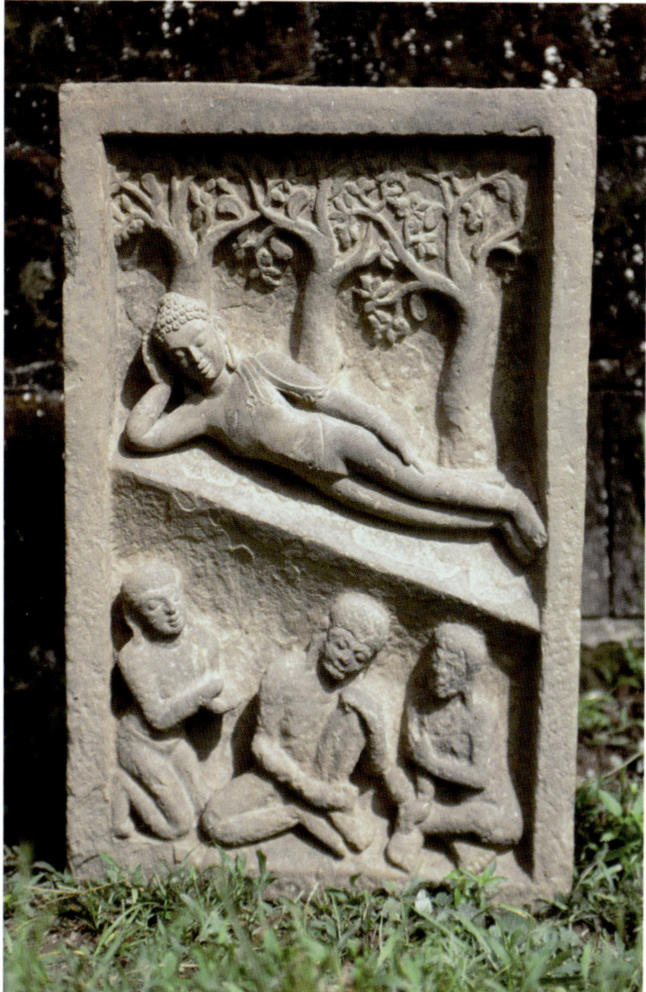

FIG. 29. The death of the Buddha, Mount Selagiri. Mahamuni site museum. Ca. 6th–7th century. Stone. Dhannavati

Other sculptures, now randomly placed within the terraces of the Mahamuni Temple, form a set of more than twenty. They are seated figures, placed against a plain background, and each is about three feet in height (fig. 30). The reverse of one bears a Sanskrit inscription (*yaksha senapati panada*) in characters attributed to the fifth century, providing a key to the entire group.[31] The set appears to be unique in Buddhist art from the first millennium. Interestingly, a closely related but not identical set is found in Myanmar

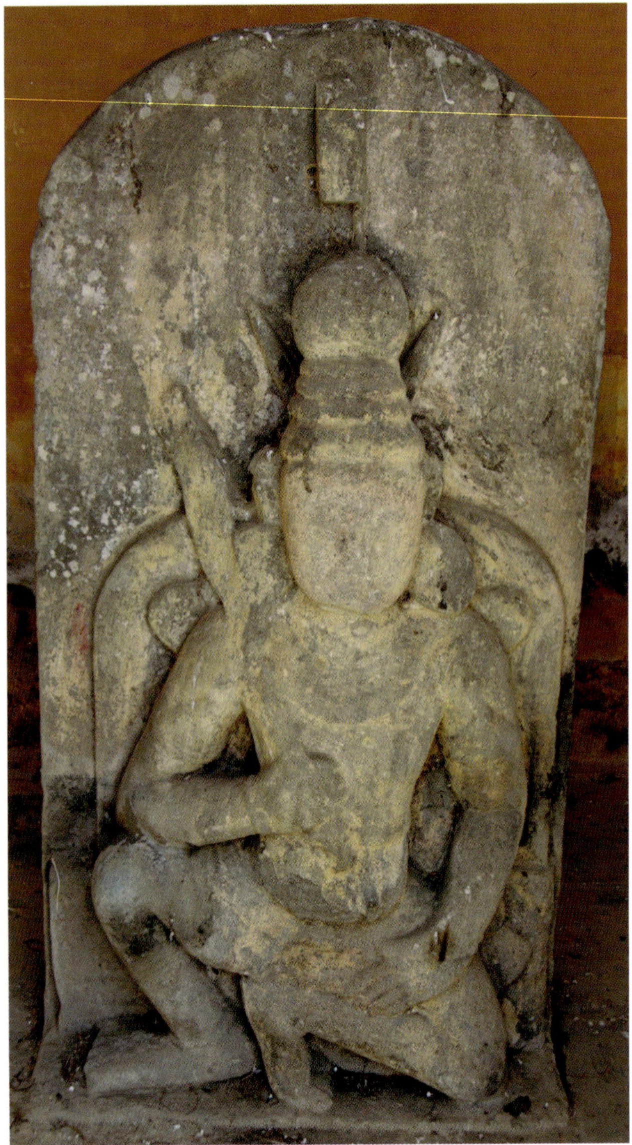

FIG. 30. More than twenty similar sculptures belonged to a set of rarely depicted Buddhist cosmological deities. Ca. 5th–7th century. Stone. Mahamuni Temple, Dhannavati

again among the glazed tiles on the eastern face of the Ananda Temple at Pagan (ca. 1100). Captions in Mon and Pali on the Pagan tiles identify the deities, with one directly recalling the much earlier example in Rakhine (*panada yakka senapati*).[32] This rarely represented group of deities underscores how communities in Myanmar borrowed from a wide variety of sources and recombined them in unique ways.

Rakhine was never absorbed into the Pagan kingdom, but by the fifteenth century the region played an active role in the vibrant commercial world of Southeast Asia. The capital, Mrauk-U, was approachable from the Kaladan River via narrow deltaic sloughs that protected the city from invaders. During the Mrauk-U period (1430–1784), the city witnessed a building frenzy rivaled only by Pagan's classic era. A strong connection with Sri Lanka was forged, especially during the fifteenth and sixteenth centuries, and many Rakhine buddha images from this period reveal Sinhala influence.[33] Mrauk-U was described in the seventeenth century by an Augustinian monk, Father Sebastian Manrique, and was also captured in seventeenth-century engravings made by Wouter Schouten, an employee of the Vereenigde Oostindische Compagnie. Rakhine enjoyed its independence until Myanmar forces from Amarapura, near modern Mandalay, annexed the region in the late eighteenth century, seized the Mahamuni Buddha, and transported it to Upper Myanmar.

THE STAGE IS SET

The reconstruction of Myanmar's history during the first millennium is in its early stages, compared to the extensive, ongoing work in surrounding countries, such as Bangladesh, Thailand, and Cambodia. Few inscriptions provide firm guides, and even the language of one major group, the Pyu, remains largely unknown. The three areas highlighted in this essay developed along separate lines but shared numerous similarities. Scholars today are charged with adding to the evidence and forming new conclusions, a process which is now producing rich results.

NOTES

1 Duroiselle, *Epigraphia Birmanica*, vol. 1, pt. 2, 113. This undated inscription from the reign of Kyanzittha is found at the Shwezigon Stupa, Pagan. The prophesy was made at the Jetavanna monastery in India.
2 An exhibition at the Metropolitan Museum of Art, New York, in 2014 focused on the art of first-millennium Southeast Asia. See Guy, *Lost Kingdoms*.
3 Moore, "Place and Space in Early Burma," 101–21.
4 Goh, "Cakkravatiy Anuruddha."
5 Aung Thaw, *Report on Excavation at Beikthano*, 64.
6 Luce, *Phases of Pre-Pagan Burma*, 1: 66.
7 Griffiths, "Early Indic Inscriptions of Southeast Asia," 55.
8 Luce, *Phases of Pre-Pagan Burma*, 2: pl. 5 (a–f).
9 Blagden, "The Pyu Inscriptions" (1913–14).
10 Luce, *Phases of Pre-Pagan Burma*, 1: 47–48.
11 Pe Maung Tin and Luce, *Glass Palace Chronicle*.

12 Aung Thaw, *Preliminary Report on the Excavation at Peikthanomyo*, and *Report on Excavation at Beikthano*.

13 Hudson, "Origins of Bagan," 127–38. The archaeological status for each of these sites is summarized here.

14 Luce, *Phases of Pre-Pagan Burma*, 1: 54.

15 Stadtner, "Art of Burma," 39–91; Pichard, "Remarques sur le chapitre 9 'The Mon Paradigm.'"

16 Duroiselle, "Excavations at Hmawza" (*Archaeological Survey of India, Annual Report, 1926–27*), 171–81.

17 Falk, "Die Goldblätter aus Śrī Kṣtra," 53–92.

18 The various scenarios that might explain this were proposed at the symposium. See ibid.; Stargardt, *Tracing Thought through Things* and "Great Silver Reliquary from Sri Ksetra."

19 Zolese, "Technical Report on Archaeological and Anthropological Activities."

20 Skilling, "Advent of Theravada Buddhism," 101.

21 Skilling, Review of *Tracing Thought through Things*, 389.

22 Galloway, "Ways of Seeing"; Brown, "Pyu Art," 35–41.

23 Myint Aung, "Excavations of Ayetthema and Winka." It has been recently proposed that the Pyu inhabited Lower Myanmar during the first millennium; see Michael Aung-Thwin, *Mists of Ramanna*. This thesis has been rebutted; see Stadtner, "Mon of Lower Burma"; an expanded article appeared in Stadtner, "Demystifying Mists." For other critiques, see Pichard, "Remarques sur le chapitre 9 'The Mon Paradigm,'" and Leider, "*Mists of Ramanna*, Compte-rendu."

24 Skilling, "Advent of Theravada Buddhism."

25 Wicks, *Money, Markets and Trade in Early Southeast Asia*.

26 Luce, *Phases of Pre-Pagan Burma*, 2: pls. 92–95.

27 Ibid., 2: pls. 88–90, 99. Three Hindu sculptures were discovered in Thaton, but all were destroyed in Yangon during World War II. Two depicted Vishu on the serpent Ananta, while the third featured Shiva and Parvati.

28 Leider, "Emergence of Rakhine Historiography."

29 Johnston, "Some Sanskrit Inscriptions of Arakan."

30 Gutman, "Series of Buddhist Reliefs from Selagiri."

31 Gutman, "Ancient Arakan," 201.

32 Shorto, "Devata Plaques of the Ananda Basement," 165.

33 Raymond, "Religious and Scholarly Exchanges."

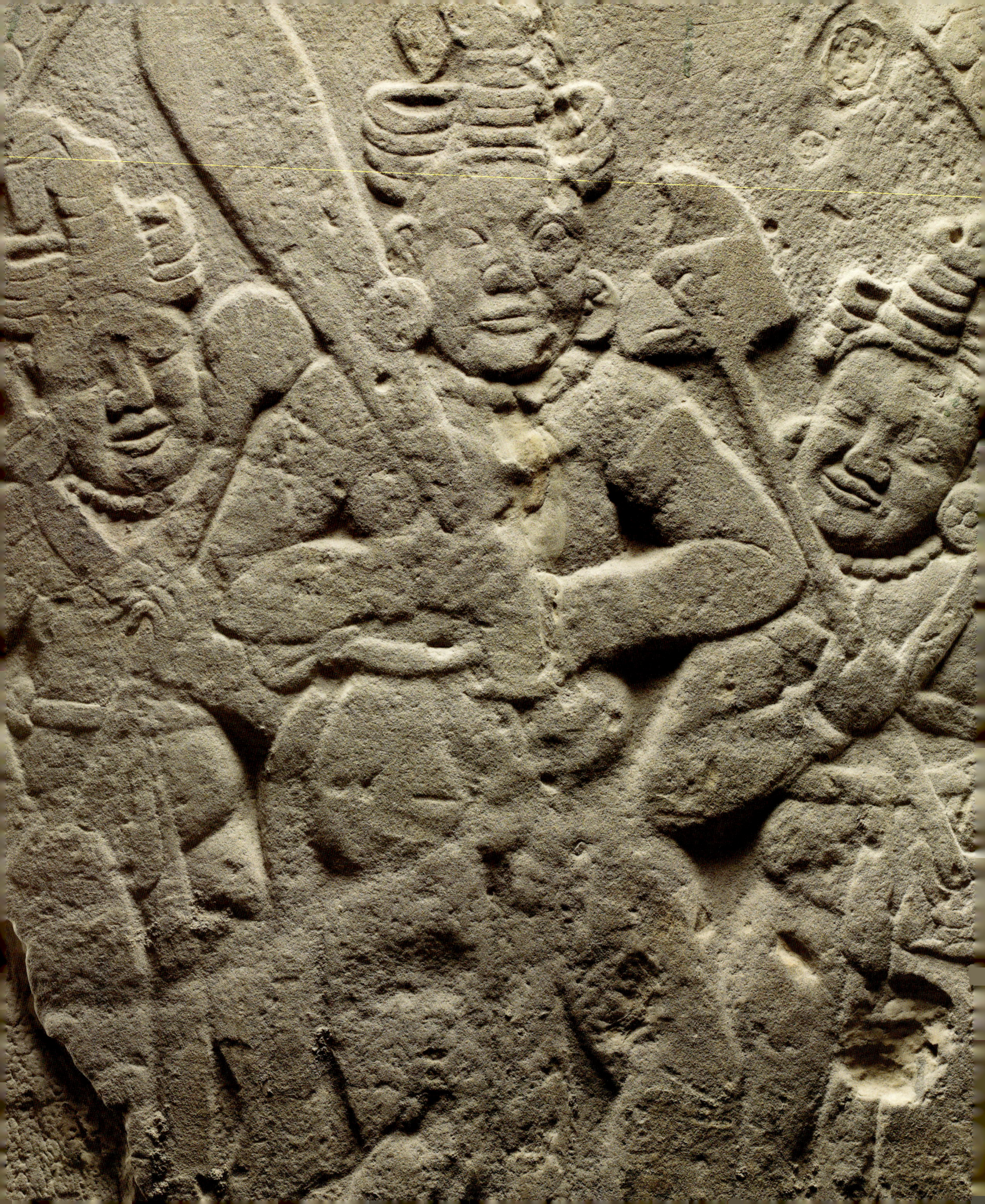

Ancient Pagan
A Plain of Merit

Donald M. Stadtner

In 1768, a royal barge traveled down the Irrawaddy River to the ancient capital of Pagan, or Bagan, for the king himself to oversee the replacement of a metal finial, or *hti*, atop the celebrated Shwezigon Stupa. Ornamented with 998 precious stones and 1,000 emeralds, the spire was described at the time as shining like a "lunar orb in a clear sky."[1] In contrast, stepping outside the stupa's compound wall, the king would have gazed upon a sea of ruinous monuments that had fallen into disuse centuries before.

The Shwezigon Stupa was one of thousands of monuments that were built during Pagan's classic era of the eleventh to the thirteenth century, a period that witnessed a construction frenzy that the Buddhist world had never seen before nor has seen since. Indeed, brick structures still dot the landscape of Pagan as far as the eye can see, along the river for six miles and inland for more than five miles (fig. 31). Construction slowed sharply, however, in the fourteenth century after the capital moved upriver to the Ava, or Inwa, area, near what in the nineteenth century became Mandalay. More than two thousand monuments were built during the city's classic phase, but fewer than two hundred were completed between the fifteenth and mid-twentieth centuries.

That Pagan still serves as a "plain of merit"[2] is proven by the hundreds of new temples built by patrons since the military government's controversial rebuilding of Pagan began in the 1990s. Reasons for the capital's relocation from Pagan to the north are unknown, but there is no evidence of pestilence, famine, or economic collapse. Older history books decry the destruction of Pagan by the Mongols from China, but no evidence supports this; the Mongols, however, probably did inaugurate a short period of turmoil in Upper Myanmar in the 1280s.

THE BEGINNINGS

Pagan represents the first Myanmar kingdom in that it was founded by Bamar-speaking people from Yunnan, China, toward the end of the second millennium. Prior to this, a group commonly known as the Pyu occupied Upper Myanmar, but little is known about their eclipse. Chinese accounts maintain that the country was invaded in the ninth century by the Nanzhao kingdom in Yunnan, but no proof exists to support this claim. The first king for whom there is historical evidence at Pagan is Aniruddha (r. ca. 1044–ca. 1077), known as Anawrahta in later chronicles.

Pagan's civilization most likely started before the appearance of Anawrahta, but it is unclear exactly when. During Anawrahta's reign, Pagan's influence extended into Lower Myanmar, which was then in the hands of the Mon. The western part of the country, modern Rakhine State, or Arakan, was never included in the Pagan realm.

OPPOSITE Detail of cat. no. 1

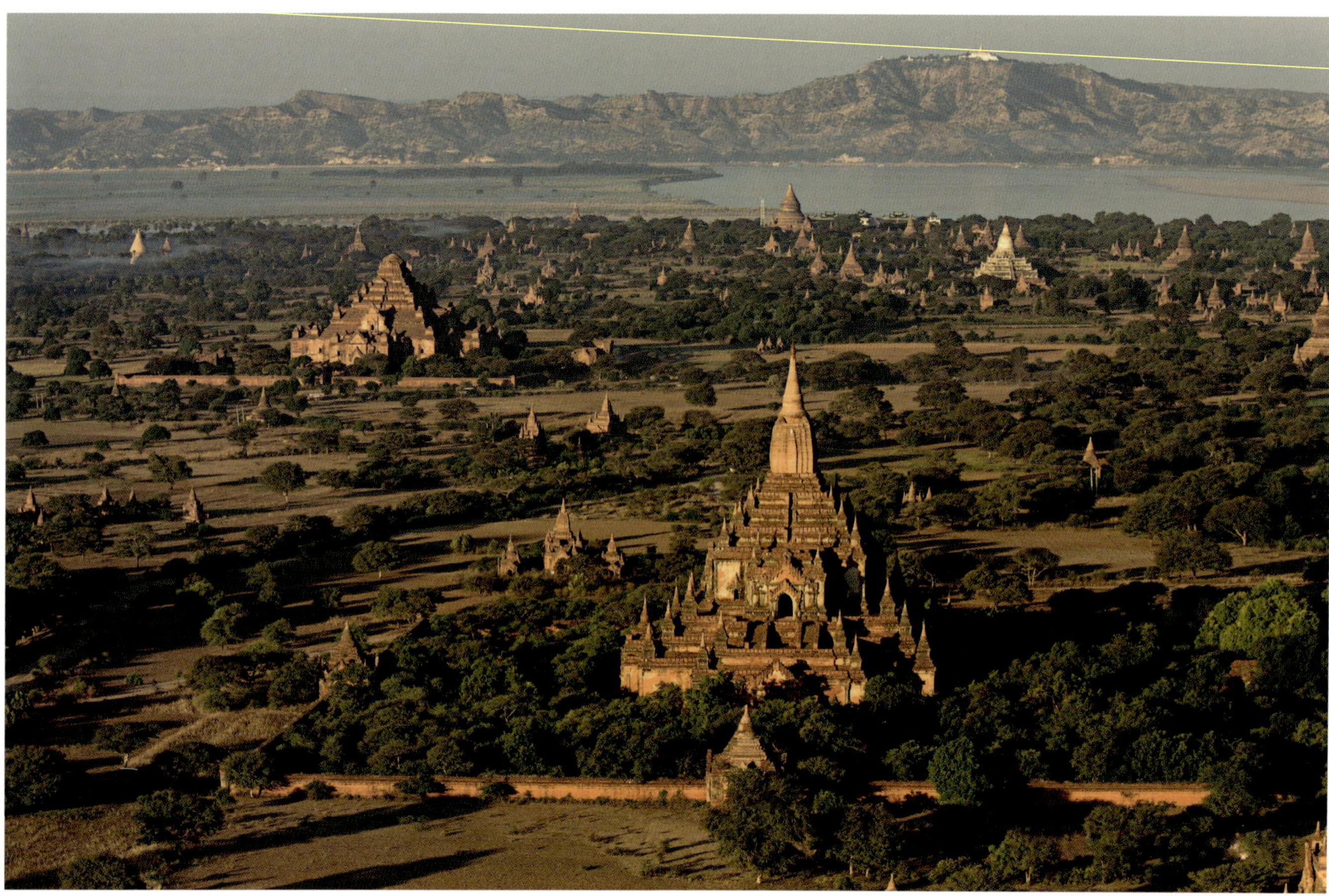

FIG. 31. The Sulamani Temple (foreground) with the Irrawaddy River and Mount Tangyi in the distance, Pagan. Photo: Dr. Kay Simon

The city's formal name was Arimaddanapura, or City of the Crusher of Foes, but was known locally as Pukam, with many variants (fig. 32). In modern times the city came to be called Pagan, but this was later changed to Bagan, conforming to the government's system of transliteration. The earliest monuments were built close to the riverbank, but by the second half of the twelfth century construction moved into the plains and further east. In the thirteenth century an explosion of activity resulted in the building of more than two thousand monuments (fig. 33). The size of the city's ancient population is unknown, since domestic architecture was made of perishable materials. The landscape was probably similar to its appearance today, with clusters of monuments surrounded by fields and villages.

PAGAN'S CIVILIZATION

Many diverse cultural strands came together at just the right moment to give birth to Pagan, beginning by the first half of the eleventh century, if not earlier. Pagan's culture blended influences from both within Myanmar and from neighboring cultures to create a unique civilization. Since existing inscriptions rarely touch upon these forces, historians are left with more questions than answers.

The Buddhism practiced in Pagan stemmed from Pali traditions, a connection proven by thousands of painted captions identifying many of the temple mural paintings. The earliest captions are in the Mon language, and by the second half of the twelfth century and thereafter the captions are in Myanmar, but in either language the captions

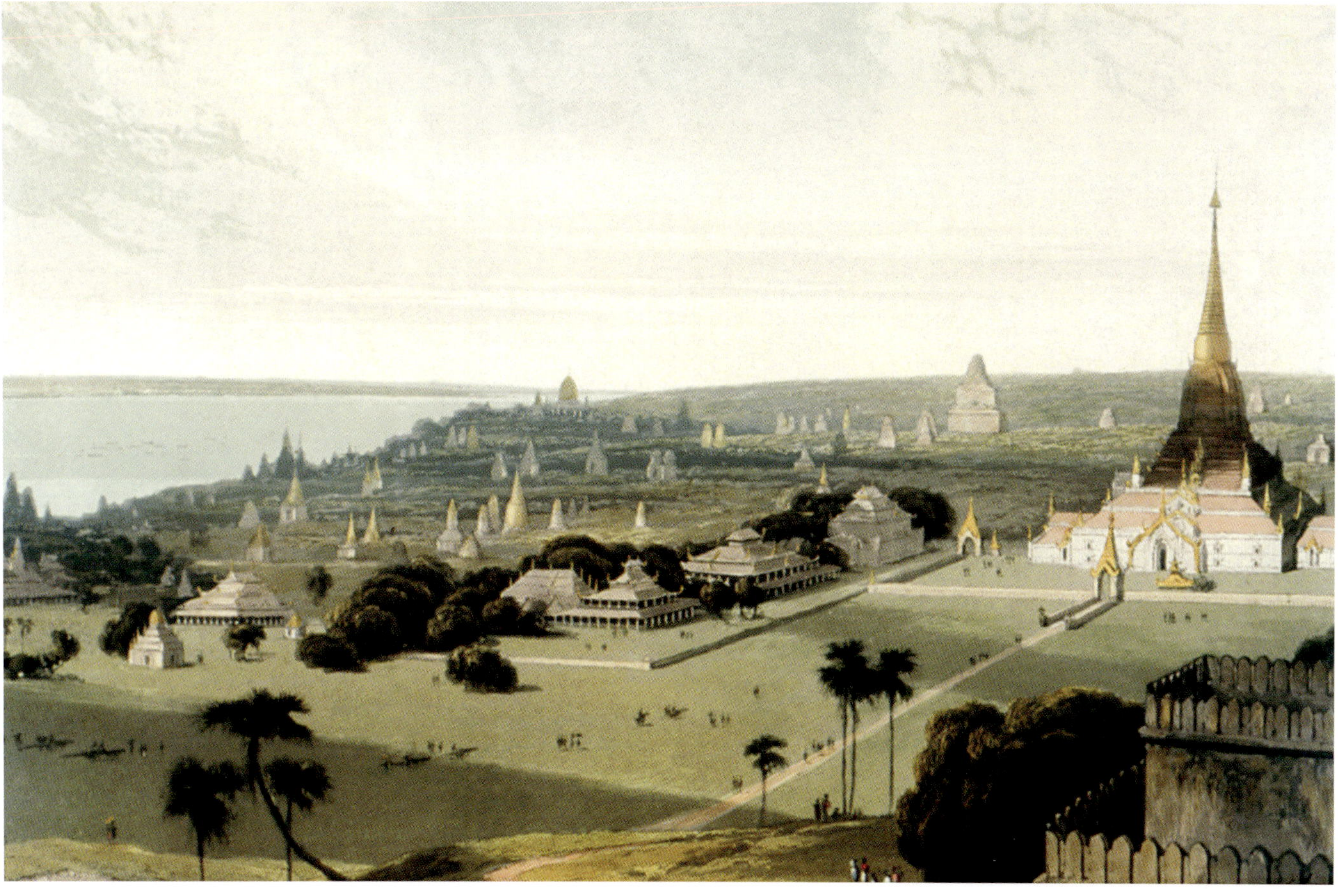

FIG. 32. Ananda Temple (right) in Pagan in the 1820s. Aquatint from Captain James Kershaw's *Views in the Burman Empire*, 1831. Courtesy of Richard M. Cooler

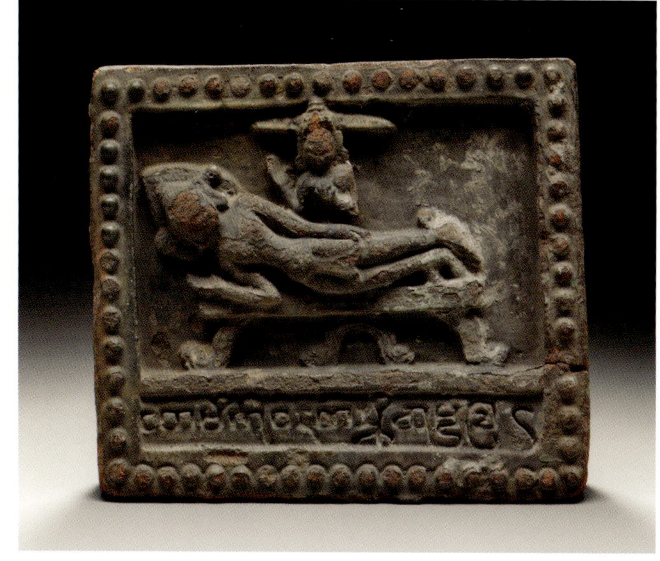

FIG. 33. The *Mughapakkha Jataka*: The Goddess Instructs Temi. Pagan period, 12th–13th century. Glazed ceramic. H. 10¾ x W. 12⅞ x D. 2⅞ in. (27.5 x 32.8 x 7.3 cm). Museum of Fine Arts, Boston: Denman Waldo Ross Collection, 17.1008. This tile was once part of a complete series of *jataka* plaques set into shallow niches within the terraces at the Mingalazedi Stupa, one of the thousands of monuments constructed between the twelfth and thirteenth centuries in Pagan.

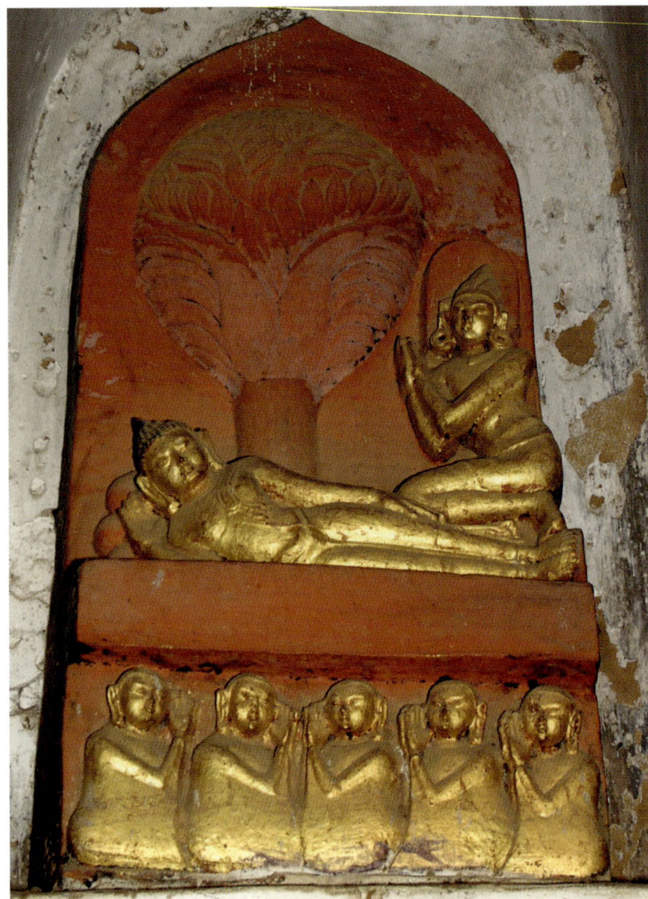

FIG. 34. The Buddha fainting after his fast; a rare if not unique depiction in Buddhist art. Ca. 11th–12th century. Stone. Ananda Temple, Pagan

draw upon the Pali canon, or *Tipitaka* (Pali). A monastery library in Pagan, dedicated in 1442, contained nearly three hundred palm-leaf manuscripts, the majority of which were in Pali, many composed in Sri Lanka. Other texts covered Hindu statecraft, medicine, astronomy, and astrology. Such a range of learning was probably no less true for the inhabitants of Pagan in its prime.

At least two divisions of Buddhism, both adhering to the Pali canon, probably existed during Pagan's classical epoch, but reconstructing their histories and interaction has yet to be done. One division seems to have been homegrown in Pagan and in later sources is called "Myanma" or Myanmar, while the other was labeled "Sinhala," an epithet for Sri Lanka. These divisions continued in succeeding centuries, in the later capital Ava.[3]

Pagan enjoyed direct political contact with Sri Lanka, but few inscriptions speak to this. One epigraph records that thirty corporal relics of the Buddha were sent to Pagan in the late twelfth century, four of which were enshrined in the royal Dhammayazika Stupa, illustrating how political and religious ties went hand in hand. Other inscriptions reveal that senior monks ventured back and forth between the two countries. Even episodes from Sri Lanka's famous chronicle, the *Mahavamsa*, were depicted in frescos within a royal temple dated to around 1112. Paradoxically, Pagan is largely free from Sri Lankan artistic influence.

The overwhelming artistic influence at Pagan originated from eastern India, which encompassed the modern states of Bihar and West Bengal, and from the area that is now Bangladesh. This vast region was in the hands of the Pala Dynasty (ca. 750–ca. 1200), but no evidence points to official diplomatic contact between Pagan and the Pala realm. The same Pala artistic styles also played an influential role in Nepal and Tibet, and the similarity between Pagan's later wall painting and certain early painted works from these Himalayan areas is uncanny, but not surprising; one is also, however, struck by significant differences.

Indian artists worked in Pagan, but from where in India they came and what was their exact status are unstated in the epigraphs. No evidence indicates that master painters or sculptors from eastern India traveled to Pagan nor that Myanmar artisans trained abroad. Artistic influence from eastern India may rather have come from traveling craftsmen and from portable religious objects, or still more likely from paintings on cloth and illustrated palm-leaf manuscripts taken to Myanmar.

Only traces of mural painting from the Pala Dynasty survive, at Nalanda, which makes Pagan's debt to Pala fresco art hard to assess. However, numerous extant Pala-period palm-leaf manuscripts reveal direct stylistic connections with Pagan's mural art. Nonetheless, many of the subjects selected for wall painting at Pagan are unknown or extremely rare in Pala art, such as the Twenty-Eight Buddhas, the Seven Weeks at Bodh Gaya, the 547 *Jatakas*, or certain episodes from the Buddha's biography.

Pagan's stone sculpture is also based loosely on Pala models, but the differences are readily apparent. The scores of stone sculptures at the Ananda Temple in Pagan illustrating the life of the Buddha up to his enlightenment draw directly upon a fifth- or sixth-century Pali text, the *Nidanakatha*, or its later recensions. The majority of the subjects are unknown in Pala sculpture but the style shares a strong affinity with Pala stylistic idioms. An example of this is the unique image of the Buddha fainting, which appears immediately after the panel showing the Buddha fasting, and is a subject that seems to be unknown elsewhere in Asian Buddhist art and was never repeated in Myanmar (fig. 34).

Mahayana Buddhism prevailed in the Pala realm, but no evidence exists of Mahayana monks or monasteries nor of the veneration of Mahayana texts in Pagan. Mahayana and even Tantric subjects are, however, present in a small number of temple murals, but exist in a thoroughly Theravada context. For example, the corridor encircling the sanctum of the twelfth-century Abeyadana Temple is filled with paintings that depict Mahayana and Tantric themes (as well as Theravada subjects), but featured in the entrance porch of the same temple is a set of painted *jatakas* with captions based on the Pali canon and therefore linked to Theravada traditions. Were worshipers adherents of Theravada Buddhism inside the entrance porch of the temple, but devotees of Mahayana and Tantric Buddhism once they crossed the threshold to the inner corridor?

The Mahayana and Tantric imagery at Pagan surely reflects sources outside of Myanmar, but it constitutes merely one aspect of borrowed subject matter within a dominant Theravada milieu. In addition, certain important Mahayana or Tantric painted imagery at Pagan cannot be identified in ancient Indian iconographic texts. For example, two fourteen-armed bodhisattvas painted prominently in one temple find no exact parallel in any surviving Indian source. The same holds true for a composition featuring scores of semidivine, semilegendary ascetics, identified as *siddhas* (Sanskrit). Such evidence suggests that artists at Pagan loosely modeled their work on certain subject matter from eastern India; the foreign subjects were probably never completely or correctly understood, since they stood outside local traditions. In addition, no identifying inscriptions accompany the Mahayana and Tantric imagery at Pagan, implying perhaps that such captions, if they indeed existed in the original models, were in Sanskrit and written in an eastern Indian script that was likely known only to a handful of the city's savants.

Lost Sanskrit texts can be invoked to explain certain iconographic anomalies found at Pagan, but it is more likely that artists mixed and matched elements from numerous sources from abroad. Such a juxtaposition of Theravada and Mahayana imagery is apt to confound the prevalent modern perspective that has drawn rigid lines among the various divisions in Buddhism. The terms Theravada and Mahayana are unknown in the inscriptions at Pagan.

Although Pagan is rightly considered the first Myanmar capital, the early stone inscriptions and the captions to wall paintings belonging to the reign of King Kyanzittha (ca. 1084–ca. 1112) are in Mon. The Mon may have formed a small religious and political elite among a dominant Myanmar community, but this does not entirely explain why Mon dominated the early inscriptional record or why its use disappeared during the second half of the twelfth century.

The early Pyu may also have contributed to Pagan's culture, but the evidence is thin. Pyu building traditions at Sri Ksetra are often said to have provided the prototypes for the monuments at Pagan, but this idea has been rightly challenged.[4] The Pyu apparently declined by the ninth or tenth century for unknown reasons, but a long gap between their decline and the rise of Pagan in the mid-eleventh century is another challenge to the idea that the Pyu influenced Pagan.

Hindu influence coexisted comfortably with Buddhism in Pagan. For example, a deity at the center of Kyanzittha's palace consecration was Nar, an abbreviation of Narayana, a common Sanskrit epithet for Vishnu. The Mon from Lower Myanmar probably also contributed to Pagan's iconography a special form of Vishnu recumbent upon a serpent. In India, this form generally shows only Brahma seated upon a lotus, its stem emerging from Vishnu's navel; however, in the handful of examples from Myanmar, the three major Hindu deities—Brahma, Vishnu, and Shiva—sit on lotuses emerging from the navel of a larger Vishnu figure below them. This special form of Vishnu, virtually unique to Myanmar, was the centerpiece of a Hindu temple in the walled city, which may have been used in court rituals.

The presence of Hindu traders from South India in Pagan is known from a thirteenth-century Tamil and Sanskrit inscription at Pagan—a dedication to a Vishnu temple—but no surviving monuments are tied to this community. One bronze Vishnu in the exhibition (see cat. no. 23) shows influence from the Chola realm of Tamil Nadu state in South India, but it is unexpectedly crude in light of Pagan's accomplished bronze work. A handful of Buddhist bronzes in the Pagan museum were likely imported from the ancient port of Nagapattinam in Tamil Nadu. Influences from southern India have been otherwise difficult to identify in artwork from Pagan.

PAGAN IN MYTH

Nearly all of Pagan's monuments lost active support after the capital relocated in the fourteenth century to the Ava area near what is now Mandalay. As patronage was curtailed so too was its handmaiden, maintenance, and thus an inexorable decline followed in which the thousands of temples, stupas, and monasteries fell into various stages of decay. A small portion of the damage can be attributed to earthquakes, which were recorded in epigraphs tied to repairs. In addition, treasure seekers from the fourteenth century onward routinely broke into stupas and hacked into large, seated brick Buddhas within temples, probably in search of interred metal objects that could likely be sold in the local market for the value of the metal. By the time British archaeologists surveyed Pagan in the early twentieth century, scarcely a single monument had not been rifled by local thieves.

Pagan's real Achilles' Heel was the thick, exterior stucco coating the monuments. Once this protective coat was chipped off, water seeped into the fabric of the building, eroded the mortar binding the bricks, and also provided a perfect environment for tenacious vegetation. By the late eighteenth century, the city's monuments had "sunk into indistinguishable masses of rubbish, overgrown with weeds," as one English envoy observed.[5] Pagan was marked by these desolate ruins until the rebuilding of the city in the 1990s.

After the capital shifted to the north in the fourteenth century, only a dozen or so major monuments received patronage. The Ananda Temple and Shwezigon Stupa received the greatest attention, while other shrines attracted far less patronage, such as the Sulamani or Abeyadana; the remaining monuments, which numbered in the thousands, fell into decay. A few new large monuments were built in this period, however, such as the Thissawadi temple, circa 1334, and a number of monastic complexes were still receiving patronage, such as the Lemyathna at Minnanthu. The donation of a monastery in the fifteenth century, together with nearly three hundred manuscripts, mentioned above, is a reminder that patronage was never completely interrupted at Pagan at any time.

After Ava eclipsed Pagan, the basic legends that may originally have been attached to the city's most sacred monuments were lost, for reasons that are not entirely clear. In their place completely new myths arose to furnish fresh meaning to the small number of temples and stupas still serving as active places of worship. These subsequent legends were then woven into a complex, historical tapestry that linked Pagan to earlier ancient centers in Myanmar, such as Sri Ksetra, and the wider Buddhist world of India, Sri Lanka, and even China. One major mythic element was the introduction of Buddhism to Myanmar by Anawrahta, who captured the *Tipitaka* from the conquered Mon in Lower Myanmar.

These later myths entered the national chronicles; today the most influential is the *Hmannam Mahayazawingyi*, begun in 1829 by thirteen savants who culled material from various sources.[6] It comprises many sections, of which only three have been translated into English and titled *The Glass Palace Chronicle* after a royal hall in Ava lined with mirrors. Not surprisingly, the temples featured in *The Glass Palace Chronicle* are the very ones that continued to be in use after Pagan's decline in the fourteenth century, such as the Ananda Temple. Moreover, all of the stupas and temples highlighted in *The Glass Palace Chronicle* are the very ones that show physical evidence of continued patronage after the fourteenth century. These new myths were probably formulated by the seventeenth century, since the majority of the temple legends are found in a chronicle that was compiled in the early eighteenth century, and which became a major source for *The Glass Palace Chronicle* in the nineteenth century.

One later legend even assigned meaning to Pagan's ruinous state, explaining that a king ordered the disassembly of a thousand stupas; ten thousand small temples; and three thousand monasteries in order to use the brick and stone to build city walls in preparation for a Chinese attack. *The Glass Palace Chronicle* reflects beliefs that were formulated long after Pagan's eclipse; these later myths therefore tell us little about the thoughts of the inhabitants during the city's classic period. Moreover, the later legends were far from uniform, and the compilers of *The Glass Palace Chronicle* grappled openly with myths that were in disagreement with each other.

Reconstructing myths from Pagan's classic period is difficult, since few inscriptions associated with the best-known monuments have survived. Also, most of the hundreds of stone epigraphs simply record the names of donors who funded the monuments and their upkeep. Occasionally the inscriptions provide a list of interred relics or precious objects. For example, the inscription recording bone relics sent from Sri Lanka did not attach a myth to the relics. In contrast, *The Glass Palace Chronicle* recounts an elaborate legend about a relic from Sri Lanka that self-replicated at Pagan, and whose copies were than dispersed by an elephant to locations in and around Pagan.

The myth that developed around the Ananda Temple is well known: King Kyanzittha was visited by eight special enlightened monks or *yahanda* (Myanmar) who descended on Pagan from the Nandamula Cave in the heavenly Mount Gandhamadana. The king fed them, and in return they "call[ed] up by their power the likeness of Nandamula grotto."[7] The king then constructed the Ananda Temple, based upon the conjured image of the Nandamula grotto. This story was likely inspired by a Sri Lankan chronicle, in which eight enlightened monks returned from a heavenly sojourn with a painted model of a celestial monument that the king then copied on earth.[8]

Later myths wove indigenous spirits, or *nats*, into Pagan's history, for example, King Anawrahta's seizure of the Pali canon at Thaton was accomplished through occult powers revealed to him by an Indian named Byatta. This same Byatta then coupled with an ogress residing near Pagan on Mount Popa and produced two sons. Later, Anawrahta sentenced Byatta to death for insubordination. Byatta's heartbroken wife and their two sons became major *nats*. Thus the introduction of Buddhism to Pagan being tied to *nats* provides a powerful context for *nat*-worship. Even such non-Buddhist lore was integrated comfortably into the national Myanmar chronicles.

When Pagan's history came under the academic microscope in the twentieth century, *The Glass Palace Chronicle* became the prism through which Pagan was interpreted. Pagan therefore came to have two histories, one based on the monuments and contemporaneous inscriptions, and another that developed following Pagan's eclipse in the fourteenth century and was known only through the chronicles. Most modern histories of Pagan mix these two indiscriminately and the result is a muddle, since Pagan's monuments are forced to conform to a history gleaned from later chronicles, which offer scant connection to the reality of the city between the eleventh and thirteenth centuries.

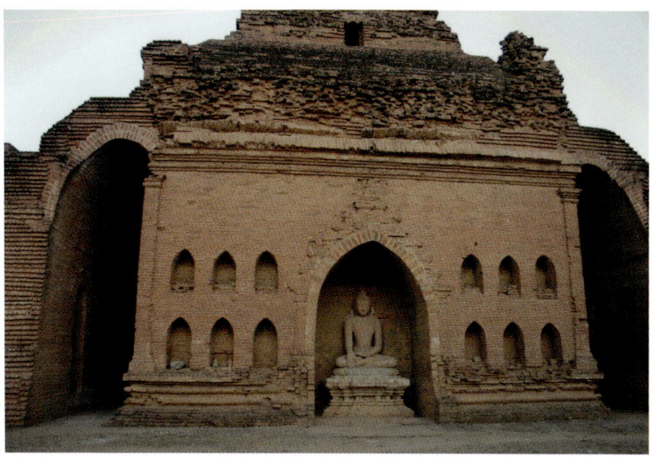

FIG. 35. The temple's collapsed entrance hall has exposed the brick vaulting system. Pathadagu Temple, Pagan

PAGAN'S TEMPLES

Wall painting and sculpture worked hand in glove with Pagan's distinctive architecture, which was based on a complexity of voussoired vaults and arches unrivalled in Asia. Vaulting may have been introduced in Pagan from the state of Orissa in coastal India, where faint traces of barrel vaults are found, but Myanmar architects quickly stretched the science of brick construction.[9] The earliest dated temple in Pagan is the royal Kubyaukgyi Temple, in Myinkaba village from circa 1112. Although it is a small temple, its vaulting displays a degree of sophistication that implies a long period of experimentation that must have begun in the previous century.

Vaulted temples allowed for large, covered interior spaces used as entrance halls, wide interior corridors, and hollow sanctums that were ideally suited for painting and sculpture contained in niches (fig. 35). Traditional Indian architecture, by contrast, favored the corbelled system of building, which restricted the size of interior spaces; the ancient Khmer architects employed corbelling too, also resulting in small temple sanctums.

The construction of Pagan is the story of converting billions of bricks into thousands of temples, and thereby transforming brick into merit. Bricks were made not only in Pagan but also at other sites along the river, judging from the names of locations sometimes stamped onto the bricks. Based on its estimated volume, about six million bricks were used to build Pagan's Dhammayazika Stupa.

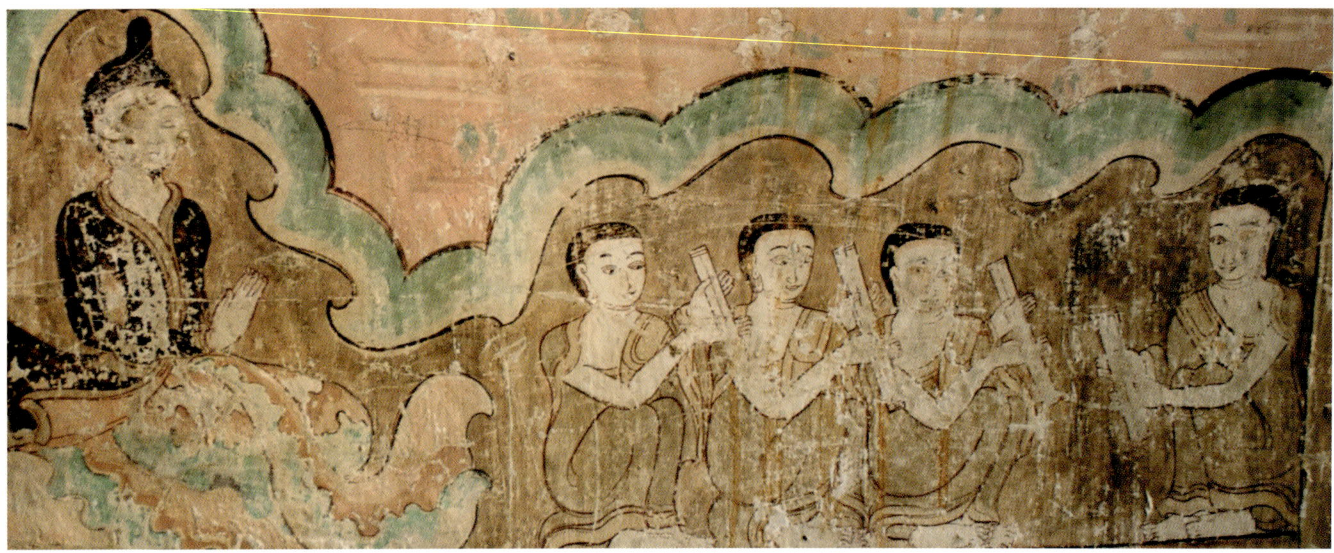

FIG. 36. King Anawrahta (left) with disciples of the Buddha and Buddhaghosa, a juxtaposition of legendary and historical characters. Mural. Ca. 1793–94. Upali Thein, Pagan

Eleven of the largest monuments built during the classic period account for roughly a quarter of the total number of bricks used in all of the structures combined. Each of these eleven monuments is attributed to royal patronage, but small or medium-sized temples were also donated by royal patrons, such as the Kubyaukgyi and the Shwegugyi, circa 1131. The majority of the city's monuments can be attributed to the thirteenth century, but they were far smaller than the earlier temples. Construction times were surprisingly short, as a few inscriptions reveal. The medium-sized Shwegugyi was built in about seven and a half months, and work on the Dhammayazika Stupa, the largest in Pagan, lasted for only two years, from 1197 to 1198.

The names of the artists who worked on Pagan's monuments rarely appear in inscriptions. One exception was a master mason named Buddhalanka, who was paid with an elephant and four pieces of cloth, and a master painter, Cittrabijann, who was given an elephant and a horse. The status of artisans was relatively high compared to unskilled laborers. Some artists were paid in units of silver, while others were rewarded with fabrics. Although cotton was grown in Myanmar, imported cotton cloth from India was always in high demand.

Stone sculpture and painting were equally dependent on eastern Indian modes at the beginning of Pagan's history. By the end of the twelfth century, however, stonework was used less often and declined in quality, while painting took a very different course and evolved into a highly controlled but flamboyant style by the thirteenth century, best demonstrated at the Payathonzu Temple in Pagan. What motivated painters to change direction and where their foreign sources, if any, originated are questions yet to be answered. The change likely took place gradually over decades and probably went unnoticed by patrons and artists alike.

Stone sculpture was reserved for Buddhist imagery placed in niches within the inner corridors of temples and entrance halls. The average height for images was between three and four feet. Stone sculpture was commonplace in the early temples, but by the end of the twelfth century architects preferred flat, painted walls without niches. The earliest stonework, for example the sculptures found at the Kubyaukgyi Temple, reveals a strong debt to Pala models; however, an indigenous direction can be detected by the second half of the century. Figures became heavier and the compositions became stiffer. This stylistic trend can be appreciated by comparing two seated Buddhas, probably from the early twelfth century, with three examples from the end of the same century from the Kubyaukgne Temple in Myinkaba village from 1198 (see cat. nos. 16, 17, and 18).

Two distinct phases of painting can easily be detected during Pagan's classic period, although the steps in this evolution remain to be charted. The two phases differ greatly: the first period is marked by bold compositions in which the subjects are confined to individual, painted frames. The wall serves merely as a surface to be covered and there is little concern for creating depth. In style, this period shows a certain affinity with eastern Indian palm-leaf painting. Examples are found at the Pathothamya Temple and the Kubyaukgyi Temple. By the end of this century painters sought to transform the wall into an illusionistic three-dimensional surface, through the use of trompe l'oeil devices, such as the dramatic overlapping of motifs. The corners of sanctums were painted with pilasters, thereby emulating architectural space and so enhancing the illusion of depth. By these contrivances the wall became an interior that the viewer could "step into."

In addition, new fanciful motifs appeared, such as foliated crocodiles from whose mouths emerge snakes ridden by frolicking armed men. Such complex compositions are small and can only be appreciated upon close examination. One temple in which all of these late characteristics appear is the Payathonzu, probably from the thirteenth century. Other compositions, including those featuring a seated Buddha within a structure resembling the Bodh Gaya Temple and surrounded by other figures in niches, share an uncanny but not unexpected resemblance to painted thangkas from the Himalayan zones. The reasons and sources for these significant changes in Pagan painting have yet to be determined, but it is clear that a complex blend of indigenous input and foreign influences was at work.

PAGAN'S LEGACY

Pagan was never completely abandoned, although following the shift of the capital to the Ava area in the fourteenth century patronage slowed to a trickle compared to its peak during the classic period. Later chronicles link Pagan to the first-millennium Sri Ksetra and to all of the capitals after Pagan, thus forever embedding the city in the nation's imagination. The art of Myanmar took new directions once the epicenter of political power and patronage shifted north. Wall painting, for example, moved away from styles that were heavily based on Indian models. Sculpture adhered somewhat more closely to earlier modes but also was subject to new approaches. Architecture proved to be more conservative, and temples continued to use many of the basic early Pagan floor plans and ornamental details.

A mural in a late eighteenth-century ordination hall in Pagan, the Upali Thein, shows the eleventh-century Pagan king Anawrahta overseeing monks reading palm-leaf manuscripts. The Myanmar caption identifies two of the monks as disciples of the Buddha, while another is labeled Buddhaghosa, a celebrated fifth-century monk-theologian from Sri Lanka. The monks and the king are shown working in harmony (the king deliberately shown sitting higher than the monks) to provide an environment in which Buddhism could flourish (fig. 36). Such an impossible juxtaposition of historical and legendary characters from the past poignantly reveals how later generations conceived of Pagan's pivotal role in the country's history.

NOTES

1 Tun Nyein, *Inscriptions of Pagan, Pinya and Ava*, 22.

2 In Buddhist practice the belief in karma is particularly emphasized. Myanmar's kings, particularly from the Pagan period on, believed in a merit path to salvation, which allowed one to enhance one's rebirths through good works and acts of devotion (the building of good karma). Myanmar's Buddhists believe that even those without means could gain merit by doing good deeds, such as feeding monks. Kings and other wealthy Buddhists built temples, monasteries, and libraries.

3 Pranke, "'Treatise on the Lineage of Elders.'" Although a brief summary, Pranke's introduction is the most reliable analysis of the development of Buddhism in Myanmar in the premodern period.

4 Pichard, "Remarks sur le chaptire 9 'The Mon Paradigm.'"

5 Cox, *Journal of a Residence in the Burmhan Empire*, 414.

6 Pe Maung Tin and Luce, *Glass Palace Chronicle*.

7 Ibid., 110.

8 Geiger, *Mahavamsa*, chap. 22.

9 Pichard, "Distinctive Technical Achievement."

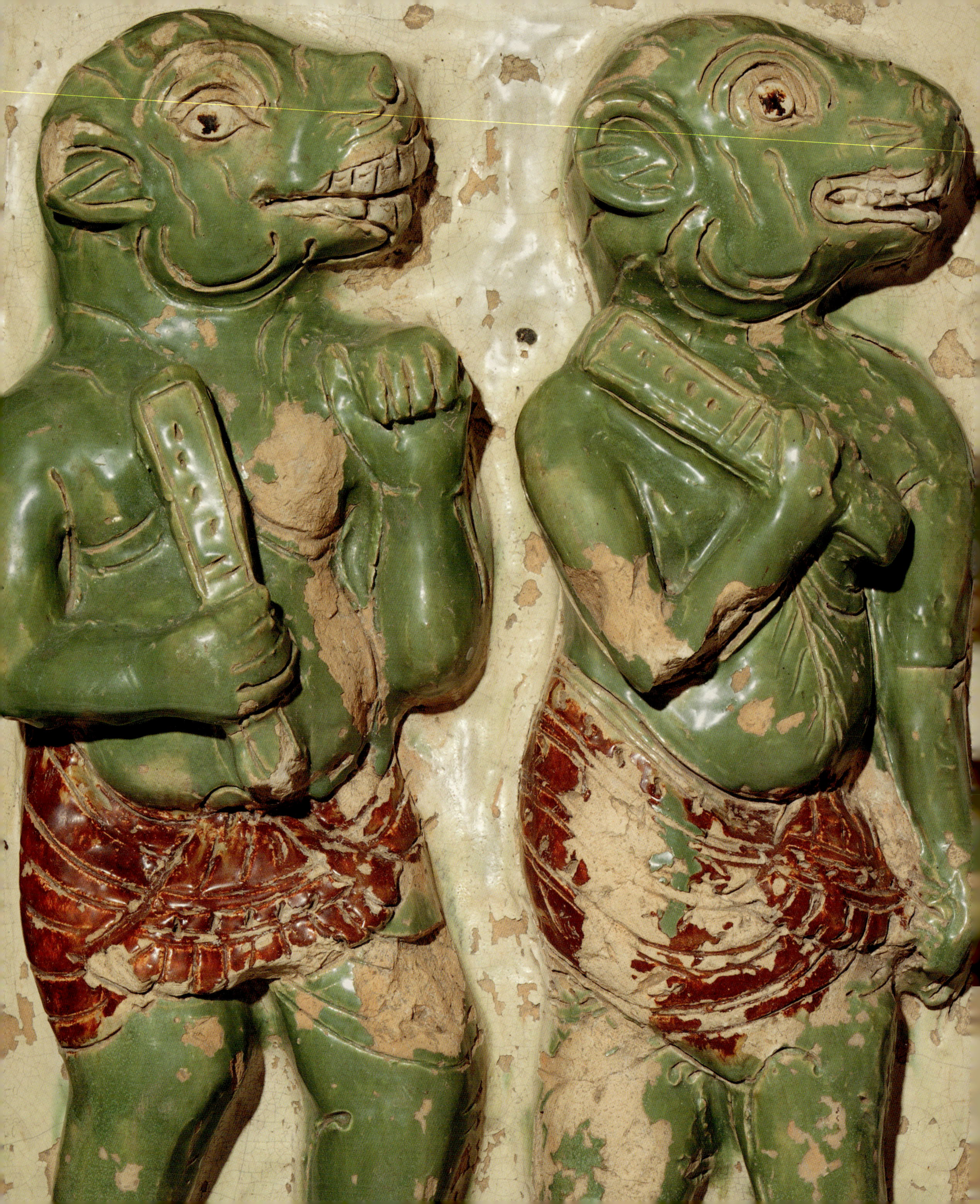

After Pagan
The Art of Myanmar, 1287–1900

Sylvia Fraser-Lu

With the decline of Pagan, or Bagan, in the late thirteenth century, the Bamar leadership moved the capital north to the Sagaing area to fend off incursions by the Mongols and the emergent Shan who had settled in the river basin of the Shan plateau. Through intrigue, strategic alliances, and judicious marriages to local nobility they had made themselves virtual masters of Upper Myanmar. Resentment against Shan domination in the north also led a number of Bamar to move south-eastward and set up a center of resistance at Taunggu. Taking advantage of weakness at the center, the restive Mon in the fourteenth century broke away to found the kingdom of Hanthawaddy in the south with its capital at Pegu (ca. 1369–1537). In legend, Rakhine resorted to carrying out raids on Pagan territory, which were beaten back, forcing the Rakhine King Min Saw Mwun to seek refuge (ca. 1406) with the Sultan of Bengal.

After nearly a century of Shan domination, the Bamar in the north eventually established their capital at Ava, or Inwa, at the confluence of the Irrawaddy and Myit-nge Rivers close to Kyaukse, a major rice-growing area. It was to serve as the Bamar capital from 1364 until about 1527 and again from 1635 to 1752, giving its name to a nearly five-hundred-year swath of Myanmar history following the fall of the Pagan dynasty.

AVA/TAUNGGU PERIOD, 1287–1752

Despite continuing instability as the Bamar, Mon, and Rakhine states competed for hegemony, the Ava period, building on the achievements and innovations of the Pagan era, developed artistic traditions that were to become more indigenous in spirit. In calm seclusion behind monastery walls, monks began writing stylistically diverse poetry, panegyrical odes, historical ballads, and chronicles in the vernacular as well as in Pali. Their efforts were emulated by the courts, which were to become major centers of patronage for Myanmar literature and the arts.

The Muslim invasions of India and a resurgence of Hinduism under the Senas led to the waning of Buddhism in India, which resulted in less regular contact with Buddhist centers of learning elsewhere. Periodic pilgrimages to sites associated with the life of the Buddha, however, continued. Sri Lanka remained Myanmar's primary source for texts, relics, and Theravada orthodoxy. Left more to its own devices, Myanmar developed a distinct style of art that owed as much to indigenous influences as to the Gupta, Pala, and other Indian styles espoused at Sri Ksetra and Pagan. Despite the fact that the architects, painters, and sculptors of religious images sought to follow the proportions and iconographic imperatives of ancient India (*shilpa*

OPPOSITE Detail of cat. no. 31

shastras) that were faithfully transmitted from craftsman to apprentice down through the ages, different styles gradually evolved in response to changing circumstances and local preferences.

The Ava period coincided with the European "Age of Discovery," which eventually was to have important far-reaching effects on the history of Myanmar. Much of what Westerners know about this period is from the accounts of European travelers, traders, and missionaries.[1] Foreign traders sought precious stones, red and black lac, ivory, horn, lead, tin, and large Martaban stoneware jars from Myanmar largely in exchange for Indian textiles. The important overland trade, particularly in cotton and silk, as well as cultural exchanges with China, continued throughout the Ava period.[2]

HANTHAWADDY, CIRCA 1369–1537

Subject to regular Bamar and Thai raids during the first century after its inception, the kingdom of Hanthawaddy, centered on Pegu, or Bago, led a precarious existence. Fortunately, the fifteenth century was followed by a period of relative peace and prosperity when devoutly Buddhist monarchs channeled their energies into works of merit on behalf of the population. Queen Shinsawbu (r. ca. 1453–1472) continued the work of her predecessors in transforming the Shwedagon Pagoda into a national shrine for the Mon by reconfiguring the site, enlarging the platform, raising the stupa's height, to 302 feet (92.04 m) and, according to later chronicles, giving the monument its first gilding.[3]

Her son-in-law and successor King Dhammazedi (r. ca. 1472–1492), a former monk, continued her work at the Shwedagon Pagoda. He also took steps to heal schisms and correct abuses that had crept into the religion by defrocking transgressors and having all monks reordained according to Sinhalese rites.[4] In addition, he built a unique complex at Payathonzu, three miles south of Pegu, to commemorate a crucial, transitional seven-week period in the life of the Buddha following his enlightenment. This time had been spent by the Buddha meditating at various sites in the vicinity of Bodh Gaya in India and culminated in his decision to embark on his teaching mission to mankind beginning at Sarnarth.[5] Illustrations of the site may be seen inscribed on a nineteenth-century palm-leaf manuscript (see cat. no. 58). Apart from the remnants of some later structures, very little remains of the original site at Payathonzu. Fortunately for posterity, examples of glazed ceramic plaques have been recovered, which at one time graced the enclosure wall of the now ruined Shwegugyi, the former central monument of the complex. They depict pairs of demon warriors dispatched by Mara, the Evil One, to derail the Buddha's quest for enlightenment (see cat. no. 31). Also, once located in niches within a wall surrounding a temple dedicated to the Buddha's fifth week were similarly glazed ceramic plaques featuring the lascivious daughters of Mara (see cat. nos. 29 and 30).

By the sixteenth and seventeenth centuries, a more abstract Mon style of Buddha image began to emerge in the Thaton-Moulmein area. Rendered mainly in wood and mounted on fairly tall-waisted thrones, the figures tended to have disproportionately large heads, hands, and feet in relation to the torso. Dyads with prominent finials, set against lotus-decorated backboards, were popular, as were crowned images replete with soaring three- to five-tiered sawtooth crowns, prominent earrings, and incised jewelry on the arms and torso.

Unfortunately for Pegu, its maritime wealth became a target of the ambitious King Tabinshwehti of Taunggu (r. 1531–1550), who dreamed of uniting all of Myanmar, Thailand, and Laos under his banner. After besieging the Mon and eventually overcoming them circa 1535–1541, he moved his capital to Pegu and succeeded in uniting much of the Myanmar heartland. However, it was left to his successor King Bayinnaung (r. 1551–1581) to consolidate his victories and complete the task of subduing the Shan states, Manipur, Chiang Mai, and Vientiane. Bayinnaung also successfully invaded Ayutthaya in 1564, which initiated two centuries of intermittent warfare between the two kingdoms.

RAKHINE MRAUK-U PERIOD, 1430–1784

King Min Saw Mwun, on regaining his throne about 1430, founded a new capital at Mrauk-U in 1433.[6] To counter possible future invasions, he sought the assistance of the Portuguese around the Bay of Bengal to help with defenses, arms manufacture, and seamanship, in return for territorial and trade concessions. Self-strengthening paid off and Mrauk-U King Min Bin (1531–1553) of Rakhine, taking advantage of a civil war in eastern Bengal, successfully made incursions into the area. A Bamar invasion was also repelled in 1546–47. Rakhine, cognizant of disturbed conditions in Lower Myan-

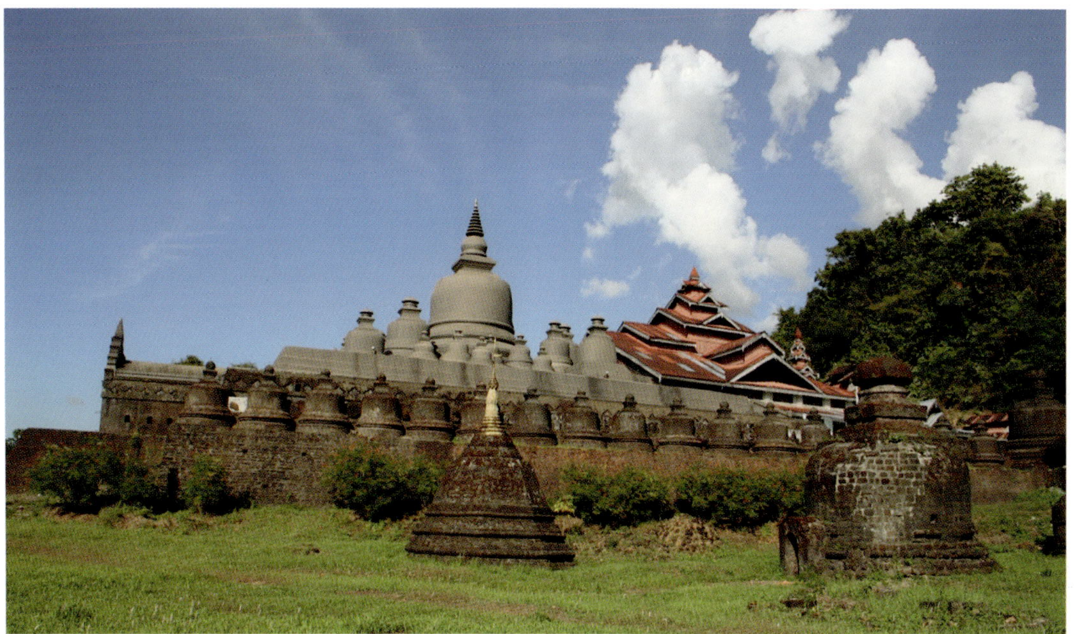

FIG. 37. The Shitthaung Temple of "Eighty Thousand Images," a fortress temple capped by a large bell-shaped stupa surrounded by smaller, similarly shaped stupas, built against a steep cliff as protection against invasions

mar, and in agreement with Taunggu invaded Pegu in 1599 and carried off much treasure.[7]

With assistance from Indian architects, Min Bin and his successors endowed Mrauk-U with some unique temples constructed of well-hewn, tightly cemented sandstone walls surmounted by plaster-covered brick superstructures of sturdy, squat stupa forms surrounded by smaller replicas of differing dimensions. The main shrines, located deep within the structures, could be accessed via stairways leading to vaulted corridors and terraces lined with numerous sculptures in both high and low relief. In addition to serving as places of worship, such temples could also function as refuges in times of siege, most notably the Shitthaung (fig. 37), the Koethaung, and the Htukanthein Temples.[8]

The solid, serene, masculine-looking Mahamuni image appeared to be the ideal for sixteenth- and seventeenth-century bronze and sandstone images from Mrauk-U, characterized by broadly round faces with a tendency toward squareness around the jaw (fig. 38).[9] Like Ava, Rakhine also produced crowned images that historically have been important. The Rakhine king at his coronation took a solemn oath, in the presence of a crowned image specially cast for the occasion, to rule wisely and support the religion.

LATE AVA/TAUNGGU PERIOD, 1531–1752

Despite inscriptions and descriptive references in chronicles to the construction of numerous works of merit, very few have survived that can be firmly assigned to the earlier Ava period (1364–1527).[10] This is not surprising given the turbulent times, periodic earthquakes, and the propensity in Myanmar for regular refurbishment of monuments at sacred sites by enlarging them or adding new structures, rather than preserving the original architecture. Much of what remains of Ava/Taunggu-period Buddhist art dates from the seventeenth and early eighteenth centuries, when calmer conditions prevailed and the capital returned to Ava.[11]

Although Pagan architecture remained the yardstick against which all later religious structures were judged, elements common to Myanmar woodcarving, such as multi-tiered structures (*pyathat*) and roof and corner antefixes, began to make their appearance in masonry during the latter part of the Ava period. Stucco decoration continued to be of a high standard and appeared especially around entranceways and windows. Florid botanical scrolling and motifs such as writhing *naga* (mythical snakes, Sanskrit), lions, ogres, *deva* (Sanskrit), and *kinnari* (Pali) replaced the *makara* (Sanskrit) and the myriad of smaller creatures popular at Pagan.

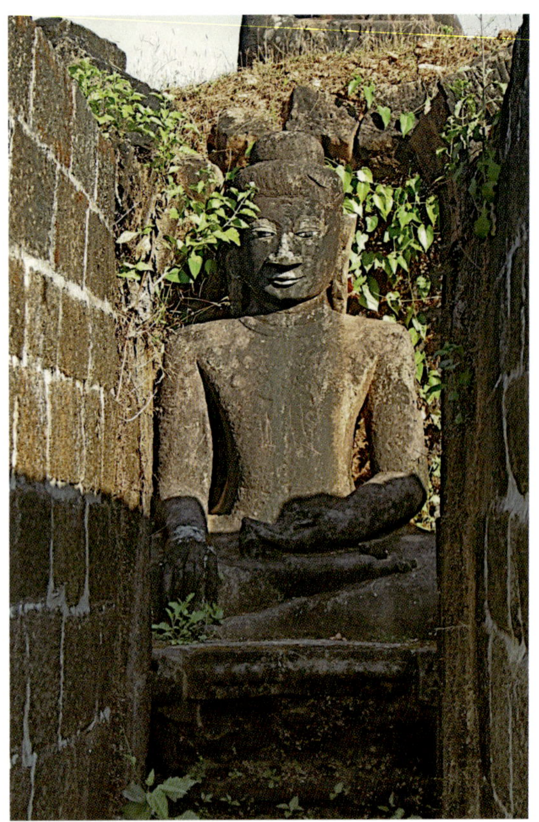

FIG. 38. Rakhine sandstone images are characterized by broad round faces with a tendency to squareness around the jaw. The arch of the brow and the distance between the brows and the eyes are more natural compared with the Bamar Ava image. Seated in *virasana* with the right hand in *bhumisparsa*; clothing lines are scarcely visible. The size and weight of such images preclude the inclusion of an example in the exhibition.

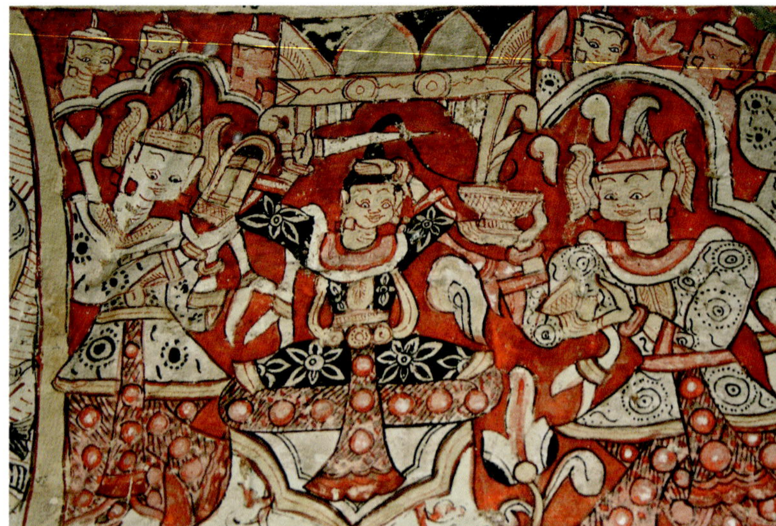

FIG. 39. This wall painting from the late seventeenth or early eighteenth century from Po Win Taung Caves depicts Prince Siddhatta, the Buddha-to-be, severing his hair to symbolize the renunciation of his princely existence in favor of the life of a mendicant. Sakka collects the hair on the right, while the brahma Ghatikara stands ready to present the Buddha-to-be with his robes.

Indian techniques, conventions, and subject matter continued to be followed with respect to Buddhist wall painting in caves and within Ava-period temples at Sagaing and Pagan, but the format had changed. Paintings of the twenty-eight Buddhas, the life of the Buddha, and *jatakas* appear in multitiered bands with short descriptive captions in Myanmar below. Scenes rendered in a palette of black, brown, green, and white against a vermillion or brownish background began to be separated by straight and wavy lines as well as—more subtly—by mountains, vegetation, and buildings. Set within distinctly local backgrounds, figures appear strongly two-dimensional, with perspective largely absent. Faces were drawn in simple, flowing lines, and dramatis personae were proudly arrayed in contemporary Myanmar dress according to their station in life (fig. 39).[12]

By the late fourteenth century, a distinct style of Ava Buddha image was evolving, which differed from the Pala ideals of Pagan. The head, with less prominent curls, has become larger in relation to the body, and the face broader and rounder. The eyes appear half-closed, the nose less aquiline, and the mouth bow-shaped. Larger ears reach the shoulders, while the head is dropped slightly forward on a shorter neck supported by a heavier torso (see cat. no. 35). Dress, where visible, continued to be the simple garb of a monk, leaving the right shoulder bare with a flap of cloth over the left. The majority of the images depict the figure seated in *padmasana* (Sanskrit) on lotus thrones with the right hand in the *bhumisparsa* (Sanskrit) or earth-touching gesture, which by that time had become the prevalent *mudra* (Sanskrit) throughout Myanmar (see cat. no. 36). Standing and reclining figures appear to be comparatively rare and continued to follow Pagan conventions. Marble had gradually supplanted sandstone in popularity as a medium.

Ava bronze images appear to be among the most elegant ever cast, particularly those where the Buddha is shown as a universal monarch, or *cakkavatti* (Pali), in a crown replete with soaring openwork flanges and a full complement of jewelry in lower relief (see cat. no. 38). Some thrones had provisions for attaching smaller effigies of disciples and other devotees as well as guardian animals such as lions (see cat. no. 35). Elephants, too, occasionally appeared as a mount or throne for Buddha images (see cat. no. 37).

During this period the Shan and Tai-Yuan states were subdued and their various rulers (*sawbwa*, Myanmar) brought into a tributary relationship with Ava. Despite incorporation into the Bamar kingdom, distance, terrain, and isolation meant that the plateau was left much to its own devices, which led to the evolution of some regional variation in art. Under influence from Thailand, stupa forms became more attenuated, and many shrines were recessed at the base. The quality of stuccowork rivaled that of Upper Myanmar. The Ava image became the model and continuing ideal for Shan images.

KONBAUNG PERIOD, 1752–1885

The Ava period was brought to a close by a Mon rebellion (1740–51). The Bamar were rescued from defeat by Alaungpaya (r. 1752–1760), the son of a hereditary official from Shwebo, who mounted a daring, vigorous campaign against the Mon. By 1757 he had united the country and founded a new dynasty. King Hsinbyushin (r. 1763–1776), his equally aggressive son, launched retaliatory raids against Manipur, the country's northwest neighbor, that resulted in the deportation of thousands of Manipuris, also known as Kathe—boatmen, cavalrymen, silk weavers, silversmiths, musicians, and court astrologers, all of whose skills were put to good use at the capital at Ava. They were soon joined by an even larger contingent of former Thai nobles and artisan prisoners-of-war following Hsinbyushin's destruction of Ayutthaya in 1767. These captive artisans have been credited with introducing many innovations in weaving, embroidery, lacquer, metalwork, and architecture. Court interest in Thai performing arts not only led to a renaissance in Myanmar literature and drama, and changes in royal costume, but also offered exciting new subject matter for artisans (see cat. no. 54). Western ideas on architecture and painting were beginning to penetrate Myanmar through regular visits from foreign envoys and Christian missionaries, some of whom were granted permission to set up schools that offered a Western education. The court also offered employment to a few Europeans familiar with modern building and engineering techniques and Western art.

After the success of his southern campaigns, Alaungpaya wasted no time in reaffirming his dominance and legitimacy over the vanquished by performing works of merit at the Shwedagon, the sacred shrine of the Mon, and turning it into a national place of worship for all Buddhist believers within the country.[13] His successors also performed notable renovations, thereby making it a key Konbaung field of merit.[14] A fourth son, King Bodawpaya, conquered Rakhine in 1785 and carried off its most sacred icon, the Mahamuni image, for veneration at his new capital at Amarapura, turning it into an important pilgrimage site.

The architecture of Pagan remained the inspiration for many Konbaung religious buildings in the Ava-Mandalay area, particularly for stupas, many of which continued to be modeled on the Shwezigon.[15] Temples such as the Ava Leihtatgyi, and the Kyauktawgyi at Amarapura, also owed much to Pagan prototypes.

Although the Konbaung monarchs expended much effort in refurbishing the shrines of their predecessors, they were also open to innovation and experimentation. Bodawpaya set out to build the world's largest pagoda at Mingun about 1790, an endeavor that was eventually abandoned, leaving behind an incomplete mass of masonry 162 feet high by 450 feet square (49.4 x 137.2 m) (fig. 40). Numerous glazed ceramic tiles intended for exterior embellishment have been recovered from the site (see cat. no. 40). The nearby Myatheindan, also known as Hsinbyume,[16] Pagoda built by King Bagyidaw (r. 1819–1837), Bodawpaya's grandson and successor, was designed to replicate the Tavatimsa Heaven.[17] King Mindon (r. 1853–1878) also commissioned a complete set of the *Tipitaka*, inscribed on 729 stone slabs sheltered by miniature shrines, in the new capital of Mandalay. Known as the Kuthodaw Pagoda, it is now a major attraction for both Buddhist scholars and tourists. He also hosted a successful Fifth Buddhist Council in 1871, and erected the Atumashi Monastery, which incorporated Italian archways into a stucco-covered masonry base.

Konbaung royalty were also avid builders of teak monasteries (*pongyi-kyaung*), which in terms of construction and layout owed more to pre-Buddhist Southeast Asian house-building practices and beliefs than to Indian prototypes. Sited on an east-west axis, such monasteries—consisting of a chapel, a room for the abbot, a multipurpose hall, and storeroom—were constructed on platforms supported on

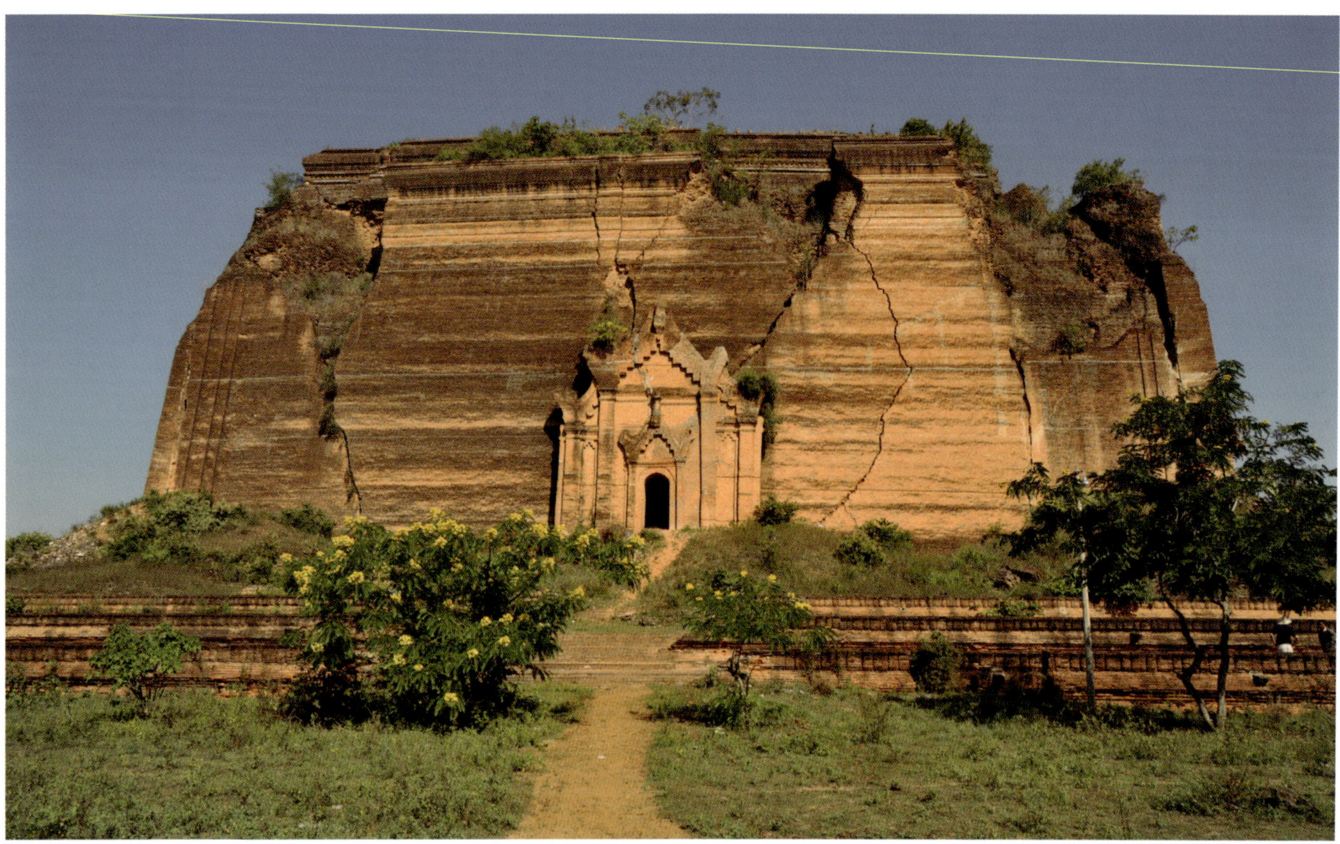

FIG. 40. This enormous cube of masonry (H. 162 x W. 450 ft.; 49.4 x 137.2 m), the unfinished Mingun Pahtodawgyi with small shrines on each of its sides, was erected under the personal supervision of King Bodawpaya (r. 1782–1819) with conscripted labor. After twenty years, the project was abandoned. Earthquakes have since caused large fissures in the brickwork.

teak piles and connected by tenon-and-mortise joints. The chief beauty of these royal monasteries lay in their carved decoration. Inspired by earthly conceptions of what the palaces of the celestials might be like, wood carvers through their collective skill and ingenuity transformed a simple wooden building into a magnificent microcosm of the Buddhist universe (see cat. no. 55). One excellent extant example is the Shwenandaw Monastery in Mandalay (fig. 41).

The monasteries, as centers of learning, possessed collections of palm-leaf books and other religious texts, such as *kammavaca*, that described ceremonies pertaining to monks (see cat. nos. 57 and 58). When not in use, such books were wrapped in bamboo-reinforced cloth covers, bound with finely woven ribbons, and stored in capacious teak chests embellished with gilded lacquer illustrations depicting Buddhist subject matter (see cat. nos. 61, 62, 63, and 64). The laity, which was responsible for supporting the monkhood, also donated alms bowls and gifts of robes and food to monasteries (see cat. no. 70). A complete meal could be brought in a pagoda-shaped receptacle known as a *hsun-ok* or served on a covered tray or *daung-baung-kalat* (see cat. nos. 68 and 69).

Although Ava-style images continued to be made, a new form of Buddha image developed during the late eighteenth and early nineteenth centuries. Referred to as the Mandalay style, this image type is noted for its blandly attractive face and horizontally emphasized features. The contours of the body are enveloped in robes that fall in thick, loose folds suggestive of the drapery on early Buddhist art from Gandhara or China—quite a contrast to the light, clinging robes of previous styles (see cat. no. 42). Although seated figures predominate, standing and reclining examples also became popular (see cat. no. 41). Besides marble and bronze, a number of images were made of dry lacquer (*man-hpaya*), many of which were sold in the Shan States. Thai influence is evident in the changing style of crowned images that became popular during the Konbaung period. Many older uncrowned images were elevated to kingly status with the addition of tiered pagoda-shaped crowns, epaulettes, and gilded metal openwork jewelry and emblems of office.

Interior paintings continued to embellish the walls of select temples built in the Pagan, Mandalay-Sagaing, and Monywa areas. A palette of red, white, and turquoise was favored for religious themes. Scenes continued to be separated by undulating lines, as well as architectural and natural features. The overlapping of figures was used to create the impression of depth. In early-nineteenth-century works, however, change becomes apparent. Narrative detail was elaborated upon and interspersed with genre scenes where the protagonists, clothed and coiffured in contemporary Konbaung fashion, go about a myriad of daily activities. Multiple perspectives were applied, allowing events inside and outside diagonally placed buildings to be viewed simultaneously (see cat. no. 59). Chinese influence is evident in the portrayal of rocks and some floral motifs. Western contact also led to outdoor scenes later coming into vogue with more centered compositions, replete with horizon lines and attempts at obtaining greater depth through diminishing perspectives and shading.[18] Western subject matter such as winged celestials, acanthus scrolling, carriages, paddle steamers, and even trains began to appear in Myanmar murals (see cat. no. 59).

Such changes were also echoed in manuscript painting, particularly in accordion folded books, called *parabaik*, made from thick mulberry paper. *Parabaik* painting was an important court art. In addition to representing religious subject matter, royal atelier artists also illustrated court customs and celebrations for posterity (see cat. no. 60). Palace artists worked in gouache in a brighter, more extensive color range than temple painters and were permitted to use gilding. *Parabaik* scenes, uninterrupted by wavy lines, unfolded from left to right. Graduated washes and lower horizon lines helped create a greater feeling of depth in later *parabaik*.

COLONIAL PERIOD, 1824–CIRCA 1900

Konbaung policies of "hot pursuit" into British territory when hunting down Rakhine, Assam, and Manipuri rebels alarmed the British authorities in India and, along with other numerous points of contention over trade and protocol, eventually culminated in three Anglo-Burmese Wars that took place in 1824–26, 1852, and 1885–86. The vanquished Myanmar were forced to pay large indemnities and cede territory to the victors—the territories of Rakhine, or Arakan, and Tenasserim in 1826, and the province of Pegu in 1852. The coup de grâce came in 1885 when the British invaded the Myanmar capital at Mandalay and dispatched King Thibaw (r. 1878–1885) and his family off to a lonely exile at Ratnagiri in western India.[19] Myanmar became a province of India.

The British, on gaining complete control of this resource-rich province, hastened to exploit its mineral wealth and bountiful reserves of teak, and opened up the deltaic lands of the south for rice production. However, they appeared unwilling to assume what was traditionally considered an essential function of Myanmar kingship in the eyes of the population—that of defender and promoter of the Buddhist faith. This entailed assuming responsibility for enforcing unity and doctrinal and ritual purity within the monkhood; erecting and repairing Buddhist shrines; and generally sponsoring conditions under which the religion could flourish.[20] The colonial administration's avowedly neutral stance with respect to the Buddhist religion and its unwillingness to provide material support led many citizens to believe that their faith was doomed to decline under an alien regime.

The Archaeological Survey of Burma established in 1902 set about drawing up a list of protected monuments considered most worthy of preservation. Compiled primarily on the basis of antiquarian and artistic interest, it did little to satisfy Myanmar Buddhists, who considered the perceived sacredness of the site of paramount importance over age and decorative merit. An endemic lack of funds meant that not all the desired conservation could be undertaken.

Such a state of affairs eventually led lay Buddhists to take matters into their own hands and to embark on a building boom at leading religious sites such as Mandalay Hill and the Shwedagon Pagoda. Ironically, the most munificent builders were the nouveau riche—rice and timber merchants, brokers, and traders, who, having taken advantage of the new opportunities offered by the colonial economy, were eager to accrue merit and respectability and to show off their new-found wealth by constructing shrines at sacred sites.

The colonial presence also brought advances in technology, which exerted an influence on Myanmar architecture. Modern mathematics and engineering, which emphasized precision and standardization, facilitated the construction of

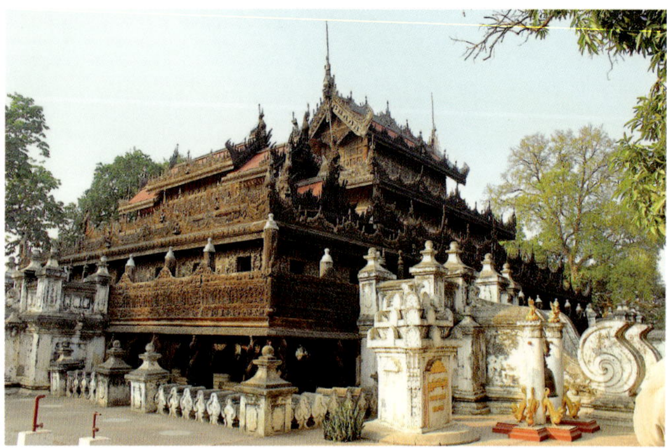

FIG. 41. The Shwenandaw Monastery of Mandalay is of great historical importance, for it is the only apartment of the former nineteenth-century Konbaung palace complex remaining. King Thibaw (r. 1878–1885) had it converted to a monastery between 1878 and 1883 in memory of his father, King Mindon.

larger buildings with more complex roofing systems, facades, and entranceways. To this was added the widespread use of steel cutting tools, templates, nails and screws, plywood, sheet and wrought iron, reinforced concrete, and glass, all of which contributed to further structural and decorative innovation. Sharper cutting tools led to more detailed paneling, lacelike woodcarving, and much finer glass mosaic inlay on lacquerware and other colonial-period works of Buddhist merit (see cat. no. 54).

The art of silverwork flourished at this time by catering to the tastes of both a Myanmar and a foreign clientele. Some of the most striking pieces combine both Myanmar and European forms and functions with decorative elements from Buddhist legends and local folklore (see cat. no. 71). Myanmar silversmiths were famous for openwork and repoussé in high relief. Some craftsmen won prizes at colonial expositions. Embroidered wall hangings (*kalaga*) depicting scenes from the life of the Buddha and *jataka* stories were also popular with both locals and Europeans (see cat. no. 66). While Westerners displayed them as tapestries, for the rest of the population they served as room dividers, furniture covers, and gifts to monasteries.

With the abolition of the monarchy, Myanmar artists had lost their most generous patrons. Some mural painters eked out a living embellishing some of the new pagoda interiors with religious themes, but commissions were hard to come by. Others managed to find design work with newly established theatrical companies, *kalaga* embroidery establishments, and *sap-bagyi* workshops that specialized in making ephemeral decorations for religious celebrations such as novitiations and monks' cremations. A number became commercial artists with foreign companies in Yangon. *Parabaiks* lost their raison d'être and some former court artists turned to portraying religious subject matter on cloth for monastic or private devotional purposes (see cat. nos. 56 and 65). The most talented made a living painting court scenes of former royalty in gouache on sized linen, which were popular with both the British and Myanmar. Such subject matter fed the nostalgia felt by many residents for former times as an independent kingdom, when life was perceived as having been simpler and more predictable.

In many cases religious pictorial art also appeared as if frozen in time. Although depictions of architectural features reflected changing styles, characters in scenes continued to be portrayed in Konbaung dress, despite notable changes in fashion. The Mandalay Buddha image remained the predominant style, although there was a tendency toward greater elaboration in the folding and decoration of the robes (see cat. no. 41). Glass mosaic decoration set in lacquer was gradually being supplanted at pagodas by Indian *shish* work—mirror mosaic inlaid in cement. Palm-leaf books were replaced by paper ones with the introduction of the printing press. Cheap editions of the *Tipitika*, as well as commercially manufactured religious wares, became readily available to all who desired them at pagoda stalls throughout Myanmar.

Despite the misgivings the Myanmar harbored toward the colonial regime for its lack of material support for the Buddhist religion, the faith continued to flourish. This resentment, however, was to manifest itself later, in the twentieth century, when Buddhism, allied to nationalism, became a potent force in the struggle for independence.

NOTES

1 Western visitors to Myanmar during the Ava period who have left accounts of their travels include the Venetian merchant Di Conti (ca. 1435), the Russian Athanasius Nitikin (ca. 1470), the Genoese Hieronimo de Santo Stephano (ca. 1496), another Italian, Ludovico de Varthema (ca. 1505–07), the Portuguese trader and merchant Duarte Barbosa (1518), Venetians Cesare Frederic (ca. 1569) and Gaspero Balbi (1583), Englishman Ralph Fitch (1586–87), as well as Portuguese priests Nicholas Pimento, who visited Pegu (1598), and the Augustinian Friar Sebastian Manrique, who was a resident in Rakhine (1628–33).

2 For an excellent account of seventeenth-century Myanmar trade, see Dijk, *Seventeenth-Century Burma and the Dutch East India Company*.
3 Queen Shinsawbu, also known in Mon as Bana Thau, had a remarkable life. She was the daughter of King Razadarit, a Mon monarch who devoted his life to fighting the Bamar. She was married to a cousin and had three children. Widowed at a young age, she became a consort to King Thihathu of Ava. After his demise, she returned to Pegu bringing with her two Mon monks. Since her brothers had died she became queen, and to ensure continuity she had Dhammazedi, one of the monks, leave the order to marry her daughter and ascend the throne. She is associated with the Shwedagon and legend has it that she passed away with her eyes transfixed upon the pagoda.
4 He sent a delegation of forty-four monks to Sri Lanka in 1475 to be reordained according to the rites of the highly revered Mahavihara sect at Kalyani in order to establish an indisputable and canonically valid monastic succession of Mon monks. Upon their return, they reordained all other monks in the Mahavihara tradition. This mission was recorded in Pali and Mon on large stone inscriptions located at Pegu near the site of the original ordination hall. They have been translated by Blagden in "Mon Inscriptions Nos. IX–XI," 53–68.
5 The seven-week period opened with the Buddha's enlightenment following the defeat of Mara while at the Bodhi Tree, where he remained seated on the Aparajita Throne for seven days. He then descended the throne to spend a week of steadfast gazing at the Bodhi Tree, followed by walking to and fro along a golden walkway built by the gods. He then proceeded to a jeweled pavilion—also provided by the gods—where he passed a further week contemplating the *Abhidhamma*. Next he proceeded to the Ajapala, or goatherd's tree. While there, he was accosted by Mara's daughters in the guise of seductive women at varying stages of life who were sent at the instigation of their father to derail the Buddha's course of action. The following seven days were spent atop the coils and under the hood of the Mucalinda Naga that sheltered him from a violent storm. The final week was passed beneath the Rajayatana tree where he was visited by the gods who jointly presented him with bowls that miraculously melded into one, in which he would receive rice cakes cooked in honey from Tapussa and Bhallika, who according to local legends were merchants from Mon country. In return, they were presented with a few strands of hair from the Buddha, which were taken back to Mon country to be enshrined in the Shwedagon Pagoda.
6 Its court was fashioned along similar lines to Indian sultanates. In addition to Rakhine names, kings assumed Muslim titles in the late sixteenth century. Muslim-style coinage was also introduced.
7 The treasure included some thirty bronzes—*dvarapala* guardians, lion, and elephant statues originally looted by the Thai from Angkor circa 1352. They were later taken from Ayutthaya to Pegu by Bayinnaung between 1564 and 1569. Minyaza-gyi of Rakhine laid claim to them in 1599 and transported them to his capital in Mrauk-U. Bodawpaya took them from Rakhine, along with the Mahamuni image, to Amarapura in 1784, where a few can still be seen in a pavilion to the rear of the Mahamuni temple complex.
8 The best known is the Shitthaung Temple (Shrine of Eighty Thousand Buddha Images) constructed in 1536 to honor Min Bin's military success in Bengal. Not to be outdone, his son Dikha (r. 1553–1556) built the even larger Koethaung (Shrine of Ninety Thousand Buddha Images), while Min Phalaung, another son (r. 1571–1593), was responsible for the forbidding Htukanthein ordination hall noted for its spiraling passageways lined with Buddha-occupied niches flanked by devotees—members of the nobility and possible donors to the project. As part of the system of fortifications, the ordination hall also sheltered the monkhood in times of siege. For descriptions of the temples of Mrauk-U, see Gutman, *Burma's Lost Kingdoms*, 94–123.
9 Rakhine historically has had the honor of being the birthplace of Myanmar's most highly revered Buddha image—the Mahamuni—originally housed near Kyauktaw, which according to a local legend is based on an actual likeness of the Buddha. Its presence over the course of history has attracted many pilgrims and aroused the envy of neighboring states, which were known to mount periodic forays with the express intention of acquiring the icon for themselves. Details of the Mahamuni legend are related in an ancient manuscript entitled *Sarvasthanaprakarana*, which gives an account of the origins of Buddhism in Rakhine. See Forchhammer, *Report on the Antiquities of Arakan*, 2–5.
10 They include two pagodas at Sagaing built by fifteenth-century kings of Ava: the Htupayon built by King Narapati of Ava (r. 1443–1469), and the Hsinmyashin Pagoda built by King Mon-hyin (r. 1427–1440), which enshrined some relics from Sri Lanka. Both were destroyed by earthquakes and refurbished. A later Sinhalese-style example is the Kaunghmudaw, built by Thalun in 1636; see Aung Thaw, *Historical Sites in Burma*, 130–31.
11 Art historians often refer to the latter part of the Taunggu era as the Nyaung-yan period, after a son of Bayinnaung who, during his short reign (1599–1606), did much to unite Upper Myanmar and the Shan States, and thereby laid the foundation for the more peaceful period that followed.
12 For an account of Ava-period painting, see Chew, *Cave-Temples of Po Win Taung*, 95–134.
13 Alaungpaya also founded Yangon (Anglicized as Rangoon) as his southern capital. It was originally known as Dagon, the site of a small fishing village.
14 "A field of merit" means an opportunity to obtain merit by, for example, refurbishing pavilions, adding new ones, or repairing or replacing wood carvings, in a particular area or within a particular complex. Traditionally at the most sacred sites such as at the Shwedagon, it was considered a prerogative of royalty to do the "hardscaping" and major refurbishments. Commoners were welcome to bring ephemeral offerings such as candles, flowers, and streamers.
15 They include the Kuthodaw and Eindawya in Mandalay, and Aungmye-lawka at Sagaing.
16 Hsinbyume is the name of the deceased wife of the Crown prince, for whom it was built. Many pagodas in Myanmar have more than one name.
17 The shrine is surrounded by seven processional terraces replete with serpentine-decorated balustrades that represent the seven oceans and mountain ranges encircling Mount Meru. There are also effigies of guardian figures that inhabit the slopes of Mount Meru.
18 The Taungthaman Kyaukdawgyi at Amarapura, inspired by the Ananda Temple at Pagan, was built in 1847 by Pagan Min (r. 1846–1853). Inspired by Western architectural drawings and outdoor vistas, the interior walls are embellished with interesting mural paintings of some of the better-known religious buildings in Myanmar, which have been depicted within a continuous panoramic landscape that includes scenes of everyday life. The skies above are enlivened by the presence of various types of celestials, along with depictions of constellations and Buddhist motifs such as a pair of footprints.
19 In Upper Myanmar local resistance was fierce, and it was not until 1890 that all of Myanmar was brought under British control.
20 Woodward, "When One Wheel Stops," 57.

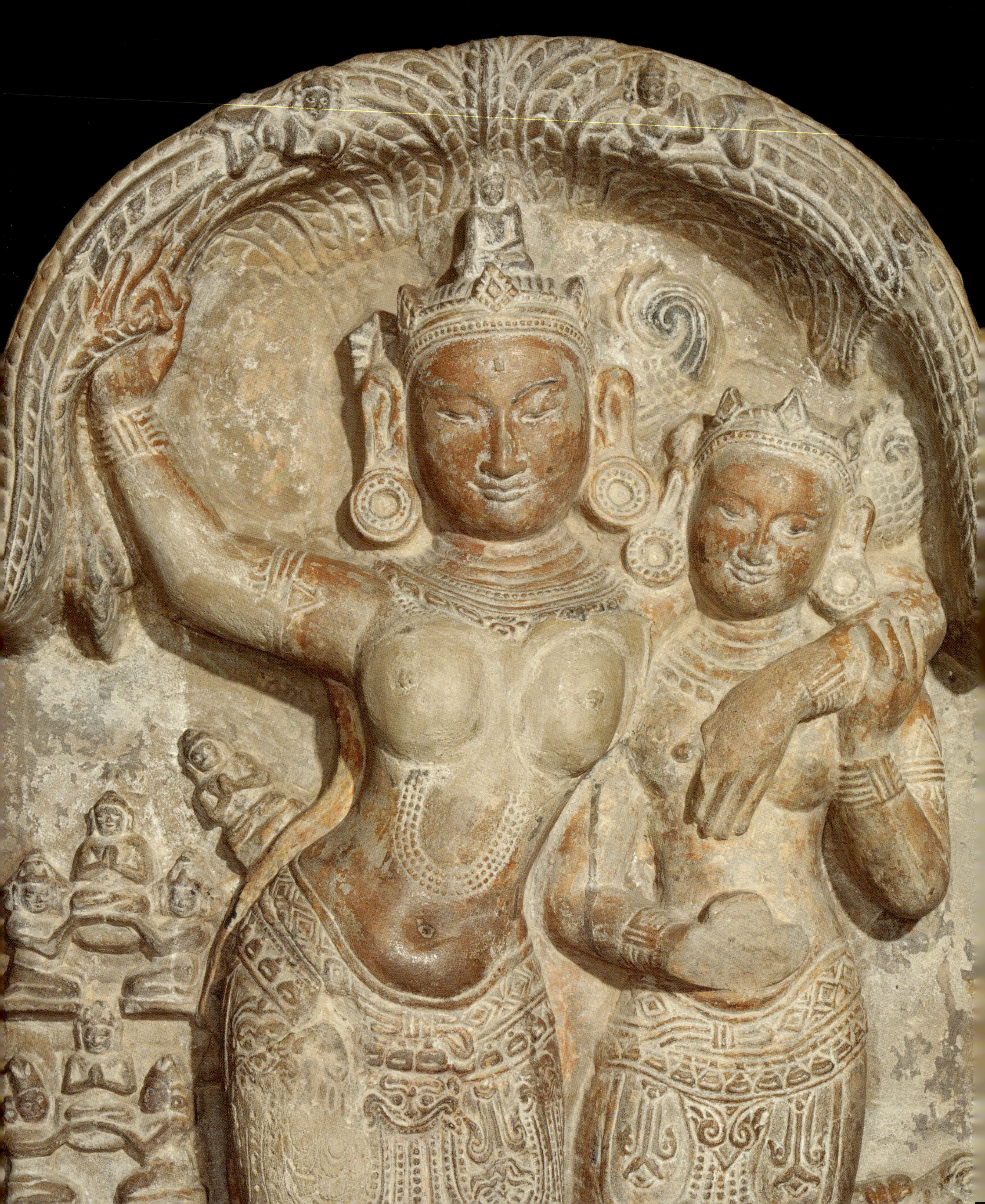

Buddhist Image Replication in Myanmar

Adriana Proser

Starting from the early story of the construction of 84,000 stupas ordered by Emperor Ashoka (304–232 BCE), the replication of imagery has been practiced throughout the Buddhist world. Such acts were integrated into Buddhist practice as a form of merit making for the benefit of the self and others. Pilgrims and merchants who traveled by land and sea to and from South, Southeast, Central, and East Asia disseminated Buddhist imagery along with the practice of replication when they carried copies of sculptures and paintings illustrating the Buddha's birth, first sermon, enlightenment, death, and other Buddhist subject matter.

Image replication is an integral part of Buddhist practice in general, and it has been and continues to be prevalent in Myanmar. Regional cultural beliefs have created a fertile atmosphere where specific images or imagery can remain both present and relevant in popular culture for hundreds of years. In addition, the nature of popular religious belief in Myanmar encourages the forgotten, neglected, or unknown image to suddenly be imbued with remarkable power in the eyes of believers, generations after craftsmen created it. This phenomenon affects the longevity of specific imagery when that image and its aesthetic characteristics are replicated over time. In this context, standard art-historical concepts like the link between chronology and stylistic development are not universally applicable. In Myanmar, therefore, it is useful to look outside of traditional modes of art-historical analysis to understand the history of images and image making.

In *The Selfish Gene* evolutionary biologist Richard Dawkins offers an intriguing model with a foundation in Darwinism that can be used as a framework to enhance the understanding of the survival and evolution of Buddhist imagery in Myanmar. Dawkins devotes his chapter "Memes: The New Replicators" to cultural transmission. He gives "tunes, ideas, catchphrases, clothes fashions, ways of making pots or of building arches" as examples of memes.[1] When an idea reappears many times it can thrive in a meme pool, he argues. For centuries, with its long history of Buddhism and myth making, Myanmar has provided a perfect environment—or meme pool—for sustaining the replication of specific Buddhist images, in media ranging from architecture to votive plaques. Myanmar's cultural environment has created a system that favors the continued replication of some Buddhist imagery such that the same or extremely similar imagery is produced hundreds of years apart. Buddhism has often been upheld and financially supported by the state, and myth and superstition, transmitted by word of mouth, have often gone hand in hand with religion. And yet in Myanmar, as elsewhere, culture does not remain static but is continually shaped by political change and population

OPPOSITE Detail of cat. no. 16

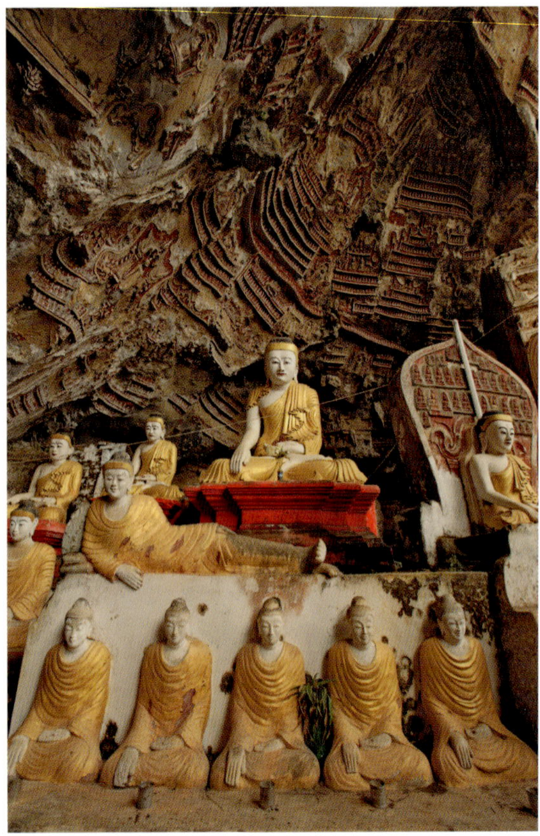

FIG. 42. Clay tablets on walls and ceiling of Kawgun Cave, near Hpa-an in Kayin State, Myanmar

shifts.[2] Therefore meme transmission has mutated, blended, and at times died out in Myanmar.

Votive plaques or impressed-clay tablets with images of the Buddha have been created en masse for use as meritorious offerings and as commemorative and auspicious objects at many Buddhist sites in Asia.[3] This practice remains common in Myanmar, where these replicated images appear in many forms (see cat. nos. 10, 26, and 27). A striking Buddhist site that may date to the seventh century is Kawgun Cave, near Hpa-an in Karen, or Kayin, State, which essentially is tiled with eighteenth-, nineteenth-, and twentieth-century impressed-clay tablets creating an impressive aesthetic atmosphere also found in other Buddhist caves in the area (fig. 42). Here a variety of replicated images were compiled over time and placed in patterns that reproduce Buddhist paradises. Today the site still contains old and new three-dimensional sculptures and is a place that continues to attract Buddhist worshipers. Replication is also evident in other parts of Myanmar, for example in Rakhine where the Shitthaung Temple is named for 80,000 Buddha images and the Koethaung for 90,000 images. On some of the corridor walls of the Koethaung Temple there are large friezes of niches occupied by small images carved in relief.[4]

A pervasive belief in the power, both benevolent and malevolent, of particular Buddhist images, especially sculpture, is as palpable in Myanmar as in any Theravada country. This power can make the acquisition of a Buddha modeled after a famously potent example particularly desirable. Replicas have been made throughout the history of Buddhism in Myanmar to fill this desire on the part of worshipers. The coexistence of replication for merit making and personal worship over many centuries makes Myanmar an especially challenging place for an art historian, hoping to pin a date on an object of a specific style, since many replica images are crafted after preexisting stylistic models.[5] Sculptures of portable size are among the objects for worship that have been replicated in multiples. These are often crafted in stone or bronze and modeled after famous Buddha sculptures (figs. 43 and 44). These smaller sculptures may be acquired by adherents for personal worship or donation to temples or pagodas. Often not exact replicas, their form or scale varies depending on where and why they were created.

There is an ongoing debate about the origins of one group of small stone sculptures, usually around seven or eight inches in height, of the seated Buddha surrounded by his life scenes (see cat. no. 28). For some time, at least some of these pieces—for example, the pyrophyllite piece now in the collection of Asia Society (fig. 45)—were believed to have originated in India and then been carried to Myanmar by traders or other travelers. However, many of the pieces show aesthetic qualities typical of sculpture from the Pagan, or Bagan, period. As Myanmar was an active and even powerful participant in international trade during the eleventh through thirteenth centuries, it is certainly feasible, and even likely, that the carvings were created in Myanmar and from there dispersed to various countries. The Asia Society example has the Tibetan letter for "a" incised onto the back just below the central Buddha. Other examples with Tibetan, Chinese, or Newari inscriptions exist. It is clear that the source for the style of this imagery is Pala-period India and Bodh Gaya in particular. In the example from the Ackland

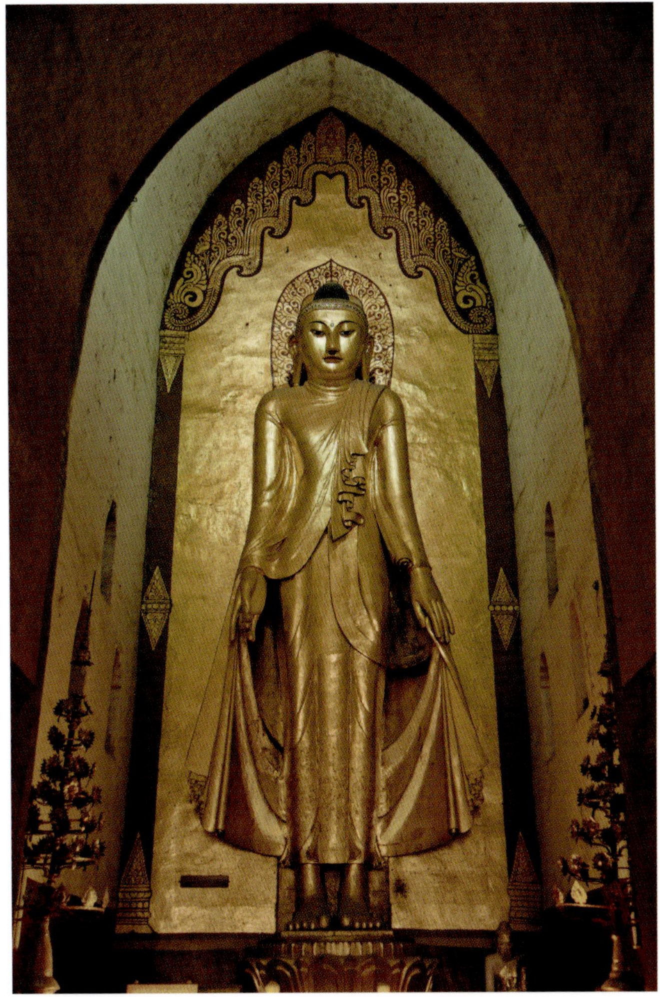

FIG. 43. Konagamana Buddha at Ananda Temple, Pagan

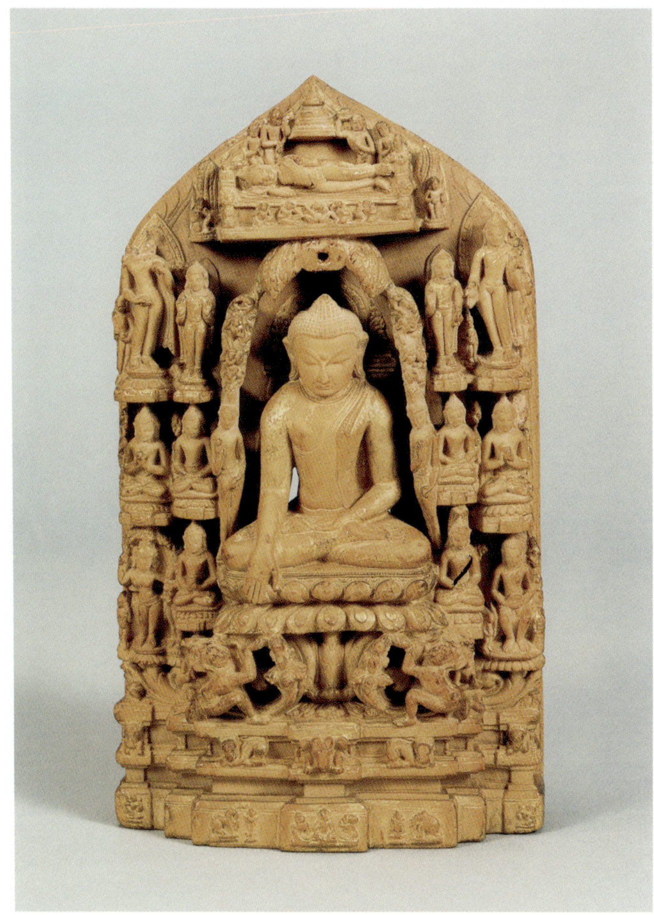

FIG. 45. Scenes of the Buddha's Life. Myanmar. 11th–12th century. Pyrophyllite with gilding. H. 7¾ x W. 4½ in. (19.7 x 11.4 cm). Asia Society, New York: Mr. and Mrs. John D. Rockefeller 3rd Collection, 1979.90

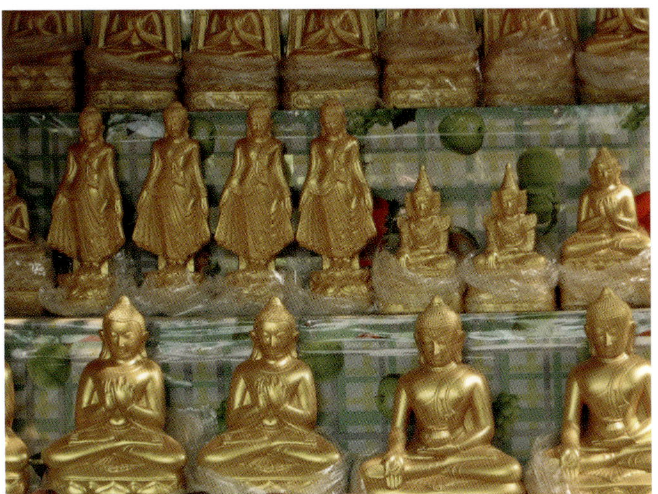

FIG. 44. Replicas of Konagamana Buddha outside of the Ananda Temple, Pagan

Museum in this catalogue (see cat. no. 28), this legacy can also be seen. While the origin for some of these images is likely to be India, a careful comparison of the physiognomy of the carved figures suggests that some are much closer to Myanmar Pagan-period sculpture than to Indian Pala-period sculpture. The articulation of the shape of the head, mouth, and eyes reveal obvious distinctions (see cat. no. 14). In the case of the Pagan sculptures, the face is broader, the "V" shape created where the upper and lower lip meet is more pronounced, and the eyes are not as heavily lidded as in most Pala examples.

According to the historical record, religious missions traveled to Bodh Gaya during this period, funds from Pagan were used to maintain the Mahabodhi Temple in Bodh Gaya, and it is certainly tenable that they brought images like those

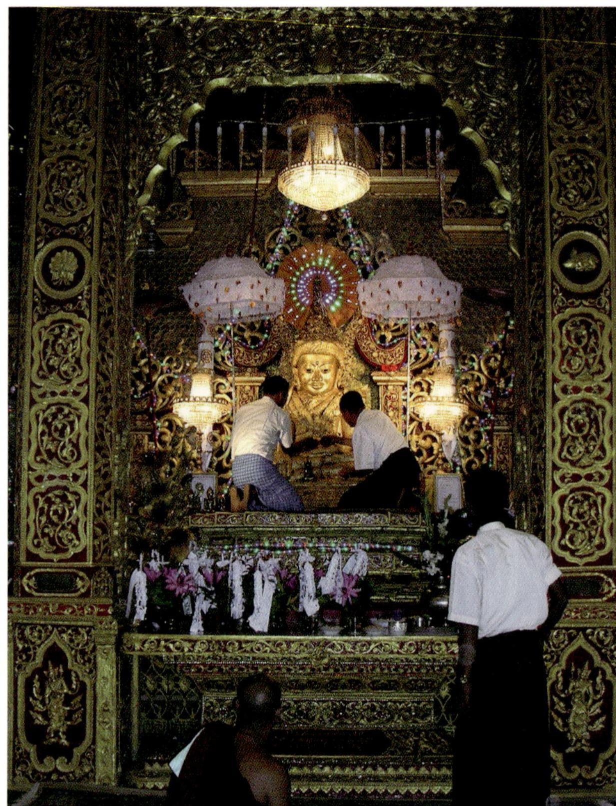

FIG. 46. "Small" Mahamuni Buddha, Kyauktaw Mahamuni Pagoda, Dhanyawadi, Rakhine

carved for the temple during Indian's Pala period back with them to Myanmar where they were replicated.[6] Myanmar's history certainly gives additional credence to this argument, and the seated Buddha figures themselves possess the somewhat broad foreheads, beaklike noses, short necks, and broad shoulders generally found on Pagan-period Buddhas. These transportable images likely replicate an original, probably of a larger scale, that either was copied in Bodh Gaya or was transported to Myanmar, became an important object of worship, and was then replicated again and again.

The best-known example of Buddha image replication in Myanmar relates to the Mahamuni Buddha, which was formerly located in the Kyauktaw Mahamuni Pagoda in Rakhine and was transported in 1794 to a new temple just south of Mandalay. The image, mythologically tied to the Buddha's own lifetime and the miraculous story of how he flew from India and landed on a hillock in Rakhine, is considered particularly potent. Even what is believed to be the original image, now in Mandalay, is difficult to date, but Donald Stadtner suggests it may have been cast in the fourteenth century.[7] Stadtner also discusses the replica images made from "great left-over" metal or *maha-kyan* (Myanmar) from the casting of the original Mahamuni Buddha. These include the "small" replica at the Kyauktaw Mahamuni Pagoda at Dhanyawadi near Mrauk-U, Rakhine, mentioned by Heidi Tan in her essay "Art, Power, and Merit" in this catalogue. Both images, embellished with gold leaf offered by worshipers, have relatively square faces with arching eyebrows that meet at the center, broad nostrils, and wide, full lips (figs. 9 and 46). They have squat bodies and wear elaborate, filigreed crowns. Today it is the small replica that worshipers consider the most potent image in the Kyauktaw Mahamuni Pagoda, not the large-scale copy of the Mahamuni Buddha, created around 1900, that shares its features and now occupies the center of the main shrine area that the two share.

The tradition of Buddhist image replication continues to this day in Myanmar. A striking recent example is the creation of a new Uppatasanti Pagoda donated by Senior General Than Shwe (b. 1933) and his wife in the newly established capital of Naypyidaw. Than Shwe announced the creation of the new capital in 2002.[8] Like the Shwedagon in Yangon, which it replicates, the Uppatasanti Pagoda rises gleaming and golden against the sky and is an important symbol of national identity (figs. 7 and 47). The Uppatasanti is slightly smaller, but both pagodas have a series of terraces from which a dome and peaked spire rises, and the similarity of their exterior structure and proportions is immediately evident. However, while Shwedagon Pagoda's central dome, or *zedi* (Myanmar), is solid, Uppatasanti Pagoda's is not. Uppatasanti, following the precedent of the Kaba Aye Stupa in Yangon of 1952, is hollow-domed, constructed to house altars with Buddha images and relics around its center. Worshipers can enter, circumambulate, view relics and Buddha images, and offer prayers within this interior space. The Shwedagon, which inscriptions indicate was in existence since at least the fifteenth century but likely had much earlier origins, houses what are said to be eight hair relics from the Buddha, among other relics. The Uppatasanti, completed in 2009, contains a Buddha tooth relic. Than Shwe and his family are reported to have donated the Buddha tooth relic so that it could be housed in the Pagoda. Tooth relics, including acknowledged

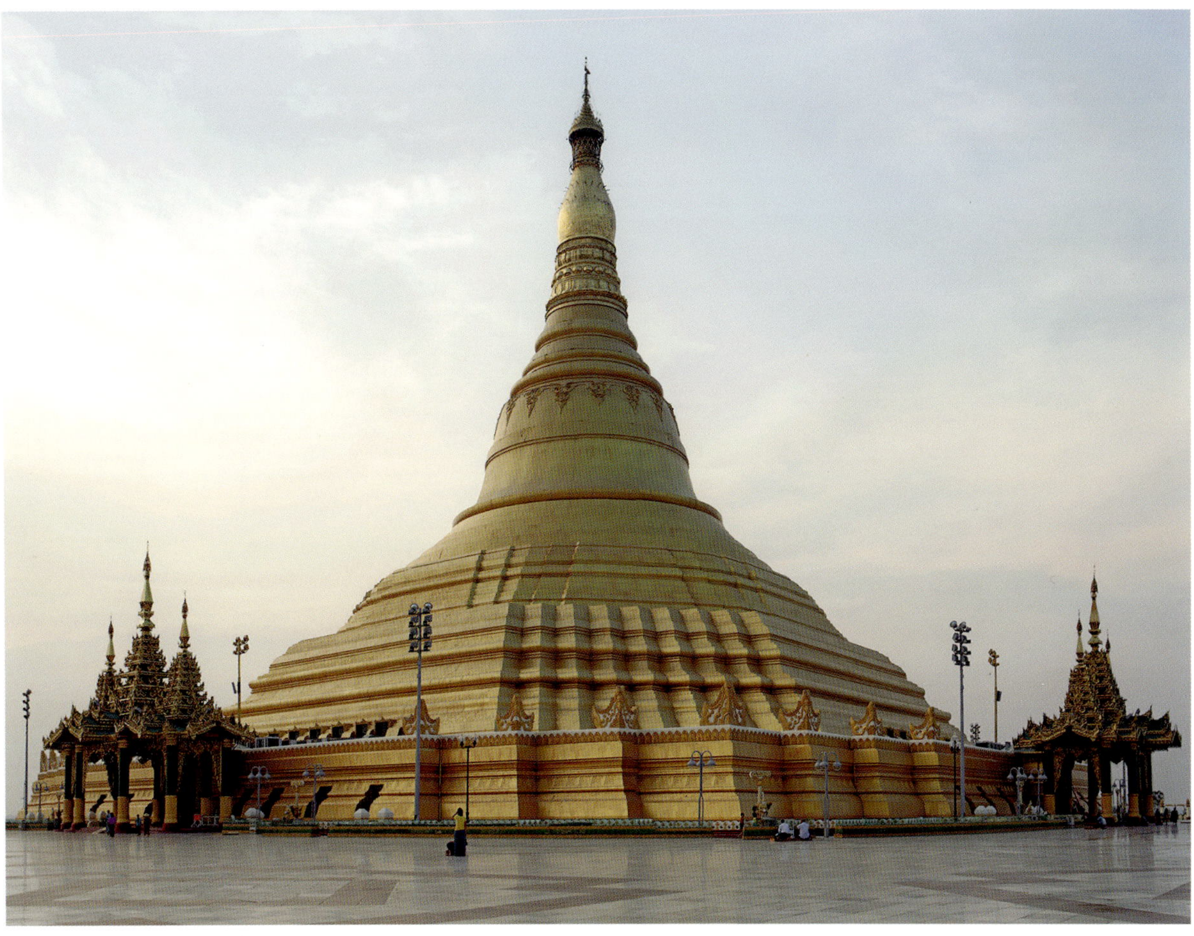

FIG. 47. Uppatasanti Pagoda, Nay Pyi Taw

replica tooth relics, have been conveyed from China to Myanmar for obeisance with some regularity over the past decades and donated tooth replicas are enshrined in a number of Myanmar's pagodas. The donation of what would be perceived as an important relic was essential to establishing the spiritual and political power of the Uppatasanti Pagoda.

As seen from the example above, the reverberations of replication continue into the present in Myanmar. Sometimes this happens on a grand scale and a big political stage, as in Naypyidaw. However, the practice of replication in Myanmar is continually fostered at major and minor sacred sites. It is at these pagodas and temples that worshipers can purchase small copies of an esteemed Buddha and then transport it and, they hope, some of the power of the original to a home shrine or another temple.

NOTES

1 Dawkins, *Selfish Gene*, 192.

2 Ibid., 194–95.

3 For a brief overview of this practice see, for example, Skilling, "Aesthetics of Devotion," 21–22.

4 Thanks to Sylvia Fraser-Lu for suggesting the importance of giving a sense of the prevalence of this practice in Myanmar. I am also grateful to Don Stadtner for his corrections and suggestions. Any errors remaining are my own.

5 Matilsky, *Buddhist Art and Ritual from Nepal and Tibet*.

6 Michael Aung-Thwin and Maitrii Aung-Thwin, *History of Myanmar*, 99.

7 Stadtner, *Sacred Sites of Burma*, 262.

8 The official reason given for this enormous project was limited space in Yangon. The people of Myanmar tell several different stories. One is the rumor of a prophecy that Than Shwe received from his astrologer that Yangon will fall.

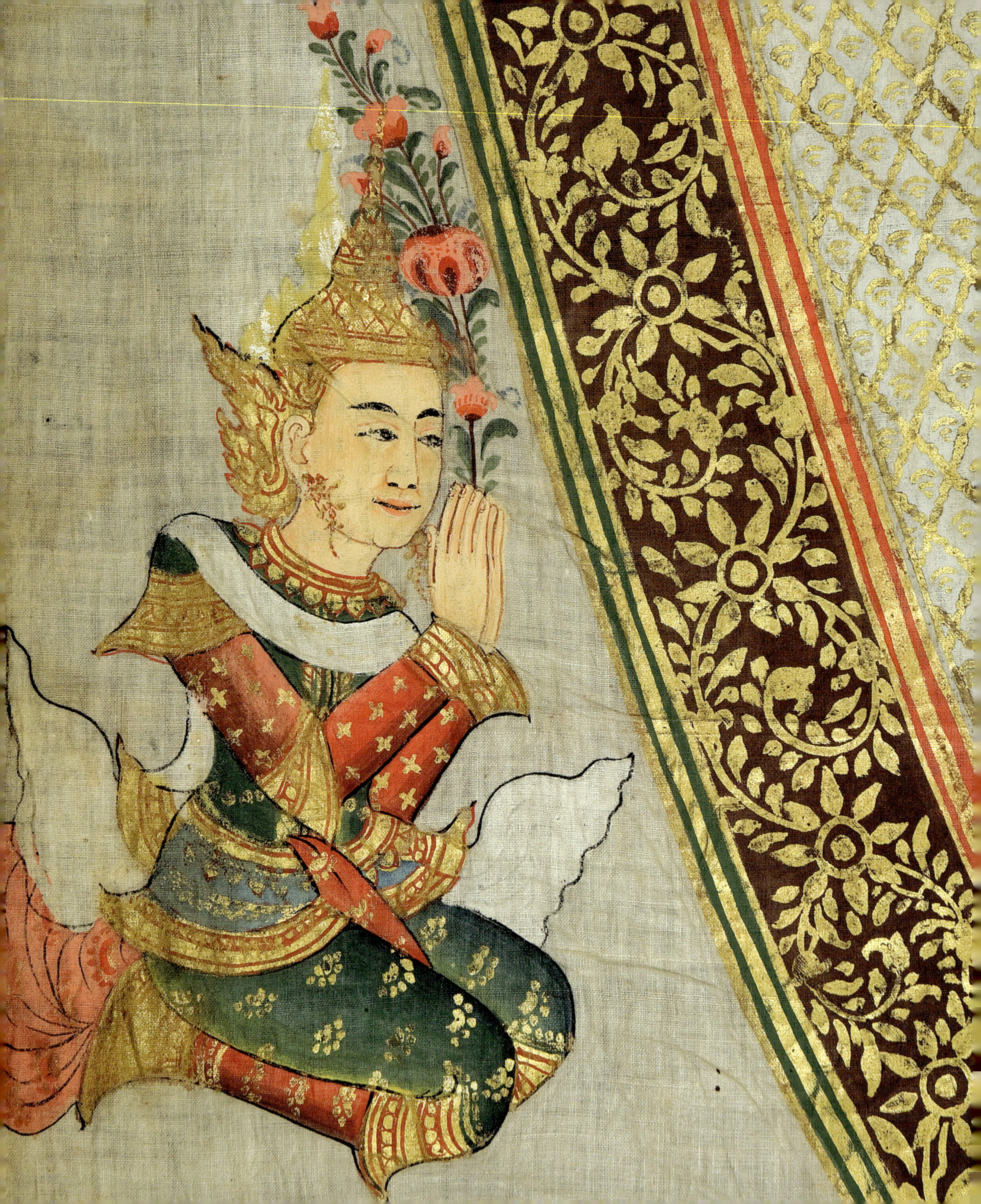

Art, Power, and Merit
The Veneration of Buddha Images in Myanmar Museums

Heidi Tan

One of the most striking aspects of Buddhist art in Southeast Asia, and in Myanmar in particular, is the way in which images of the Buddha can have multiple meanings. They are usually encountered in groups, with multiple forms depicting different ages and postures, and they frequently appear in close proximity to other images, including those of the Brahmanic deities, the spirits, or *nats*, and cult images of hermits with occult powers called *weikza*. The multiplication and grouping of images reflect their key role as agents in the process of merit making, and imply a fundamental need to cultivate multiple sources of divine power, for the welfare of the devotee and others.[1]

Informants often make clear distinctions, however, between what they see as pure Theravada Buddhism and other traditions, when describing rituals performed at the temples. One in particular is that the Buddha, or rather his *Dhamma*, or teachings, is venerated in hopes of a better rebirth and ultimately the path to *nibbana*, while the *nats* are propitiated by some in order to achieve more worldly goals focused around protection against malevolent forces, wealth, and good health. In practice, though, Buddhist rituals take place in many different contexts and can be transactional and syncretic in nature. In such cases worship may involve seeking supernatural assistance with practical matters. A poignant example is the casting of bronze Buddha images. Metalworkers pray to the Buddha and then make offerings to the household *nat* known as Maung Tint Te at the start of the smelting process when the fire is first lit. Buddhist monks sometimes come to the workshop to chant *paritta*, or protective verses, to further ensure the successful pouring of molten metals, especially for more complex or large images.[2]

The objects in this exhibition come largely from state museums, where they appear to be celebrated mainly for their artistic merit. However, within the context of these museums, it is also possible to witness their value as sacred objects. Ritual behavior within museum galleries—both those associated with Buddhist edifices and sites as well as state museums—and the perpetuation of local stories of objects' repute, show how a vibrant, living culture exists around Buddhist art in Myanmar. Although museums typically impose limits on the extent of ritual behavior, officially sanctioned consecration rituals for certain images are further evidence of the belief in their potency and the importance of merit making.

Rituals such as merit making and consecrations, or *anekazar* (Pali), more often acknowledge the potency of Buddha images, which can be appropriated in many ways. At the Kyauktaw Mahamuni Pagoda, a smaller copy of the original Mahamuni Buddha is now a potent source of merit. New bronze images are placed around the base in order to draw from its powers (fig. 48).[3]

OPPOSITE Detail of cat. no. 65

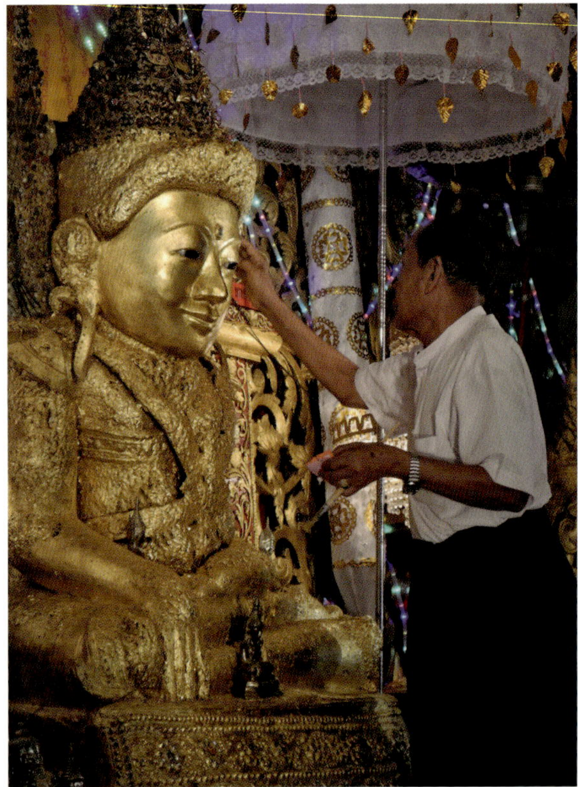

FIG. 48. Gold leaf is applied to the Mahamuni Buddha, Kyauktaw Mahamuni Pagoda. Note the smaller images around the base.

MATERIALITY AND SPIRITUAL POWER

At the soteriological level, the image of Buddha is also symbolic of the Theravada ideal of the Three Jewels, or *Tiratana* (Pali): the historical Buddha, the *Dhamma* or his teachings, and the *Sangha* or community of monks. Beyond this, however, an image of Buddha acquires multiple meanings over the course of its life. All images start out as raw materials to be transformed by artists. As Alexandra de Mersan shows for the production of images in Rakhine, from the moment raw materials are gathered to the final stages of consecration, the energetic potential or power, or *tan khoe* (Rakhine), of a new image is made manifest. Myanmar legend also speaks of the intention on the part of artists to achieve a perceived likeness to the historical Buddha. The Mahamuni Buddha's legendary fame derives from its raw materials, which were brought from across the region, as well as its association with the historical Buddha and that it was said to bear a strong likeness to him.[4] According to a Rakhine chronicle, the Buddha allowed King Chandrasuriya to make a metal replica of him and even breathed life into the image.[5]

An image therefore stands for the Buddha and his Buddhahood, but its power is also derived from many other factors. For example, Steven Collins points out that while statues in essence enable the Buddha to be seen, this experience is stronger if an image is reinforced with relics.[6] These can take various forms, from bodily relics to objects associated with the Buddha. The image is in itself a form of commemorative relic.

MULTIPLE MEANINGS

The historical and spiritual importance of sites, local knowledge, ritual, and patronage create multiple meanings and make manifest the powers of Buddhist images and allow them to acquire potency as their life story progresses. This can be observed whether in the privacy of a home shrine, or in a temple or a museum. Unlike state-sponsored institutions, the home shrine is more homogenous terrain and reflects the domestic realities of family life. Images of Buddha can also embody family memories and provide a focal point for fears and dreams to be expressed in private.

PAGODA MUSEUMS: BUDDHIST ART MUSEUM, KABA AYE PAGODA

The temple grounds are consecrated space, in which merit making attracts and perpetuates the cycle of donations and the veneration of new as well as old Buddha images, relics, and other sacred objects. Situated within the grounds of many pagodas and monasteries are small museums that house Buddha images and a plethora of donated objects that have over time acquired merit.

The Kaba Aye, or World Peace Pagoda, built in Yangon in 1952 in the independence years, became a focal point for the Buddhist world. In 1951, Prime Minister Nehru of India gave a gift of a portion of the relics of Buddha's two disciples—Sariputta and Moggallana—to Prime Minister U Nu. These relics had been excavated near Sanchi in India and kept at the Victoria and Albert Museum in London, until their return in 1947. The inspiration drawn from the ancient Buddhist world of India continued in the form of additional buildings at Kaba Aye. In 1956, the complex became the site of a historical gathering of international Buddhist leaders, known as the Sixth Buddhist Council,

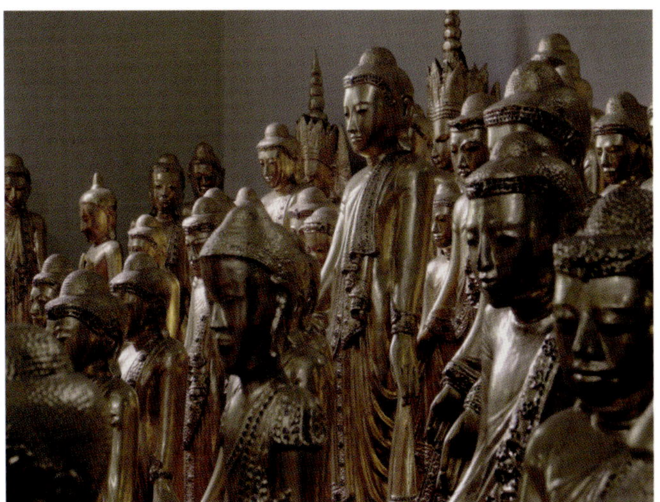

FIG. 49. Regilded Buddha images of diverse styles and ages at Kaba Aye Pagoda Buddhist Art Museum

which was housed in a hall known as the Great Cave (Maha Pasana Guha).[7]

The Buddhist Art Museum was built as an annex to the Buddhist library on the grounds of the Kaba Aye Pagoda in 1954. Designed by Benjamin Polk, a partner of the Indian architectural firm Mehandru and Polk in New Delhi, it drew inspiration from Myanmar architectural forms. The museum was set up to collect, research, and exhibit Buddhist art, including images, ritual utensils, and other monastic objects. The permanent display aims to show the stylistic developments of Buddha images and explain their iconographic features. Models of famous stupas were also collected to demonstrate the development of architectural forms. Cultivating relations with other Buddhist countries is also one of the aims.[8] After the Sixth Council the museum received gifts from India and neighboring Southeast Asian countries.

In more recent times, the collection has been boosted by significant numbers of Buddha images that have been restored from illegal exportation. In seeking to bring these unprovenanced collections into public view, the museum created a new display in 2008. Not only was the gallery reconceived, but the images themselves underwent a process of restoration and regilding. This ritual attracted the support of local patrons, who funded the supply of new lacquer and gold leaf. In this way, the images were ritually brought back to life with merit making.

Images are arranged in a gleaming array of tiered rows, and their new gilding provides an overall unifying effect that masks distinctiveness of style and age (fig. 49). At the center resides a marble image that was donated in the mid-1950s. Previously situated at the Great Cave at the center of the Kaba Aye complex, it was replaced at that location in 2004 by a new image carved in jade. Although not old, the original marble image is said to have demonstrated a certain power, which resulted in 2006 in its reconsecration at the Shwedagon Pagoda, and its subsequent reinstallation at the museum.[9]

Local patrons include the religious establishment, government officials, and members of the military, as well as pilgrims from all over the country. The addition of this contextual display, complete with an altar, means that the museum becomes an extended field of merit, especially during the full moon when large Buddhist groups request to visit.

SHWEDAGON PAGODA MUSEUM

Pagoda museums usually originate as repositories to house meritorious gifts. The museum at the Shwedagon Pagoda was situated along the southern terrace in the 1970s and was known as the Ancient Buddha Image Pavilion. The current building was constructed during the late 1980s and opened to the public in 1992, in order to house a growing collection of gifts and other ritual objects.[10] Situated at the northwestern terrace, the museum is set back, suggesting that it is an adjunct to the varied routes that one might take around the main stupa. The complexity of this ritual space is explored by Elizabeth Moore, who identifies four main routes that are usually taken by pilgrims: circumambulation of the main stupa, veneration of the four Buddhas of the Current Era (situated at the cardinal entrances), wish offerings made to the planetary shrines, and respects paid to the various cult images.[11]

How visits to the museum are incorporated into a pilgrim's itinerary has yet to be studied. It is likely that one would encounter the museum after visiting the shrine to the Eight Week Days or the Great Bell (also known as Mahaghanta or Singu's Bell), behind which it is situated. At times the museum seems like a quiet space for contemplation and prayer, but often it is alive with the sounds of school parties, groups of monks, visiting families, and pilgrims who show demonstrable interest in the displays.[12]

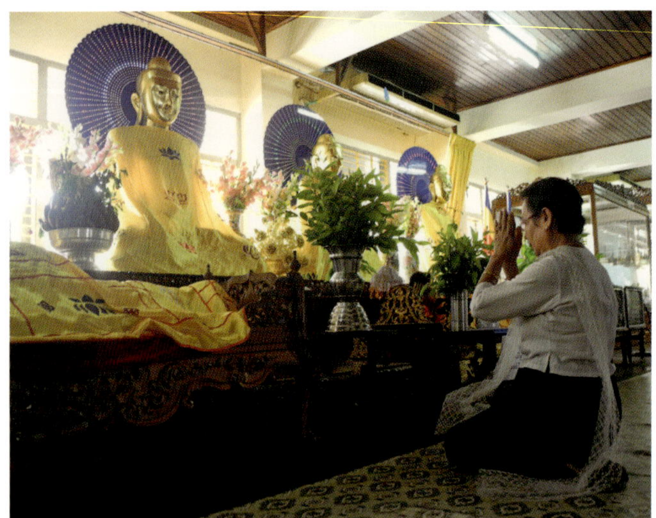

FIG. 50. Offerings made by museum staff, Shwedagon Pagoda Museum, Yangon

Arranged densely in showcases protected by iron bars, the displays are grouped mainly by material categories. They include Buddha images in various materials, silver money trees, reliquary boxes, gold jewelry, lacquerware, manuscripts, weaponry, colonial crockery, and woodcarvings from the pagoda's many pavilions. They provide an experiential database of merit making and imply lifetimes of good karma for the donors. The sheer volume is testimony to the power of the Shwedagon, which has touched countless lives and continues to attract pilgrims from all over the country and the wider Buddhist world.

Along the outer wall of the main gallery is a narrow prayer space with an altar for five large, seated Buddha images and two reclining figures. Visitors can stop to pray or meditate here at any point during their visit. A young couple that had taken the day off work to pay respects to an ancestor on the anniversary of her death made a fairly lengthy visit to admire the display of silver gifts before stopping at the altar. Museum rules prohibit visitors from making offerings, although there is a donation box for the collection of funds for the museum's maintenance. Staff, however, make daily offerings of cooked rice, water, and bunches of *thapye-pan* or "victory leaves" (eugenia) (fig. 50). Plans are underway to make modifications to the prayer space so that in the future small ceremonial occasions can be held more comfortably.[13]

PILGRIMAGING TO THE BAGAN (PAGAN) ARCHAEOLOGY MUSEUM

Among other factors, the enduring appeal of particular images relies on the patronage of the famous and successful. An eleventh-century stone image of the Buddha seated in *dharmacakra mudra* (see cat. no. 14) has become popular with visitors who travel on pilgrimages through the area. Its potency has grown through its purported association with the Alodawpyi Pagoda, an ancient, neglected temple that became famous under the patronage of Secretary 1 Lieutenant General Khin Nyunt. During the 1990s when it was extensively renovated, the Alodawpyi Pagoda was endorsed as an important pilgrimage site that promised wishes to be fulfilled in keeping with its name.[14] Although the pagoda's popularity apparently declined after the General's removal from office in 2004, it appears to have retained a following; for example, signature offerings of Nine Fruits, which were previously promoted, are still made in quantity during the pilgrimage season today (fig. 51). The Bagan Archaeology Museum has also become a destination for pilgrims who visit to view the seated stone Buddha image that is reportedly the prototype for a copy that was installed at the Alodawpyi Pagoda (see cat. no. 14). While art historians may fret over the lack of clear provenance for this image, in this case it is the image's spiritual authenticity that matters most for the devotee (fig. 52). Tour guides usually stop at the image to explain its significance, after which visitors prostrate themselves and offer prayers.

One group from Taunggyi in Shan State had yet to visit the Alodawpyi Pagoda, but had been brought to the museum by their guide. Prayers were said in front of the stone image after it was introduced as the original, as well as in front of a large lacquer Ava image where rubbing the figure's knees was believed to cure knee pain. Finally, at the front of a small room enclosed by iron bars, respects were paid to a classic Pagan-period Buddha. Said to be cast from the auspicious mix of metal alloys known as Five Metals, or *pyinsa-lawha* (Myanmar),[15] with its right hand in *abhaya mudra* (for another, similar example, see cat. no. 19), this unprovenanced Pagan-period image remains important to local visitors. It was deemed beautiful by this particular group of well-traveled pilgrims, who compared it to the Sukhothai sculptural tradition of north-central Thailand.

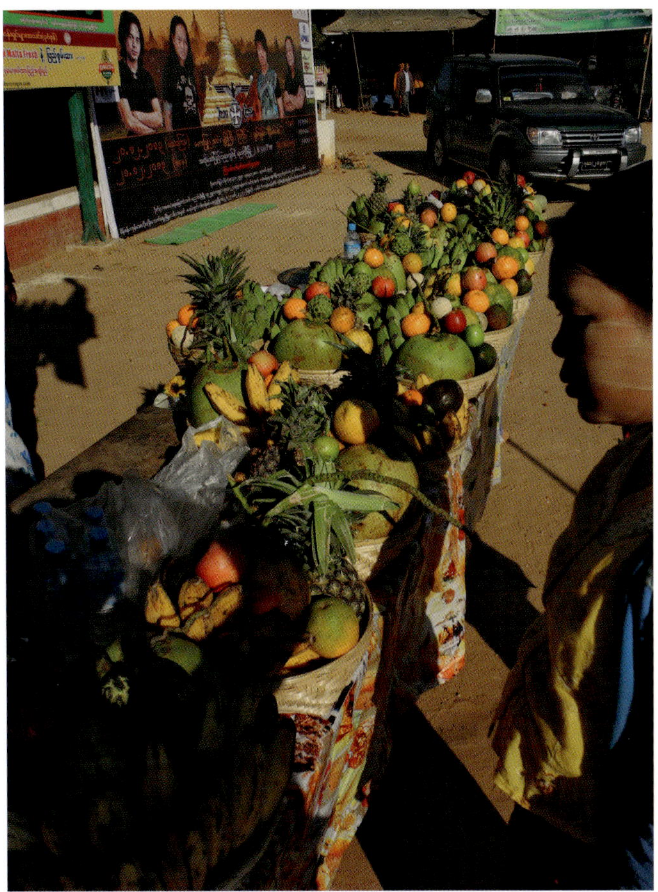

FIG. 51. Offerings of Nine Fruits, Alodawpyi Pagoda, Pagan

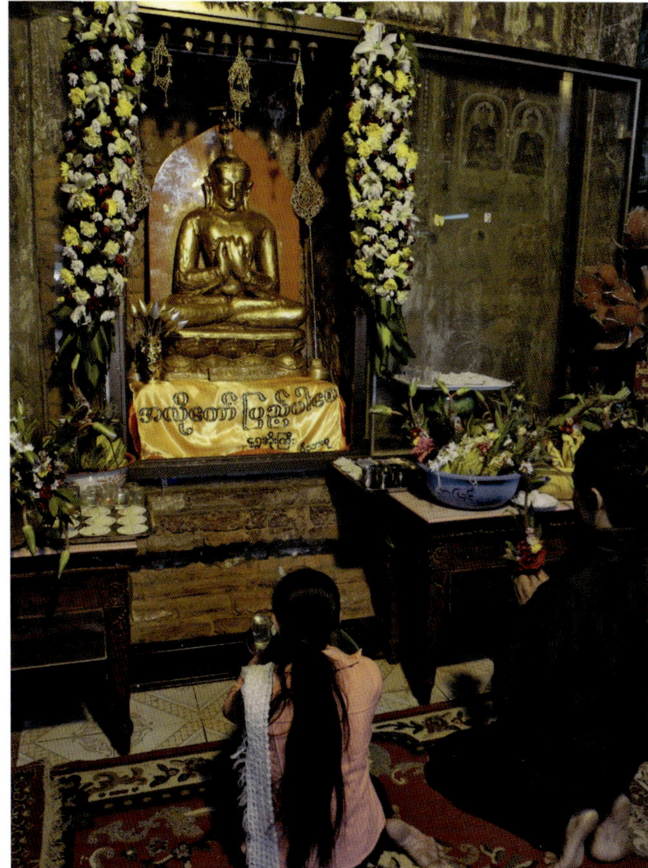

FIG. 52. Gilded copy of the stone image, Alodawpyi Pagoda, Pagan

Old images are sometimes considered problematic if they accumulate too much power, or may be agents of curses made by their owners. In this respect, it is believed that old images should not be kept in the home.[16] Consecration rituals are undertaken to neutralize such powers, or at least to limit potential latent powers. A ritual was undertaken a few years ago for the stone image at the Bagan museum, for example. While this image is not known to have any problematic history, other more famous images have legendary histories that illustrate a causal link between deeds done in previous lives and their consequences. Angela Chiu cites the karmic retribution that manifested itself in the Mahamuni Buddha's biography. Believed to have been made in Rakhine during the Buddha's lifetime, the Buddha foretold that the image would suffer consequences, since in a previous life he had broken the leg of a man and cut flesh from another's back. The image went missing in the mid-seventeenth century, and when it was found, it had a damaged right leg and was missing sections of its back.[17]

The museum context presents a different kind of religious terrain—suspended, as it were, between temple and home. It is a space where the visual language of image making and art history are conventionally presented, although vestiges of the living culture frequently seep through, revealing surprising insights that would otherwise be absent.

For example, at the National Museum in Yangon, the Buddha Image Gallery presents the narrative of iconographic and stylistic developments over the course of two millennia. One of the most popular since the Pagan period is the image of Buddha seated in the earth-touching gesture, or *bhumisparsa mudra* (Sanskrit), also known as *maravijaya* (Sanskrit), in reference to the moment when the historical

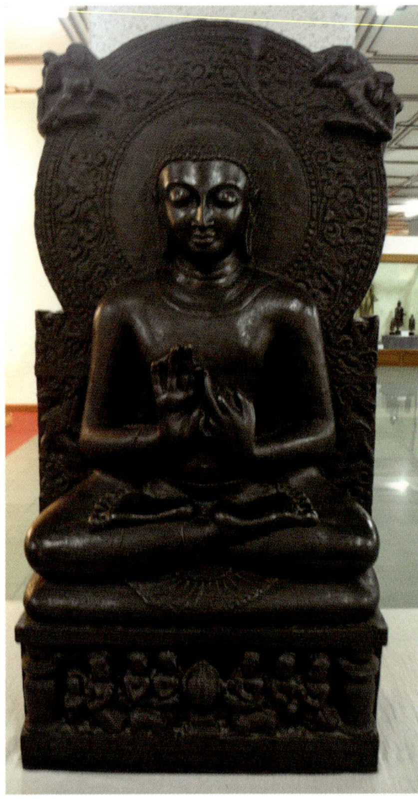

FIG. 53. Modern bronze replica of Sarnath-style Buddha, National Museum, Yangon

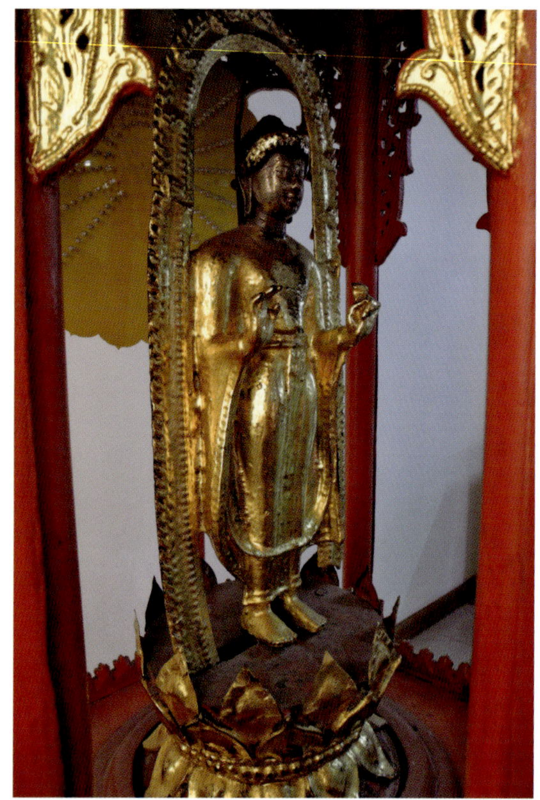

FIG. 54. Standing Pyu image from Thegone, Bago

Buddha overcomes the demon Mara, a potent metaphor for mental obstacles and delusions. Informants say that this type of image is an important reminder to follow the path to enlightenment. However, visitor behavior indicates that beyond beauty, iconography, and age, the physical presence of the image can have significance of a therapeutic kind. A modern bronze replica of an Indian Sarnath-style Buddha provides a means not only to pay respects but also to ask for assistance. In this case, a shiny patina has resulted from frequent touching, and as one local tour guide shared, this is done in the belief that it will relieve ailments in corresponding parts of the visitor's body (fig. 53).

On the other hand, an older, Pyu-period image said to be cast in Five Metals is venerated daily at the National Museum. This image of Buddha standing with his right hand in the fearlessness gesture (*abhaya mudra*) has a reputation for answering prayers, particularly among museum staff since its retrieval from a small village in Thegone, near Pegu, or Bago, in 2004 (fig. 54). The memories of its ceremonial journey to Yangon and the ritual consecration after its arrival persist in the minds of many who were involved at the time.[18] It has become a focal point for early morning prayers, and its spiritual presence enhances the museological value of the gallery by revealing aspects of intangible heritage that otherwise would remain largely invisible.[19] Intentional or not, the museum can therefore be a contested space in which historical, artistic, and religious ideals and local practice vie for expression.

CONCLUSION

Images symbolize the Theravada ideal of the Three Jewels. In practice, they have a multivalent existence, as merit making and other rituals draw on their power for assistance in many of life's endeavors as well as otherworldly aims. It remains to be seen how the introduction of these Buddha images to new audiences around the world will add a new dimension to the images' life histories. Their enduring appeal as objects of art, merit, and power will surely take on a new significance in a global context.

NOTES

I would like to thank Daw Nu Mra Zan, U Ngwe Tun Myint and National Museum staff in Yangon; Daw Nwe Nwe at the Buddha Image Museum, Kaba Aye Pagoda; Daw Nyo Nyo Win at the Shwedagon Pagoda Museum; Daw Baby at Bagan Archaeology Museum; U Thaw Kaung, U Moe Aung Lwin, Daw Khin Phyu Win, Ko San, Ma Lily and family, and especially Ma Ohnmar Myo, for generously sharing their knowledge and experiences on so many levels, as scholars and Buddhist practitioners.

1 This syncretic experience is often explained by local informants as being two or three separate traditions—an older *nat* worship tradition, a pure Theravada Buddhist religion, and more recent unorthodox cult practices. The spatial arrangement of images in pagodas, for example with the Buddha always placed at a higher level, is usually cited as an example of the overriding importance of Buddhism. Bénédicte Brac de la Perrière ("Burmese *Nats*") points out that rather than being pre-Buddhist, the national pantheon of *nat* spirits actually evolved alongside Buddhism, the two being part of a system of royal patronage.

2 Ko San, Mandalay bronze caster, personal communication, December 2013. Swearer (*Buddhist World of Southeast Asia*, 18) describes the many occasions, including those which are not necessarily Buddhist, at which *paritta* are chanted by monks in Thailand.

3 The term "pagoda" is conventionally used in Myanmar to denote temples that house one or more religious images as well as stupas (Moore, "Unexpected Spaces," 197, n. 1).

4 De Mersan, "'Land of the Great Image,'" 97–100.

5 Stadtner, *Sacred Sites of Burma*, 318.

6 Collins, *Nirvana*, 243. A hierarchy of relics according to late Theravada sources includes bodily relic shrines (*saririka-cetiya*) such as stupas, shrines of use (*paribhoga-cetiya*) such as Bodhi Trees, and commemorative shrines (*uddesika-cetiya*) that represent Buddha (Strong, *Relics of the Buddha*, 19).

7 Ostensibly inspired by a dream by U Nu, who had visited the cave in Rajghir in India that was the site of the First Council, supported by the great Buddhist patron Emperor Ashoka (Stadtner, *Sacred Sites of Burma*, 63–64).

8 *A History of the Buddhist Art Museum*, Buddhist Art Museum leaflet.

9 Nwe Nwe, personal communication, December 2013.

10 According to Nu Mra Zan, the earlier pavilion's displays were arranged less systematically and had the appearance of a cabinet of curiosities. Personal communication, December 2013.

11 Moore, "Unexpected Spaces," 183.

12 Interviews with visitors undertaken in December 2013 found a group of secondary school girls who confirmed that they felt the museum was more extensive in its exhibits compared to the national museum.

13 Nu Mra Zan and Nyo Nyo Win, personal communication, December 2013.

14 Stadtner (*Sacred Sites of Burma*, 22) relates how job promotions for military personnel and new claims of ancient rulers' successes fueled pilgrims' interest in the site, which became the only pagoda at Bagan to be air-conditioned.

15 The origins of this composition of alloys remain unclear. Juliane Schober ("Venerating the Buddha's Remains," 118) discusses the practice by alchemists and practitioners of *samatha*, or concentration meditation, of making images from metal alloys, in the belief that these alloys will lend power to the image. The practice of women and children throwing additional silver and gold jewelry into the molten bronze was remarked on by Sir James George Scott (Shwe Yoe) in the late nineteenth century (*Burman*, 206). The alloy is said to comprise gold, silver, copper, iron, and lead and was used to cast important images as well as large bells that were donated to temples (ibid., 207). A large Buddha image now at the Botataung Pagoda in Yangon was made by King Mindon in 1859 of five metals and contained relics. It was taken to England after Upper Myanmar was annexed in 1885 and was returned in 1951.

16 Nu Mra Zan, personal communication, December 2013. Paritta Chalermpow Koanantakool ("Contextualising Objects," 159) discusses the consecrated space of a temple as being able to neutralize such powers in the Thai context.

17 Chiu ("Social and Religious World," 70) cites Tun Shwe Khine (*A Guide to Mrauk-U*, 103) on the possibility that the chronicle may have added this comment by the Buddha to account for the damage incurred to the Mahamuni image.

18 Museum staff recall a ritual procession by car back to Yangon and the consecration ritual after its installation, which involved the chanting of *paritta*, or protective verses, by monks and the making of offerings. There is a real sense in which this gallery is a focal point for museum staff, whose daily inspection rounds include prayers here for the security of the museum. During the Nargis storm of 2008, it is reported that the gallery remained unscathed despite damage incurred elsewhere in the building.

19 State museum protocols limit obeisance to prostrations, prayers, and meditation. Making offerings is not allowed. Pagoda museums make allowances for offerings, which in some cases can be made by visitors as well as staff.

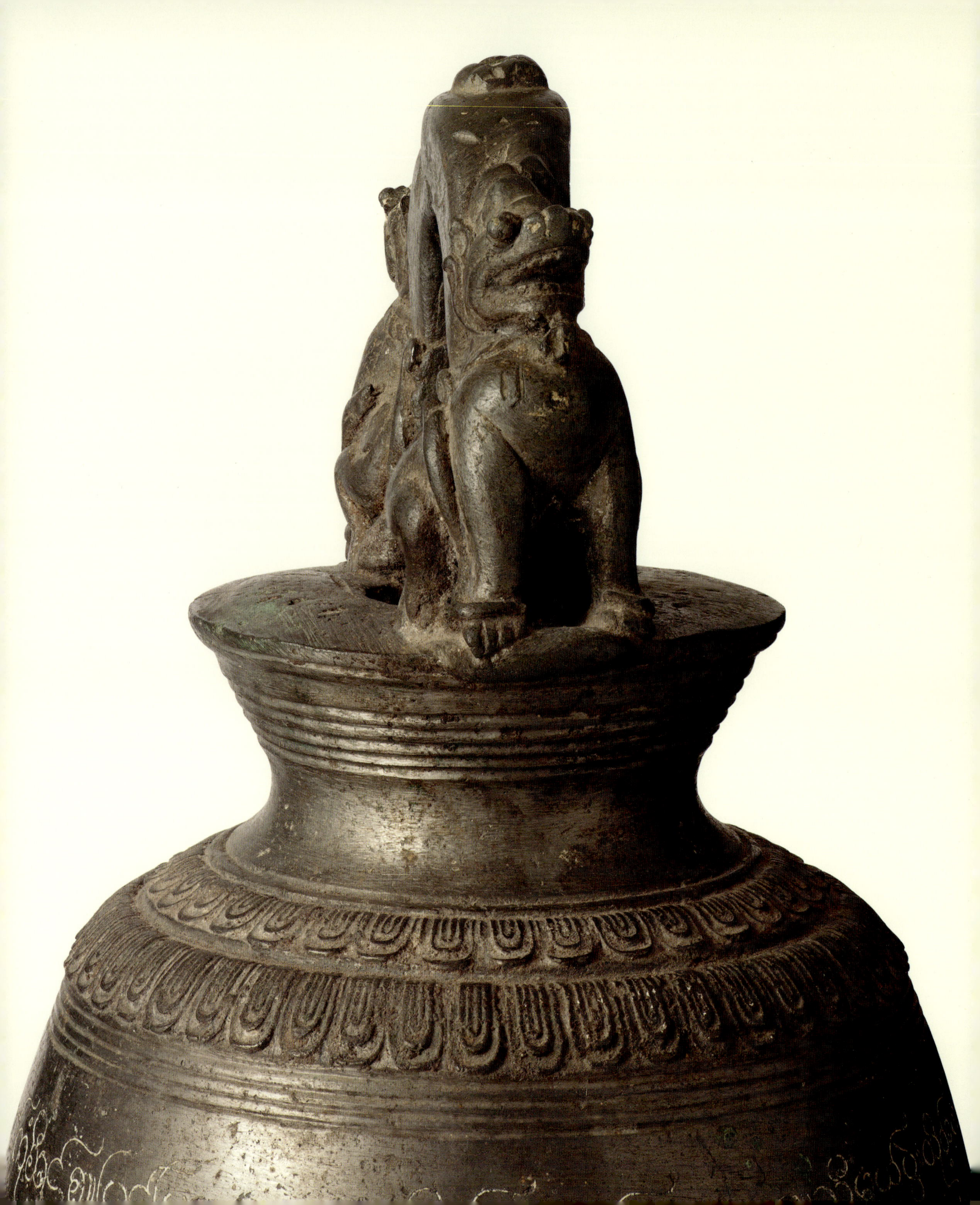

Catalogue

RB	Robert L. Brown
SFL	Sylvia Fraser-Lu
AP	Adriana Proser
CR	Catherine Raymond
DS	Donald M. Stadtner
TK	U Thaw Kaung

OPPOSITE Detail of cat. no. 67

1.

Double-sided stele

Excavated northwest of Sri Ksetra palace complex, Hmawza
Ca. 4th–6th century
Sandstone
H. 59 1/16 x W. 27 9/16 x D. 7 7/8 in. (150 x 70 x 20 cm)
National Museum, Yangon, 1649

Discovered within the walled city of Sri Ksetra in the 1970s, this stele has raised more questions than it has provided answers. The central figure carries a large tapered club in both hands. His attendant on the right holds a Garuda standard, or *garudadhvaja* (Sanskrit), a staff topped with the face of a Garuda, Vishnu's avian vehicle. The third figure holds a *cakradhvaja*, or standard crowned by a discus, or *cakra*. The trio seems to be in procession, facing right. The panel's reverse shows two females, whose lowered hands appear to support an empty throne.

The stele cannot be tied directly to Buddhism or Hinduism in as much as there are too few defining attributes; also, no convincing parallels are known in the art of India or Southeast Asia. It has been suggested that the empty throne depicted on one side of the stele is an aniconic reference to the Buddha and that the stele should date to the early centuries BCE.[1] It has also been more plausibly argued that the stele should be dated to about the fourth century and that its iconography highlights the connections between India and early Southeast Asia.

The panel's shallow relief and somewhat clumsy figural style contrast sharply with more refined and well-known works at Sri Ksetra. Perhaps this stele represents the earliest phase of lithic art at Sri Ksetra, say from the fifth or early sixth century, before the apogee of Pyu art represented by the objects in the Khin Ba trove. Two fragmentary stone panels in the Sri Ksetra museum, also depicting a single figure supporting a club on the right shoulder, perhaps relate stylistically to this same early phase of Pyu art.[2]

RB & DS

NOTES

1 For an extensive discussion of this stele see Guy, *Lost Kingdoms*, 40–44.

2 Luce, *Phases of Pre-Pagan Burma*, 1: 171, 2: pl. 91 (a, b).

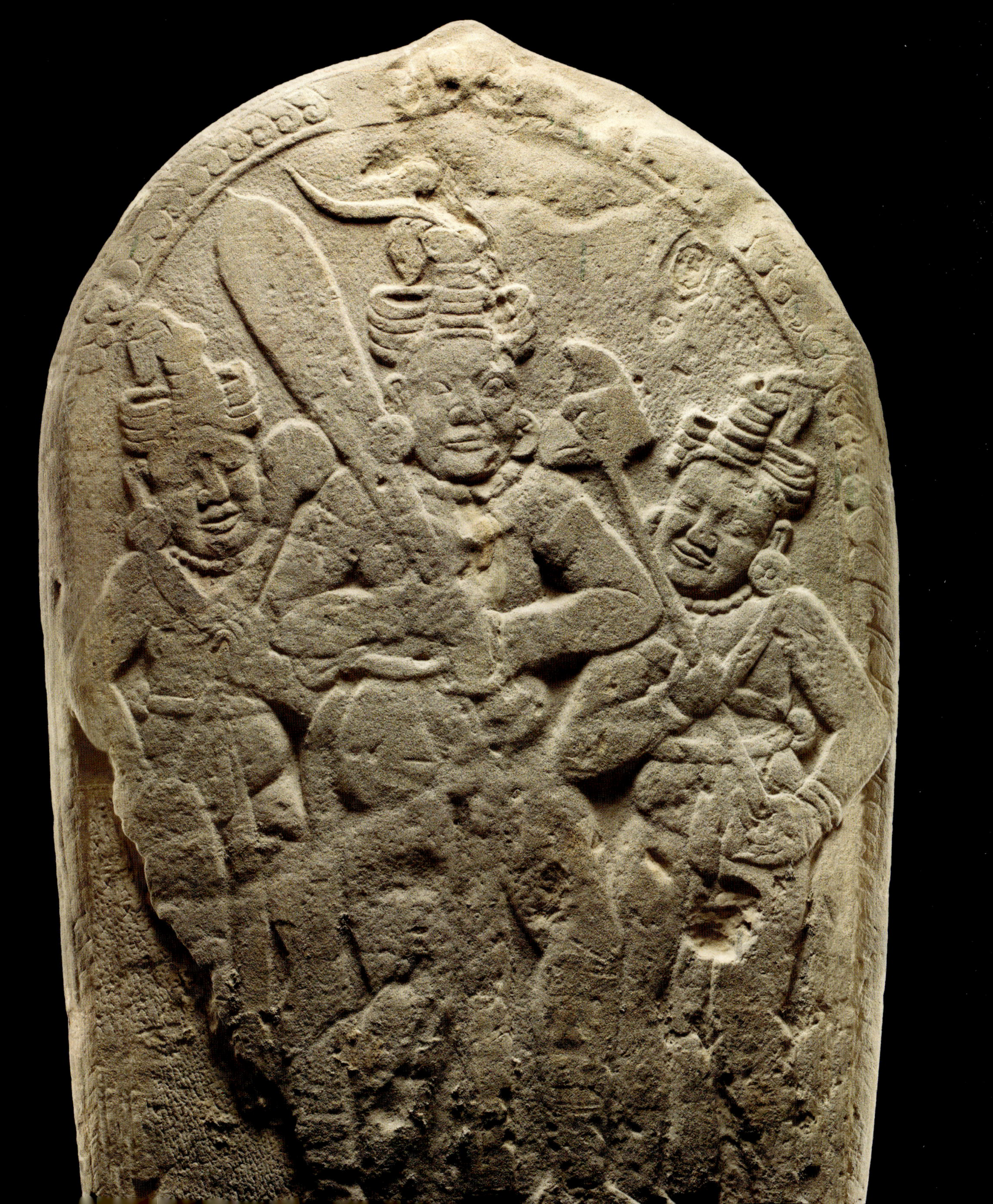

2.

Hollow cube

Khin Ba Stupa relic chamber
Pyu period, ca. 7th century
Silver
H. 5¾ x W. 5 x D. 5 in. (14.6 x 12.7 x 12.7 cm)
National Museum, Yangon

This hollow cube was among hundreds of objects discovered within the Khin Ba Stupa relic chamber at Sri Ksetra in 1926.[1] This spectacular trove remains the most significant group of objects associated with the Pyu in Upper Myanmar. Like the centerpiece of this trove—a circular silver casket—this cube is adorned with four repoussé Buddhas in *bhumisparsa mudra*. Inscriptions on the reliquary casket indicate that the four represent the historical Buddha Sakyamuni and his three immediate predecessors.[2] However, their hands are all in the meditation gesture, or *dhyana mudra*. Nothing distinguishes one from the other. A comparative group of five seated Buddhas is depicted at the bottom of the two large stone slabs excavated in the Khin Ba Stupa mound. The fifth seated figure was likely the Buddha of the future, Metteyya. All five Buddhas are shown in the *dhyana mudra* position, resembling the four found on the silver cube.[3]

The craftsmanship in this example is significantly less refined than the circular casket. For example, the fanciful crocodiles, or *makara* (Sanskrit), on the thrones' crossbars are scarcely readable, with no attention to detail. This discrepancy in craftsmanship suggests that artists of widely differing skills contributed to objects that found their way into the same relic chamber at the time of their single interment.

DS

NOTES

1 Duroiselle, "Excavations at Hmawza" (*Archaeological Survey of India, Annual Report, 1926–27*), 176, pl. XL (f); Luce, *Phases of Pre-Pagan Burma*, 1: 137, 2: pl. 30 (a, b).

2 The four Buddhas are named in an inscription on the rim on the top of the reliquary casket.

3 One of these slabs is discussed by Guy, *Lost Kingdoms*, 78–80.

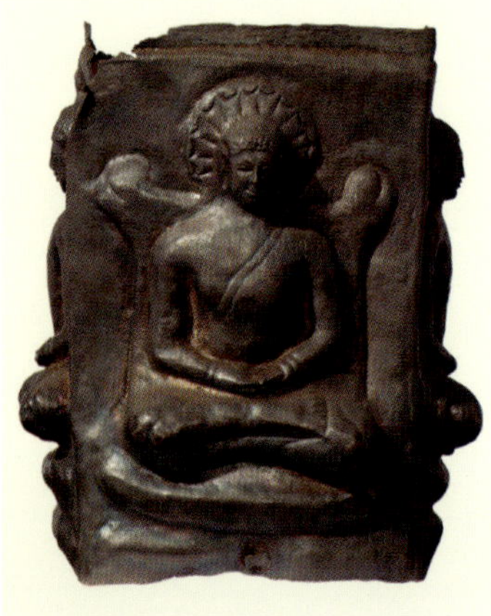
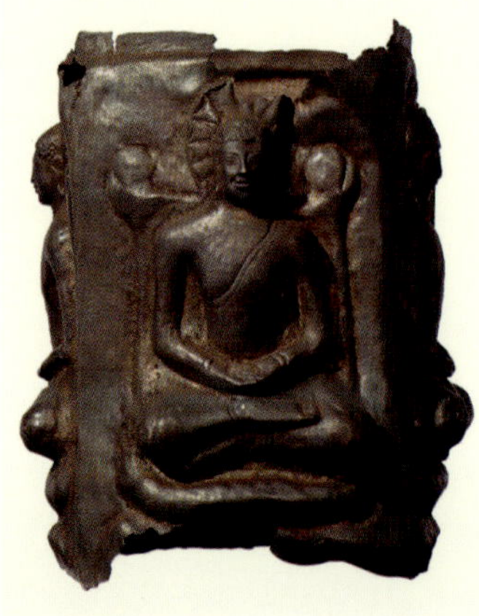
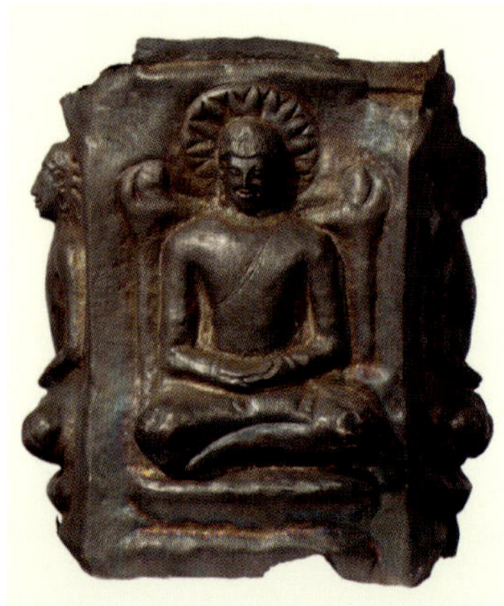

SIDE VIEWS

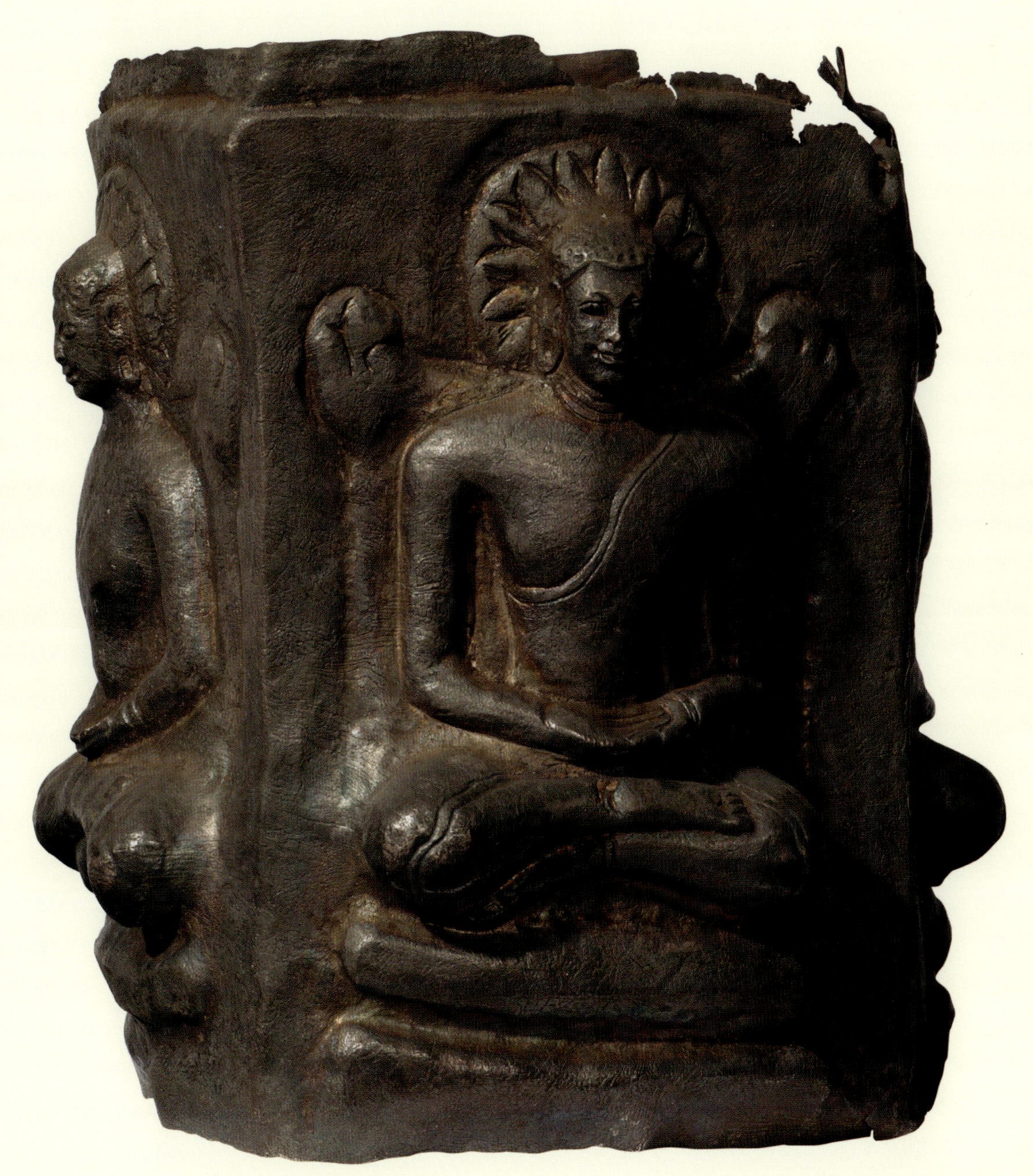

3.

Buddha

Pyu period
Stone
Approx. H. 45 x W. 44 x D. 9 in. (114.3 x 111.8 x 22.9 cm)
Sri Ksetra Archaeological Museum, Hmawza, 2013/1/41

Large sculpted stone panels, arranged in rows of three and facing one another, were popular at Sri Ksetra, judging from two sets noted by archaeologists in the early twentieth century. Each group of three panels was separated by nearly a hundred yards and organized on a north–south axis; each triad was enclosed within a U-shaped brick wall.[1] The function of these paired triads is unknown, but the complex certainly demarcated sacred space.

The middle panel is always slightly larger than the two flanking it. In the two surviving complete groupings, the central panel of one of the triads was inscribed on its base, but the inscriptions have never been deciphered. Each panel has a central seated Buddha at the base, with hands in the meditation gesture, or *dhyana mudra* (Sanskrit), with seated figures on either side, usually shown with both hands placed together in homage.

This panel, discovered in 1910 near the Bawbawgyi Stupa, may well have once belonged to a triad that was dispersed long ago.[2] The indistinct object held by the central Buddha was perhaps a bowl. The flanking figure on one side has chipped off; the companion figure has his left hand raised.

DS

NOTES

1 The triads were first noted by General Léon de Beylié, *Prome et Samara*, 82–84, figs. 56 and 57. For an illustration of one triad placed long ago in a shed beside the museum at Sri Ksetra, see Stadtner, "Art of Burma," fig. 237; this complex was labeled the Kyaukka Thein. The two sets of triads are treated by Luce, *Phases of Pre-Pagan Burma*, 1: 129–30, 2: pls. 12–13. The best-known panel that once belonged to a triad is the main object of worship in the post-Pyu-period Bebe Pagoda at Sri Ksetra.

2 Taw Sein Ko, "Excavations at Hmawza near Prome," 121, pl. XLVII (5).

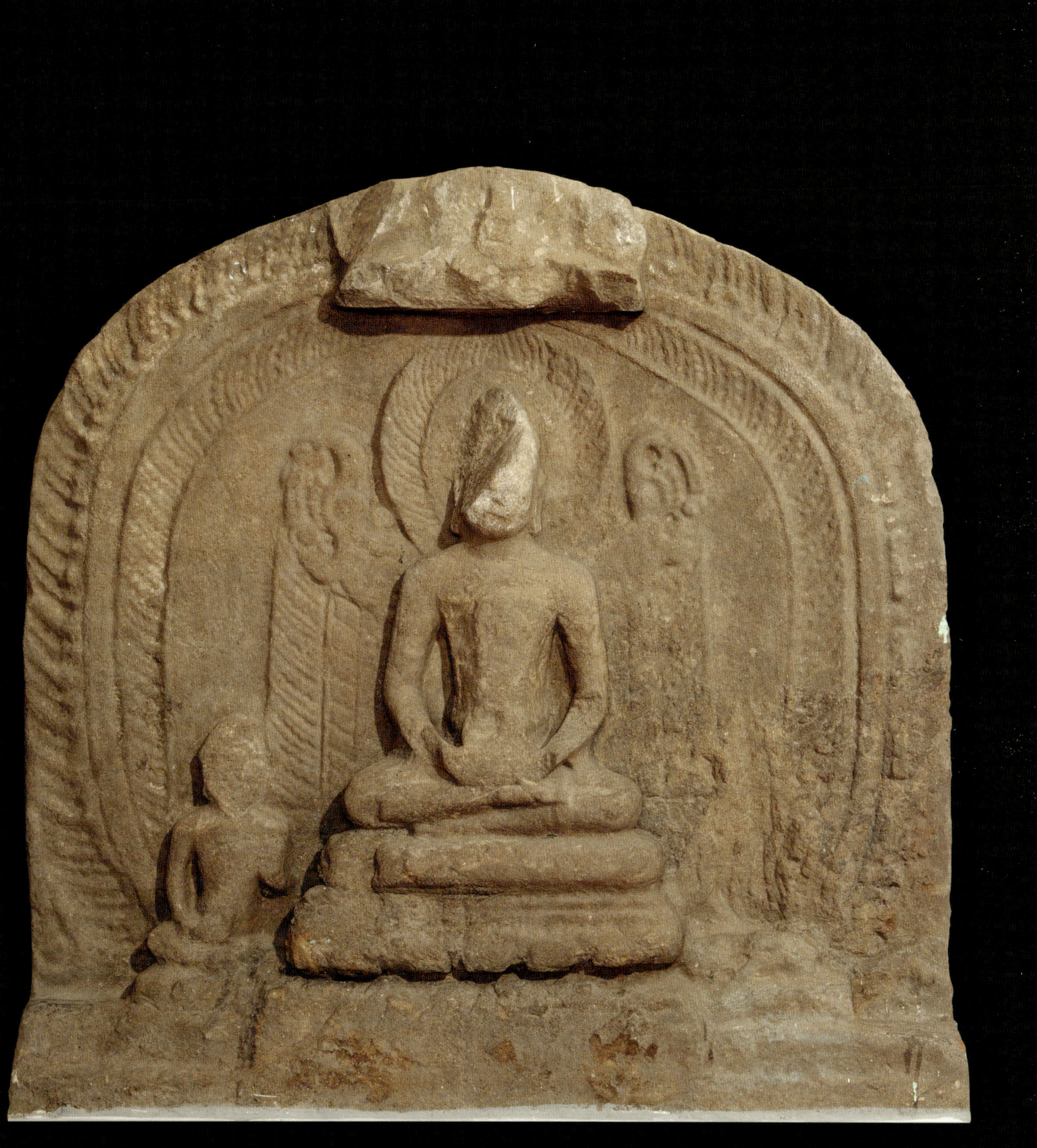

4.

Buddha preaching

Excavated from the relic chamber of Khin Ba Stupa, Sri Ksetra, Hmawza
Pyu period, ca. 7th century
Silver
H. 3¾ x W. 2¾ x D. 2 in. (9.5 x 7 x 5 cm)
National Museum, Yangon, 4585

This seated silver Buddha was one of hundreds of precious objects discovered in 1926 amidst debris within the relic chamber of the Khin Ba Stupa at Sri Ksetra.[1] The Buddha's right hand is raised, with the tip of the forefinger touching the thumb, in the *vitarka mudra* (Sanskrit), or the hand gesture of teaching. The bottoms of the feet and the palms of the hands are incised with *cakras*, a canonical attribute of the Buddha.

The centerpiece of the Khin Ba trove was a silver casket, inscribed with the names of its donors, Sri Prabhuvarma and Sri Prabhudevi. Whether all of the objects were placed in the chamber together at one time or there were two or more later interments is debated. However, the difficulty of removing thousands of bricks and at least one immense stone lid in proximity to such fragile metal objects and then completely resealing the chamber suggests that a single interment is far more likely. All agree however that the Khin Ba trove represents the zenith in the art of Sri Ksetra.

The only dated objects from Sri Ksetra are four inscribed stone urns with the names of individual rulers. One king, Harivikrama, who died in 695, is the same king whose name appears on the base of a headless seated Buddha, a masterpiece in the corpus of Pyu sculpture. If this inscribed stone Buddha belongs to the reign of Harivikrama and the seventh century, then the Khin Ba objects, including this Buddha, which also represents a high peak in the art of the site, probably date to the same general period.

RB & DS

NOTE

1 Duroiselle, "Excavations at Hmawza" (*Archaeological Survey of India, Annual Report, 1926–27*), 171–75, pl. XLI (e). This object is treated in Guy, *Lost Kingdoms*, 84–85. The dynastic history of the Pyu remains stubbornly unclear and subject to debate, with much of the puzzle centered on comparing the inscriptions of Upper Myanmar with more securely dated epigraphs from neighboring civilizations. The Chulasakaraja era, beginning in 638, was almost certainly started at Sri Ksetra, a date providing an anchor for the city's principal kings, such as King Harivikrama, who ruled during the site's artistic peak in the seventh century.

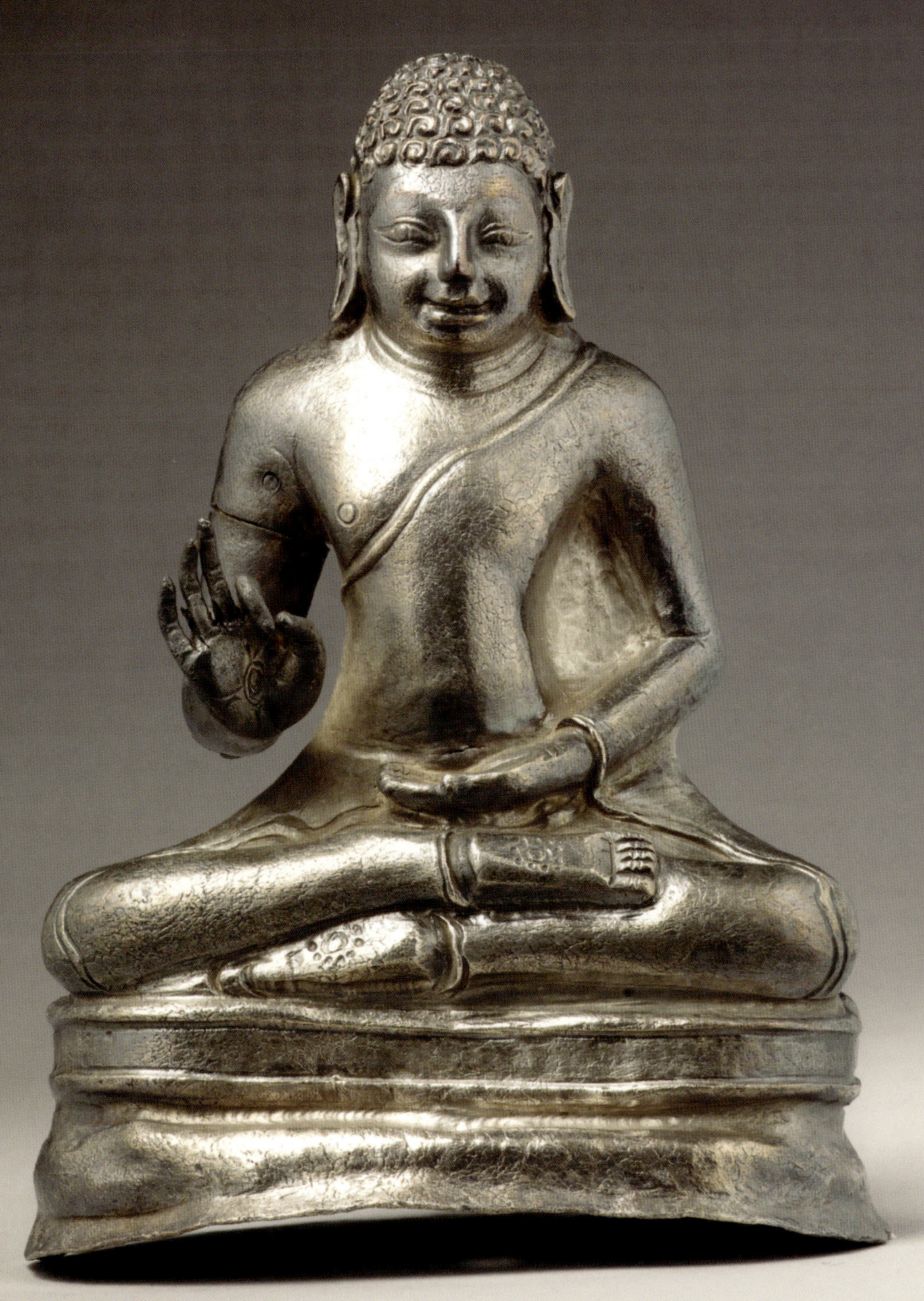

5.

Buddha

Ca. 7th century
Sandstone
H. 14 x W. 7 x D. 2 in. (35.6 x 17.9 x 5.1 cm)
Sri Ksetra Archaeological Museum, Hmawza, 2013/1/56

This Buddha is one of twenty-three nearly identical seated Buddhas that were recovered when a mound known as the Kanwetkhaungkon was excavated at Sri Ksetra in 1927. Each holds an alms bowl in his open palm, while the right hand assumes the earth-touching gesture, or *bhumisparsa mudra* (Sanskrit). They were excavated in situ surrounding the base of a low octagonal brick monument in which each side had four images, making up a total of thirty-two.[1] This mound also yielded the headless stone Buddha incised with an inscription referring to Harivikrama, a Pyu ruler of the late seventh century. It is therefore tempting to postulate a seventh-century date for these images.

The bowl that the Buddha is holding may represent the episode following the enlightenment when four directional guardian deities presented him with bowls. Examples of flanking figures offering the Buddha bowls are rare but not unknown at Sri Ksetra. Bronze buddhas from Sri Ksetra perhaps also depict this theme, although in these examples the bowl is more spherical and therefore possibly represents not a bowl but something different, perhaps the myrobalan medicinal fruit given to the Buddha by Indra.[2]

DS

NOTES

1 This group was first described by Duroiselle ("Excavations at Hmawza," in *Archaeological Survey of India, Annual Report, 1927–28*, 128). Many years before Duroiselle's excavation of this mound, one of these seated Buddhas was found at Sri Ksetra by Taw Sein Ko ("Excavations at Hmawza near Prome," pl. XLVIII [10]). Two from the group are illustrated in H. R. H. Prince Damrong Rajanubhab, *Journey through Burma*, 197, fig. 5 (the photo is reversed). One in the series, from the National Museum, Yangon, is discussed by Guy (*Lost Kingdoms*, 109). The lotus base on these stone images strongly resembles the bases beneath the four seated Buddhas on the Khin Ba silver reliquary casket. For an image of this casket, see Guy, *Lost Kingdoms*, cat. 27, 80.

2 Luce, *Phases of Pre-Pagan Burma*, 1: 47, 145, 147; 2: figs. 45 (a, b), 48 (a–c).

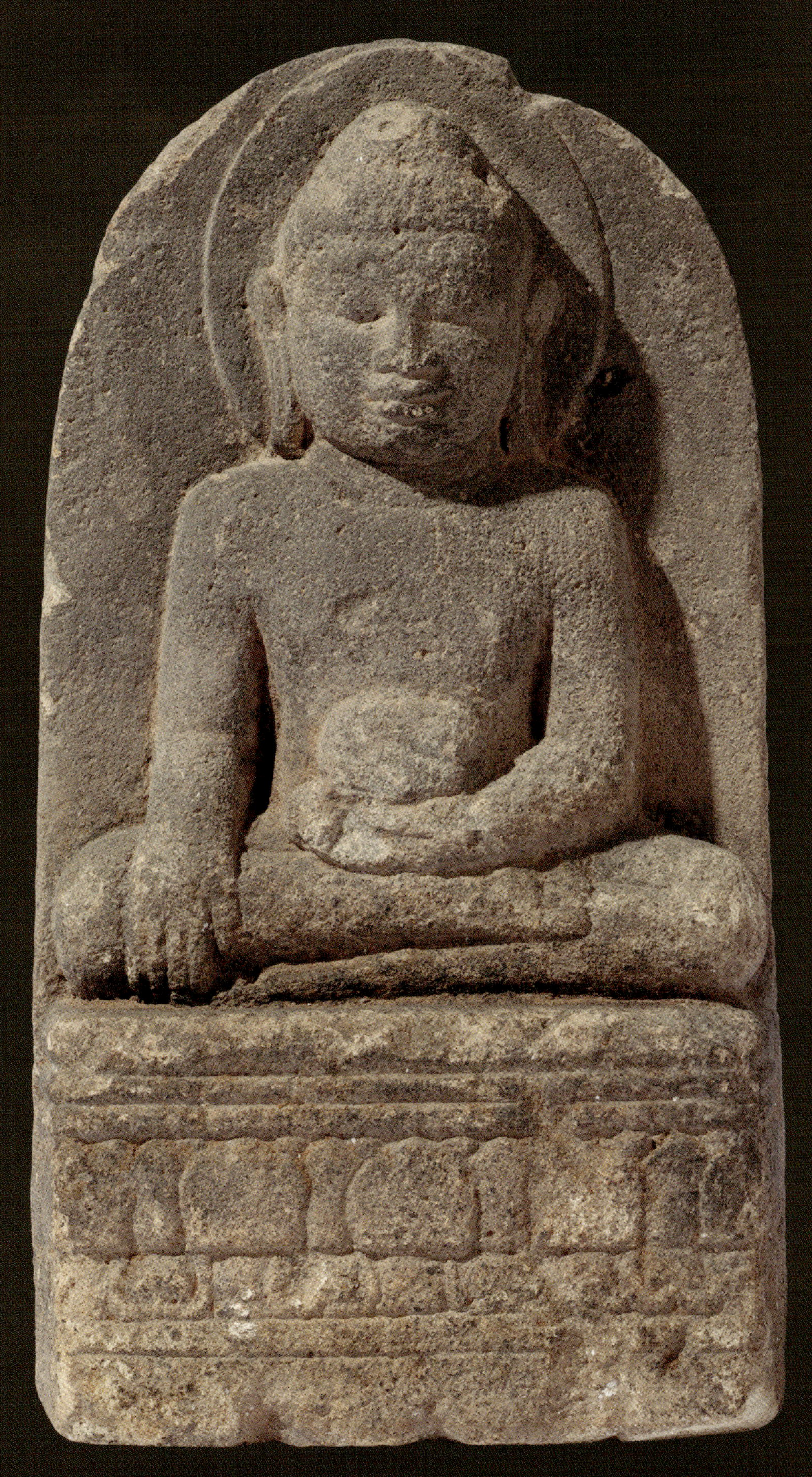

6.

Buddha

Pyu period, ca. 8th–9th century
Copper alloy
H. 18½ x W. 12½ x D. 9½ in. (47 x 31.8 x 24.2 cm)
Sri Ksetra Archaeological Museum, Hmawza, 2013/2/2

This Buddha image with two raised hands and forefingers touching thumbs (*vitarka mudra*) is one of seven objects discovered accidentally beneath the ground within the walled city at Sri Ksetra in 2005.[1] Six were bronze and one was a small standing Buddha made of quartz.[2] Why such objects were placed together is uncertain but they were not found in connection with an ancient brick structure nor do they appear to have been interred as relics.

It is reasonable to conclude that all of the objects belong to the same age, at least within a hundred-year period. They include a Buddhist ritual implement, a *vajra-ghanta*, that was likely brought to Myanmar, possibly from Java or India, and is perhaps datable to the eighth or ninth century (see cat. no. 7). Another slightly smaller seated Buddha, with the same iconography and in identical style, was found with the Buddha in this exhibition.[3]

DS

NOTES

1 This iconography was known not only at Sri Ksetra, among the Pyu, but also in Lower Myanmar, controlled by the Mon. It is also found in first-millennium Sri Lanka. Luce, *Phases of Pre-Pagan Burma*, 1: 165, 2: pl. 76 (b, c).

2 The discovery was made near the Shwedaga Gate, in the western part of the walled city. Now in storage at the museum in Sri Ksetra, the objects are not yet properly published and recorded. The hoard contained a small Buddha image, in white-colored quartz, three seated Buddhas, each of a different size, a standing Buddha, a ritual implement (*vajra-ghanta*), and what is perhaps a bronze lid with a thin circular handle. Bob Hudson kindly shared a photograph, taken in July 2007, showing the seven objects. The Buddha chosen for the exhibition is the largest of the seated bronzes and is much larger than the standing Buddha.

3 Guy, *Lost Kingdoms*, 89–90, cat. no. 38.

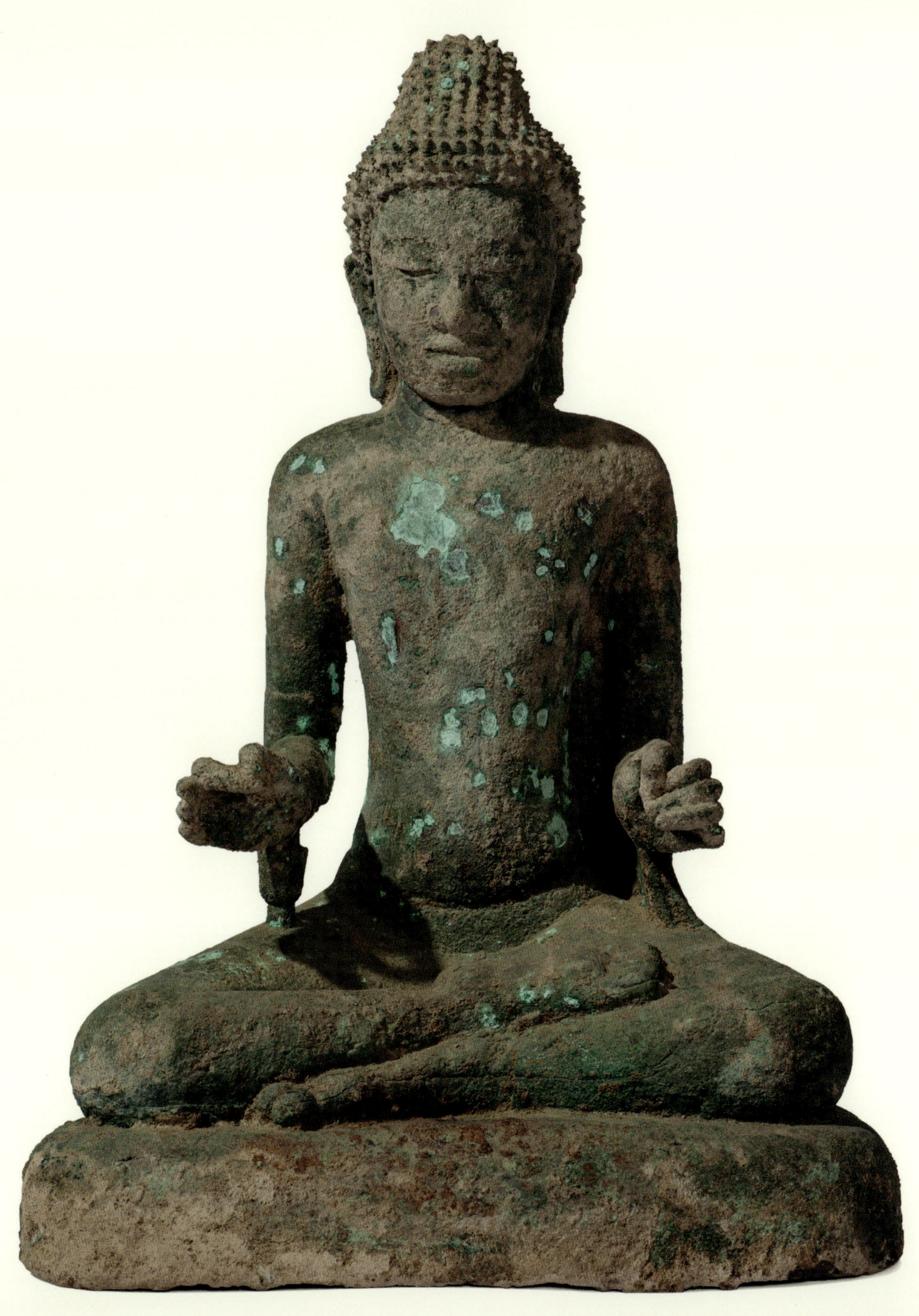

7.

Vajra-ghanta

Pyu period, ca. 8th–9th century
Copper alloy
H. 6 x Diam. 2¼ in. (15.2 x 5.7 cm)
Sri Ksetra Archaeological Museum, Hmawza, 2013/2/5

This bronze ritual implement combining the thunderbolt, or *vajra* (Sanskit), and the bell, or *ghanta* (Sanskrit), was discovered in 2005 buried together with six first-millennium objects within the walled city at Sri Ksetra. The *vajra* is a symbol of Vajrayana Buddhism and refers to the immutable, adamantine nature of the universe. The bell can symbolize wisdom, or *prajna* (Sanskrit). A single face divides the two sections.

This is the only known *vajra-ghanta* implement to have been found in early Myanmar, suggesting that it was likely brought to Sri Ksetra, perhaps from Java or India. More elaborate and refined examples attributed to first-millennium Java provide the wider Asian context for this bronze in Myanmar.[1]

How this ritual implement was used at Sri Ksetra is unknown, but the overarching nature of Buddhism at Sri Ksetra was based on the Pali canon, to judge from gold sheets from Sri Ksetra incised with passages taken from Pali texts. This ritual implement's presence in Sri Ksetra indicates Myanmar's link to other Southeast Asian communities and the eclectic religious environment in the first millennium.

DS

NOTE

1 Zwalf, *Buddhism*, 190. Another example from Java is now in the Cleveland Museum of Art (acc. no. 1989.355). Both these examples have four small heads separating the bell from the *vajra*.

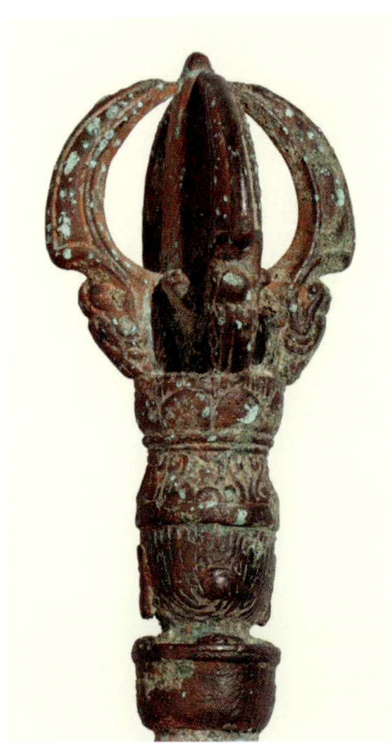

DETAIL OF VERSO

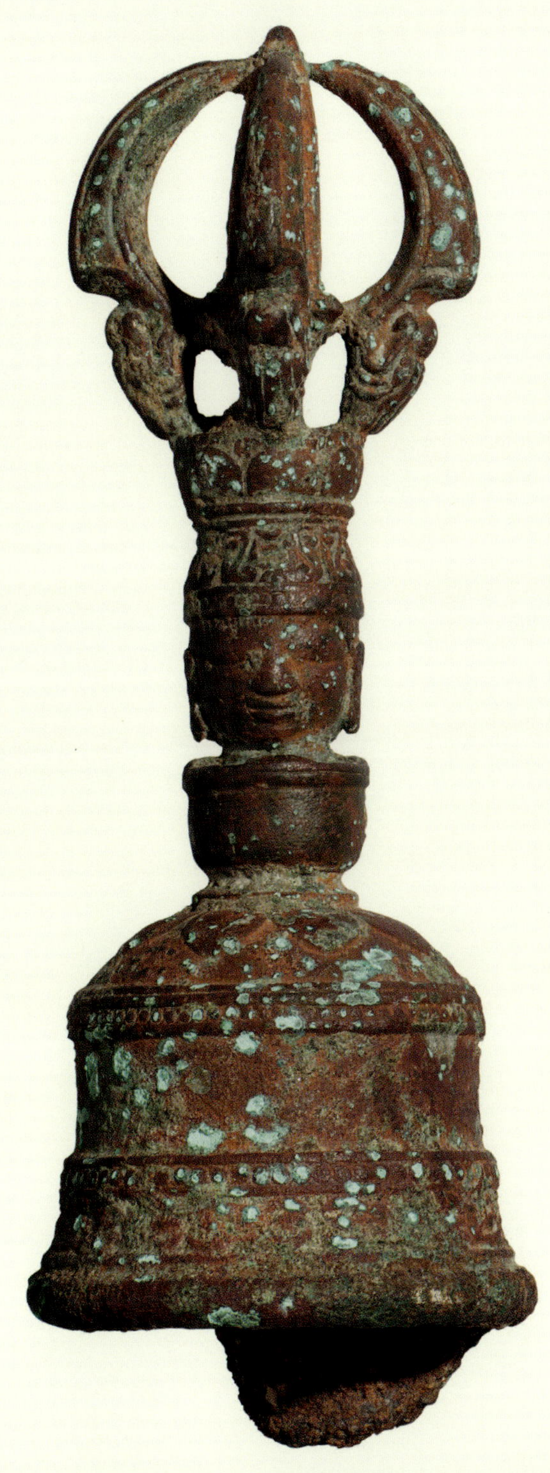

8.

Buddha

Pyu period, ca. 8th–9th century
Quartz
H. 5 x W. 2 x D. 1¼ in. (12.7 x 5 x 3.2 cm)
Sri Ksetra Archaeological Museum, Hmawza, 2013/1/106

This white quartz standing Buddha was found in 2005 buried with six other first-millennium objects within the walled city at Sri Ksetra. It appears to be the only known quartz Buddha image from first-millennium Myanmar.

The lowered hand is in the boon-bestowing gesture, or *varada mudra*, while the other hand, upraised, grasps the end of the long monastic robe. Standing buddhas with hands disposed in this fashion were well known in India and throughout Southeast Asia during the first millennium. However, no major standing stone buddhas have survived in Upper or Lower Myanmar from the first millennium. Standing metal buddhas are known in Myanmar, with one recently discovered bronze in Lower Myanmar, with hands disposed in this same position (see fig. 26). One standing Buddha also in this pose appears in a rare Pyu votive tablet.[1]

There are other rare examples of quartz carvings from the first millennium. A miniature stupa "cut out of crystal" was discovered at Sri Ksetra in the early twentieth century, but its whereabouts is unknown.[2] This stupa was probably placed in a relic chamber and likely resembled quartz stupas known from early Sri Lanka. Numerous quartz beads have also been located at Sri Ksetra. Quartz, however, was more commonly used in the Mekong delta area during the first millennium. Quartz buddhas were likely known at Pagan, or Bagan, and are recorded in lists of objects interred in stupas. During this period clear quartz was also used within small metal reliquaries, allowing the central relics to be viewed; at least one example of this has survived.[3]

DS

NOTES

1 Luce, *Phases of Pre-Pagan Burma*, 1: 154, 2: pl. 58 (b). A fragmentary tablet, probably made from the same mold, is on display at the Sri Ksetra site museum. For more on the standing bronze Buddha from near Twante in Lower Myanmar, see Moore, *Early Landscapes of Myanmar*, 202.

2 Taw Sein Ko, "Excavations at Hmawza near Prome," 123; Bob Hudson, personal communication.

3 Stadtner, *Sacred Sites of Burma*, 220.

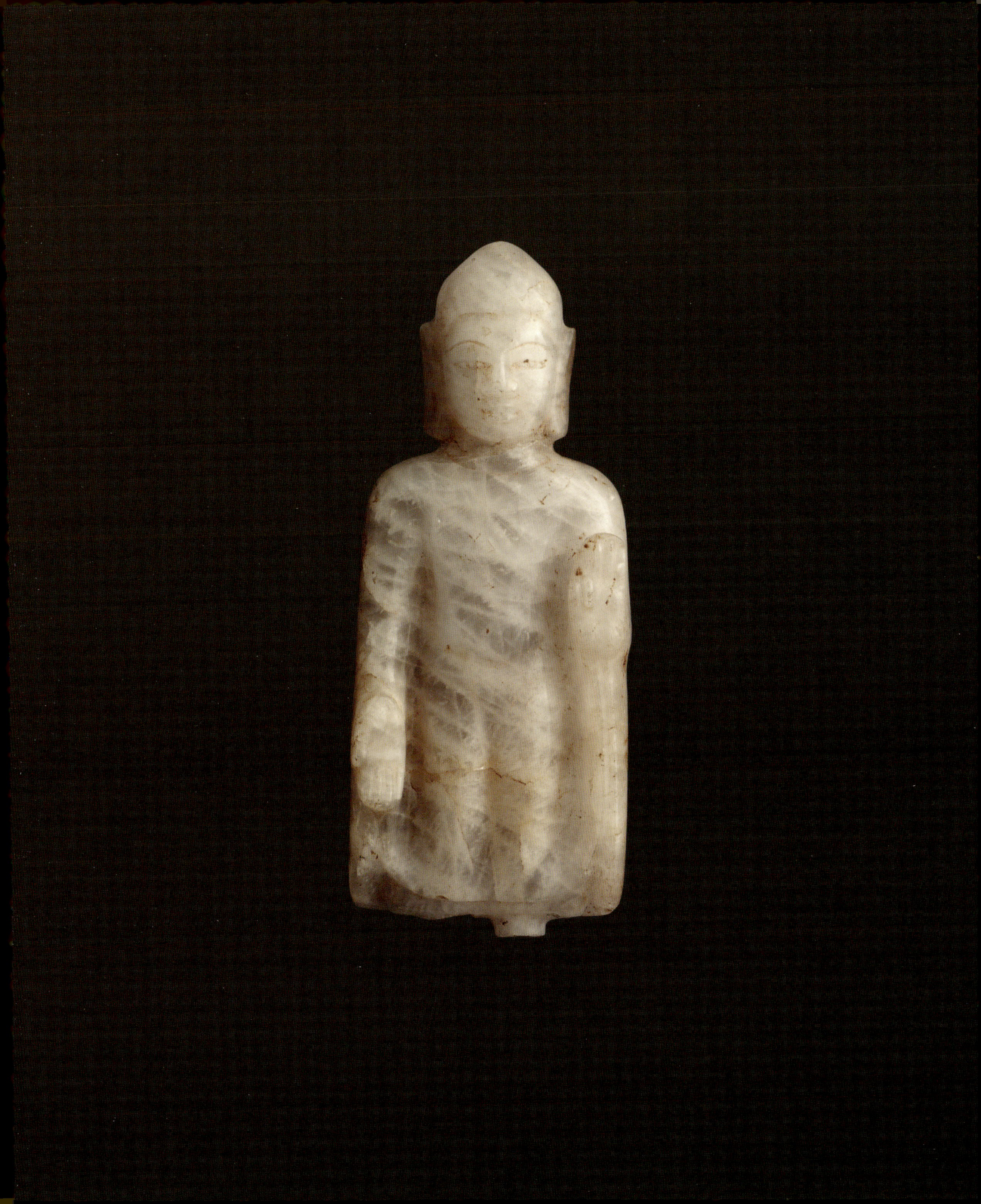

9.

Metteyya

Ca. 8th–9th century
Copper alloy
H. 18½ x W. 12½ x D. 9½ in. (47 x 31.8 x 24.1 cm)
Sri Ksetra Archaeological Museum, Hmawza, 3013/2/5

This fragmentary Metteyya (Pali), or the Buddha of the future, was found in 2004 near the Shwedaga Gate, in the western section of Sri Kshetra. Most metal images from Sri Ksetra are seated Buddhas, but a small number are bodhisattvas.[1]

This two-armed figure is a seated Metteyya, based upon a comparison with seven known examples. The angle of the break in the right leg indicates that the figure was originally seated in the royal ease posture, or *rajalilasana* (Sanskrit), also featured on a well-known Pyu-period Metteyya in the Victoria and Albert Museum, London; four first-millennium bronze Metteyyas found at Pagan; and one example was recently acquired by the Art Institute of Chicago.[2] The identification of Metteyya is based on a reading long ago of a short Pyu inscription on the base of one of the four bronzes at Pagan. The dating of this group is tentative, in as much as the chronology of the art of Upper Myanmar in the first millennium has yet to be fully charted.

The circular earrings recalling Gupta conventions, the elaborate, staged headdress, the heavy necklace, and the waistband secured with an unusual, wide sash are features on this piece that all of the previously known Metteyya bronzes share. Even the sparse ornament on the reverse is nearly identical. The similarity among these bronzes suggests that a single workshop conservatively repeated the same motifs over generations or that perhaps there were similar models used in different ateliers in different locations.

DS

NOTES

1 The most elegant is a four-armed Avalokiteshvara that may have been produced at Sri Ksetra or was perhaps imported from southern Thailand sometime during the seventh century. Guy, *Lost Kingdoms*, 238–39.

2 For the four examples in Pagan, see Luce, *Old Burma—Early Pagan*, 3: pls. 443 (e) and 444 (a–f). Another possible bronze Metteyya from Sri Ksetra is illustrated in Luce, *Phases of Pre-Pagan Burma*, 2: pl. 44 (f). The Victoria and Albert Metteyya is discussed by Guy, *Lost Kingdoms*, 239–40. The example in the Art Institute is unpublished (acc. no. 2001.300). Charles Duroiselle was the first to discuss the inscription on the inscribed example, found at Pagan; see Duroiselle, "Excavations at Pagan," 165.

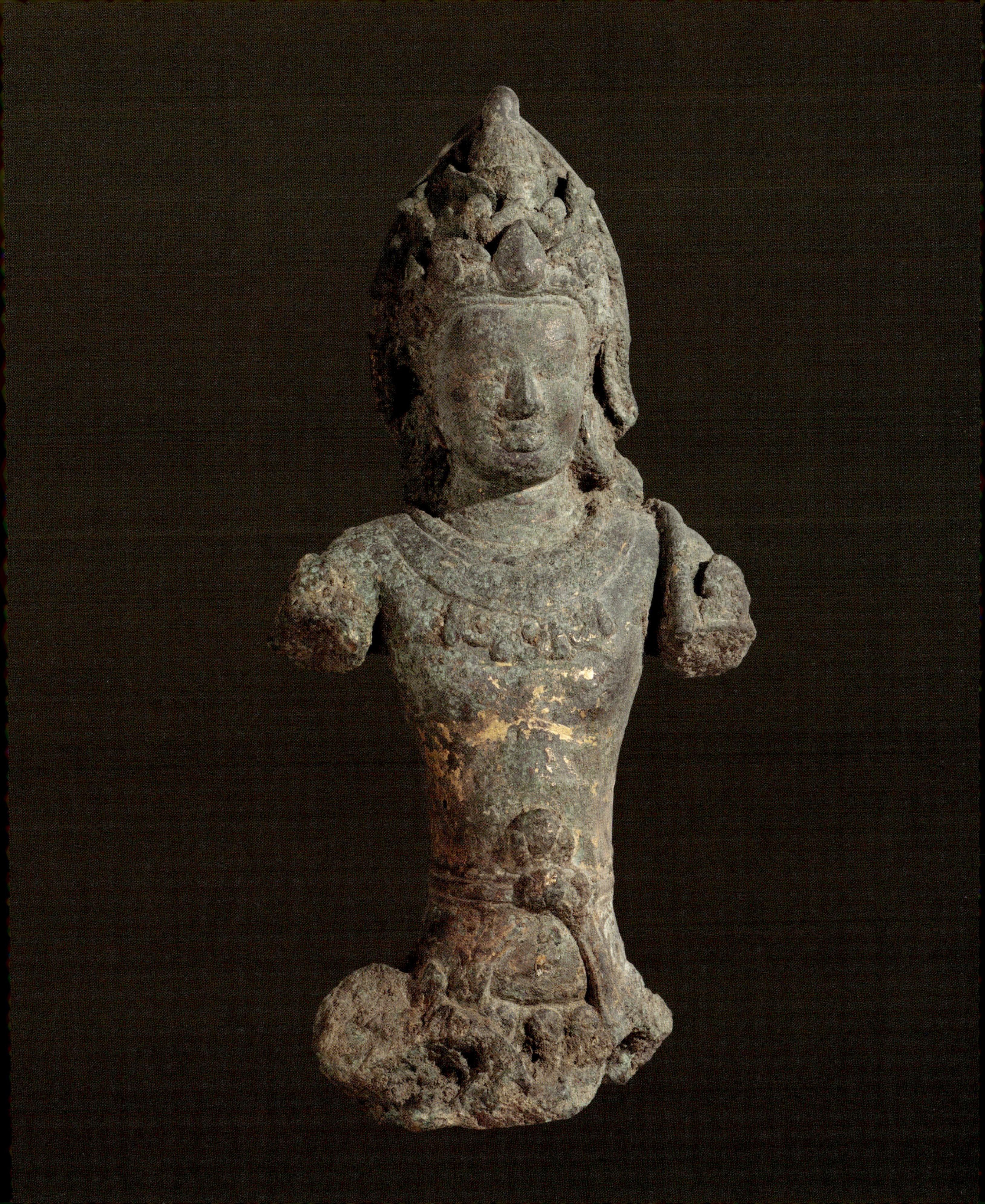

10.

Votive tablet

Pyu period
Terracotta
H. 3¾ x W. 3 x D. ¾ in. (9.5 x 7.6 x 1.9 cm)
Sri Ksetra Archaeological Museum, Hmawza, 2013/6/92

Thousands of terracotta votive tablets from the first millennium have been discovered throughout Myanmar, with even more belonging to the second millennium. Pressed from metal or baked-clay molds, these sealings were generally interred within stupas. The tradition of votive tablets in Myanmar and in many Southeast Asian regions was adopted from India.

Sri Ksetra alone has yielded many hundreds of examples, made from dozens of different molds produced over centuries. Some tablets, while the clay was still moist, were marked with short hand-written inscriptions in the Pyu language, presumably commissioned by the donors.[1] This practice continued for centuries, into the Pagan era, as a later inscribed tablet indicates (see cat. no. 26).

The Buddha pictured on this votive tablet sits on a double-lotus base, with his hands in the teaching gesture, or *dharmacakra mudra*. The right hand supported on the palm of second hand is reminiscent of a seated bronze Buddha whose base is incised with a Pyu inscription.[2] Two elephants with their forelegs stretched out also appear on the tablet. Using their trunks, they support lotuses bearing stupas with a cylindrical shape that is close to that of the Bawbagyi Stupa at Sri Ksetra. Rampant lions facing frontally make up the sides of the Buddha's throne and *makaras* ornament its top. A number of examples made from this same mold, or one that is nearly identical, have survived.

DS

NOTES

1 For many illustrations of Pyu votive tablets, see Luce, *Phases of Pre-Pagan Burma*, 1: 150–59, 2: pls. 55–63; and Mya, "Beginnings of Jambhupati Images." See also Guy, *Lost Kingdoms*, 106–9.

2 Guy, *Lost Kingdoms*, 90.

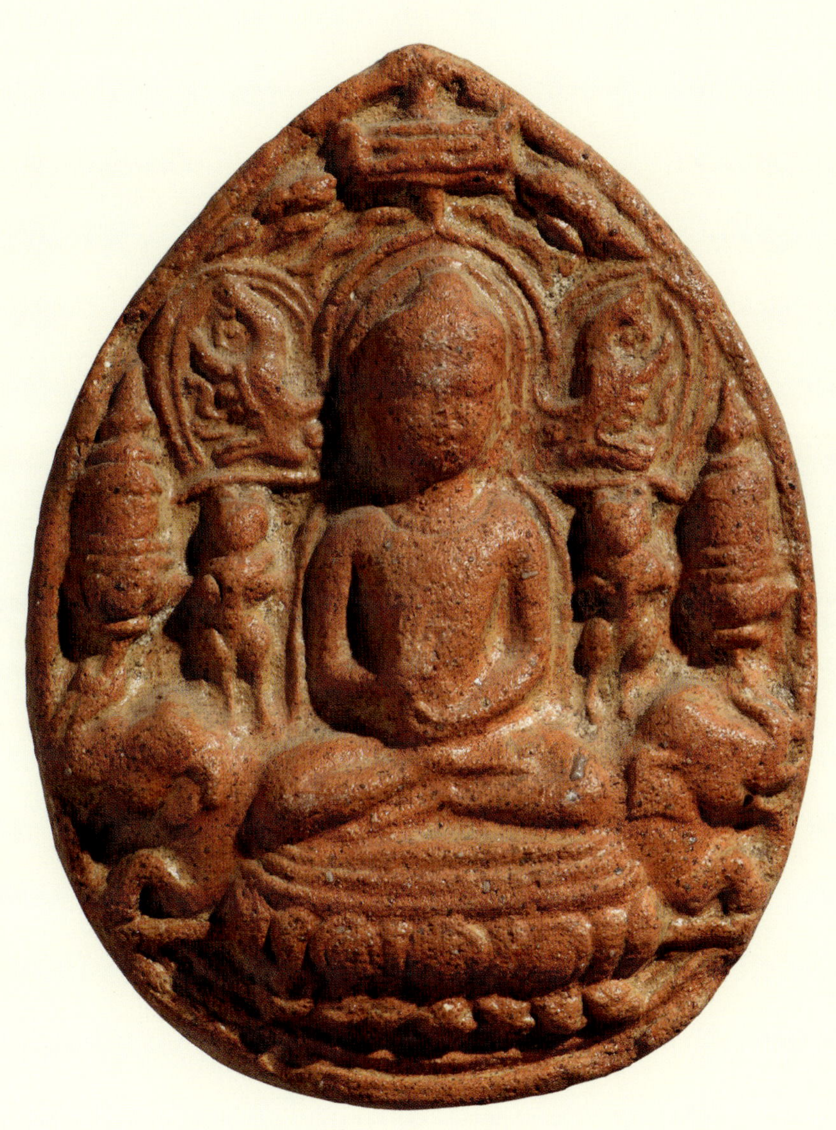

11.

Roundel with figures

Kyontu
Ca. 5th–6th century
Terracotta
H. 17 x W. 18 x D. 5½ in. (43.2 x 45.7 x 14 cm)
National Museum, Nay Pyi Taw

This roundel, with dwarfish musicians goading two bulls, was once set into the base of a brick stupa near the village of Kyontu, about twenty miles northeast of Pegu, or Bago, in Lower Myanmar. Kyontu was controlled by the Mon in the first millennium. The stupa base measured 240 feet square, with roundels placed roughly five feet apart; approximately fifteen have survived, some only in fragments. That these multiple figures burst with energy, despite being cramped into such a restricted space, indicates that the art of Lower Myanmar was on equal footing with the art produced at Sri Ksetra.[1]

Some of the other tiles feature impish male musicians and dancers, with no animals, while others show mounted horses and elephants. One depicts a lion mauling a prone figure.[2] The diverse subjects suggest that there was no overarching narrative for the tiles and that secular topics were considered appropriate for religious architecture. A somewhat smaller roundel with lions, in nearly identical style and with the same decorative motifs as the one pictured here, was recovered from Winka, an excavated brick monastic site north of Thaton, suggesting a cultural link between the Pegu area and the area much farther down the coast.[3]

DS

NOTES

1 These tiles were first noted in the 1930s; see Duroiselle, "Explorations in Burma," 80–83, pls. XXXI–XXXIII. Duroiselle records that the tiles are placed three feet apart from each other. The best summary is by Luce, *Phases of Pre-Pagan Burma*, 1: 166–68, 2: pls. 77–81; Luce includes one photo of two medallions in situ within the brick base, pl. 77 (a).

2 This tile was not included in Luce's discussion but for many years remained at Kyontu; see Stadtner, *Sacred Sites of Burma*, 153. It has now been shifted to the Bago Archaeology Museum. One previously unrecorded tile was discovered in 2013 in the Waw Township in the vicinity of Kyontu, suggesting that perhaps there was a second stupa. This tile, now in the Bago museum, is virtually identical to the aforementioned tile with the lions.

3 For a photograph of this tile from Winka, together with a treatment of all of the major first-millennium sites in Lower Myanmar, see Moore, *Early Landscapes of Myanmar*, 195–218. See also Stadtner, "Demystifying Mists," 25–60. Another large stupa base from the first millennium is in the village of Zothoke, but the base is entirely faced with large laterite blocks.

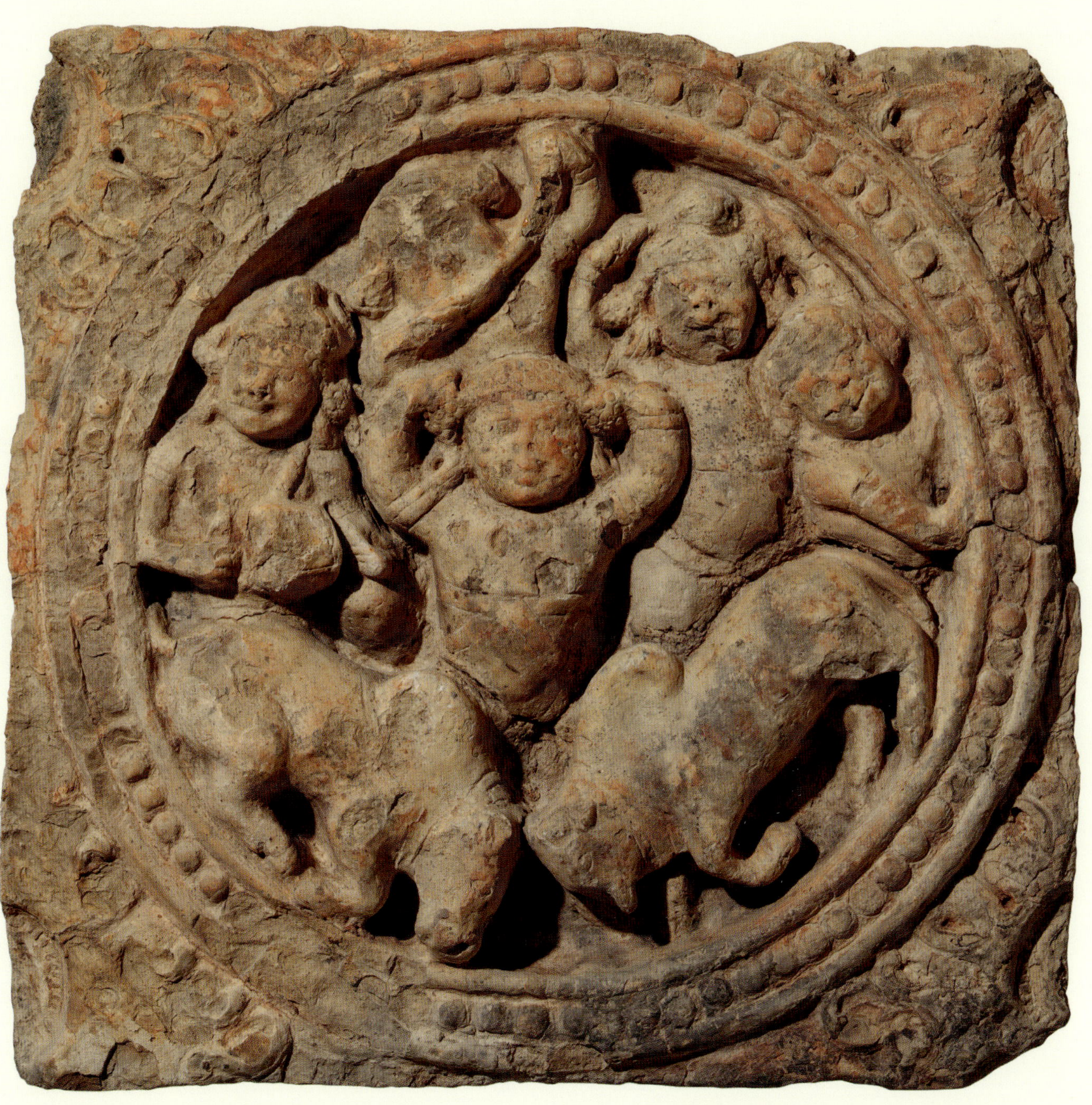

12.

Plaque with image of seated Buddha

Pagan period, 11th–13th century
Gilded metal with polychrome
H. 7 x W. 6¼ x D. ¼ in. (17.8 x 15.9 x 0.6 cm)
Bagan Archaeological Museum

Few earthquakes have silver linings, but the tremor that rocked Pagan in July 1975 unlocked a number of treasures and relics hidden within the city's monuments. Among the most exciting were five gilded, metal repoussé plaques, each featuring a seated Buddha, flanked by two disciples.[1] This plaque and one other depict the Buddha in the teaching gesture, *vitarka mudra*, while another pair is in the earth-touching gesture, *bhumisparsa mudra*. The fifth raises his right hand in instruction, with the other hand resting on folded legs. Pictured here is one of three of the Buddhas that rest upon a double-lotus. The two other Buddhas sit upon formal thrones. On each plaque a prominent tree is above each figure, delicately painted. In one case, the leaves are not painted but are raised in shallow relief. It is tempting to identify the set as representing the four buddhas of our era and the Buddha of the future, Metteyya, but the evidence is insufficient. Moreover, none of the trees can be identified as the "tree of enlightenment," or the Bodhi Tree (*Ficus religiousa*) associated with Gotama Buddha. Perhaps these five once belonged to a complete set of plaques depicting the Twenty-Eight Buddhas. However, for depictions of the Twenty-Eight Buddhas at Pagan, each is usually in the earth-touching gesture. Small holes in the corners of each plaque suggest that they were pinned to a surface. Only one similar plaque is known, showing the Buddha in the earth-touching gesture with two seated disciples; found in the early twentieth century, it has been missing for decades.[2]

DS

NOTES

1 All five are on display at the Bagan Archaeological Museum. All were found at the Myinpyagu Temple (Pichard, *Inventory*, no. 1493), a temple south of the city walls. Four were first published by Than Tun in *Some Observations*. Subsequently, two additional plaques from the same temple were recovered, and are also from the same set to judge by their size and style, but these were not gilded; they have been recently placed on display in the Bagan Archaeological Museum. Therefore, a total of seven are known.
2 Luce, *Old Burma—Early Pagan*, 2: frontispiece. It is described as gold.

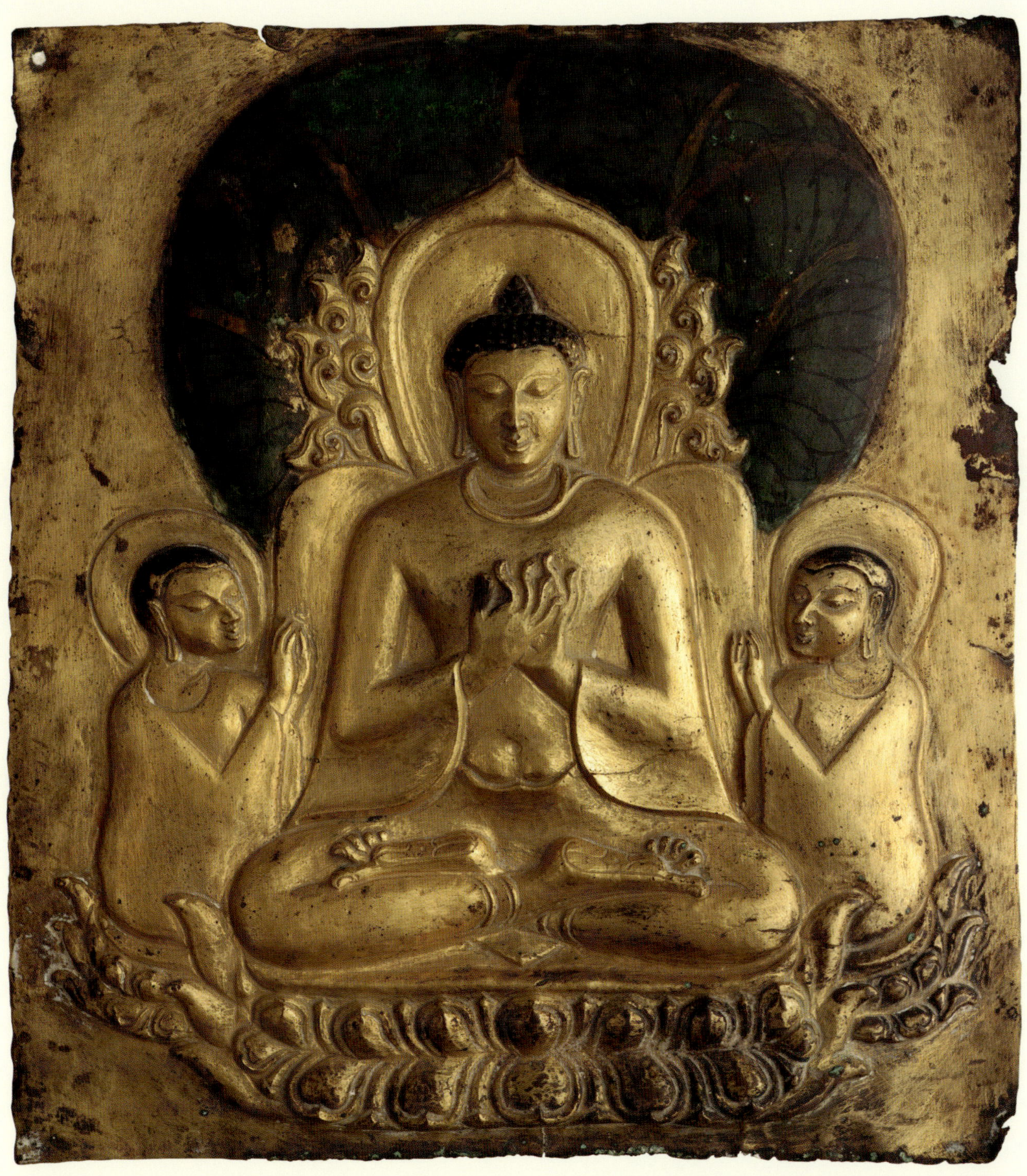

13.

Parinibbana

Pagan period, 11th–13th century
Copper
H. 4¾ x W. 11¼ x D. ¼ in. (12.1 x 28.6 x 0.6 cm)
Bagan Archaeological Museum

This repoussé plaque was found in the early 1970s while clearing debris on the floor inside Pagan's thirteenth-century Thayanbu Temple (Pichard, *Inventory*, no. 1554). The setting is the Buddha's death, or the *parinibbana*. Two monks hover above, with one placing his hand on the Buddha's forearm; another two monks are at the base. The figure on the far left has been identified as Sakka, king of the gods, although he is usually shown crowned at Pagan; however, this figure is perhaps the Buddha of the future, Metteyya, particularly if the object held in his suspended right hand is a water container, one of this deity's attributes.[1] Next in the panel is the god Brahma. On the far right is Vishnu, his upper left hand holding a discus, while his upper right grasps what may be a lotus. The figure next to him is Shiva, in his horrific form known as Bhairava, identified by his corpulence and his flame-like pointed hair, attributes found in Pala sculpture depicting this deity.[2] At each end of the relief there are two sala trees.

Numerous examples of this theme exist at Pagan, both in sculpture and mural painting, each example remarkably different.[3] None, for example, has this same configuration of auxiliary deities. The wide margin on the bottom, ornamented with a row of lotus leaves, and the uneven and jagged surface on the top suggest that this formed the bottom of a larger panel.

DS

NOTES

1 This panel is briefly treated in Aung Thaw, *Historical Sites in Burma*, 80.
2 Huntington and Huntington, *Leaves from the Bodhi Tree*, fig. 28, 154–55.
3 Bautze-Picron, *Buddhist Murals of Pagan*, 63–67.

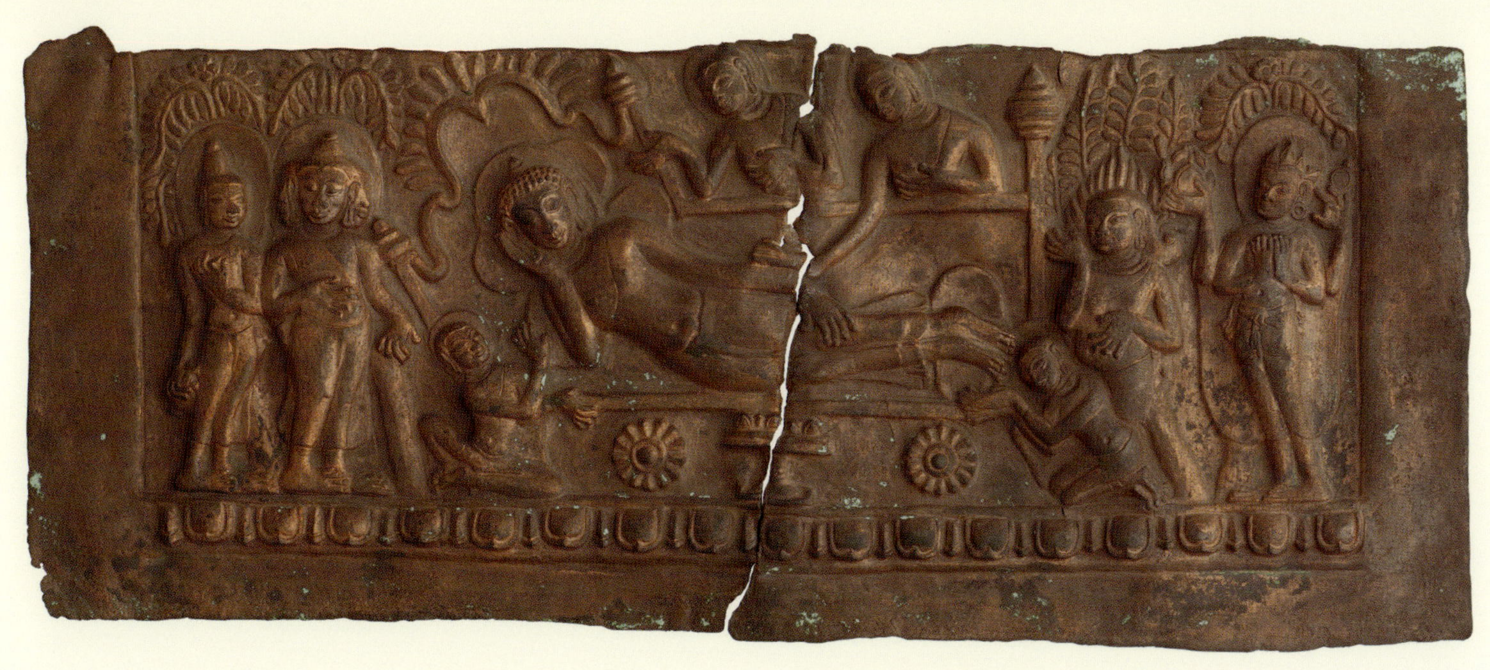

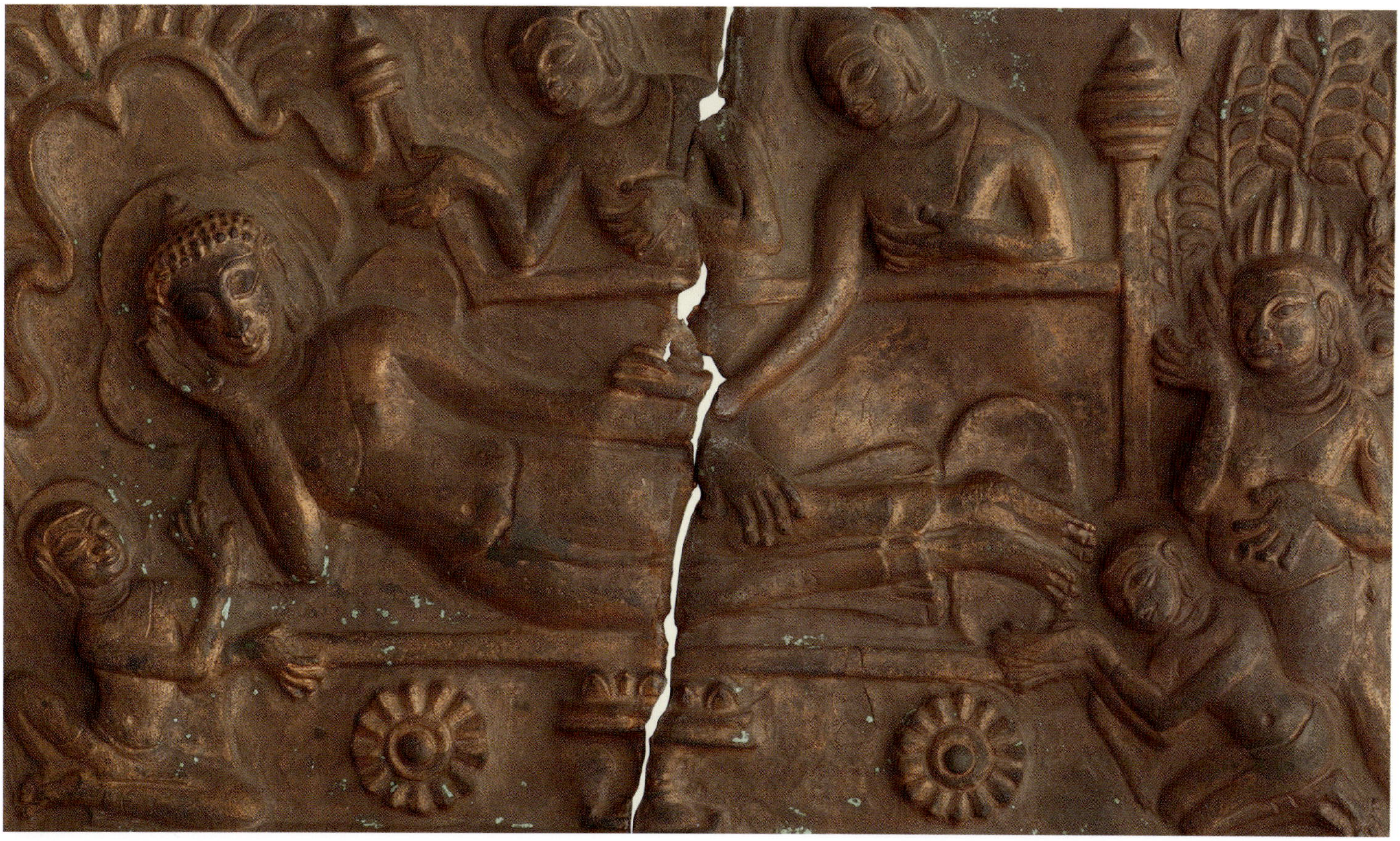

DETAIL

14.

Buddha seated in *dharmacakra mudra*

Pagan period, 11th century
Sandstone
H. 42 x W. 27 x D. 10 in. (106.7 x 68.6 x 25.4 cm)
Bagan Archaeological Museum

Buddha holds his hands together at chest level to signify the teaching gesture, or *dharmacakra mudra*, commonly associated with the Buddha's first sermon at the deer park at Sarnath. The middle finger of the left hand bends sharply behind the other fingers to touch the end the thumb. Seated Buddhas with this hand gesture at Pagan, or Bagan, are also associated with two separate episodes: defeating the heretics at Savatthi and the demon Alavaka. This hand gesture was used with some standing images also at Pagan, but the meaning is unclear.

This seated figure was discovered in the early twentieth century and deposited in the Bagan Archaeological Museum. An old photograph reveals that the flat slab forming the background was originally painted with an elaborate throne. The image was cleaned at some early stage and the painting is now missing. It has been suggested that it was collected from the Kubyauknge Temple near the village of Wetkyi-in, Pagan, but this is improbable.[1]

The figure belongs to Pagan's early phase of sculpture, with affinities to images in the Kubyaukgyi Temple in the village of Myinkaba, Pagan, dated by an inscription to circa 1112, and to sculpture at Pagan's Ananda and Nagayon Temples. The motifs and style reveal a debt to the art associated with Pala India but with numerous differences.[2] For example, both traditions share the use of the double lotus at the bottom, but Pala sculpture often has far more complex bases, including multiple recessed, horizontal registers occupied by numerous auxiliary figures. When extra figures are added to the bases of Pagan images, they are normally sculpted within a framed, flat, rectangular panel in shallow relief.

DS

NOTES

1 The sculpture was illustrated by Spooner, "Annual Report of the Director-General of Archaeology for the Year 1917–18," 28, pl. XVII. It is said here that the object was collected "among the ruins of a temple" at the village of Wetkyi-in. Later, G. H. Luce (*Old Burma—Early Pagan*, 2: 177) opined that the image may belong to the Kubyauknge Temple, but no stone images were found at this temple, nor are there niches for stone images.

2 A preliminary survey of Pagan images, Pala stone sculpture, and manuscript painting suggests that the two hands could be placed together in widely diverse ways. In Pala sculpture, for example, it seems that the middle finger of the left hand that bends to touch the end of the thumb in Pagan sculpture is substituted for another finger. Also, the left hand in Pala sculpture is placed at an oblique angle to the chest, unlike most Pagan examples where the hand rests flat against the chest. Also, there are painted examples and metal buddhas at Pagan, such as one repoussé plaque discussed in this publication (see cat. no. 12). Another example reveals yet other ways in which the hands were held (see cat. no. 13).

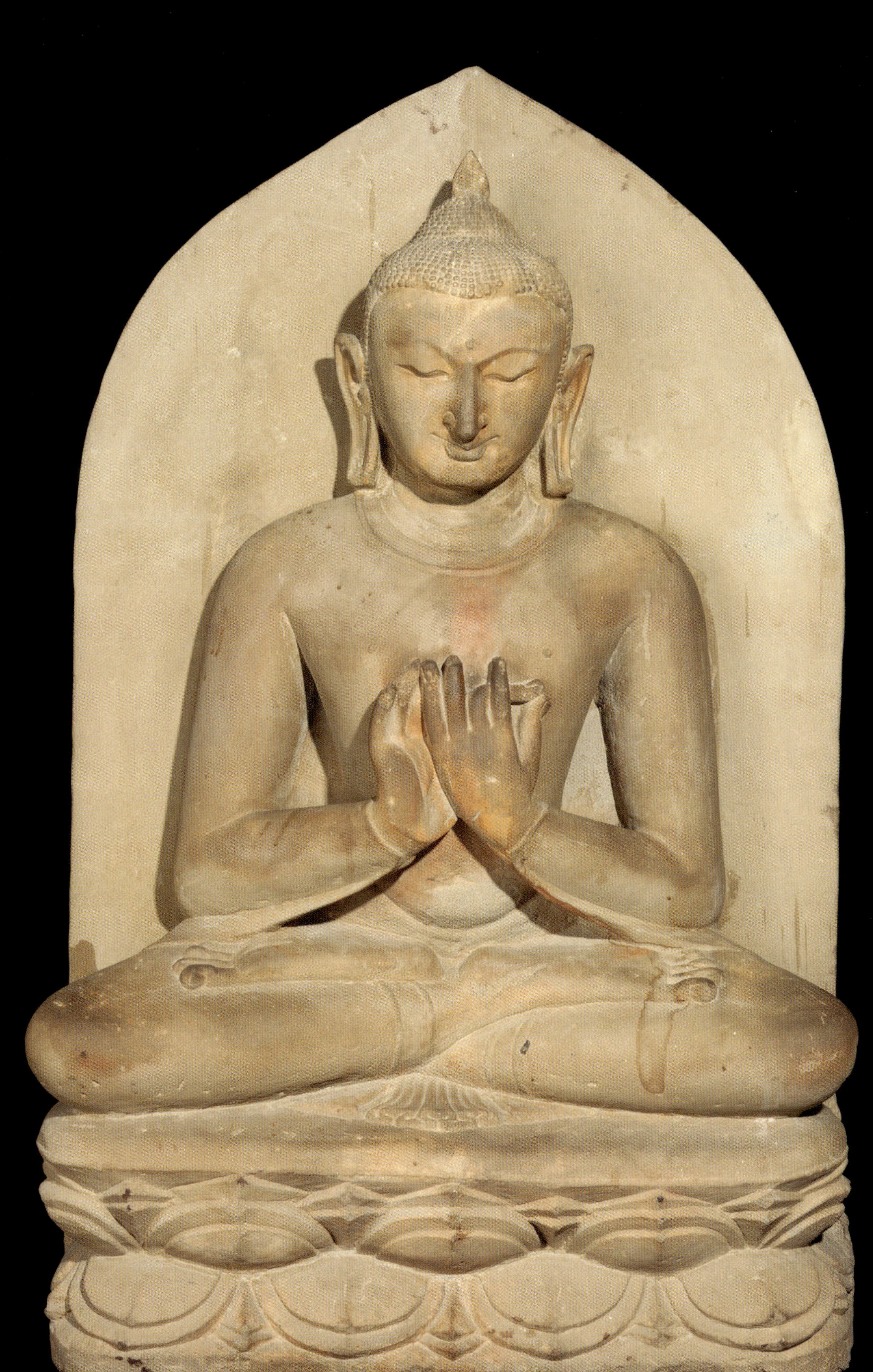

15.

Buddha Severing His Hair

Pagan period, ca. 11th–12th century
Sandstone with traces of pigment
H. 31 x W. 18 x D. 9 in. (78.7 x 45.7 x 22.9 cm)
Bagan Archaeological Museum

A pivotal moment in the Buddha's early life was his poignant withdrawal from his father's kingdom and from his wife and newborn son. After departing from the palace, the man who was to become the Buddha soon realized: "These locks of mine do not become a monk."[1] This theme was a popular one in ancient Pagan, or Bagan, as it is today in Myanmar. In this Pagan-period example, the long tubelike shape forming the Buddha's hair probably represents the unwound, twisted coiffeur, or topknot, associated with royalty. Such an elaborate headdress is sometimes seen at Pagan in connection with this same episode.[2] The Buddha cast his topknot into the air, vowing: "If I am to become a Buddha let it remain in the sky; if not, let it fall to the ground."[3] In some examples, the god Sakka, or Indra is shown hovering above the Buddha, ready to catch it and then enshrine it in a stupa in heaven.

DS

NOTES

1 Jayawickrama, *Story of Gotama Buddha*, 86.

2 This example from the Pagan museum is said to have come from the Kubyauknge Temple in Wetkyi-in village, Pagan; see Luce, *Old Burma—Early Pagan*, 2: 179, and 3: pl. 410 (c). This is unlikely, however, since the original niches inside this early temple were found to be filled with fragmentary sculptures made of brick, covered with stucco. Our image belongs probably to the early period at Pagan, together with a piece from the Kyauk Ummin Cave Temple. In this latter work, the strands making up the unraveled topknot can be seen. For this example and others, see ibid., 3: pls. 141 (c), 289 (c), 312 (a), and 313 (c); pl. 313 (d) is a much later addition.

3 Jayawickrama, *Story of Gotama Buddha*, 86.

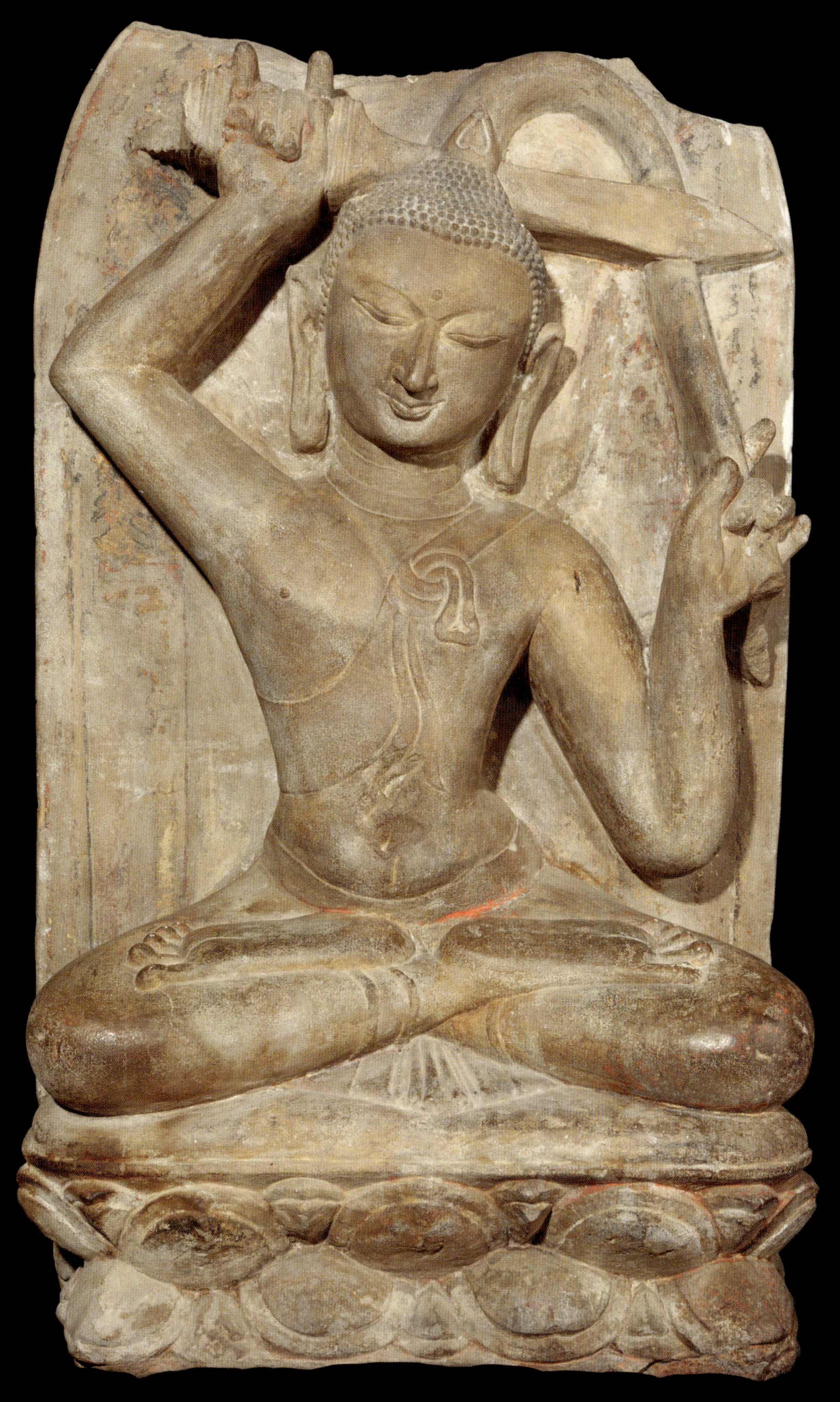

16.

Birth of the Buddha

Kubyauknge Temple, Myinkaba village
Pagan period, 1198
Sandstone
H. 43¾ x W. 25¾ x D. 15½ in. (111.1 x 65.4 x 39.4 cm)
Bagan Archaeological Museum

Grasping a flowering tree with her right hand, Queen Maya, the Buddha's mother, gave birth to the future Buddha, who emerged from her right side, "unsmeared with any impurity arising from the mother's womb."[1] Queen Maya expired seven days later, and her sister, Prajapati, shown standing on the right in this sculpture, stepped into the role of stepmother. Four events related to the birth are featured on the left. The topmost shows two *brahmas*, a class of Buddhist deity, supporting the newborn in a golden net. Next are the World Guardians (*Lokapalas*) with the infant sitting upon antelope skins, while below mortals hold the child aloft in a cloth. On the base are gods and humans observing the Buddha taking his legendary seven strides.[2]

This image once belonged to a niche within the Kubyauknge Temple, in Myinkaba village at Pagan, dated by an inscription to 1198 (Pichard, *Inventory*, no. 1391).[3]

DS

NOTES

1 Jayawickrama, *Story of Gotama Buddha*, 70. The depictions at Pagan featuring the Buddha's life up to his enlightenment conform most closely to the circa fifth-century Pali text *Nidana-katha*, or its later recensions.

2 In rare examples at Pagan, Maya is shown holding a branch, but no child is seen emerging from her side. One example is a stone sculpture in storage at the Bagan Archaeological Museum, while the other is a recently exposed painting inside the Pathodhammya Temple within the walled city at Pagan. In Pala manuscripts, Maya is generally shown with her legs crossed.

3 This image, in its original niche, can be seen in Pichard, *Inventory*, 8: fig. 1391.

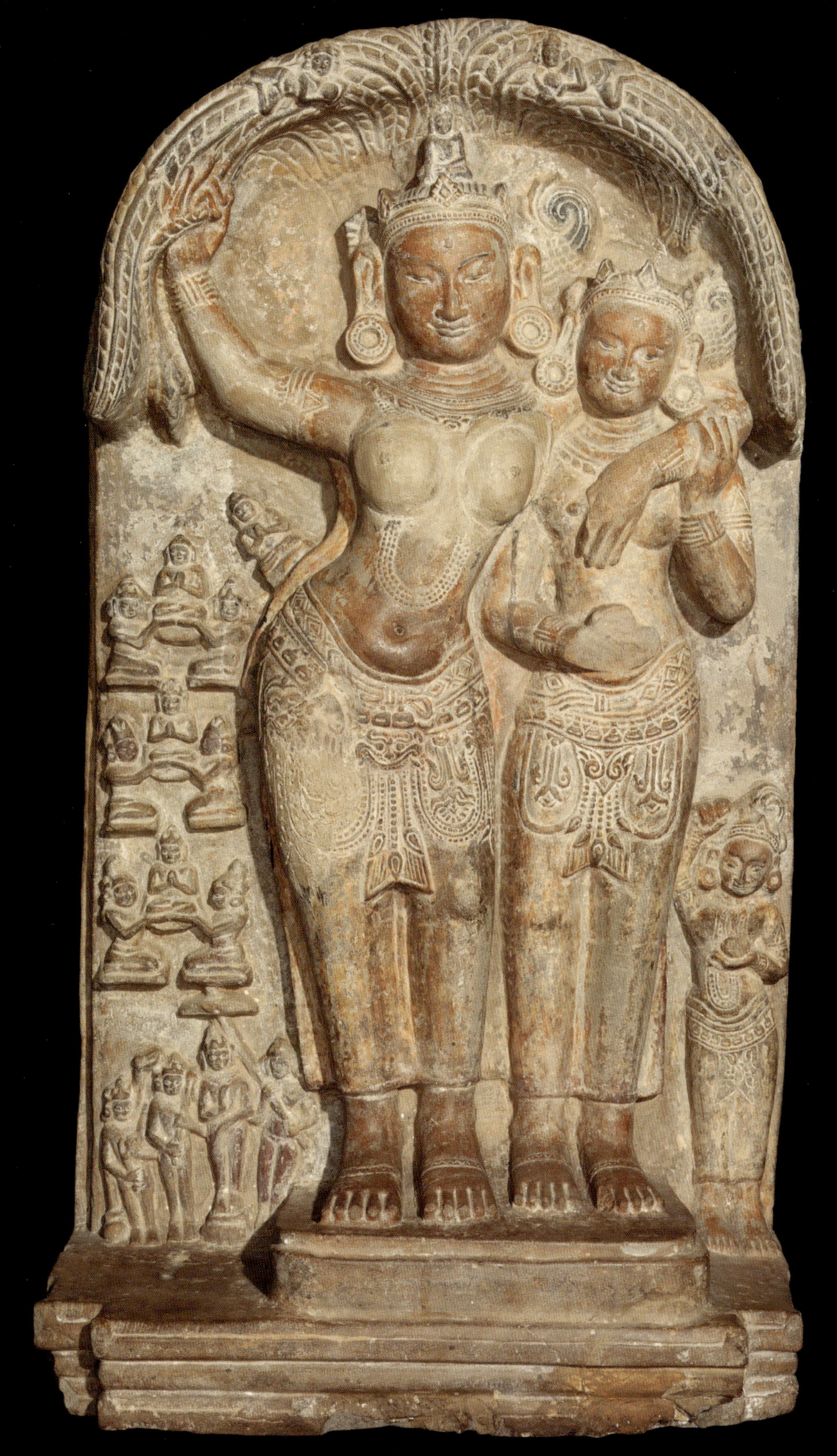

17.

Parinibbana

Kubyauknge Temple, Myinkaba village
Pagan period, ca. 1198
Sandstone with pigment
H. 35½ x W. 51 x D. 13 in. (90.2 x 129.5 x 33 cm)
Bagan Archaeological Museum

The Buddha's death, or *parinibbana*, was a popular subject for sculptors and painters at Pagan, or Bagan. The best known are the stone images inside the four entrance halls of the Ananda Temple, probably created at the opening of the twelfth century. That the motifs and the style of the four images are so similar suggests that the artists based their work on a single model. The painted examples at Pagan show a great deal of diversity, however, with no two alike, and none close to the four stone sculptures at the Ananda Temple.[1]

This panel was until recently in its original niche within the Kubyauknge Temple dated by an inscription to 1198.[2] Its composition reveals striking parallels with the four examples at the Ananda Temple of a much earlier date, suggesting that sculptors used pattern books that were handed down for generations within workshops. In all of the stone examples, the gods Brahma and Sakka appear above the Buddha on the left, with a row of gods on the upper right and a row of monks beneath. The three-tiered shrine is probably a reference to the worship of relic monuments that would follow the Buddha's cremation.[3] The figures in royal attire along the base show some variation in their placement and number, but they perhaps represent the Malla chiefs in whose kingdom the Buddha's death occurred.

DS

NOTES

1 Luce, *Old Burma—Early Pagan*, 3: pls. 302 and 319 (c).
2 Pichard, *Inventory*, 5: fig. 1391 (s).
3 The Buddha's death appears in Pala palm-leaf manuscripts, but the depictions are far simpler, probably reflecting the small frames available to painters. The theme was not common in Pala sculpture, but the compositions had far fewer figures than these examples at Pagan. In the Pala works, a stupa often replaces the tiered shrines found among these works at Pagan.

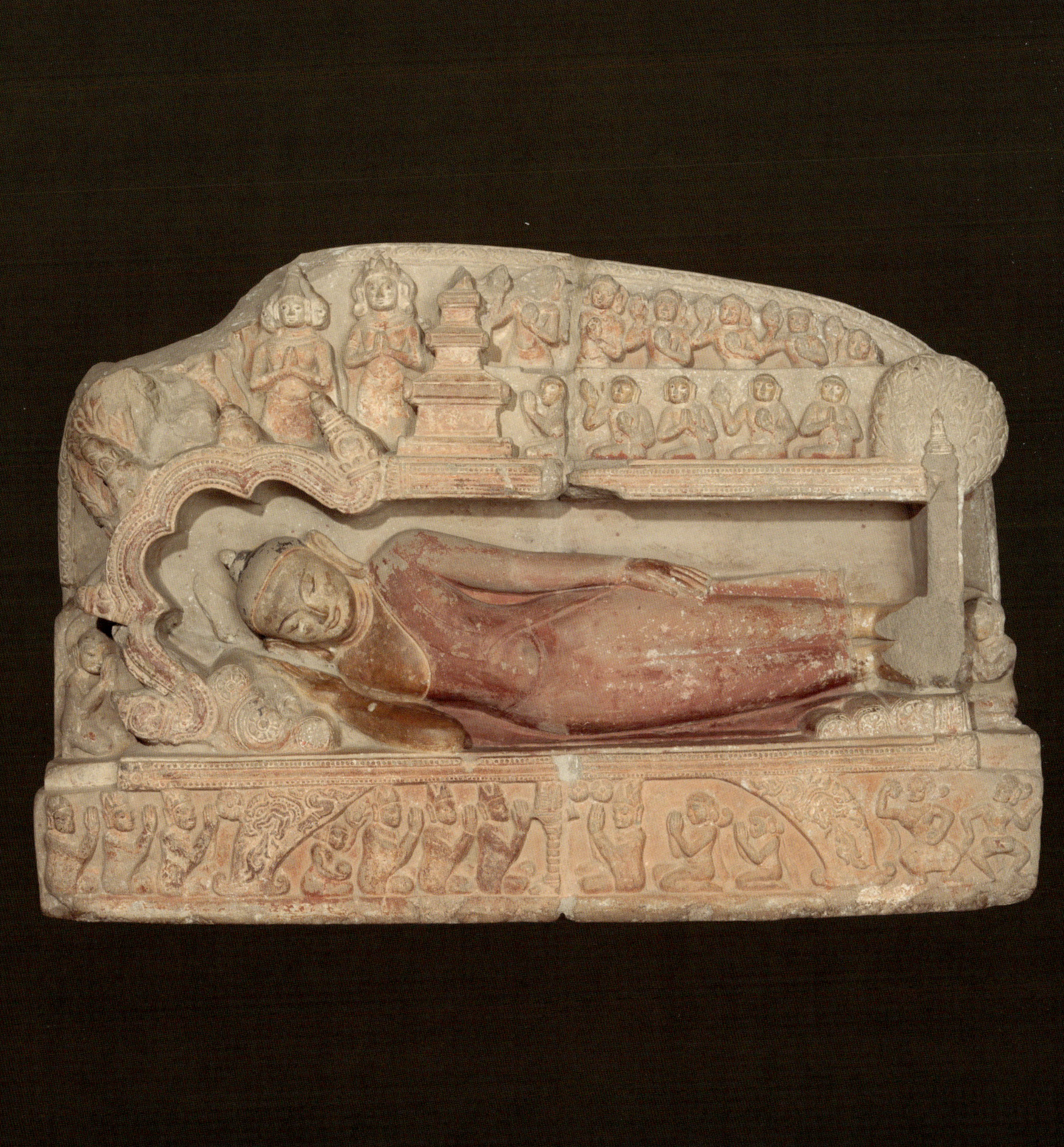

18.

Monkey Making Offering of Honey to the Buddha

Kubyauknge Temple, Myinkaba village
Pagan period, 1198
Sandstone with polychrome
H. 45½ x W. 27 x D. 9½ in. (115.6 x 68.6 x 24.1 cm)
Bagan Archaeological Museum

A monkey and an elephant accrued merit by presenting the Buddha food offerings, suggesting that even animals, as sentient beings, are subject to the law of karma (Sanskrit). In this rendering, the monkey holds his hands aloft and a bowl is seen in the Buddha's lap. A monkey honoring the Buddha also appears in early Indian art, for example in one gateway at the Great Stupa at Sanchi and also in Gandhara reliefs. Later, following the seventh century, the monkey was shown falling down a well, intoxicated with joy at serving the Buddha, and then depicted rising to the heavens, a reward for his selflessness. The theme became especially popular in the art of the Pala dynasty in eastern India since it was included in the Eight Great Events. The elephant is rarely paired together with a monkey in Indian Buddhist art, but the two are regularly placed together in Myanmar art and in the later art of Thailand, reflecting a tradition found in a commentary on a famous Buddhist text, the *Dhammapada*. In this version, the monkey becomes ecstatic by his donation and jumps from a tree, falls, and impales himself on a cut tree trunk but is then reborn in heaven.[1] In this panel the monkey is also shown in a dance pose, suggesting his joy at serving the Buddha; the pose, with the left arm raised, is identical to a scene in an illustrated Pala manuscript belonging to Asia Society, New York, dated to circa 1105.[2]

Until recently this sculpture was in its original niche within the inner corridor of the Kubyauknge Temple at Pagan, or Bagan, dated by an inscription to 1198.[3] Compared to Pagan's sculpture from the early twelfth century, the poses are stiff and less buoyant.

DS

NOTES

1 This theme in Buddhist art and literature has been examined recently in Brown, "Telling the Story."

2 Huntington and Huntington, *Leaves from the Bodhi Tree*, pl. 57, 185–89. Mr. and Mrs. John D. Rockefeller 3rd Collection, 1987.1.

3 Pichard, *Inventory*, no. 1391, with a photograph of this work in its original niche, vol. 5, fig. 1391(r). Eight stone panels were noted within their original niches at this temple; the walls had eleven niches in total. All eight were removed to the Pagan museum in 1993.

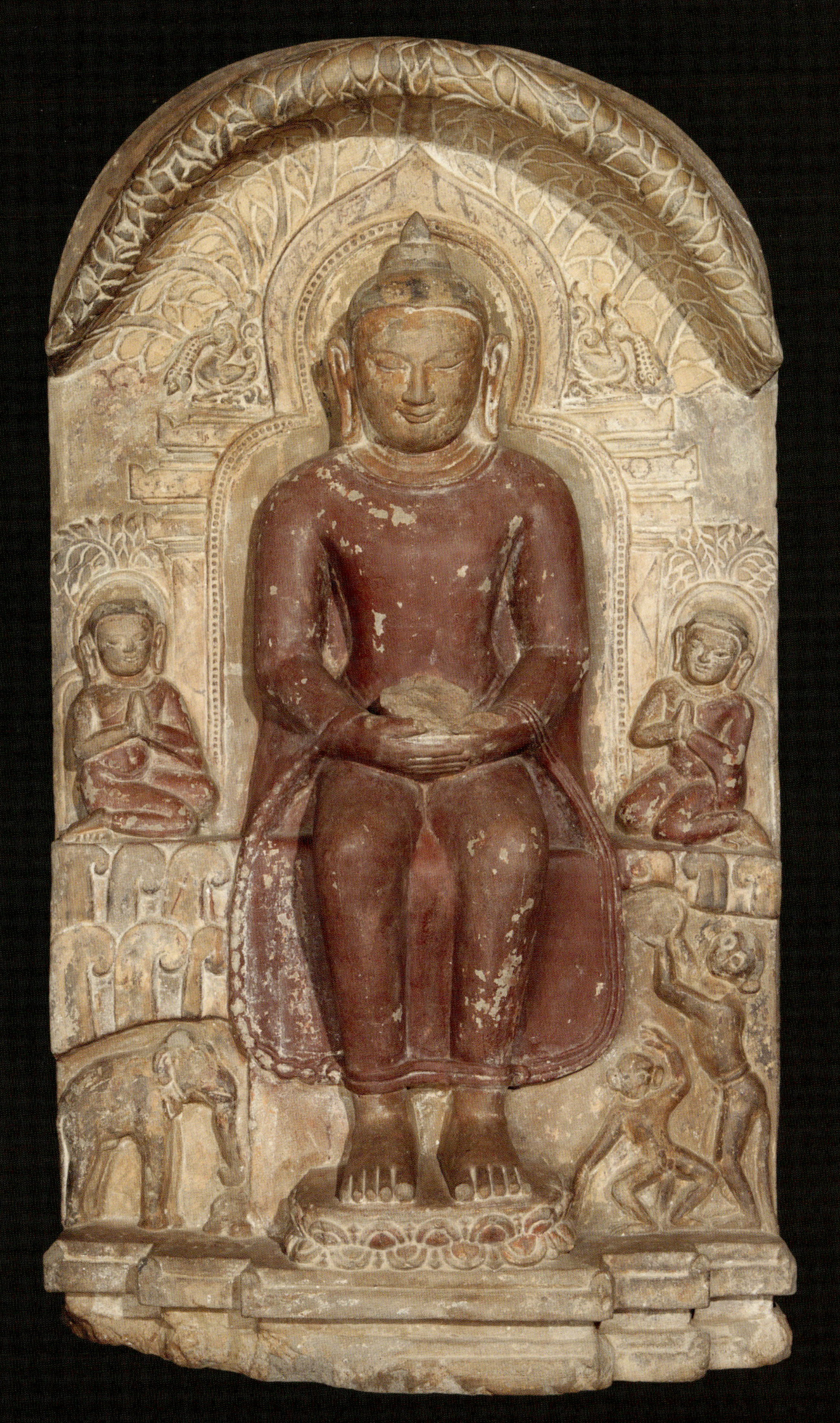

19.

Buddha

Pagan period, ca. 11th–12th century
Bronze
H. 27¼ x W. 9 x D. 4 in. (69.2 x 22.9 x 10.2 cm)
National Museum, Yangon

This bronze and two others were found accidentally in 1937 when a brick wall of a temple "canted outwards" and a "wide vertical crack" appeared, revealing a chamber about two feet square and located about ten feet above the floor level.[1] The practice of interring bronzes within the brick fabric of temple walls and even towers or superstructures was probably intended not to hide or conceal the bronzes but to enhance the efficacy of the donation, much like terracotta votive tablets placed within stupas or even under the floors of temples. Stone inscriptions at Pagan, or Bagan, record that metal objects were interred within stupas and even encased within large Buddhas made of brick inside temples. Some are described as silver or gold but none have survived; only those in bronze like this one, cast in the lost-wax process, remain. Treasure seekers, probably beginning in the fourteenth century, removed virtually all of these objects in the ancient period; they were presumably sold in local markets for the value of the metal.[2] Even in the late nineteenth century, it was difficult to locate a single monument that did "not show the marks of these marauders."[3]

That this Pagan bronze and others exhibit so little sign of wear is another reason to think that they were never under active worship but were interred within chambers. The famous inscription associated with the Kubyaukgyi Temple, Myinkaba village, Pagan, mentions a donated metal Buddha, and perhaps this bronze is still somewhere within the brick fabric of the temple. People in Myanmar today commission metal figures that are worshiped in shrines at home or donated to monasteries.

DS

NOTES

1 Duroiselle, "Explorations in Burma," 78. For photos of all three bronzes located in this chamber, see Luce, *Old Burma—Early Pagan*, 2: pl. 429.

2 Than Tun, *Some Observations*, 165–244.

3 Oertel, *Notes on a Tour in Burma*, 16.

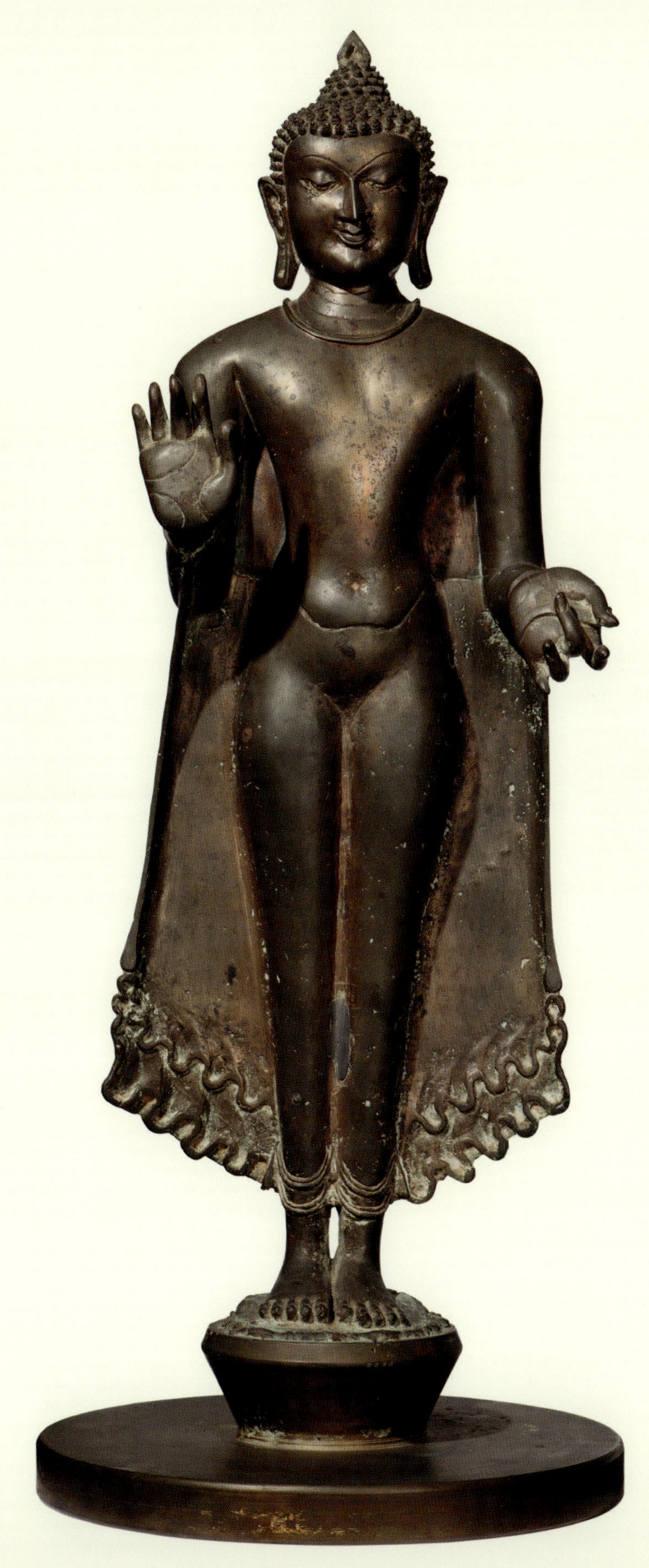

20.

Buddha Descending from Tavatimsa

Pagan period, 12th century
Wood
H. 27¾ x W. 17½ x D. 9 in. (70.5 x 44.5 x 22.9 cm)
Bagan Archaeological Museum

The Buddha rose to the Heaven of the Thirty-Three Gods, or Tavatimsa, in order to teach an important division of the Pali canon, the *Abhidhamma*, to his reborn mother. On this sculpture, the descent from this heaven is suggested by a triple ladder in low relief, set diagonally at the panel's edge. The god Brahma holds an umbrella, while Indra carries a bowl. The Buddha grasps the end of his robe in the upraised hand, while the other hand once extended with an open palm. The kneeling figure is probably Sariputta, a disciple who greeted the Buddha upon his descent, near the city gates of Sankassa in northern India. The Buddha posed questions to the assembled monks at Sankassa, but only Sariputta answered correctly.[1] While the basic composition of this sculpture derives from Pala examples from eastern India, Indra is usually the one holding the umbrella in Pala examples.[2]

No ancient wooden sculptures have been found in situ at Pagan, or Bagan, so the placement and function of wooden images from this period is unknown. The largest surviving wooden work from ancient Pagan is an immense doorway now displayed in the compound of the Shwezigon Temple. A sculpted wooden doorway lintel remains in place at the Nagayon Temple at Pagan. One remarkable large wooden throne has survived from the ancient period and is now preserved in a monastery museum in Sale, a town south of Pagan.[3] These few surviving examples prove that wood sculptors were equal to Pagan's stone artisans.

DS

NOTES

1 A kneeling monk appears also in some painted examples showing this same theme. Bautze-Picron, *Buddhist Murals of Pagan*, 53, pl. 52.

2 For a discussion of this theme in Pala sculpture, see Huntington and Huntington, *Leaves from the Bodhi Tree*, 132–33, fig. 9.

3 This is in the Yok-son monastery museum. It stands at least nine feet high and is made of multiple pieces fastened together by metal clamps. Stadtner, *Ancient Pagan*, 52.

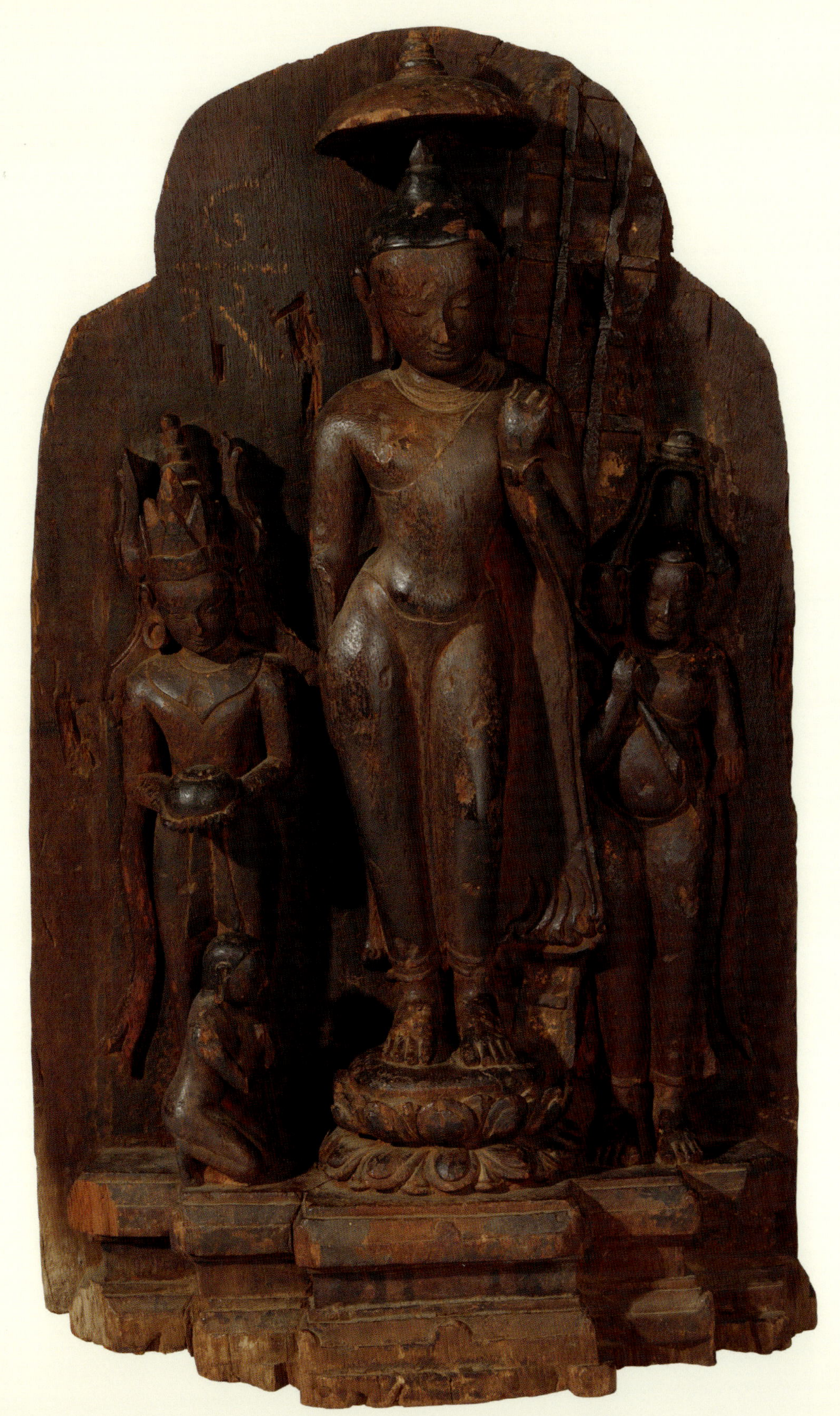

21.

Buddha

Pagan period, 12th–13th century
Wood with traces of red lacquer, gesso, and gold leaf
H. 78 x W. 20 x D. 10 in. (198.1 x 50.8 x 25.4 cm)
Metropolitan Museum of Art: Anonymous Gift, 1992; 1992.382

There are scores of examples of life-size wooden standing buddhas, crowned and bejeweled, both in Myanmar and in museums worldwide. The arms are closely wedded to the torso in this example and others because the sculpture is created from a single piece of wood. The right hand is suspended, with palm outward, while the other arm is sharply bent, with the palm inward, and from which protrudes a small segment of the robe.

None of these sculptures were found in contexts indicating that they were part of the original design of temples. Instead, these figures were likely set inside temples sometime after the original construction date. Pagan's later history is marked by countless donations made by diverse pilgrims to previously built temples, and these wooden images probably fit into this category. Placing privately commissioned Buddha figures within temples is a practice widely continued in Southeast Asia today.

G. H. Luce thought that these figures may represent deceased kings, but they probably should be identified as crowned and bejeweled Buddhas, an uncommon theme for Pagan's stone sculpture but widely found in Pala art.[1] The vertical lancet-like projections forming the crowns on the wooden images have forerunners among certain stone sculpture at Pagan, the most well known of which is a seated figure in a small shrine within the compound of the Ananda Temple.[2] Radiocarbon testing on two of the crowned Buddhas suggests a circa twelfth- to thirteenth-century date for the group as a whole.[3]

DS

NOTES

1 Luce, *Old Burma—Early Pagan*, 1: 291. Luce recorded that these types of objects were also found at other sites in Upper Myanmar. The religious meaning of crowned Buddhas in Buddhist art has generated much debate. Two paired standing wooden images were recovered from one Pagan temple (Pichard, *Inventory*, no. 778), each with a pronounced sway to the hips in opposite directions. These may have been *bodisattas* (Pali) that flanked a central Buddha image; they are now in the Bagan Archaeological Museum.

2 Pichard, *Inventory*, 8: 136, fig. 2163 (c). This large, seated stone figure, bejeweled and crowned, is now inside a small modern wooden shrine known as the Tothwegyi, on the western side of the platform.

3 None of the wooden sculptures within Myanmar have been scientifically tested. For an excellent study on these images, see Brown, "Three Wood Buddha Sculptures." Radiocarbon tests conducted on two Pagan-period images belonging to the Los Angeles County Museum of Art returned a range between the twelfth and thirteenth centuries. One is crowned and bejeweled, while the other is a standing Buddha depicted in monk's garb. A third crowned Buddha, belonging to the Asian Art Museum, San Francisco, was tested with results beginning somewhat earlier, ca. 1043–ca. 1290; Forrest McGill kindly shared the museum's scientific report. All of the tested images are made of teak wood.

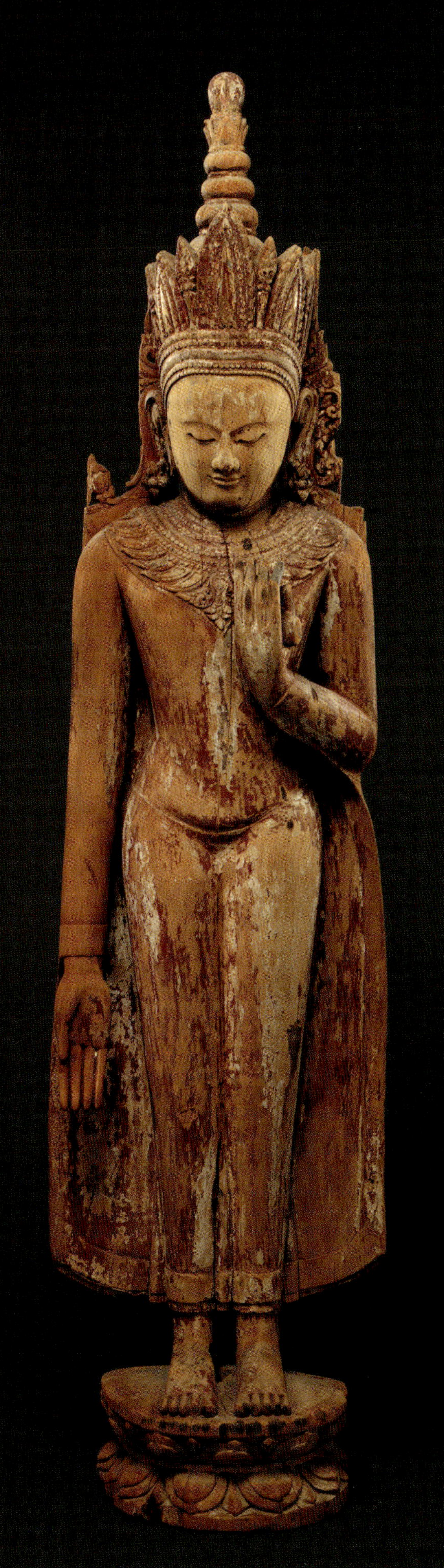

22.

Brahma

Pagan period, ca. 11th–13th century
Sandstone
H. 13¼ x W. 10 x D. 4¾ in. (33.7 x 25.4 x 12 cm)
Bagan Archaeological Museum

The three faces on this sculpture belong to the god Brahma. Both the faces and figure bear a debt to the Pala-period sculpture of India, but features of Pagan-period sculpture are highlighted by the figure's compact body and generous U-shaped lower lips. The Hindu god Brahma played an auxiliary role to the Buddha, both in early Indian art and at Pagan. In Buddhist thought there is a World of Brahma, or *Brahmaloka* (Pali), made up of twenty heavens inhabited by many *brahmas*; the best known in this class was Brahma Sahampati, who persuaded the Buddha to launch his teaching mission following the enlightenment. At Pagan, Brahma's importance was highlighted when enormous painted images of Brahma within the entrance chambers at the Ananda Temple came to light after layers of whitewash were recently removed. Other examples are the life-size seated stone Brahmas on the four piers of Pagan's Nanpaya Temple.

This small sculpture belongs to a dispersed set that once numbered at least seven.[1] Their exact find spot at Pagan was never recorded. This carving is one of five now in the collection of the Bagan Archaeological Museum. Another from the series almost certainly is a sculpture collected by a Scottish zoologist, John Anderson, on his mission to Upper Myanmar and Yunnan in 1867, and is now in the Victoria and Albert Museum, London. Another, in the Indian Museum, Kolkatta, was probably also collected by Anderson on the same journey, since he served as the museum's first director (1865–87).[2] The set likely formed the base of a large brick throne that supported a seated Buddha within a brick temple, judging from a series of similar stone Brahmas found in a row beneath the central seated brick Buddha at the Myebontha Temple at Pagan.[3]

DS

NOTES

1 Luce, *Old Burma—Early Pagan*, 3: pl. 416 (a–c).

2 For the example in Calcutta, see ibid., pl. 416 (b). One example has been incorrectly attributed to Thaton in Lower Myanmar, pl. 416 (c).

3 Pichard, *Inventory*, no. 1512. See Luce, *Old Burma—Early Pagan*, 3: pl. 251, for photographs of the stone Brahmas in situ beneath the main image in the Myebontha Temple.

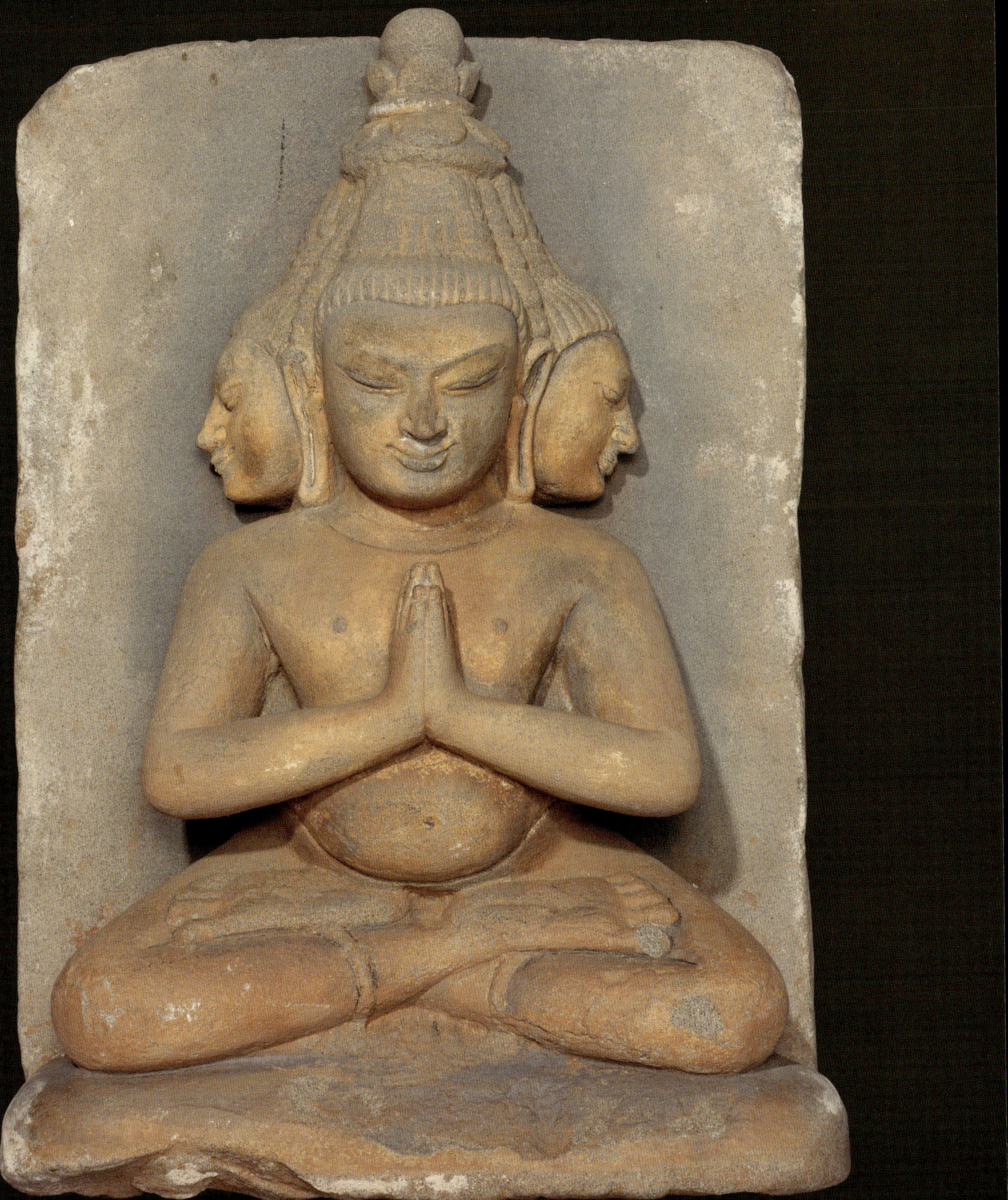

23.

Vishnu

Pagan period, 11th–12th century
Bronze
H. 14 x W. 7 x D. 4 in. (35.6 x 17.8 x 10.2 cm)
National Museum, Yangon

This bronze Vishnu is a reminder that Hinduism has always played a significant role in religious life in Myanmar, coexisting with Buddhism. Indeed, court rituals from the Pagan period onward were steeped in Hindu practices. One inscription at Pagan, or Bagan, for example invoked the deity Vishnu during ceremonies consecrating wooden pillars used in a possible palace.

This bronze was found in a field south of the walled city near the village of Myinkaba in 1913. It shares important parallels with bronze Vishnu images from the Chola period (ca. mid-9th to 13th century) in Tamil Nadu, but is extremely crude in light of Pagan's outstanding metalworking traditions. Its function and context remain unknown, but perhaps it was commissioned by South Indian traders whose presence at Pagan is proved by a Sanskrit and Tamil inscription attributed to the thirteenth century.[1] The upper right hand supported a discus, long since missing but visible in old photographs, while the upper left grasps a conch.[2] The other right hand displays the reassurance-gesture, while the other left hand supports a thin club. The discus and the conch are held by two raised fingers, a feature of many Vishnu bronzes from the Chola period. Another connection with Chola traditions is the looped band around the torso's midsection, a feature occasionally found on Vishnu bronzes from Tamil Nadu. Vishnu images from north India generally hold the club in the upper right hand, with the discus in the upper left. The long bands of hair resting on both shoulders can also be found among the Hindu bronzes of South India and in the Buddhist images from Nagapattinam, Tamil Nadu.[3]

DS

NOTES

1 Hultzsch, "Vaishnava Inscription at Pagan," 197–98. The inscription has been dated to the thirteenth century on the basis of its paleography. It records the gift of a door and a lamp to a temple.

2 Luce, *Old Burma—Early Pagan*, 3: pl. 448; for two small stone Vishnus with the discus, or *cakra*, raised in the upper right hand, see pl. 417.

3 For Chola Vishnu bronzes, see Dehejia, *Sensuous and the Sacred*, 171–79. An example with a looped belt around the midsection is found on a standing Chola Vishnu bronze in the Metropolitan Museum of Art, New York (62. 265). For Nagapattinam examples, see Ramachandran, *Nagapattinam and Other Buddhist Bronzes*.

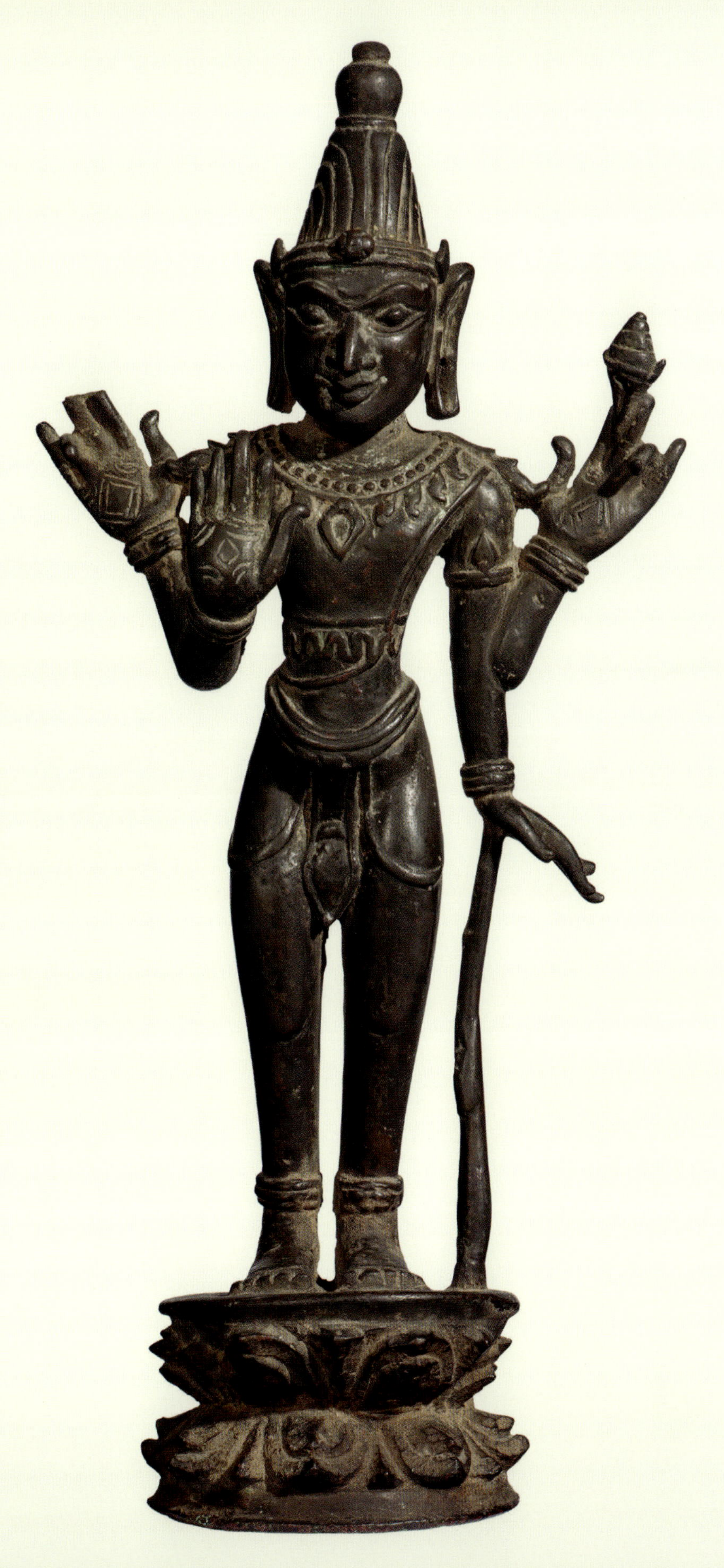

24.

Lotus shrine

Pagan period, 11th–13th century
Bronze with stone inlay
H. 15¼ x Diam. 9 in. (38.7 x 22.9 cm) when petals are open
Bagan Archaeological Museum

This shrine, together with another, was recovered in 1955 amidst the ruins of a brick structure near Pagan's eighteenth-century Upali Thein ordination hall. A third came to light much earlier, in 1927, when it was accidently discovered in the ground at Tawin Taung, a sacred hill twelve miles east of Pagan, or Bagan.[1] The function of these lotus shrines is uncertain, but they were likely interred in relic chambers. Their prototypes were probably from eastern India and Bangladesh, where a handful of similar shrines have been found.[2] In the Myanmar examples, separately cast lotus petals fixed to the rim at the bottom can be folded inward and closed by means of a metal ring. On the inner face of each petal is a small seated figure dressed as a monk. The centerpiece in this example is a replica of the tower, or superstructure, of the temple at Bodh Gaya, with depictions of the Eight Great Events placed around the base. In the other examples at Pagan, one has a seated Buddha in its center and the other depicts a stupa.

DS

NOTES

1 All three examples at Pagan are discussed and illustrated in Luce, *Old Burma—Early Pagan*, 3: pls. 425–28. In two of the examples, numerals are inscribed on the backs of the leaves, presumably to indicate their position.

2 The two best-known examples of lotus shrines from India—from Patharghata in Bihar and the Faridpur District, Bangladesh—feature images of Tara at their centers. There is also one in the British Museum with a seated Buddha at its center. These are discussed as a group in Jinah Kim, *Receptacle of the Sacred*, 65–70.

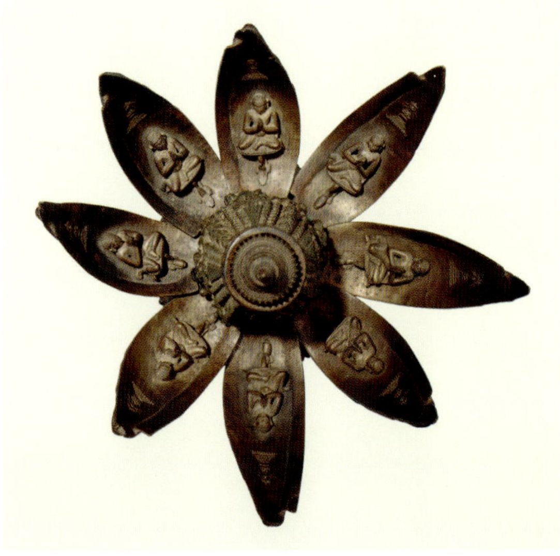

TOP VIEW OF PETALS

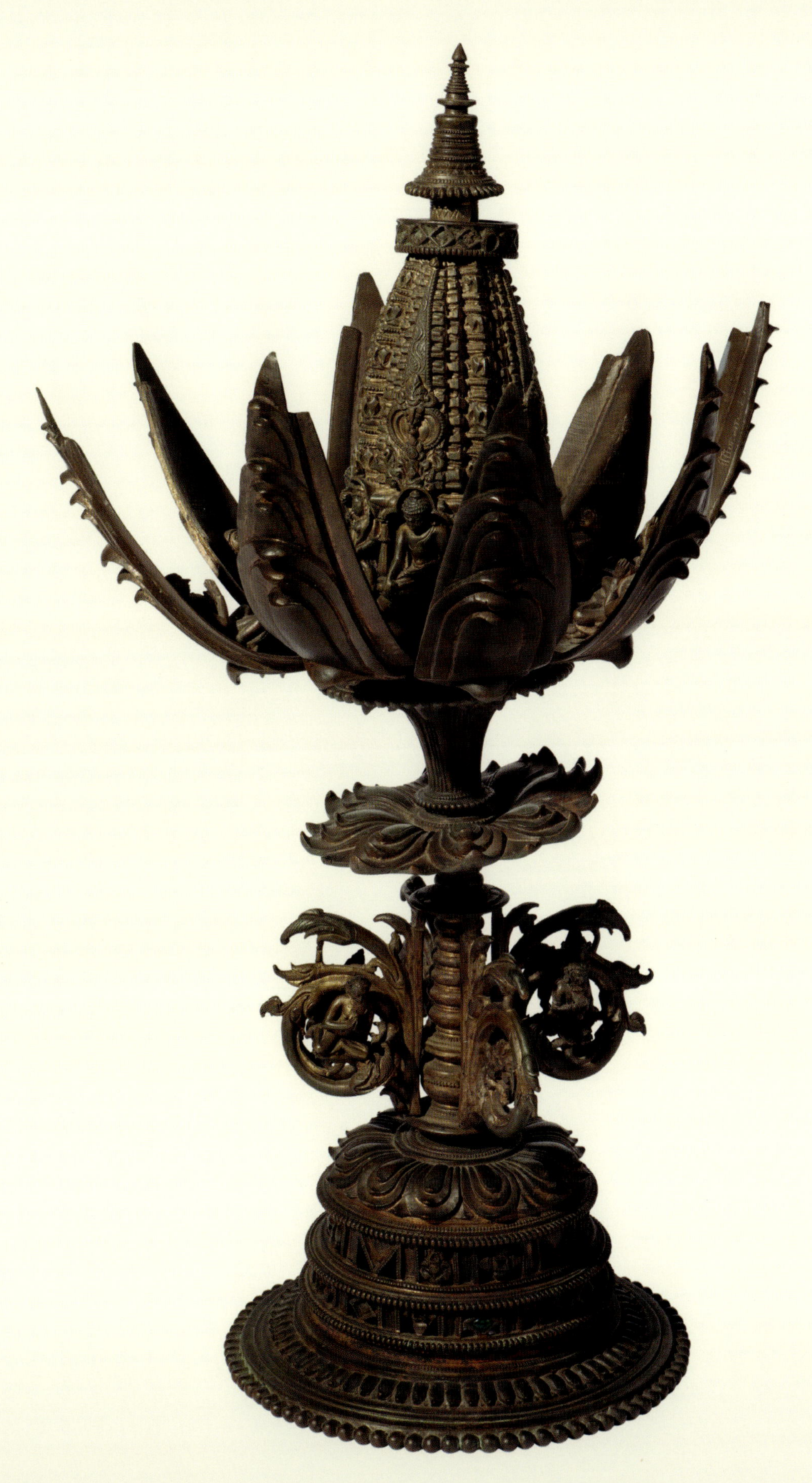

25.

Jataka stories [The Telapatta *Jataka* (*Jataka* no. 96)]

Pagan period, ca. 12th century
Pigment on cloth
H. 66¼ x W. 38 in. (168.3 x 96.5 cm)
Bagan Archaeological Museum

This unique work highlights the quality of cloth painting likely once prevalent at Pagan and also in eastern India. Recovered in over thirty fragments, it was discovered in 1984 rolled up and concealed by debris on the floor of a temple (Pichard, *Inventory*, no. 315). Restored in Rome in 1986–87, it is now a centerpiece in the Bagan Archaeological Museum.[1] This type of painting may have been hung and displayed or have been presented to a monastic library and stored there, like palm-leaf manuscripts.

The subject is the *Telapatta Jataka* (*Jataka* no. 96), divided into five horizontal registers, starting from the top, with identifying captions in Myanmar beneath each row.[2] Each *jataka* story is always preceded by a separate preamble spoken by the Buddha that sets the narrative of the *jataka* tale into a broader didactic context. However, with the exception of this painting, these important introductory sections of each *jataka* appear never to be represented in Buddhist art, suggesting that this example is unique. The preamble appears in the uppermost register showing the Buddha propounding the *jataka* tale to monks in a forest near the town of Desaka; this is the context for the telling of the *Telapatta* story. The *jataka* is an allegory about mindfulness, brought to life by the beautiful seated female on the far left and two standing men facing her. The man beside the damsel holds aloft a pot, filled with oil, while the other, bearing a sword, has been instructed to slay the man if the oil spills. The concentration required was therefore a matter of life and death, echoing the *jataka* tale, which highlights the fate of five brothers who were devoured by ogresses who disguised themselves as alluring ladies. An ogress is seen at the lower right munching on the loose limbs of the brothers. The inclusion of the preamble was perhaps an innovation at Pagan, or perhaps artists were indebted to lost traditions from India, Sri Lanka, or Southeast Asia.

DS

NOTES

1 The painting was restored under the auspices of UNESCO. Pierre Pichard, *The Pagan Newsletter*, 1988. It was discussed in detail by Pratapaditya Pal in "Fragmentary Cloth Painting from Early Pagan." The artists began by priming the surface with gypsum or light clay, followed by drawing the outline in black. Colors included cinnabar, red, yellow ocher, and copper green.

2 This *jataka* is a cautionary tale about the danger of the five senses. The Buddha-to-be, as a prince, traveled with his five brothers for further education to Taxila. On the way, each brother was ensnared by different damsels, each representing one of the five senses. Later, the ladies transformed themselves into ogresses and feasted on all five brothers. Even the king of Taxila was seduced and consumed, leaving the Buddha-to-be to become king. This *jataka* is a favorite in Myanmar today, often painted on thin metal sheets suspended along the corridors of pagodas. This *jataka* was combined with the *Valahassa-jataka* in the *Mulasarvastivada-vinaya* and the *Divyavadana*; see Appleton, *Jataka Stories*, 23.

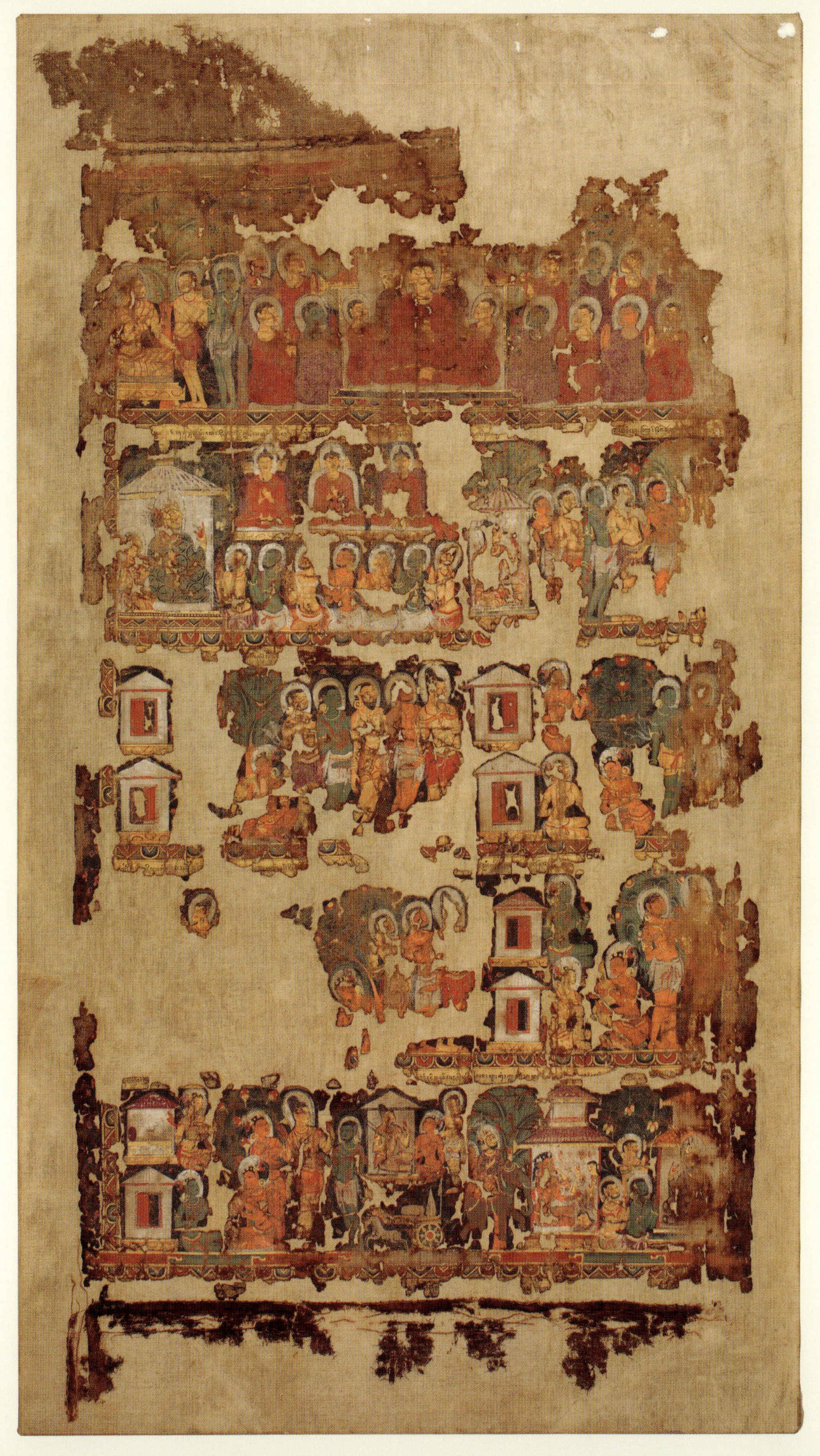

26.

Votive tablet

Pagan period, late 11th or 12th century
Terracotta
H. 7¾ in. (19.68 cm)
Museum of Fine Arts, Boston: Marshall H. Gould Fund, 1976.62

Thousands upon thousands of small terracotta tablets have been recovered at Pagan, or Bagan, often found interred within the brick fabric of stupas and temples. In view of this tile's rich iconography, its royal inscription on the reverse, and its size and condition, it is likely the most important surviving tile from the entire Pagan period. A small number of unpublished tiles produced from the same mold are known to be at Pagan, but they are fragmentary.

The central seated Buddha, combined with the seven small surrounding scenes, represents the familiar Eight Great Events. The miniscule dancing monkey, a reference to the episode of the monkey offering the Buddha honey, exhibits a remarkable degree of detail and intricacy.

Figures arranged along the base are devoted to the seven weeks that the Buddha resided at Bodh Gaya, beginning with his enlightenment during the first week. The events are not depicted in chronological order but are paired. From right to left: the shielding of the Buddha by the snake-king Mucalinda (sixth week), gazing at the Bodhi Tree without blinking (second week), defeating Mara's daughters (fifth week), obtaining enlightenment (first week), residing in a jeweled house (fourth week), walking east and west on a promenade (third week), and the gifting of hairs to two merchants (seventh week).

An inscription in Myanmar on the tile's reverse, incised by hand, states that the image was made by the son-in-law of King Kyanzittha (ca. 1084–ca. 1112) in order to gain deliverance. The inscription along the bottom edge contains the so-called "Buddhist Creed" ("*ye dhamma hetu . . .*") in Pali, in Mon-Myanmar script, and is followed by a repetition of the donor's name and his wish for deliverance.[1]

DS

NOTE

1 A translation, provided by U Tun Aung Chain, reads, "The beloved son-in-law of Shri Tribhuvanadityadhammaraja [Kyanzittha] named Trelokasinghavijeya [Tilokasinhavijaya: Pali] made this image of the Buddha to gain deliverance."

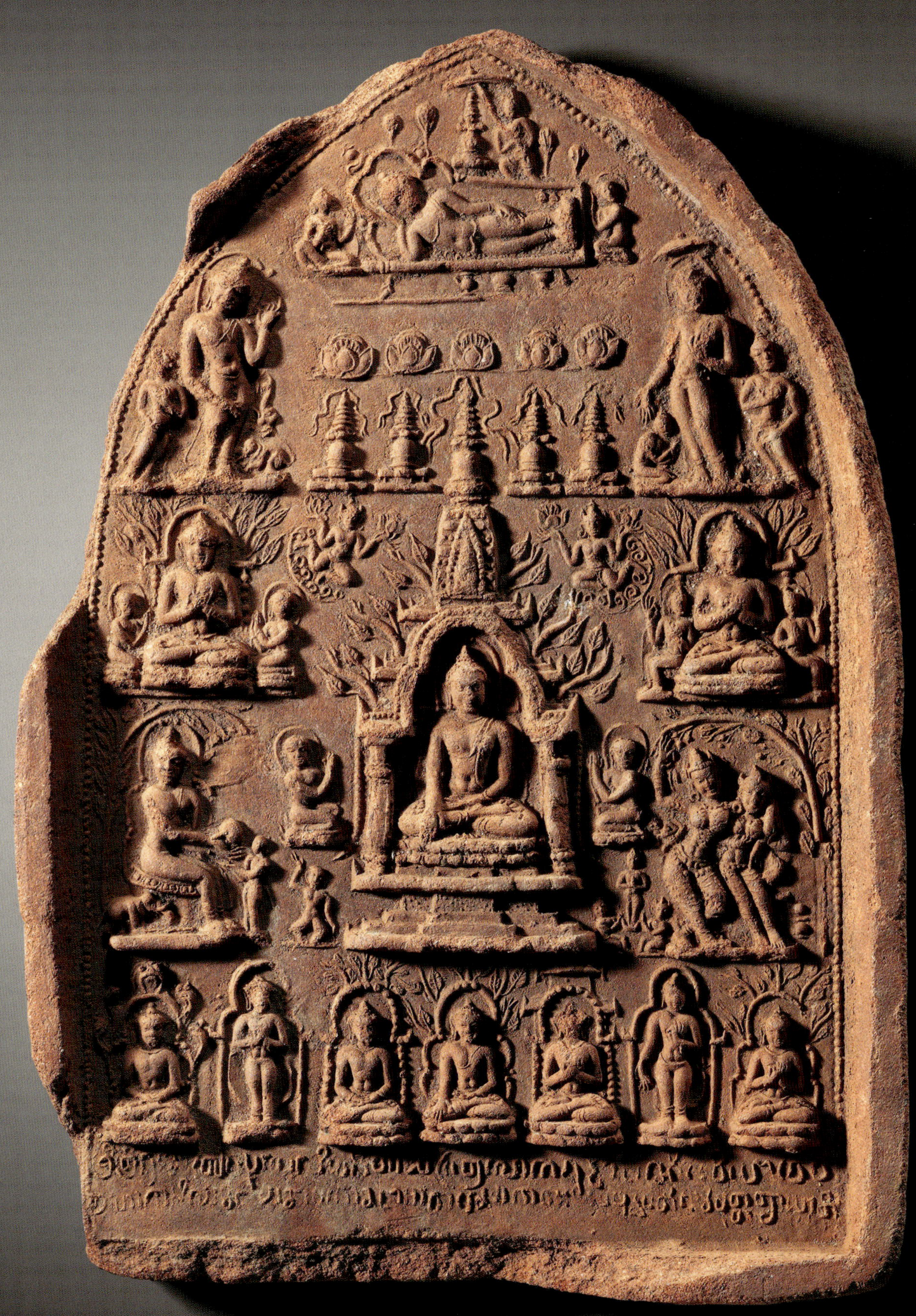

27.

Mold for votive tablets

Pre-Pagan or Pagan period
Metal
H. 3½ x W. 2⁵⁄₁₆ x D. 2 in. (8.9 x 5.9 x 5 cm)
National Museum, Yangon

This simple mold for creating clay tablets with images of the Buddha likely dates to the first millennium. The tradition of using metal molds for this purpose began in South Asia and was transmitted from there to Myanmar, where the practice continues to this day.

AP

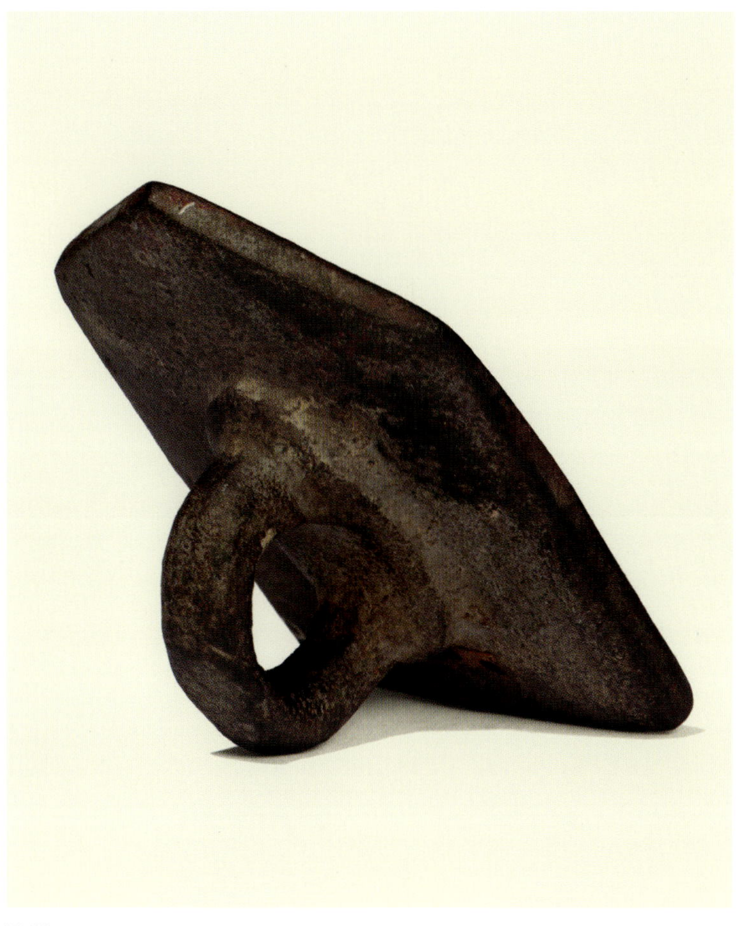
BACK

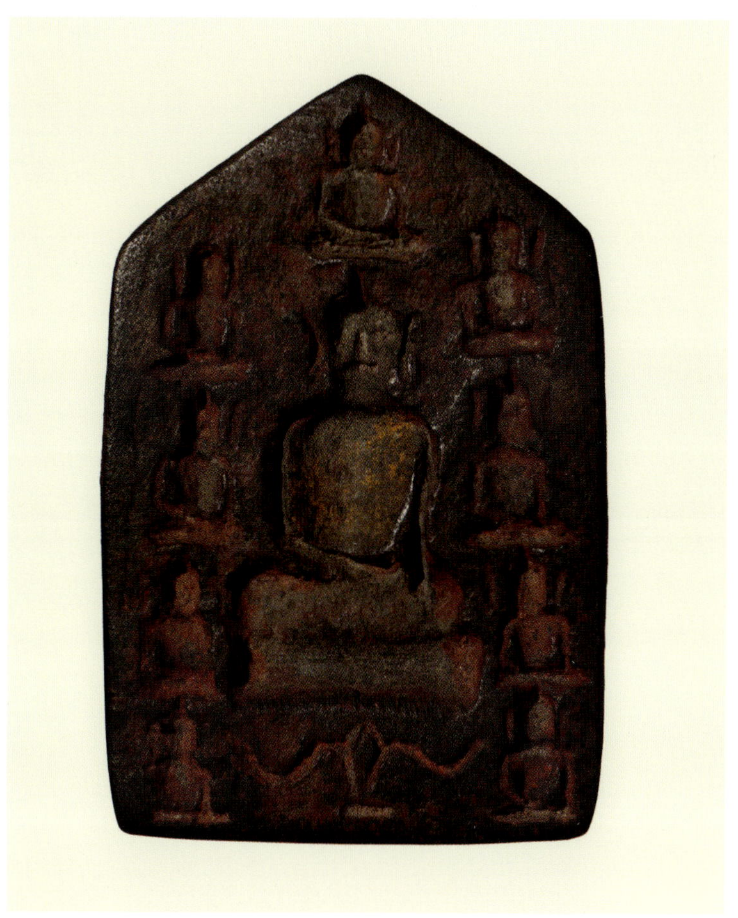
FRONT

28.

Buddha Calling the Earth to Witness

Ca. 12th–13th century
Pyrophyllite
H. 6½ x W. 4⅛ x D. 1⅝ in. (16.5 x 10.4 x 4.1 cm)
Ackland Art Museum, University of North Carolina at Chapel Hill: Ackland Fund, 97.14.1

This remarkable plaque features a seated Buddha surrounded by two vertical rows of small figures, the outer one dedicated to the Eight Great Events and the inner row representing a special seven-week period that the Buddha spent at Bodh Gaya. Similar small sculptures, numbering at least two dozen, have been noted in widely separated parts of Asia.[1] Few are tied to excavations, and therefore their find spots, original context, and function are as yet unknown. Some are four inches in height, while others are nearly twice as large. Some are crudely executed, while others bespeak the dexterity of an ivory carver. None have dated inscriptions, but they likely were created between the eleventh and thirteenth centuries, based on their style. Two basic categories are distinguished: one class has only the Eight Great Events, while the other, to which this example belongs, is supplemented with the Seven Weeks. Many variations within these two categories have been noted. For example, on this carving an episode of two youths tormenting the emaciated Buddha by thrusting spikes in his ears is seen in the lower left, a rare theme at Pagan, or Bagan, but known in Pala manuscripts and hanging cloth scrolls from Nepal and Tibet.

Many of the finest examples have come from Pagan, which has suggested to some that Pagan is the source for all these related objects. Whether the plaques were crafted in Myanmar, or in India, or in both countries, is a subject of lively debate. The stone type provides little help in localizing the tradition, since this soft, yellow-beige stone is found widely in nature. However, an excavated example at Sarnath may provide pivotal evidence to suggest that most of the objects, if not all, were produced in India.[2] Moreover, in certain examples found outside of Myanmar, the reverse side is inscribed with Tibetan characters, suggesting that they were acquired by Tibetan pilgrims who were more likely to have visited India than Myanmar.[3] In Myanmar, the greatest number were located at Pagan, although two were found in Rakhine and one near Mandalay.

DS

NOTES

1 Bautze-Picron, "Between India and Burma," 37–52.

2 This Sarnath example is fragmentary but includes images depicting the Seven Weeks, a theme unknown in Pala art but popular at Pagan. If this was created in Pagan, then it makes little sense for a pilgrim from Myanmar to convey it to India; hence it was probably made in India for pilgrims from Myanmar; see Oertel, "Excavations at Sarnath," 84, fig. 8. In addition, objects sculpted in this type of stone feature a number of Hindu and Mahayana deities, subjects that are associated with North India and not Myanmar. See also Woodward, "The Indian Roots of the 'Burmese' Life-of-the-Buddha Plaques." I wish to thank Forrest McGill for sharing his insights on the origins of these objects.

3 Many of the examples with Tibetan inscriptions are noted in Bautze-Picron, "Between India and Burma."

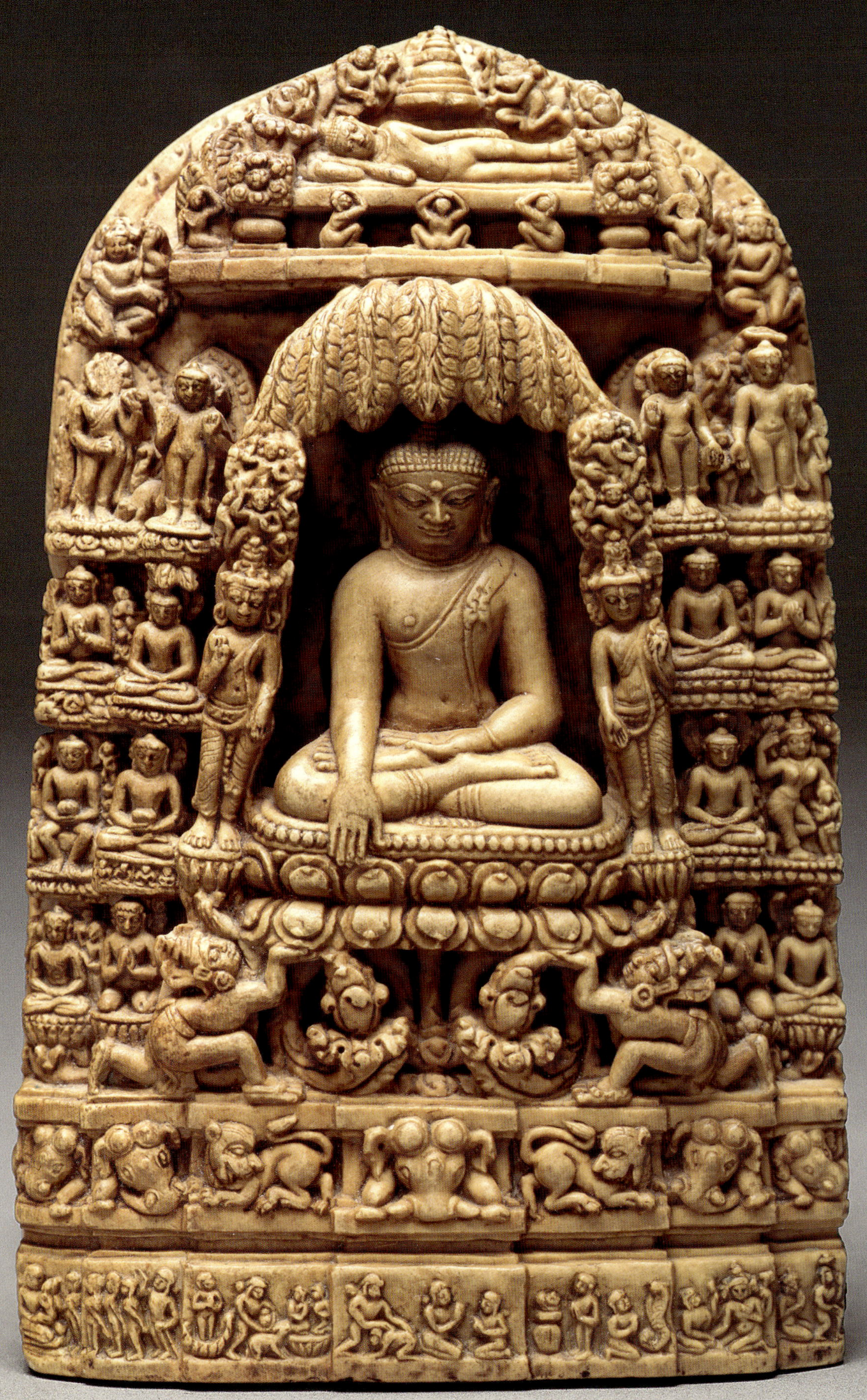

29.

Mara's daughters

From Shwegugyi Temple complex, Ajapala Shrine, Pegu
Ca. 1479
Glazed terracotta
H. 17½ x W. 13 x D. 3 in. (44 x 33 x 7.6 cm)
© Asian Art Museum, Museum purchase, B86P14

30.

Mara's daughter

From Shwegugyi Temple complex, Ajapala Shrine, Pegu
Ca. 1479
Glazed terracotta
H. 18 x W. 13 x D. 4 in. (45.7 x 33 x 10.2 cm)
National Museum, Nay Pyi Taw

After Mara's minions were defeated at the end of the Buddha's first week of meditation at Bodh Gaya, the demon's three daughters advanced coquettishly toward the Buddha during his fifth week at Bodh Gaya. Allegorically representing Desire, Aversion, and Lust, the daughters, as early Pali texts recount, cleverly reasoned that men's tastes varied, with some "attracted by virgins . . . [and others] . . . by older women."[1] The daughters therefore replicated themselves in six different ways, from young, childless girls to older women. Each form is enumerated in a Mon stone inscription at the temple in Pegu, or Bago, dedicated to the fifth week at Bodh Gaya.

Over 160 tiles with female figures were found in the debris within the vicinity of the Shwegugyi Temple complex and were originally placed within two rows of parallel horizontal niches set into the inner face of the temple compound wall. Like this one, all of the tiles feature two women, facing toward the right, as if in procession, similar to the demons that are also depicted on tiles from this site. Only two known tiles depict a single female facing to the right, one is in this exhibition and the other is in the Kambazathadi Golden Palace Museum (see cat. no. 30). Perhaps these two rare tiles began and closed the series. That the backgrounds are cream colored and not green surely distinguished them from the others.

Many of the Shwegugyi Temple complex tiles bear Mon inscriptions along the top edge, each referring to one of the six categories found in the nearby stone inscription.[2] The background is green, with figures in browns and cream colors. Whether the appearances among these females can be matched with the six categories of females noted in the descriptive captions has yet to be determined. Their poses and penetrating glances are no less alluring today than when they emerged from the kiln in Pegu in the middle of the second millennium.

DS

NOTES

1 Jayawickrama, *Story of Gotama Buddha*, 106. This text refers to six forms that the daughters assumed, exactly paralleling the six types found in the fifteenth-century Mon stone inscription and the inscriptions on the tiles. The fifth week takes place in the vicinity of a goatherd's banyan tree, or Ajapala (Pali).

2 The Mon inscription was edited and translated by Blagden, "Mon Inscriptions Nos. IX–XI," 1–16. The inscription's date is missing the last of its three numerals, but it probably was dedicated on the same day and year (1479) as an inscription at the site connected to the sixth week commemorating the snake-king shielding the Buddha. Charles Duroiselle "unearthed over 160" tiles in the compound of this shrine in 1914; see *Archaeological Survey of India 1914–1915*, pt. 1: 23, pl. XX (a). Today the locations of no more than fifty tiles depicting the daughters of Mara are known. A literal translation of the inscription on our tile ("Mara's daughters assuming the shape of not having a child") has been provided by Christian Bauer. Other inscriptions record daughters with one child or two children.

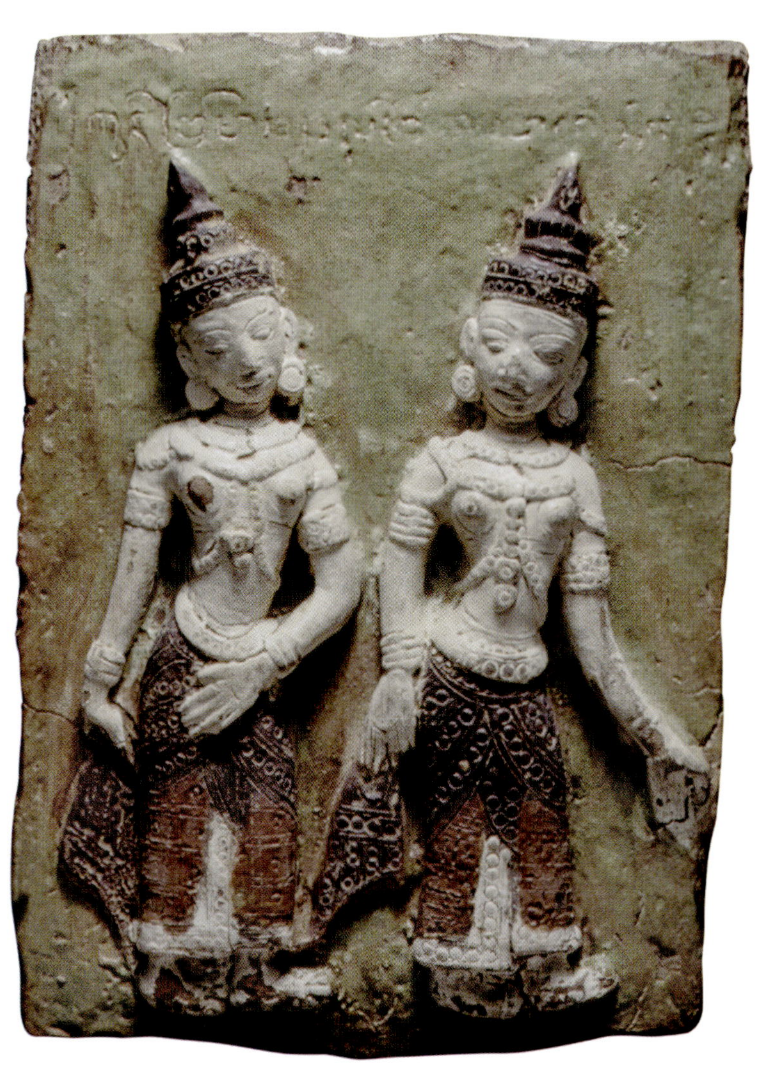

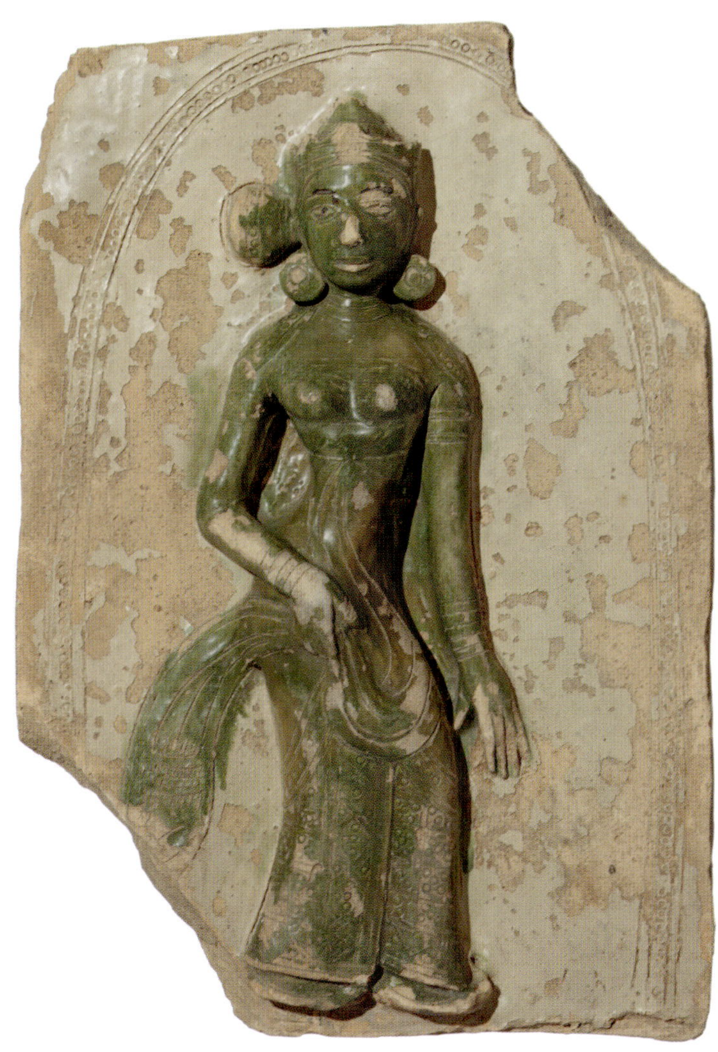

31.

Mara's demons

Shwegugyi Temple, Pegu
Ca. 1479
Glazed earthenware
H. 18½ x W. 13 x D. 4 in. (47 x 33 x 10.2 cm)
National Museum, Nay Pyi Taw

Two beastly brutes enlisted in Mara's army are featured in this tile from Pegu in Lower Myanmar. This was one of two to three hundred demon tiles that were once set into niches on the inner face of a compound wall that encompassed the Shwegugyi Temple, Pegu's replica of the Mahabodhi Temple in India.

The ruling Mon king, Dhammazedi (ca. 1472–ca. 1492), sponsored a huge complex of brick monuments commemorating certain episodes in the Buddha's biography, such as the Buddha receiving washing stones from the god Indra. The centerpiece was a group of monuments dedicated to the special seven-week period that the Buddha spent at Bodh Gaya at the time of the enlightenment, with the Mahabodhi Temple placed in the center. Most of the brick shrines are now in ruins, while a few have been rebuilt in modern times.[1]

The demons are shown paired, advancing toward the right, usually with weapons drawn. Some tiles bear short Mon captions incised along the upper edge that describe the nature of their weaponry. A smaller number of tiles show the demons in retreat. These two types of tiles were placed within two parallel, horizontal rows of niches, but old descriptions make it unclear if there was a special order in their placement. The palette for the figures is restricted to mainly brown and green, juxtaposed against a buff-colored surface.[2]

DS

NOTES

1 Stadtner, "King Dhammaceti's Pegu" and "Fifteenth-Century Royal Monument in Burma." No more than a hundred tiles from this site can be traced today in Myanmar and abroad.

2 In the late 1980s, a second set of demons from the same period came onto the international art market; these probably surrounded a large, damaged reclining brick Buddha located near Pegu's famous recumbent Buddha known as the Shwethalyaung. Yamamura Michio, *Nazo no seramikku roodo ten*. A handful of tiles that were not smuggled to Thailand and abroad are displayed next to the newly rebuilt recumbent Buddha.

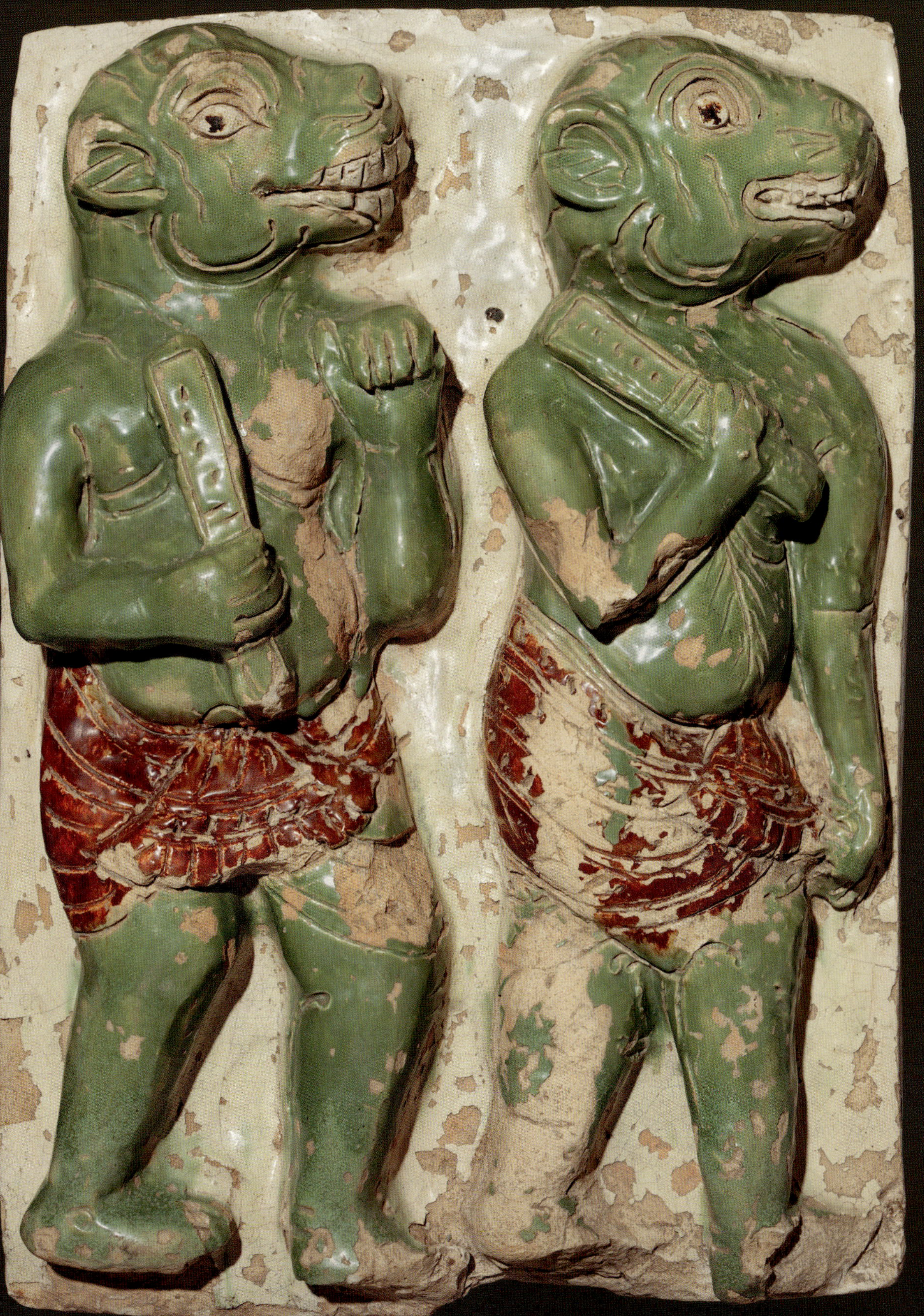

32.

Buddha

Rakhine
Ca. 16th–17th century
Silver-plated bronze
H. 3½ x W. 2⅜ in. (9 x 6 cm)
National Museum, Nay Pyi Taw

This diminutive Buddha sits with his legs folded and with his hands in the meditation gesture, or *dhyana mudra* (Sanskrit). Bronze buddhas of this size or larger are usually placed on a metal altar framed by an ornamented arch with *makara* crowning the twin pillars supporting the arch.

This bronze reflects a period of Rakhine art that reveals a strong debt to Sri Lanka, underpinned by both commercial and religious ties, particularly from the close of the sixteenth century and throughout the seventeenth century. Much of the communication between these two coastal communities at this time was in the hands of the Dutch United East India Company (Vereenigde Oostindische Compagnie, or V.O.C.), whose ships transported not only delegations of Rakhine monks to Sri Lanka but also Sinhalese Buddha images to Rakhine, as ship manifests have revealed.

Characteristic Sinhalese motifs include the cranial protuberance, or *ushnisha* (Sanskrit), in the form of a tapered flame; the treatment of the robe; and the lotus base. The tuft of hair, or *urna* (Sanskrit), on the forehead is also in a Sri Lankan mode. These characteristics evolved during the Divided Kingdoms Period (1232–1596) in Sri Lanka, which partially overlapped with the Buddhist kingdom of Rakhine (ca. 1404–1784) with its capital in Mrauk-U.

CR

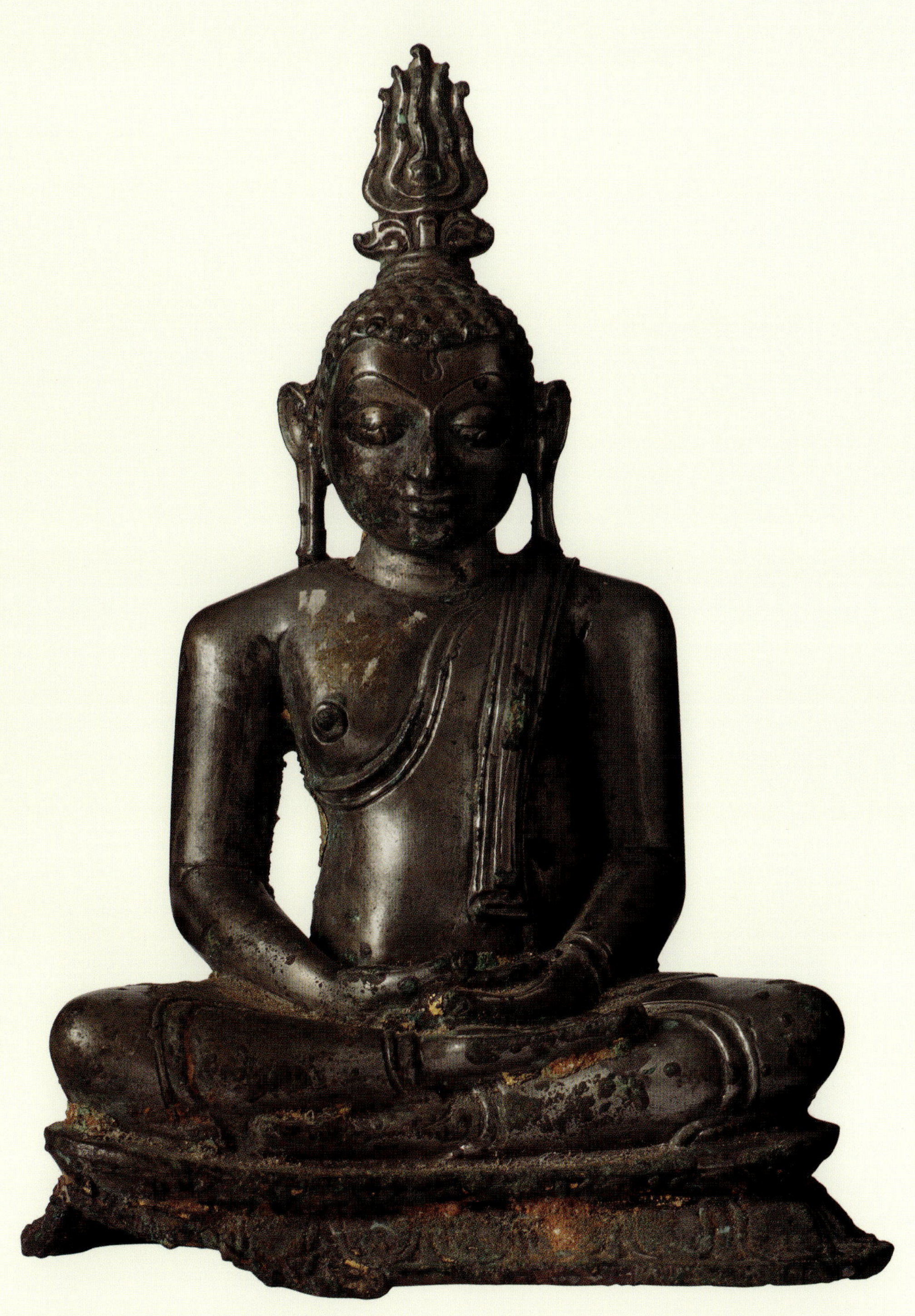

33.
Buddha seated in *bhumisparsa mudra*

Nyaung-yan period, 17th–18th century
Bronze, with silver pigment
H. 21 x W. 13 x D. 7¾ in. (53.3 x 33 x 19.7 cm)
National Museum, Yangon

Cast in bronze and partially covered with silver pigment, this image with its rounded face, shoulder-touching earlobes, narrow band separating the forehead from the hair curls, and lotus bud finial atop a broad low *ushnisha* is typical of the late Ava Dynasty. The simple robe covering the left shoulder is also characteristic. The image is mounted on a high-waisted double lotus throne with prominently molded petals edged with beading. At one time it was flanked by a pair of small separately cast adorants or disciples in *namaskara mudra*, the tangs of which were inserted through the rings toward the base.

This image, like many others discussed in this catalogue, has the right hand in the "earth-touching" *bhumisparsa* position—also known as "calling the earth to witness," which represents the moment when the Buddha, seated in meditation under the Bodhi Tree on the eve of enlightenment, is challenged by Mara (the Evil One) to prove that he had given alms. At that point the Buddha touched the ground with his right hand, asking the earth to bear witness to his good deeds in previous existences. In response the earth quaked, causing Mara and his hosts to flee.[1] This *mudra* may also be referred to as *maravijaya*, meaning "victory over Mara."

SFL

NOTE

1 This version of the attainment of enlightenment is from Indian sources and differs in details from popular Southeast Asian versions. Here the Earth Goddess is not mentioned. See Warren, *Buddhism in Translations*, 80–81. This version is also known in Myanmar.

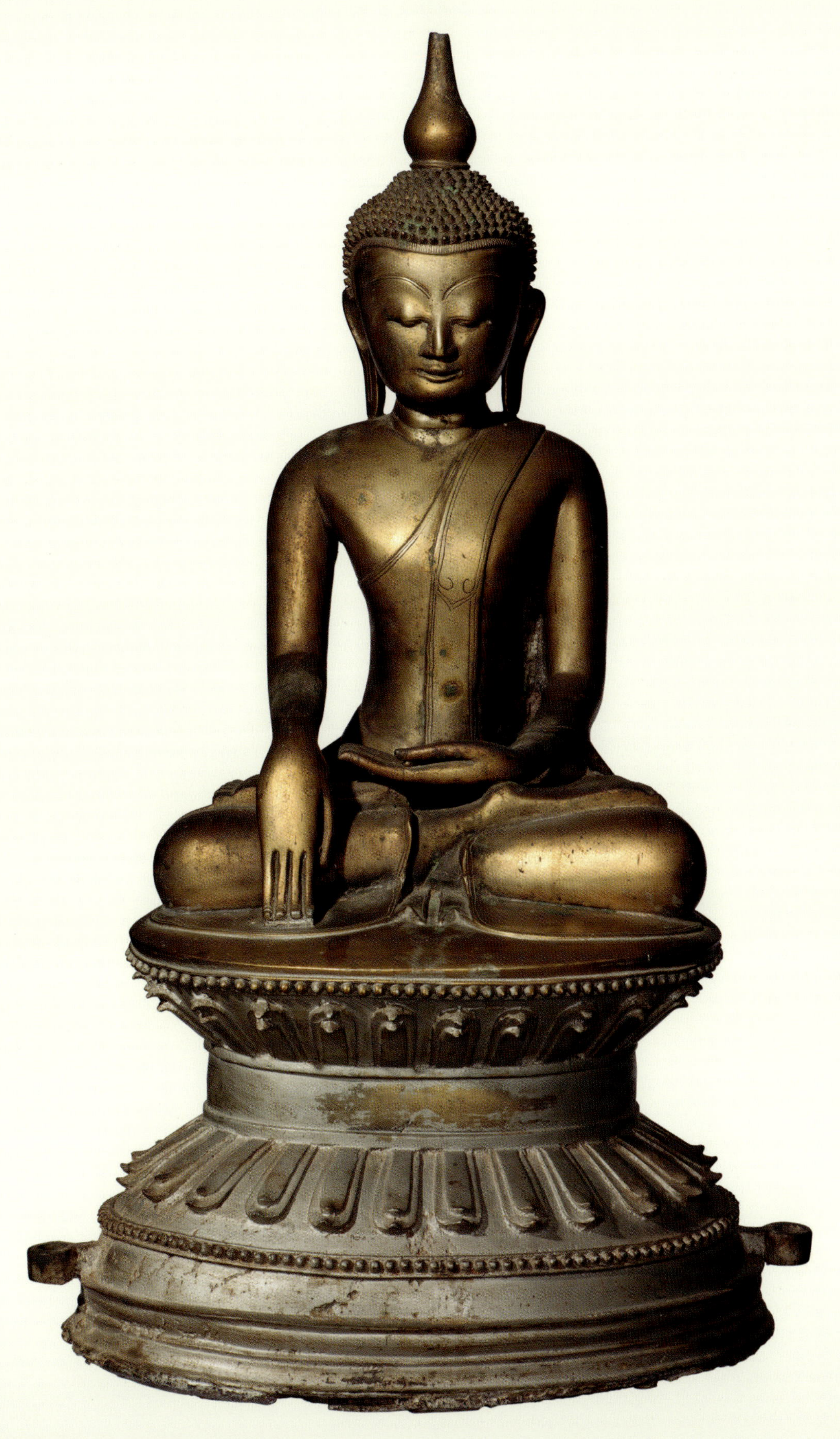

34.

Crowned bejeweled Buddha

Myanmar
Ca. 1600–1700
Copper alloy
H. 12¾ x W. 5½ x D. 3¾ in. (32.4 x 14.0 x 9.5 cm)
© Asian Art Museum: Gift of the Donald W. Perez Family in memory of Margaret and George W. Haldeman, 2010.341

This serene Ava-style kingly image of the Buddha is set upon an hourglass-shaped throne that has been cinched at the center by a clearly defined band of upward- and downward-facing lotus petals. The Buddha is seated in *padmasana*, showing small slablike feet resting on the thighs. The right hand in *bhumisparsa* has fingers of equal length that barely touch the ground. The left hand, showing the presence of a monk's robe at the wrist, lies open at the waist supported from below by a small prop of metal.

The soaring crown is composed of vertical leaflike triangular elements that arise from a beaded band encircling the forehead to enclose an abstract elongation of a former Indian-derived chignon. Tall, graceful, butterfly-wing-like openwork appendages that dwarf the crown extend as far as the shoulders. These developed from the lateral Pala-style ribbons that prior to the Ava period are seen securing headdresses on Buddhas.[1] On this bejeweled example, extended ear lobes support tasseled plug ornaments that cascade to the chest, and between them may be seen an elaborately embellished Indian-style double stringed necklace.

In keeping with many Myanmar images, the figure's verso is quite plain. Apart from the hairline and the outline of a monk's shoulder robe, the torso shows little in the way of modeling and additional decoration. The petals encircling the throne also do not extend all the way around, leaving a space for an inscription if desired by the donor.

SFL

NOTE

1 For some interesting observations on Myanmar crowned images, see Blurton, "Burmese Bronze Sculpture in the British Museum"; also Green and Blurton, *Burma*.

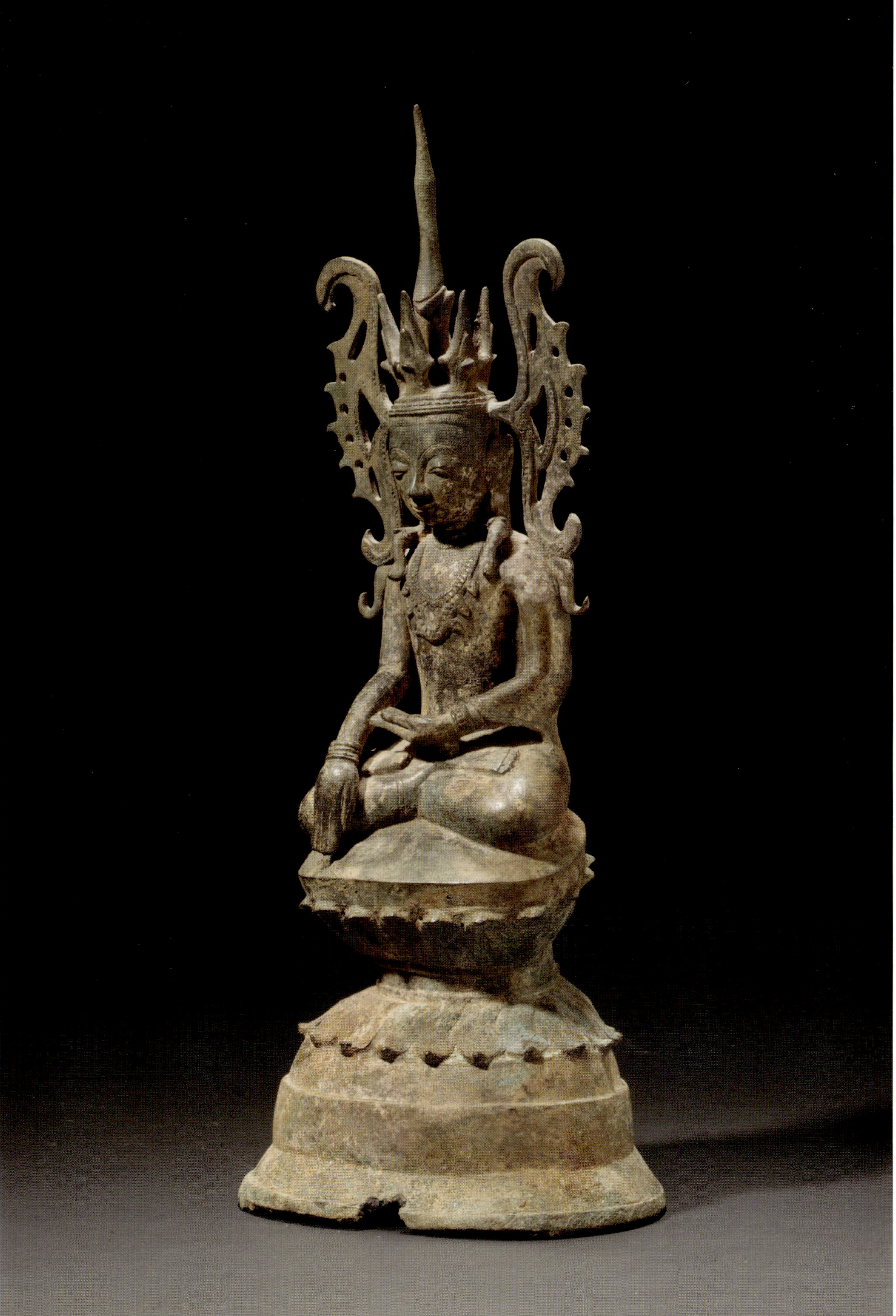

35.

Buddha image

Ava period, dated 1628
Bronze, gold leaf
H. 16 x W. 12½ x D. 9 in. (46.8 x 31.8 x 22.9 cm)
Denison Museum: Gift of William A. Hensley, 1989.25

This simply clad bronze image is inscribed and dated to the early seventeenth century. With its full face, caplike head of curls, crowning bud above the *ushnisha*, ears that fall short of touching the shoulders, and short triple-lined neck set on plump rounded shoulders, along with slablike feet in *padmasana*, and right hand resting on a prop in *bhumisparsa*, this important sculpture clearly demonstrates the changes that took place in the portrayal of the Buddha icon following the fall of Pagan.[1] This image also shares more characteristics common to the stone sculpture of the period rather than with features associated with the more slender bronze images of the late Ava era.[2]

The flaring, waisted throne embellished with lotus petals and beading supports a pair of lateral loops for the placement of a pair of devotees. The two that came with the image probably represent the Buddha's chief disciples Sariputta and Moggallana, but it is doubtful that they are the original pair. Nestled in the corners of the base is a quartet of seated guardian *chinthe* lions. In the front is an unusual squatting figure that appears to be a male earth god wringing out two braids of hair. It has also been suggested that this could be *youkkhazou*, a Myanmar nature spirit rather than an earth god.[3]

SFL

NOTES

1 See Bailey, "Addendum," 79–88.

2 For seventeenth-century marble examples, see Bailey, "Some Seventeenth Century Images from Burma."

3 See F. K. Lehman's comments in Bailey, "Addendum." *Youkkhazou* in Myanmar is regarded as the *nat* spirit guardian of trees and forests. In local legends he is understood to have guarded the Bodhi Tree, under which the Buddha sat while meditating to achieve final enlightenment.

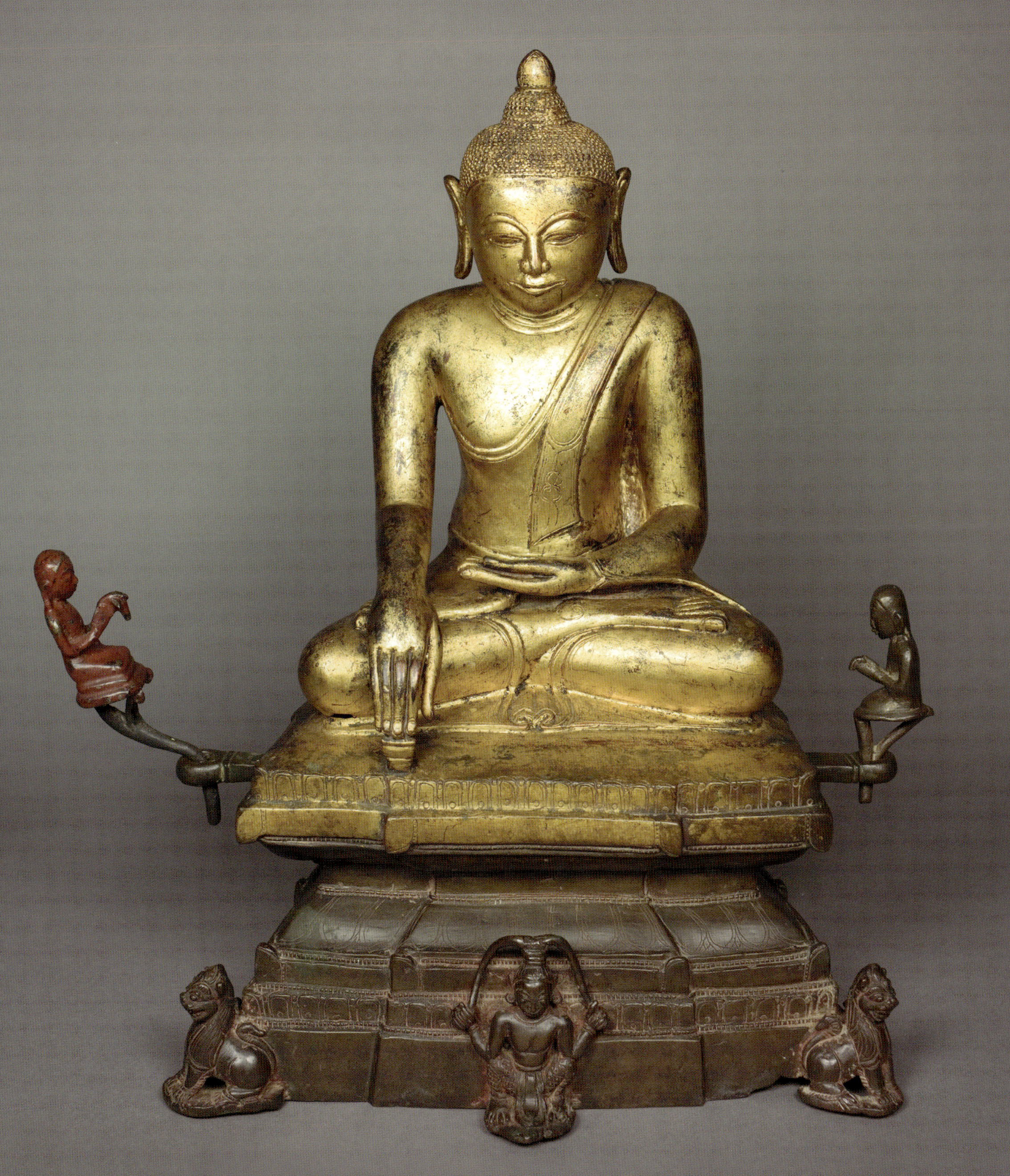

36.

Buddha seated in *bhumisparsa mudra*

From the Kyaung-U Temple, Pagan
Late Ava period, 18th century
Marble with traces of lacquer
H. 33½ x W. 20 x D. 9 in. (85 x 50.8 x 22.9 cm)
Bagan Archaeological Museum

The stylistic qualities of this seated Buddha exemplify those that evolved during the Ava period. The face is oval to square and flattish in contour with little attempt to show the underlying bone structure. Large, curving ears, placed well back from the face, touch the shoulders. Sweeping bowlike brows, set high on the forehead above half-closed eyes, gaze past a long nose terminating in well-defined nostrils above a small, thin-lipped and smiling mouth. A narrow incised band separates the forehead from the hair, formerly completely covered in small black raised lacquer curls. Atop a truncated *ushnisha* rests a lotus bud finial. The figure is seated in *padmasana*, the right hand with fingers of equal length extends over the knee in the *bhumisparsa mudra*. The left hand rests in the lap, supported by a small plug of stone left uncut below the wrist. A further prop of stone separates the thumb from the fingers. The right shoulder is bare, and clothing has been emphasized by incised double lines and the remains of red lacquer. Incising also indicates the presence of a flap of cloth over the left shoulder that extends to the waist. The simple throne has been finished with a band of lotus petals.[1]

SFL

NOTE

1 For a description of some seventeenth-century Myanmar marble images, see Bailey, "Some Seventeenth Century Images from Burma," 219–27.

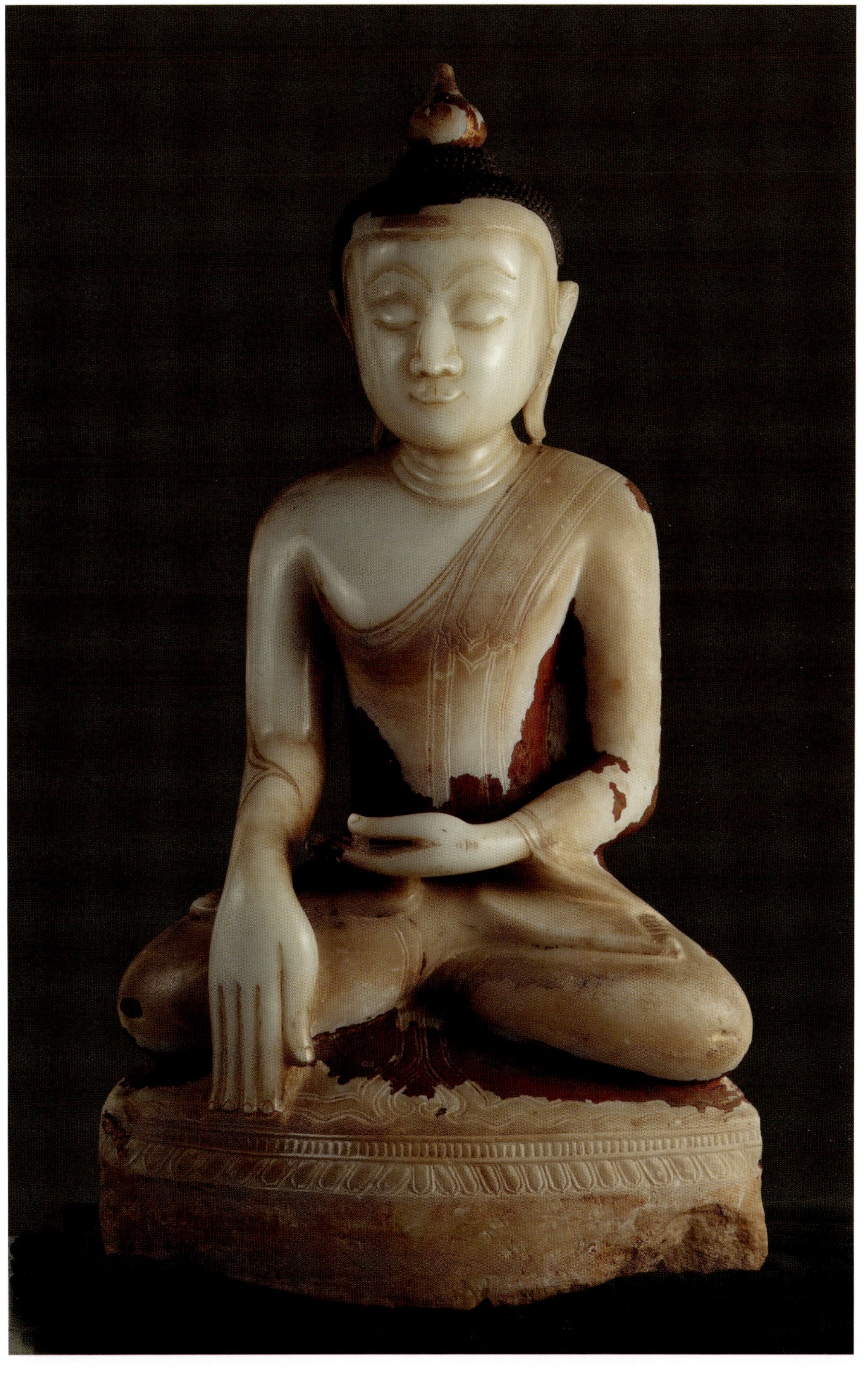

37.

Buddha seated on three elephants (*gajasana*)

18th century
Wood, traces of lacquer and gilt
H. 38 x W. 20 x D. 19 in. (96.5 x 50.8 x 48.3 cm)
Kaba Aye Buddhist Art Museum, Yangon, 71-1421

This serene Buddha image is seated in *padmasana* with the left hand resting at the waist and right hand extending over knee in the *bhumisparsa mudra*. The erectly held head, framed by large curved ears and tall *ushnisha* surmounted by a lotus-bud-shaped finial, has the sharply chiseled features and downcast eyes associated with late Ava-period images. The figure is seated on a scalloped lotus leaf that rests on a magnificent throne formed by the broad shoulders of a trio of caparisoned elephants (*gajasana*).

Elephant imagery appears in Myanmar in both foreign and local contexts. In Indian literature elephants have been associated with rain, abundance, fertility, boldness, strength, and sagacity. A triple-headed elephant (Airavata) is the mount of the Hindu god Indra, a god co-opted by Buddhism to become Sakka the chief deity of the Tavatimsa Heaven. A number of *jataka* stories feature elephants in major roles.[1] The Buddha entered his mother's womb in the form of an elephant. In South and Southeast Asia elephants have traditionally served as the mounts of kings, and the possession of numerous elephants is one of the prerequisites of a universal monarch. White elephants are considered sacred and are regarded as emblems of power and prosperity by Buddhist monarchs, and in Myanmar in particular the desire to acquire a rival's white elephants historically has been a factor in a king's decision to go to war.[2]

SFL

NOTES

1 Examples include the *Chaddanta Jataka* (no. 514), *Dalhadhamma Jataka* (no. 409), *Somadatta Jataka* (no. 410), *Matti Posaka Jataka* (no. 455); see Cowell, Chalmers, Rouse, Francis, Alexander, and Freer, *Jātaka*, vols. 3–4.
2 In some chronicles and legends of Myanmar history, Anawrahta of Pagan desired the king of Thaton's white elephants. During the Ava period, monarchs in Myanmar were known to be envious of the Thai kings' white elephants and were keen to acquire them as part of the spoils of war.

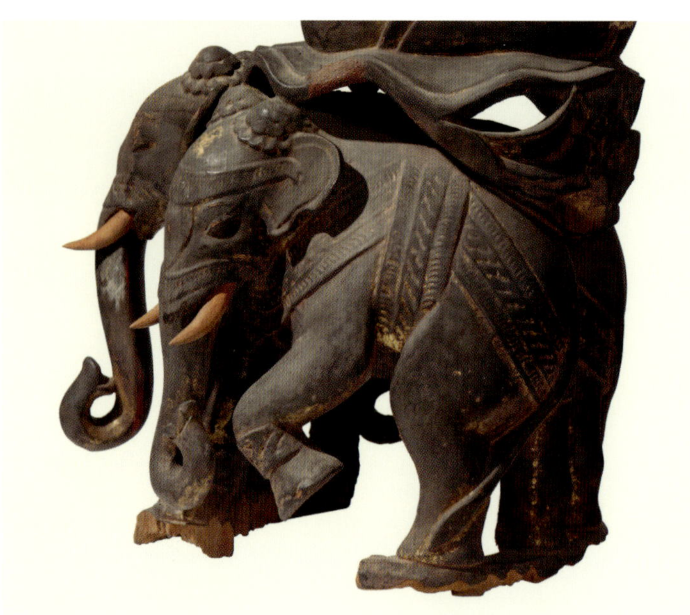

DETAIL OF SIDE VIEW

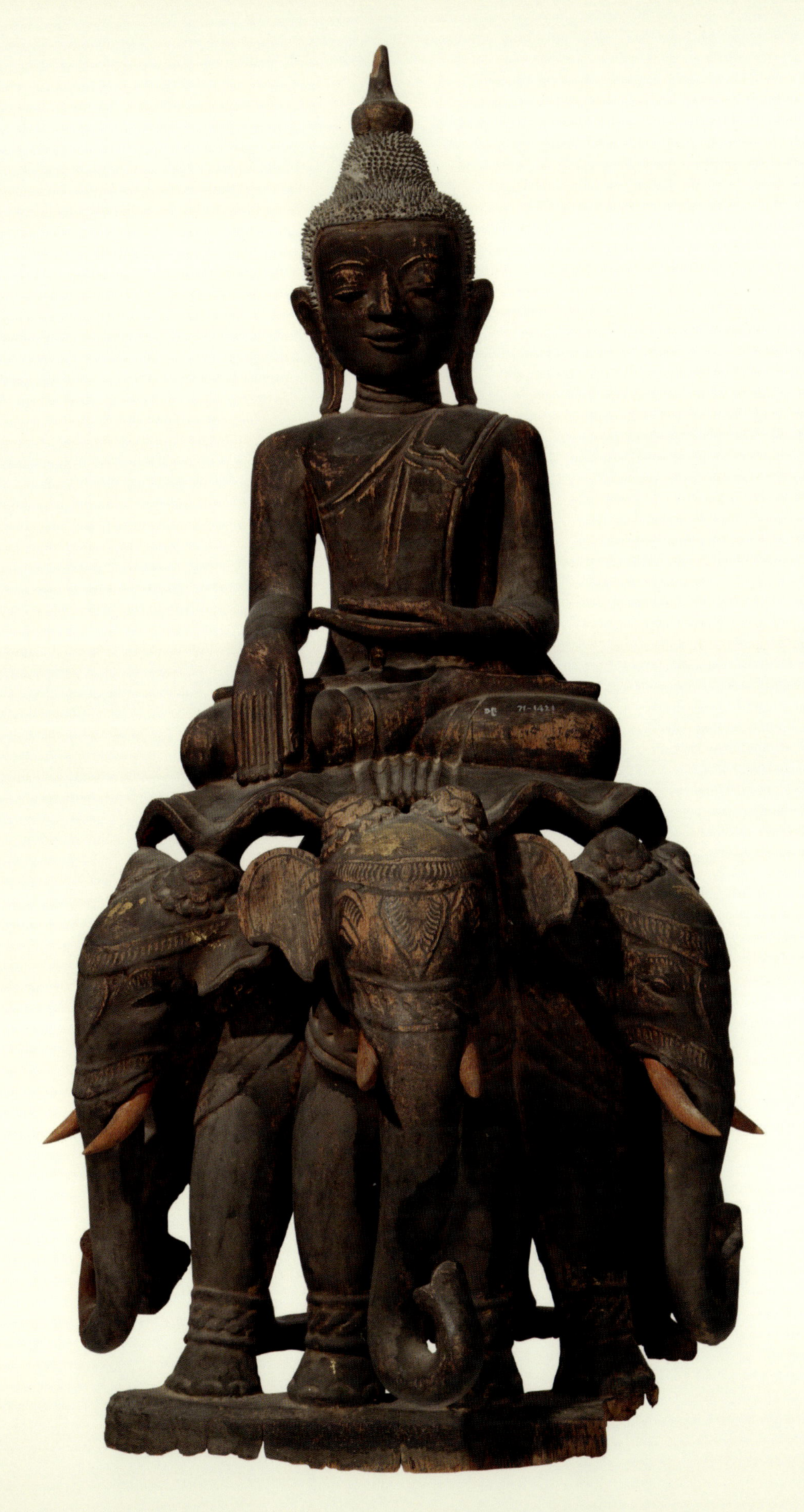

38.

Crowned seated Buddha (*Jambupati*)

Ava period, 18th century
Wood, traces of lacquer and gilt
H. 39 x W. 15 x D. 9 in. (99.1 x 38.1 x 22.9 cm)
Kaba Aye Buddhist Art Museum, Yangon, 71-1387

This provincial example of a crowned image from the Ava, or Inwa, period is notable for its large head that rests on a very short neck. A headband supports a very elaborate headdress that is half the size of the image. The crown, composed of a circlet of foliate triangular blades enclosing a high chignon-like finial, derives from art at Pagan, or Bagan, that was inspired by Indian Pala-period art.[1] In the Ava crowned image, the ribbons, formerly seen flowing from the base of Pala-period crowns, have evolved into huge curving lateral winglike appendages that soar above the central crown and extend downward behind the ears to partially cover the shoulders. Large drooping ear ornaments spring from the lobes to touch the chest, which is also embellished with a long necklace. The Buddha is seated in *padmasana* with the right hand in the *bhumisparsa mudra*. Jewelry also adorns the limbs, while clothing lines are scarcely visible. The image rests on a small, unassuming throne.

This crowned type of image is referred to as *Jambupati* in Southeast Asia after a legend that does not appear to be part of the Indian Pali canon. The story tells of Jambupati, an overly ambitious ruler who intimidated the monarchs of neighboring states until he was humbled and converted by the Buddha, who appeared before him resplendently attired and bejeweled as a powerful universal monarch and world conqueror (*cakkavatti*).

SFL

NOTE

1 See Mya, "Beginnings of Jambhupati Images," an article in Myanmar language on the development of crowned images in Myanmar.

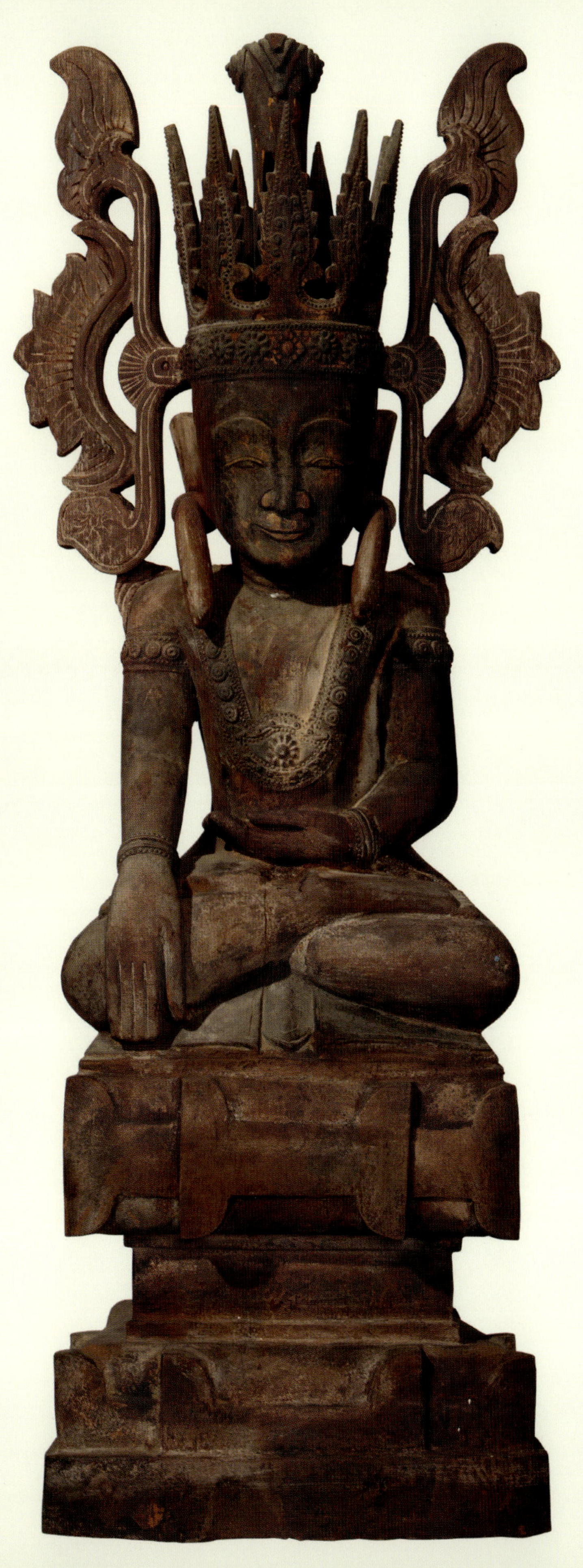

39.

Bodhisatta Lokanatha

Mandalay
Ca. late 18th century
Marble
H. 21½ x W. 13½ x D. 9 in. (54.6 x 34.3 x 22.9 cm)
Los Angeles County Museum of Art: Gift of Louis R. Mosbrooker, AC1995.103.1

Lokanatha, a form of the Mahayanan Avalokiteshvara, the god of compassion and mercy, is the designated guardian of the Buddhist faith and welfare of the world from the time of the *parinibbana* of Gotama Buddha until the appearance of Metteyya, the Buddha of the future. Images of this deity began appearing on votive tablets around the seventh century, but with the waning of northeast Indian influence they seemed to go out of vogue after the Pagan period. During the Ava era, the iconography underwent a change from the Indianized traditions of Pagan, or Bagan.[1] The central portion of the crown, set above a plump face of Ava, or Inwa, style supported by an extremely short neck, bears some resemblance to the miterlike cap of a Konbaung period royal minister, while the remains of lateral ribbons are suggestive of royalty. The ears support drooping *karnapura* floral ornaments. Incised Indian-style necklaces adorn the torso, while bangles and anklets encircle the limbs, and the legs are set in the *lalitasana* pose. The right arm, bent at the elbow, supports a flowering lotus stem resting on the shoulder, while the left hand is resting on the calf rather than with the palm facing outward in the *varada mudra*, the latter being common in Indian images. The upper front portion of an uneven base is incised with lotus petals.

SFL

NOTE

1 For a description of the Avalokiteshvara image in Myanmar, see Nandana Chutiwongs, *Iconography of Avalokiteśvara in Mainland South East Asia*, 95–211; and Lowry, *Burmese Art*, 10. For a description of Avalokiteshvara in India, see Donaldson, *Iconography of the Buddhist Sculpture of Orissa*, 178–214.

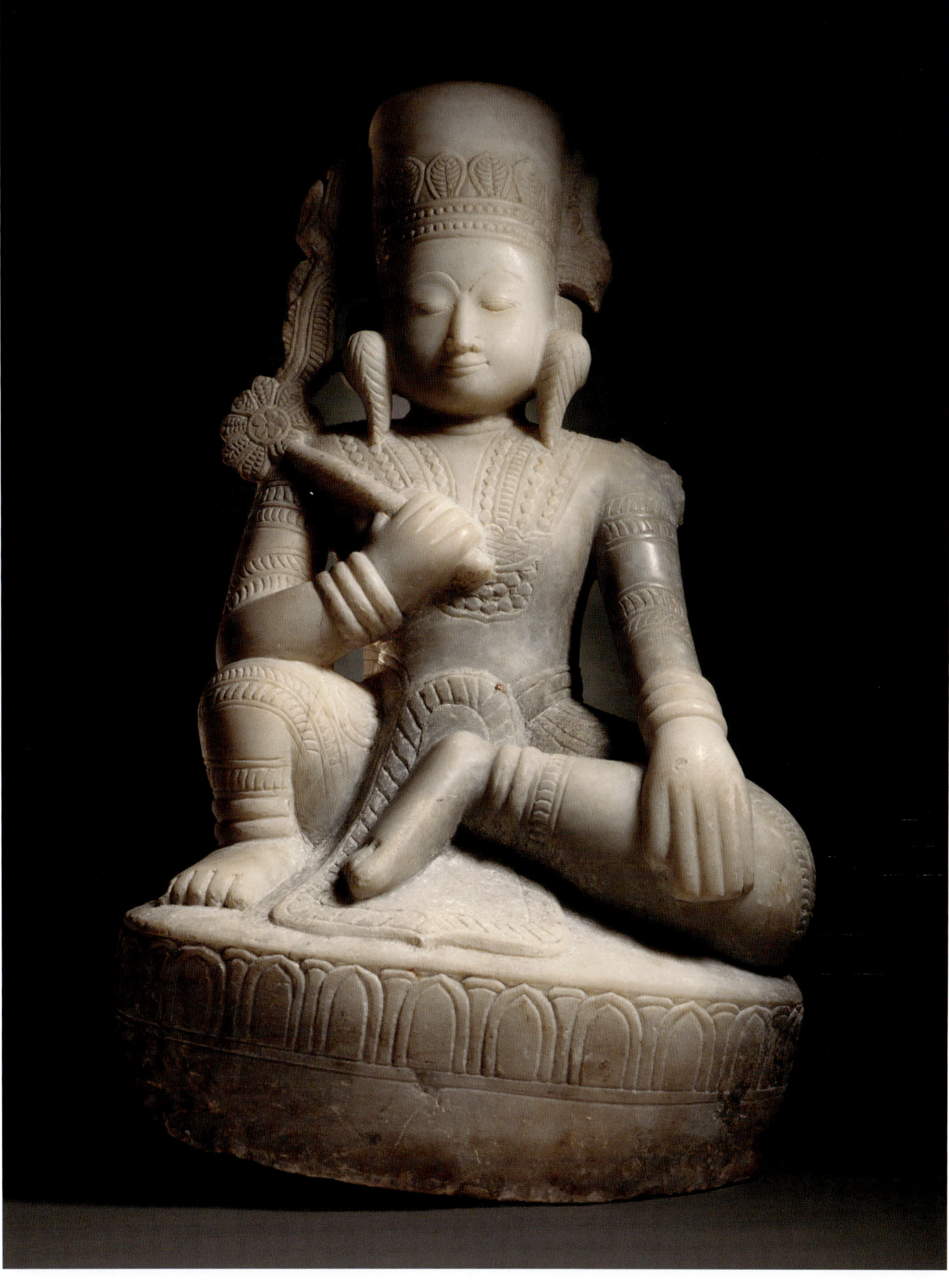

40.

Tile with Mara's soldiers with parrot heads

Mingun Pagoda, Sagaing Region
Ca. 1792
Glazed terracotta
H. 9 x W. 9 x D. 1¾ in. (22.9 x 22.9 x 4.4 cm)
National Museum, Nay Pyi Taw

This tile is one of a series made for Mingun Pagoda. Ground breaking for the pagoda, which is Myanmar's largest brick monument, started on January 9, 1791, and work continued to 1812.[1] The series was modeled on over fifteen hundred glazed plaques at the Ananda Temple in Pagan, or Bagan, from seven hundred years earlier. Drawings of the Ananda tiles were prepared by artists and then evaluated in February 1791 by a learned monk whose criteria for the Mingun series was conformity to the Pali canon. The compositions of a number of Ananda *jataka* tiles were therefore rejected because they drifted too far from Pali orthodoxy, and fresh compositions were prepared for some of the Mingun series. The tile series was finished in the following year by March 25. Captions on the tiles in Myanmar identify the subjects, many categories of which went beyond those of the Ananda Temple.[2]

In addition, the hundreds of demon tiles on the west basement of the Ananda were copied, together with the same number of minor deities on the eastern face. This impressed tile is glazed in white—craftsmen also created brown and green glazed tiles for Mingun—and the frame surrounding the pair of club-wielding soldiers is ornamented with an appliqué of lotus flowers, as is typical of Mingun tiles. Many of the tiles bear numerals beneath the captions that relate to the sequence of tiles at the Ananda or their intended ordinal position at Mingun. This tile is identified in the caption below as, "Mara's soldiers with parrot head and human body." Below that are three numerals. Only the first can be recognized: the number 4. Each of the two recessed terraces has a single row of niches. The size of the niches matches those of the tiles. The tile series was never installed, for unknown reasons. The Mingun tiles provide a rare instance of archaizing in Myanmar art, or the deliberate probing of antiquity to shape the present.

DS

NOTES

1 The Mingun Pagoda's solid brick core conceals at least sixteen relic chambers sunk into the basement terraces and filled with nearly forty thousand objects, including a tooth relic from China. An English mission to Upper Myanmar in 1855 spun a tale that claimed the monument was unfinished, abandoned by its royal patron, Bodawpaya (r. 1782–1819). His failure was added to an elastic myth that painted this king as a debauched, corrupt "Oriental monarch." In fact, the monument may have been considered finished in 1812, but no conclusive evidence has settled the issue. For an overview, see Stadtner, *Sacred Sites of Burma*, 246–59.

2 Stadtner, "'Questions and Answers' of Maungdaung Sayadaw," 97–109. See also Stadtner, "Glazed Tiles at Mingun," 169–85.

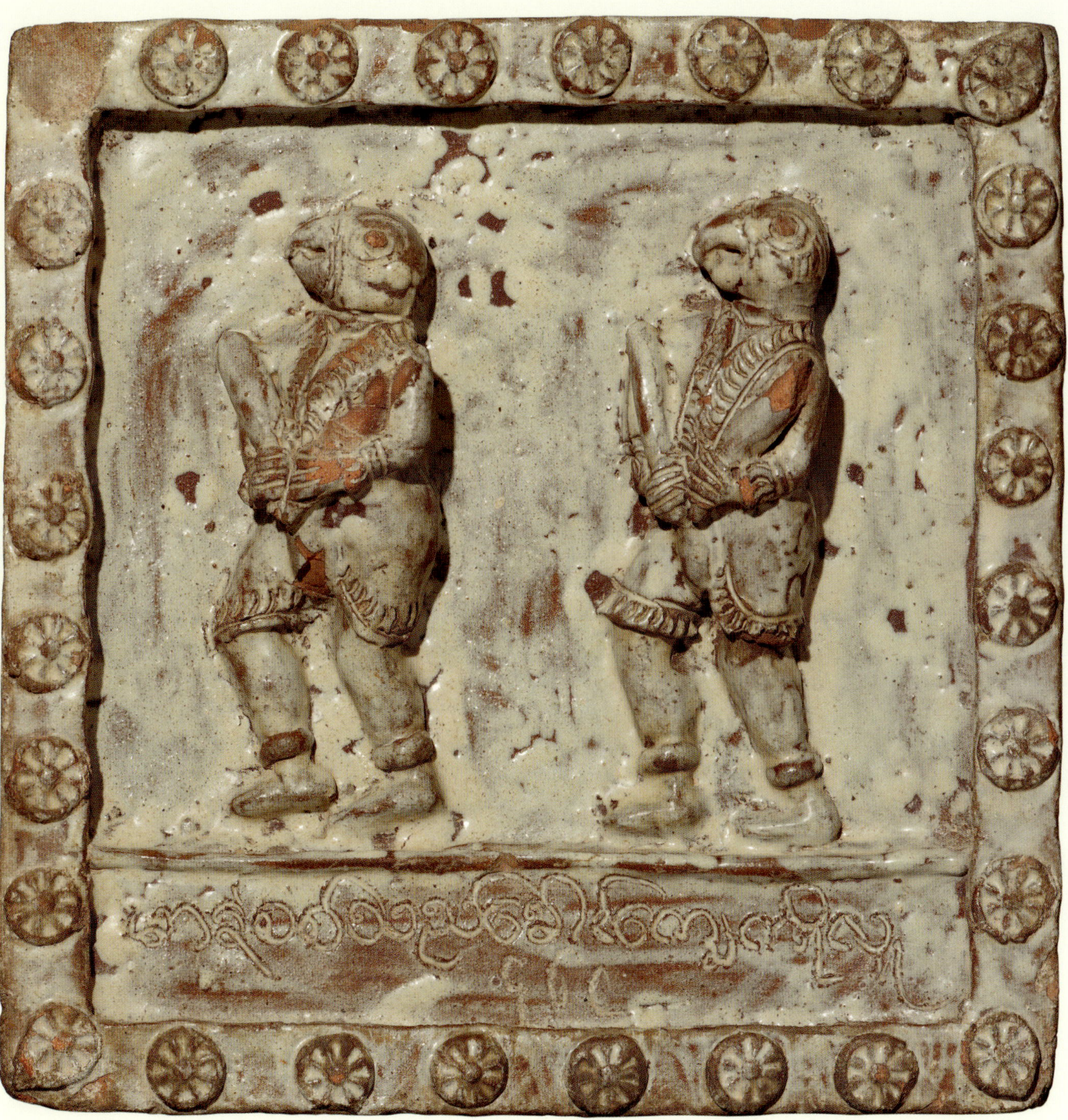

41.

Standing Buddha

Konbaung period, mid- to late 19th century
Wood, lacquer, gold leaf, and glass inlay
H. 48½ in. (123.2 cm)
Denison Museum: Gift of William A. Hensley, 1989.79

Mounted on a simple lotus base, this standing image is in the classic Mandalay style—a more naturalistic mode of portraying the Buddha image's facial features and robes that developed during the late eighteenth century and continues to be the prevalent mode of representation today. Unlike earlier images, such standing figures were not always carved from a single block of wood. The hands and/or flared sides of the lower robe were often carved separately and later dovetailed with joins filled in and lacquered over. The torso of the Buddha is completely enveloped in an elaborately draped capelike outer robe (*uttarasanga*) that terminates around the hemlines in cascades of flaring overlapping folds finished with bands of raised lacquer scrolling inlaid with rosettes in mirror and glass mosaic. The shoulder cloth (*sanghati*) is similarly decorated. Monks in Myanmar wear their robes in this covered mode when going outside the monastery on the morning alms rounds and to other events. The hands are in a variant of the *varada mudra*—a gesture of benevolence. The right hand of the image holds the myrobalan fruit (*Terminalia chebula*), suggestive of the physical and spiritual healing powers of the Buddha.[1]

SFL

NOTE

1 This image has also been described in Green, *Eclectic Collecting*, 201–2. For another excellent example, see Zwalf, *Buddhism*, 163, fig. 232.

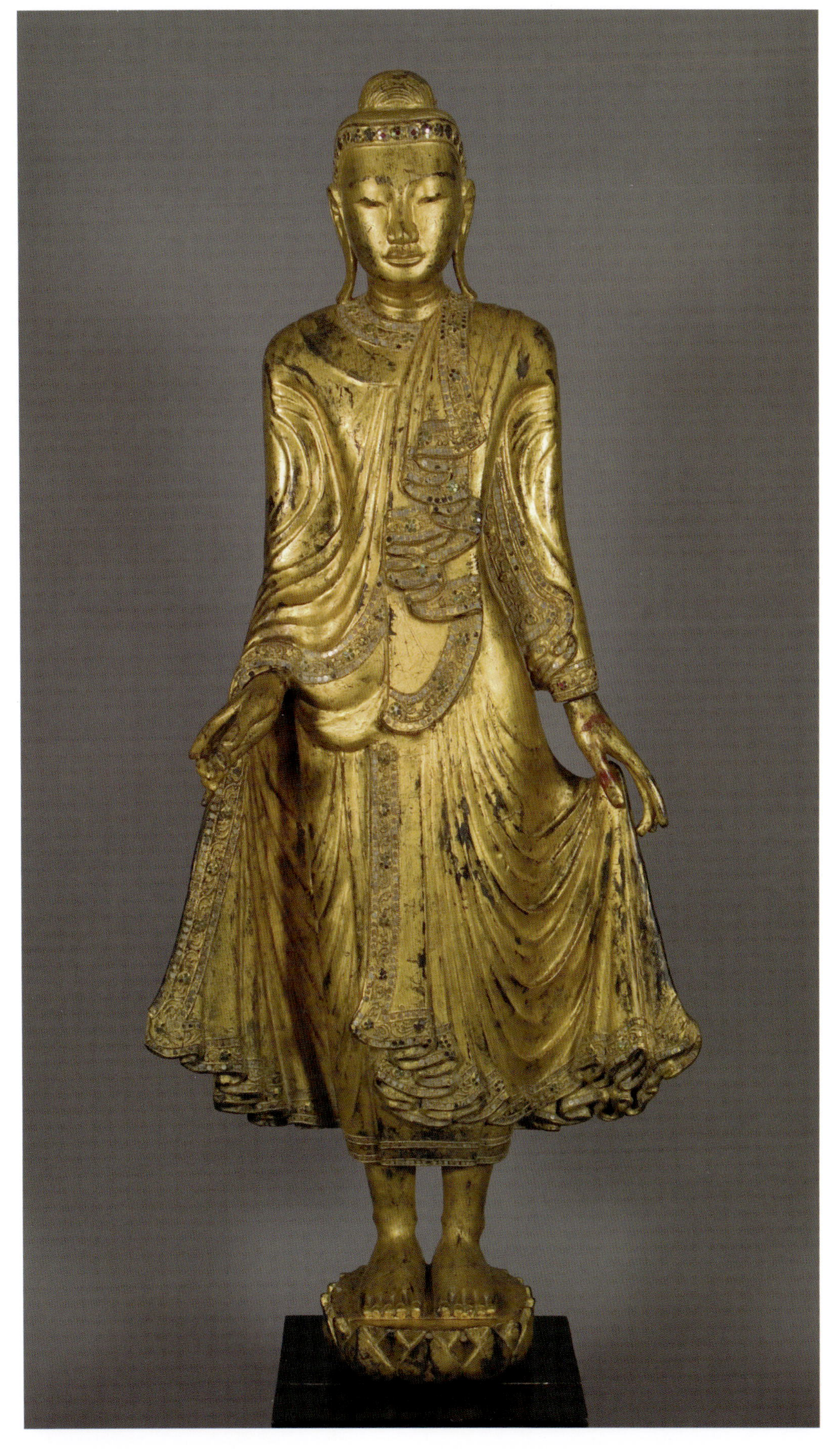

42.

Seated Buddha

Mandalay era, ca. 1860–1900
Copper alloy
H. 18½ x W. 15½ in. (47 x 39.4 cm)

Since the colonial period, the naturalistic style characterized by this image, with its gentle, benign expression, has come to be the quintessential icon for the Buddhist art of Myanmar. The oval face with its naturally arched brows, downward-focused eyes with a slight slant, and long slender nose with flaring nostrils set above a slightly smiling mouth is typical of the Mandalay image. Also characteristic is the head marked by even rows of slightly raised curls surmounted by a thick fleshy *ushnisha*. A plain, undecorated raised band separates the hairline from the face. The earlobes, the right one of which is supported by an extra prop of metal, flare outward to touch gently sloping shoulders. Apart from unusually long thumbs seen here, the hands and the feet (in *padmasana*) show more modeling than is found on Ava images. The right hand, in the *bhumisparsa mudra*, the earth-touching gesture, does not quite touch the ground. In metal Mandalay-era images the left hand resting at the waist was often cast separately and inserted later. The creases and folds of drapery, which flare slightly at the ends, tend to follow the contours of the body. The image is seated on a plain triangular-shaped throne.[1]

SFL

NOTE

1 This image is also referred to in McGill, *Emerald Cities*, 76.

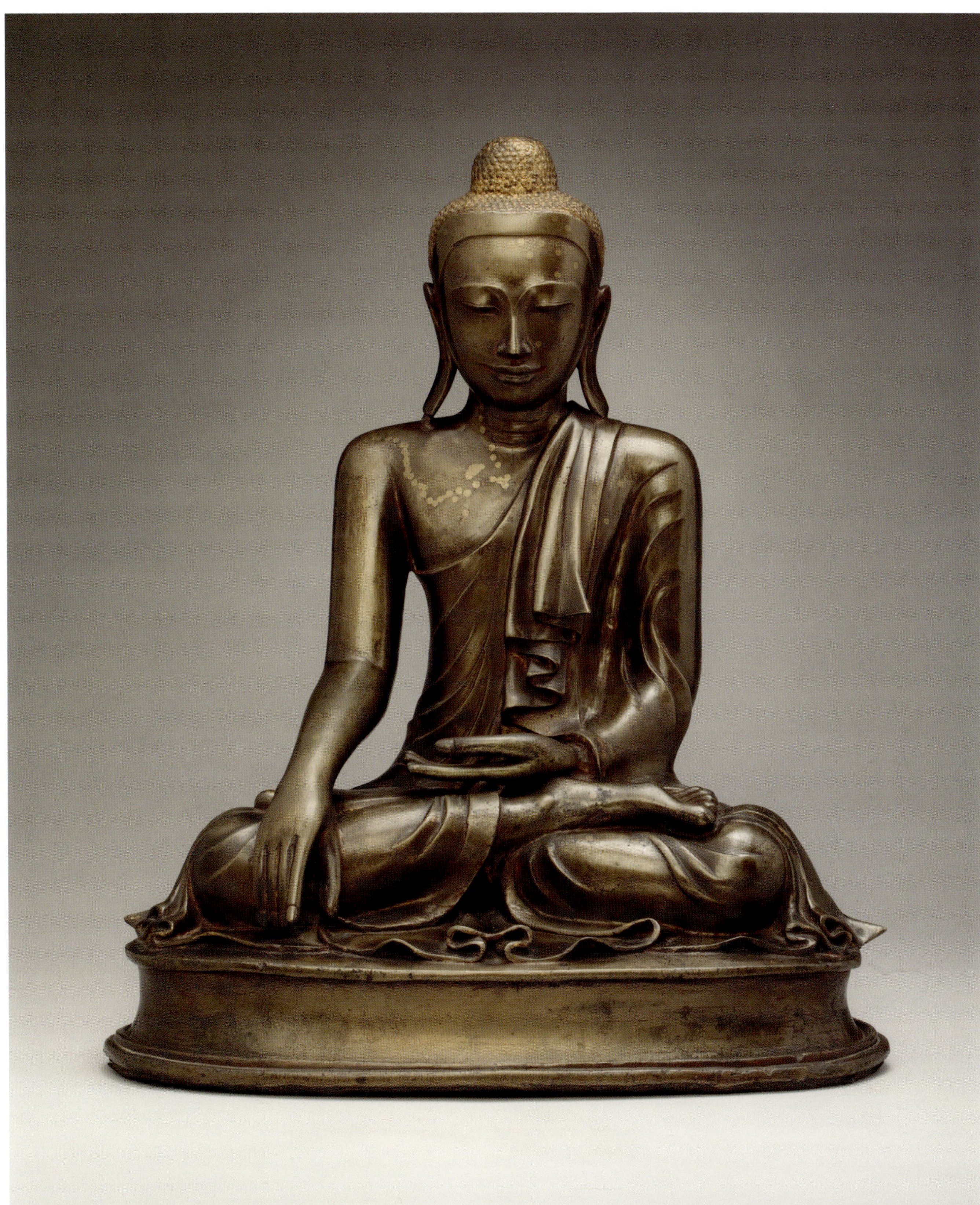

43.

The Great Departure

19th century
Bronze
H. 12 x W. 9½ x D. 4 in. (30.5 x 24.1 x 10.2 cm)
Private Collection

This exceptionally fine narrative bronze tableau has been artfully assembled from separately cast figures. The individual components have tangs that are inserted into a rectangular openwork base to hold them in place. Dressed in Konbaung court costume, they comprise the dramatis personae of the Great Departure, the important scene that captures the Buddha-to-be as Prince Siddhatta, renouncing his privileged existence by escaping from the palace on horseback in the dead of night to become an ascetic in search of the cessation of suffering. To facilitate his escape, a pair of torch-bearing *devas* illuminate the way, while four others support the horse's hooves to muffle the sound. Mara, at the head of the group, accosts the prince in an effort to dissuade him from his course of action.

Narrative bronzes traditionally portray effigies of praying devotees, small images of the previous twenty-eight buddhas, the Dipankara Buddha's prophesy, and seminal events in the life of the present Buddha.[1] The majority of them are small, and in their manufacture show more devotion than skill. They appear to have been largely destined for relic chambers. This example, however, given its large size and excellent workmanship, could have been used for didactic purposes.

SFL

NOTE

1 For excellent photographs of a wide variety of narrative bronzes, see Karow, *Burmese Buddhist Sculpture*, pls. 1–40.

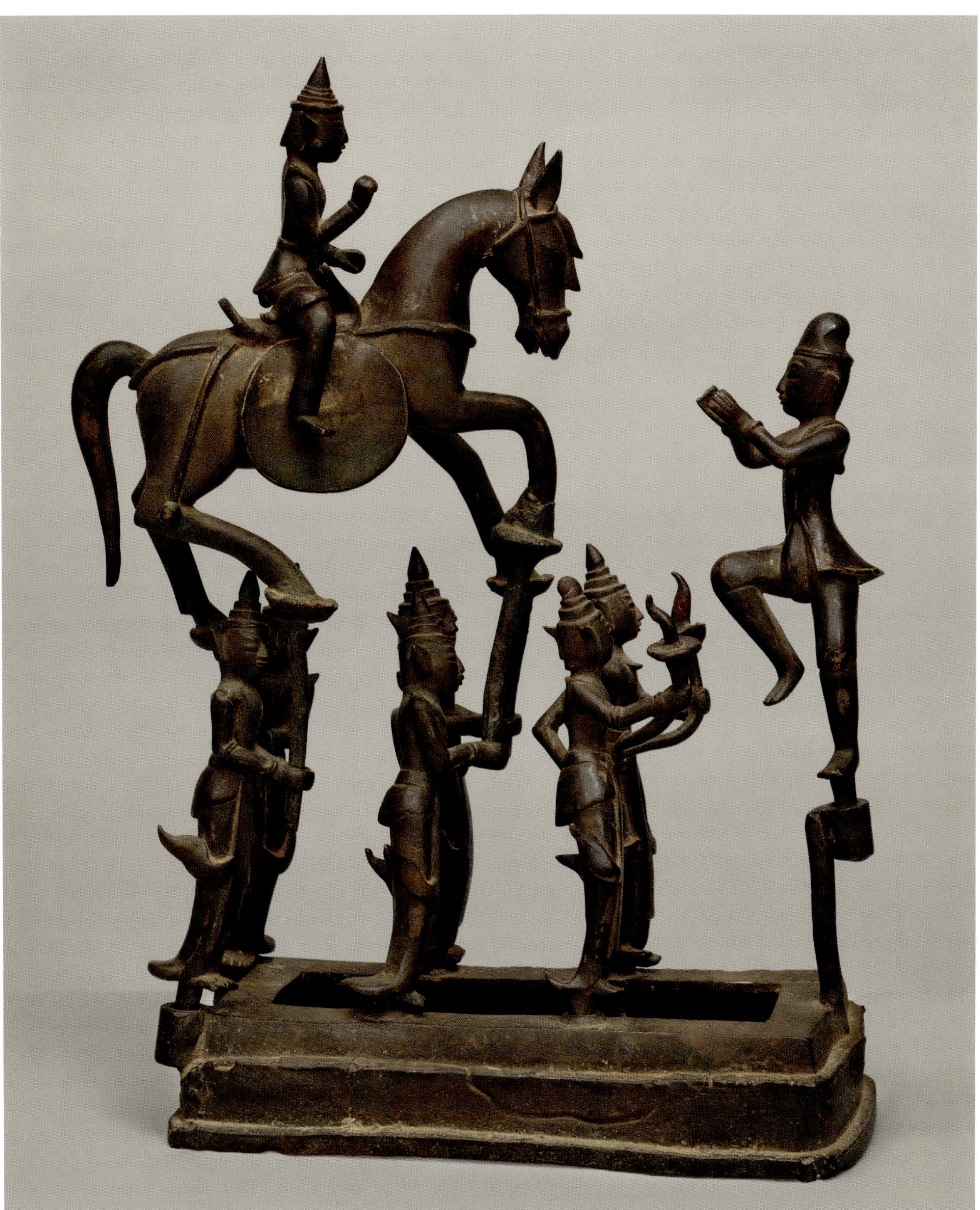

44.

Seated Buddha

19th century
Dry lacquer, traces of gold leaf
H. 30 x W. 21 x D. 17 in. (76.2 x 53.3 x 43.2 cm)
Collection of Ronald L. Krannich

This Buddha image with eyebrows set high on the forehead well above downcast eyes, sharply chiseled nose, and a small slightly puckered mouth displays features typical of Ava-style images. Framing the facial features and neck are ears with very long lobes that touch the shoulders. The head and *ushnisha* are covered with a cap of small spikes of lacquer sometimes referred to as "Shwebo thorns."[1] The usual wooden bud-shaped finial surmounting the *ushnisha* is missing. Outlines of clothing have been indicated by a diagonal line across the chest and a flap over the left shoulder, as well as by small ridges at the wrists and ankles; the feet are locked in the *padmasana* position. The left hand, with very long digits, rests palm upward in the lap. The right hand, with fingers of equal length, is in the *bhumisparsa mudra* touching the upper surface of what remains of the base of the throne, where light outlines of the lower robe can be seen fanning out between the legs.

This example is typical of images made in the dry lacquer medium known as *man-hpaya*. Light and hollow inside, such images were portable. Although easily damaged, they could also be repaired, restored, and refurbished with *thayo* and glass inlay by skilled lacquer artisans.[2]

SFL

NOTES

1 Such spiky *thayo* lacquer decoration resembling thorns was named after Shwebo, the largest town in the district where such images were made.
2 For an excellent article on the subject of dry lacquer images, see Than Tun, "Lacquer Images of the Buddha."

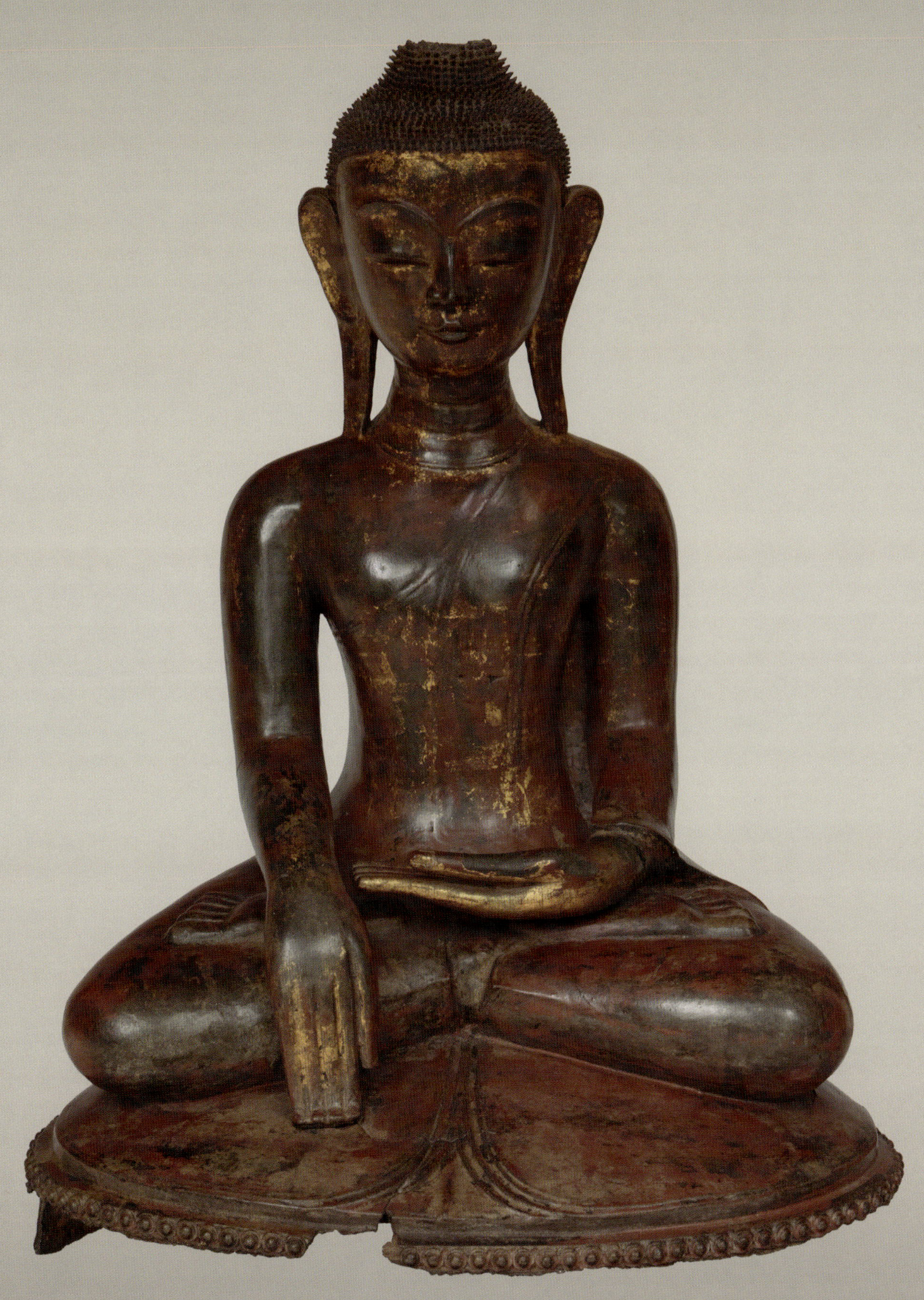

45.
Buddhist shrine

Second half of the 19th century
Wood, metal, lacquer, gold leaf, and mirror glass inlay
H. 106 in. (269.2 cm)
© Asian Art Museum: Gift from Doris Duke Charitable Foundation's Southeast Asian Art Collection, 2006.27.1

45A.
Buddha

Second half of the 19th century
Wood, metal, lacquer, gold leaf, and mirror glass inlay
H. 20 x W. 15 x D. 10 in. (50.8 x 38.1 x 25.4cm)
© Asian Art Museum: Gift from Doris Duke Charitable Foundation's Southeast Asian Art Collection, 2006.27.17

This seated Mandalay-style Buddha image, with the right hand in the *bhumisparsa* (earth-touching) *mudra*, is resplendent in royal Konbaung period (1752–1885) gem-studded raiment, which with its upturned epaulettes, owes much to Thai royal costume. The soaring pagoda-shaped crown with its lateral flanges, long drooping earrings, and *sa-lwe* chest ornament portray the Buddha as a universal monarch (*cakkavattin*).[1]

Designed to set the Buddha image well above the viewer, the gilded wooden throne-like shrine is embellished with glass inlay and shows some similarities to the thrones of the former Konbaung kings. The footed dais supporting the structure is recessed at the corners and finished with a band of upturned, flared decoration that stops a few inches above the floor. Rising from the base is an hourglass-shaped pedestal embellished with horizontal rows of upturned and pendant lappet decoration representing lotus petals. Atop the pedestal rests a throne for the image that is housed within a columned aedicule surmounted by a finely carved pediment similar to those found over Konbaung-period monastic windows and doorways. The foliate carving trails down the sides to terminate in *naga* figures at the base.[2]

Such lavishly embellished thrones housing Buddha images continue to be an important focal point for worship in Buddhist temples and monasteries throughout Myanmar.

SFL

NOTES

1 The original crown, which had disappeared, has been replaced with a replica made by Tampawaddy U Win Maung, a leading traditional craftsman and expert on Myanmar art. It is a gift in memory of M. T. Vadhanathorn Chirapravati. For donation details: http://searchcollection.asianart.org/view/objects/asitem/search$0040/0/title-asc/designation-asc?t:state:flow=c31e9154-b871-4d79-92bb-9aab4d4d775d

2 For photographs of a similar throne, see Lowry, *Burmese Art*; also Isaacs and Blurton, *Visions from the Golden Land*, 127.

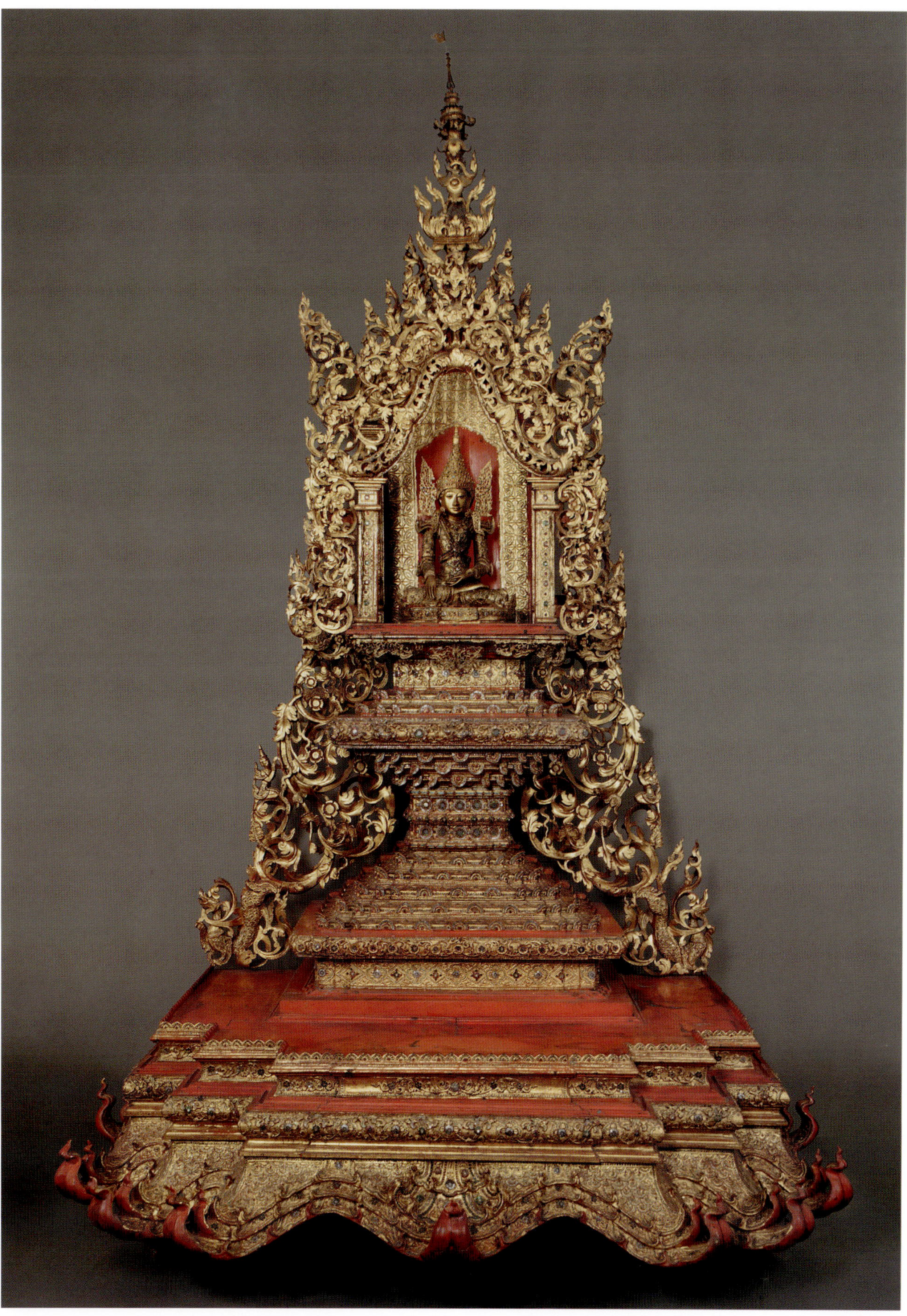

46.
Crowned Buddha

Shan State, Myanmar
Ca. 1895
Wood, dry lacquer, gold leaf, and glass inlay
H. 51½ x W. 39 x D. 21½ in. (130.8 x 99.1 x 54.6 cm)

This image was created with dry lacquer, using a technique originally from China, which became a popular medium for seated images during the eighteenth and nineteenth centuries. Made from an armature or a clay core covered with lacquer-soaked cloth and a putty of lacquer resin and ash (*thayo*), many such images were destined for a Shan clientele who favored an Ava-style image.

This slender Buddha image inscribed in the Khun language of the Kaingtong (Kengtung) area is atypical.[1] The serene attractive face has more in common with the Mandalay style of icon than the Ava image, while the soaring, multitiered crown and bejeweled clothing have been strongly influenced by neighboring Thailand. Apart from a scarcely visible Myanmar *sa-lwe* chest ornament of rank, the closely patterned costume inlaid with slivers of cut glass closely resembles that of the Thai monarchy prior to sartorial changes made by Chulalongkorn (1853–1910).[2] A layered waistcloth reappears from between the feet locked in *padmasana* and cascades down a pedestal with a flaring base.

Former rulers of the states of eastern Myanmar historically enjoyed close ties with the Lan Na kingdom of northern Thailand, a relationship that greatly influenced eastern Shan architecture and crafts. Two inscriptions on the base express the desire of the donor's family to support the religion and acquire merit through the sponsorship of this image.

SFL

NOTES

1 The Khun language and its dialects are spoken in the Kaingtong (Kengtung) Valley area of eastern Shan State by approximately a hundred thousand people. There are also a few thousand speakers in Chiang Mai and Chiang Rai provinces of Thailand, and a few hundred speakers in Luang Prabang province in Laos; see Lewis, Simons, and Fennig, *Ethnologue*.

2 For costume similarities, see the photograph of King Chulalongkorn in formal attire for his second coronation in 1783 in McQuail, *Treasures of Two Nations*, 34.

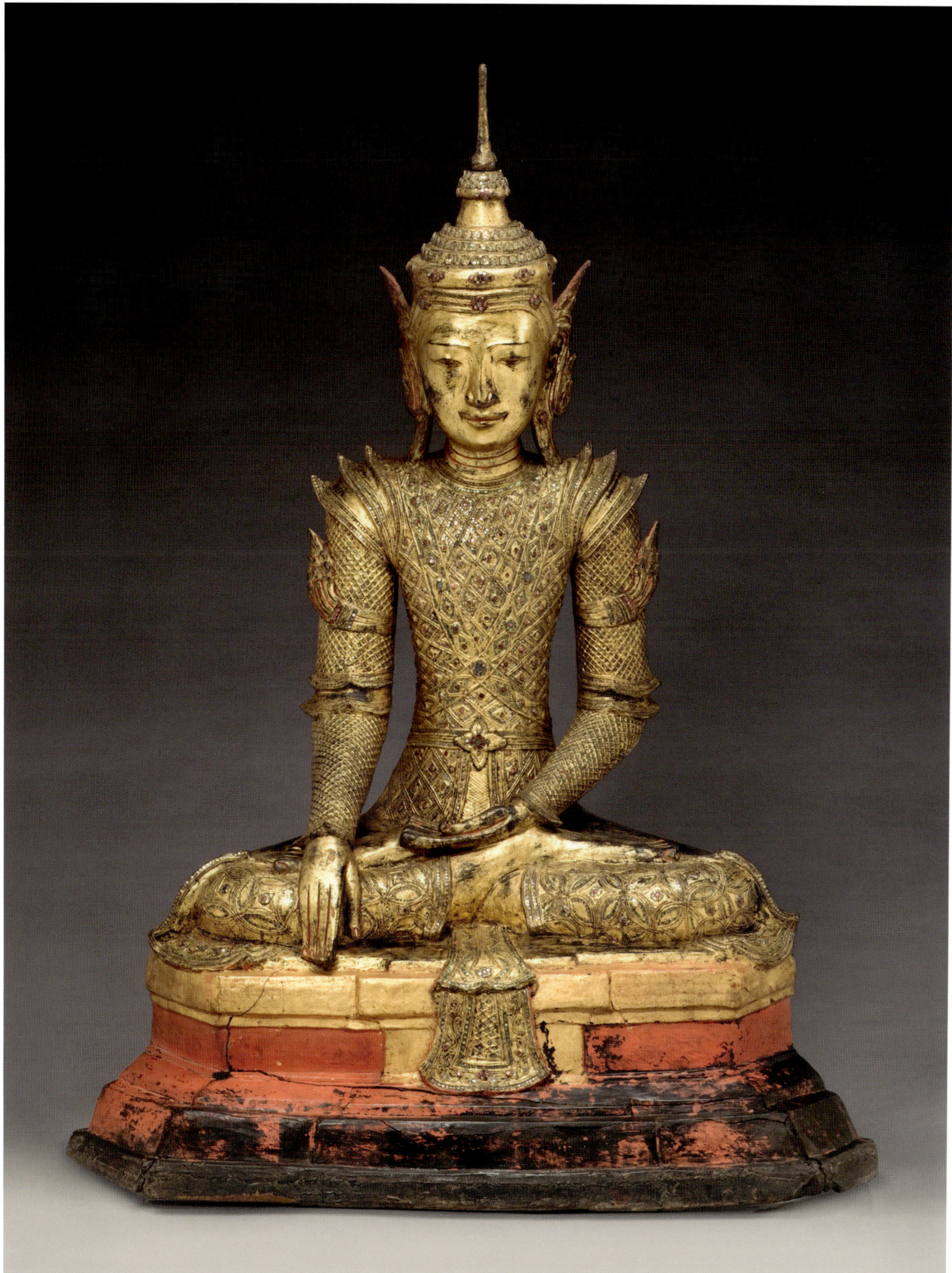

47.

Earth Goddess (Vasudhara)

19th century
Wood, lacquer, and gold leaf
H. 30 x W. 9¾ x D. 14 in. (76.2 x 24.8 x 35.6 cm)
Bagan Archaeological Museum

This serene, elegantly clad, kneeling female figure has extremely long tresses that extend over the left shoulder, traverse diagonally across the torso, and touch the ground on the right. She is Vasudhara the Earth Goddess, or Wathundaye, as she is known in Myanmar. Her timely appearance and subsequent actions in response to an urgent plea from the meditating Buddha under attack from Mara, the Evil One, enabled the Blessed One to attain enlightenment under the Bodhi Tree. On placing his right hand to the ground to summon the earth to bear witness to his good deeds from previous existences, the Earth Goddess emerged and placed herself before the Buddha as if to say, "Oh Great Man I know that thou hast fulfilled the necessary conditions for the attainment of supreme enlightenment. My hair is soaked with the water poured on the earth to ratify thy gifts." With that she wrung out her hair and water flowed like "waves of the Ganges," causing the hosts of Mara to flee in disarray in the ensuing flood.[1] This legend does not appear in the Pali or Sanskrit literature of India, but is popular among believers in mainland Southeast Asia.[2] In Myanmar, the goddess is depicted either sitting or standing.[3]

SFL

NOTES

1 The quotations come from a recounting of the story in one of the short-lived magazines that sprang up after independence (copy at Rangoon University), *Burma* 2, 1951–52, 47.

2 Duroiselle ("Wathundaye, the Earth Goddess of Burma," 6) notes that the legend does appear in a few Pali works in Southeast Asia such as *Pathamasambodhi*, which is popular in Cambodia and Thailand. He goes on to say that the legend is also briefly mentioned in a Myanmar work, the *Tathagata-udana-dipani*, 1: 99.

3 In some instances in Myanmar the figure might be male. Instead of being Mother Earth bearing witness, the male figure could be considered a steward of the earth recording and testifying offerings made by worshipers.

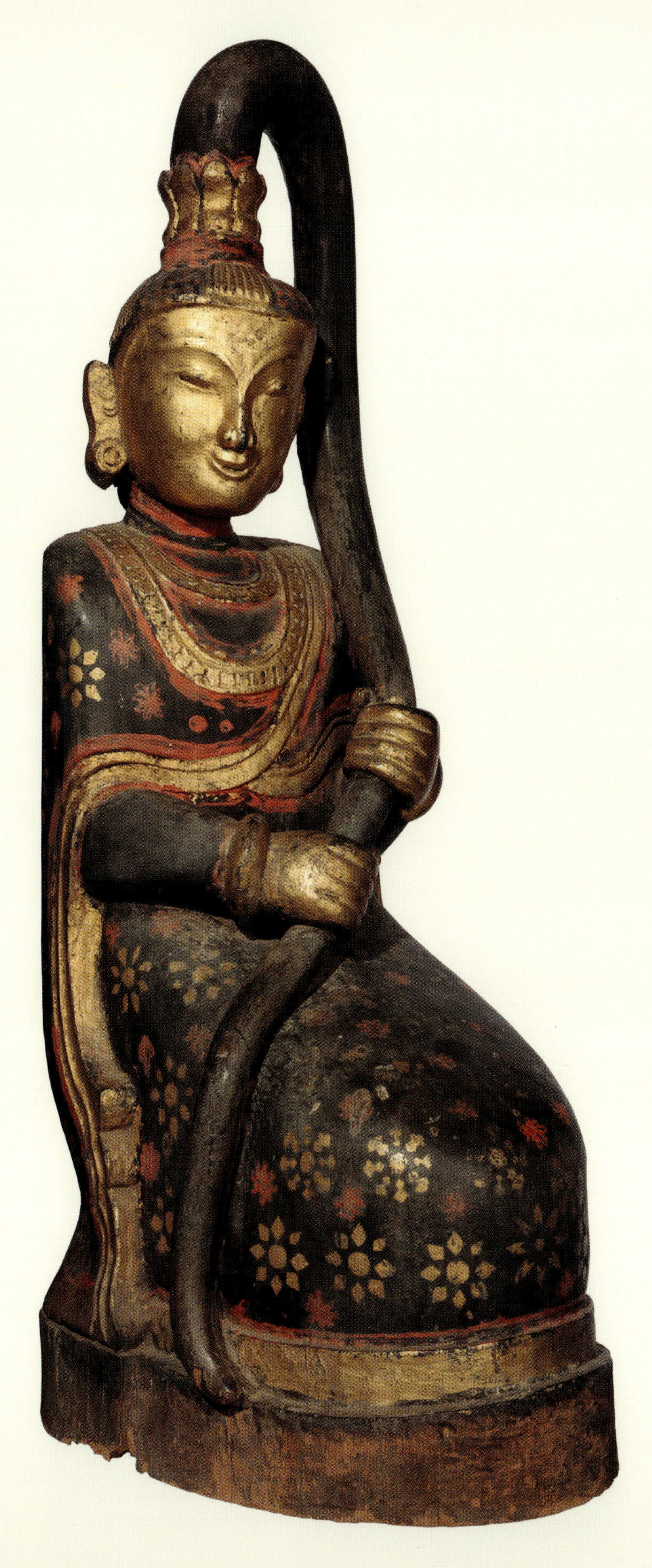

48.

Monk Upagutta (*Upagok*)

Late 19th century
Wood, lacquer, gold leaf, and glass inlay
H. 32 x W. 17 x D. 12 in. (81.3 x 43.2 x 30.5 cm)
Private Collection

Shin Upagutta, a popular saint, is not mentioned in the Pali scriptures and commentaries, but his supernatural powers and various exploits such as a Homeric fight with Mara at the behest of the Mauryan emperor Ashoka (304–232 BCE) came to Myanmar in a Pali work, the *Lokapannatti*, also popular in other parts of Theravadin Southeast Asia.[1] A potpourri of legends has sprung up surrounding this saint, and he has become a cult figure to many lay people who consider him to be immortal. Thought to be living in a palace in the Southern Ocean, he is usually shown domiciled in a small open pavilion or shrine surrounded by water.[2] Dressed as a monk he sits in *padmasana* on a waisted lotus pedestal with his left hand cradling his alms bowl, while the right hand appears to be in the act of taking food. The upraised head looks into the distance as if expecting the sun to appear from behind the clouds. Thought to be able to control rain, he is propitiated with food offerings when fine weather is desired such as prior to a festival or theatrical performance. In the Tenasserim region, small rafts of lighted candles might be floated downstream in his honor in December.[3]

SFL

NOTES

1 Upagupta (Sanskrit) was a saint in the Sanskrit tradition who was born in Mathura and lived around the time of Emperor Ashoka. A great teacher of meditation and insight, he became the fifth Buddhist patriarch.

2 For an excellent account of the various legends surrounding this saint, see Strong, *Legend and Cult of Upagupta*. See also Brown, *Burma as I Saw It*, 105–9.

3 Charles Duroiselle also cites other sources besides the *Lokapannatti* for the Upagutta legend; see Duroiselle, "Four Burmese Saints."

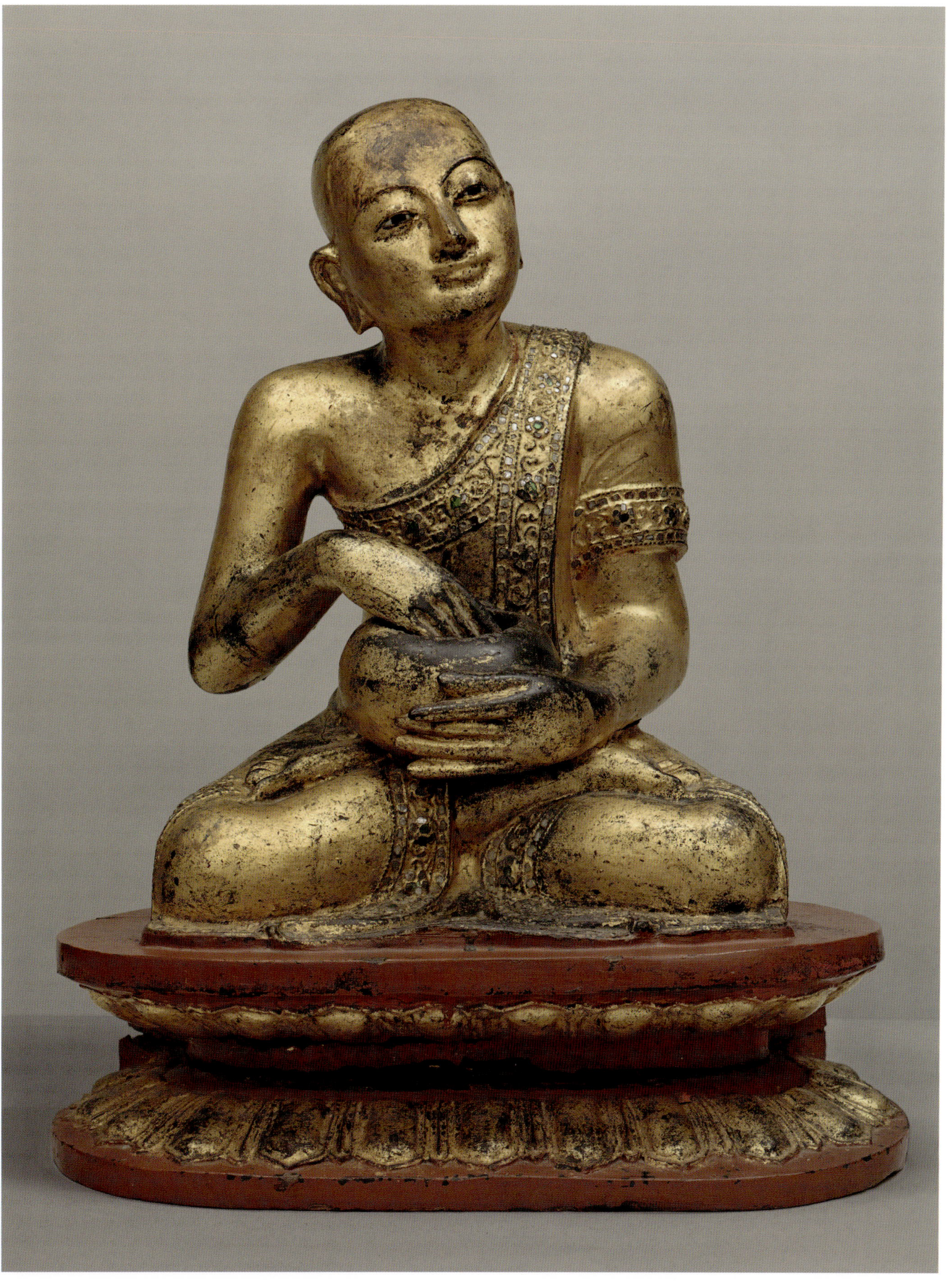

49.

Monk Sariputta, chief disciple of the Buddha

Late 19th–early 20th century
Wood, lacquer, gold leaf, and glass
H. 22 x W. 14 in. (55.9 x 35.6 cm)

Although the Buddha has been regularly portrayed in bas reliefs surrounded by disciples and devotees since the Pyu era, by late Konbaung times it became popular to show the Blessed One in temple and monastic shrines flanked by seated sculptures of his two chief disciples—Sariputta on his right and Moggallana to the left. Born in adjacent villages north of Rajagaha, the pair grew up together and were ascetics before becoming followers of the Buddha. Through their piety and superior intellect they became *arahants*. Sariputta was to become second to the Buddha in wisdom and his knowledge of the *Dhamma*, while Moggallana was gifted with supernatural powers. Both are usually shown kneeling with legs gracefully folded toward the right. Moggallana is usually depicted with hands in the praying position (*namaskara mudra*) while Sariputta leans forward with his head inclined toward the left shoulder as if listening intently to the Buddha. His left hand is pressed on the thigh for support, while the right hand reaches back to clasp the ankle. The robe, worn in the open mode, is draped in naturalistic folds terminating in a ripple of small S-shaped pleats at the back. The flowing shoulder cloth, like the edge of the main robe, is finished with a band of inlaid glass rosette decoration.[1]

SFL

NOTE

1 This image has been discussed in McGill, *Emerald Cities*, 77. See Nyanaponika and Hecker, *Great Disciples of the Buddha*, for further details on the lives and associated legends of the disciples of the Buddha.

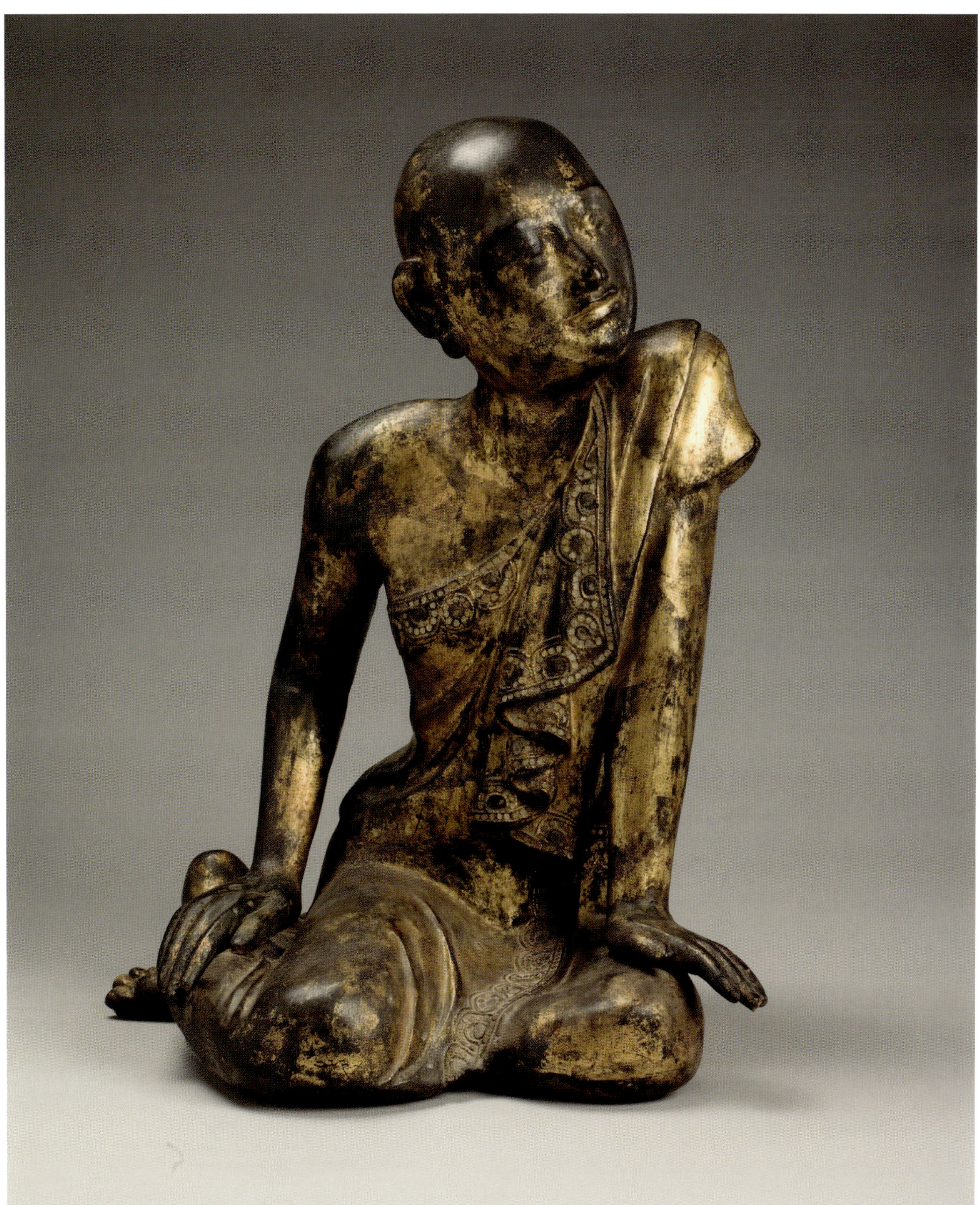

50.

Ogress (*bilu-ma*)

Konbaung Mandalay period (1857–85)
Wood, lacquer, gold leaf, and glass inlay
H. 35 x W. 14½ x D. 18 in. (88.9 x 36.8 x 45.7 cm)
Burma Art Collection at Northern Illinois University, Gift of Konrad and Sarah Bekker, BC87.01.03

Ogres, which may be male (*bilu*) or female (*bilu-ma*) in Myanmar art, are usually depicted in human form with the fierce, deeply lined, and whiskered visage of a monster, replete with black or red eyes and protruding, curved, boarlike canines.[1] A stock character of Myanmar theater and folklore, ogres are often, as here, shown in Konbaung court costume—large collar, upturned shoulder epaulettes, *sa-lwe* cross-over chest ornaments, and long flowing waistcloth with flaring edges, the lines of which have been picked out by neat rows of colored glass inlay. The rather flat head has been crowned with a pagoda-like finial, reminiscent of royal crowns. The even kneeling position and plainer clothing compared with the other *bilu* example in the exhibition (see cat. no. 51) suggests that this figure is possibly female.

Despite the fearsome reputation of ogres for devouring human flesh and striking terror in the minds of wayward Myanmar children, this kneeling ogress, leaning forward with upward gaze and hands together in *namaskara*, the *mudra* of prayer and devotion, is portrayed here as an adorant. The hands at one time might also have held some sort of offering. Buddhist teachings are not limited to the human sphere and the *deva* heavens, but extend to all sentient beings, including those of the lower regions, where ogres are thought to dwell. Ogres may also serve a protective function within pagoda precincts. In such a capacity they are believed to become animated if a sacrilege occurs.

SFL

NOTE

1 Popular stories in Myanmar featuring ogres and ogresses are derived from Hindu Buddhist mythology and local legends. They include Ravanna of the Hindu epic the *Ramayana*, Punnaka in *Vidhura-pandita Jataka* (no. 545), and the Taming of Avalaka the Ogre by the Buddha. For local legends, a few of which feature ogres, see Khin Myo Chit, *Wonderland of Burmese Legends*, 7, 57–59.

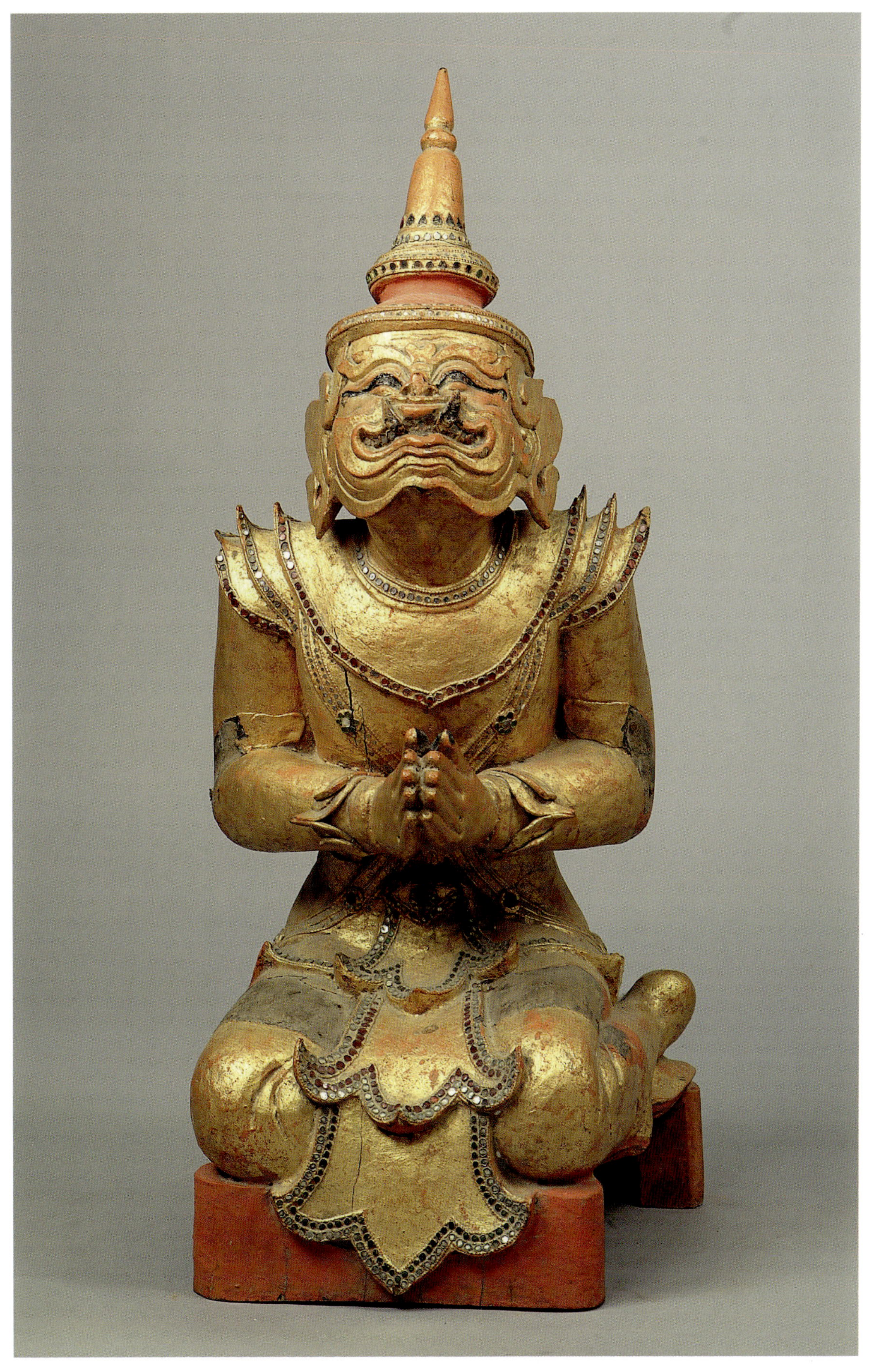

51.

Ogre (*bilu*)

Konbaung Mandalay period (1857–85)
Wood, lacquer, gold leaf, and glass inlay
H. 38 x W. 14 x D. 22 in. (96.5 x 35.6 x 55.9 cm)
Burma Art Collection at Northern Illinois University: Gift of Konrad and Sarah Bekker, BC87.01.04

This male *bilu* exhibits a few differences from the female included in this exhibition (see cat. no. 50) evident in the kneeling pose and the embellishment of the robe. The head is crowned by a distinctive backward curving, wedge-shaped finial emerging from an hourglass-shaped form, rather than a pagoda-like crown as is seen on the female, the *bilu-ma*. The Konbaung court costume, although virtually identical in style to the female's, has an overall surface more densely embellished with lappets of raised decoration highlighted by slivers of mirror glass. The diagonally crossed *sa-lwe* ornament over the chest and back has been further emphasized by larger inlays of colored cut glass.

Neither ogre sits on a throne, but each is supported by a block of red lacquered wood. This male ogre, although in a kneeling pose, has his higher-placed right knee supported by an extra slab of wood. Despite being depicted here as an adorant, ogres on pagoda platforms are often shown seated in the "hunter," *ardhaparyankasana*, pose with the right knee raised and bent and the left leg folded and crossed under the heel. Ogres may sometimes be seen in this pose in a supportive role behind the *chinthe* lions that guard the entranceways to pagodas throughout Myanmar.

SFL

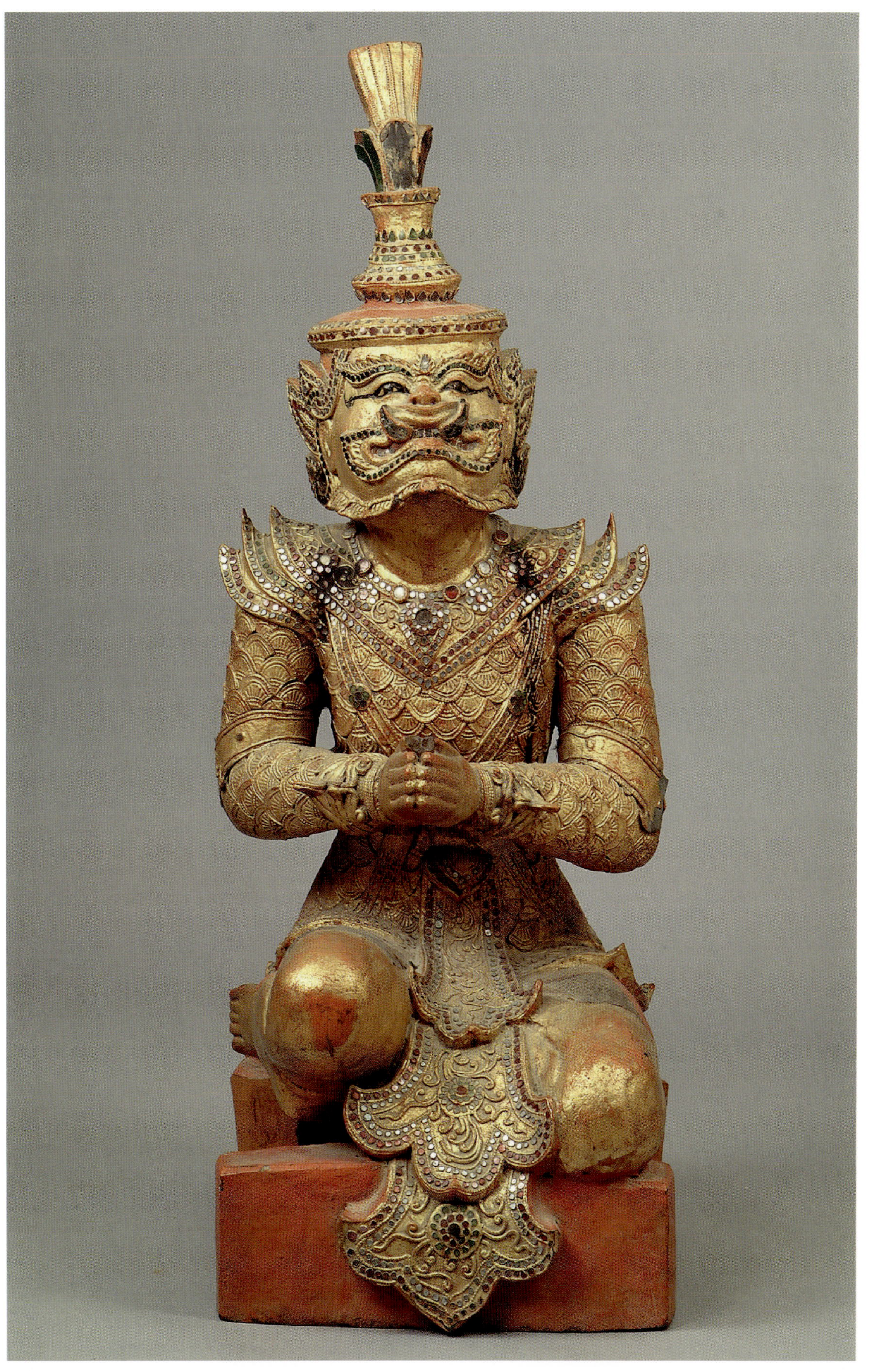

52 and 53.
Pair of *kinnara* and *kinnari* (*keinaya*)

Konbaung Mandalay period (1857–85)
Wood, lacquer, gold leaf, and glass inlay
Kinnara: H. 56½ x W. 22⅝ x D. 26⅜ in. (143.5 x 57.5 x 67 cm); *Kinnari*: H. 38³⁄₁₆ x W. 14³⁄₁₆ in. (97 x 36 cm)
Burma Art Collection at Northern Illinois University: Gift of Konrad and Sarah Bekker, BC87.01.01 and BC87.01.02

These magical hybrid half-human half-bird figures, splendidly attired in Thai-inspired late Konbaung court costume, are locally known as *keinaya*. The species most likely came to Myanmar through Indian literature and the spread of Buddhism. Such creatures are thought to inhabit a mythical semicelestial region in the Himalayas. They are noted for their physical beauty, glorious plumage, grace, and gentle ways, as well as for their sweet voices and dancing abilities. In literature they have occasionally interacted with humans, not always happily, as evident in the popular *Manohra* play (*Dwemenaw*), in which a *kinnari* married to a prince is forced to return to her abode to avoid being sacrificed.[1]

Kinnari have also become emblems of marital fidelity thanks to the popularity of the *Canda-kinnara Jataka* (no. 485).[2] The grace and beauty of these mythical creatures has been well expressed in this dancing couple. The *kinnara* (male) with slightly leaning torso and feet in a ballet-like position is particularly arresting, as his arms and upraised hands in a popular Myanmar dance pose compliment and mirror the upper-body stance of the *kinnari* (female). *Kinnari* sometimes are placed as welcoming figures on pagoda platforms both as adorants and as a subtle reminder and possible link to the celestial regions that eventually await those who keep the precepts.

SFL

NOTES

1 The *Manohra* appears to have come to Myanmar via Thai sources. It was originally part of the Panji cycle of legends and dramas popular in Malaysia and Indonesia.

2 For details of this particular story, see Cowell, Chalmers, Rouse, Francis, Alexander, and Freer, *Jātaka*, 4: 179–82.

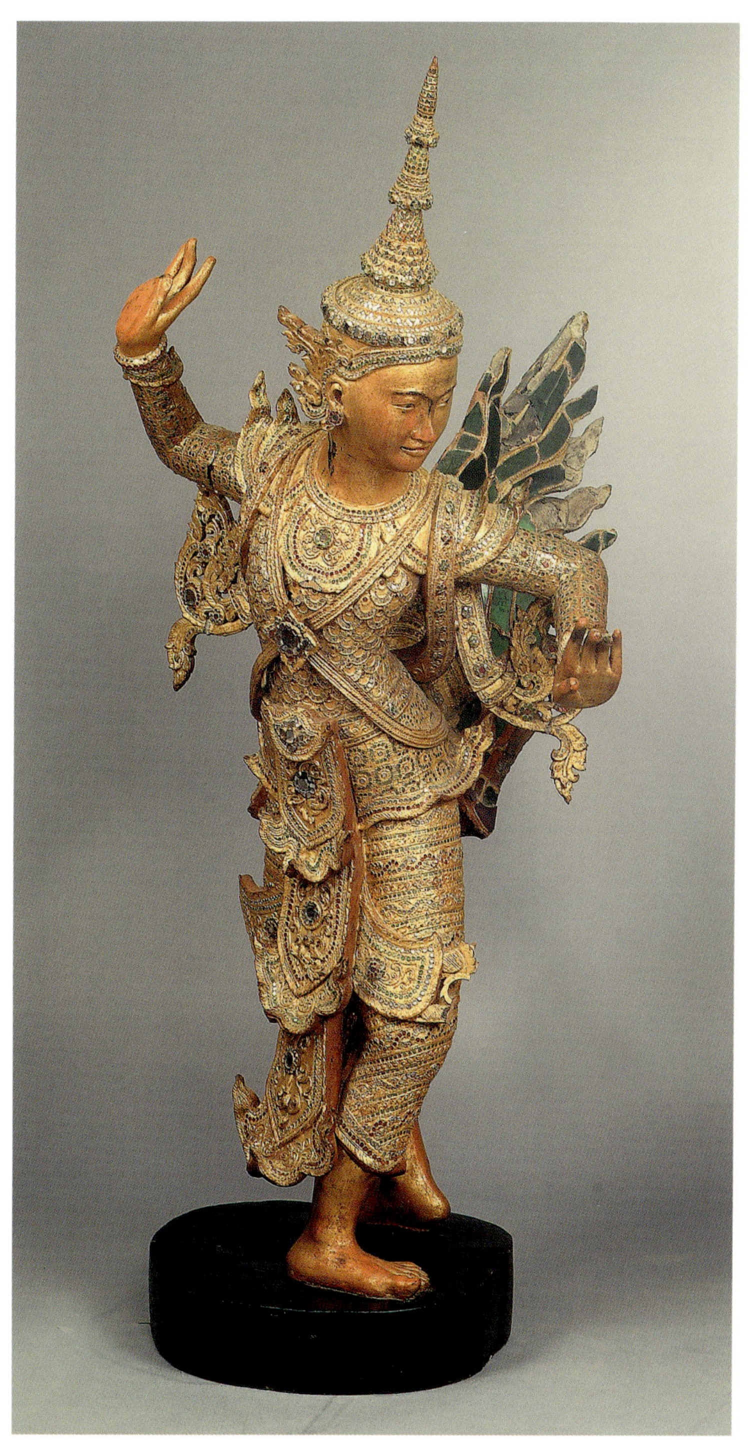

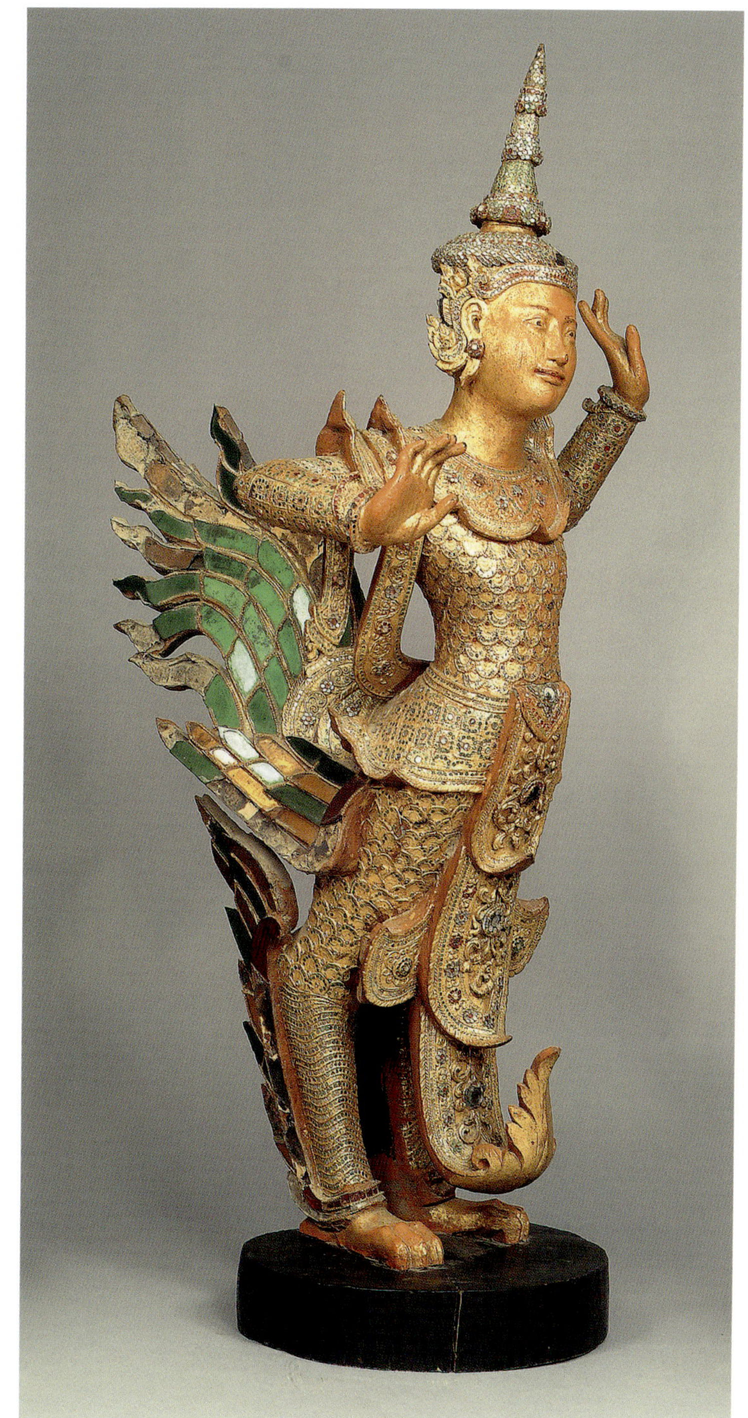

54.

Wood carving of the *Ramayana*

Late 19th century
Teak wood
H. 31 x W. 28 in. (78.7 x 71.1 cm)
Private Collection

In form, this wood carving resembles a lintel ornament or the upper portion of a backboard for an image. The subject matter is from the *Ramayana*, a Hindu epic that has been pictorially represented in Myanmar since Pagan times.[1] Despite its non-Buddhist origins, it has in some instances been incorporated into depictions of *jataka* tales.[2] Scenes from this epic have also appeared as stone reliefs at the Mahalawkamayazein Pagoda near Budalin.[3] In this example, no particular episode is represented, but the presence of a graceful Rama in Konbaung court costume bearing his bow, immediately below a menacing ogre mask, identifies the subject matter.[4]

Myanmar craftsmen excelled at carving relief on two or more planes, and in this example this skill is showcased in the surrounding architectural elements framing the central figure. Rama, balancing delicately on a lotus, has been carved fully in the round, with careful attention to surface detail, and attached separately. The appendages of the *kinnari* that embellish the sides have been artfully integrated with the surrounding upward-pointing vegetal decoration known as *a-saw*. Good use has also been made of the interplay of light and shadow and the use of openwork in the surrounding foliate elements to give added depth to the carving.[5]

SFL

NOTES

1 For details of the *Ramayana* in Myanmar, see Thaw Kaung, "Ramayana Drama in Myanmar," 55–82; and Thein Han and Khin Zaw, "Ramayana in Burmese Literature and Arts."

2 A version of the *Ramayana* story appears in no. 431, *Dasaratha-Jataka*. See Cowell, Chalmers, Rouse, Francis, Alexander, and Freer, *Jākata*, 4: 78–82.

3 The Mahalawkamayazein Pagoda at Thakhut Ta-nyei, approximately thirteen miles north of Butalin, was built in 1847–49 and has 347 relief-carved marble plaques devoted to the *Ramayana* epic.

4 The depiction of *Ramayana* characters in court dress is due to the fact that when Myanmar destroyed Ayutthaya in 1767, Thai versions of the *Ramayana* as a dance drama were introduced to the court of Myanmar by captive Thai nobles. See Singer, "Ramayana at the Burmese Court," 90–103. For an account of the history and evolution of the Ramayana drama in Myanmar, see Htin Aung, *Burmese Drama*, 31–49.

5 For an excellent account and photographs of late Konbaung and colonial period woodcarving, see Tilly and Klier, *Wood-Carving of Burma*.

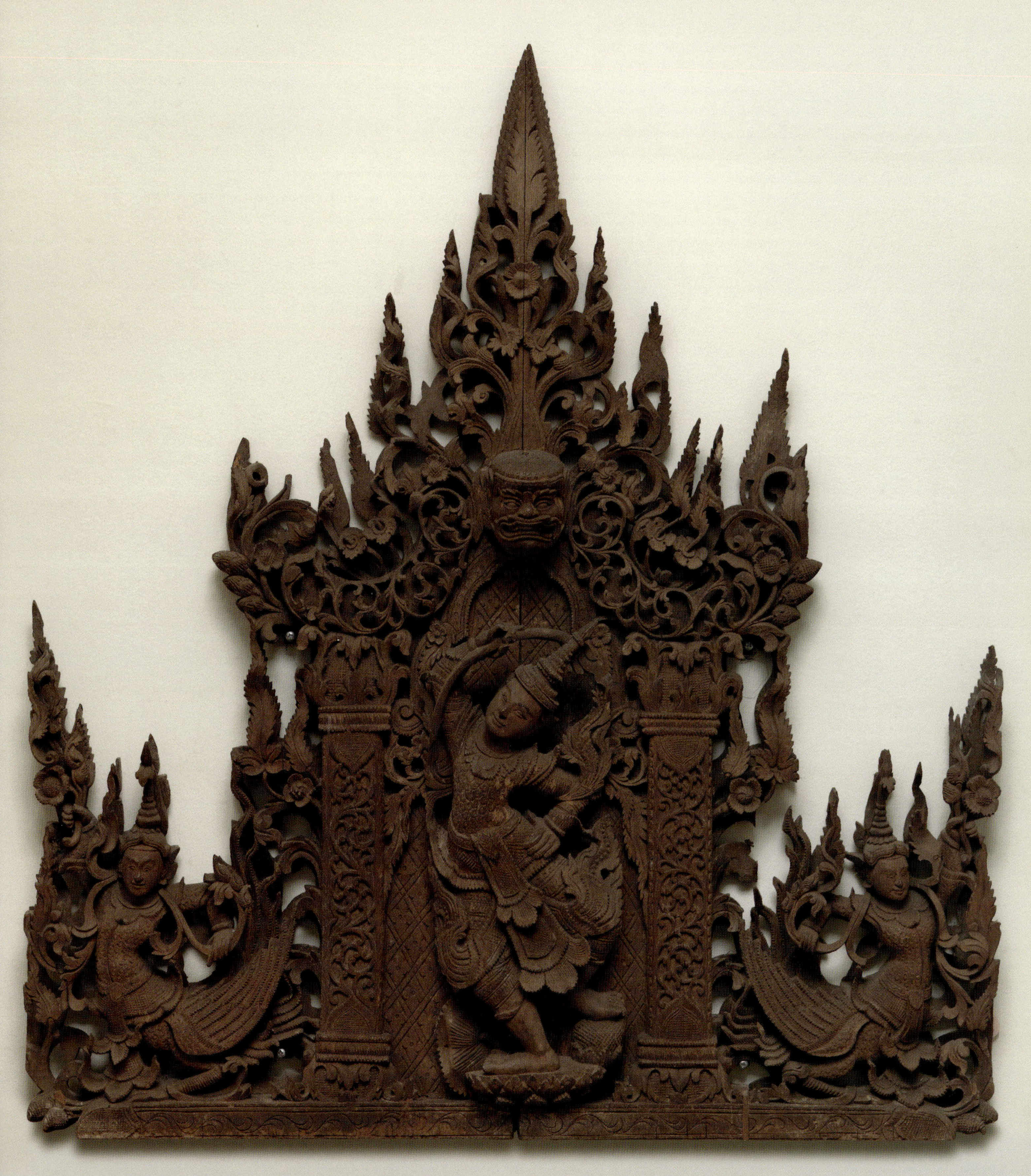

55.

Ceiling board

Late 19th–early 20th century
Wood, lacquer, and glass inlay
H. 70 x W. 70 in. (177.8 x 177.8 cm)
Collection of Ronald L. Krannich

This ceiling board was used to hide the internal view of the carpentry involved in the construction and support of triple-tiered *zetuwan*, or towering multitiered *pyathat* roofing structures, which crowned traditional religious wooden architecture such as pagoda pavilions (*tazaung*) and monasteries (*pongyi-kyaung*). European-inspired innovation is evident in the application of traditional *chu-pan* openwork arabesques, lotus petal bands of scrolling, and *leik-pya/linno-daung* leaflike corner ornament, cut from thin sheets of wood with narrow, fine-toothed fretsaws, rather than carved from a single slab of teak. Divisions between the various bands of scrolling have been highlighted by glass inlay imbedded in lacquer and arranged in concentric lines of diminishing dimensions that serve to frame the raised central motif—a lotus in full bloom, also embellished at the center with slivers of glass. Such a ceiling board usually appears above the most sacred area of a building, such as over a shrine or hall where sermons are delivered. As a leitmotif for purity and the Buddhist religion, the open lotus continues to serve as a reminder to adherents to slough off the bonds of greed, anger, lust, passion, and ego and grow toward becoming truly enlightened beings.[1]

SFL

NOTE

1 For further examples of carved ceiling boards in monasteries, see Fraser-Lu, *Splendour in Wood*, 95, 99, and 202.

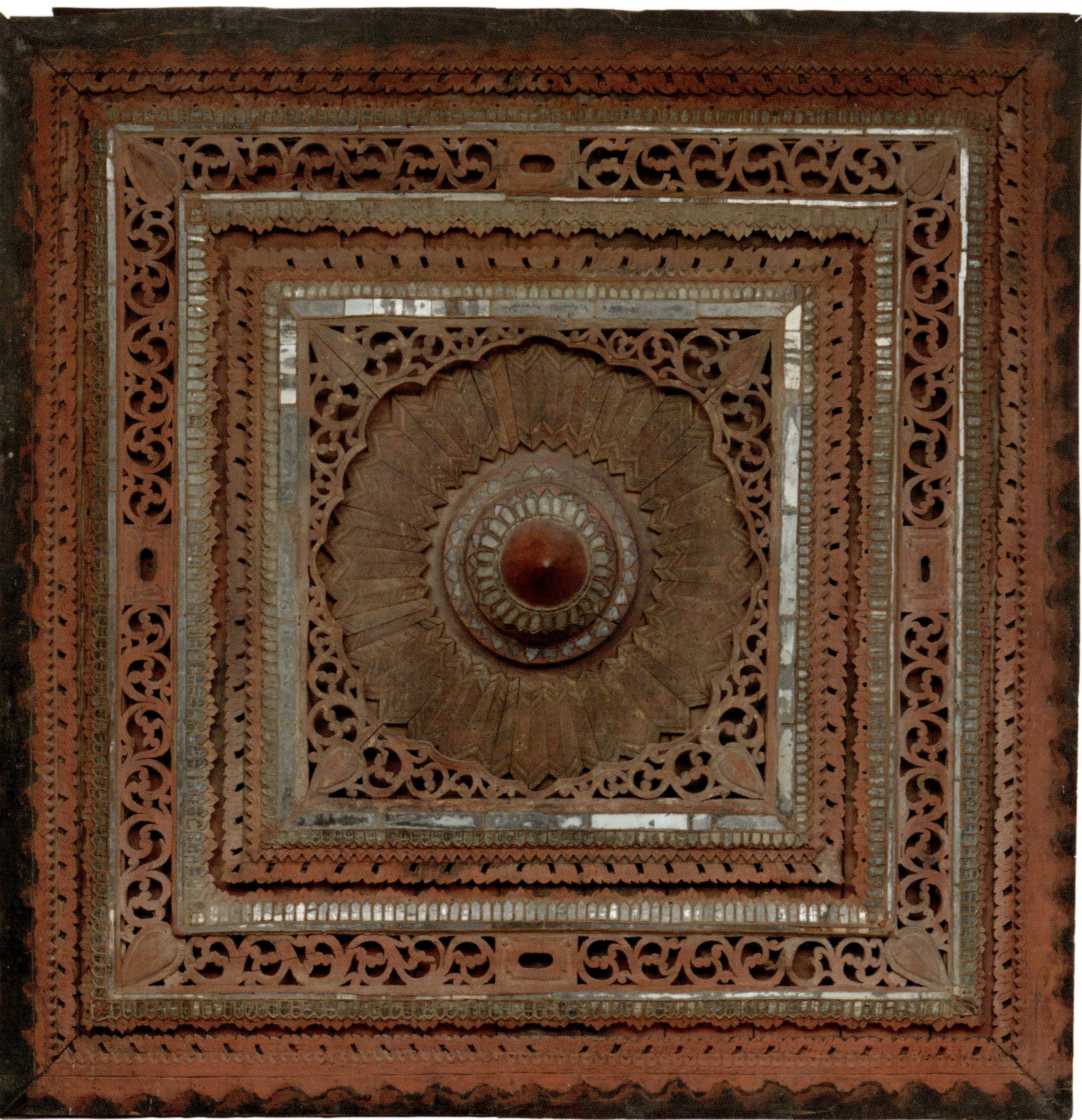

56.

The Buddha's Descent from the Tavatimsa Heaven

Late Konbaung period
Tempera on cotton cloth
H. 32½ x W. 39 in. (82.6 x 99.1 cm)
Burma Art Collection at Northern Illinois University: Gift of William Wise, BC2007.03.01

This late-nineteenth-century cloth painting narrates an important event in the life of the Buddha in the form of a continuous narration. A sequence of events is portrayed within a single frame. The Buddha is depicted three times: first, in the upper left, where he is shown seated within a pavilion in the Tavatimsa Heaven at the summit of Mount Meru, the center of the Buddhist universe. He went there to preach the *Abhidhamma* to his mother, Mayadevi, who had died shortly after his birth and had not had the opportunity to hear him preach. In the middle section, the Buddha is returning to earth by means of a triple ladder made by Sakka, ruler of the Tavatimsa. The Buddha's loyal disciples wait below. In the middle section on the right, he is shown preaching to his earthly followers amid great rejoicing, as evident in the presence of a Myanmar orchestra and *devas* in the sky.

The Buddha's three-month absence from the earth is known as *vassa*, or Lent. It is the monsoon season, when monks are confined to their monasteries and celebrations for the laity are banned. Austerities end with a colorful three-day festival of lights to celebrate the Buddha's return to earth during which people pay obeisance to monks, parents, and teachers.[1]

SFL

NOTE

1 For details of festivities, see Khin Myo Chit, *Flowers and Festivals Round the Burmese New Year*, 54–58.

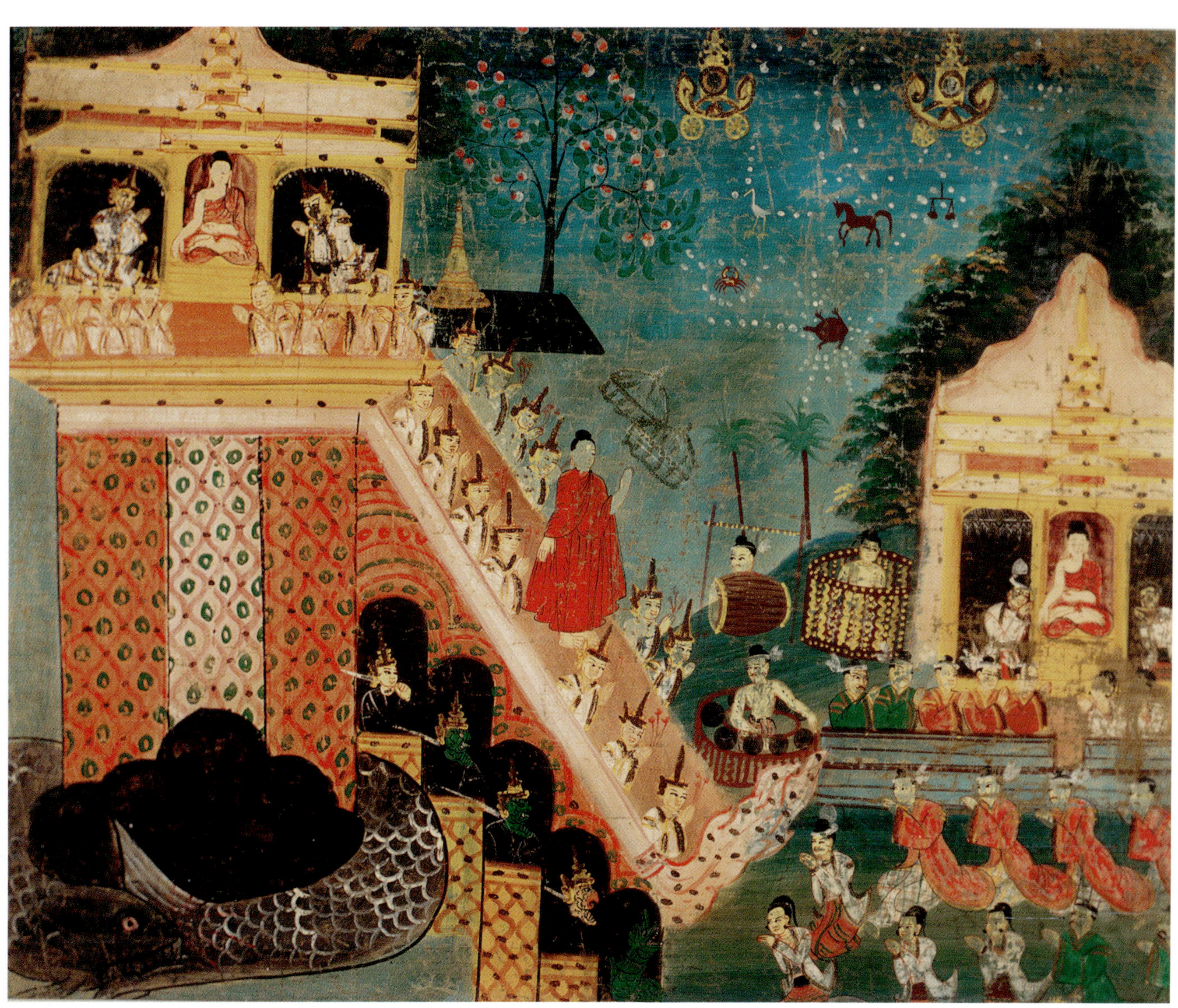

57.

Religious manuscript (*kammavaca/kammawa*)

1914
Teak, cotton cloth, lacquer, gold leaf
H. 6 x W. 24½ x D. 2 in. (15.2 x 62.2 x 5.1 cm)
Private Collection

According to the inscription on the inside front cover, this *kammavaca* manuscript was commissioned as an act of merit by U Soe Pe and Daw Khaw Gyi. It consists of sixteen consecutive unbound pages inscribed with an extract from one of the nine *khandhakas*, a section of the Pali *Vinaya* that prescribes the conduct of ceremonies pertaining to monks.[1] Made from layers of lacquered cloth, the orange-colored pages, read from left to right, are inscribed on both sides with six lines of text written in thick, lustrous black lacquer in a square "tamarind seed" script.[2]

The intervening spaces and margins have been ornamented with delicate wisps of foliage and birds in gold leaf against a fine hatch-stroke ground. The pages are enclosed by a pair of teak covers embellished with a horizontal frieze of interlocking space cells that enclose lively effigies of sword-bearing *devas*, alternating with a composite animal known in Myanmar as *pyinsa-yupa*. The end papers are similarly decorated. The underside of the front cover has been inscribed with the date and the donors' aspirations for *nibbana*. In keeping with palm-leaf conventions, the first and last pages of text have wider decorative margins. A small hole at the left of each page allows for a bamboo pin to be drawn through to secure the text when not in use.[3]

SFL

NOTES

1 The *khandhakas* include ceremonies to be observed for ordination (*Usampada*), the presentation of robes (*Kathina* and *Ticavarena Avippavassa*), designating sacred ground—for fasting and meditation (*Upsathagara*), acquiring land for a monastery (*Kutivatthuolokanasammuti*), and its dedication (*Kappyiabhumisammuti*), the election of a senior monk (*Therasammuti*), the naming of a monk (*Namasammuti*), and the expulsion of a monk from the order (*Nissayamuttisammuti*).

2 Lacquer needs a substrate to adhere to, which in this case consists of a few layers of folded lacquered cloth finished with *thayo* to create a smooth surface on which to write and draw.

3 For an account of the evolution of *kammavaca* in Myanmar, see Singer, "Kammavaca Texts." Originally made of palm leaf, *kammavaca* were also made from thin sheets of wood, metal, and ivory. *Kammavaca* may be written in Pali or the local vernacular such as Myanmar or Mon.

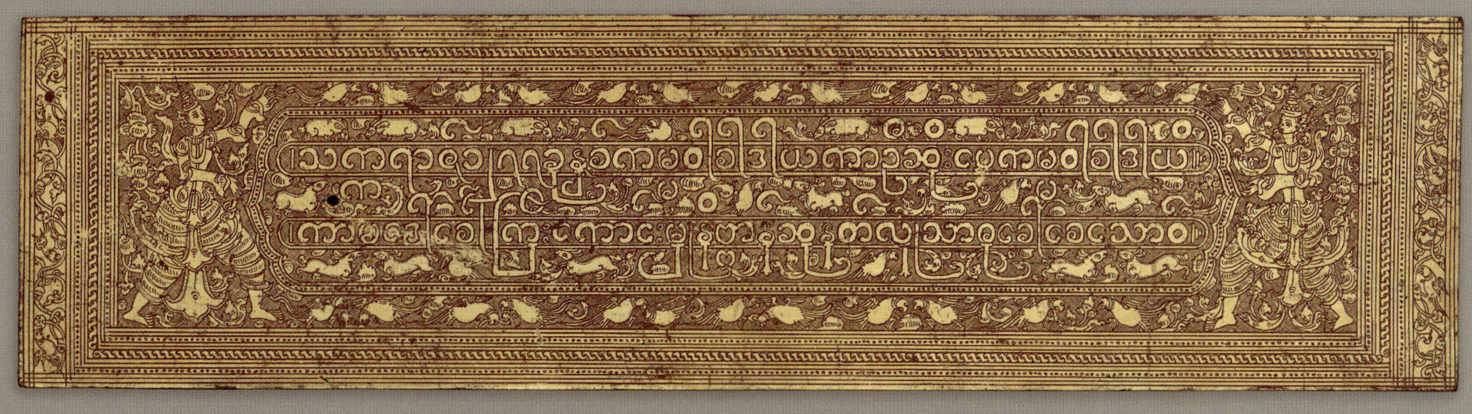

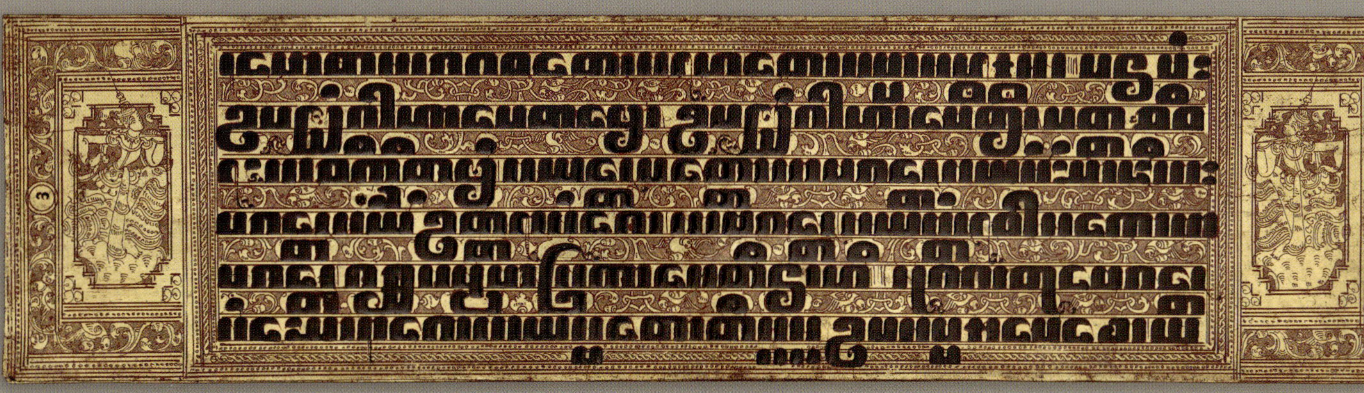

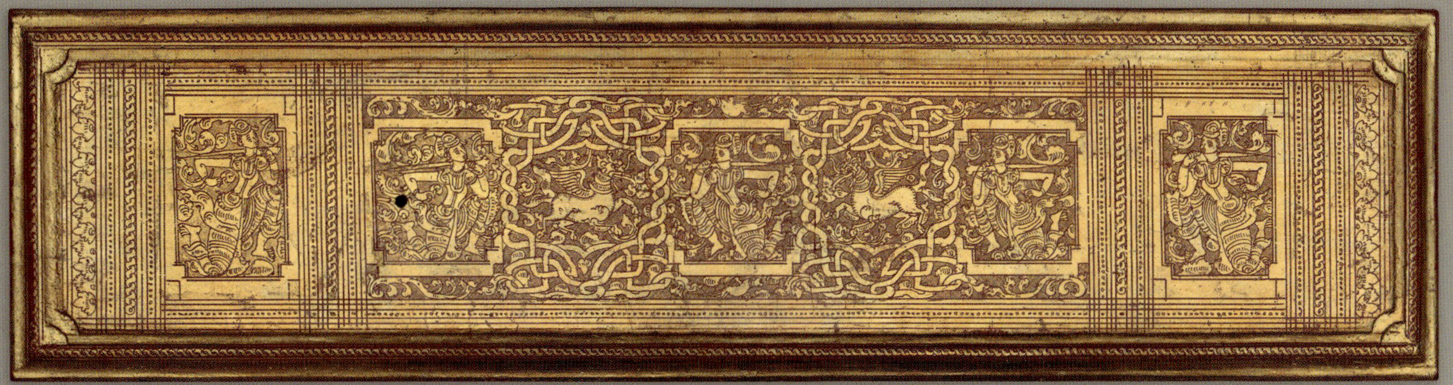

58.

Cosmology palm-leaf manuscript (*pe-za*)

1894
Palm leaf, cotton thread
H. 2½ x W. 20 in. (6.4 x 50.8 cm) when closed
Rare Books and Special Collections, Founders Memorial Library
Northern Illinois University Rare Book Collection, Northern Illinois University, De Kalb
Gift of Friends of Burma, BC: 9641A-025-031

This palm-leaf manuscript (*pe-za*) is composed of fifty-five leaves, inscribed and illustrated on both sides, that have been stitched and interlaced with cotton thread to enable each folio to unfold downward to reveal a vertical annotated diagram of the Buddhist universe. One face is devoted to the thirty-one planes of existence extending from the highest heavens in the formless realm and the realms of form—*arupaloka* and *rupaloka* respectively—down to the lowest hells in the realm of desire (*kamaloka*). The reverse features a Buddha's footprint (*buddhapada*), Lake Anotatta, where the Four Great Rivers originate, a cross section of the Four Islands at the cardinal points of the Buddhist universe, and the life of the Buddha prior to and following his enlightenment.

Of special interest is one mandala-like illustration covering seven leaves that depicts the Seven Weeks, the period after enlightenment. The Buddha is shown seated under the Bodhi Tree at the center, in *bhumisparsa mudra*, with spokes radiating out to the Sixteen Sacred Lands—small kingdoms in eastern India (identified by captions), which were the sites of important events in the life of the Buddha. Illustrations of the events that took place during the Seven Weeks have been placed between the spokes.[1]

SFL

NOTE

1 Raymond ("Seven Weeks") has an excellent description of the contents of this manuscript pertaining to the seven sites. For further information on the cosmological manuscripts of Myanmar, see Herbert, "Burmese Cosmological Manuscripts."

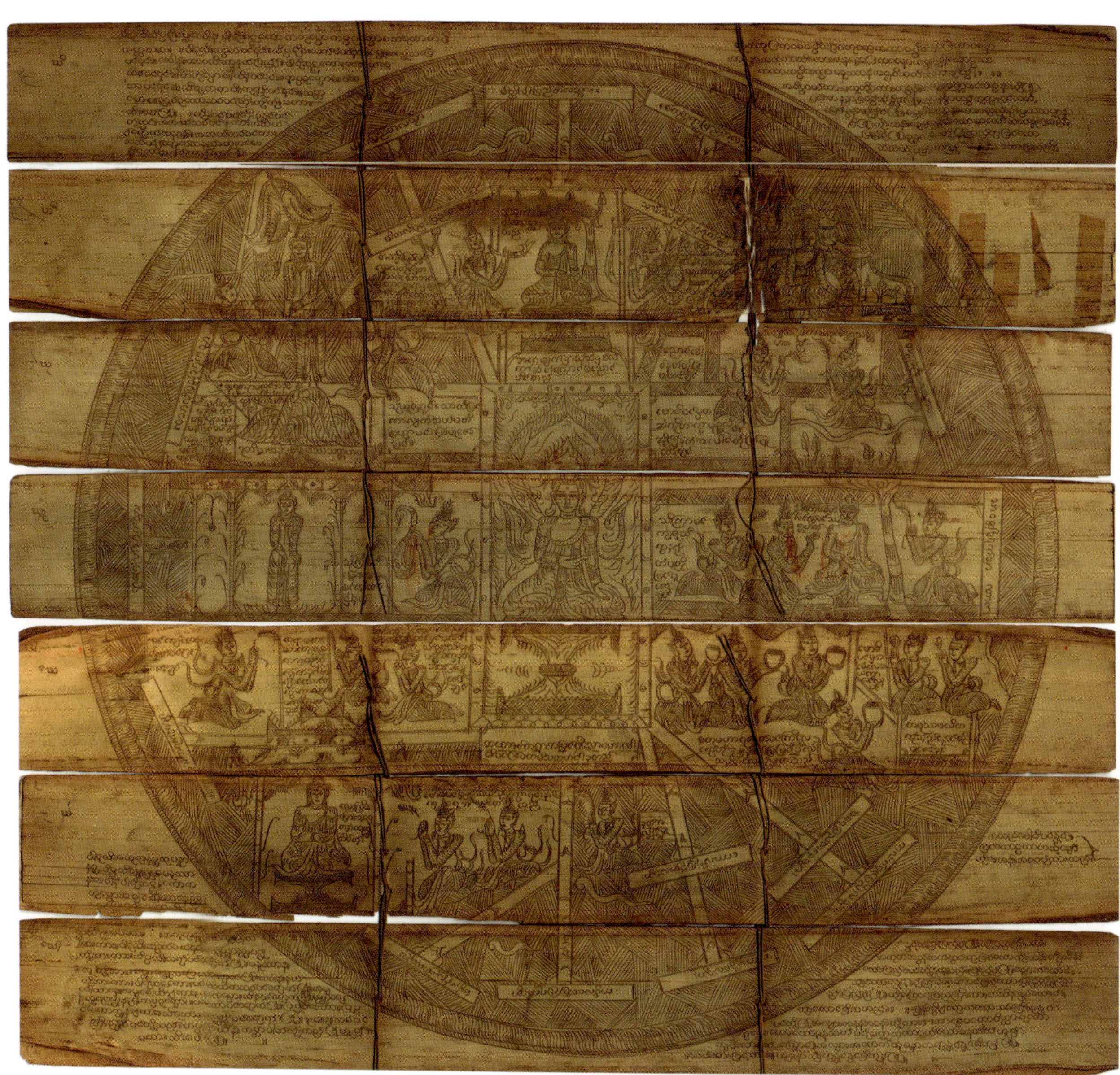

59.

Illustrated Konmara folding book (*parabaik*)

Ca. late 19th century
Mulberry paper, watercolor, gouache, and ink
H. 16 x W. 7 x D. 1½ in. (40.6 x 17.8 x 3.8 cm) when closed
Spencer Collection, The New York Public Library, Astor, Lenox and Tilden Foundations, Burmese MS No. 2

This folding book (*parabaik*) illustrates some episodes of the *Konmara* story, a *jataka*-inspired folktale that tells of a recently appointed crown prince who has been prevailed upon to find a suitable consort. Prince Konmara and his entourage take leave of the palace and on their travels hear of the beautiful and spirited Kharamai, a daughter of prosperous peasants. He enlists the help of a wily, unscrupulous matchmaker to arrange a tryst, despite the fact that the young woman is betrothed to another (albeit unhappily). The prince and peasant girl fall in love, but their future together is thwarted by Kharamai's father and jilted fiancé who complain to the king. The prince is banished until his father's death, Kharamai is shunned, and the matchmaker is confined to a nunnery, reinforcing important axioms of traditional Myanmar society—that of obeying one's parents, keeping the Buddhist precepts, and behaving according to society's expectations.[1]

Despite the use of Pali names, the story has been given a distinctly Myanmar setting, as is apparent in the opening scene, which features the king and courtiers inside a typical Konbaung palace replete with open verandah, tiered roofs, and supplementary pavilions. Scenes in the panoramic mode are rendered from a bird's-eye perspective. The diagonal placement of architecture indicates an attempt at Western perspective. Hills, embankments, and trees have also been shaded to indicate depth.

SFL & TK

NOTE

1 This story and its variants became particularly well known in the late nineteenth century when it became a popular play performed with a variety of songs that helped convey the pathos of the story line. Most highly acclaimed was a version known as *Konmara Pya Zat*, which was written in 1875 by U Pok Ni (1849–after 1875) and published by printing press—a new method of dissemination for plays. The play is set in colonial period Lower Myanmar, and the characters have been given Myanmar names. References to Buddhist beliefs and mores abound in the dialogue, along with the occasional reference to objects that had come into vogue during the colonial period. This play has been translated and annotated by Hla Pe, former professor of Burmese literature at SOAS; see Hla Pe and Pok Ni, *Konmara Pya Zat*, vols. 1 and 2.

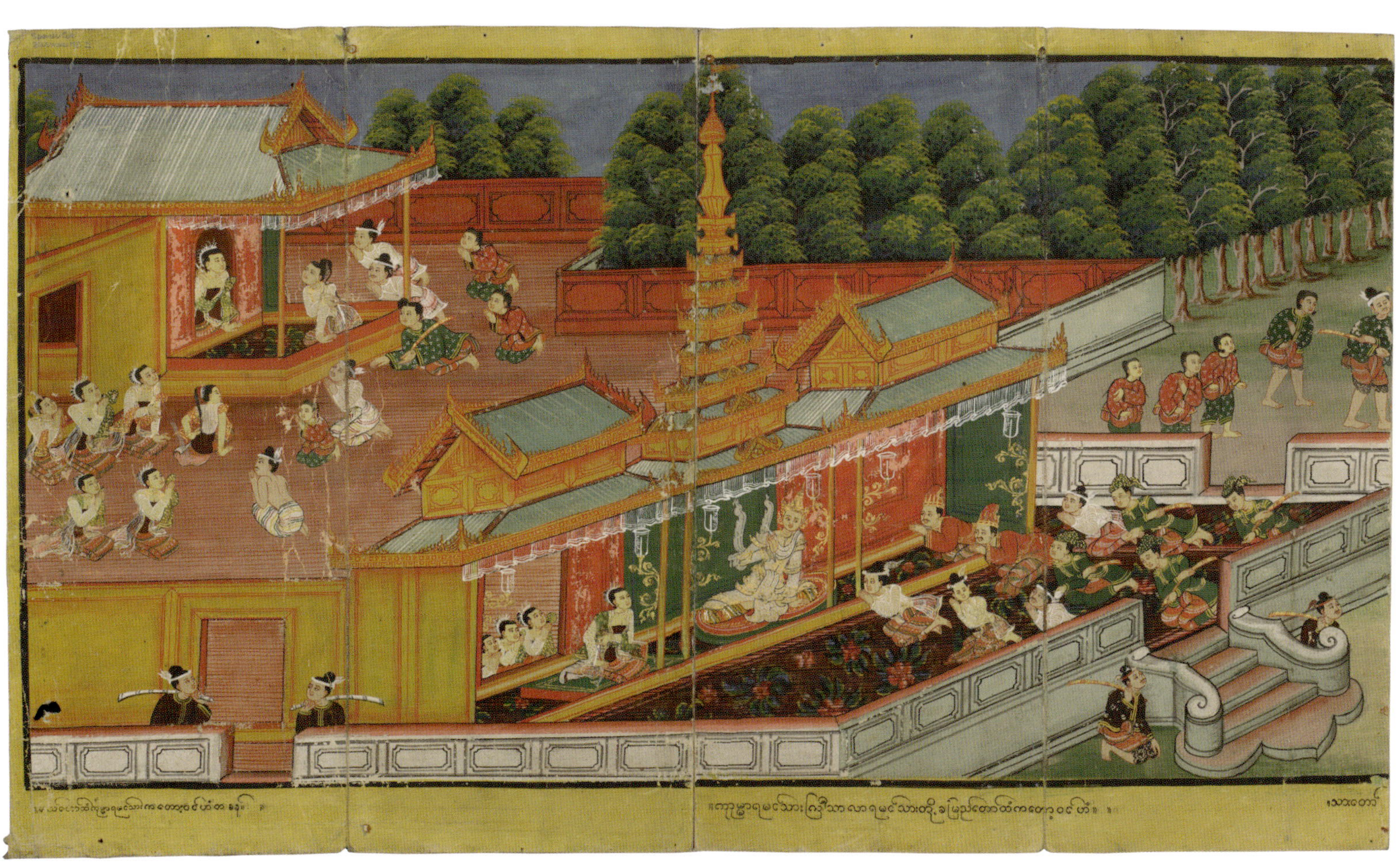
သားတော်

60.

Illustrated folding book (*parabaik*)

Ca. 1875–1900
Mulberry paper, watercolor and gouache, ink, and gold paint
H. 6¾ x L. 15⅞ in. (17.2 x 40.3 cm)
Denver Art Museum Collection: Museum Purchase, 1951.20

This late-nineteenth-century illustrated folded book (*parabaik*), made from thick mulberry paper, provides a colorful record of court ceremonies at the time of Thibaw, Myanmar's last king (r. 1875–1885). While some depictions in this manuscript are of pleasances and pastimes, the majority of activities focus on the monarch's solemn duties as secular head of the Buddhist religion. He is shown presiding over various processions and events associated with the conclusion of the Buddhist Lent, such as the Festival of Light (*Thadingyut*) in October, the offering of requisites to monks *Kathina* (*kahtein*) in November, and the watering of the Banyan tree in May. Some scenes are incomplete, while other seemingly related paintings do not appear to be placed in sequential order. A series of small paintings on the reverse offers vignettes of people of different classes and ethnic groups in Myanmar going about their daily lives.[1]

The featured illustration shows the king and his consort, sheltered by a white umbrella as they proceed by elephant to a pagoda to observe the distribution of votive gifts of food and flowers, which are tastefully arrayed in vases and stands on display in the foreground. Armed and uniformed soldiers line the route, while dignitaries preceding the royal couple on foot proudly bear accouterments of office.

SFL & TK

NOTE

1 For a more detailed description of the Denver *parabaik*, see Fraser-Lu, "Burmese Art at the Denver Art Museum."

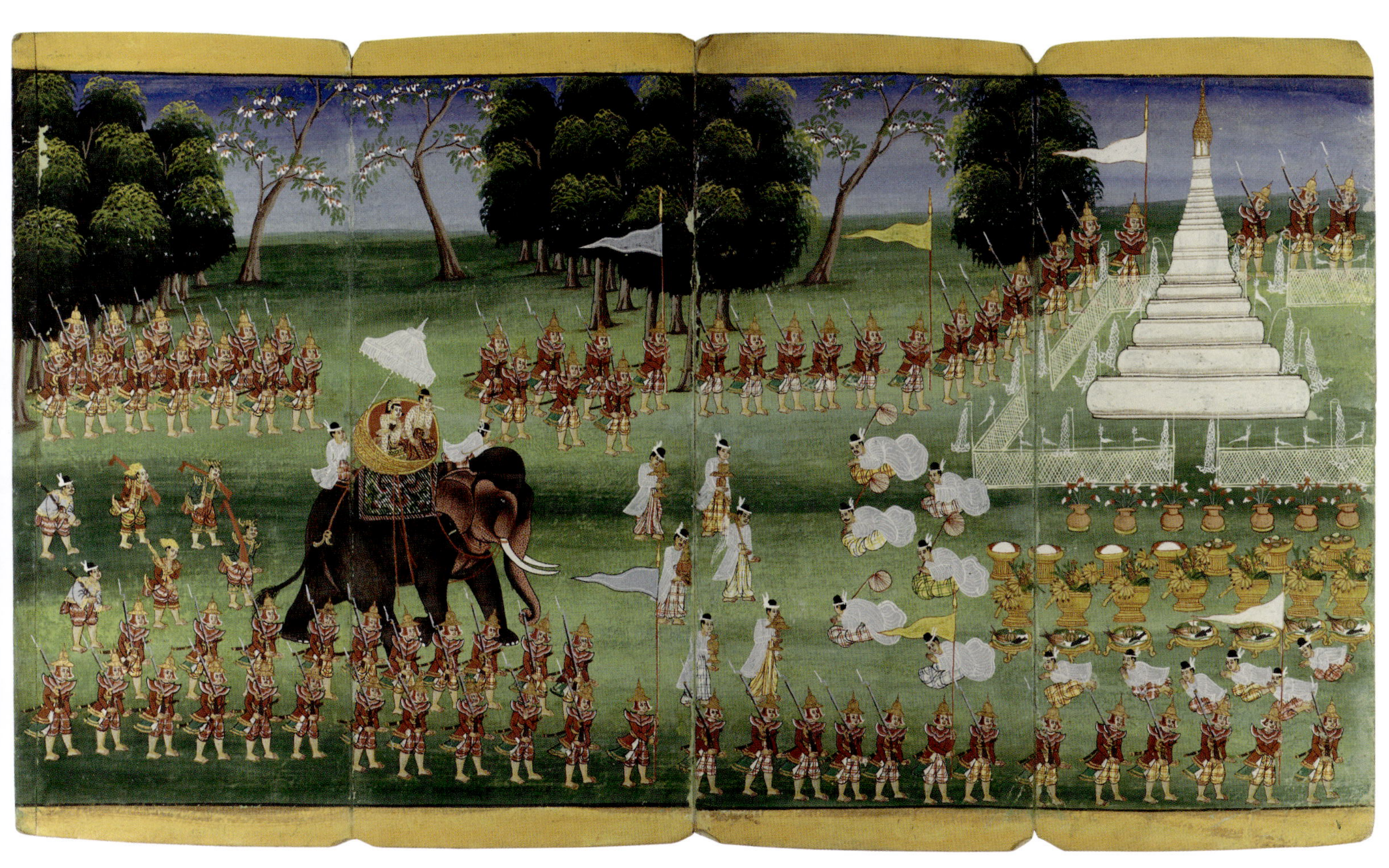

61.

Manuscript wrapper (*sapa-lwe*)

Late 19th–early 20th century
Bamboo, cotton cloth, and silk thread
L. 20½ x H. 11½ in. (52.1 x 29.2 cm)
Private Collection

Before the introduction of the printing press to Myanmar, all religious manuscripts were laboriously written by hand, often by lay scribes in the employ of monasteries. Such texts, often representing hours of toil, were considered sacred and were among the most valuable items a monastery possessed. When in use, manuscripts were handled with great respect. As protection against dust, insects, and moisture, they were carefully wrapped in special covers known as *sapa-lwe* made from a skeleton of bamboo, interlaced with strips of cloth such as chintz, remnants of monks' robes, or velvet. In addition, the bamboo strips were often wrapped and interlaced with silk thread of varying hues in a variety of geometric surface designs—zigzags, crosses, and Chinese-inspired key fret patterns. Some have lateral strips of cloth sewn to two opposite edges, which fold over to offer extra protection to the sides of the manuscript enclosed. *Sapa-lwe* edges were finished with binding and the back reinforced with a cotton lining. No longer produced today, *sapa-lwe* are thought to have been made largely by the Shan of the Inle Lake region, having at some point learned the craft from their northern Thai compatriots, who call such wrappers *phaa hau khampii*.

SFL

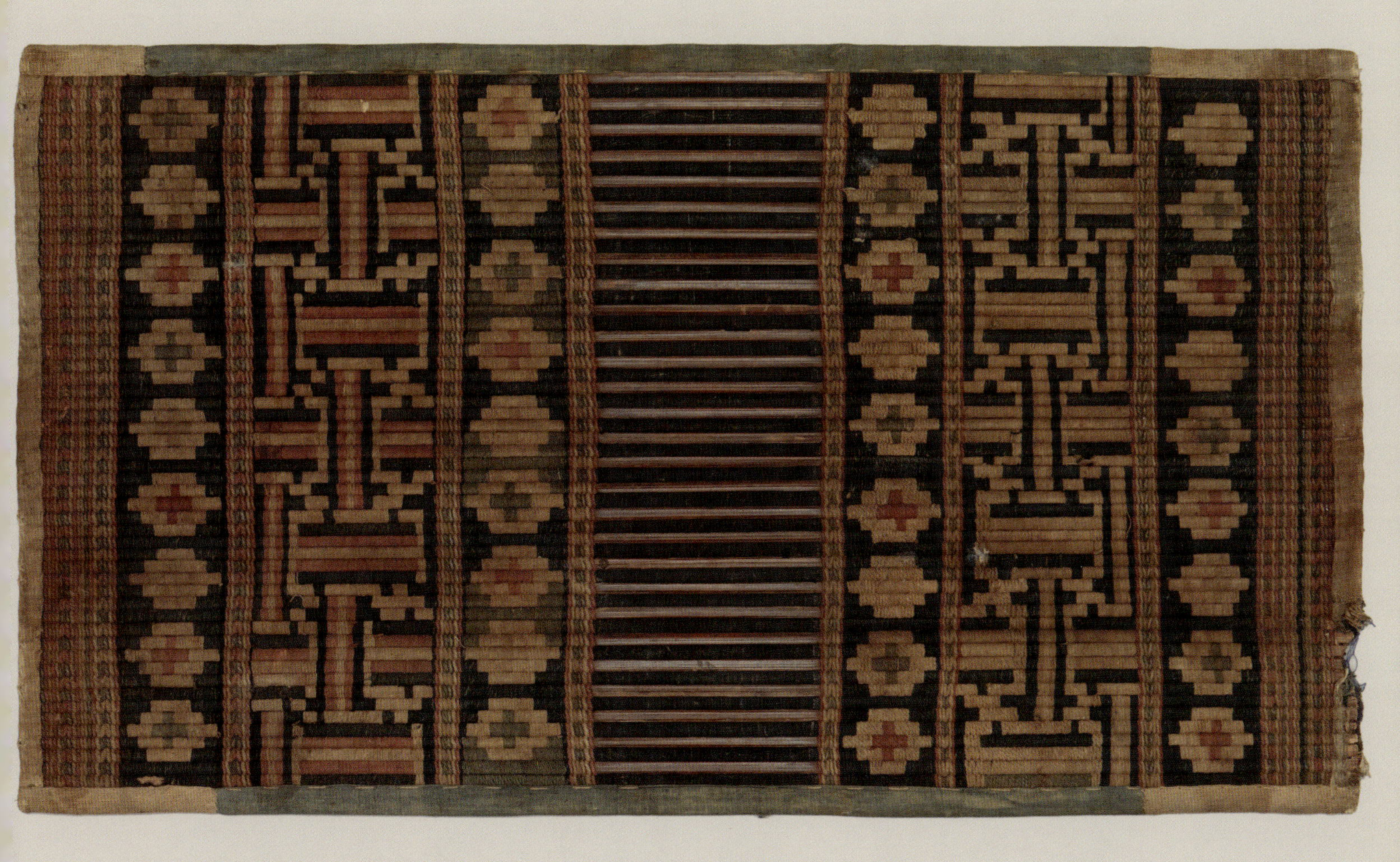

62.

Manuscript binding ribbon (*sazi-gyo*)

Early 20th century
Cotton
L. 236 x W. ¾ in. (599.4 x 1.9 cm)
Private Collection

Intricately crafted *sazi-gyo* ribbons, like the religious manuscripts they enclosed, were commissioned as works of merit by the faithful.[1] Woven on a tablet loom, *sazi-gyo* were patterned with a variety of religious symbols, such as the Myanmar flagstaff (*tagundaing*) that heralded the presence of a sacred compound, along with various *devas*, birds, animals, and objects synonymous with the Buddhist religion, such as bell and gong stands. The text in the vernacular usually had a dedication that included the name and titles of the donor and members of his family, along with the date of the donation, pious aspirations for *nibbana*, and a desire to share the merit accrued with others.

This very fine later example from Pyun Tan Za village, Taik-U quarter, Pegu, or Bago has made use of milled yarns in a variety of colors, which by the late nineteenth century had become readily available in bazaars throughout the country, resulting in very legible lettering and finely rendered motifs. According to the woven inscription, it was donated to a highly revered senior monk by a U Myat Tha Dun, his good wife, and their three beautiful, virtuous daughters, all of whom hoped that by taking refuge in the Three Jewels, they would eventually experience the bliss of *nibbana*.

SFL

NOTE

1 A recently published volume by Isaacs, *Sazigyo, Burmese Manuscript Binding Tapes*, is a comprehensive study of the subject. Singer ("Kammavacca Texts, Their Covers and Binding Ribbons") provides an account of *sazi-gyo* history and development.

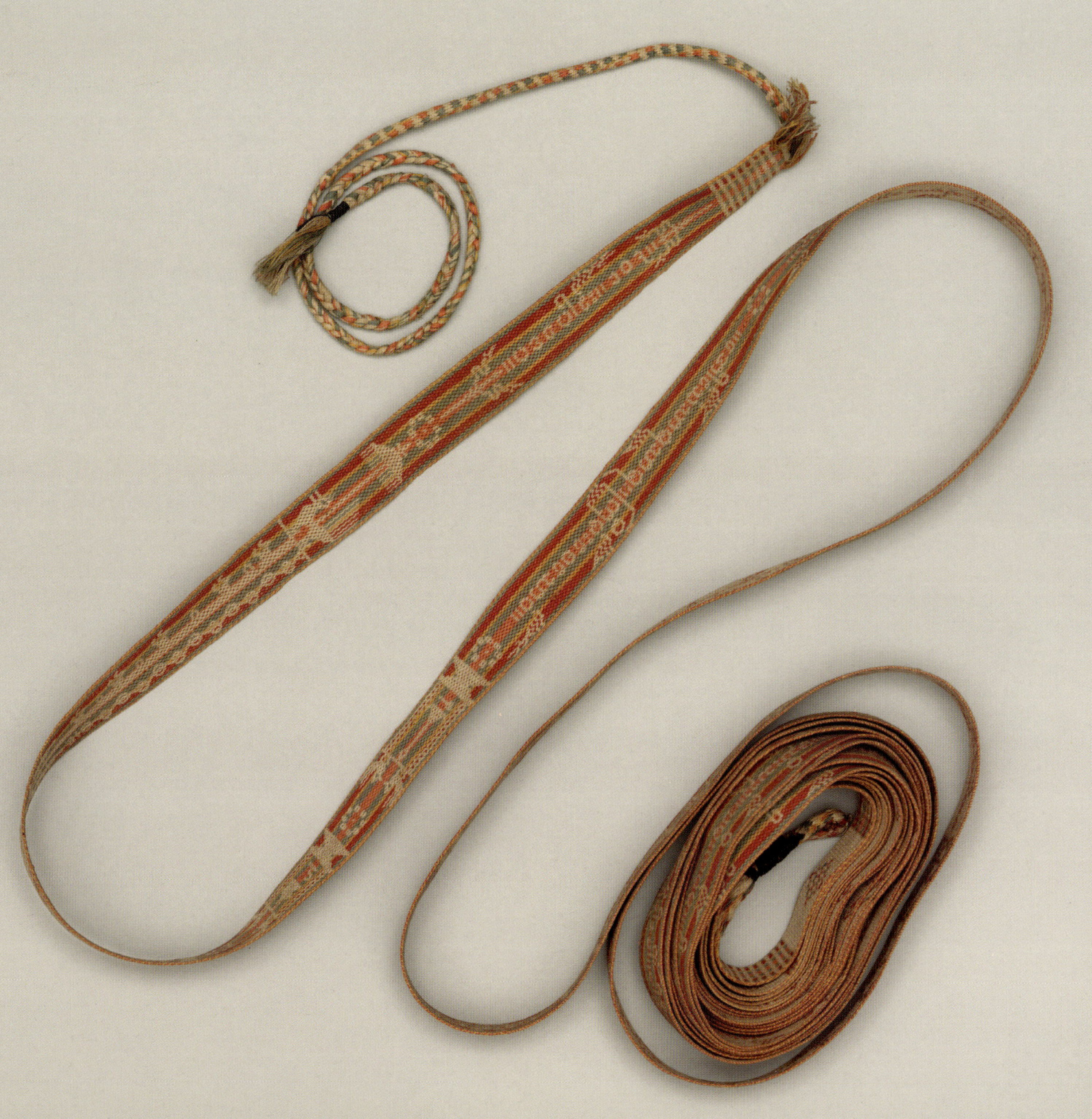

63.

Scripture chest (*sa-daik*)

Early 19th century
Wood, metal, lacquer, gold leaf, and glass
H. 24 x W. 45½ x D. 25 in. (61 x 115.6 x 63.5 cm)
Collection of Ronald L. Krannich

The front panel of this teak scripture chest (*sa-daik*) has been embellished in lacquer and cut glass with a rendition of Mount Meru, the center of the Buddhist universe, which rests in a vast ocean with a gigantic fish encircling the base. Instead of the usual schema of mountains, oceans, and guardians and gods in their dwellings, the summit of Mount Meru here is occupied by a pair of adorants flanking a stupa, possibly the Culamani, which according to the biography of the Buddha, enshrines the locks of the Buddha's hair severed at the Great Renunciation and a tooth taken by Dona at the distribution of the relics following the *parinibbana*. Flanking Mount Meru are two-storied and triple-tiered pavilions that house a standing Buddha in the central pavilion on the right and a seated effigy in the upper story on the left. The other rooms in the pavilions and the surrounding courtyards are filled with devotees oriented toward the two Buddha figures in worshipful attitudes. Trailing sprigs of foliage fill the background. The thick chunks of glass backed by sheet metal and cemented in place with ribbons of *thayo* lacquer suggest an early-nineteenth-century date.[1]

SFL

NOTE

1 For more conventional and detailed depictions of Mount Meru, see Herbert, "Burmese Cosmological Manuscripts."

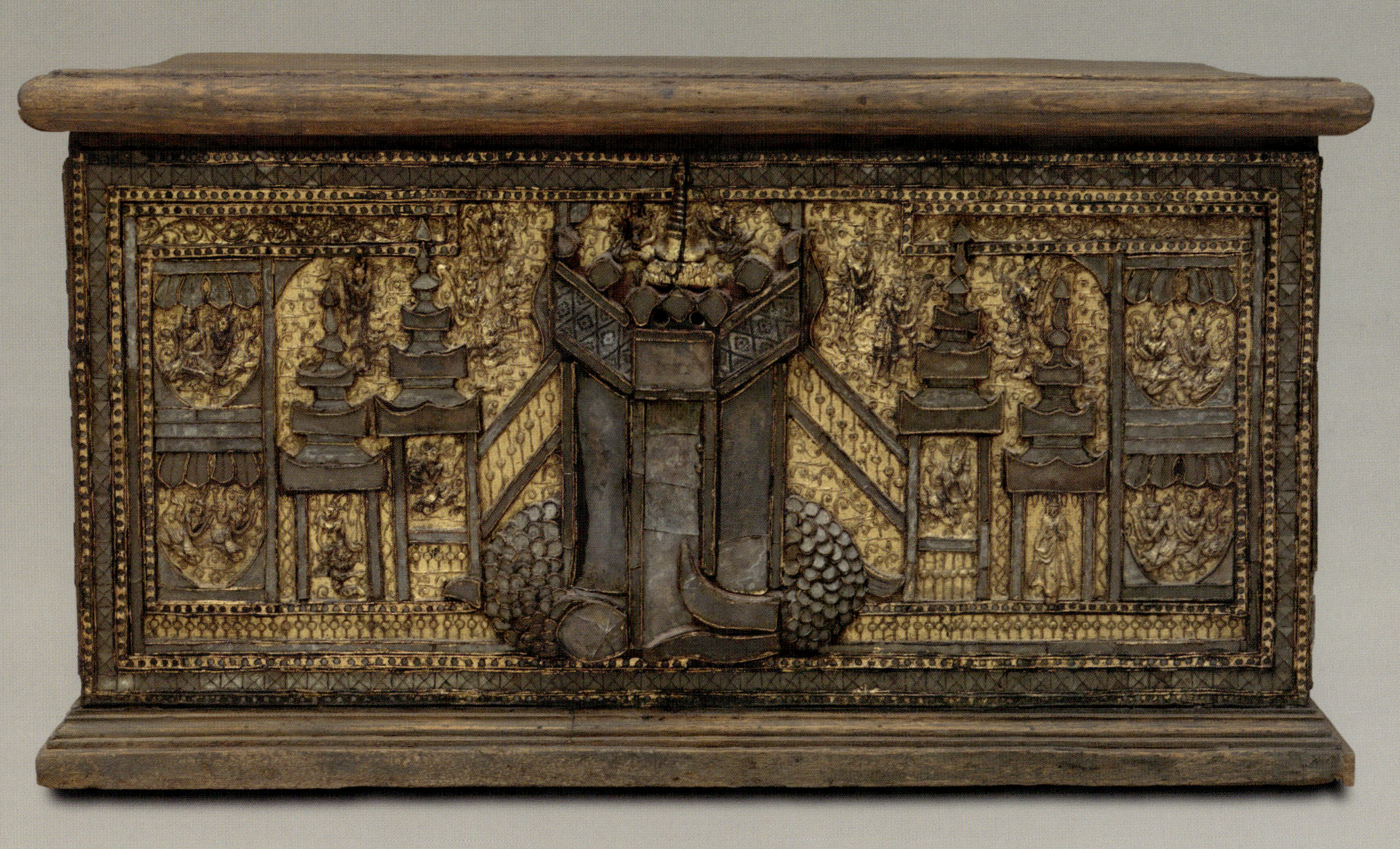

64.

Scripture chest (*sa-daik*) depicting the Death of the Buddha

Late 19th century
Wood, iron, lacquer, gold leaf
H. 22½ x W. 44 x D. 22 in. (57.2 x 111.8 x 55.9 cm)
Private Collection

In Myanmar, teak chests (*sa-daik*) were used to store sacred religious manuscripts donated to monasteries. As a work of merit, the sides were often embellished in gold leaf and/or raised lacquer, with scenes from the life of the Buddha or *jataka* stories of previous existences.

This particular example depicts episodes from the death of the Buddha (*parinibbana*) on three faces of the chest. The side panels portray a prologue of events pertaining to his demise, while the larger central panel shows a closely patterned panorama of the death and funeral events.[1] Episodes are separated by small rocklike wavy lines above a blank space. In the upper left corner, Kassapa, the Buddha's de facto chief disciple, sees an ascetic carrying a *mandarava* flower, a portent that the demise of his leader is at hand. There are two similar scenes where the Buddha is lying in a grove at Kushinagara surrounded by monks. In one he receives medicine and in the other he converts a rival. In the upper right quadrant, Kassapa pays homage to the deceased. Dona apportions the relics to the Malla kings immediately below. At lower left, King Ajatsattu honors the relics. The center and lower right depict the funeral procession, with monks surrounding the catafalque preceded by an orchestra.

SFL

NOTE

1 Bigandet (*Life, or Legend, of Gaudama*, 2: 28–75) gives a detailed description of the demise of the Buddha.

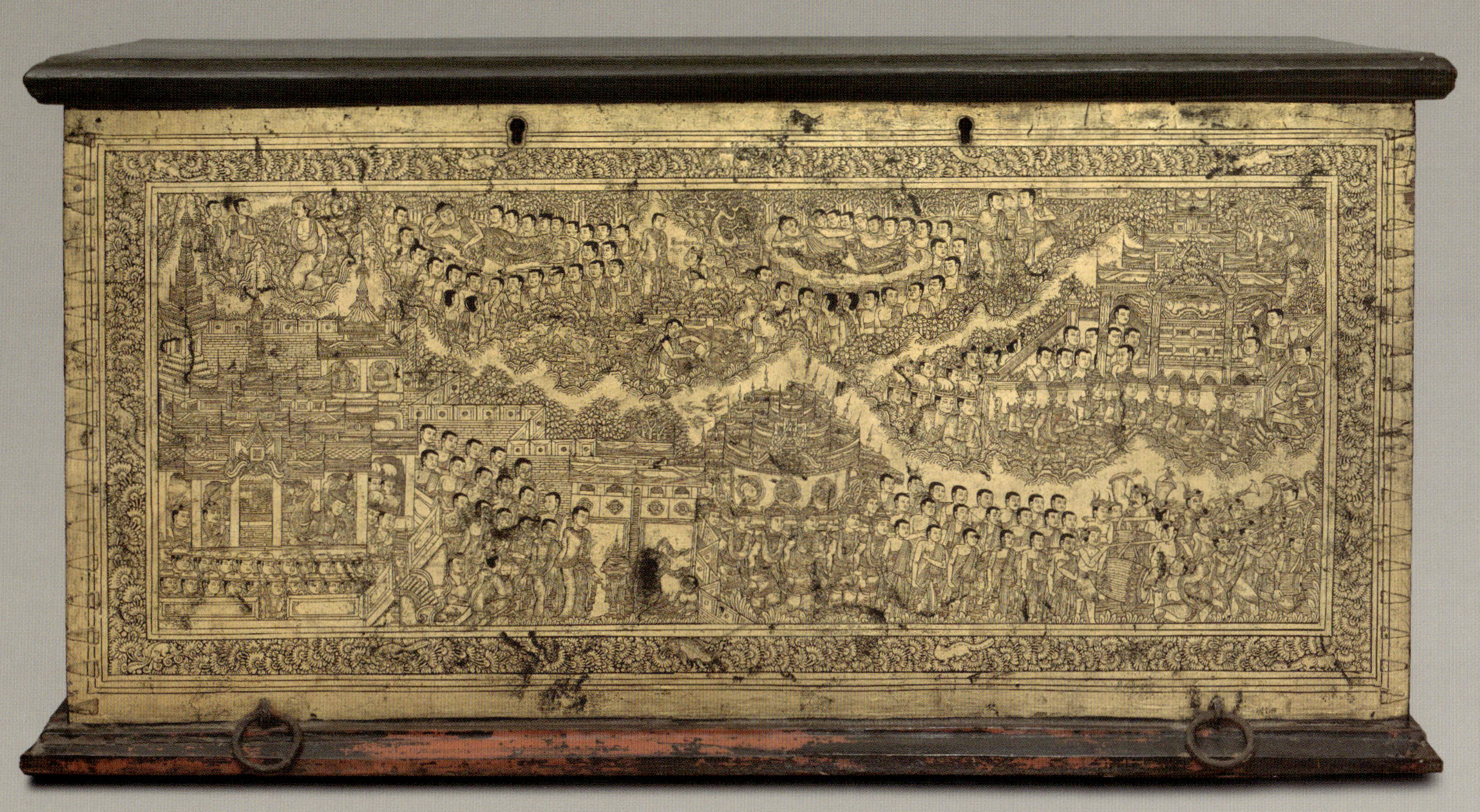

65.

Footprint of the Buddha (*buddhapada*)

Late 19th century
Cotton, tempera, and gold paint
H. 80 x W. 29 in. (203.2 x 73.7 cm)
Burma Art Collection at Northern Illinois University, BC2004.5.1

The footprint (*buddhapada*) had its origins in India and Sri Lanka as an aniconic symbol for the Buddha. Despite the eventual appearance of images of the Buddha, in Buddhist lands the footprint continued to be an object of veneration and worship in its own right. It served as a reminder of the Buddha's life on earth, his enlightened nature, the *Dhamma*, and his continuing presence in the lives of believers. *Buddhapada* in most cases are characterized by toes of equal length, parallel sides, rounded heels, and the presence of a wheel (*cakka*) on the sole, which later came to enclose, or be surrounded by 108 symbols associated with Buddhist cosmological ideas of the Three Worlds, royal insignia, religious paraphernalia, and associated animals.[1]

In this particular example, the 108 symbols have been placed within three concentric circles of the wheel. At the center of the circle is a Rahu mask.[2] At the base of the heel is an open lotus, a motif standing for the Buddha himself and the potential for all sentient beings to grow beyond the mundane desires of earthly existence to become truly enlightened beings, as expressed in the proliferation of smaller upward extending lotuses. The conch shells refer to the proclamation of Buddhism throughout the world spreading to the lower regions, as represented by the *naga*, and extending to the upper realms occupied by worshipful, flower-bearing *devas*.

SFL

NOTES

1 For an examination of various Buddha footprints, including some in Myanmar, see Di Crocco, *Footprints of the Buddhas*; see also Selig Brown, *Eternal Presence*.

2 In Indian mythology, a Rahu mask represents the head of an *asura* demon, which swallows the sun and causes eclipses.

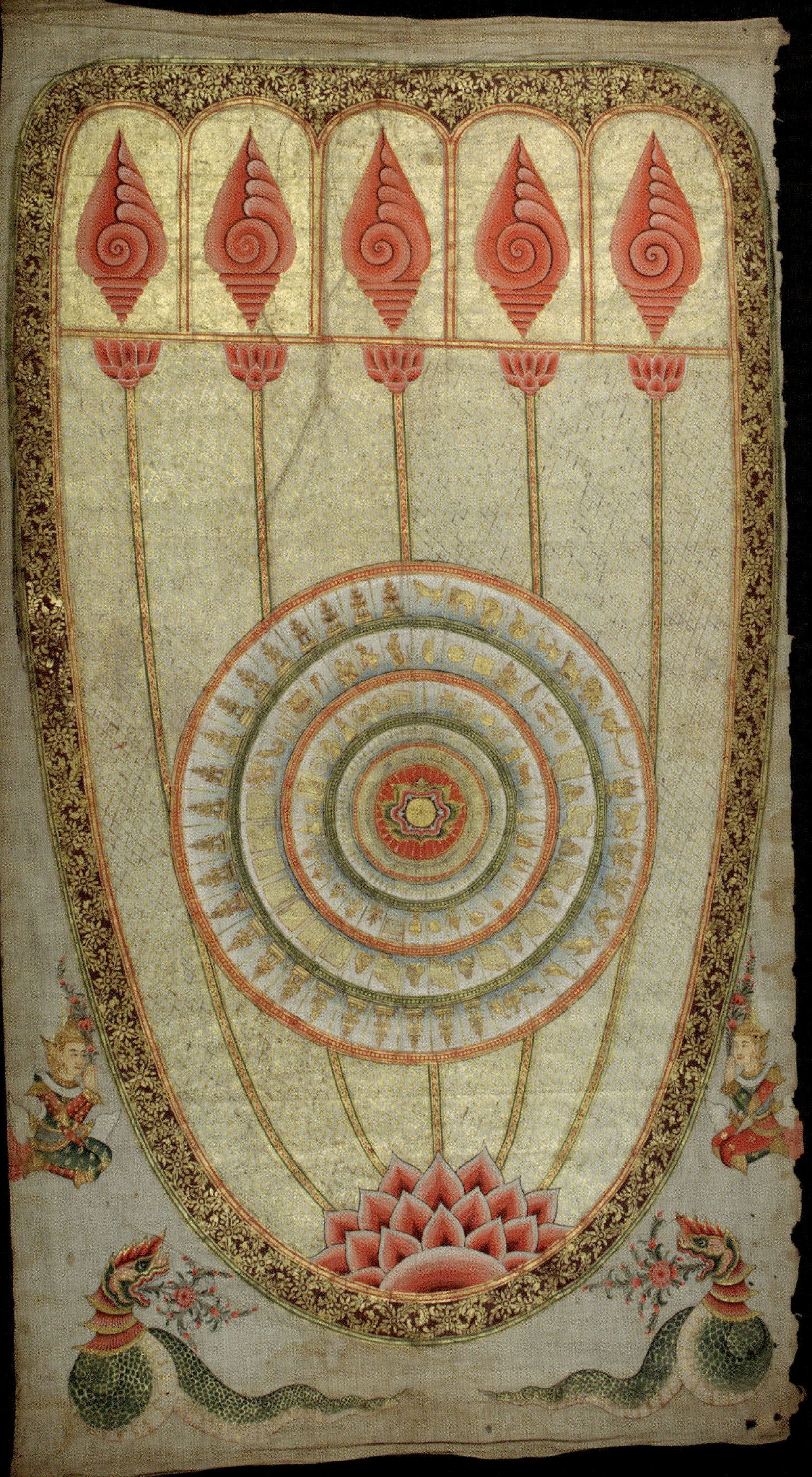

66.

Wall hanging depicting the *Vessantara Jataka* (*Wethandaya Zat*)

Late 19th–early 20th century
Velvet, cotton and flannel cloth, wool, sequins, and metal-wrapped thread
H. 17½ x W. 138½ in. (44.5 x 351.8 cm)
Burma Art Collection at Northern Illinois University: Gift of Paul J. Bennett, BC90.4.275

This embroidered wall hanging depicts episodes from the *Vessantara Jataka*, the last great *jataka* (no. 547) of the Buddha's previous existences, which emphasizes the Buddhist virtue of boundless generosity. It is the most popular and beloved of the *jatakas* in the Theravada Buddhist world of Southeast Asia. In the first panel (not shown), Prince Vessantara was sent into exile for giving away the country's revered white elephant. In the second panel, shown here, the prince has given away his beloved children Jali and Kanhajina to Jujaka, a Brahmin who treats them harshly. The story continues to the left with the Brahmin en route to his home resting overnight in a tree. The children left below are protected from harm by a pair of *devas*. The third and final panel (not shown here) depicts the children being rescued and Vessantara reconciled with his family in his parents' palace.[1]

Depicting narratives on wall hangings became popular during the colonial period when a wider variety of imported embroidery materials such as velvet, flannel, lace, sequins, glass beads, gold-wrapped thread, and mercerized silk and colorful wool yarns became readily available at bazaars throughout the country. The addition of a swag along the base of the hanging has also been adapted from European furnishings.

SFL

NOTE

1 There is an excellent account of the episodes depicted on all panels by Raymond, "Notes on a Burmese Version of the Vessantara Jataka." For a translation of the story from the Pali, see Cowell, Chalmers, Rouse, Francis, Alexander, and Freer, *Jātaka*, 6: 246–305. For an account of embroidery (*shwe-chi-doe*) techniques practiced in Myanmar see Tin Myaing Thein, *Old and New Tapestries of Mandalay*, 43–55. Myanmar tapestries are also referred to as *kalaga* in much of the colonial-period literature.

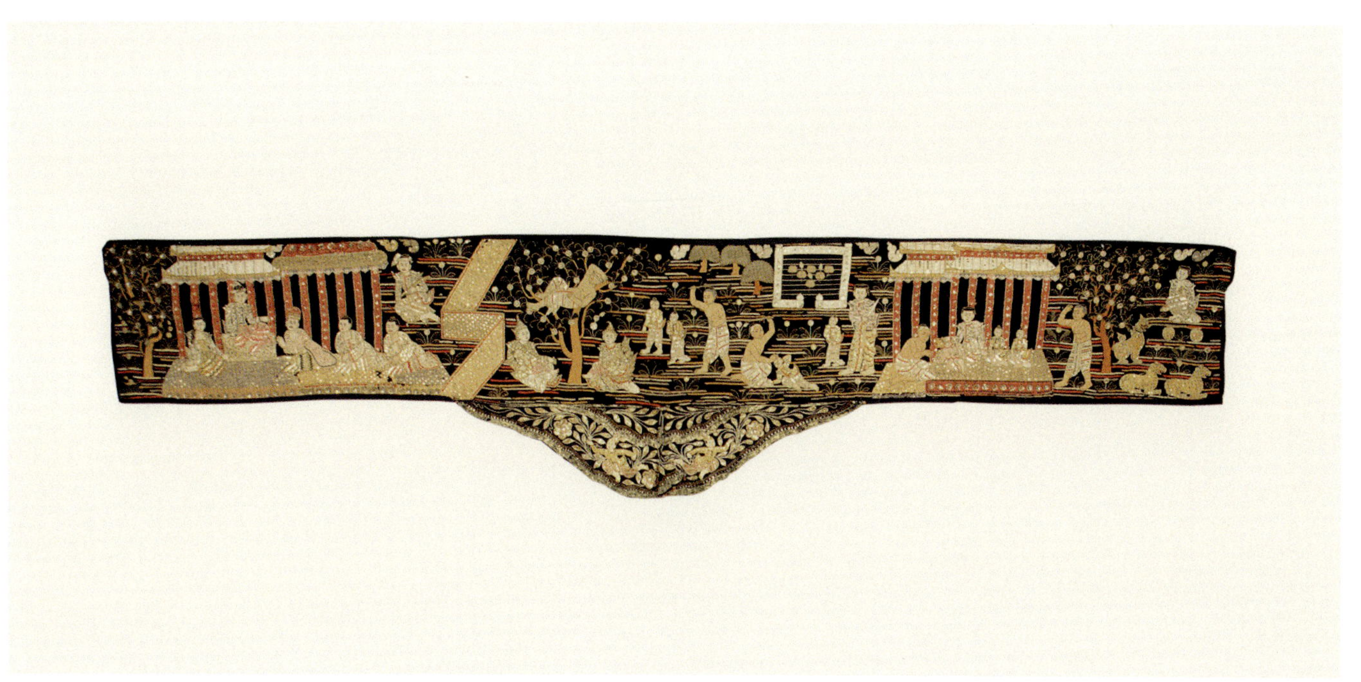

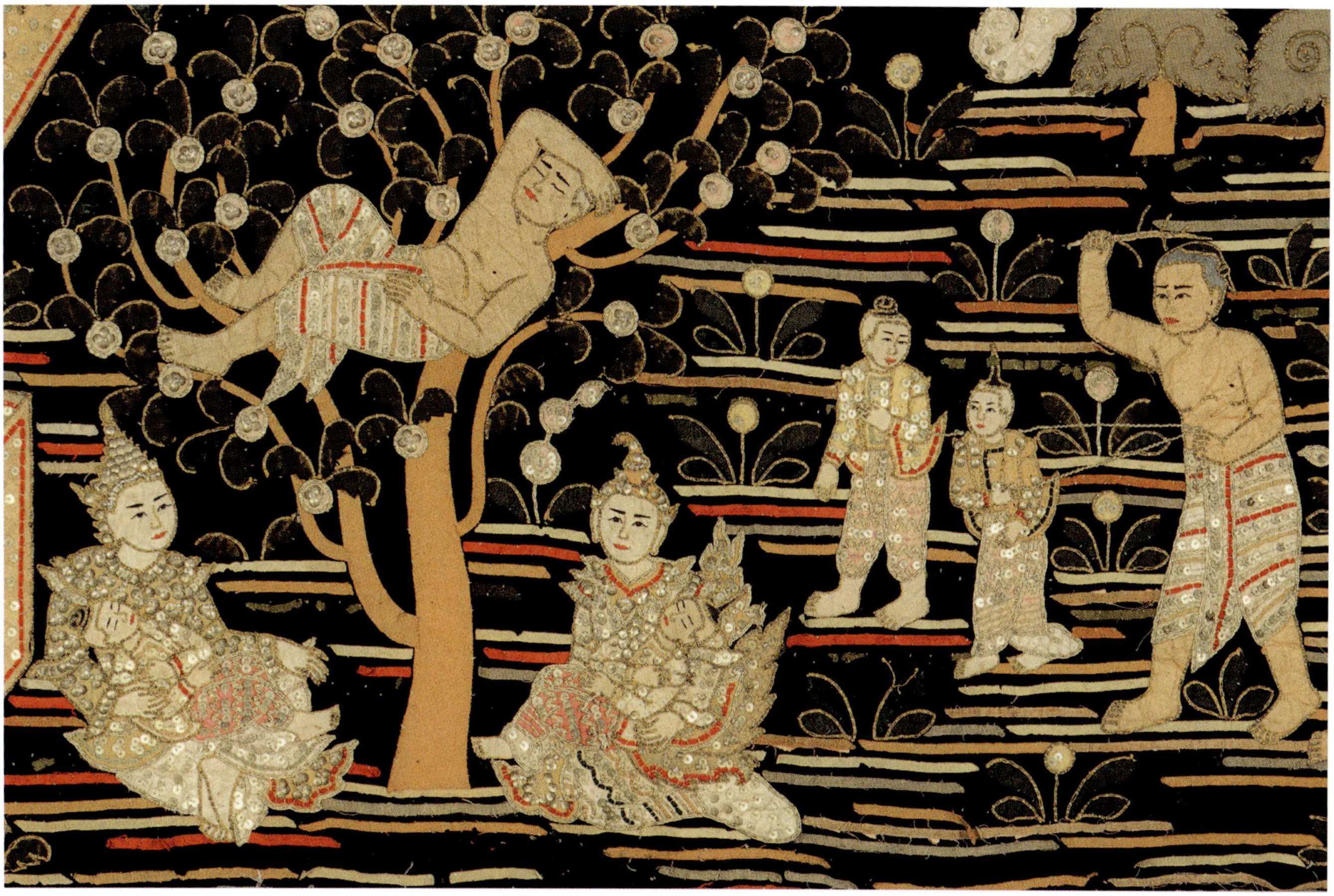

DETAIL

67.
Bell

1884
Bronze
H. 16 x Diam. 9 in. (40.6 x 22.9 cm)
National Museum, Nay Pyi Taw

Sturdy bells suspended on a crossbar with wooden supports are a ubiquitous feature of pagoda platforms throughout Myanmar.[1] As works of merit, they were manufactured with great care, using the *cire perdue* method, and a successful casting was traditionally cause for a village-wide celebration.[2]

The holding ring surmounting the bell in this example is flanked by a pair of sturdy seated lions (*chinthe*), which perform a guardian function.[3] The body of this bell has been divided into sections by bands of concentric lines. A double row of lappet-like lotus petals adorns the shoulder, below which is a three line inscription that may be summarized as: This donation of a bell by a mother and daughter (Ma Khin and May Pwe respectively) of Pin-bya village, Thing-gon district, was made with a clear, detached mind full of good intentions with a desire for their beloved family and friends to follow the precepts, escape the cycle of life, pay homage to Metteyya the future Buddha, and to ascend to the blissful state of *nibbana*.[4]

SFL

NOTES

1 Having no clapper, pagoda bells are sounded on the outside with a wooden striker at the conclusion of personal devotions as open invitation for all to share in the merit. Nearby onlookers usually respond with the refrain *thadu, thadu, thadu*, meaning "well done."

2 Smith-Forbes, *British Burma and Its People*, 130–31.

3 The *chinthe* is a mythical creature resembling a lion and is usually found in pairs guarding pagoda entranceways throughout Myanmar. As king of the beasts, denoting courage, strength, endurance, and power, the lion is considered a worthy guardian of sacred places. The Buddha has also been referred to as Sakyasiha or "Lion of the Sakya clan," as well as a "lion" among men and first among spiritual teachers, with his sermons, like a "lion's roar," spreading his authority to the four corners. See *Annual Report of the Archaeological Survey of India, 1902–1903*, 99.

4 Information about the inscription was provided by a member of staff of the National Museum, Nay Pyi Taw. U Zaw Win of Washington, D.C., also assisted with translating. Besides the aspirations of the donors, inscriptions on bells often provide interesting information on historical towns, economic conditions, customs, and the orthography of the period in which the bell was cast.

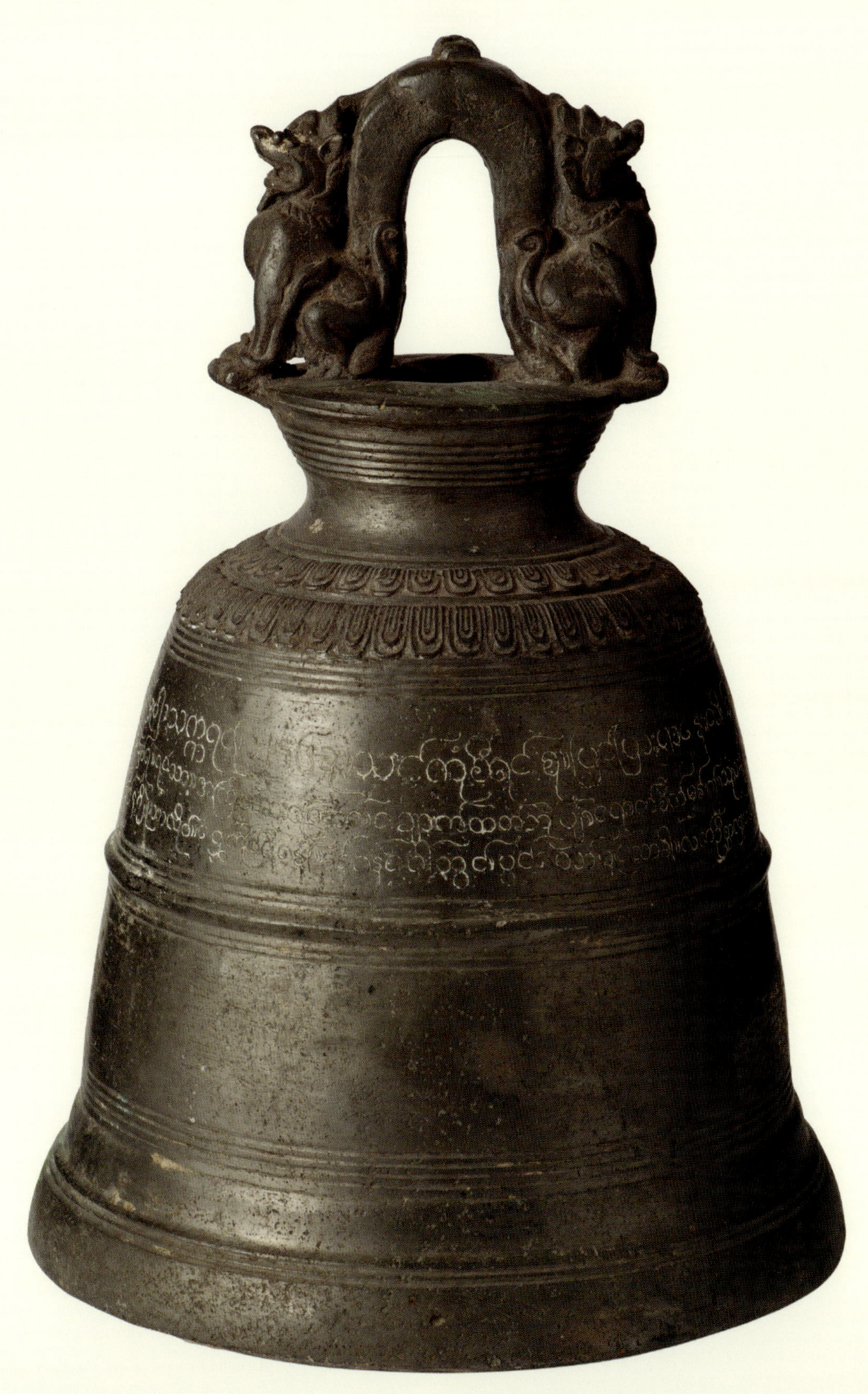

68.

Cover for a food platter with episodes from *Vidhura-pandita Jataka*

Late 19th century
Wood, lacquer, gold-leaf mirror, and colored glass inlay
H. 26¼ x Diam. 26¼ in. (66.7 x 66.7 cm)
Burma Art Collection at Northern Illinois University: Gift of Konrad and Sarah Bekker, BC87.01.45

This gilded wooden dome-shaped lid once covered a large footed tray (*daung-baung kalat*) on which food could be placed for offerings or for a meal prepared for important personages such as members of royalty or highly revered senior monks.[1] A separate finial crowns the apex, which at one time probably incorporated a small *hintha* bird. Artfully embellished with molded lacquer, the upper section consists of a network of foliate patterns picked out in green glass inlay, while the lower part features episodes from the *Vidhura-pandita Jataka* (no. 545), the last but two of the *jatakas*, which emphasizes the virtue of truth. In this story the *bodhisatta* (Buddha-to-be) has been born as Vidhura, a wise minister to King Dhananjaya of Indapatta. The extent of the sage's learning reached the ears of the Queen of the *nagas*, who desired his heart. She sent Punnaka the ogre on a quest to capture him. A win at dice led the ogre to claim Vidhura as the prize. Hanging on to the back of the horse's tail, Vidhura is taken to the *naga* kingdom. Despite attempts en route to kill him, the sage arrives safely to preach a sermon to the *naga* queen, who is converted to the true path.[2]

SFL

NOTES

1 For other examples of *daung-baung kalat*, see Lowry, *Burmese Art*, 5.

2 For an account of the *Vidhura-pandita Jataka*, see Cowell, Chalmers, Rouse, Francis, Alexander, and Freer, *Jātaka*, 6: 126–56. For a succinct summary, see Stanislaw, *Kalagas*, 30–31.

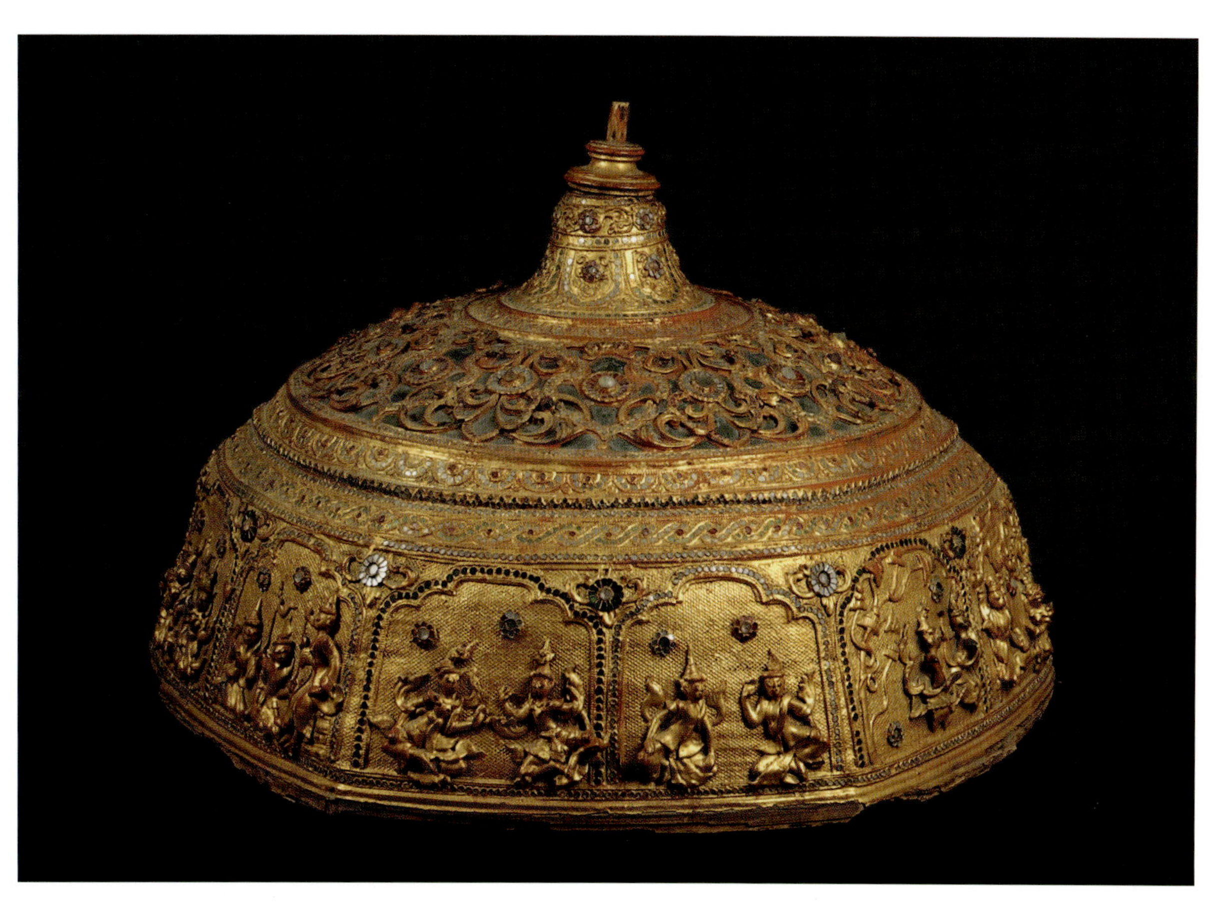

69.

Offering vessel (*hsun-ok*)

Mandalay
Late 19th–early 20th century
Bamboo, wood, sheet metal, lacquer, gold leaf, and cut glass
H. 38 x Diam. 18½ in. (96.5 x 47 cm)

This distinctive spired vessel known as *hsun-ok* was traditionally used to transport food to a monastery. Manufactured from split coiled bamboo, it is made up of three parts: a bowl attached to a pedestaled flaring stand, a pagoda-shaped cover, and an internal plainly lacquered tray on which food such as soup, curries, pickles, and rice might be placed. In addition to circular moldings, the external surface of this example has been lavishly embellished with bands of gilded raised lacquer decoration in the form of rhythmic twirling foliage that springs from regular, centrally placed rosettes of cabochons and slivers of colored glass. Midway up the tapering spire rests an effigy in wood and openwork sheet metal of a *hamsa*, or *hintha*, a semidivine bird whose presence reiterates the sacred nature of the vessel. The tip of the finely turned wooden spire appears to be missing.

Hsun-ok come in all sizes, forms, and modes of decoration, ranging from the tall and slender to the short and squat. Embellishment may be in monotones of red and black as well as in multicolored incised designs.[1] Those of miniscule size might be designated for the family shrine. A well-crafted example such as this was probably donated for display rather than for the presentation of food.[2]

SFL

NOTES

1 For a variety of *hsun-ok* shapes, see Capelo, *A Arte da Laca na Birmânia e na Tailândia*, 61–105.

2 For similar examples, see Isaacs and Blurton, *Visions from the Golden Land*, 201; and Than Htun (Dedaye), *Lacquerware Journeys*, 167.

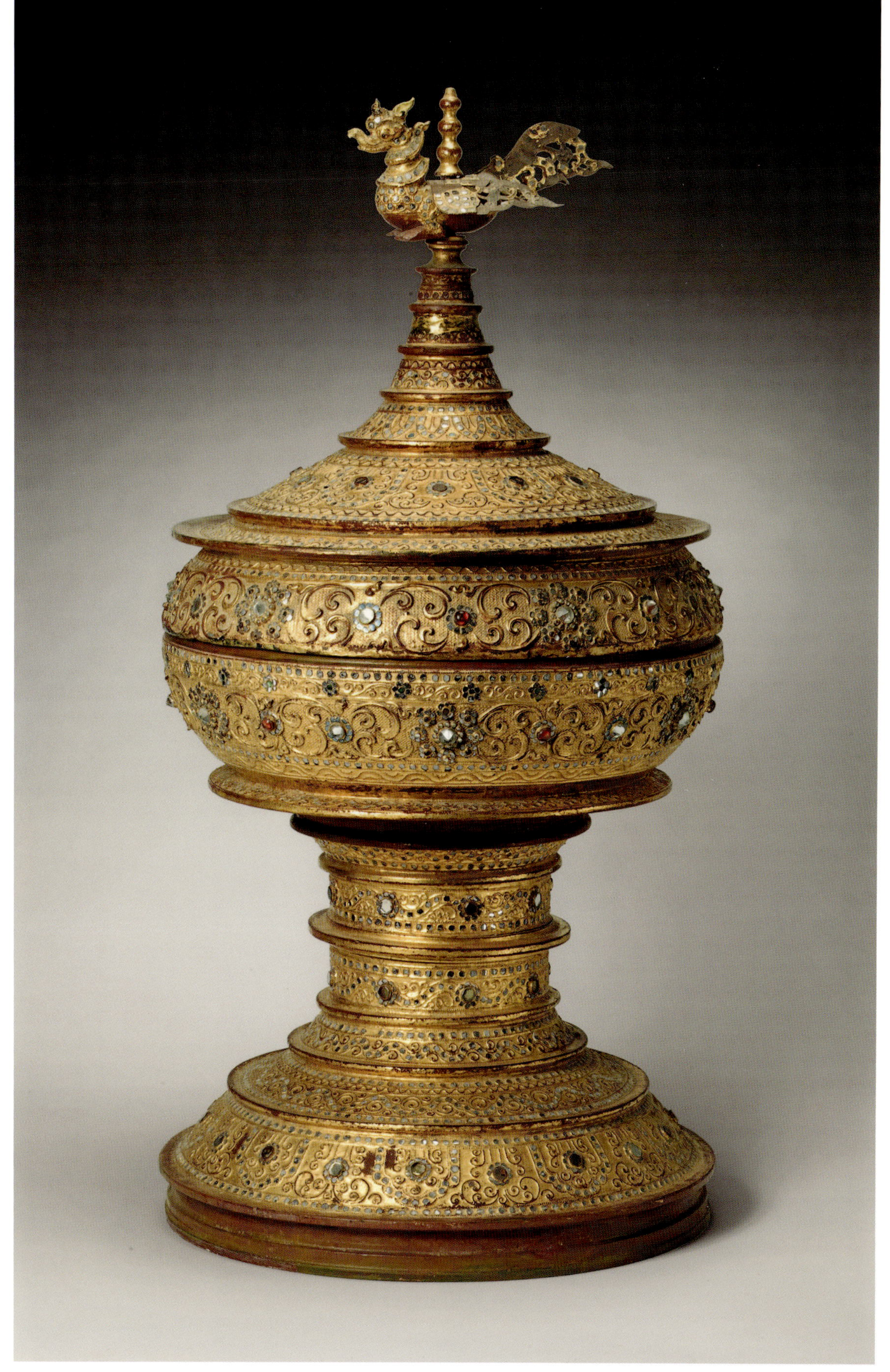

70.

Covered bowl on stand (*thabeik*)

Early 20th century
Wood, bamboo, lacquer, colored cut glass, and gold leaf
H. 24½ in. (62.2 cm)
Denison Museum: Gift of Ann Rohrer, 1968.78

This highly decorated covered receptacle mounted on a matching hourglass-shaped stand is a ceremonial replica of the monk's alms bowl (*patta*), or *thabeik*, which is globular in shape and curves inward toward the rim. Such a bowl, made of clay or iron and intended for gathering food, is one of the "eight requisites" (*attha parikkhara*) that a Buddhist monk is permitted to personally own.[1] The flat-topped lid made from a substrate of coiled bamboo and matting protects the contents and serves as a tray if necessary.

In this particular example, the botanical-inspired decoration has been placed within concentric bands of molded lacquer (*thayo*) and is composed of various designs that have been artfully inlaid with slivers of blue, red, and green mirrored glass, along with rows of cabochon beading and floral centers of faceted glass (*hman-zi shwe-cha*).[2] The underlying green glass mosaic around the body of the bowl has been overlain with rhythmic scrolling alternating with *bilu-gwin*, quatrefoil space cells enclosing floral motifs, suggestive of Shan rather than Bamar craftsmanship. Such bowls with matching stands were commissioned and donated for display purposes at pagoda and monastery shrines.[3]

SFL

NOTES

1 The other "requisites" include the three robes, the *antaravasaka* worn around the hips, the *uttarasanga* large outer cloth, and the *sanghati* shoulder cloth; a razor for shaving; a needle and thread for repairs to the robes; a waistband to secure the *antaravasaka*; and a strainer for filtering impurities from drinking water. For details concerning what monks are permitted with respect to bowls, see Rhys Davids and Oldenberg, *Vinaya Texts*, pt. 3, 81–88.

2 For details of the *hman-zi shwe-cha* technique, see Fraser-Lu, *Burmese Lacquerware*, 49–50.

3 This bowl has also been described in Green, *Eclectic Collecting*, 174–75.

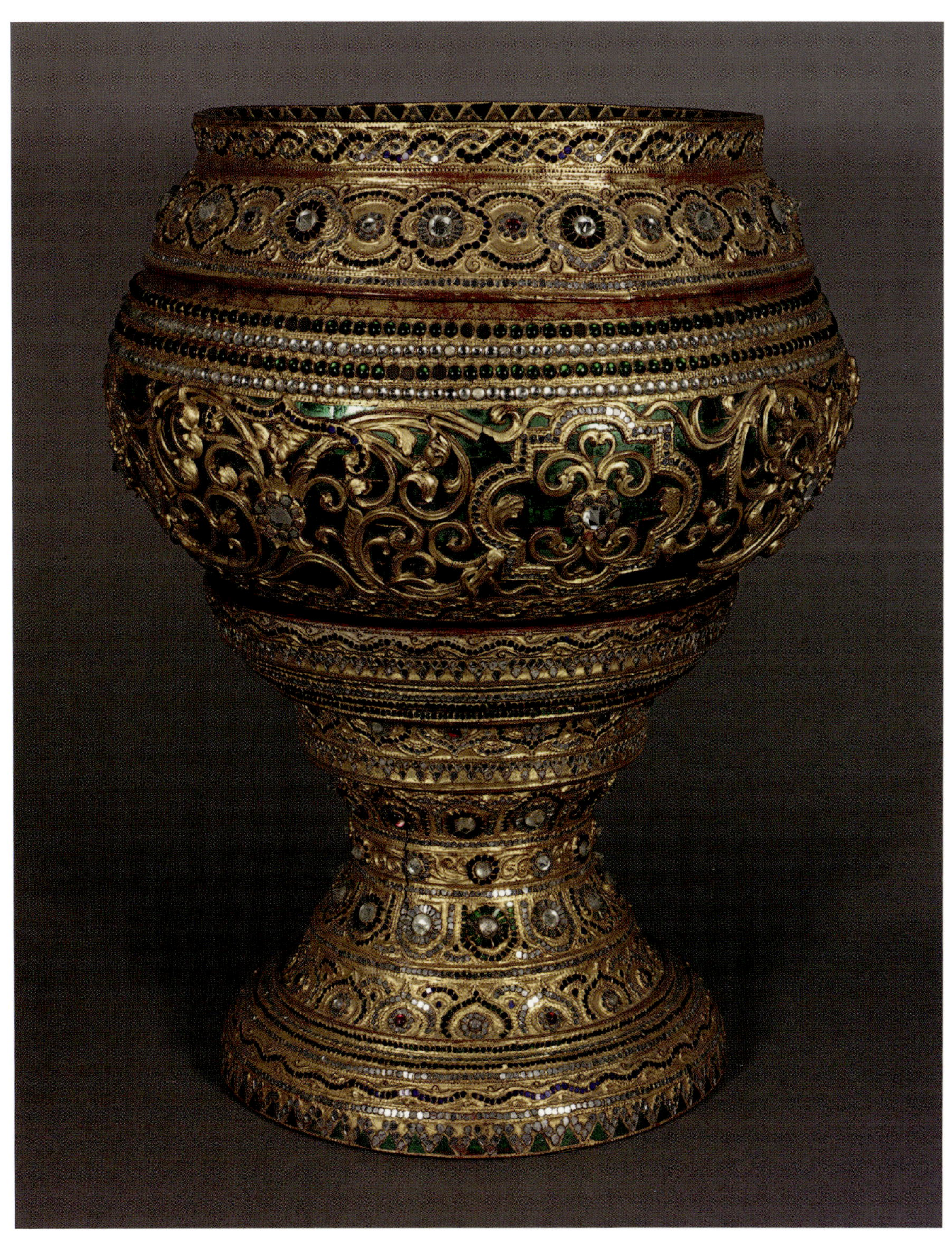

71.

Covered box with *Vessantara Jataka*

Early 20th century
Silver
H. 8 x Diam. 6 in. (20.3 x 15.2 cm)
Burma Art Collection at Northern Illinois University: Gift of John Lacey, BC97.2.46

This lidded silver box with its shallow inner tray very much resembles a *betel* box (*kun-it*), which was formerly an important item of hospitality in every Myanmar home. Bamar and Shan silversmiths were masters of the repoussé technique and excelled at embellishing objects in closely patterned high relief, as seen in this example depicting episodes of the *Vessantara Jataka* around the sides of the box. Scenes include the family being sent into exile and the prince giving away the horses and chariot that carried them, Jujaka the Brahmin asking Vessantara for his children, Vessantara's wife Maddi collecting food and being prevented from returning home by a lion, and the Brahmin sleeping in a tree. The lid is decorated with closely patterned floral and vegetal scrolling interrupted by small shield-shaped space cells containing figures. These may refer to the family's life in exile in the forest. A small, separately cast effigy of a dancing female half-human, half-bird *kinnari* figure crowns the cover. A band of lotus petals embellishes both the rim of the lid and the base of the box, a characteristic feature of Myanmar silverwork. European influences may be seen in the outlines of the space cells and in the smoothly polished edges.[1]

SFL

NOTE

1 For accounts of Myanmar silver, see Fraser-Lu, "Burmese Silverware"; and Wilkinson, Wilkinson, and Harding, "Burmese Silver of the Colonial Period," 69–81.

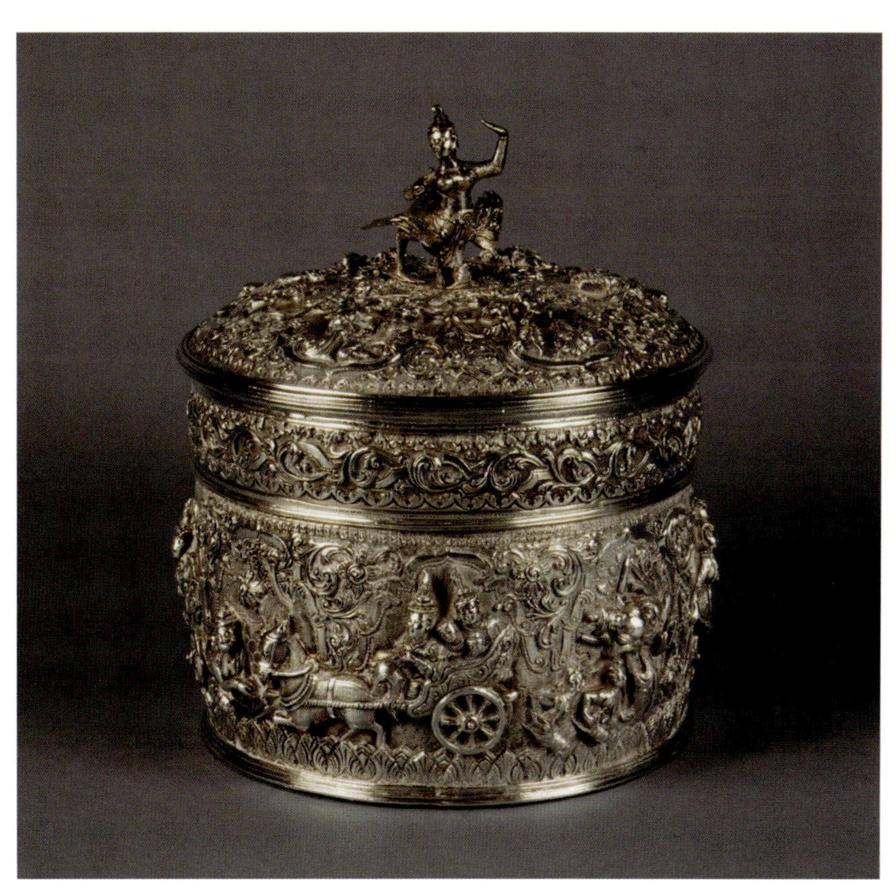

Myanmar and Surrounding Countries

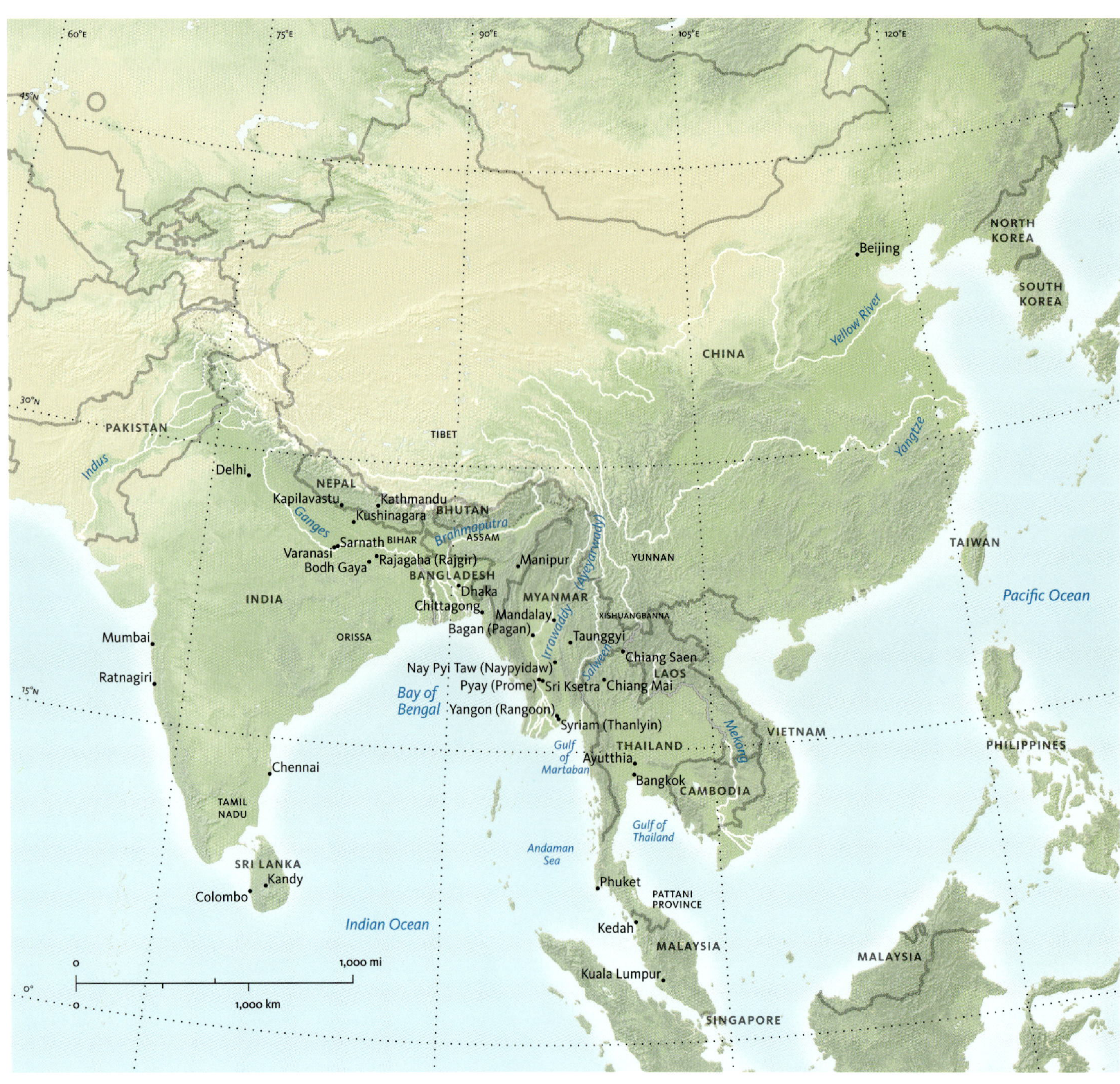

CARTOGRAPHIC DATA AND COUNTRY BORDERS DERIVED FROM NATURAL EARTH (WWW.NATURALEARTHDATA.COM), WHICH MAY BE REFERENCED FOR ADDITIONAL INFORMATION

Myanmar

90°E
100°E
BHUTAN
INDIA
CHINA
BANGLADESH
KACHIN
SAGAING
MYANMAR
Myit-ng
Budalin
Monywa
Mingun
Mandalay
Sagaing
Amarapura
Ava (Inwa)
CHIN
SHAN
VIETNAM
Bagan (Pagan)
MANDALAY
Chiang Tung
Kyauktaw
Mount Selagiri
Mount Popa
Taunggyi
Vesali
Mrauk-U
Irrawaddy (Ayeyarwady)
20°N
Sittwe (Akyab)
Magwe
Salween
MAGWAY
Nay Pyi Taw (Naypyidaw)
Bay of Bengal
RAKHINE
KAYAH
LAOS
Pyay (Prome)
Sri Ksetra
Thegone
Sittang
BAGO
KAYIN
Kyontu
Kyaikto
Aythema
Bago (Pegu)
Thaton
Hpa-an
Yangon (Rangoon)
YANGON
Syriam (Thanlyin)
Mottama (Martaban)
AYEYARWADY
Mawlamyine (Moulmein)
MON
Gulf of Martaban
THAILAND
CAMBODIA
TANINTHARYI
Gulf of Thailand
0
200 mi
200 km
Andaman Sea
10°N

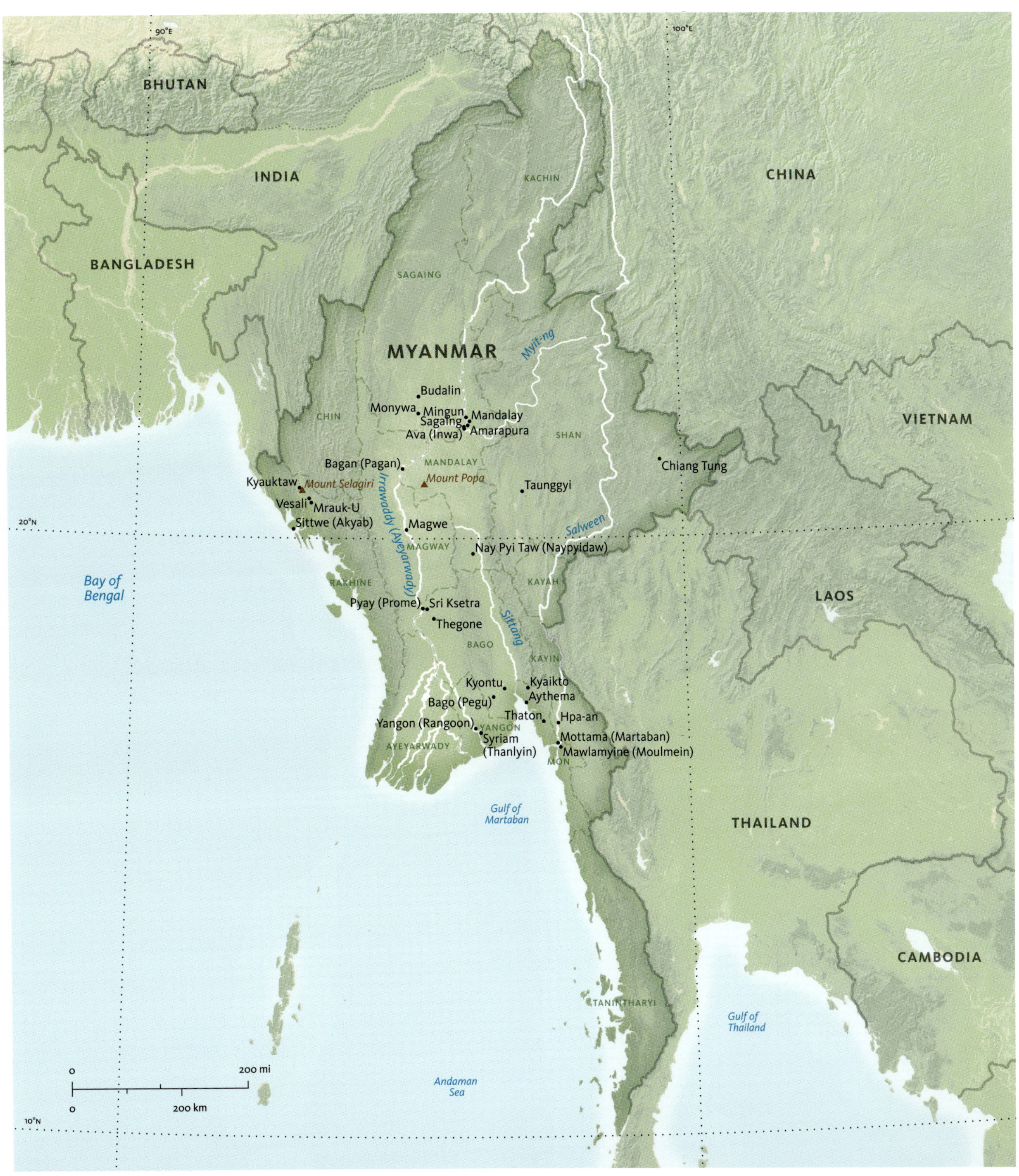

Chronology

Jacques Leider

	WEST/NORTHWEST MYANMAR	CENTRAL AND UPPER MYANMAR	EAST/SOUTHEAST/SOUTH MYANMAR
700,000 BCE	700,000–4,000 BCE Hunter-Gatherer Period		
4,000 BCE	4,000 BCE–1st century CE Neolithic Period		
100 CE	2nd–10th century CE Emergence of urban civilizations Rakhine Dhanyawadi-Vesali	2nd–10th century CE Emergence of urban civilizations Pyu (Beikthano-Sri Ksetra)	2nd–10th century CE Emergence of urban civilizations Mon (Thaton)
1000 CE	11th–14th century Rakhine Lemro Period	11th–13th century Bamar Pagan Period	
1400	1430–1784 Rakhine Mrauk-U Period	1364–1527 Bamar Ava Period	1369–1537 Mon Hanthawaddy Pegu Period
1500		1531–99 Taunggu Period	
1700		1599–1752 Restored Taunggu/Nyaung-yan Period	1740–57 Restored Hanthawaddy
	1752–1885 Konbaung Dynasty		
	1784 Konbaung conquest of Rakhine	1767 Konbaung conquest of Ayutthaya	
1800	1813 Konbaung conquest of Manipur	After 1784–1804 Konbaung loss of control over Chiang Mai and northwestern Laos	
	1824–26 First Anglo-Burmese War British gain control of Rakhine		1824–26 First Anglo-Burmese War British gain control of Tenasserim
	1852 Second Anglo-Burmese War British gain control of Lower Myanmar		
	1884–85 Third Anglo-Burmese War British gain control of Upper Myanmar		
1900	1942–45 Japanese Occupation		
	January 4, 1948 Independence—Union of Burma		
	1962–88 General Ne Win Burma Socialist Program Party Period		
2000	1988–2011 Union of Myanmar State Law and Order Restoration Council/State Peace and Development Council		
	After 2011 new elected government		

Glossary

The glossary has been divided into the following four sections: Terms; Geographical Names; Historical and Mythical Figures; and Pagodas, Temples, and Monuments. The glossary entries are in alphabetical order within each section.

Terms

a-saw (Myanmar). A pointed flame-like leaf decoration in plaster or woodcarving which may be repeated along the upper periphery of railings, doorways, and gables.

abhaya mudra (Sanskrit, *abhaya mudrā*). A hand gesture of protection, benevolence, and the dispelling of fear. In Theravada the gesture is made with bent elbow and right hand raised to shoulder level with straight fingers and palm facing outwards.

Abhidhamma (Pali). The third section of the Pali ***Tipitaka*** containing the profound moral philosophy (ethics and epistemology) and psychology of the Buddha's teaching as expounded by the Buddha's disciples and great scholars. The *Abhidhamma* contains higher philosophical teachings and is greatly venerated in Myanmar.

Airavata (Sanskrit, Airāvata). A mythical, triple-headed white elephant, the mount of the Hindu god Indra.

Ajatasattu (Pali, Ajātasattu/Sanskrit, Ajātaśatru). Son of King Bimbisara, an early fervid supporter of the Buddha. Ajatasattu ruled ca. 492–460 BCE. Impatient for his inheritance, he imprisoned his father and followed a policy of conquest and expansion making the kingdom of Magadha the most powerful state in northern India. Repenting of his ways, he too became an avid supporter of the Buddha.

Ambwe ko-pa (Myanmar). The Nine Wonders, nine Buddha statues at the **Shwedagon Pagoda**, each associated with a legend of its creation.

Ananta (Sanskrit). Serpent associated with **Vishnu**.

antaravasaka (Pali and Sanskrit, *antaravāsaka*). The lower garment of a monk that extends from the waist to below the knees. It is secured with a waistband.

arahant (Pali/Sanskrit, *arhat*/Myanmar, *yahanda*). A person who has attained enlightenment through practicing the teachings of the Buddha and is no longer subject to rebirth. To reach the state of an *arahant* is the proper goal of a Buddhist in the Theravada tradition. Mythical *arahants* appear often in Myanmar Buddhist legends.

ardhaparyankasana (Sanskrit, *ardhaparyaṅkāsana*). A semi-sitting posture where one thigh is raised and bent at the knee with the foot resting on the seat or pedestal. The other leg is pendant and may rest on a support.

arupaloka (Pali, *arūpaloka*/Sanskrit, *arūpyaloka*). The highest of three planes of existence in Buddhist thought, a world without form, consisting of four realms of neither perception nor nonperception, nothingness, infinite consciousness, and infinite space.

asana (Sanskrit, *āsana*). A seat or throne; leg positions assumed by deities.

attha parikkhara (Pali, *aṭṭha parikkhāra*). Buddhist monks are permitted to have eight requisites as personal property. They include the three robes (the *uttarasanga* outer robe, the *antaravasaka* inner robe, and *sanghati* shoulder robe) along with a belt to secure the inner robe to the waist, and a needle for repairs. A *patta* alms bowl is permitted for receiving food, as is a razor for shaving, and a water strainer to filter impurities from the water.

ayedawbon (Myanmar/Mon, *akruin*). A form of royal chronicle that details a single reign.

Bamar. Ethnic Burman. Held kingdoms in **Pagan**, **Ava**, and **Taunggu**.

Banyan tree (*Ficus benghalensis*). Tree belonging to a goatherd who appeared during the fifth week that the Buddha remained at Bodh Gaya.

***betel* box** (Myanmar, *kun-it*/*betel* is Portuguese from Malayalam). Lidded box used to store the ingredients essential to a *betel* chew: chopped areca nut, lime paste, fresh betel leaves, and other ingredients. An item of hospitality in a Myanmar home.

Bhairava (Sanskrit). A wrathful and powerful form of the god Shiva, one of the three most important deities of the Hindu pantheon. Bhairava is also sometimes identified as a form of Shiva himself.

bhikkhu (Pali/Myanmar, *yahan*). Buddhist monk.

bhumisparsa mudra (Sanskrit, *bhūmisparśa*). An earth-touching gesture in which the right hand extends downward, palm inward to touch the ground or base of a throne with the fingers. The fingers may be naturalistic or of equal length. The use of this *mudra* is confined to seated images usually in the *padmasana* or *virasana* pose. The gesture symbolizes "calling the earth to witness" at the moment of enlightenment when the Buddha called upon the Earth Goddess to verify his perfections of previous existences. Also known as *maravijaya*, the gesture also symbolizes victory over Mara (the Evil One). This *mudra* has been the prevalent pose for Myanmar Buddha images since the Pagan period. Also spelled *bhumisparsha mudra*. See ***maravijaya***.

bilu (Myanmar). A male ogre.

bilu-gwin (Myanmar). A term for a four-lobed floral pattern. The design shape may also be used as a space cell for another design or to enclose a group of figures in a narrative.

bilu-ma (Myanmar). An ogress.

bodawin (Myanmar). Buddha chronicle.

Bodhi Tree. *Ficus religiousa*, the tree under which Gotama Buddha achieved enlightenment.

bodhisatta (Pali/Sanskrit, *bodhisattva*). A being ultimately destined for Buddhahood. May serve as a guide to others on the Buddhist path.

bodhisattva (Sanskrit). See ***bodhisatta***.

buddhanana (Pali, *buddhañāṅa*). Buddha knowledge. There are fourteen kinds of Buddha knowledge possessed by all Buddhas.

buddhapada (Pali and Sanskrit, *buddhapāda*). Footprint of the Buddha.

Burman. Equivalent in meaning to **Bamar**.

cakka (Pali, *cakka*/Sanskrit, *cakra*). In Buddhism, the "wheel of the law." At the first sermon in a deer park at Sarnath, the Buddha began to preach to mankind, so setting the wheel of the law (his doctrine) in motion.

cakkavatti (Pali /Sanskrit, *cakravartin*). An Indian term for an ideal monarch, who has both the temporal and spiritual power to rule wisely and benevolently over the whole world.

chinthe (Myanmar). A mythical lionlike creature, which is a popular fixture for guarding temples and pagodas throughout Myanmar.

chu-pan (Myanmar). A popular coil-like foliage design seen on woodcarving, lacquerwork, and metalwork.

cire perdue (French). An ancient metal casting process whereby an object is formed by melting out the wax cast and replacing it with molten metal.

contrapposto. A position in which the human body is twisted on the vertical axis, with the result that the hips, shoulders, and head are turned in different directions.

Culamani (Pali, Cūḷāmaṇi/Myanmar pronunciation Sulamani). A type of pagoda that enshrines Buddha's hair.

daung-baung-kalat (Myanmar). Votive stand of lacquered wood supported on small feet, which may sometimes be zoomorphic. A lacquered bamboo conical or dome-shaped cover protects the contents of the tray.

deva (Pali and Sanskrit/Myanmar, *nat*). Celestials inhabiting the lower heavens of the Hindu-Myanmar cosmos; the "angels" of Buddhism. In Myanmar the term *nat* may also refer to animistic nature spirits, mytho-biological guardian figures, and former humans who died unnatural deaths and are propitiated for various reasons.

Dhamma (Pali/Sanskrit *Dharma*). The natural and moral law of the universe. In Buddhism it refers to the foundation and essence of the religion itself. The teachings of the Buddha.

dhammayon (Myanmar). Buddhist preaching hall.

dharmacakra mudra (Sanskrit, *dharmacakra mudrā*). "Wheel of the Dharma" gesture. A symbol of teaching the Dharma. Both hands are held close to the chest and touch one another in various ways.

dhyana mudra (Sanskrit, *dhyāna mudrā*). A gesture indicating a state of meditation, with hands placed one upon the other, resting on the folded legs in a seated position.

Dipavamsa (Pali, *Dīpavavaṃsa*). Fourth-century chronicle of Sri Lanka.

dvarapala (Sanskrit, *dvārapāla*). Male guardian figure. They are often placed in pairs flanking doorways in Hindu and Buddhist temples.

Dvaravati. The Mon culture of Thailand during the first millennium.

Eight Great Events. Also called the Eight Great Miracles. They are eight major events in the life of the Buddha: the birth, the first sermon, the taming of the elephant Nalagiri, the enlightenment, the descent from Tavatimsa Heaven, the miracle at Shravasti, the gift of honey by a monkey, and the death.

gajasana (Sanskrit, *gajāsana*). Elephant throne. Also a position in yoga.

ghanta (Sanskrit, *ghaṇṭā*). Bell.

Gotama (Pali/Sanskrit, Gautama). The name of the historical Buddha's clan, or *gotra* (Sanskrit), to which the Buddha and the Sakyans belonged. The name is used to distinguish the historical Buddha from the Buddhas of other eras.

Gupta period. North Indian dynasty (ca. 300–500) noted for its architecture, sculpture, and paintings.

hamsa (Pali, *haṃsa*). Species of goose (*Tadorna ferruginea*) associated with the Mon civilization of Lower Myanmar.

hintha (Myanmar). See ***hamsa***.

hman-zi shwe-cha (Myanmar). Gilded lacquer relief work inlaid with colored glass.

hpaya (Myanmar). Also anglicized as *paya*. Literally meaning Lord, *hpaya* can refer to a Buddhist temple or pagoda, a Buddha image, or be used as an honorific for a monk.

Hpo-u (Myanmar). A hill on the west bank of the Irrawaddy (Ayeyarwady) River near Prome (Pyay) where the Buddha prophesied the founding of Sri Ksetra.

hsun-ok (Myanmar). A pagoda-shaped, pedestalled votive vessel with a distinctive tapering lid.

hti (Myanmar). Metal finial, often translated as "umbrella," crowning the top of a pagoda.

Jambudipa (Pali, Jambudīpa/Sanskrit, Jambudvīpa). The great continent south of the cosmic Mount Meru in Buddhist cosmology.

Jambupati (Pali). The name of an arrogant expansionist monarch who was humbled by the Buddha. The term has come to mean a crowned Buddha image.

jataka (Pali and Sanskrit, *Jātaka*/Myanmar, *Zat*). A canonical collection of 547 stories of the Buddha's former lives in divine, human, and animal form, which were originally written in stanzas. Each story is also called a *jataka/zat* and opens with a prologue that relates to the particular circumstance in the Buddha's life that led him to tell a particular birth story. The purpose of these stories was to emphasize a particular virtue illustrated by the Buddha's actions in his numerous reincarnations, and so to serve as a example for others.

Jataka-nidana (Pali, *Jātaka-nidāna*). Also known as *Nidana-katha*, introduction to the fifth-century *jataka* commentary by Buddhaghosa.

kalaga (Myanmar). A term that became popular during the colonial period to describe a Myanmar wall hanging embellished with applique, couched gold and silver thread, colored yarns, and sequins.

kamaloka (Pali and Sanskrit, *kāmaloka*). The world of desire, consisting of eleven realms dominated by the senses. Seven of these realms are favorable places to be and include the human realm, with its balance of pleasure and pain that offers the possibility of acquiring virtue, wisdom, and compassion to escape the cycle of rebirths. The four lowest realms are reserved for demons, ghosts, animals, and those who merit time in hell.

kammavaca (Pali, *kammavācā*/Myanmar, *kammawa*). Ritual texts recited during formal monastic ceremonies often preserved in finely embellished manuscripts with pages made from lacquered cloth, metal, or ivory inscribed with extracts pertaining to monastic ritual.

kanot (Myanmar). Flowing floral and vegetal forms in Myanmar art. *Kanot* forms in later Myanmar art have been influenced by flamelike forms from Thailand.

Karen. See **Kayin**.

karma (Sanskrit/Pali, *kamma*). "Action" or "deed" in this life on earth. Ultimately determines the form in which the individual will be reborn in the next life. In Buddhism, karma refers to the universal law of cause and effect.

karnapurna (Sanskrit, *karṇapūrṇa*). A pendulous flower.

Kathe. See **Manipuri**.

kathina (Pali/Myanmar, Kahtein). A festival that occurs shortly after the end of the Buddhist Lent (late October–November) where the faithful show their gratitude to monks by replenishing their requisites such as robes and alms bowls. They also make gifts of sandals, umbrellas, water flasks, and other objects that a monk might have use for. "Padetha," treelike stands, are erected in public places on which donations may be placed before being conveyed to a monastery in a grand procession.

Kayin (Myanmar). Ethnic group, also anglicized as Karen.

keinaya (Myanmar). See ***kinnara***.

khandhaka (Pali). A chapter or section of scripture from the ***Tipitaka***, such as the nine *khandhakas* of the Pali *Vinaya*.

kinnara (Pali, *kinnara*/Sanskrit, *kiṃnara*/ Myanmar, *keinaya*). A mythical creature with a human face and torso and a bird's legs and wings.

kinnari (Pali, *kinnarī*/Sanskrit, *kiṃnarī*). Female form of a ***kinnara***, a mythical, hybrid half-human, half-bird creature.

Konagamana (Pali, Koṇāgamana). The twenty-third of twenty-four Buddhas listed chronologically in the Buddhavamsa, and the second of five Buddhas to appear in the current "auspicious eon."

Konbaung dynasty (1752–1885). Myanmar kingdom from the mid-eighteenth to the late nineteenth century, with capitals in **Shwebo**, **Sagaing**, **Ava**, **Amarapura**, and **Mandalay**. (See Chronology.)

Konmara (Myanmar). A ***jataka***-inspired folktale.

kou-za (Myanmar). A physical representation or stand-in for the Buddha in the form of a relic or icon.

koyin (Myanmar). See ***samanera***.

kun-it (Myanmar). See **betel box**.

lalitasana (Sanskrit, *lālitāsana*). A seated posture of "royal ease" in which the left leg is folded while the right leg is pendent, suggestive of serenity.

leik-pya (Myanmar). Literally "butterfly." A leaf-like or outspread butterfly/bat-wing design that fills a right angle corner decoration in Myanmar woodwork and other media.

linno-daung (Myanmar). Literally "bat wing." See ***leik-pya***.

Lokapannati (Pali, *Lokapaññati*). A pivotal text pertaining to the cult of Upagutta.

lotus (Sanskrit, *padma*). The flower that symbolizes the beauty and purity of the Buddhist faith.

magyi-zi (Myanmar). "Tamarind seed." A square style of script, used for ***kammavaca*** manuscripts. A style of writing popular during the Pagan period.

maha-kyan (Myamar). Prized leftover gold from the casting of the Mahamuni statue.

Mahakarmavibhanga (Sanskrit, *Mahākarmavibhaṅga*). The name of a widely known Sanskrit Buddhist text in which **Gavampati** is referred to.

Mahaparinibbana Sutta (Pali, *Mahāparinibbāna Sutta*). *The Discourse on the Great Passing Away*, a famous ***sutta*** recounting the Buddha's last year of life and attainment of ***parinibbana***.

Mahavamsa (Pali, *Mahāvaṃsa*). An influential fifth-century chronicle of Sri Lanka.

Mahavihara (Pali, Mahāvihāra). Influential Sri Lankan monastery and monastic lineage.

Mahayana (Sanskrit, Mahāyāna). "Great Vehicle." Emerging in India in the first century, it is the form of Buddhism that flourishes in Nepal, Tibet, China, Korea, Japan, and Vietnam. It contrasts with the **Theravada** Buddhism of Sri Lanka, Myanmar, Thailand, Laos, and Cambodia.

Majjhimadesa (Pali). Mythical-cum-historical middle land of Buddhist canonical texts.

makara (Pali and Sanskrit). A mythic acquatic creature resembling a crocodile and a symbol of water in Indian mythology. It is a widely used artistic motif in India and Southeast Asia and may assume a protective function over entranceways of temples. The *makara* was popular over doorways during the Pagan period.

Malla princes/kings. Rulers of the territory around Kushinagara where the Buddha passed into ***nibbana***. They were on the verge of going to war with neighboring kingdoms over the division of the relics until Dona, a clever Brahmin, agreed to apportion them equally.

man-hpaya (Myanmar). A hollow Buddha image made with the dry lacquer technique.

mandarava (Sanskrit, *māndārava*). A scarlet flower (*Erythrina indica*) of the coral tree, which in Buddhist mythology bloomed as a portent to an event. It was also one of the fabled trees that grew in paradise.

Manipuri. People from Manipur, also called **Kathe**.

Manohra (Thai, Myanmar, *Dwei Mei Naw* or *Dwemenaw*). A popular dance drama, which appears to have come to Myanmar via Thai sources. Thought to be part of the *panji* cycle of legends popular in Indonesia that spread to Malaysia and southern Thailand where it became a major theatrical genre. It depicts the love story between Prince Suthon and the *kinnari* Manohra. While away at war, unscrupulous courtiers led the king to believe that only the way to ensure the safety of his son was to sacrifice Manohra. The distraught *kinnari*, on becoming aware of her fate, flees the palace and returns to her father's domain, where Prince Suthon, after much trial and tribulation, seeks her out and they are reunited.

Mara (Pali and Sanskrit, Māra/Myanmar, Marnat). The god of desire in Buddhism and the personification of selfish worldly desires and delusions.

maravijaya (Pali and Sanskrit, *māravijaya*). The Buddha's victory over Mara at the moment of enlightenment. See ***bhumisparsa mudra***.

matha (Sanskrit, *maṭha*). Hindu monastery.

matho thingan (Myanmar). New robes offered to the main Buddha images at the Shwedagon Pagoda at the end of Buddhist Lent. In precolonial times this event was held in many villages throughout Myanmar.

Mon (Myanmar). Ethnic group in Lower Myanmar, now centered in Mon State, Myanmar, responsible for important myths, such as the Shwedagon legend.

Mount Meru (Pali, Sineru/Sanskrit, Sumeru). The central axis or cosmic mountain at the center of the Hindu-Buddhist universe, surrounded by seven seas and seven mountain chains, with a continent at each cardinal point, one of which is Jampudipa to the south where mortals are believed to dwell. Above the summit of Mt. Meru are a series of heavens, home to various celestials.

mudra (Sanskrit, *mudrā*). Position of the arms, hands, and fingers of a deity to convey a symbolic or ritual gesture.

Mugapakkha Jataka (Pali, *Mūgapakkha Jātaka*). Jataka number 538, known in Myanmar as the *Temi Jataka*, in which a prince vowed never to assume the throne of his father.

myrobalan (*Terminalia chebula*). A medicinal fruit.

naga (Pali and Sanskrit, *nāga*). A serpent deity in Hindu/Buddhist mythology that is regarded as a guardian of the earth's waters. *Nagas* may also be considered symbols of abundance and fertility.

namaskara mudra (Sanskrit, *namaskāra mudrā*). A gesture made with the palms together at the chest with fingers pointing upward in an act of devotion or worship.

nat (Myanmar). Nonhuman beings ranging from gods in Buddhist heavens (*devas* and *brahmas*) to the thirty-seven *nats* of the Myanmar royal pantheon, to local spirits and sprites. See also ***deva***.

nibbana (Pali, *Nibbāna*/Sanskrit, *Nirvana*). A state of extinction devoutly wished for by all Buddhists; a release from suffering, delusion, and future births. The attainment of perfect knowledge and peace. See also ***parinibbana***.

Nidana-katha (Pali, *Nidāna-kathā*). See ***Jataka-nidana***.

Nirvana (Sanskrit, *nirvāṇa*). See ***nibbana***.

Pa-O (Myanmar). One of the ethnic groups that make up the citizenry of Myanmar, located in Shan State around the Inle area.

padmasana (Sanskrit, *padmāsana*). A seated position in which the legs are crossed and the feet rest on opposite thighs with soles facing upwards. Also known as the lotus pose.

Pala (Sanskrit, Pāla). Name of an Indian dynasty that ruled much of northern India along the Gangetic Plain from the eighth to the twelfth century.

Pali. An ancient Indo-Aryan language used by the followers of Theravada Buddhism in writing the scriptures and in various liturgies. It continues to be learned by monks and scholars in Myanmar today. Over the centuries the people of Myanmar have developed an extensive body of Pali literature.

Panji cycle of legends (Indonesian). Panji is a legendary East Javanese prince whose adventures, along with the ***Ramayana*** and *Mahabharata*, provide much of the subject matter for Indonesian theater.

parabaik (Myanmar). A book of paper (usually of mulberry) folded in accordion style to create pages to be inscribed in ink with text and/or illustrations.

paribhoga-ceti (Pali, *paribhoga-cetiya*). Shrine for relics of use or contact in Buddhism. Can also refer to the relics themselves.

parinibbana (Pali, *Parinibbāna*/Sanskrit, *Parinirvāṇa*). The death and passage of the Buddha into final ***nibbana*** and his liberation from the cycle of rebirths.

Parinirvana (Sanskrit, *Parinirvāṇa*). See ***parinibbana***.

paritta (Pali). A collection of ***suttas*** that are recited as protective spells.

paso (Myanmar). A man's voluminous lower garment.

Paticcasamuppada Sutta (Pali, *Paṭiccasamuppāda Sutta*/Sanskrit, *Pratītyasamutpāda Sūtra*). Discourse on Dependent Origination.

patta. See ***thabeik***.

pe-za (Myanmar). Manuscript composed of palm leaves that have been dried, smoothed, polished, and trimmed, before being inscribed with text and/or illustrations using an iron stylus.

phaa hau khampii (Thai). Manuscript covers.

pitaka (Pali, *piṭaka*). See ***Tipitaka***.

pongyi-kyaung (Myanmar). A Buddhist monastery.

ponna (Myanmar). Hindu Brahmin ritualists serving in Myanmar courts.

prajna (Sanskrit, *prajñā*/Pali, *paññā*). Liberating wisdom.

Punnovada Sutta (Pali, *Puṇṇovāda Sutta*). A ***sutta*** in the Pali ***Tipitaka***.

pyathat (Myanmar/Sanskrit, *prāsāda*). A spire composed of a series of roofs that diminish in size with ascent. Its presence marks a sacred or important ritual area in a palace or monastery.

pyinsa-lawha (Myanmar/Pali and Sanskrit, *pañca-loha*). The "five metals." An alloy of gold, silver, copper, iron, and lead.

pyinsa–yupa (Myanmar/Pali and Sanskrit, *pañca-rūpa*). A popular composite animal composed of the "five virtues": avian wings, piscine-like tail, herpian torso, the hooves and antlers of a stag, and trunk and tusks of a pachyderm.

Pyu. Early inhabitants of central Myanmar.

Rahu (Pali and Sanskrit, Rāhu/Myanmar, Yahu). One of the nine planets in Hindu and Buddhist astrology.

rajalilasana (Sanskrit, *rājalīlāsana*). The posture of royal ease.

rajawan (Mon). See **yazawin**.

Ramayana (Sanskrit, *Rāmāyana*). An Indian epic ascribed to the poet Valmiki that relates the struggles of Rama, a prince of Ayodhaya and seventh incarnation of Vishnu, to save the world from destruction by the multi-headed demon Ravanna. The story centers around the hero Rama's search for his wife Sita, who has been abducted by Ravanna.

repoussé (French). A method of embellishing metal in which parts of a design are raised in relief from the back or inside of an object by hammering with punches and bossing tools.

rupaloka (Pali and Sanskrit, *rūpaloka*). The world of form, with sixteen planes of existence in which beings who have renounced sensual desire, hatred, and ill will may be reborn. The world of the *brahma* gods who enjoy varying degrees of bliss. Note: In Buddhist cosmology, the gods of the *rupa-* and *arupalokas* all receive the appellation *brahma* (Pali *brahmā*) to distinguish their superior status from that of the *devas*. *Devas* are lesser gods who dwell in the upper strata, the ***kamaloka***.

sa-daik (Myanmar). A chest, usually of teak, to hold manuscripts. It may be embellished with lacquer decoration, gold leaf, and glass inlay.

sa-lwe (Myanmar). A royal official's chain of office, which was worn diagonally over the shoulder(s). Rank was evident in the number of strands permitted and the size and embellishment of the clasps used to secure them.

sala/sal (Pali, *sāla*/Sanskrit, *śāla*). A type of tree also known by the Latin name *Shorea robusta*. The Buddha was born under a sal tree and passed into ***nibanna*** between two such trees.

samanera (Pali, *sāmaṇera*/Myanmar, *koyin*). Buddhist novice.

samatha (Pali). Tranquility meditation. One of two types of meditation recognized in Theravada, the other being ***vipassana***, insight meditation.

samsara (Pali and Sanskrit, *saṃsāra*). The endless cycle of death and rebirth.

san-daw (Myanmar). Hair relic of the Buddha.

Sangha (Pali, *Saṅgha*/Sanskrit, Saṃgha). Community of ordained monks, one of the Three Jewels.

sanghati (Pali, *saṅghāṭi*/Sanskrit, *saṃghāṭi*). A monk's upper robe worn folded over the left shoulder.

sap-bagyi (Myanmar). Ephemeral constructions made from bamboo and paper for processions, celebrations, and funerals.

sapa-lwe (Myanmar/Thai, *phaa hau khampii*). A cloth wrapper for sacred books.

saririka-ceti (Pali, *sārīrika-cetiya*). Shrine for bodily relics. Can also refer to the relics themselves.

sasana (Pali, *Sāsana*). The Buddha's teachings and dispensation as an historical entity. The Buddhist religion.

sattasahana (Sanskrit/Pali). The seven sites in Bodh Gaya where the Buddha spent a week each, following his englightenment beneath the Bodhi Tree.

sawbwa (Myanmar). A **Shan** ruler.

sazi-gyo (Myanmar). Narrow ribbons woven on a card loom, which are used to secure sacred manuscripts within their cloth covers.

Senas. Dynastic family that ruled in a region of northeastern India during the eleventh and twelfth centuries.

Sentient beings. In Buddhism the term generally refers to conscious beings, all of whom have the potential for eventual enlightenment.

Shan. An ethnic group in Upper Myanmar divided into numerous polities which were often subject to vassal status by Bamar kingdoms. Also one of the ethnic classifications in contemporary Myamar.

shilpa shastras (Sanskrit, *śilpa śāstra*). A general term for the numerous Hindu texts and manuals that describe the standards, proportions, and iconography for the sculpting of religious objects such as icons, statues, and murals.

shin-pyu (Myanmar). Ordination of novices.

shish (Urdu). An Indian decorative technique in which mirror glass designs may be inlaid into stone or set in an aggregate such as plaster or cement.

shwe-chi-doe (Myanmar). A style of Myanmar embroidery that includes applique, couching, and quilting with metallic thread, colored yarns, sequins, and slivers of glass.

siddha (Sanskrit). Buddhist adept possessed of supernormal powers.

Siddhattha (Pali/Sanskrit, Siddhartha). The personal name of the prince before he renounced the palace and became the Buddha. See **Gotama**.

Sinhala. Theravada Buddhist people and culture of contemporary Sri Lanka.

stupa (Sanskrit/Pali, *thūpa*/Myanmar, *zedi*). Originally a circular domed burial mound, adapted by Buddhists as a monument to enshrine relics of the Buddha.

Sukhothai. Kingdom in north-central Thailand that ruled between the first half of the thirteenth and the first half of the fifteenth century.

Sumana (Pali). The leader of a group of ogres encountered by the Buddha at Martaban in Lower Burma, in Mon chronicles.

sutta (Pali/Sanskrit, *sūtra*). Sermon or discourse of the Buddha. The sermons are collected into the *Suttapitaka*, the Basket of Discourses, one of three main divisions of the ***Tipitaka***.

tagundaing (Myanmar). A tall, sixty- to eighty-foot-high gilded column found with pagoda and monastery precincts. Originally placed to celebrate the submission of animistic elements, today they herald a religious site. Some may be surmounted by a sacred ***hamsa*** bird while at the base there may be one to four ***deva*** guardian figures in Konbaung royal dress.

Tai-Yuan. A branch of the Tai ethnicity living in northern Thailand and eastern Myanmar in the Chaing Tung area.

Tanka. See ***thangka***.

tan khoe (Rakhine). The energetic potential or power of an image.

Tathagata-udana-dipani (Pali, *Tathāgata-udāna-dīpanī*). One of several popular Buddha chronicles (*bodawin*) written in Myanmar during the eighteenth and nineteenth centuries.

Tavatimsa (Pali, Tāvatiṃsa/Sanskrit, Trāyastriṃśa). The second of the six *deva* worlds in Buddhist cosmology. Located on the summit of Mt. Meru, and presided over by Sakka, it is the highest of the heavens that maintains a physical connection to the world. Also known as the Abode of the Thirty-Three Devas, using a generic number for the number of *devas* who live there.

tazaung (Myanmar/Sanskrit, *prāsāda*). An open-sided pavilion with a tiered roof found in the vicinity of pagodas and monasteries. *Tazaungs* were multifunctional and could be used to house images for veneration and serve as assembly halls for listening to sermons, reciting prayers, and holding feasts for monks.

Tazaungmon (Myanmar). The eighth month of the Myanmar lunar calendar, overlapping October–November.

thabeik (Myanmar/Pali, *patta*/Sanskrit, *pātra*). A monk's alms bowl, made from clay or metal.

thamaing (Myanmar). Pagoda history. In modern Myanmar usage it also means history in general.

Thadingyut (Myanmar). The seventh lunar month of the Myanmar calendar, overlapping September–October. Festival of Light marking the end of the Buddhist Lent and welcoming the return of the Buddha from the Tavatimsa Heaven after preaching the Abhidamma to his mother.

thadu (Myanmar/Pali and Sanskrit, *sādhu*). Literally means "well done!" It is a congratulatory refrain said by on-lookers in acknowledgment of the performance of a deed of merit.

thangka (Tibetan). Buddhist painting on cotton or silk.

thapye-pan (Myamar). "Victory leaves." Eugenia leaves, regarded as particularly auspicious, may be used at various ceremonies, both religious and secular, to sprinkle water as a blessing.

Thathanalinkara-sadan (Myanmar). *The Ornament of the Religion*, a nineteenth-century Myanmar Buddhist chronicle.

thathanawin (Myanmar/Pali, *sāsanavaṃsa*). Monastic chronicle.

thayo (Myanmar). A pliable substance of lacquer resin mixed with finely sifted sawdust, rice straw, cow dung, or bone ash; can be molded and sculpted. A thinner application of *thayo* may be used as an undercoat to lacquer.

Theravada (Pali, Theravāda). "School of the Elders." An ancient school of Buddhism that stresses monasticism, the importance of Pali scripture and commentary, and merit making through good works and meditation. Practiced today in Sri Lanka, Myanmar, Thailand, Cambodia, and Laos. Compare **Mahayana**.

thila-shin (Myanmar). Myanmar Buddhist nun.

Three Jewels or Three Gems. See ***Tiratana***.

Three Worlds. The three planes of existence in Buddhist cosmology composed of the formless realm or *arupaloka*, the form realm or *rupaloka*, and the desire realm or *kamaloka*.

Tipitaka (Pali, *Tipiṭaka*/Sanskrit, *Tripiṭaka*). Buddhist scriptures composed of three collections or baskets (*pitaka*) of texts, namely: the *Suttas*, the *Vinaya*, and the *Abhidhamma*. The term *Tipitaka* literally means "three baskets."

Tiratana (Pali). The Three Jewels, also called the *Tisarana* (Pali, *Tisaraṇa*) or the Three Refuges composed of the Buddha, the ***Dhamma***, and the ***Sangha***.

Tisarana. See ***Tiratana***.

uddissa-ceti (Pali, *uddissa-cetiya*). Shrine for relics of commemoration in Buddhism. Can also refer to the relics themselves.

upasaka (Pali, *upāsaka*). Buddhist layman.

upasika (Pali, *upāsikā*). Buddhist laywoman.

ushnisha (Sanskrit, *uṣṇīṣa*/Pali, *uṇhīsa*). A fleshy protuberance at the crown of the head of Buddha images, one of the thirty-two special physical markings of Buddha found in Buddhist texts.

uttarasanga (Pali, *uttarāsaṅga*/Sanskrit, *uttarāsaṃga*). The outer robe of a Buddhist monk, which is worn over the chest and shoulders. It may be worn like a cloak when appearing in public.

vajra (Sanskrit). Diamond, lightning bolt.

vajra-ghanta (Sanskrit, *vajra-ghaṇṭā*). *Vajra*: thunderbolt; *ghanta*: bell. An implement, usually metal, used in esoteric Buddhist rituals.

varada (Sanskrit). A *mudra* where the arm lies pendant along the side of the body with palm outwards in a boon- or gift-giving gesture. In some Buddha images from Myanmar there may be a small fruitlike offering in the hand.

Vassa (Pali). Buddhist Lent. See **Waso**.

Vasudhara (Pali, Vasudhārā/Myanmar, Wathundaye). The Earth Goddess, who may be invoked as a witness at the ceremonial pouring of water at the conclusion of donation celebrations to share the merit accrued with other sentient beings.

Vessantara (Pali/Sanskrit, Viśvantara/Myanmar, Wethandaya). The last incarnation of the Buddha (*Jataka* no. 547) prior to his rebirth as Prince Siddhatta. In this best-known and most-beloved *jataka*, the Buddha-to-be as Prince Vessantara is of such an excessively generous disposition that he gives away his kingdom's highly prized white elephant, an act that forces him and his family into exile. En route to his forest retreat he gives away his carriage and horses and is not beyond giving his children as servants to a Brahmin who requests them and is even tempted to give up his wife. Fortunately the children are recognized by the *devas* and returned to their grandparents and the family recalled from exile.

Vidhura-pandita Jataka (Pali, *Vidhura-paṇḍita Jātaka*). In this *jataka* tale (no. 545) the wife of the ***naga*** king, desirous of attaining wisdom, seeks the heart of wise minister Vidhura. The king, anxious to please his spouse, promises a daughter's hand in marriage to Punnaka the ogre, if he can return with the heart of Vidhura. Punnaka defeats the king of the wise minister at dice and claims Vidhura as his prize. En route back to the *naga* kingdom, he attempts to kill the wise minister by various means, without success. The wise minister preaches the law to the *naga* queen, who becomes a follower.

Vinaya (Pali). The second section of the Pali ***Tipitaka***, pertaining to the rules and regulations governing the conduct of Buddhist monastic life.

vipassana (Pali, *vipassanā*). Insight meditation. One of two types of meditation recognized in Theravada, the other being ***samatha***, tranquility meditation.

virasana (Sanskrit, *vīrāsana*). A seated posture in which the legs are crossed with the left foot resting on the right thigh. The left thigh rests against the right foot. Known as the hero pose in yoga.

vitarka mudra (Sanskrit, *vitarka mudrā*). One or both hands raised, with a forefinger touching the thumb. The teaching gesture.

Waso (Myanmar/Pali, Vassa). Fourth lunar month of the Myanmar calendar, overlapping June–July. The Buddhist Lent has also come to be called Waso because it begins with this month.

Wathundaye (Myanmar). See **Vasudhara**.

weikza (Myanmar). Buddhist wizard, often engaged in alchemy and other occult arts to obtain a form of immortality and serve as a supernatural protector of Buddhism.

yahan (Myanmar). See ***bhikkhu***.

yahanda (Myanmar). See ***arahant***.

yathei (Myanmar). Buddhist hermit.

yazawin (Myanmar/Mon, *rajawan*/Pali, *rājavaṃsa*). Royal chronicle.

Yazawin-gyaw (Myanmar). *The Celebrated Chronicle*.

yokkhazo (Myanmar). A guardian spirit (***nat***) of trees and the forest who is traditionally propitiated prior to traveling through a wooded area or prior to felling trees.

zawgyi (Myanmar). A well-known character in Myanmar mythology and folkore associated with alchemy.

zedi (Myanmar/Pali, *cetiya*). See **stupa**.

zetuwan (Myanmar). A palace or religious building with a triple-tiered roof. The term comes from Jetavana, a famous monastery built during the time of the Buddha, where the Blessed One spent many rainy seasons.

Geographical Names

Amarapura. A capital of the **Konbaung dynasty** twice during the eighteenth and nineteenth centuries, located a short distance south of Mandalay, in contemporary central Myanmar.

Andaman Sea. Part of the Indian Ocean, a sea adjacent to the southernmost part of Myanmar running south along the west edges of Thailand and Malaysia.

Anuradhapura. Ancient capital of a Sri Lankan kingdom in the first millennium.

Arakan. See **Rakhine**.

Arimaddanapura. City of the Crusher of the Foes. Formal Pali name for the city of **Pagan**.

Assam. Modern state in eastern India.

Ava. Seat of the **Konbaung** and **Nyaung-yan** dynasties in the period of the fourteenth to the sixteenth century. Also called Inwa. In contemporary central Myanmar.

Ayeyarwady. See **Irrawaddy**.

Ayodhya. Name of both the birthplace of Rama in Indian myths and the capital of a Thai kingdom from the fourteenth to the eighteenth century.

Aythema (Golikamatta-nagara). **Mon** brick-walled city on the Gulf of **Martaban**, north of Thaton in contemporary Myanmar.

Ayutthaya. Capital of a Thai kingdom from the fourteenth to the eighteenth century. Also known as Yodhya, in Myanmar, and **Ayodhya**.

Bagan. See **Pagan**.

Bago. See **Pegu** and **Hanthawaddy**.

Banares. See **Varanasi**.

Beikthano. Ancient **Pyu** city that flourished in the first millennium. Also a city in contemporary Myamar.

Bodh Gaya. Site of the Buddha's enlightenment. A pilgrimage site and location of monuments. Located in contemporary Bihar, India.

Budalin. A small town north of Mandalay in the Monywa district.

Burma. See **Myanmar**.

Chiang Mai. Capital of the **Lan Na** kingdom from the thirteenth to the eighteenth century. In contemporary northern Thailand.

Chiang Saen. City and district of the same name located in Chiang Rai Province, contemporary northern Thailand.

Chiang Tung. Seat of important **Shan** rulers (***sawbwa***) located in contemporary Shan State. It is in the easternmost part of Myanmar and is part of the Golden Triangle. Also called Kengtung.

Chittagong. Coastal capital of the Chittagong Division in contemporary southeast Bangladesh.

Dhannavati (Myanmar/Pali, Dhaññavatī). First-millennium city in **Rakhine**, also called Dhanyawadi.

Dhanyawadi. See **Dhannavati**.

Gandhara. Region in ancient northwest India, now in northern Pakistan and northeastern Afghanistan. It was an important center of Buddhist culture under the Kushans from the first to the fifth century. Peshawar and Taxila were major centers at that time.

Golden Triangle. A vast mountainous region encompassing Myanmar, Laos, and Thailand.

Halin. Ancient **Pyu** city that flourished in the first millennium. In contemporary Myanmar.

Hanthawaddy (Pali, Haṃsāvati). **Mon** kingdom of the period of the fourteenth to the sixteenth century. Centered on what is now **Pegu**.

Hpa-an. City in contemporary **Karen State**, Myanmar.

Indapatta. Town in Kuru Country in the Pali canon, such as in the *Jatakas*. One of the three chief cities of **Jambudipa**.

Inwa. See **Ava**.

Irrawaddy. The river whose valley forms the center of many Myanmar civilizations; also spelled Ayeyarwady.

Kaladan River. Major river in northern Rakhine.

Kandy. Site of an important Buddhist kingdom in the period of the fifteenth to the nineteenth century, and of The Temple of the Tooth Relic. In contemporary Sri Lanka.

Kapilavastu (Sanskrit/Pali, Kapilavatthu). Home of the Sakya clan of the Buddha; see **Gotama**. In contemporary Nepal.

Karen State. See **Kayin State**.

Kayin State. State in contemporary southeast Myanmar, where many **Kayin**, or Karen, groups live. Also spelled Karen State.

Kedah. A modern state in northern Malaysia.

Kengtung. See **Chiang Tung**.

Kushinagara (Sanskrit, Kuśinagara/Pali, Kusinārā). The site in India marking the Buddha's death.

Kyaikhtiyo. Site of the Golden Rock Pagoda in contemporary Mon State, Myanmar.

Kyaikkatha. Mon brick-walled city on the Gulf of **Marataban**.

Kyaukse. Rice-growing region at the confluence of the **Irrawaddy** and **Myit-nge** rivers near **Ava**. In the contemporary **Mandalay** region of Myanmar.

Kyauktaw. Site of the original Mahamuni Pagoda in **Rakhine**, Myanmar.

Kyontu. Location of terracotta roundels from the first millennium, northeast of **Pegu**.

Lan Na. Northern Thai kingdom from the thirteenth to the eighteenth century. See also **Chiang Mai**.

Lower Myanmar. Home of the Mon **Hanthawaddy** kingdom and later British Burma from 1852 to 1885.

Madras. City known as Chennai in contemporary India.

Magwe. City on the **Irrawaddy** River in Myanmar, located near Shwesettaw.

Maingmaw. Ancient **Pyu** city.

Mandalay. Capital of the last two kings of the Konbaung dynasty.

Manipur. A small state in northeastern India.

Martaban (English/Myanmar, Mottama). English name given to the town of Mottama, a formerly important port in Lower Myanmar. Also the name given to large ceramic jars made in Myanmar for local use and for export. Historically many were exported from the port of Martaban, hence the name.

Martavan. See **Martaban**.

Mawlamyine. See **Moulmein**.

Mekong River. River that runs from China through Myanmar, Thailand, Laos, and Cambodia.

Mingun. Site of massive brick pagoda begun in the late eighteenth century, located in Sagaing region.

Minnathu. A village within the larger area known as **Bagan** or **Pagan**.

Monywa. Town northwest of Mandalay in central Myanmar.

Mottama. See **Martaban**.

Moulmein. In contemporary Mon State, Myanmar. Also called Mawlamyine.

Mount Gandhamadana. A mythical mountain in Buddhism.

Mount Popa. Traditional sacred home of the ***nats***. In central Myanmar.

Mount Selagiri. A hill in **Rakhine** where the Buddha met king Chandrasuriya.

Mrauk-U. Capital of **Rakhine** kingdoms from the fifteenth to the late eighteenth century. In contemporary Rakhine State, Myanmar.

Mro-haung. See **Mrauk-U**.

Myanmar. Official English name of the country since 1989 and indigenous term for civilization and kingdoms. Also the official language of Myanmar, often referred to as Burmese. Also known as Burma.

Myinkaba. A village within the larger area known as Bagan or **Pagan**.

Myit-nge River. A tributary of the **Irrawaddy** River, near **Ava**.

Nagapattinam (Sanskrit, Nāgapāṭaṇam). Important ancient trading center on India's east coast.

Nalanda. Ancient center of learning during the Pala dynasty period, in modern Bihar state, India.

Nanzhao. A kingdom formed by six Tai kingdoms in 729. It was located in what is now the western part of Yunnan province, China.

Naypyidaw (Nay Pyi Taw). New capital of contemporary Myanmar, founded in 2005.

Negrais. Trade settlement located in coastal western Myanmar.

Okkalapa. Transposed version of the place-name **Utkala**, which appears in Pali sources. Identified in Myanmar myths as **Yangon**.

Pagan. The first capital of the Myanmar people, between the eleventh and thirteenth centuries. Located on the **Irrawaddy** River in Upper Myanmar, also called Bagan.

Pattani. Modern province in southern Thailand.

Pegu. Seat of **Mon** kingdoms in the period of the fourteenth to the sixteenth century. Also called Bago. See also **Hanthawaddy**.

Penang. Port city in contemporary northwestern Malaysia.

Phuket. The largest island in Thailand. It was formerly known as **Thalang** and was located along a major trade route between India and China.

Piao. Chinese term for **Pyu**.

Prome. See **Pyay**.

Puer. City in southern Yunnan (China). In early modern times Myanmar and Chinese rulers rivaled to establish power over the region. Myanmar influence declined after the First Anglo-Burmese War (1824–26).

Pukam. See **Pagan**.

Pyay. A small town near ancient Sri Ksetra, located on the Irrawaddy River in the Bago Division. Also called Prome.

Pyu. Civilization in ancient Myanmar in the first millennium. In Chinese, Piao. See also **Tircul**.

Rajagaha. See **Rajgir**.

Rajgir. City in contemporary Bihar State, India.

Rakhine. A state in western Myanmar, bordering Bangladesh, also known as Arakan.

Ramannya. Traditional name for the **Mon** kingdom in Lower Myanmar.

Rangoon. See **Yangon**.

Ratnagiri. City of the the Bamar king **Thibaw**'s exile during British colonial rule. In western India.

Sagaing. City in Upper Myanmar, near Mandalay.

Sankassa (Pali). A town in northern India visited by the Buddha.

Sarnath. Site of the deer park near present-day Varanasi (Benares), India, where the Buddha gave his first sermon.

Shan State. Region in contemporary eastern Myanmar that was home to a number of different local polities once ruled by Shan ***sawbwa*** chieftans.

Shwebo. Town in central Myanmar that was the first capital of the Konbaung dynasty 1752–60. A notable region for crafts, pottery, metalwork, woven palm-leaf boxes, and formerly dry lacquer.

Siam. Traditional name for the Thai kingdom and nation state.

Sipsong Panna. Theravada Buddhist kingdom. Now part of the Xishuangbanna Dai Autonomous Prefecture in Yunnan Province, China. Also called Xishuangbanna.

Sri Ksetra (Sankrit, Ṣrī Kṣetra). **Pyu** city that flourished in the first millennium. Site of important archaeological finds.

Sunaparanta (Pali, Sunāparanta). Identified as the Bamar homeland of Upper Myanmar in the ***Yazawin-gyaw***.

Suvannabhumi (Pali, Suvaṇṇabhūmi/Sanskrit, Suvarṇabhūmi). "The Golden Land." A region in Buddhist geography that was identified by the **Mon** as their homeland.

Syriam. Port city in contemporary southeast Myanmar. Also called Thanlyin.

Tamil Nadu. State in modern southern India.

Taunggu. Briefly the seat of the Bamar Taunggu dynasty in the second millennium. Also spelled Toungoo.

Taunggyi. Capital of modern Shan State.

Tavoy. British spelling of Dawei Port, a city in southeastern Myanmar.

Tenasserim. Coastal division of southeastern Myanmar on the isthmus of Kra, now known as Tanintharyi.

Thalang. An island and southern province of Thailand. See **Phuket**.

Thanlyin. See **Syriam**.

Thaton. Walled city in **Mon** territory associated with the myth of **Suvannabhumi**. In contemporary Mon State, Myanmar.

Thegone. Village south of Prome, with Pyu antiquities.

Tircul. A word that may refer to the ancient **Pyu** people.

Toungoo. See **Taunggu**.

Twante. A town about fifteen miles west of Yangon.

Upper Myanmar. Usually defined as anything north of Prome (Pyay).

Utkala (Sanskrit/Pali, Ukkala). Old name for Orissa State, in contemporary India, appearing in Pali sources as Ukkala. Later transposed to **Okkalapa** and identified as **Yangon**, Myanmar.

Varanasi. Modern name for Benares, India.

Vesali. A town in India visited by the Buddha.

Vientiane. Capital city of modern Laos.

West Bengal. Modern state in India.

Winka. First-millennium brick monastic site north of **Thaton**.

Xishuangbanna. See **Sipsong Panna**.

Yangon. Home of the **Shwedagon Pagoda** and capital of the British Colonial government and independent nation-state until 2005. Also called Rangoon.

Yodaya (Myanmar). The Myanmar name for the Thai kingdom of **Ayutthaya/Ayodhya**.

Yunnan. A province in southern China.

Zothoke. First-millenneium archaeological site in Lower Myanmar, north of Thaton.

Historical and Mythical Figures

Alaungmintaya. See **Alaungpaya**.

Alaungpaya. Founder of the Konbaung dynasty (r. 1752–1760). Also know as Alaungmintaya.

Ananda (Pali and Sanskrit, Ānanda). One of the major disciples of the Buddha. He was the personal attendant of the Buddha, noted for his kindness to all. After the demise of the Buddha he became important in the transmission and preservation of the ***Dhamma***.

Anawrahta. King of **Pagan** (ca. 1044–ca. 1077). Also known as Aniruddha.

Aniruddha (Pali). See **Anawrahta**.

Anjanadevi (Pali, Añjanadevī). A female character in a ***jataka*** and who played a role in the founding of a mythical kingdom in **Rakhine**.

Ashoka (Sanskrit, Aśoka/Pali, Asoka). A Mauryan emperor (304–232 BCE) who came to rule much of India through conquest. After embracing Buddhism he dedicated himself to spreading its doctrines thoughout India and neighboring states.

Avalokiteshvara (Sanskrit, Avalokiteśvara). A highly revered and often prayed to ***bodhisatta*** who embodies the compassion and mercy of the Buddha.

Bagyidaw (r. 1819–1837). **Konbaung** king.

Bana Thau. See **Shinsawbu**.

Banya Barow (r. 1446–1450). **Mon** king of **Hanthawaddy**.

Banya Dala (r. 1747–1757). **Mon** king of **Hanthawaddy**.

Bayinnaung (r. ca. 1551–ca. 1581). **Taunggu** king who, through conquest, assembled the largest empire known in Southeast Asia that included much of Myanmar, Shan States, Laos, Siam, and Manipur.

Bhallika (Pali). Brother of Tapussa. Both brothers play an important role in the Shwedagon legend.

Bo Bo Gyi. Guardian of pagoda platforms in Myanmar.

Bodawpaya (r. 1782–1819). **Konbaung** king.

Brahma (Sanskrit and Pali, Brahmā). In Hinduism one of the three major Hindu gods: Brahma, Vishnu, and Shiva. In Buddhism a species of god superior to the ***devas*** who dwells in the form and formless realms.

Buddhaghosa. Fifth-century Pali commentator on the ***Tipitaka***.

Byatta. Indian who helped King **Anawrahta** seize **Thaton** using his occult powers. Through a liaison with the Flower Ogress on **Mount Popa** he came to father a pair of powerful ***nats***, the Taung-byon brothers.

Chakri dynasty. Founded in Bangkok, Thailand, in 1782; still exists today.

Chandrasuriya. Mythic **Rakhine** king who cast the Mahamuni bronze Buddha, with the Buddha's consent.

Dhammazedi (r. ca. 1472–ca. 1492). **Mon** king of **Hanthawaddy**, responsible for the Shwedagon and Kalyani Inscriptions. Also known as Dhammaceti.

Dikha (r. 1553–1556). Rakhine monarch.

Dipankara Buddha (Pali, Dīpaṅkara Buddha/Sanskrit, Dīpaṅkara Buddha). This Buddha was known as the first of twenty-eight of this present world cycle. While on a visit to Paduma, he encountered Sumedha, a rich Brahmin turned hermit, who lay prostrate on the ground with his hair covering the mud so that the Buddha would not soil his feet. For his selflessness, Dipankara prophesied that Sumedha would become a Buddha in a future existence. He became **Gotama** Buddha.

Dona (Pali, Doṇa/Sanskrit, Droṇa). Brahmin who distributed the Buddha's relics among rival kings. See **Malla princes/kings**.

Duttabaung. Legendary founder and king of the **Pyu** kingdom of **Sri Ksetra**.

Gavampati. A disciple of the Buddha important for the **Mon** in the introduction of Buddhism to Lower Myanmar.

General Than Shwe. Head of state in Myanmar from 1992 to 2011.

Harivikrama. **Pyu** ruler in the late seventh century.

Hsinbyushin (r. 1763–1776). **Konbaung** king.

Indra. See **Sakka**.

Kakusandha. First of the five Buddhas of the present world cycle (*kalpa*).

Kassapa (Pali/Sanskrit, Kaśyapa). The preeminent disciple of the Buddha following the deaths of Sarriputta and Moggallana. Also the name of the third Buddha of the present world cycle (*kalpa*).

Kavila. Northern Thai ruler who defeated the **Bamar** in **Chiang Mai**.

Konagamana. Second of the five buddhas of the present world cycle (*kalpa*).

Konbaung dynasty (1752–1885). Myanmar kingdom from the mid-eighteenth to the late nineteenth century, with capitals in **Shwebo**, **Sagaing**, **Ava**, **Amarapura**, and **Mandalay**. (See Chronology.)

Kyanzittha (ca. 1084–ca. 1112). King of **Pagan**.

Lokanatha. A form of the Mahayana **Avalokiteshvara**, Bodhisattva of Compassion.

Lord Curzon (1859–1925). Viceroy of India 1899–1905.

Luce, Gordon (1889–1979). A major figure in Buddhist history and archaeology of Myanmar.

Mahadhammayazadhipati (r. 1733–1752). **Ava** king; last king of the **Nyaung-yan dynasty**, overthrown by the **Mon**.

Mahapunna. Mythic saint who asks the Buddha to visit **Sunaparanta** (identified as Upper Myanmar) in Myanmar chronicles.

Mahasammata. Original king of the first humans in Buddhist myths.

Mahasilavamsa (1452–1520). Monastic author of the ***Yazawin-gyaw***, the Celebrated Chronicle.

Mahasithu (1726–1806). Royal tutor to King **Bodawpaya,** who authored the *Yazawinthit*, the New Chronicle.

Maung Tint Te. A ***nat*** of the household.

Mayadevi (Pali, Māyādevī). The mother of the Buddha.

Metteyya (Pali/Sanskrit, Maitreya). The Buddha of the Future, who is believed to be the successor of the present Buddha.

Min Bin (r. 1531–1553). **Rakhine** king.

Mindon (r. 1853–1878). **Konbaung** king.

Mingaung (r. 1401–1422). **Bamar** king of **Ava**.

Min Phalaung (r. 1571–1593). **Mrauk-U** king.

Min Saw Mwun (r. ca. 1404–1406, ca. 1429–1433). **Rakhine** king and founder of **Mrauk-U**. Also known as Narameikhla.

Moggallana (Pali, Moggallāna/Sanskrit, Maudgalyāyana). One of two chief disciples of the Buddha, the other being Sariputta.

Mon-hyin (r. 1426–1439). King of **Ava**.

Mucalinda Naga (Pali, Mucalinda Nāga). A snake-king, who shielded the Buddha from a storm at **Bodh Gaya** in the sixth week after his enlightenment.

Nar. See **Narayana**.

Narameikhla. See **Min Saw Mwun**.

Narapati (r. 1443–1469). King of **Ava**.

Narathihapate (r. 1256–1287). The **Pagan** king who is credited in later myths with constucting the **Mingalazedi Stupa**, Pagan.

Narayana. Shortened to Nar. Epithet for **Vishnu**.

Ne Win. A military ruler from 1962 to 1988.

Nyaung-yan dynasty. Myanmar kingdom from the seventeenth to eighteeth century. Also known as Restored Taunggu dynasty. (See Chronology.)

Pagan Min (r. 1846–1853). **Konbaung** king.

Pe Maung Tin (1888–1973). A Pali scholar in Myanmar who translated *The Glass Palace Chronicle* and the Shwedagon Inscription into English.

Qianlong (r. 1735–1796). Chinese Qing dynasty emperor.

Rajadhiraj (r. 1384–1420). **Mon** king of **Hanthawaddy** who repelled **Bamar** advances; Father of Queen **Shinsawbu**. Also spelled Razadarit.

Razadarit. See **Rajadhiraj**.

Saccabandha. Legendary disciple of the Buddha who was presented by the Buddha with a footprint.

Sakka (Pali/Sanskrit, Śakra or Indra/Myanmar, Thagya-min). King of gods who, according to Hindus and Buddhists, dwells in **Tavatimsa**, or Heaven of the Thirty-Three Gods. Also referred to as Indra or Thagya-min.

Sariputta (Pali, Sāriputta). One of two chief disciples of the Buddha, the other being Moggallana.

Shariputra (Sanskrit, Śāriputra). See **Sariputta**.

Shinsawbu (r. ca. 1453–1472). **Mon** queen of **Hanthawaddy**. Also known in Mon as Bana Thau.

Sona and Uttara. Buddhist saints said to have converted the people of **Suvannabhumi** to Buddhism during the reign of Emperor **Ashoka**.

Sri Prabhuvarma (Sanskrit, Śrī Prabhuvarman). A **Pyu** personage whose name is incised on the famous silver casket found at **Sri Ksetra**.

Tabinshwehti (r. 1531–1550). King of **Taunggu**.

Tapussa (Pali). Legendary figure who, together with Bhallika, were merchants who received hair relics from the Buddha that, according to **Mon** and **Bamar** legend, are enshrined in the **Shwedagon Pagoda**.

Thagya-min. See **Sakka.**

Thalun (r. 1629–1648). Bamar **Taunggu** king, who ruled from **Ava**.

Thibaw (r. 1878–1885). Last **Konbaung** king, reigned in Mandalay and was exiled to India.

U Kala. Author of the *Mahayazawingyi*, the Great Chronicle.

Upagok (Myanmar). See **Upagutta**.

Upagutta (Pali/Sanskrit, Upagupta/Myanmar, Upagok). A popular saint credited with the power to facilitate fine weather. Buddhist monk born in Mathura who lived during the reign of Emperor **Ashoka**.

Vasudhara (Pali and Sanskrit, Vasudhārā). The Earth Goddess. She assisted the Buddha in his defeat of the demon **Mara**. Also called Wathundaye.

Vishnu. One of the three major deities in the Hindu pantheon.

Wareru (r. 1287–1307). Semi-legendary founder of the **Mon** kingdom in **Martaban**.

Wathundaye (Myanmar). See **Vasudhara**.

Xuanzang (602–664). Chinese Buddhist monk and translator who traveled to India and Southeast Asia.

Yijing (635–713). Chinese Buddhist monk who traveled to India and Southeast Asia.

Pagodas, Temples, and Monuments

Abeyadana Temple. Twelfth-century temple in **Pagan** with Tantric and Mahayana themes.

Ananda Temple. Twelfth-century temple in **Pagan**. Continues to be an important pilgrimage site.

Atumashi Monastery. Monastery built by King **Mindon** in **Mandalay**.

Bawbawgyi Stupa. **Pyu** monument in **Sri Ksetra**.

Botataung Pagoda. Major pagoda in **Yangon**. Rebuilt after bombing in 1944.

Dhammayazika Stupa. Twelfth- to thirteenth-century **Pagan** temple. The largest in Pagan.

East Hpetleik Stupa. In **Pagan**. Paired with the West Hpetleik, these two stupas showcase early unglazed ***jataka*** tiles (ca. 11th–12th century).

Hsinbyume Pagoda. See **Myatheindan Pagoda**.

Htukanthein. **Mrauk-U** ordination hall known for passageways with niches. **Rakhine**.

Kaba Aye Stupa. Built in 1952 for the Sixth Buddhist Council. In Rangoon (**Yangon**).

Kalyani Inscription. Erected by King **Dhammazedi** to celebrate his purification of the Mon ***Sangha*** circa 1479. The inscription is incised on ten stones: three in Pali, seven in Mon. It is preserved in the compound of the Kalyani Vihara, Pegu.

Kawgun Cave. Cave in **Kayin State**, Myanmar, containing three first-millennium stone sculptures and thousands of clay votive tablets dating from the eighteenth through the twentieth century.

Khin Ba Stupa. In **Sri Ksetra**.

Khin Ba trove. Pyu archealogical site discovered in 1926. In contemporary central Myanmar. Hundreds of objects were excavated from the Khin Ba Stupa relic chamber.

Koethaung Temple. Mrauk-U shrine of ninety thousand images in **Rakhine**.

Kubyaukgyi Temple, Myinkaba village, Pagan. Earliest dated Pagan temple (ca. 1112).

Kubyaukgyi Temple, Wetkyi-in village, Pagan. Thirteenth-century temple.

Kubyauknge Temple, Myinkaba village, Pagan. Temple dated to 1198.

Kubyauknge Temple, Wetkyi-in village, Pagan. Late-eleventh- or early-twelfth-century temple.

Kuthodaw Pagoda. Built by King **Mindon** and surrounded by a full copy of the ***Tipitaka*** inscribed on marble slabs. **Mandalay**.

Kyaikhtiyo. Golden Rock Pagoda. Associated with the Buddha's conversion of the king of **Thaton** and hair relics bestowed to hermits. In contemporary Mon State, Myanmar.

Kyauktaw Mahamuni Pagoda. Thought to be the original site of the Mahamuni bronze image. In contemporary **Rakhine** State, Myanmar.

Kyauktawgyi Temple. Located on the shore of Taungthaman Lake, bordering **Amarapura** to the south (ca. 1848–50).

Kyauk Ummin Cave Temple. Circa eleventh to twelfth century, among the earliest temples built in **Pagan**.

Leihtatgyi Temple. Ava temple of around the eighteenth century built in **Pagan** style. Myanmar.

Lemyathna Monastery. Pagan monastery complex built in the thirteenth century.

Lemyathna Temple. Modern name for one of the later, post-**Pyu** temples at **Sri Ksetra**.

Lingguang Temple. Temple with Buddha's tooth relic in Beijing, China.

Lokananda Pagoda (Pali, Lokānanda). A stupa thought to contain a tooth relic of the Buddha.

Mahabodhi Temple. A temple in Bodh Gaya, Bihar State, marking the site where the Buddha obtained enlightenment.

Mahaghanta Bell. At Shwedagon Pagoda, also known as King Singu's Bell or the Great Bell.

Mahalawkamayazein Pagoda. Near Budalin, noted for its marble reliefs of the ***Ramayana*** epic.

Maha Pasana Guha. Great Cave that housed the recitation of the ***Tipitaka*** for the Sixth Buddhist Sinod in 1956. Rangoon (**Yangon**).

Mingalazedi Pagoda. Built by King Narathihapate in the thirteenth century, **Pagan**.

Mingalazedi Stupa. Contains a full set of glazed ***jataka*** tiles. **Pagan**, circa twelfth to thirteenth century.

Mingun Pagoda. A brick pagoda, possibly unfinished, constructed during the reign of **Bodawpaya**, near Mandalay.

Minnanthu. A village within **Pagan**.

Myatheindan Pagoda. Also known as Hsinbyume. Built during the reign of King **Bagyidaw** at Mingun.

Myebontha Temple. In **Pagan**.

Myinpyagu Temple. Built in the eleventh or twelfth century, **Pagan**.

Nagayon Temple. Built in the eleventh or twelfth century, **Pagan**.

Nandamula Cave. A mythical cave visited by the eight **arahants** who appear before King Kyanzittha and provide the king with a model for the Ananda Temple.

Nanpaya Temple. Built in the eleventh or twelfth century, **Pagan**.

Pahtodawgyi Stupa. Built 1820–24 in **Amarapura** by King **Bagyidaw**. The lower terraces have marble reliefs illustrating ***jataka*** tales.

Pathodhammya Temple. Built in the eleventh or twelfth century, **Pagan**.

Payagyi Stupa. Monument in **Sri Ksetra** attributed to the **Pyu**.

Payama Stupa. Monument in **Sri Ksetra** attributed to the **Pyu**.

Payathonzu Temple. Temple from circa the thirteenth century, **Pagan**. Best example of later painting style.

Sanchi. Major early Buddhist stupa site in central India.

Shitthaung Temple. Mrauk-U shrine of eighty thousand images.

Shwedagon Pagoda. One of the most important pilgrimage sites, said to contain hair relics of the Buddha enshrined by **Sona and Uttara**. Patronized by **Mon** monarchs including Queen **Shinsawbu**.

Shwegugyi Temple. Pagan temple built about 1131.

Shwemawdaw Pagoda. Mon pagoda in **Pegu**, established by the Mon probably in the fourteenth century. Once thought to enshrine a tooth relic in the fifteenth century, now thought to contain two hair relics.

Shwenandaw Kyaung. Originally an apartment in the Mandalay Palace, it was refurbished as a monastery around 1880 by King **Thibaw** in honor of his father King **Mindon**.

Shwesettaw Pagoda. Golden Footprint Pagoda and pilgrimage site near contemporary Magwe, Myanmar. Associated with the legend of **Mahapunna** and **Saccabandha**.

Shwethalyaung. Recumbent Buddha sculpture in **Pegu**.

Shwezigon Pagoda. Stone stupa in **Pagan** thought to contain a tooth relic and a bone of the Buddha, from circa the eleventh or twelfth century.

Sulamani Temple. A temple constructed in 1183 in **Pagan** containing later **Konbaung** period murals.

Sule Pagoda. Central pagoda in Yangon, commemorating the home of the deity who indicated the location where the Shwedagon should be built.

Thayanbu Temple. Temple (no. 1554) built in the thirteenth century in **Pagan**.

Thissawadi Temple. Temple (no. 918) built circa 1334 in **Pagan**.

Upali Thein. Ordination hall at **Pagan** constructed in the late eighteenth century, with murals.

Uppatasanti Pagoda. Replica of the **Shwedagon Pagoda**, with a tooth relic, built in 2006 in Naypyidaw by Senior **General Than Shwe** and his wife.

Bibliography

Appleton, George. *Buddhism in Burma*. No. 3 of *Burma Pamphlets*. London: Longmans, Green & Co. Ltd., 1943.

Appleton, Naomi. *Jataka Stories in Theravada Buddhism: Narrating the Bodhisatta Path*. Farnham, Surrey, England: Ashgate Publishers, 2010.

Aung Thaw. *Historical Sites in Burma*. Rangoon: Ministry of Union Culture, Government of the Union of Burma, 1972.

——. *Preliminary Report on the Excavation at Peikthanomyo*. Rangoon: Directorate of Archaeological Survey, 1958.

——. *Report on Excavation at Beikthano*. Government of the Union of Burma, Ministry of Culture, 1968.

Aung Thein (Phra Phraison Salarak). "Intercourse between Siam and Burma." *Journal of the Burma Research Society* 25, no. 2 (1935): 49–108.

——. "Intercourse between Siam and Burma." *Journal of the Burma Research Society* 28, no. 2 (1938): 109–76.

Aung-Thwin, Michael. "Burma before Pagan: The Status of Archaeology Today." *Asian Perspectives* 25, no. 2 (1982–83): 1–21.

——. "Burmese Historiography-Chronicles (*Yazawin*)." In *Making History: A Global Encyclopedia of Historical Writing*, edited by D. R. Woolf. New York: Garland, 1998.

——. "Divinity, Spirit, and Human: Conceptions of Classical Burmese Kingship." In *Centers, Symbols and Hierarchies: Essays on the Classical States of Southeast Asia*, edited by Lorraine Gesick. New Haven: Yale University South East Asian Studies, 1983.

——. "Heaven, Earth and the Supernatural World: Dimensions of the Exemplary Center in Burmese History." In *The City as a Sacred Center: Essays on Six Asian Contexts*, edited by Holly Baker Reynolds and Bardwell Smith. Leiden: E. J. Brill, 1987.

——. "Lower Burma and Bago in the History of Burma." In *The Maritime Frontier of Burma: Exploring Political, Cultural and Commercial Interaction in the Indian Ocean World, 1200–1800*, edited by Jos Gommans and Jacques Leider. Leiden: KITLV Press, 2002.

——. *The Mists of Ramanna: The Legend That Was Lower Burma*. Honolulu: Hawai'i University Press, 2005.

——. "Mranma Pran: When Context Encounters Notion." *Journal of Southeast Asian Studies* 39, no. 2 (2008): 193–217.

——. *Myth and History in the Historiography of Early Burma: Paradigms, Primary Sources, and Prejudices*. Athens, Ohio: Ohio University Press, 1998.

——. "The Myth of the 'Three Shan Brothers' and the Ava Period in Burmese History." *Journal of Asian Studies* 55, no. 4 (1996): 881–901.

——. *Of Monarchs, Monks, and Men: Religion and the State in Myanmar*. ARI Working Paper Series, no. 127 (2009): 2–31.

——. *Pagan: The Origins of Modern Burma*. Honolulu: University of Hawai'i Press, 1985.

——. "Spirals in Burmese and Early Southeast Asian History." *Journal of Interdisciplinary History* 21, no. 4 (1991): 575–602.

——. "A Tale of Two Kingdoms: Ava and Pegu in the Fifteenth Century." *Journal of Southeast Asian Studies* 42, no. 1 (2011): 1–16.

Aung-Thwin, Michael, and Maitrii Aung-Thwin. *A History of Myanmar since Ancient Times*. London: Reaktion Books, 2012.

Bailey, Jane Terry. "Some Seventeenth Century Images from Burma." *Artibus Asiae* (1971): 219–27.

——. "Addendum: Some Seventeenth Century Images from Burma with an Appendix by F. K. Lehman: The Inscription." *Artibus Asiae* 48, no. 1/2 (1987): 79–88.

Bautze-Picron, Claudine. "Between India and Burma: The 'Andagu' Stelae." In *The Art of Burma: New Studies*, edited by Donald Stadtner, 37–52. Bombay: Marg Publications, 1999.

——. *The Buddhist Murals of Pagan: Timeless Vistas of the Cosmos*. Trumbull, Conn.: Weatherhill, 2003.

Beemer, Bryce. "The Creole City in Mainland Southeast Asia: Slave Gathering, Warfare and Cultural Exchange in Burma, Thailand and Manipur, 18th–19th c." PhD diss., University of Hawai'i, Manoa, 2013.

Beylié, Léon de. *Prome et Samara: Voyage archéologique en Birmanie et en Mésopotamie*. Paris: E. Leroux, 1907.

Bigandet, Paul Ambroise. *The Life, or Legend, of Guadama, the Buddha of the Burmese*. 2 vols. London: Trübner & Co., 1880.

Blackburn, Anne M., and Jeffery Samuels, eds. *Approaching the Dhamma: Buddhist Texts and Practices in South and Southeast Asia*. Seattle: Pariyatti Publishing, 2003.

Blackburn, Terrence. *A Report on the Locations of Burmese Artifacts in Museums*. Kiscadale Asia Research Series, Gartmore, Scotland: Kiscadale Publications, 1994.

Blagden, C. O. "Mon Inscriptions Nos. IX–XI." *Epigraphia Birmanica*, vol. 3, pt. 1. Rangoon: Superintendent, Government Printing, 1923.

——. "The Pyu Inscriptions." *Epigraphia Indica*, vol. 12. Calcutta: Superintendent, Government Printing, 1913–14.

——. "The 'Pyu' Inscriptions." *Journal of the Burma Research Society* 7, no. 1 (1917): 37–44.

Blurton, Richard T. "Burmese Bronze Sculpture in the British Museum." In *Burma Art and Archaeology*, edited by Alexandra Green and Richard T. Blurton, 55–65. London: British Museum Press, 2002.

Bode, Mabel Haynes. *The Pali Literature of Burma*. London: Royal Asiatic Society, 1909.

Brac de la Perrière, Bénédicte. "The Burmese Nats: Between Sovereignty and Autochthony." *Diogenes 174*, 44, no. 2 (1996): 45–60.

Brown, George E. R. Grant. *Burma as I Saw It, 1889–1917, with a Chapter on Recent Events*. New York: Frederick A. Stokes Company, 1925.

Brown, Robert L. "Pyu Art: Looking East and West." *Orientations* 32, no. 4 (2001): 35–41.

——. "Telling the Story in Art of the Monkey's Gift of Honey to the Buddha." *Bulletin of the Asia Institute*, New Series/23 (2009): 43–52.

——. "Three Wood Buddha Sculptures from Myanmar (Burma) in the Los Angeles County Museum of Art." *Artibus Asiae* 73, no. 1 (2013): 219–29.

Burma Research Society. *Fiftieth Anniversary Publications No. 2*. Rangoon: Burma Research Society, 1960.

Capelo, Francisco. *A Arte da Laca na Birmânia e na Tailândia*. Lisbon, Portugal: Instituto Português de Museus, 2004.

Carbine, Jason A. *Sons of the Buddha: Continuities and Ruptures in a Burmese Monastic Tradition*. New York: Walter de Gruyter, 2011.

Catalogue of Burmese Art and Its Influences: An Exhibition Held at 16 Saville Row, London W.1, 18–25 April 1981. Exh. cat. London: Beurdeley, Matthews and Co., 1981.

Census of India 1911, Volume IX, Burma, Part 1 (report by C. Morgan Webb). Rangoon: Office of the Superintendent, Government Printing Burma, 1912.

Charney, Michael. "Centralizing Historical Tradition in Precolonial Burma: The Abhiraja/Dhajaraja Myth in Early Kon-baung Historical Texts." *South East Asia Research* 10, no. 2 (2002): 185–215.

——. *Powerful Learning: Buddhist Literati and the Throne in Burma's Last Dynasty, 1752–1885*. Ann Arbor: University of Michigan, 2006.

Chew, Anne-May. *The Cave-Temples of Po Win Taung, Central Burma: Architecture, Sculpture and Murals*. Bangkok: White Lotus Press, 2005.

Chit Thein. *Shei-haung Mon Kyauksa Paungkhuyup*. Yangon: Shei-haung Thudethana Htana-khwe, 1965.

Chiu, Angela. "The Social and Religious World of Northern Thai Buddha Images: Art, Lineage, Power and Place in Lan Na Monastic Chronicles (Tamnan)." PhD diss., School of Oriental and African Studies, London, 2012.

Coedes, George. *The Indianized States of Southeast Asia*. 3rd edition, Paris, 1964. Edited by Walter F. Vella. Translated from the French by Susan Brown Cowing. Honolulu: University of Hawai'i Press, 1969.

Collins, Steven. *Nirvana and Other Buddhist Felicities*. Cambridge: Cambridge University Press, 1998.

Coomaraswamy, A. K. "Burmese Glazed Tiles." *Museum of Fine Arts Bulletin* 16, no. 98 (December 1918): 85.

Cowell, Edward B., Robert Chalmers, W. H. D. Rouse, H. T. Francis, Robert Alexander Neil, and Charles Lang Freer. *The Jātaka; or, Stories of the Buddha's Former Births*. 6 vols. Cambridge: Cambridge University Press, 1895–1913.

Cox, Hiram. *Journal of a Residence in the Burmhan Empire*. London: John Warren, 1821. Reprinted Gregg International Publishers, 1971.

Dai, Yingcong. "A Disguised Defeat: The Myanmar Campaign of the Qing Dynasty." *Modern Asian Studies* 38, no. 1 (2004): 145–90.

Damrong Rajanubhab, Prince, son of Mongkut, King of Siam. *A Journey through Burma in 1936: A View of the Culture, History and Institutions.* Reprinted Bangkok: River Books, 1991.

Dawkins, Richard. *The Selfish Gene.* Oxford: Oxford University Press, 1976.

Dehejia, Vidya. *The Sensuous and the Sacred: Chola Bronzes from South India*. Seattle: American Federation of Arts and University of Washington Press, 2002.

De Mersan, Alexandra. "'The Land of the Great Image' and the Test of Time: The Making of Buddha Images in Arakan (Burma/Myanmar)." In *The Spirit of Things: Materiality and Religious Diversity in Southeast Asia*, edited by Julius Bautista. Ithaca, N.Y.: Cornell University, Southeast Asia Program Publications, 2012.

Dhar, Parul Pandya, and Anupa Pande, eds. *Cultural Interface of India with Asia: Religion, Art and Architecture*. New Delhi: D.K. Printworld & National Museum Institute, 2004.

Di Crocco, Virginia McKeen. *Footprints of the Buddhas of This Era in Thailand and the Indian Subcontinent, Sri Lanka, Myanmar*. Bangkok: Siam Society, 2004.

Dijk, W. O. *Seventeenth-Century Burma and the Dutch East India Company, 1634–1680*. Singapore: National University of Singapore Press, 2006.

Donaldson, Thomas E. *Iconography of the Buddhist Sculpture of Orissa*. New Delhi: Indira Gandhi National Centre for the Arts, 2001.

Duroiselle, Charles, ed. *Epigraphia Birmanica*, vol. 1, pt. 2. Rangoon: Superintendent, Government Printing, 1917.

——. "Excavations at Hmawza." In *Archaeological Survey of India, Annual Report, 1926–27*, 171–83. Calcutta: Government of India, Central Publications Branch, 1930.

——. "Excavations at Hmawza." In *Archaeological Survey of India, Annual Report, 1927–28*, 127–35. Calcutta: Government of India, Central Publications Branch, 1931.

——. "Excavations at Hmawza, Prome." In *Archaeological Survey of India, Annual Report, 1911–12*, 141–48. Calcutta: Government of India, Central Publications Branch, 1915.

——. "Excavations at Pagan." In *Archaeological Survey of India, Annual Report, 1926–27*, 161–71. Calcutta: Government of India, Central Publications Branch, 1930.

——. "Explorations in Burma." In *Archaeological Survey of India, Annual Report, 1936–1937*, 75–84. Calcutta: Superintendent, Government Printing, 1940.

——. "Four Burmese Saints." In *Archaeological Survey of India, Annual Report 1922–1923*, 174–76. Calcutta: Superintendent of Government Printing, 1926.

——, ed. *A List of Inscriptions Found in Burma*. Rangoon: Superintendent Government Printing, Archaeological Survey of Burma, 1921.

——. *Note on the Ancient Geography of Burma*. Rangoon: Government Printing Office, 1906.

——. "The Rock-Cut Temples of Powun-daung." In *Archaeological Survey of India, Annual Report, 1936–1937*, 42–55. Calcutta: Government Printing Office, 1920.

——. "Wathundaye, the Earth Goddess of Burma." In *Archaeological Survey of India, Annual Report 1921–1922*, 144–46. Calcutta: Superintendent of Government Printing, 1925.

Edwards, Penny. "Relocating the Interlocutor: Taw Sein Ko (1864–1930) and the Itinerancy of Knowledge in British Burma." *South East Asia Research* 12, no. 3 (2004): 277–335.

Encyclopedia of Buddhism. 2 vols. Edited by Robert E. Buswell Jr. New York: Macmillan Reference USA, 2004.

Falconer, John, Luca Invernizzi, and Kim Inglis. *Myanmar Style: Art, Architecture and Design of Burma*. Hong Kong: Periplus Editions, 1998.

Falk, Harry. "Die Goldblätter aus Śrī Kṣtra" [The gold foils from Sri Ksetra]. *Weiner Zeitschrift für die Kunde Südasians* 41 (1997): 53–92.

Forchhammer, Emmanuel. *Report on the Antiquities of Arakan*. Rangoon: Superintendent, Government Printing, 1892.

Franklin, Frances, Noel Singer, and Deborah Swallow. "Burmese Kalagas." *Arts of Asia* 33, no. 2 (March–April 2003): 57–69.

Frasch, Tilman. "The Making of a Buddhist Ecumene in the Bay of Bengal." In *Pelagic Passageways: The Northern Bay of Bengal Before Colonialism*, edited by Rila Mukherjee, 383–405. New Delhi: Primus Books, 2011.

Fraser-Lu, Sylvia. "Ancient Arakan." *Arts of Asia* 17, no. 2 (March–April 1987): 96–109.

——. "Buddha Images from Burma, Part One: Sculptured in Stone." *Arts of Asia* 11, no. 1 (January–February 1981): 72–82.

——. "Buddha Images from Burma, Part Two: Bronze and Related Metals." *Arts of Asia* 11, no. 2 (March–April 1981): 62–72.

——. "Buddha Images from Burma, Part Three: Wood and Lacquer." *Arts of Asia* 11, no. 3 (May–June 1981): 129–36.

——. "Burman Textiles." In *Eclectic Collecting: Art from Burma in the Denison Museum*, edited by Alexandra Green, ch. 8. Honolulu: University of Hawai'i Press, 2008.

——. "Burmese Art at the Denver Art Museum." *Arts of Asia* 37, no. 1 (January–February 2007): 116–25.

——. *Burmese Crafts: Past and Present*. Singapore: Oxford University Press, 1993.

——. *Burmese Lacquerware*. Revised and expanded edition. Bangkok: Orchid Press, 2000.

——. "Burmese Silverware." *Arts of Asia* 10, no. 2 (March–April 1980): 77–83.

——. "Lacquer." In *Eclectic Collecting: Art from Burma in the Denison Museum*, edited by Alexandra Green, ch. 9. Honolulu: University of Hawai'i Press, 2008.

——. "Robes for the Buddha." *Asia Magazine*. December 20, 1981: 34–36.

——. "Sadaik: Burmese Manuscript Chests." *Arts of Asia* 14, no. 3 (May–June 1984): 69–74.

——. *Silverware of South-East Asia*. Singapore: Oxford University Press, 1989.

——. *Splendour in Wood: The Buddhist Monasteries of Burma*. Bangkok: Orchid Press, 2001.

——. "Stemming from the Lotus: Sacred Robes for Buddhist Monks." In *Material Choices: Refashioning Bast and Leaf Fibers in Asia and the Pacific*, edited by Roy Hamilton and B. Lynne Milgram, 93–105. Los Angeles: Fowler Museum, 2007.

——. "Visual Narratives in Burmese Lacquer." *Arts of Asia* 43, no. 3 (May–June 2013): 82–94.

Furnivall, John S. *Colonial Policy and Practice: A Comparative Study of Burma and Netherlands India*. New York: New York University Press, 1948.

——. *The Fashioning of Leviathan*. Rangoon: Zabu Meitswe Pitaka Press, 1939.

——. *The Government of Modern Burma*. New York: International Secretariat, Institute of Pacific Relations, 1958.

——. *An Introduction to the Political Economy of Burma*. Rangoon: Burma Book Club, 1931.

Galloway, Charlotte. "Ways of Seeing a Pyu, Mon and Dvaravati Artistic Continuum." *Bulletin of the Indo-Pacific Prehistory Association* 30 (2010): 70–78.

Geiger, Wilhelm, trans. *The Mahavamsa of the Great Chronicle of Ceylon*. Colombo: Government Information Department, 1950.

Goh, Geok Yian. "Cakkravatiy Anuruddha and the Buddhist Oikoumene: Historical Narratives of Kingship and Religious Networks in Burma, Northern Thailand, and Sri Lanka (11th–14th Centuries)." PhD diss., University of Hawai'i, 2007.

Grabowski, Volker, and Renoo Wichasin. *Chronicles of Chiang Khaeng, A Tai Lü Principality of the Upper Mekong*. Chiang Mai: Silkworm Press, 2011.

Granoff, Phyllis. "Karma, Curse or Divine Illusion: The Destruction of the Buddha's Clan and the Slaughter of the Yadavas." In *Epic and Argument in Sanskrit Literary History: Essays in Honor of Robert P. Goldman*, edited by Sheldon Pollock, 75–91. Delhi: Manohar, 2010.

Green, Alexandra, ed. *Eclectic Collecting: Art from Burma in the Denison Museum*. Honolulu: University of Hawai'i Press, 2008.

——. "From Gold Leaf to Buddhist Hagiographies: Contact with Regions to the East Seen in Late Burmese Murals." *Journal of Burma Studies* 15, no. 2 (2011): 337–46.

Green, Alexandra, and Richard T. Blurton, eds. *Burma: Art and Archaeology*. London: British Museum Press, 2002.

Griffiths, Arlo. "Early Indic Inscriptions of Southeast Asia." In *Lost Kingdoms: Hindu-Buddhist Sculpture of Southeast Asia*, edited by John Guy. New York: Metropolitan Museum of Art, 2014.

Gutman, Pamela. "Ancient Arakan: With Special Reference to Its Cultural History between the 5th and 11th Centuries." PhD diss., Australian National University, 1976.

——. *Burma's Lost Kingdoms: Splendours of Arakan*. Bangkok: Orchid Press, 2001.

——. "A Series of Buddhist Reliefs from Selagiri." In *Etudes birmanes en homage a Denis Bernot*, edited by P. Pichard and F. Robinne. Paris: Bulletin de l'École française d'Extrême-Orient, 1998.

Gutman, Pamela, and Bob Hudson. "The Archaeology of Burma, from the Neolithic to Pagan." In *Southeast Asia: From Prehistory to History*, edited by Ian Glover and P. Bellwood, 149–76. New York: Routledge, 2004.

Guy, John, ed. *Lost Kingdoms: Hindu-Buddhist Sculpture of Southeast Asia*. New York: Metropolitan Museum of Art, 2014.

Halliday, R., trans. and notes. "Slapat Rājāwan Datow Smin Ron, A History of Kings." *Journal of the Burma Research Society* 13 (1923): 9–67.

Hamilton, Francis. "Account of a Map Drawn by a Native of Dawae or Tavay." *The Edinburgh Philosophical Journal* 9 (1823): 228–36.

——. "Account of a Map of the Countries Subject to the King of Ava, Drawn by a Slave of the King's Eldest Son." *The Edinburgh Philosophical Journal* 3 (1820): 89–95; 4 (1820): 262–77.

——. "Description of the Ruins of Buddha Gáya." In R. Montgomery Martin, *The History, Antiquities, Topography, and Statistics of Eastern India: Report of a Survey of South Bihar*, 1: 40–51. London: William. H. Allen, 1838.

Harvey, Geoffrey E. *History of Burma: From the Earliest Times to 10 March 1824, the Beginning of the English Conquest*. London: Frank Cass & Co. Ltd., 1967. First published 1925.

Hazra, Kanai Lal. *Buddhism and Pali Literature of Myanmar*. Delhi: Buddhist World Press, 2011.

Herbert, Patricia M. "Burmese Cosmological Manuscripts." In *Burma: Art and Archaeology*, edited by Alexandra Green and Richard T. Blurton, 77–98. London: British Museum Press, 2002.

——. *Life of the Buddha*. London: The British Library, 1993.

Hla, Myint Swe. *Buddham, Dhammam, Samghan: Buddhist Faith in Myanmar*. Singapore: Spirit Asia, 2009.

Hla Pe. *Burma: Literature, Historiography, Scholarship, Language, Life and Buddhism*. Singapore: Institute of Southeast Asia Studies, 1985.

Hla Pe and Pok Ni. *Konmara Pya Zat: An Example of Popular Burmese Drama in the XIX Century*. London: Luzac, 1952.

Hoffenberg, Peter. *An Empire on Display: English, Indian, and Australian Exhibitions from the Crystal Palace to the Great War*. Berkeley: University of California Press, 2001.

Hoke Sein. *Pali-Myamma Abhidhan*. Yangon: Pyi-daung-su Myamma Naingan-daw A-sau-ya Sa-pon-hneit-ye hning Sa-yei kiriya htana, 1954.

——. *Universal Burmese-English-Pali Dictionary*. Rangoon: Daily Gazette Press, 1981.

Hpe Aung. "Selected Lectures and Papers on Buddhism." Rangoon: A Buddhist Scholars Society Publication, 1958–59.

Htin Aung. *Burmese Drama: A Study, with Translations, of Burmese Plays*. London: Oxford University Press, 1937.

——. *Burmese Monk's Tales*. New York: Columbia University Press, 1966.

——. *Folk Elements in Burmese Buddhism*. London: Oxford University Press, 1962.

Hudson, Bob. "The King of 'Free Rabbit' Island: A GIS-Based Archaeological Approach to Myanmar's Medieval Capital, Bagan." In *Proceedings of the Myanmar Two Millennium Conference*, 3: 10–20. Yangon, 2000.

——. "The Nyaungyan 'Goddesses': Some Unusual Bronze Grave Goods from Upper Burma." *Journal of the Asian Arts Society of Australia* 10, no. 2 (June 2001): 4–7.

——. "The Origins of Bagan: The Archaeological Landscape of Upper Burma to AD 1300." PhD diss., University of Sydney, 2004.

Hultzsch, E. "A Vaishnava Inscription at Pagan." *Epigraphia Indica* 7 (1902–3): 197–98.

Huntington, Susan L., and John C. Huntington. *Leaves from the Bodhi Tree: The Art of Pala India (8th–12th Centuries) and Its International Legacy*. Dayton, Ohio: Dayton Art Institute in association with the University of Washington Press, 1990.

Isaacs, Ralph. *Sazigyo, Burmese Manuscript Binding Tapes: Woven Miniatures of Buddhist Art*. Bangkok: Silkworm, 2014.

Isaacs, Ralph, and T. Richard Blurton. *Visions from the Golden Land: Burma and the Art of Lacquer*. Chicago: Art Media Resources, 2000.

Jayawickrama, N. A., trans. *The Story of Gotama Buddha: The Nidana-katha of the Jatakatthakatha*. Oxford: Pali Text Society, 1990.

Jinah Kim, *Receptacle of the Sacred: Illustrated Manuscripts and the Cult of the Book in South Asia*. Berkeley: University of California Press, 2013.

Johnston, E. H. "Some Sanskrit Inscriptions of Arakan." *Bulletin of the School of Oriental and African Studies* 11 (1944): 357–85.

Judson's Burmese-English Dictionary. Edited by Robert C. Stevenson and F. H. Eveleth. Rangoon: Baptist Board of Publications, 1966.

Karow, Otto. *Burmese Buddhist Sculpture: The John Moger Collection*. Bangkok: White Lotus, 1991.

Keck, Stephen L. "'It Has Passed Forever into Our Hands': Lord Curzon and the Construction of Imperial Heritage in Colonial Burma." *Journal of Burma Studies* 11 (2007): 49–83.

———. "Recovering a Lost Genealogy: Taw Sein Ko and the Colonial Roots of 'Myanmar Studies.'" In the proceedings of *The 2011 International Conference of ISEAS/PUFS*, Institute for Southeast Asian Studies, cosponsored by the National Research Foundation of Korea and Pusan University of Foreign Studies, June 2–3, 2011, 59–78.

Keyes, Charles F. *The Golden Peninsula: Culture and Adaptation in Mainland Southeast Asia*. New York: Macmillan, 1977.

Khin Myo Chit. *Flowers and Festivals Round the Burmese New Year*. Rangoon, 1980.

———. *A Wonderland of Burmese Legends*. Bangkok: Tamarind Press, 1984.

Koenig, William J. *The Burmese Polity, 1752–1819: Politics, Administration and Social Organization in the Early Kon-baung Period*. Ann Arbor: Center for South and Southeast Asian Studies, University of Michigan, 1990.

Krishnan, Gauri Parimoo. *On the Nalanda Trail: Buddhism in India, China and Southeast Asia (Fo Xue Zhi Guang: Yindu, Zhongguo he Dongnanya de foJiao Chuan Cheng)*. Singapore: Asian Civilisations Museum, 2008.

Law, Bimala Churn. *The History of Buddha's Religion, Sasanavamsa*. Delhi: Sri Satguru Publications, 1986.

Leider, Jacques. "The Emergence of Rakhine Historiography: A Challenge for Myanmar Historical Research." In *Myanmar Historical Commission Conference Proceedings*, pt. 2, 38–59. Yangon: Universities Press, 2005.

———. "The *Mists of Ramanna*, Compte-rendu." *Aséanie* 18 (2006).

Lester, Robert C. *Theravada Buddhism in Southeast Asia*. Ann Arbor: University of Michigan Press, 1973.

Lewis, M. Paul, Gary F. Simons, and Charles D. Fennig, eds. *Ethnologue: Languages of the World*. 17th ed. Dallas: SIL International, 2014. Online version: http://www.ethnologue.com/language/kkh.

Lieberman, Victor B. *Burmese Administrative Cycles*. Princeton, N.J.: Princeton University Press, 1982.

———. "Excising the 'Mon Paradigm' from Burmese Historiography." *Journal of Southeast Asian Studies* 38 (2007): 377–83.

———. *Strange Parallels: Southeast Asia in the Global Context, c. 800–1830*, vol. 1: *Integration on the Mainland*. Cambridge: Cambridge University Press, 2003.

———. "The Transfer of the Burmese Capital from Pegu to Ava." *Journal of the Royal Asiatic Society of Great Britain and Ireland* 1 (1980): 64–83.

Lowry, John. *Burmese Art*. London: Her Majesty's Stationery Office, 1974.

Luce, G. H. "The Ancient Pyu." *Fiftieth Anniversary Publications*, 1: 307–21. Rangoon: Burma Research Society, 1960.

———. "Dvaravati and Old Burma." *Journal of the Siam Society* 53, no. 1 (1965): 9–26.

———. "The Early Syam in Burma's History: A Supplement." *Journal of the Siam Society* 47, no. 1 (1959): 59–101.

———. "The Greater Temples of Pagan." *Journal of the Burma Research Society* 8, pt. 3 (1918): 189–98.

———. "Mons of the Pagan Dynasty." *Journal of the Burma Research Society* 36, no. 1 (1953): 1–19.

———. "Note on the Peoples of Burma in the 12th–13th Century AD." *Census of India* 11, no. 1 (1931): 296–306.

———. *Old Burma—Early Pagan*. 3 vols. New York: Artibus Asiae and the Institute of Fine Arts, New York University, 1969–70.

———. *Phases of Pre-Pagan Burma: Languages and History*. 2 vols. Oxford: Oxford University Press, 1985.

———. "The Smaller Temples of Pagan." *Journal of the Burma Research Society* 10, pt. 2 (1920): 41–48.

———. "Sources of Early Burma History." In *Southeast Asian History and Historiography: Essays Presented to D. G. E. Hall*, edited by C. D. Cowan and O. W. Wolters. Ithaca, N.Y.: Cornell University Press, 1976.

Luce, G. H., and Pe Maung Tin, eds. *Inscriptions of Burma*. 5 vols. Rangoon: University of Rangoon Oriental Studies Publication, 1933–56.

———. *Selections from the Inscriptions of Pagan*. Rangoon: British Burma Press, 1928.

Mahadhamma-thingyan. *Thathanalinkara-sadan*. Yangon: Hanthawaddy Pitaka Ponnaik Taik, 1956.

Mahasilavamsa. *Yazawin-gyaw*. Yangon: Hanthawadi Ponnaik Taik, 1965.

Malalsekera, G. P. *Dictionary of Pali Proper Names*. 2 vols. London: Pali Text Society, 1974.

Marshall, John. *Annual Report of the Director-General of Archaeology for the Year 1914–15*. Part 1. Superintendent, Government Printing, Archaeological Survey of India, 1916.

Matilsky, Barbara C. *Buddhist Art and Ritual from Nepal and Tibet*. Ackland Art Museum, 2001.

McGill, Forrest. *Emerald Cities: Arts of Siam and Burma 1775–1950*. San Francisco: Asian Art Museum, 2009.

McQuail, Lisa. *Treasures of Two Nations: Thai Royal Gifts to the United States of America*. Washington, D.C.: Asian History Program, Smithsonian Institution, 1997.

Moilanen, Irene, and Sergey Ozhegov. *Mirrored in Wood: Burmese Art and Architecture*. Bangkok: White Lotus Press, 1999.

Monier-Williams, M. *Sanskrit-English Dictionary*. New Delhi: Manshiram Manoharlal Publishers, 1976.

Moore, Elizabeth H. *Early Landscapes of Myanmar*. Bangkok: River Books, 2007.

———. "Place and Space in Early Burma: A New Look at 'Pyu Culture,'" *Journal of the Siam Society* 97 (2009): 101–28.

———. "Unexpected Spaces at the Shwedagon." In *A Companion to Asian Art and Architecture*, edited by Rebecca M. Brown and Deborah S. Hutton. London: Blackwell Publishing Ltd., 2011.

Morris, A. P. "The Lacquerware Industry of Burma." *Journal of the Burma Research Society* 9, pt. 1 (1919): 1–14.

———. "Pottery in Burma." *Journal of the Burma Research Society* 8, pt. 3 (1918): 213–21.

Morris, T. O. "Copper and Bronze Antiquities from Burma." *Journal of the Burma Research Society* 28 (1938): 95–99.

Mus, Paul. "Lecture at Yale," November 8, 1966, quoted in Yves Goudineau, "Généalogie des formes et scénarios rituels dans l'Asie des Moussons: L'orientalisme de Paul Mus entre sociologie et iconologie." In *L'espace d'un regard: Paul Mus et l'Asie*, edited by D. Chandler and C. Goscha, 133–46. Paris: Les Indes savantes, 2006.

Musée des Arts Asiatiques, Nice. *Laque et Or de Birmanie*. Exh. cat. Milan: Silvana Editoriale, 2011.

Mya. "Beginnings of Jambhupati Images." In *Report of the Director, Archaeological Survey of Burma* (in Myanmar language). 1959.

Myanmar-English Dictionary. Yangon: Department of the Myanmar Language Commission, 1993.

Myint Aung. "The Development of Myanmar Archaeology." *Myanmar Historical Research Journal* 9 (2002): 11–29.

——. "The Excavations of Ayetthema and Winka (? Suvannabhumi)." In *Studies in Myanmar History*, vol. 1: *Essays Given to Than Tun on His 75th Birthday*, 17–64. Yangon: Inwa House, 1999.

Nandana Chutiwongs. *The Iconography of Avalokiteśvara in Mainland South East Asia*. New Delhi: Aryan Books International, 2002.

Nash, Manning. "Burmese Buddhism in Everyday Life." *American Anthropologist* 65, no. 2 (February–June 1963): 285–95.

Nyanaponika, Bodhi, and Hellmuth Hecker. *Great Disciples of the Buddha: Their Lives, Their Works, Their Legacy*. Boston: Wisdom Publications, 1997.

Nyanatiloka, *Buddhist Dictionary: Manual of Buddhist Terms and Doctrines*. Kandy: Buddhist Publication Society, 1980.

O'Connor, V. C. Scott. *Mandalay and Other Cities of the Past in Burma*. London: Hutchinson & Co., 1907.

Oertel, E. O. "Excavations at Sarnath." In *Archaeological Survey of India, Annual Report, 1904–1905*, 59–104. Calcutta: Superintendent, Government Printing, 1908.

——. *Notes on a Tour in Burma in March and April 1892*. First published 1892; reprinted Bangkok: White Orchid Press, 1995.

Oshegowa, Nina, and Sergej Oshegow. *Kunst in Burma*. Leipzig: E. A. Seemann Verlag, 1988.

Pal, Pratapaditya. "Fragmentary Cloth Painting from Early Pagan and Their Relations with Indo-Tibetan Traditions." In *The Art of Burma: New Studies*, edited by Donald Stadtner, Mumbai: Marg Publications, 1999: 79–88.

Paritta Chalermpow Koanantakool. "Contextualising Objects in Monastery Museums in Thailand." In *Buddhist Legacies in Mainland Southeast Asia. Mentalities, Interpretations and Practices*, edited by Francois Lagirarde and Paritta Chalermpow Koanantakool. Bangkok: Princess Maha Chakri Sirindhorn Anthropology Centre, 2006.

Parker, Edward Harper. *Burma: With Special Reference to Her Relations with China*. Rangoon: Rangoon Gazette Press, 1893.

Pasquet, Sylvie. "Quand l'Empereur de Chine écrivait à son jeune frère, Empereur de Birmanie. . . . Analyse d'une correspondance diplomatique sur 'feuilles d'or' (XVIIIe siècle)." *Journal Asiatique* 300, no. 1 (2012): 269–317.

Pe Maung Tin. "The Shwe Dagon Pagoda." *Journal of the Burma Research Society* 24, no. 1 (1934): 1–91.

Pe Maung Tin and G. H. Luce, trans. *The Glass Palace Chronicle of the Kings of Burma*. London: Oxford University Press, 1923.

Phayre, Sir Arthur Purves. *History of Burma: Including Burma Proper, Pegu, Taungu, Tenasserim, and Arakan; From the Earliest Time to the End of the First War with British India*. London: Trübner and Co., 1883.

——. "History of Pegu." *Journal of the Asiatic Society of Bengal* 42, no. 1 (1873): 23–57.

Pichard, Pierre. "A Distinctive Technical Achievement: The Vaults and Arches of Pagan." In *The Art of Burma: New Studies*, edited by Donald Stadtner. Mumbai: Marg Publications, 1999.

——. *Inventory of Monuments of Pagan*. 8 vols. Gartmore, Scotland: Kiscadale; and Paris: UNESCO, 1992–2000.

——. "Remarques sur le chapitre 9 'The Mon Paradigm and the Evolution of the Pagan Temple.'" *Aséanie* 18, 2006.

Poungpattana, Rattanaporn. "King Bodawhpaya of Konbaung in a Testimony of Ayudhya War Captives." Paper presented at the *Golden Jubilee Conference of the Myanmar Historical Commission,* Yangon, January 12–14, 2005.

Pranke, Patrick Arthur. "The 'Treatise on the Lineage of Elders' (*Vaṃsadīpanī*): Monastic Reform and the Writing of Buddhist History in Eighteenth-Century Burma." PhD diss., University of Michigan, 2004.

Princeton Dictionary of Buddhism. Edited by Robert E. Buswell Jr. and Donald S. Lopez Jr. Princeton, N.J.: Princeton University Press, 2013.

Ramachandran, T. N. *The Nagapattinam and Other Buddhist Bronzes in the Chennai Museum*. Chennai: Director of Museums, Government of Tamil Nadu, 2005.

Ranard, Andrew. *Burmese Painting: A Linear and Lateral History*. Thailand: Silkworm Books, 2009.

——. "Burmese Painting: River of Unknowns." *Arts of Asia* 43, no. 3 (May–June 2013): 95–109.

Ray, Niharranjan. *An Introduction to the Study of Theravada Buddhism in Burma: A Study in Indo-Burmese Historical and Cultural Relations from the Earliest Times to the British Conquest*. Calcutta: University of Calcutta, 1946.

——. *Sanskrit Buddhism in Burma*. Calcutta: University of Calcutta, 1936.

Raymond, Catherine. "Notes on a Burmese Version of the Vessantara Jataka as Represented on Three Shwe Chi Doe in the NIU Art Collection." *Journal of Burma Studies* 16, no. 1 (June 2012): 123–48.

——. "Religious and Scholarly Exchanges between the Singhalese Sangha and the Arakanese and Burmese Theravadin Communities: Historical Documentation and Physical Evidence." In *Commerce and Culture in the Bay of Bengal, 1500–1800*, edited by Om Prakash and Denys Lombard, 87–114. New Delhi: Manohar, 1999.

——. "The Seven Weeks: A 19th-Century Burmese Palm-leaf Manuscript." *Journal of Burma Studies* 14 (2010): 255–65.

Reid, Anthony. *Southeast Asia in the Age of Commerce: 1450–1680*, vol. 1: *The Lands below the Winds*. New Haven: Yale University Press, 1988.

Reynolds, Frank E., and Jason A. Carbine. *The Life of Buddhism*. Berkeley: University of California Press, 2000.

Rhys Davids, T. W., and William Stede. *Pali-English Dictionary*. Delhi: Motilal Banarsidass, 1993.

Rhys Davids, T. W., Hermann Oldenberg, and F. Max Mueller. *Vinaya Texts*, Part 3, *Sacred Books of the East*, Vol. 40. Oxford: Clarendon Press, 1881–85. Reprinted Delhi: Motilal Banarsidrass, 1965.

Robbine, Francois. "Early Myanmar Myths and History as Revised by the Minorities in the Oral Tradition." In *Views and Visions*, 1: 34–37. Yangon: Universities Historical Research Centre, 2001.

Rodrigues, Yves. *Nat-Pwe: Burma's Supernatural Culture*. Gartmore, Scotland: Kiscadale Publications, 1992.

Saibaba, V. V. S. *Theravada Buddhist Devotionalism in Ceylon, Burma, and Thailand*. New Delhi: DK Printworld, 2005.

San Lwin, trans. *The Campaigns of Razadarit*, by Binnya Dala. Bangkok: Institute of Asian Studies, Chulalongkorn University, 2007.

San Tha Aung. *The Buddhist Art of Arakan (An Eastern Border State Beyond Ancient India, East of Vang and Samatata)*. Rangoon: Government Press, 1979.

Sao Saimong. "The Phaungtaw-U Festival." *Journal of the Siam Society* 68, no. 2 (1980): 70–81.

Sao Saimong Mangrai. *The Padeaeng Chronicle and the Jengtung State Chronicle Translated*. Ann Arbor: Center for South and Southeast Asian Studies, University of Michigan, 1981.

Saya Pwa. *Mahazayawin-gyi*, vol. 1. Yangon: Myanmar Thudethana Athin, 1924.

Schober, Juliane. "In the Presence of the Buddha: Ritual Veneration of the Burmese Mahamuni Image." In *Sacred Biography in the Buddhist Traditions of South and Southeast Asia*, edited by Juliane Schober. Honolulu: University of Hawai'i Press, 1997.

——. "Venerating the Buddha's Remains in Burma: From Solitary Practice to the Cultural Hegemony of Communities." *Journal of Burma Studies* 6 (2001): 111–39.

Scott, James George (Shwe Yoe). *The Burman: His Life and Notions*. Gartmore, Scotland: Kiscadale Publications, 1989. First published 1882; reprinted from revised 1910 Macmillan edition.

Selig Brown, Katheryn H. *Eternal Presence: Handprints and Footprints in Buddhist Art*. Katonah, N.Y.: Katonah Museum of Art, 2004.

Shorto, H. L. "The Devata Plaques of the Ananda Basement." *Artibus Asiae: Supplementum* 23 (1966): 156-65.

——. "The Gavampati Tradition in Burma." In *R. C. Majumdar Felicitation Volume*, edited by H. B. Sarkar, 15–30. Calcutta: Firma K. L. Mukhopadhyay, 1970.

Singer, Noel F. *Burmah: A Pictorial Journey 1855–1925*. Gartmore, Scotland: Kiscadale Publications, 1993.

——. "Kammavaca Texts, Their Covers and Binding Ribbons." *Arts of Asia* 23, no. 3 (May–June 1993): 97–106.

——. "The Ramayana at the Burmese Court." *Arts of Asia* 19, no.6 (November–December 1989): 90–103.

Sirisaddhammabhilankara, *Tathagata-udana-dipani-kyam*. 2 vols. Yangon: Hanthawaddy Thadinza Pon-hneit-daik, 1914.

Sivasundaram, Sujit. "Buddhist Kingship, British Archaeology and Historical Narratives in Sri Lanka c. 1750–1850." *Past and Present* 197 (2007): 111–42.

Skilling, Peter. "The Advent of Theravada Buddhism to Mainland South-East Asia." *Journal of the International Association of Buddhist Studies* 20, no. 1 (1997): 93–107.

——. "The Aesthetics of Devotion: Buddhist Arts of Thailand." In Heidi Tan et al., *Enlightened Ways: The Many Streams of Buddhist Art in Thailand*. Singapore: Asian Civilizations Museum, 2013.

——. Review of Janice Stargardt, *Tracing Thought through Things: The Oldest Pali Texts and the Early Buddhist Archaeology of India and Burma*. In *Asian Perspectives* 44, no. 2 (Fall 2005): 386–90.

Slater, Robert Lawson. *Paradox and Nirvana: A Study of Religious Ultimates with Special Reference to Burmese Buddhism*. Chicago: University of Chicago Press, 1951.

Smith-Forbes, Charles James Forbes. *British Burma and Its People: Being Sketches of Native Manners, Customs, and Religion*. London: J. Murray, 1878.

Snellgrove, David, ed. *The Image of the Buddha*. London: Serindia Publications/UNESCO, 1978.

Somkiart Lopetcharat. *Myanmar Buddha: The Image and Its History*. Bangkok: Siam International Books, 2007.

Spiro, Melford E. *Buddhism and Society: A Great Tradition and Its Burmese Vicissitudes*. New York: Harper & Row, 1970.

——. *Burmese Supernaturalism*. Englewood Cliffs, N.J.: Prentice-Hall, 1967.

Spooner, D. B. "Annual Report of the Director-General of Archaeology for the Year 1917–18." *Archaeological Survey of India 1917–18*. Calcutta: Superintendent Government Printing, India, 1920.

Stadtner, Donald Martin. *Ancient Pagan: Buddhist Plain of Merit*. Thailand: River Books, 2005.

——. "The Art of Burma." In *Art of Southeast Asia*, edited by Maude Girard-Geslan. New York: Harry N. Abrams, 1998.

——, ed. *The Art of Burma: New Studies*. Mumbai: Marg Publications, 1999.

——. "Burma on the Eve of the Modern Era." *Orientations* 32, no. 4 (2001): 50–56.

——. "Demystifying Mists: The Case for the Mon." In *The Mon over Two Millennia: Monuments, Manuscripts, Movements*, edited by Patrick McCormick, Mathias Jenny, and Chris Baker. Bangkok: Chulalongkorn University, 2011.

——. "The Enigma of the Mingun Pagoda: Is the Pagoda Really Unfinished?" In *Proceedings of the Myanmar Two Millennium Conference*, 3. Yangon, 2000.

——. "An 'Extraordinary Folly'?" *Archaeology* 53, no. 3 (May–June 2000): 54–59.

——. "A Fifteenth-Century Royal Monument in Burma and the Seven Stations in Buddhist Art." *Art Bulletin* 73, no. 1 (1991): 39–52.

——. "The Glazed Tiles at Mingun." In *Etudes Birmanes en hommage à Denise Bernot*, edited by Pierre Pichard and Francois Robinne, 165–85. Paris: Ecole Française d'Extrême-Orient, 1998.

——. "King Dhammaceti's Pegu," *Orientations* 21, no. 2 (1990): 53–60.

——. "The Lost Legend of the Shwemawdaw Pagoda." In *The Mon over Two Millennia: Monuments, Manuscripts, Movements*, edited by Patrick McCormick, Mathias Jenny, and Chris Baker. Bangkok: Institute of Asian Studies, Chulalongkorn University, 2011.

——. "The Mon of Lower Burma." *Journal of the Siam Society* 96 (2008): 198–215.

——. "New Approaches to South Asian Art." *Art Journal* 49, no. 4 (Winter 1990): 359–62.

——. "'The Questions and Answers' of Maundaung Sayadaw and the Confluence of the Ananda Temple, Bagan, and the Mingun Pagoda." In *Texts and Contexts in Southeast Asia: Proceedings of the Texts and Contexts in Southeast Asia Conference, 12–14 December 2001, Part 3*. Yangon: Universities Historical Research Centre, 2003.

——. *Sacred Sites of Burma: Myth and Folklore in an Evolving Spiritual Realm*. Bangkok: River Books, 2011.

——. "The Three Jewels at Pagan." In *In the Footsteps of the Buddha: An Iconic Journey from India to China*, edited by Rajeshwari Ghose. Hong Kong: University Museum and Art Gallery, University of Hong Kong, 1998.

——. "The Three Jewels in Burma: Tarnished But Still Shining." *National Palace Museum Bulletin* 28 (2006).

Stanislaw, Mary Anne. *Kalagas: The Wall Hangings of Southeast Asia*. Menlo Park, Calif.: Ainslies, 1987.

Stargardt, Janice. *The Ancient Pyu of Burma*. Cambridge: Publications on Ancient Civilisations in South East Asia, 1990.

——. "The Great Silver Reliquary from Sri Ksetra: The Oldest Buddhist Art in Burma and One of the Two Oldest Pali Inscriptions in the World." In *Festschrift for Professor J. G. de Casparis*, edited by K. van Kooij and M. Klokke, 487–519. Groningen: Egbert Forster, 2001.

——. *Tracing Thought through Things: The Oldest Pali Texts and the Early Buddhist Archaeology of India and Burma*. Amsterdam: Royal Netherlands Academy of Arts and Sciences, 2000.

Stark, Miriam T., and Michael Aung-Thwin. "Recent Developments in the Archaeology of Myanmar Pyay (Burma): An Introduction." *Asian Perspectives* 40, no. 1 (Spring 2001): 6–34.

Strachan, Paul. *Pagan: Art and Architecture of Old Burma*. Whiting Bay, Scotland: Kiscadale Publications, 1989.

Strong, John. "Gavampati in Pali and Sanskrit Texts: The Indian Background to a Southeast Asian Cult." Unpublished conference paper, The International Association of Buddhist Studies. London, 2005.

——. *The Legend and Cult of Upagupta: Sanskrit Buddhism in North India and Southeast Asia*. Princeton, N.J.: Princeton University Press, 1992.

——. *Relics of the Buddha*. Princeton, N.J.: Princeton University Press, 2004.

Surakiat, Pamaree. *The Changing Nature of Conflict between Burma and Siam as Seen from the Growth and Development of Burmese States from the 16th to the 19th Centuries*. ARI Working Paper no. 64. Singapore: Asia Research Institute Working Paper Series, 2006.

Swearer, Donald, K. *Becoming the Buddha*. Princeton, N.J.: Princeton University Press, 2004.

——. *Buddhism and Society in Southeast Asia*. Chambersburg, Pa.: Anima Books, 1981.

——. *The Buddhist World of Southeast Asia*. Chiang Mai: Silkworm Books, 2009; and Albany: State University of New York Press, 2010.

Symes, Michael. *An Account of an Embassy to the Kingdom of Ava, Sent by the Governor-General of India, in the Year 1795*. London: J. Debrett, 1800.

Taw Sein Ko. "Excavations at Hmawza near Prome." In *Archaeological Survey of India, Annual Report, 1909–1910*. Calcutta: Superintendent, Government Printing, 1914.

——. *The Kalyani Inscriptions Erected by King Dhammaceti at Pegu in 1476 A.D.: Text and Translation*. Rangoon: Superintendent, Government Printing, Burma, 1892.

Tet Htoot. "The Nature of the Burmese Chronicles." In *The Historians of Southeast Asia*, edited by D. G. E. Hall, 50–62. London: Oxford University Press, 1961.

Thakur, Upendra. *Indian Missionaries in the Land of Gold*. Patna: Kashi Prasad Jayaswal Research Institute, 1986.

Than Htun (Dedaye). *Lacquerware Journeys: The Untold Story of Burmese Lacquer*. Bangkok: River Books, 2013.

Than Tun. "The Buddhist Church in Burma During the Pagan Period: 1044–1287." PhD diss., University of London, 1955.

——. *Essays on the History and Buddhism of Burma*. Arran, Scotland: Seven Hills Books, 1988.

——. "History of Buddhism in Burma: A.D. 1000–1300." *Journal of the Burma Research Society* 62, nos. 1 & 2 (1978): 1–266.

——. "History of Burma: A.D. 1300–1400." *Journal of the Burma Research Society* 42, no. 2 (1959): 119–33.

——. "Lacquer Images of the Buddha." *Shiroku* 13 (1980): 21–36.

——, ed. *The Royal Orders of Burma, A.D. 1598–1885*, 10 vols. Kyoto: Centre for Southeast Asian Studies, Kyoto University, 1983–90.

——. *Some Observations on History and Culture of Early Myanma*. Yangon: Myanmar Historical Commission, 2004.

Than Tun (Shwebo). *The Hindu-Buddhist Impact on Myanmar Culture*. Rangoon: Pinyan Myanma Sape Taik, 2009.

Thant Myint-U. *The Making of Modern Burma*. Cambridge: Cambridge University Press, 2001.

Thaw Kaung. *Aspects of Myanmar History and Culture*. Yangon: Loka Ahlin Publishing House, 2010.

——. "The Ramayana Drama in Myanmar." *Journal of the Siam Society* 40, nos. 1 & 2 (2002): 55–82.

Thein Han and Khin Zaw. "Ramayana in Burmese Literature and Arts." *Journal of the Burma Research Society* 59, nos. 1 & 2 (December 1976): 137–54.

Thomann, Theodor Heinrich. *Pagan, Ein Jahrtausend buddhistischer Tempelkunst*. Stuttgart: W. Seifert, 1923.

Tilly, Harry L., and Philipp Klier. *Wood-Carving of Burma: With Photographs*. Rangoon: Superintendent, Government Printing, 1903.

Tin Hla Thaw. "History of Burma: A.D. 1400–1500." *Journal of the Burma Research Society* 42, no. 2 (1959): 135–51.

Tin Myaing Thein. *Old and New Tapestries of Mandalay*. Kuala Lumpur: Oxford University Press, 2000.

Tingley, Nancy. *Doris Duke: The Southeast Asian Art Collection*. New York: The Foundation for Southeast Asian Art and Culture, 2003.

Tun Aung Chain, trans. *A Chronicle of the Mons*. Yangon: SEAMEO Regional Centre for History and Tradition, 2010.

——. "The Kings of the Hpayahtaung Urn Inscription." In *Selected Writings of Tun Aung Chain*, 18–32. Yangon: Myanmar Historical Commission, 2004.

——. "Yadanabon Remembered: The Maung Maung Tin Chronicle." In *Texts and Images: Glimpses of Myanmar History*, 24–52. Yangon: SEAMEO Regional Centre for History and Tradition, 2011.

Tun Aung Chain and Thein Hlaing. *Shwedagon*. Yangon: Universities Press, 1996.

Tun Nyein. *Inscriptions of Pagan, Pinya and Ava: Translations, with Notes*. Rangoon: Superintendent, Government Printing, 1899.

Tun Shwe Khine. *A Guide to Mrauk-U: An Ancient City of Rakhine, Myanmar*. Sittwe: Sittwe Degree College, 1992.

Upasak, C. S. *Dictionary of Early Buddhist Monastic Terms (Based on Pali Literature)*. Varanasi: Bharati Prakashan, 1974.

Wales, H. G. Quaritch. "Dvaravati in South-East Asian Cultural History." *Journal of the Royal Asiatic Society* 1–2 (1966): 40–52.

Walshe, Maurice. *The Long Discourses of the Buddha: A Translation of the Digha Nikaya*. Boston: Wisdom Publications, 1995.

Warren, Henry Clark, ed. *Buddhism in Translations*. New York: Atheneum, 1973.

Wicks, Robert. *Money, Markets and Trade in Early Southeast Asia: The Development of Indigenous Monetary Systems to AD 1400: Studies on Southeast Asia*. Ithaca, N.Y.: Cornell University, Southeast Asia Program Publications, 1992.

Wilkinson, Wynyard R. T., Mary-Louise Wilkinson, and Barbara Harding. "Burmese Silver from the Colonial Period." *Arts of Asia* 43, no. 3 (2013): 69–81.

Win, Sao Htun Hmat. *The Initiation of Novicehood and the Ordination of Monkhood in the Burmese Buddhist Culture*. Rangoon: Department of Religious Affairs, 1986.

Woodward, Hiram J., Jr. "The Indian Roots of the 'Burmese' Life-of-the-Buddha Plaques." *Silk Road Art and Archaeology* 5 (1997–98), 395–407.

Woodward, Mark R. "When One Wheel Stops: Theravada Buddhism and the British Raj in Upper Burma." *Crossroads: An Interdisciplinary Journal of Southeast Asian Studies* 4, no. 1 (Fall 1988): 57–91.

Yamamura Michio, ed. *Nazo no seramikku roodo ten: ima, yomigaeru Tai, Biruma no kokkyō: Yamamura korekushon* [Riddle of the ceramic road: the Thai-Burmese borderland returns to life: the Yamamura collection]. Beppu, Oita prefecture: Yamamura Michio, 1989.

Zolese, Patrizia. "Technical Report on Archaeological and Anthropological Activities Carried out at Pyay School of Field Archaeology Training Course." 2012.

Zollner, Hans-Bernd. "Germans in Burma 1837–1945." *Journal of Burma Studies* 7 (2000): 29–69.

Zwalf, W., ed. *Buddhism: Art and Faith*. London: British Museum Publications, 1985.

Contributors

Robert L. Brown graduated from the University of California, Los Angeles (UCLA), with a Ph.D. in Indian art history in 1981. He became Curator of Indian and Southeast Asian Art at the Los Angeles County Museum of Art (LACMA) in 1984. In 1986 he began teaching at UCLA, where he is now Professor of Art History. In 2001 he was reappointed as Curator in the Department of South and Southeast Asian Art at LACMA. His research extends over broad geographical areas and chronological periods. Recent publications include three edited books, *Art from Thailand* (1999), *Roots of Tantra* (2002), and the *Encyclopedia of India*, 4 vols. (senior editor, Stanley Wolpert; 2005), as well as *Studies on the Art of Ancient Cambodia* (translated and edited with Natasha Eilenberg; 2008).

Sylvia Fraser-Lu has an M.A. in history from Otago University in New Zealand. She has lectured and presented papers on various subjects pertaining to Southeast Asian arts and crafts at major museums and universities in the United States, Europe, Australia, and Southeast Asia. Fraser-Lu has published widely on Southeast Asian art, including books on the crafts of Myanmar, Buddhist monasteries in Myanmar, and Myanmar lacquerware. During the 1980s she served as series advisor for Oxford University Press's *Images of Asia*, and she is the author of *Indonesian Batik: Processes, Patterns and Places*, *South-East Asian Silverware*, and *Handwoven Textiles of South-East Asia*, among other books. She currently is working on a book on Myanmar textiles.

Jacques Leider obtained his doctorate from the Institut National des Langues et Civilisations Orientales in 1998, having completed a study on the kingdom of Arakan and its political history between the start of the fifteenth and the end of the seventeenth centuries. In 2001 he joined the Ecole française d'Extrême-Orient, where he oversaw the newly created branch in Yangon. His research focuses on Myanmar and the history of Rakhine, as well as on the cultural and political relations between the ancient kingdom of Arakan and the Irrawaddy valley.

Patrick Pranke is Assistant Professor of Religious Studies in the Department of Humanities at the University of Louisville, where he teaches Asian religions with a focus on Theravada Buddhism and Myanmar. Pranke received his doctorate in Buddhist studies from the University of Michigan in 2004, and is affiliated with the Buddhist academy Thitagu Kaba Buddha Takkatho in Sagaing, Myanmar. His research interests include Myanmar Buddhist monastic history and historiography, sangha-state relations, Buddhist scholasticism, and popular religion in Myanmar. Pranke was an assistant editor for the *Princeton Dictionary of Buddhism* (2014), and his articles and chapters have appeared in the *Journal of Burma Studies*, the *Journal of the International Association for Buddhist Studies*, *Buddhism in Practice* (2007), the *Encyclopedia of Buddhism* (2004), and *Champions of Buddhism: Weikza Cults in Contemporary Burma* (2014).

Adriana Proser is John H. Foster Senior Curator for Traditional Asian Art at Asia Society Museum, New York. A specialist in Chinese art, she has organized, co-organized, and managed more than forty exhibitions featuring diverse works from all over Asia over the past fourteen years. Her recent publications include an essay in *Revolutionary Ink: The Paintings of Wu Guanzhong* (2012) and contributions to *Pilgrimage and Buddhist Art* (2010), for which she served as editor. Proser was formerly Assistant Curator of East Asian Art at the Philadelphia Museum of Art. In 1995 she received a Ph.D. in Chinese art and archaeology from Columbia University.

Catherine Raymond is Director of the Center for Burma Studies at Northern Illinois University (NIU). She holds a Ph.D. in art and archaeology and in Indian and Southeast Asian studies from La Sorbonne (Université de Paris). Her special interest is the arts of Myanmar as more broadly interactive with South and Southeast Asian civilization. Her research subjects include the art of the former Buddhist kingdom of Arakan. She also is curator for the extensive Myanmar collection at the NIU Art Museum, where she is presently developing new digital approaches to teaching Myanmar art at all levels.

Donald M. Stadtner received his Ph.D. in Indian art history at the University of California, Berkeley, and was for many years Associate Professor in the Department of Art at the University of Texas, Austin. His publications include *Ancient Pagan: Buddhist Plain of Merit* (2005) and *Sacred Sites of Burma* (2011). His early research trips to Myanmar were sponsored by the Smithsonian Institution (1985, 1987), the National Endowment for the Humanities (1987), the Luce Foundation (1989–90), and the Association for Asian Studies (1991–92).

Heidi Tan was Deputy Director of the Curatorial, Collections and Exhibitions Department at the Asian Civilisations Museum in Singapore. She also was Chief Curator at the museum, and was responsible for the development of its collections over the past eighteen years. She has curated several exhibitions, notably "Viet Nam! From Myth to Modernity" (2008) and "Enlightened Ways: The Many Streams of Buddhist Art in Thailand" (2012). Tan is one of the first Alphawood Foundation scholars at the School of Oriental and African Studies in London, and is pursuing postgraduate research on curating Buddhist art in Myanmar.

U Thaw Kaung is a leading authority in the field of library studies in Asia, with a focus on Myanmar. His specialty is the preservation of traditional documents. He has studied rare Buddhist texts and other valuable palm-leaf manuscripts as historical and cultural records. Thaw Kaung received a degree in librarianship from the University of London and was appointed Chief Librarian of the Universities Central Library, Yangon, in 1969. He served as a consultant librarian to the British Library in 1984 and 1991, and to the Institute of Southeast Asian Studies in Singapore in 1989. In recent years, with Myanmar and Thai collaborators, he has translated palm-leaf manuscripts in Myanmar about Chiang Mai into English. Thaw Kaung is winner of the Academic Prize of the Fukuoka Asian Culture Prizes.

U Tun Aung Chain is former Secretary of the Myanmar Historical Commission, former Director of the South East Asian Ministers of Education Organization's Regional Center for History and Tradition, and retired Professor of History at Yangon University. He is a prolific leading scholar of Myanmar's history, and his publications include *Selected Writings of Tun Aung Chain* (2004), *Broken Glass: Pieces of Myanmar History* (2004), and *Flowing Waters: Dipping into Myanmar History* (2013).

Index

Note: Pages with images are given in *italic*.

Photography Credits

figs. 1, 21: © The British Library Board, WD 540 (84) © The British Library Board, WD 540 (91); fig. 2: Paisarn Piemmattawat, River Books, Bangkok; figs. 3, 4, 37–39, 41: Sylvia Fraser-Lu; figs. 5, 6, 8, 10, 11, 13–15, 17–20, 24, 27, 28, 30, 34–36: Donald M. Stadtner; figs. 7, 9, 12, 16, 40, 42, 43: Perry Hu; fig. 22: Gottfried Wilhelm Leibniz Bibliothek-Niedersächsische Landesbibliothek, Hanover, Germany; fig. 23: Image copyright © The Metropolitan Museum of Art. Image source: Art Resource, NY; fig. 25: © Victoria and Albert Museum, London; fig. 26: U Win Maung; fig. 29: Pamela Gutman; fig. 31: Dr. Kay Simon; fig. 32: Courtesy Richard M. Cooler; fig. 33: Photograph © 2015 Museum of Fine Arts, Boston; figs. 44, 46: Adriana Proser; fig. 45: Susumu Wakisaka, Idemitsu Museum of Arts, Tokyo; fig. 47: Sean Dungan; figs. 48–54: Heidi Tan, Asian Civilisations Museum, Singapore; cat. nos. 1, 4: Thierry Ollivier; cat. nos. 2, 3, 5, 6–20, 22–25, 27, 30–33, 36–38, 40, 47, 67: Sean Dungan; cat. no. 21: Image copyright © The Metropolitan Museum of Art. Image source: Art Resource, NY; cat. no. 26: Photograph © 2015 Museum of Fine Arts, Boston; cat. no. 28: Courtesy of the Ackland Art Museum at The University of North Carolina at Chapel Hill; cat. nos. 29, 34, 42, 45, 46, 49, 69: © Asian Art Museum, San Francisco; cat. nos. 35, 41, 70: Jens Johansen, 2008; cat. no. 39: Digital Image © 2014 Museum Associates / LACMA. Licensed by Art Resource, NY; cat. nos. 43, 44, 48, 54, 55, 57, 61–64: Alex Jamison; cat. nos. 50–53, 56, 58, 65, 66, 68, 71: Northern Illinois University media services; cat. no. 59: Courtesy of the New York Public Library; cat. no. 60: Photograph © Denver Art Museum